Lecture Notes in Artificial Intell...

T0238691

Subseries of Lecture Notes in Computer Science

LNAI Series Editors

Randy Goebel
University of Alberta, Edmonton, Canada
Yuzuru Tanaka
Hokkaido University, Sapporo, Japan
Wolfgang Wahlster
DFKI and Saarland University, Saarbrücken, Germany

LNAI Founding Series Editor

Joerg Siekmann
DFKI and Saarland University, Saarbrücken, Germany

Leszek Rutkowski   Marcin Korytkowski
Rafał Scherer   Ryszard Tadeusiewicz
Lotfi A. Zadeh   Jacek M. Zurada (Eds.)

Artificial Intelligence and Soft Computing

11th International Conference, ICAISC 2012
Zakopane, Poland, April 29 - May 3, 2012
Proceedings, Part I

 Springer

Series Editors

Randy Goebel, University of Alberta, Edmonton, Canada
Jörg Siekmann, University of Saarland, Saarbrücken, Germany
Wolfgang Wahlster, DFKI and University of Saarland, Saarbrücken, Germany

Volume Editors

Leszek Rutkowski
Marcin Korytkowski
Rafał Scherer
Częstochowa University of Technology, Poland
E-mail: lrutko@kik.pcz.czest.pl,
{marcin.korytkowski, rafal.scherer}@kik.pcz.pl

Ryszard Tadeusiewicz
AGH University of Science and Technology, Kraków, Poland
E-mail: rtad@agh.edu.pl

Lotfi A. Zadeh
University of California, Berkeley, CA, USA
E-mail: zadeh@cs.berkeley.edu

Jacek M. Zurada
University of Louisville, KY, USA
E-mail: jacek.zurada@louisville.edu

ISSN 0302-9743   e-ISSN 1611-3349
ISBN 978-3-642-29346-7 e-ISBN 978-3-642-29347-4
DOI 10.1007/978-3-642-29347-4
Springer Heidelberg Dordrecht London New York

Library of Congress Control Number: 2012934672

CR Subject Classification (1998): I.2, H.3, F.1, I.4, H.4, I.5

LNCS Sublibrary: SL 7 – Artificial Intelligence

Typesetting: Camera-ready by author, data conversion by Scientific Publishing Services, Chennai, India

Printed on acid-free paper

Springer is part of Springer Science+Business Media (www.springer.com)

Preface

This volume constitutes the proceedings of the 11th International Conference on Artificial Intelligence and Soft Computing, ICAISC 2012, held in Zakopane, Poland, from April 29 to May 3, 2012. The conference was organized by the Polish Neural Network Society in cooperation with the SWSPiZ Academy of Management in Łódź, the Department of Computer Engineering at the Czesto-chowa University of Technology, and the IEEE Computational Intelligence Society, Poland Chapter. The previous conferences took place in Kule (1994), Szczyrk (1996), Kule (1997) and Zakopane (1999, 2000, 2002, 2004, 2006, 2008, 2010) and attracted a large number of papers and internationally recognized speakers: Lotfi A. Zadeh, Igor Aizenberg, Shun-ichi Amari, Daniel Amit, Piero P. Bonissone, Jim Bezdek, Zdzislaw Bubnicki, Andrzej Cichocki, Wlodzislaw Duch, Pablo A. Estévez, Jerzy Grzymala-Busse, Martin Hagan, Akira Hirose, Kaoru Hirota, Janusz Kacprzyk, Jim Keller, Laszlo T. Koczy, Soo-Young Lee, Robert Marks, Evangelia Micheli-Tzanakou, Erkki Oja, Witold Pedrycz, Jagath C. Rajapakse, Sarunas Raudys, Enrique Ruspini, Jorg Siekman, Roman Slowinski, Igor Spiridonov, Ryszard Tadeusiewicz, Shiro Usui, Jun Wang, Ronald Y. Yager, Syozo Yasui and Jacek Zurada. The aim of this conference is to build a bridge between traditional artificial intelligence techniques and novel soft computing techniques. It was pointed out by Lotfi A. Zadeh that "soft computing (SC) is a coalition of methodologies which are oriented toward the conception and design of information/intelligent systems. The principal members of the coalition are: fuzzy logic (FL), neurocomputing (NC), evolutionary computing (EC), probabilistic computing (PC), chaotic computing (CC), and machine learning (ML). The constituent methodologies of SC are, for the most part, complementary and synergistic rather than competitive." This volume presents both traditional artificial intelligence methods and soft computing techniques. Our goal is to bring together scientists representing both traditional artificial intelligence approach and soft computing techniques. This volume is divided into five parts:

- Neural Networks and Their Applications
- Fuzzy Systems and Their Applications
- Pattern Classification
- Computer Vision, Image and Speech Analysis
- The 4th International Workshop on Engineering Knowledge and Semantic Systems

The conference attracted a total of 483 submissions from 48 countries and after the review process 212 papers were accepted for publication. ICAISC 2012 hosted the Symposium on Swarm Intelligence and Differential Evolution, the Symposium on Evolutionary Computation and the 4th International Workshop on Engineering Knowledge and Semantic Systems (IWEKSS 2012). A special theme of IWEKSS 2012 was "Nature-Inspired Knowledge Management Systems."

I would like to thank two main IWEKS 2012 organizers: Jason J. Jung from Korea and Dariusz Krol from Poland. I would also like to thank our participants, invited speakers and reviewers of the papers for their scientific and personal contribution to the conference. Several reviewers were very helpful in reviewing the papers and are listed herein.

Acknowledge

Finally, I thank my co-workers Łukasz Bartczuk, Agnieszka Cpałka, Piotr Dziwiński, Marcin Gabryel, Marcin Korytkowski and the conference secretary Rafał Scherer, for their enormous efforts to make the conference a very successful event. Moreover, I would like to acknowledge the work of Marcin Korytkowski, who designed the Internet submission system and Patryk Najgebauer, Tomasz Nowak and Jakub Romanowski who created the web page.

April 2012   Leszek Rutkowski

Organization

ICAISC 2012 was organized by the Polish Neural Network Society in cooperation with the SWSPiZ Academy of Management in Łódź, the Department of Computer Engineering at Częstochowa University of Technology, and the IEEE Computational Intelligence Society, Poland Chapter.

ICAISC Chairs

Honorary Chairs	Lotfi Zadeh (USA)
	Jacek Żurada (USA)
General Chairs	Leszek Rutkowski (Poland)
Co-Chairs	Włodzisław Duch (Poland)
	Janusz Kacprzyk (Poland)
	Józef Korbicz (Poland)
	Ryszard Tadeusiewicz (Poland)

ICAISC Program Committee

Rafał Adamczak - Poland
Cesare Alippi - Italy
Shun-ichi Amari - Japan
Rafal A. Angryk - USA
Jarosław Arabas - Poland
Robert Babuska - The Netherlands
Ildar Z. Batyrshin - Russia
James C. Bezdek - USA
Marco Block-Berlitz - Germany
Leon Bobrowski - Poland
Leonard Bolc - Poland
Piero P. Bonissone - USA
Bernadette Bouchon-Meunier - France
James Buckley - Poland
Tadeusz Burczynski - Poland
Andrzej Cader - Poland
Juan Luis Castro - Spain
Yen-Wei CHEN - Japan
Wojciech Cholewa - Poland
Fahmida N. Chowdhury - USA
Andrzej Cichocki - Japan
Paweł Cichosz - Poland
Krzysztof Cios - USA

Ian Cloete - Germany
Oscar Cordón - Spain
Bernard De Baets - Belgium
Nabil Derbel - Tunisia
Ewa Dudek-Dyduch - Poland
Ludmiła Dymowa - Poland
Andrzej Dzieliński - Poland
David Elizondo - UK
Meng Joo Er - Singapore
Pablo Estevez - Chile
János Fodor - Hungary
David B. Fogel - USA
Roman Galar - Poland
Alexander I. Galushkin - Russia
Adam Gaweda - USA
Joydeep Ghosh - USA
Juan Jose Gonzalez de la Rosa - Spain
Marian Bolesław Gorzałczany - Poland
Krzysztof Grąbczewski - Poland
Garrison Greenwood - USA
Jerzy W. Grzymala-Busse - USA
Hani Hagras - UK
Saman Halgamuge - Australia

Enrique H. Ruspini - USA
Khalid Saeed - Poland
Dominik Sankowski - Poland
Norihide Sano - Japan
Robert Schaefer - Poland
Rudy Setiono - Singapore
Paweł Sewastianow - Poland
Jennie Si - USA
Peter Sincak - Slovakia
Andrzej Skowron - Poland
Ewa Skubalska-Rafajłowicz - Poland
Roman Słowiński - Poland
Tomasz G. Smolinski - USA
Czesław Smutnicki - Poland
Pilar Sobrevilla - Spain
Janusz Starzyk - USA
Jerzy Stefanowski - Poland
Pawel Strumillo - Poland
Ron Sun - USA
Johan Suykens Suykens - Belgium
Piotr Szczepaniak - Poland
Eulalia J. Szmidt - Poland
Przemysław Śliwiński - Poland
Adam Słowik - Poland
Jerzy Świątek - Poland
Hideyuki Takagi - Japan

Yury Tiumentsev - Russia
Vicenç Torra - Spain
Burhan Turksen - Canada
Shiro Usui - Japan
Michael Wagenknecht - Germany
Tomasz Walkowiak - Poland
Deliang Wang - USA
Jun Wang - Hong Kong
Lipo Wang - Singapore
Zenon Waszczyszyn - Poland
Paul Werbos - USA
Slawo Wesolkowski - Canada
Sławomir Wiak - Poland
Bernard Widrow - USA
Kay C. Wiese - Canada
Bogdan M. Wilamowski - USA
Donald C. Wunsch - USA
Maciej Wygralak - Poland
Roman Wyrzykowski - Poland
Ronald R. Yager - USA
Xin-She Yang - UK
Gary Yen - USA
John Yen - USA
Sławomir Zadrożny - Poland
Ali M.S. Zalzala - United Arab Emirates

SIDE Chairs

Janez Brest, University of Maribor, Slovenia
Maurice Clerc, Independent Consultant
Ferrante Neri, University of Jyväskylä, Finland

SIDE Program Chairs

Tim Blackwell, Goldsmiths College, UK
Swagatam Das, Indian Statistical Institute, India
Nicolas Monmarché, University of Tours, France
Ponnuthurai N. Suganthan, Nanyang Technological University, Singapore

SIDE Program Committee

Ashish Anand, India
Borko Boskovic, Slovenia
Jagdish Chand Bansal, India
Carlos Coello Coello, Mexico
Iztok Fister, Slovenia
Bogdan Filipic, Slovenia
Sheldon Hui, Singapore
Peter D. Justesen, Denmark
Nicolas Labroche, France
Jane Liang, China
Hongbo Liu, China
Efren Mezura Montes, Mexico
A. Nakib, France
Rammohan Mallipeddi, Korea
Slawomir Nasuto, UK
Jouni Lampinen, Finland

Mirjam Sepesy Maucec, Slovenia
Marjan Mernik, Slovenia
Godfrey Onwubolu, Canada
Jérôme Emeka Onwunalu, Canada
Quanke Pan, China
Gregor Papa, Slovenia
Boyang Qu, China
Shahryar Rahnamayan, Canada
Jurij Silc, Slovenia
Josef Tvrdik, Czech Republic
M. N. Vrahatis, Greece
Daniela Zaharie, Romania
Ales Zamuda, Slovenia
Qingfu Zhang, UK
Shizheng Zhao, Singapore

IWEKSS Program Committee

Jason J. Jung, Korea
Dariusz Krol, Poland
Ngoc Thanh Nguyen, Poland
Gonzalo A. Aranda-Corral, Spain
Myung-Gwon Hwang, Korea
Costin Badica, Romania
Grzegorz J. Nalepa, Krakow, Poland

ICAISC Organizing Committee

Rafał Scherer, Secretary
Łukasz Bartczuk, Organizing Committee Member
Piotr Dziwiński, Organizing Committee Member
Marcin Gabryel, Finance Chair
Marcin Korytkowski, Databases and Internet Submissions

Reviewers

R. Adamczak
M. Amasyal
A. Anand
R. Angryk
J. Arabas

T. Babczyński
M. Baczyński
C. Badica
Ł. Bartczuk
M. Białko

A. Bielecki
T. Blackwell
L. Bobrowski
A. Borkowski
L. Borzemski

B. Boskovic

J. Brest

T. Burczyński

R. Burduk

K. Cetnarowicz

M. Chang

W. Cholewa

M. Choraś

R. Choraś

K. Choros

P. Cichosz

R. Cierniak

P. Ciskowski

M. Clerc

O. Cordon

B. Cyganek

R. Czabański

I. Czarnowski

B. De Baets

J. de la Rosa

L. Diosan

G. Dobrowolski

W. Duch

E. Dudek-Dyduch

L. Dymowa

A. Dzieliński

P. Dziwiński

S. Ehteram

J. Emeka Onwunalu

N. Evans

A. Fanea

I. Fister

M. Flasiński

D. Fogel

M. Fraś

M. Gabryel

A. Gawęda

M. Giergiel

P. Głomb

F. Gomide

M. Gorzałczany

E. Grabska

K. Grąbczewski

W. Greblicki

K. Grudziński

J. Grzymala-Busse

R. Hampel

C. Han

Z. Hasiewicz

O. Henniger

F. Herrera

Z. Hippe

A. Horzyk

E. Hrynkiewicz

S. Hui

M. Hwang

A. Janczak

N. Jankowski

S. Jaroszewicz

J. Jung

W. Kacalak

W. Kamiński

A. Kasperski

W. Kazimierski

V. Kecman

E. Kerre

H. Kim

F. Klawonn

P. Klęsk

J. Kluska

A. Kołakowska

L. Kompanets

J. Konopacki

J. Korbicz

P. Korohoda

J. Koronacki

M. Korytkowski

M. Korzeń

W. Kosiński

J. Kościelny

L. Kotulski

Z. Kowalczuk

J. Kozlak

M. Kraft

D. Krol

R. Kruse

B. Kryzhanovsky

A. Krzyzak

J. Kulikowski

O. Kurasova

V. Kurkova

M. Kurzyński

J. Kusiak

H. Kwaśnicka

N. Labroche

S. Lee

Y. Lei

J. Liang

A. Ligęza

H. Liu

B. Macukow

K. Madani

K. Malinowski

R. Mallipeddi

J. Mańdziuk

U. Markowska-Kaczmar

A. Martin

J. Martyna

A. Materka

T. Matsumoto

V. Medvedev

J. Mendel

E. MezuraMontes

Z. Michalewicz

J. Michalkiewicz

Z. Mikrut

W. Mitkowski

W. Moczulski

W. Mokrzycki

N. Monmarche

T. Munakata

A. Nakib

G. Nalepa

S. Nasuto

E. Nawarecki

A. Nawrat

F. Neri

M. Nieniewski

A. Niewiadomski

R. Nowicki

A. Obuchowicz

M. Ogiela

G. Onwubolu

S. Osowski

M. Pacholczyk

Table of Contents – Part I

Part I: Neural Networks and Their Applications

Part II: Fuzzy Systems and Their Applications

Part III: Pattern Classification

Part IV: Computer Vision, Image and Speech Analysis

Part V: The 4th International Workshop on Engineering Knowledge and Semantic Systems

Table of Contents – Part II

Part I: Data Mining

Part II: Hardware Implementation

Part III: Bioinformatics, Biometrics and Medical Applications

Part IV: Concurrent Parallel Processing

Part V: Agent Systems, Robotics and Control

Part VI: Artificial Intelligence in Modeling and Simulation

Part VII: Various Problems od Artificial Intelligence

Part I

Neural Networks and Their Applications

Neural Network-Based PCA:
An Application to Approximation
of a Distributed Parameter System

Krzysztof Bartecki

Opole University of Technology, Institute of Control and Computer Engineering,
ul. Sosnkowskiego 31, 45-272 Opole, Poland
k.bartecki@po.opole.pl

Abstract. In this article, an approximation of the spatiotemporal response of a distributed parameter system (DPS) with the use of the neural network-based principal component analysis (PCA) is considered. The presented approach is carried out using two different neural structures: single-layer network with unsupervised, generalized Hebbian learning (GHA-PCA) and two-layer feedforward network with supervised learning (FF-PCA). In each case considered, the effect of the number of units in the network projection layer on the mean square approximation error (MSAE) and on the data compression ratio is analysed.

Keywords: principal component analysis, neural networks, distributed parameter systems.

1 Introduction

Principal Component Analysis (PCA) is one of the main approaches to reduce the dimensionality of data, losing the least amount of information. It can be applied in many fields such as pattern recognition, computer vision, signal processing, data compression, etc. The advantages of PCA result from its optimality properties in maximization of variance as well as in minimization of mean square error [5,7]. However, numerical calculations of the data covariance matrix and its eigenvectors being the main feature of the PCA can achieve considerable computational complexity, particularly at the high dimensionality of the input data. In this case, it may be preferable to employ methods that do not require explicit determination of the covariance matrix. Such an approach can rely e.g. on the well-known properties of artificial neural networks. Their learning algorithms directly process the input vectors, which can be delivered either off- or on-line [2,10,15,17,19]. Therefore, when the online scheme is taken into account, or when only a few principal components are required, the neural network-based PCA technique tends to be the good solution [8,13,14,18].

In this paper neural networks are proposed to be used as a tool for the PCA-based approximation of spatiotemporal responses of a distributed parameter system (DPS). A mathematical description of this class of systems takes most

L. Rutkowski et al. (Eds.): ICAISC 2012, Part I, LNCS 7267, pp. 3–11, 2012.

often the form of partial differential equations (PDEs), which lead to the infinite-dimensional state space and irrational transfer function representations. Therefore, due to the mathematical complexity, these models are often approximated by finite-dimensional ones. Among many approximation techniques, an important role is played by the so-called reduction methods, consisting in the replacement of the high-order model of DPS by a lower-order one, mapping the most relevant aspects of the dynamical properties of the system. A significant role is played here by the reduction methods based on the PCA approach [6,11,12,16]. This paper proposes PCA-based DPS approximation to be carried out using two different neural network structures: single-layer network with unsupervised, generalized Hebbian learning (GHA-PCA) and two-layer feedforward network with supervised autoassociative learning (FF-PCA).

2   Neural Network-Based PCA Schemes

In this section, the abovementioned neural network-based PCA techniques are introduced, with particular emphasis on their use in the approximation of the DPS spatiotemporal response.

Assume that as a result of the measurement or numerical simulation experiment, we have obtained a discrete set of values $y(l_m, t_n)$, representing the spatiotemporal distribution of a one-dimensional DPS process variable $y \in \mathbb{R}$, where $t_n = n \cdot \Delta t$ for $n = 1, 2, \ldots, N$ and $\Delta t = T/N$ is a discrete independent variable representing time, $l_m = m \cdot \Delta l$ for $m = 1, 2, \ldots, M$ and $\Delta l = L/M$ is a discrete independent variable representing spatial position. $T \in \mathbb{R}^+$ and $L \in \mathbb{R}^+$ denote temporal and spatial observation horizons, while $N \in \mathbb{N}$ and $M \in \mathbb{N}$ are number of observations and number of spatial positions, respectively. After initial processing, involving subtracting from each sample $y(l_m, t_n)$ the time average for the m-th spatial position, given by

$$\bar{y}(l_m) = \frac{1}{N} \sum_{n=1}^{N} y(l_m, t_n), \tag{1}$$

the DPS response will be represented by the matrix $Y = [y(l_m, t_n) - \bar{y}(l_m)] \in \mathbb{R}^{M \times N}$.

PCA can be seen as optimal factorization of Y into two matrices:

$$\hat{Y} = \Phi_K \Psi_K \tag{2}$$

where $\hat{Y} \in \mathbb{R}^{M \times N}$ denotes the approximated matrix Y, $\Phi_K \in \mathbb{R}^{M \times K}$ is matrix consisting of $K < M$ orthogonal column eigenvectors $\varphi_1, \varphi_2, \ldots, \varphi_K \in \mathbb{R}^M$ of the response covariance matrix C calculated as:

$$C = \frac{1}{N} Y Y^T, \tag{3}$$

corresponding to its K largest eigenvalues, $\lambda_1, \lambda_2, \ldots, \lambda_K$. The matrix $\Psi_K \in \mathbb{R}^{K \times N}$ in (2) can be determined from the following relationship [3]:

$$\Psi_K = \Phi_K^T Y. \tag{4}$$

Optimality condition for the factorization (1) means that the Frobenius norm $\|E\|_{\mathrm{F}}$ of the approximation error matrix $E = Y - \hat{Y}$ must be minimized for the given value of the model order K.

In the following subsections two neural network-based PCA techniques are discussed: a single-layered neural network with unsupervised Hebbian learning and a feedforward neural network with supervised autoassociative learning.

2.1 Single-Layered Network with Supervised Training (GHA-PCA)

A single neuron acting as a principal component analyzer was first proposed by Oja in [13]. Its extension to a network consisting of many neurons, known as Generalized Hebbian Algorithm (GHA) or Sanger's rule, enabling the estimation of the subsequent principal components, was presented in the works of Oja and Sanger [14,18]. In this case, the PCA task is performed by the use of a single-layered neural network consisting of K linear neurons, corresponding to the subsequent principal components.

The structure of the GHA-PCA network used for the approximation of the spatiotemporal DPS response is presented in Fig. 1. The number of network inputs is equal to the number of M spatial positions for which the value of the process variable y is determined, whereas number of network outputs is equal to the number of the K principal components.

According to the GHA, modification of the weight coefficients of the k-th neuron is performed after each presentation of the input patterns corresponding to the time instant t_n, based on the following expression [15,18]:

$$w_{k,m}(t_{n+1}) = w_{k,m}(t_n) + \eta v_k(t_n) \left[y(l_m, t_n) - \sum_{h=1}^{k} w_{h,m}(t_n) v_h(t_n) \right] \quad (5)$$

where $w_{k,m}(t_n)$ is the value of the weight coefficient connecting the k-th neuron

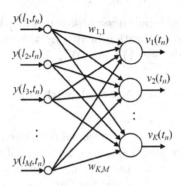

Fig. 1. Structure of the GHA-PCA neural network

with the m-th network input, $v_k(t_n)$ is the output signal of the k-th neuron, both calculated for the time instant t_n, and η is the network learning rate. Denoting by $w_k(t_n)$ vector containing all weight coefficients of the k-th neuron at the time instant t_n, i.e. vector of the following form:

$$w_k(t_j) = \left[w_{k,1}(t_n)\, w_{k,2}(t_n) \,\ldots\, w_{k,M}(t_n) \right], \tag{6}$$

by $y(t_n)$ the input vector representing the distribution of the process variable y for all M spatial positions at the time instant t_n:

$$y(t_n) = \left[y(l_1, t_n)\, y(l_2, t_n) \,\ldots\, y(l_M, t_n) \right]^T \tag{7}$$

and introducing the following notation:

$$y'(t_n) = y(t_n) - \sum_{h=1}^{k-1} (w_h(t_n))^T v_h(t_n), \tag{8}$$

the relationship (5) can be written in the compact vector form:

$$w_k(t_{n+1}) = w_k(t_n) + \eta v_k(t_n) \left[(y'(t_n))^T - w_k(t_n) v_k(t_n) \right], \tag{9}$$

analogous to the Oja algorithm for a single neuron, for which self-normalization of weight coefficients is carried out.

As mentioned in Sec. 1, one of the main applications of PCA is lossy data compression. In the case under consideration, the compression task should be understood as follows: a large input data set represented by the matrix $Y \in \mathbb{R}^{M \times N}$ is replaced by the reduced data set consisting of the network weight matrix $W = [w_{k,m}] \in \mathbb{R}^{K \times M}$, the network responses matrix $V = [v_k(t_n)] \in \mathbb{R}^{K \times N}$ and the vector of time averages $\bar{y} = [\bar{y}(l_m)] \in \mathbb{R}^M$. The data compression ratio C_K can be thus calculated as:

$$C_K = \frac{M \times N}{M \times K + K \times N + M}. \tag{10}$$

Approximation of the spatiotemporal response is possible due to the "decompression", realized as simple multiplication of W^T by V and adding time-averaged values of $\bar{y}(l_m)$ to the result (see (1) and (2)).

2.2   Two-Layer Feedforward Network with Supervised Training (FF-PCA)

An alternative approach to extracting principal components from the data set is based on a feedforward, two-layer linear neural network of the structure shown in Fig. 2. The number of the network outputs (i.e. number of neurons in its second layer, hereinafter referred to as a *reconstruction layer*) is equal to the number of its inputs and represents the number M of spatial positions of the process variable y. Furthermore, the number of $K < M$ units in the first network layer, called the *projection layer*, represents the number of the principal components to be extracted. For the structure presented here, the acronym FF-PCA (*Feed-Forward Principal Component Analysis*) neural network will be used later in the article.

The role of the network input patterns will be taken over, as in the case of the GHA-PCA network, by the vectors representing distribution of the process variable y at the successive time instants t_n, i.e. by the subsequent columns of the matrix Y. In the considered case of the auto-associative network learning, the output patterns are equal to the input ones, and the learning procedure consists in the iterative modifications of all weight coefficients in order to minimize the network error function of the following well-known form [10,15,17,19]:

$$E(w) = \frac{1}{M \cdot N} \sum_{m=1}^{M} \sum_{n=1}^{N} (y(l_m, t_n) - \hat{y}(l_m, t_n))^2. \tag{11}$$

Denoting by $W^{(1)} \in \mathbb{R}^{K \times M}$ the weight matrix of the projection layer, by $W^{(2)} \in \mathbb{R}^{M \times K}$ the weight matrix of the reconstruction layer and by $V \in \mathbb{R}^{K \times N}$ the matrix of the projection layer responses to the input patterns Y, we obtain the following relationships describing the operation of the network of Fig. 2:

$$V = W^{(1)}Y \tag{12}$$

and

$$\hat{Y} = W^{(2)}V = W^{(2)}W^{(1)}Y. \tag{13}$$

As can be easily seen, (13) is equivalent to (2) and (4), wherein $W^{(1)}$ corresponds to ${\Phi_K}^T$ and V corresponds to Ψ_K. In order to determine the optimal values of the weight coefficients, a supervised learning procedure has to be applied – e.g. gradient descent or Levenberg-Marquardt algorithm [2,15,17,19].

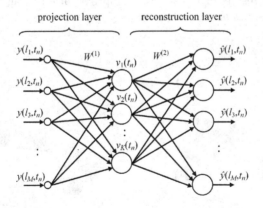

Fig. 2. Structure of the FF-PCA neural network

3   Example: Spatiotemporal Response of Hyperbolic DPS

Among many different kinds of DPS, an important class is constituted by the processes in which the phenomena of mass and energy transport take place. One can mention here e.g. electrical transmission lines, transport pipelines or heat exchangers [1,3,4,9]. Their mathematical description takes the general form of the following two coupled partial differential equations of hyperbolic type:

$$
\begin{aligned}
\frac{\partial y_1\,(l,t)}{\partial t} + f_1 \frac{\partial y_1\,(l,t)}{\partial l} &= g_{11} y_1\,(l,t) + g_{12} y_2\,(l,t), \\
\frac{\partial y_2\,(l,t)}{\partial t} + f_2 \frac{\partial y_2\,(l,t)}{\partial l} &= g_{21} y_1\,(l,t) + g_{22} y_2\,(l,t),
\end{aligned}
\tag{14}
$$

where $y_1(l,t) \in \mathbb{R}$ and $y_2(l,t) \in \mathbb{R}$ are functions representing spatiotemporal distribution of the process variables, defined on the set $\Omega \times \Theta$, where $\Omega = [0, L]$ is the domain of the independent spatial variable l, while $\Theta = [0, T]$ is the domain of the independent variable t representing time. The constant coefficients $f_1, f_2 \in \mathbb{R}$ usually represent the transport or wave propagation velocities, whereas the constants $g_{11}, g_{12}, g_{21}, g_{22} \in \mathbb{R}$ depend on the geometrical and physical parameters of the plant.

In order to determine the numerical solutions of (14), the *method of lines* has been applied for the following values of the equation parameters, the domain of the solution and the spatial discretization step: $f_1 = 1$, $f_2 = 0.5$, $g_{11} = -0.0638$, $g_{12} = 0.0638$, $g_{21} = -0.0359$, $g_{22} = 0.0359$, $L = 5$, $T = 50$, $\Delta l = 0.1$. The simulations were carried out assuming zero initial conditions, $y_1(l,0) = 0$ and $y_2(l,0) = 0$, as well as two different forms of boundary conditions: the Kronecker delta impulse and the Heaviside step function for the control variable $y_1(0,t)$. The solutions of (14) representing spatiotemporal distribution of the controlled variable $y_2(l,t)$ for both types of boundary conditions are shown in Fig. 3. In the following, the results of the response approximation using aforementioned neural PCA techniques are presented.

a)   b)

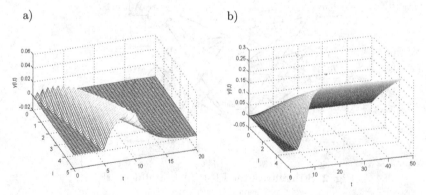

Fig. 3. Impulse (a) and step (b) spatiotemporal responses $y_2(l,t)$ of the system (14)

The results of the application of the GHA-PCA network with three neurons ($K = 3$) in the approximation of the step response of Fig. 3b are presented in Fig. 4. In Fig. 4a weight vectors of individual neurons are plotted, whereas Fig. 4b shows original step responses (solid line), obtained by the numerical solution of (14) and the responses of the GHA-PCA approximation model (dashed line), compared for six different spatial positions l.

Furthermore, Fig. 5 shows approximation results analogous to those presented in Fig. 4, obtained as a result of the use of the FF-PCA method discussed in Sec. 2.2. As can be seen, in contrast to the case of the GHA-PCA network, the weight vectors w_1, w_2 and w_3 of the projection layer of the FF-PCA network are not orthogonal – their values have somewhat "chaotic" distribution. This is mainly due to the fact that the network learning algorithm generates random initial values of the weight coefficients, and, moreover, it does not impose the orthogonality condition on the weight vectors as opposed to the GHA-PCA method.

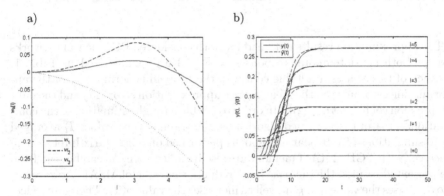

Fig. 4. GHA-PCA approximation results for the step response and $K = 3$: a) weight vectors w_1, w_2 and w_3, b) exact and approximate responses, $y(l, t)$ and $\hat{y}(l, t)$

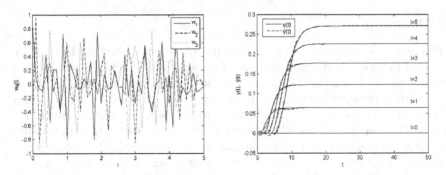

Fig. 5. FF-PCA approximation results for the step response and $K = 3$: a) weight vectors w_1, w_2 and w_3, b) exact and approximate responses, $y(l, t)$ and $\hat{y}(l, t)$

Table 1. Approximation results for GHA-PCA and FF-PCA neural networks (after 1000 training epochs)

		impulse response			step response		
		number of neurons K			number of neurons K		
		$K=1$	$K=3$	$K=5$	$K=1$	$K=3$	$K=5$
	$\|E\|_{\mathrm{F}}$	0.335	0.111	0.074	0.820	0.689	0.680
GHA-PCA	MSAE	$2.18{\cdot}10^{-5}$	$2.38{\cdot}10^{-6}$	$1.07{\cdot}10^{-6}$	$1.33{\cdot}10^{-4}$	$9.23{\cdot}10^{-5}$	$8.98{\cdot}10^{-5}$
	C_K	25.37	10.16	6.35	25.37	10.16	6.35
	T_t	1.9 s	2.5 s	3.1 s	1.9 s	2.5 s	3.1 s
	$\|E\|_{\mathrm{F}}$	0.337	0.147	0.143	0.773	0.724	0.650
FF-PCA	MSAE	$2.21{\cdot}10^{-5}$	$4.20{\cdot}10^{-6}$	$4.00{\cdot}10^{-6}$	$1.04{\cdot}10^{-4}$	$1.02{\cdot}10^{-4}$	$8.2{\cdot}10^{-5}$
	C_K	25.37	10.15	6.35	25.37	10.16	6.35
	T_t	1.0 s	1.7 s	2.4 s	1.0 s	1.7 s	2.4 s

The approximation results obtained for both considered PCA neural networks and for both spatiotemporal responses of Fig. 3 are summarized in Table 1. For each of these cases, the table contains: the Frobenius norm $\|E\|_{\mathrm{F}}$ of the approximation error matrix, the mean square approximation error (11) and the data compression coefficient C_K (10). In order to enable a rough estimation of the computational cost of the proposed algorithms, the training time values T_t averaged for 10 simulations of 1000 learning epochs performed on a 2.27 GHz Intel Core i5 processor with 4 GB of RAM memory are also included here. As can be seen from the presented results, the increase in K reduces the value of MSAE, however, it also decreases the value of C_K as well as increases the value of T_t. Therefore, selection of the appropriate value for K should take into account the tradeoff between an assumed (reasonably low) value for the approximation error, and a sufficiently high value for the compression ratio as well as low computation time.

4   Summary

In this paper, neural network-based PCA techniques as applied to the approximation of the spatiotemporal responses of a distributed parameter system have been discussed. A positive aspect of using artificial neural networks as a tool for extracting principal components from a spatiotemporal data set is that they do not require calculating the correlation matrix explicitly, as in the case of the classical PCA approach. For this reason, they can be used e.g. in the on-line data acquisition scheme, when calculation of the data correlation matrix in the explicit form is impossible. The neural approach presented in the paper may act as a good starting point for further research concerning, for example, approximation of nonlinear DPS using nonlinear PCA method, based on the function approximation properties of neural networks with nonlinear, sigmoidal units.

References

1. Bartecki, K.: Frequency- and time-domain analysis of a simple pipeline system. In: Proceedings of the 14th IEEE IFAC International Conference on Methods and Models in Automation and Robotics, Miedzyzdroje (August 2009)
2. Bartecki, K.: On some peculiarities of neural network approximation applied to the inverse kinematics problem. In: Proceedings of the Conference on Control and Fault-Tolerant Systems, Nice, France, pp. 317–322 (October 2010)
3. Bartecki, K.: Approximation of a class of distributed parameter systems using proper orthogonal decomposition. In: Proceedings of the 16th IEEE International Conference on Methods and Models in Automation and Robotics, Miedzyzdroje, pp. 351–356 (August 2011)
4. Bartecki, K., Rojek, R.: Instantaneous linearization of neural network model in adaptive control of heat exchange process. In: Proceedings of the 11th IEEE International Conference on Methods and Models in Automation and Robotics, Miedzyzdroje, pp. 967–972 (August 2005)
5. Berkooz, G., Holmes, P., Lumley, J.L.: The proper orthogonal decomposition in the analysis of turbulent flows. Annual Review of Fluid Mechanics 25, 539–575 (1993)
6. Bleris, L.G., Kothare, M.V.: Low-order empirical modeling of distributed parameter systems using temporal and spatial eigenfunctions. Computers and Chemical Engineering 29(4), 817–827 (2005)
7. Chatterjee, A.: An introduction to the proper orthogonal decomposition. Current Science 78(7), 808–817 (2000)
8. Diamantaras, K.I., Kung, S.Y.: Principal Component Neural Networks - Theory and Applications. John Wiley, New York (1996)
9. Friedly, J.C.: Dynamic Behaviour of Processes. Prentice Hall, New York (1972)
10. Hertz, J., Krogh, A., Palmer, R.: Introduction to the Theory of Neural Computation. Addison Wesley, Redwood City (1991)
11. Hoo, K.A., Zheng, D.: Low-order control-relevant models for a class of distributed parameters system. Chemical Engineering Science 56(23), 6683–6710 (2001)
12. Li, H.X., Qi, C.: Modeling of distributed parameter systems for applications - A synthesized review from time-space separation. Journal of Process Control 20(8), 891–901 (2010)
13. Oja, E.: A simplified neuron model as a principal component analyzer. Journal of Mathematical Biology 15(3), 267–273 (1982)
14. Oja, E.: Neural networks, principal components, and subspaces. International Journal of Neural Systems 1(1), 61–68 (1989)
15. Osowski, S.: Neural Networks for Information Processing. Warsaw University of Technology Press, Warsaw (2000)
16. Qi, C., Li, H.X.: A time-space separation-based Hammerstein modeling approach for nonlinear distributed parameter processes. Computers and Chemical Engineering 33(7), 1247–1260 (2009)
17. Rojas, R.: Neural networks: a systematic introduction. Springer, Berlin (1996)
18. Sanger, T.D.: Optimal unsupervised learning in a single-layer linear feedforward neural network. Neural Networks 2(6), 459–473 (1989)
19. Zurada, J.: Introduction to artificial neural systems. West Publishing Company, St. Paul, MN (1992)

Parallel Realisation of the Recurrent Multi Layer Perceptron Learning

Jarosław Bilski and Jacek Smoląg

Department of Computer Engineering,
Częstochowa University of Technology,
Częstochowa, Poland
{Jaroslaw.Bilski,Jacek.Smolag}@kik.pcz.pl

Abstract. This paper presents the parallel architecture of the Recurrent Multi Layer Perceptron learning algorithm. The proposed solution is based on the high parallel three dimensional structure to speed up learning performance. Detailed parallel neural network structures are explicitly shown.

1 Introduction

The RMLP network is an example of dynamical neural networks. Dynamical neural networks have been investigated by many scientists for the last decade [4], [5]. To train the dynamical networks the gradient method was used eg. [8]. In the classical case the neural networks learning algorithms are implemented on serial computer. Unfortunatelly, this method is slow because the learning algorithm requires high computational load. Therefore, high performance dedicated parallel structure is a suitable solution, eg. [1] - [3], [6], [7]. This paper contains a new concept of the parallel realisation of the RMPL learning algorithm. A single iteration of the parallel architecture requires much less computation cycles than a serial implementation. The efficiency of this new architecture is very satisfing and is explained in the last part of this paper. The structure of the RMPL network is shown in Fig. 1.

The RMLP network has K neurons in the hidden layer and one neuron in the network output. The input vector contains input signal, its N previous values and M previous outputs. Note, the previous signals from input and output are obtained through unit time delay z^{-1}. Therefore, the network function is

$$y^{(2)}(t+1) = f\begin{pmatrix} x^{(1)}(t), x^{(1)}(t-1), \ldots, x^{(1)}(t-(N-1)), \\ y^{(2)}(t-1), \ldots, y^{(2)}(t-M) \end{pmatrix} \tag{1}$$

In the recall phase the network is described by

$$\begin{aligned} s_i^{(1)} &= \sum_{j=0}^{N+M} w_{ij}^{(1)} x_j^{(1)} \\ y_i^{(1)} &= f\left(s_i^{(1)}\right); \quad x_i^{(2)} = y_i^{(1)} \\ s^{(2)} &= \sum_{i=0}^{K} w_i^{(2)} x_i^{(2)} \\ y^{(2)} &= f\left(s^{(2)}\right) \end{aligned} \tag{2}$$

L. Rutkowski et al. (Eds.): ICAISC 2012, Part I, LNCS 7267, pp. 12–20, 2012.

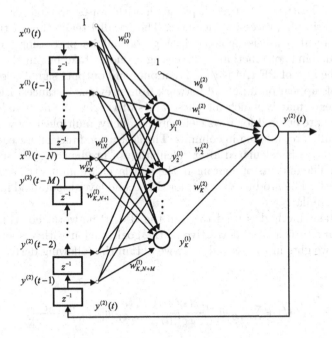

Fig. 1. Structure of the RMLP network

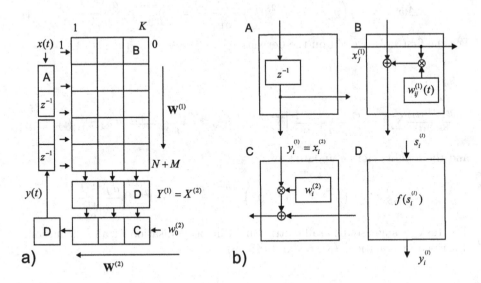

Fig. 2. Recal phase of the RMLP network and the structures of processing elements

Parallel realisation of the recall phase algorithm uses architecture which requires many simple processing elements. The parallel realisation of the RMLP network in recal phase is depicted in Fig. 2a and its processing elements in Fig. 2b. Four kinds of functional processing elements take put in the proposed solution. The aim of PE (A) is to delay inputs and outputs signals, so that values of signals appear on inputs of network from previous instances. Elements of type (B) create matrix which includes values of weights of the first layer. The input signals are entered for rows elements parallelly, multiplied by weights and received results are summed in columns. The activation function for each neuron un the first layer is calculated after calculation of product $\mathbf{w}_i^{(1)}\mathbf{x}^{(1)}$ in element of type (D). The outputs of neurons in the first layer are inputs the second layer simultaneously. The product $\mathbf{w}^{(2)}\mathbf{x}^{(2)}$ for the second layer is obtained in elements of type (C) similarly.

The gradient method is used to train the RMLP network. For this purpose it is nesessary to calculate derivative of the goal funcion with respect to each weight. For weights in the second layer we obtain the following derivative

$$\frac{dy^{(2)}(t)}{dw_\alpha^{(2)}} = $$
$$\frac{df\left(s^{(2)}(t)\right)}{ds^{(2)}(t)} \left[y_\alpha^{(1)}(t) + \sum_{i=0}^{K} w_i^{(2)} \frac{df\left(s_i^{(1)}(t)\right)}{ds_i^{(1)}(t)} \sum_{j=1}^{M} w_{i,j+N}^{(1)} \frac{dy^{(2)}(t-M-1+j)}{dw_\alpha^{(2)}} \right] \tag{3}$$

Weights are updated according to the steepest descent algorithm as follows

$$\Delta w_\alpha^{(2)} = -\eta \left(y^{(2)}(t) - d^{(2)}(t) \right) \frac{dy^{(2)}(t)}{dw_\alpha^{(2)}} = -\eta \varepsilon^{(2)}(t) \frac{dy^{(2)}(t)}{dw_\alpha^{(2)}} \tag{4}$$

For the first layer we obtain the derivative

$$\frac{dy^{(2)}(t)}{dw_{\alpha\beta}^{(1)}} = $$
$$\frac{df\left(s^{(2)}(t)\right)}{ds^{(2)}(t)} \sum_{i=1}^{K} w_i^{(2)} \frac{df\left(s_i^{(1)}(t)\right)}{ds_i^{(1)}(t)} \left[\sum_{j=1}^{M} w_{i,j+N}^{(1)} \frac{dy^{(2)}(t-M-1+j)}{dw_{\alpha\beta}^{(2)}} + \delta_{i\alpha} x_\beta^{(1)}(t) \right] \tag{5}$$

and the weights can be updated by

$$\Delta w_{\alpha\beta}^{(1)} = -\eta \left(y^{(2)}(t) - d^{(2)}(t) \right) \frac{dy^{(2)}(t)}{dw_{\alpha\beta}^{(1)}} = -\eta \varepsilon^{(2)}(t) \frac{dy^{(2)}(t)}{dw_{\alpha\beta}^{(1)}} \tag{6}$$

The task of suggested parallel structure will be realisation of all calculations described by equations (3), (4) and (5), (6).

2   Parallel Realisation

In order to determine derivative in the second layer it is required to know its previous values. Derivative values will be stored in (E) PE Fig. 3b. These elements will create matrix of the dimension $M(K+1)$ Fig. 3a. They will be useful

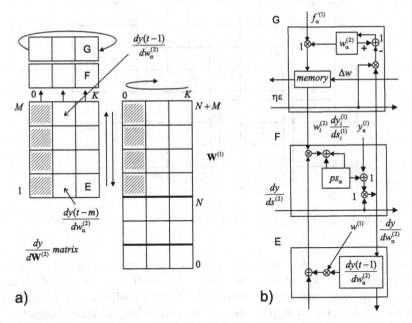

Fig. 3. Idea of learning the second layer and the processing elements

for realizing operations given by equations (5) and (6). Presented idea relies on multiplication of respondent elements of derivative matrix $\frac{dy}{dw_\alpha}$ by corresponding to them weights of the first layer Fig. 3a. Then, received produtcts in the entire column are added to each other. At the same time, the result obtained is multiplied by $w_i^{(2)} \frac{dy_i^{(1)}}{ds_i^{(1)}}$ and accumulated. In the next step, first column is moved to the extreme right position (as a result of the rotation to the left) $W^{(1)}$ matrix. After a rotation of columns the previous actions are repeated. These operations are repeated $(K+1)$ times until the first column of the matrix will revert to the original place. The value of $y_\alpha^{(1)}$ is added to accumulated value and next the sum is multiplied by derivative $\frac{dy}{ds^{(2)}}$. In this way the new value of the derivative $\frac{dy}{dw_\alpha^{(1)}}$ is obtained.

The calculated value of the derivative is placed in the top row of the array, and then is moving down. This newly calculated derivative is used in PE (G) to update the second layer weights according to the equation (4). Suggested solution leads to acceleration of calculations, but it is not optimal solution yet. It results from the fact that after multiplication of both matrices, serial summation follows. In this case multiplication and addition is realized in $M(K+1)$ steps. It is easily seen that changing manner of entering of values from weights matrix to derivatives matrix we can reduce the amount of steps required for execution of the multiplication and addition operations to $M + (K+1)$. The manner of weights entering is presented in Fig. 4. The multiplication is realised only for elements depicted by the thick line. In the first step only last row is taken into

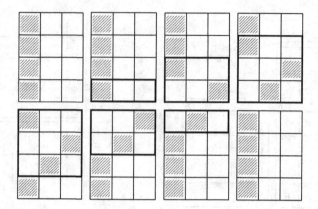

Fig. 4. Method of entering weights for the second layer learning

account. In the next cycles the number of rows is incremented, and the rows that have participated in multiplication are subject to rotation. Rotation is done from step one to the left until all rows reach the starting position. The rows are no longer included in the multiplication. As a result, the proposed modifications in subsequent steps, making the multiplication and summation, as described in the first scenario. In this case we will receive the sum of the new inner product without waiting the M steps. For the first layer the derivatives $\frac{dy(t-j)}{dw_{\alpha\beta}}$ are placed

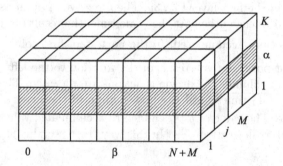

Fig. 5. Cuboid matrix of the derivatives $\frac{dy(t-j)}{dw_{\alpha\beta}}$ for first layer learning

in the cuboid matrix of the processing elements, see Fig. 5. It can be splited into K matrices (Fig. 6) which are parallely processed. For simplicity next figures show structures only for one such matrix. The architecture of processing elements dedicated to realization of first layer lerning is shown in Fig. 7a. In this case weights are given step by step to the derivatives matrix, in which the total sums are calculated according to eq. (5). Then, in the elements (F), see Fig. 3b, above the array new values of derivatives are calculated. These values are sent back to

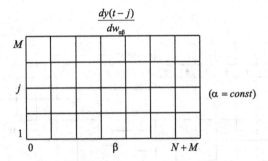

Fig. 6. Single matrix (2D) of the cuboid matrix (3D)

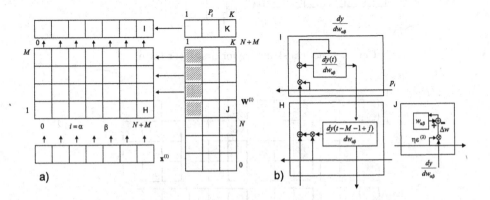

Fig. 7. Idea of learning for first layer and the processing elements

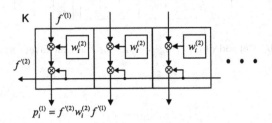

Fig. 8. The auxiliary vector

the derivatives matrix, and in this way the new value of derivatives overrides the previous etc. The newly obtained values of derrivatives from all two dimensional matrices are used to updating weights (6). This is done in elements of the type (J), see Fig. 7b. The use of these elements simplifies the calculation of the vector P see (5) and Fig. 8.

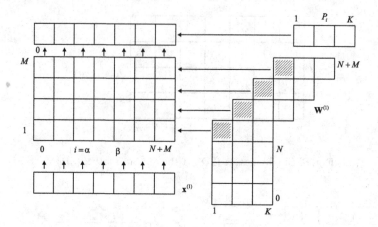

Fig. 9. Practical structure for first layer learning

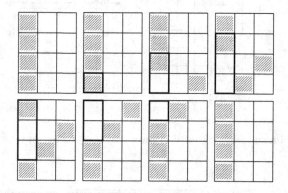

Fig. 10. Method of entering weights for the first layer learning

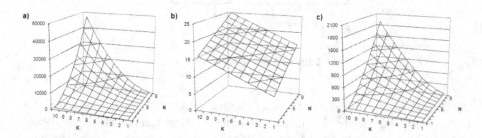

Fig. 11. Number of times cycles in a) classical, b) parallel implementation and c) performance factor classical/parallel

The optimal performance of the structure is obtained by the specific way of sending weight values. The practical structure for the first layer learning is shown in Fig. 9. Weights are sent in the following steps as indicated by the thick line in Fig. 10 The layout of all weights is identical in Fig. 10 and Fig. 4 which means that weights of the first layer, necessary for the calculations in the first and second layers can by sent fully paralelly.

3 Conclusion

In this paper the parallel realisation of the RMLP neural network was proposed. We assume that all multiplications and additions operations take the same time unit. For simplicity of the result presentation we suppose that M=N in the input vector of the network.

We can compare computational performance of the RMLP parallel implementation with sequential architectures up to N=M=10 for inputs and 10 neurons (K) in the hidden layer of neural network. Computational complexity of the RMPL learning is of order $\mathcal{O}(K^4)$ and equals $4M^2K^2 + 6MK^2 + 10MK + K^2 + 2M + 9K + 8$. In the presented parallel architecture each iteration requires only $K + M + 5$ time units (see Fig. 11). Performance factor (see Fig. 11) of parallel realisation of the RMLP algorithm achieves nearly 1900 for N=M=10 inputs and K=10 of neurons in the hidden layer and it grows fast when those numbers grow. We observed that the performance of the proposed solution is promising. In the future research we plan to design parallel realisation of learning of neuro-fuzzy structures [9], [10], [11], [12], [13], [14], [15], [16], [17], [18], [19].

References

1. Bilski, J., Litwiński, S., Smoląg, J.: Parallel Realisation of QR Algorithm for Neural Networks Learning. In: Rutkowski, L., Siekmann, J.H., Tadeusiewicz, R., Zadeh, L.A. (eds.) ICAISC 2004. LNCS (LNAI), vol. 3070, pp. 158–165. Springer, Heidelberg (2004)
2. Bilski, J., Smoląg, J.: Parallel Realisation of the Recurrent RTRN Neural Network Learning. In: Rutkowski, L., Tadeusiewicz, R., Zadeh, L.A., Zurada, J.M. (eds.) ICAISC 2008. LNCS (LNAI), vol. 5097, pp. 11–16. Springer, Heidelberg (2008)
3. Bilski, J., Smoląg, J.: Parallel Realisation of the Recurrent Elman Neural Network Learning. In: Rutkowski, L., Scherer, R., Tadeusiewicz, R., Zadeh, L.A., Zurada, J.M. (eds.) ICAISC 2010. LNCS (LNAI), vol. 6114, pp. 19–25. Springer, Heidelberg (2010)
4. Kolen, J.F., Kremer, S.C.: A Field Guide to Dynamical Recurrent Neural Networks. IEEE Press (2001)
5. Korbicz, J., Patan, K., Obuchowicz, A.: Dynamic neural networks for process modelling in fault detection and isolation. Int. J. Appl. Math. Comput. Sci. 9(3), 519–546 (1999)
6. Smoląg, J., Bilski, J.: A systolic array for fast learning of neural networks. In: Proc. of V Conf. Neural Networks and Soft Computing, Zakopane, pp. 754–758 (2000)
7. Smoląg, J., Rutkowski, L., Bilski, J.: Systolic array for neural networks. In: Proc. of IV Conf. Neural Networks and Their Applications, Zakopane, pp. 487–497 (1999)

8. Williams, R., Zipser, D.: A learning algorithm for continually running fully recurrent neural networks. Neural Computation, 270–280 (1989)
9. Korytkowski, M., Scherer, R., Rutkowski, L.: On Combining Backpropagation with Boosting. In: International Joint Conference on Neural Networks, IEEE World Congress on Computational Intelligence, Vancouver, BC, Canada, pp. 1274–1277 (2006)
10. Korytkowski, M., Rutkowski, L., Scherer, R.: From Ensemble of Fuzzy Classifiers to Single Fuzzy Rule Base Classifier. In: Rutkowski, L., Tadeusiewicz, R., Zadeh, L.A., Zurada, J.M. (eds.) ICAISC 2008. LNCS (LNAI), vol. 5097, pp. 265–272. Springer, Heidelberg (2008)
11. Nowicki, R.: Rough Sets in the Neuro-Fuzzy Architectures Based on Monotonic Fuzzy Implications. In: Rutkowski, L., Siekmann, J.H., Tadeusiewicz, R., Zadeh, L.A. (eds.) ICAISC 2004. LNCS (LNAI), vol. 3070, pp. 510–517. Springer, Heidelberg (2004)
12. Nowicki, R.: Rough Sets in the Neuro-Fuzzy Architectures Based on Non-monotonic Fuzzy Implications. In: Rutkowski, L., Siekmann, J.H., Tadeusiewicz, R., Zadeh, L.A. (eds.) ICAISC 2004. LNCS (LNAI), vol. 3070, pp. 518–525. Springer, Heidelberg (2004)
13. Rutkowski, L., Cpałka, K.: A general approach to neuro - fuzzy systems. In: Proceedings of the 10th IEEE International Conference on Fuzzy Systems, Melbourne, December 2-5, vol. 3, pp. 1428–1431 (2001)
14. Rutkowski, L., Cpałka, K.: A neuro-fuzzy controller with a compromise fuzzy reasoning. Control and Cybernetics 31(2), 297–308 (2002)
15. Scherer, R.: Boosting Ensemble of Relational Neuro-fuzzy Systems. In: Rutkowski, L., Tadeusiewicz, R., Zadeh, L.A., Żurada, J.M. (eds.) ICAISC 2006. LNCS (LNAI), vol. 4029, pp. 306–313. Springer, Heidelberg (2006)
16. Scherer, R.: Neuro-fuzzy Systems with Relation Matrix. In: Rutkowski, L., Scherer, R., Tadeusiewicz, R., Zadeh, L.A., Zurada, J.M. (eds.) ICAISC 2010. LNCS (LNAI), vol. 6113, pp. 210–215. Springer, Heidelberg (2010)
17. Starczewski, J., Rutkowski, L.: Neuro-Fuzzy Systems of Type 2. In: Proc. 1st Int'l Conf. on Fuzzy Systems and Knowledge Discovery, Singapore, vol. 2, pp. 458–462 (2002)
18. Starczewski, J., Rutkowski, L.: Interval type 2 neuro-fuzzy systems based on interval consequents. In: Rutkowski, L., Kacprzyk, J. (eds.) Neural Networks and Soft Computing, pp. 570–577. Physica-Verlag, Springer-Verlag Company, Heidelberg, New York (2003)
19. Starczewski, J.T., Rutkowski, L.: Connectionist Structures of Type 2 Fuzzy Inference Systems. In: Wyrzykowski, R., Dongarra, J., Paprzycki, M., Waśniewski, J. (eds.) PPAM 2001. LNCS, vol. 2328, pp. 634–642. Springer, Heidelberg (2002)

An Innovative Hybrid Neuro-wavelet Method for Reconstruction of Missing Data in Astronomical Photometric Surveys

Giacomo Capizzi[1], Christian Napoli[2], and Lucio Paternò[3]

[1] Dpt. of Electric, Electronic and Informatic Eng., University of Catania, Italy
gcapizzi@diees.unict.it
[2] Department of Physics and Astronomy, University of Catania, Italy
chnapoli@gmail.com
[3] Astrophysical Observatory of Catania, National Institute for Astrophysics, Italy
lucio.paterno@oact.inaf.it

Abstract. The investigation of solar-like oscillations for probing the star interiors has encountered a tremendous growth in the last decade. For ground based observations the most important difficulties in properly identifying the true oscillation frequencies of the stars are produced by the gaps in the observation time-series and the presence of atmospheric plus the intrinsic stellar granulation noise, unavoidable also in the case of space observations. In this paper an innovative neuro-wavelet method for the reconstruction of missing data from photometric signals is presented. The prediction of missing data was done by using a composite neuro-wavelet reconstruction system composed by two neural networks separately trained. The combination of these two neural networks obtains a "forward and backward" reconstruction. This technique was able to provide reconstructed data with an error greatly lower than the absolute a priori measurement error. The reconstructed signal frequency spectrum matched the expected spectrum with high accuracy.

Keywords: Kepler Mission, Recurrent Neural Networks, Wavelet Theory, Photometry, Missing Data.

1 Introduction

The investigation of solar-like oscillations for main sequence, sub giant and red giant stars for probing the star interiors has encountered a tremendous growth in the last decade. This science, known as Asteroseismology, is fairly increasing our knowledge about stellar physics, especially after the launch of the NASA space mission Kepler in 2009 [1]. The data acquired for the study of solar-like oscillations are mainly of two different types, spectroscopic and photometric. Although in both cases they are in the form of a temporal sequence of measurements (time-series) and are able to probe the same physical quantities, the information carried on is not equivalent and their usage appears to be complementary. Ground-based observations, which usually detect oscillations by exploiting very

L. Rutkowski et al. (Eds.): ICAISC 2012, Part I, LNCS 7267, pp. 21–29, 2012.
© Springer-Verlag Berlin Heidelberg 2012

high-precision Doppler shift measurements of the spectroscopic lines, can probe a wider number of modes of oscillations because of their high sensitivity to spatial resolution upon the stellar disk. Nonetheless, ground-based projects are able to follow up one target per time and heavily suffer the alternating of day and night due to Earth's rotation, which hence does not allow for continuous-time observations. Furthermore, the effort and workload required for assembling the spectrometers used to acquire the data do not allow to use such systems on space. For ground-based observations the most important difficulties in properly identifying the true oscillation frequencies of the stars are produced by the gaps in the observation time-series and the presence of atmospheric plus the intrinsic stellar granulation noise, the latter unavoidable also in the case of space observations. The gaps are caused by the alternation of day and night and casual interruptions of data flow due to bad weather conditions; the first introduces possible shifts of 11.57 μHz in the identified frequencies and the second spurious frequencies. The noise can produce peaks whose amplitude is even larger than the real stellar frequencies. All the mentioned disturbs make the identification of stellar oscillations uncertain in several cases. In this paper the problem of data prediction in order to reconstruct the gaps present in the observation time-series has been addressed by using an hybrid computation methods based on wavelet decomposition and recurrent neural networks (RNNs). Wavelet analysis has been used in order to reduce the data redundancies and selectively remove stellar granulation noise so obtaining a representation that can express their intrinsic structure, while the neural networks (NNs) are used for the exploiting the complexity of non-linear data correlation and to perform the data prediction. In order to minimize the error propagation, we designed a composite network, with doubled neural paths, to obtain a "forward and backward" reconstruction. This composite WRNN uses as input several time steps of the signal, in the past and in the future with respect to the gap.

2   Kepler Data as a Probe for Testing WRNN Method

New missions based on photometric acquisitions have been launched on space in the few past years. The latest one in particular, the NASA *Kepler* mission, which is presently in the middle of its running, is providing an enormous amount of an unprecedented quality data, with a combined differential photometric precision high to $2 \cdot 10^{-6}$ for a 12th magnitude solar-like star for a 6.5 hour integration [2]. In fact, the photometric observations allow the great advantage of acquiring brightness measurements on hundred of targets at the same time and, most of all, they can be carried out directly from space, allowing scientists to weed out the problem of the daily gap, which strongly hampers the quality of the results, but not the problem of granulation noise. Long term acquisitions of brightness variations on the surface of stars are able to tell us a lot about solar-like oscillations as they are directly correlated to variations in temperature of the surface layers. By the continuous production of new data sets, many interesting studies can be made upon the stars falling in the Kepler field o view (FOV), from early

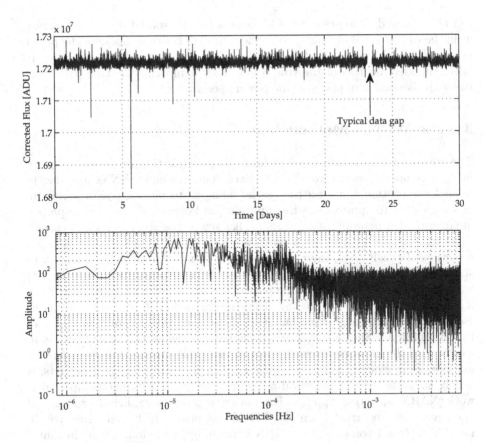

Fig. 1. The light flux time-series and the relative power spectrum

main sequence to red giants stars. The data used in this paper were collected
by Kepler satellite with a sampling rate of about 58.7 s, as light flux measurement and corrected flux estimation with the related absolute error. The data
were relative to the star KIC 3102411 measured at short cadence in the season
Q2.2. The most common way to analyze a time-series and thus to derive the
frequencies of oscillations is to convert the data acquired on the time domain to
a set of values that range in a frequency domain (the Power Spectrum). This
is done in general by adopting a Fourier analysis on the time-series, both of
radial velocities (from Doppler shift measurements) and of radiation flux counts
(from photometric acquisitions) [3]. The result is shown in Fig. 1, where the
upper panel represents the light-curve, i.e. a time-series of radiation flux counts,
for a star observed by Kepler and the lower panel is its relative Fourier transform reported in a logarithmic scale. As clearly visible, a bump of power arises
around 150 μHz, showing the typical pattern for a set of p-mode frequencies
that roughly follows a gaussian shape peaked at its maximum frequency ν_{max}.
As one can intuitively understand, the longer is the observation run, the higher
is the frequency resolution at which the frequency peaks in the power spectrum

can be measured. The presence of huge gaps equally spaced in the time-series, as in the case of the daily gap, causes the arising of fictitious peaks in the power spectrum, which are not real frequencies of oscillation and that consequently affect the identification of the true p modes by hampering the true pattern of the solar-like excess of power in the power spectrum.

3   The WRNN Methodology

The reconstruction of missing data from photometric time-series was done by using a composite neuro-wavelet reconstruction technique. RNNs are able to predict the continuation of a time series amounts to picking one of a class of functions so as to approximate the input-output behavior in the most appropriate manner. For deterministic dynamical behaviors, the observation at a current time point can be modeled as a function of a certain number of preceding observations. In such cases, the model used should have some internal memory to store and update context information [4],[5]. This is achieved by feeding the network with a delayed version of the past observations, commonly referred to as a delay vector or tapped delay line. These networks do not try to achieve credit assignment back through time but instead use the previous state as a part of the current input. Such a simple approach may be seen as a natural extension to feedforward the networks in much the same way that ARMA models generalize autoregressive models. A network with a rich representation of past outputs, is a fully connected recurrent neural network, known as the Williams-Zipser network (NARX networks) [6],[7],[8]. For stochastic phenomena, like the considered ones, real time recurrent learning (RTRL) has proven to be very effective, in fact RTRL based training of the RNN is made upon minimizing the instantaneous squared error at the output of the first neuron of the RNN [6],[9]. The reconstruction system is composed by two NARX RNNs with the same topology and number of neurons but separately trained with RTRL algorithm (Fig. 4). A complete description of RTRL algorithm, NARX and RNNs can be found in [8]. The first one is trained to predict the signal samples one step ahead in the future, while the second one is trained to predict the signal samples one step backward in the past. The combination of these two neural networks obtains a "forward and backward" reconstruction (Fig. 4). This reconstruction technique was able to minimize the error propagation and, also, the possibility to conduct a double check verification of the reconstructed data. At a first time the selected neural networks were trained to reconstruct missing data from a photometric time-serie which was yet proven to have an high cross-correlation degree. Although different kinds of topology and size variations were implemented, the system was not able to provide predictions with enough accuracy. On the other hand, there was evidence of misleading data sequences avoiding a correct training of the networks. At a successive step the same procedure was adopted, but, this time, providing as input the wavelet decompositions of the signal. A function $\psi \in L^2(\mathbb{R})$ that exhibit the following properties:

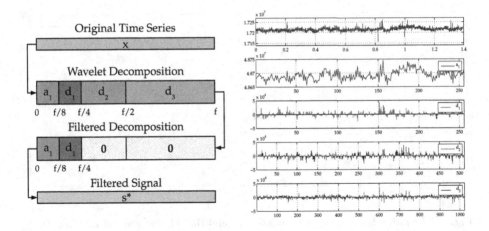

Fig. 2. Wavelet decomposition and thresholding

$$\int\limits_{-\infty}^{+\infty} \psi(x)\ dx = 0. \tag{1}$$

$$\|\psi(x)\|^2 = \int\limits_{-\infty}^{+\infty} \psi(x)\psi^*(x)\ dx = 1. \tag{2}$$

is called wavelet if it can be used to define a Hilbert basis, that is a complete system, for the Hilbert space $L^2(\mathbb{R})$ of square integrable functions. The Hilbert basis is constructed as the family of functions $\{\psi_{j,k} : j, k \in \mathbb{Z}\}$ by means of dyadic translations and dilations of ψ, $\psi_{j,k}(x) = \sqrt{2^j}(2^j x - k)$. For an extended treatment one can consult [10],[11],[12]. It is known in literature that the star granulation produces temporal variations in the light flux. These variations, at frequencies greater than 100 μHz, produce a quasi-white signal-related noise effect. Even if it is not possible to adapt a neural network to this kind of noise, the used wavelet decomposition permits to locate the coefficients bands related to frequencies from about 4250 μHz to higher frequencies. Thresholding to zeros these two related bands (Fig. 2), the resulting coefficients and residuals carries the relevant information for the predictions. These wavelet coefficients were so provided as input $(u_i(t))$ to the system. Another positive effect is that these wavelet coefficients provide a less redundant representation of the information carried out by the signal. This effect was proven to be an advantage for a correct and efficient training of recurrent neural networks [13],[14],[15]. As yet shown by a previous work of the authors [16], a properly designed hybrid neuro-wavelet recurrent network is able to execute wavelet reconstruction and prediction of a signal. The selected neural networks are composed by two hidden layers of 16 neurons and a single output neuron. The wavelet decomposition of the time

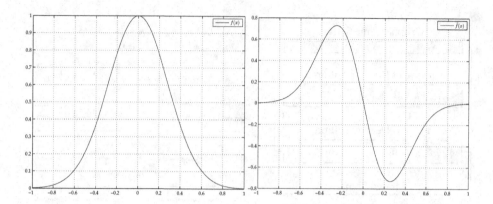

Fig. 3. The radial basis transfer function $f(x)$ and the relative wavelet function $\tilde{f}(x)$

series is given as N × 4 input vectors with a 3-step delay and a 1-step output feedback. While the forward network was trained with coefficients at time t_0 to predict output signals $s(t_0 + 1)$, the backward network was trained to backward reconstruct the signal at a previous time $(t_0 - 1)$ in the past. For clarity, on describing the forward neural network with a functional of the type $F[u(t)] = y(t + 1)$, it follows that the backward network will be described by a similar $\tilde{F}[u(-t)] = \tilde{y}(-t - 1)$. In this manner, at the end of a correct training of the selected neural networks, it will be possible to reconstruct missing part of the data series using both the neural networks. The forward network will reconstruct forward in time the missing part from the beginning to his mid-point. The backward network will reconstruct backward in time from the ending to the same mid-point of the same gap. The resulting reconstructed signal $\tilde{s}$, from a signal s with missing data in the interval $[t_1; t_3]$ will be:

$$\tilde{s}(t) = \begin{cases} s\,(t) & t \in\,]-\infty\,,\,t_1 \quad [\\ y\,(t) & t \in [\quad t_1\,,\,t_2 \quad [\\ \tilde{y}\,(t) & t \in\,]\quad t_2\,,\,t_3 \quad] \\ s\,(t) & t \in\,]\quad t_3\,,\,+\infty\,[\end{cases} \tag{3}$$

In the present paper the implemented WRNN is able to reconstruct a signal from wavelet coefficients, but it is also capable to predict these wavelet coefficients, and, then, to reconstruct the predicted signal. To obtain this behavior some rules had to be applied during the design and implementation work. For reasons that will be cleared ahead, all the hidden layers have a pair neuron number, and, also, to permit in sequence the wavelet coefficient exploitation and the signal reconstruction, a double hidden layer is required in the proposed architecture. As for the hidden layers the neurons activation function (transfer function) have to simulate a wavelet function. It is not possible to implement a wavelet function itself as transfer function for a forecast oriented time predictive neural network,

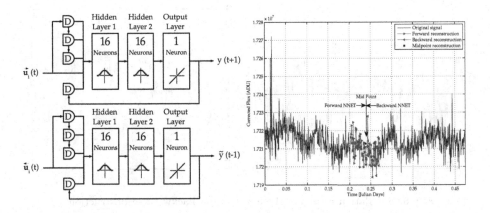

Fig. 4. Neural networks structures (left), Forward and Backward reconstruction (right)

this because wavelets do not verify some basic properties such as the absence of local minima, and does not provide by itself a sufficiently graded response [17]. In the existent range of possible transfer functions only some particular classes approximate the functional form of a wavelet. In this work the radial basis functions (radbas) were chosen as transfer functions, indeed this particular kind of functions well describes in first approximation half of a wavelet, even if these functions do not verify the properties shown by (1) and (2). Anyway, after scaling, shift and repetition of the chosen activation function, it is possible to obtain several mother wavelet filters. Let $f : [-1; 1] \to \mathbb{R}^+$ to be the choosen transfer function, then

$$\tilde{f}(x) = \tilde{f}(x + 2k) = \begin{cases} + f(2x + 1) & x \in [-1, 0] \\ - f(2x - 1) & x \in [0, 1] \end{cases} \quad \forall k \in \mathbb{Z} \qquad (4)$$

verifies all the properties of a wavelet function. So it is possible for the selected neural networks to simulate a wavelet by using the radbas function defined in the $[-1; 1]$ real domain. It is indeed possible to verify that

$$\int_{2h+1}^{2k+1} \tilde{f}(x) \, dx = 0 \ \forall \, h < k \in \mathbb{Z} \qquad (5)$$

It was shown that, in order to simulate a wavelet function, the chosen transfer functions must be symmetrically periodical to emulate a wavelet. This is the reason for choosing a pair number of neurons in the aim to have the same number of positive and negative layer weights in the reconstruction layer. Theoretically, if this happens, then the neuron pairs of the second layer are emulating exactly a reconstruction filter. Althoug this was a theoretical schema, there are strong reasons for the weights, in this experimental setup, to have a non-zero sum, because the neural network beyond to perform the inverse wavelet transform must perform also the signal prediction.

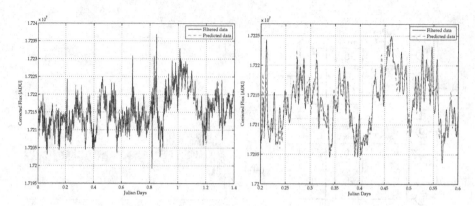

Fig. 5. Simulation results of the forward and backward reconstruction

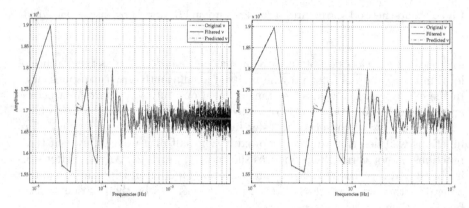

Fig. 6. Simulation results in the frequency domain

4   Results and Conclusion

We performed simulations on one month photometric survey of the star KIC 3102411 observed during the season Q2.2 from the Kepler orbital telescope with a sampling rate of about 58.847 s and so a sampling frequency of almost $1.7 \cdot 10^{-2}$ Hz. Wavelet analysis was used in order to remove the data sparsity and to threshold the higher frequencies (mostly characteristic of the star granulation and intrinsically affected by a signal-correlated time-evolving noise). In particular the lower two sub-bands of the decomposition were substituted with zero-vectors. In this manner the filtered reconstructed signal was transferred to the neural networks. To test the capabilities of the system, several gaps, ranging from 2 to 10 samples, were artificially placed at random positions in the data series. The trained forward and backward reconstruction system was able to reconstruct the missing data with an error greatly lower than the absolute a priori measurement error. The reconstructed signal frequency spectrum matches the expected spectrum with high accuracy, as shown in Figs. 5 and 6. This paper has outlined the advantage of a composite hybrid neuro-wavelet system as advanced reconstruction tool for photometric time-series. This technique leads to implement a new generation of tools based on recurrent neural networks with the future possibility of further developments such as embedded system for data reconstruction of corrupted time-series for noise-affected survey contests.

References

1. Chaplin, W.J., et al.: Ensemble Asteroseismology of Solar-Type Stars with the NASA Kepler Mission. Science 332(6026) (2011)
2. Koch, D.G., et al.: Kepler Mission Design, Realized Photometric Performance, and Early Science. The Astrophysical Journal Letters 713(2) (2010)
3. Gray, D.F.: The Observation and Analysis of Stellar Photospheres, 3rd edn. Cambridge Press (2005)
4. Lapedes, A., Faber, R.: A self-optimizing, nonsimmetrical neural net for content addressable memory and pattern recognition. Physica D 22, 247–259 (1986)
5. Connor, J.T., Martin, R.D., Atlas, L.E.: Recurrent Neural Networks and Robust Time Series Prediction. IEEE Trans. on Neural Networks 5(2), 240–254 (1994)
6. William, R.J., Zipser, D.: A learning algorithm for continually running fully recurrent neural networks. Neural Comput. 1(1), 270–280 (1989)
7. William, R.J., Zipser, D.: Experimental analysis of the real-time recurrent learning algorithm. Connection Sci. 1(1), 87–111 (1989)
8. Mandic, D.P., Chambers, J.A.: Recurrent Neural Networks for Prediction: Learning Algorithms, Architectures and Stability. Wiley, New York (2001)
9. Haykin, S.: Neural Networks and Learning Machines. Prentice-Hall, Englewood Cliffs (2008)
10. Strang, G., Nguyen, T.: Wavelets and Filter Banks. Wellesley-Cambridge Press (1996)
11. Sweldens, W.: The lifting scheme: A construction of second generation wavelets. SIAM J. Math. Anal. 26(2), 511–546 (1997)
12. Mallat, S.: A Wavelet Tour of Signal Processing, The Sparse Way, 3rd edn. Academic Press (2009)
13. Napoli, C., Bonanno, F., Capizzi, G.: An hybrid neuro-wavelet approach for long-term prediction of solar wind. In: IAU Symposium No. 274, Advances in Plasma Astrophysics, Giardini Naxos, Italy, pp. 247–249 (2010)
14. Napoli, C., Bonanno, F., Capizzi, G.: Exploiting solar wind time series correlation with magnetospheric response by using an hybrid neuro-wavelet approach. In: IAU Symposium No. 274, Advances in Plasma Astrophysics, Giardini Naxos, Italy, pp. 250–252 (2010)
15. Bonanno, F., Capizzi, G., Napoli, C.: A wavelet based prediction for Wind and Solar Energy for Long-Term simulation of integrated generation systems. In: 20th IEEE International Symposium on Power Electronics, Electrical Drives, Automation and Motion, Pisa, Italy, pp. 586–592 (2010)
16. Bonanno, F., Capizzi, G., Napoli, C., et al.: An Innovative Wavelet Recurrent Neural Network Based Approach for Solar Radiation Prediction. Submitted to IEEE Transaction on Sustainable Energy
17. Gupta, M.M., Jin, L., Homma, N.: Static and Dynamic Neural Networks. Wiley, New York (2003)

Speeding Up the Training of Neural Networks with CUDA Technology

Daniel Salles Chevitarese, Dilza Szwarcman, and Marley Vellasco*

Department of Electrical Engineering, Pontifical Catholic University,
Rua Marquês de São Vicente, 225, Gávea - Rio de Janeiro, Brazil
daniel@ele.puc-rio.br
http://www.puc-rio.br

Abstract. Training feed-forward neural networks can take a long time when there is a large amount of data to be used, even when training with more efficient algorithms like Levenberg-Marquardt. Parallel architectures have been a common solution in the area of high performance computing, since the technology used in current processors is reaching the limits of speed. An architecture that has been gaining popularity is the GPGPU (General-Purpose computing on Graphics Processing Units), which has received large investments from companies such as NVIDIA that introduced CUDA (Compute Unified Device Architecture) technology. This paper proposes a faster implementation of neural networks training with Levenberg-Marquardt algorithm using CUDA. The results obtained demonstrate that the whole training time can be almost 30 times shorter than code using Intel Math Library (MKL). A case study for classifying electrical company customers is presented.

Keywords: Artificial Neural Networks, Software Engineering, High Performance Com-puting, GPGPU, CUDA.

1 Introduction

Neural networks are very useful for solving complex problems (pattern recognition, forecasting, classification) and there are already many software libraries that support the modeling, creation, training and testing of various types of known networks. However, the available libraries present limitations when the problem size or complexity exceeds certain threshold, such as the case when the database used in the early stages of training, validation and testing contains a huge amount of information (patterns/attributes).

Besides the database size, there is also a tradeoff between the complexity of the algorithm used for training and the number of iterations needed to reach the network's performance goal, which greatly affects the total training time. For example, if a neural network is trained by an algorithm of back propagation with gradient descent, the cost of each step is relatively small; however, many steps are required to train the network. On the other hand, a greater order gradient algorithm requires much less iterations, but with a much greater computational cost for each iteration [5].

There are already several studies using graphics cards to propagate input data through feedforward neural networks, but the learning algorithm is not implemented in CUDA.

---

* IEEE Senior Member.

L. Rutkowski et al. (Eds.): ICAISC 2012, Part I, LNCS 7267, pp. 30–38, 2012.

For example, [2] and [7] have used neural networks for character recognition. In the second paper, the program implemented in CUDA was almost six times faster than the same program running on the CPU. In [1] a program for training neural networks was implemented using the gradient descent algorithm, which was compared to Matlab and resulted in tens of times faster.

This work proposes a faster implementation of neural networks training with Levenberg - Marquardt algorithm (LMA) using CUDA and compares its performance with an implementation using Intel MKL [6], a math library which is known for its outstanding efficiency.

The results obtained with the execution on the GPU of the training phase using LMA were very promising. Although only part of the algorithm was processed on the graphics card, again of almost 30 times faster was obtained when compared with the same algorithm running with the help of MKL.

This paper has been organized as follows: Section 2 presents an overview of CUDA Architecture; Section 3 describes the architecture proposed for solving the problem; Section 4 demonstrates the experiments performed and lastly, Section 5 presents the conclusions drawn from this work.

2 GPGPU and CUDA

While parallel solutions are becoming more common, graphics cards are becoming powerful computers and highly parallel, mostly because of the digital entertainment industry and its demand for high definition graphics. The reason for the huge discrepancy between conventional processors and graphics processors is that a GPU (Graphics Processing Units), unlike the CPU, uses more transistors for processing than for flow control or cache memory [8].

The GPU architecture is better suited to problems whose data can be broken into smaller pieces and be processed in parallel. As these pieces are processed by the same program and at the same time, they do not require a sophisticated flow control. Moreover, as there are many arithmetic calculations to be performed, the latency of memory access is diminished by data buffering instead of the use of great cache memories.

The NVIDIA architecture has three types of abstraction: the hierarchy of thread groups, the shared memories and synchronization barriers. This architecture makes the learning time relatively small and requires few extensions to programming languages. Moreover, the abstractions provide parallelism both in data and in threads, requiring, from the programmer, only a simple division of tasks and data [8].

Another advantage of the abstractions is that they help the developer divide the problem into smaller tasks that can be solved independently and, therefore, in parallel. This decomposition is made so as the threads can cooperate to solve the subtasks, and, at the same time, make scalability possible, since the threads can be scheduled to be resolved in any available core. A program compiled in CUDA, which is also called kernel, may, in that case, run on a machine regardless of the number of processors, which will be checked at runtime [8]. Thus, the programming model comprises several types of clients, supporting cards with different number of processors (this number can vary from ten to thousands of processors).

3   The Proposed LMA in CUDA

In this work, neural network training is carried out by the Levenberg - Marquardt Algorithm, which calculates the neuron's errors in a way equivalent to conventional back - propagation, but based on the Jacobian [4]. In order to combine a reduced number of epochs with low time cost iteration, this study proposes a new design of a Levenberg - Marquardt training which runs on a GPU (Graphic Processor Unit) supporting CUDA. The new model uses the computational power of graphics cards to calculate the critical point of the training algorithm, that is, the change in the network's weights given in Equation (1) [4]. Its processing time generally represents more than 70% of the total training time if the training data set is small, and can reach almost 90% of the time for larger sets. This is because Equation (1) includes the computation of a Jacobian matrix of size (w, p), where w is the number of network weights and p is the number of patterns. In this equation, x is the weights vector of the network and $\underline{e}(\underline{x})$ is the error vector, while μ is a parameter that controls the balance between speed and stability. This matrix can easily contain millions of elements even if the training data includes just a few thousand patterns.

$$\triangle x = -\left[J\left(\underline{x}\right)J^T\left(\underline{x}\right) + \mu I\right]^{-1}J^T\left(\underline{x}\right)\underline{e}\left(\underline{x}\right) \tag{1}$$

The use of graphics cards has been proved promising, since the number of processing cores on a single card can be up to hundreds. In addition, the time to manage threads in conventional languages can cost more than 10% of the total training time, while the NVIDIA architecture can handle CUDA threads without additional cost. Another positive point of NVIDIA technology is the possibility of working with multiple graphics cards, allowing the execution of several concurrent trainings.

Initially, this work proposed the use of the graphics card to calculate the Jacobian square matrix $(J(\underline{x})J^T(\underline{x}))$, which is a part of Equation (1). For that matter, a function (from NVIDIA) copies all data to the global memory. Once in global memory, a kernel calculates it and, after that, another CUDA function transfers the result back to the RAM of the CPU. The second model was to create a kernel that calculates the whole equation in the GPU, so the vector with the weights variation is obtained directly from it, as shown in Figure 1. In this figure, the black box indicates the training starting point or a new epoch, including the patterns propagation through the neural network. The following stages calculate the squared errors of the network, as shown in equation (2).

$$E\left(x\right) = \sum_{i=1}^{N} e_i^2\left(\underline{x}\right) \tag{2}$$

In order to calculate $\triangle x$ from the Jacobian matrix, Equation (1) has been divided in three major steps: the calculation of $(J\left(\underline{x}\right)J^T\left(\underline{x}\right) + \mu I)$, the calculation of the inverse resultant matrix by Gaussian Decomposition, and the multiplication of the previous result with $J^T\left(\underline{x}\right)\underline{e}\left(\underline{x}\right)$. To calculate the first and the third steps, this work used the library CUBLAS from NVIDIA, which implements levels 1, 2 and 3 of the known library BLAS (Basic Linear Algebra Subroutines) to run in GPU. The second step of this kernel is described below:

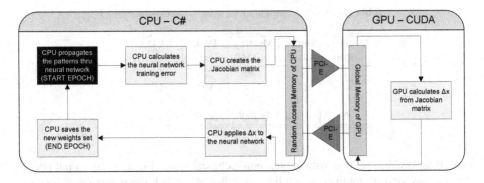

Fig. 1. Proposed model, which performs a major portion of the code in the graphics card. In this picture, PCI-E means PCI-Express bus.

1. Divide the matrix $(J(\underline{x}) J^T(\underline{x}))$ in sub matrixes (squared) in order to have these parts in blocks of shared memory. Using this technique, the global memory is read and written only once per sub matrix;
2. The Gaussian Decomposition is applied on those sub matrices and the pivots are calculated. The pivots here have the same function as on LU decomposition, for example;
3. Using the pivots, the adjacent rows are updated. In this step it is necessary to synchronize all blocks, because the pivots calculated in the first block are also used to update the other block and generates its respective pivots;
4. At the end, all elements above the principal diagonal are equal to zero.

4   Main Results

This section presents 7 experiments where the proposed model was used to train networks and ensembles of neural networks. On these experiments, ensembles of neural networks were used to classify customers of a Brazilian electricity distribution company (Light) as regular or irregular. Four types of NVIDIA graphics cards were used, as shown in Table 1, where Gflop means how many floating-point operations, in billions, can be performed per second, Number of SP means the number of Stream Processors onboard, and CUDA capability means which version of the architecture is supported by the graphics card (Min 1.1 and Max 1.3) [8]. Computer specification I is an Athlon 6000 with 1GB RAM and a GeForce 8400 GS; specification II is an Athlon 6000 with 2GB RAM and a GeForce 8800 GT; specification III is an Athlon 6000 with 2GB RAM; and a GeForce 260 GTX and specification IV is a Phenom II with 16GB RAM and four Tesla c1060.

4.1   Problem Description

Light is a company with 3.79 million consumers divided in 5 regions (East, West, Coastal, Interior, Lower Region) in 31 cities of Rio de Janeiro. The company loses

Table 1. Computer configurations used in the experiments

Computer Spec	Number of SP	Memory size (MB)	Peak (Gflop/s)	CUDA Capability
I	8	256	2, 5	1.1
II	112	512	194	1.1
III	192	896	310	1.3
IV	4x240	4x4096	4x340	1.3

more than US$400 million with annual non-technical losses [3]. In order to put pressure on this kind of companies to adjust their prices through the reduction of losses, the Regulatory Agency for Electric Energy of Brazil (ANEEL) introduced new rules to limit the amount of non-technical losses, fraud and theft that can be charged to the customer. In addition, ANEEL is treating the issue as a priority and intends to adopt a policy of no tolerance [3], forcing companies to clearly specify goals for reducing these losses.

Currently, Light uses a set of methodologies and is associated with a reporting service to help identify low-voltage customers suspected of committing any type of fraud. These customers are classified as suspect by these methodologies and a specialist company selects a particular set of customers to be inspected. Through this process, Light has obtained an average of 25% successes in the verification of fraudulent customers [3]. In this experiment, a prototype of an intelligent computer system for identifying the fraudulent customer profile was developed, providing information to help select customers to inspect, increasing the effectiveness of energy recovery actions. In this experiment, we developed a prototype of an intelligent computer system for identifying the customer profile fraudsters, providing information to help a selection of customers to inspect, increasing the productivity of recovery actions energy.

4.2 System Architecture

The system structure is divided in three modules: (a) Preprocessing, (b) Filtering and (c) Classification. The module (a) includes data cleaning, where duplicated or corrupted data, missing values and outliers are removed, codification and normalization of categorical attributes and selection of those attributes. The Filtering (b) and Classification (c) modules use Ensembles composed of five MLP neural networks and 28 input attributes, one hidden layer and one neuron in the output layer. The whole process is shown in Figure 2.

This case study was chosen to prove the efficiency of the proposed model because of the high computational cost it demands. The Filtering module has to process all database in order to provide a new base with less noise to be processed by the Classification module, which can take almost 3 days (tested environment).

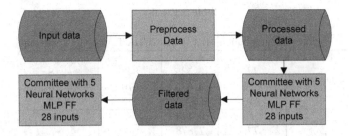

Fig. 2. Overview of system architecture

4.3   Results

The results of this experiment refer only to the performance of the two architectures described earlier, one where a $\triangle x$ calculation running on the CPU making the use of MKL library, and another where the most expensive code is handled by the video card. To calculate, approximately, the training time of one network, you have to get the showing times and multiply by the number of epochs, by ±50 (adjust of μ) and by 10% (the time to process the rest of the code). The times in the tables refer to the training time of a ensemble and are in milliseconds.

Since commercial customers of all regions have similar profiles, only one ensemble was created to classify all of them, independently of their region. Other customers, such as residencial and industrial, where divided by region, with a different ensemble for each of the five existent regions. Table 2 presents the configuration for each region as well as for commercial customers.

Table 2. Regions properties

Region	Number of customers	Number of hidden neurons	Number of epochs	Jacobian Size (bytes)
Commercial	53, 307	12	50	148, 406, 688
East	98, 983	14	50	321, 496, 784
West	123, 272	15	50	428, 986, 560
Coastal	52, 217	10	50	212, 143, 440
Interior	27, 353	12	50	76, 150, 752
Lower	203, 704	14	50	661, 630, 592

The results in Table 3 show the training times using the Intel MKL and the times using the CUDA architecture. The number of neurons in hidden layer was defined by testing many other possibilities and the number of epochs was defined as 50, but the algorithm always get the network with the lowest validation error. This technique has a similar effect of early stopping. In addition, the speedup is shown in the last column meaning how many times one architecture is faster than the other. Some times could not be measured, because the matrixes' size was bigger than the graphic board memory.

Table 3. Results

Region	Configuration	MKL Time	CUDA Time	CUDA Speedup
Commercial	I	4, 855	–	–
	II	3, 535	843	4.18
	III	3, 535	670	5.26
	IV	1, 906	213	8.95
East	I	9, 744	–	–
	II	7, 878	–	–
	III	7, 878	889	8.27
	IV	4, 427	232	19.08
West	I	13, 275	–	–
	II	11, 372	1, 140	9.98
	III	11, 372	1, 138	9.99
	IV	6, 203	274	22.64
Coastal	I	3, 217	1, 922	1.67
	II	2, 542	499	3.53
	III	2, 542	312	5.45
	IV	1, 475	202	4.91
Interior	I	3, 217	1, 922	1.67
	II	1, 700	499	3.53
	III	1, 762	312	5.45
	IV	992	202	4.91
Lower	I	16, 200	–	–
	II	16, 255	–	–
	III	16, 255	1, 482	10.97
	IV	9, 363	333	28.12

The results of training the network with the commercial customer database already show a considerable difference between CPU and GPU, even though the base is not very large. Configuration I could not be assessed because the graphics card has failed reading one of the matrices. This error may be caused by the operating system that restarts the graphics card driver after 3 seconds if GPU stays unresponsive during that time. In Microsoft Windows, this feature is within the WDDM (Microsoft Display Driver Model) and is known as TDR (Timeout Detection and Recovery). The same problem occurred with East, West and Lower, but it was expected since those database are bigger than the commercial customer base. An important point that can be noticed in the results for East customers is the increased difference between the training time on the CPU and on the GPU. One of the factors that can explain this result is that, by doing the calculation for $\triangle x$ in the GPU, the CPU needs to transfer all matrices to global memory on graphic card every epoch. It is also important to notice the difference between the CPU and GPU clocks; some CPU has a frequency almost five times greater than some GPU. In the experiments conducted in this paper, this difference reached three times.

The customer database of region West is even larger than the customer base of region East. As was expected, the difference of training times between CPU and GPU has increased. However, the first GPU configuration could not be used due to memory size. As indicated above, this graphic card has only 256 MB of global memory and the required memory to calculate $\triangle x$ is at least 450 MB. The customer base of region Coastal presents an important result related to the speedup of the first configuration. The training time in CPU and on the GPU are virtually tied. The causes have been described previously, but this fact indicates that an assessment regarding the problem complexity must be made to verify if the architecture running on a GPU is recommended.

When running the training base for customers of region Interior, even configuration I shows a performance gain of almost 200% higher compared to the CPU. Moreover, the cost of the graphics card used in configuration I is approximately US$ 30, while the computer can cost more than US$ 300.

The largest customer base is the one of Lower region, with more than 200,000 customers. On this last experiment the great difference between configurations III and IV can be noticed, as configurations I and II could not be assessed due to memory size. The training time of configuration IV is almost three times faster than the time of configuration III, and the reason for this difference is the number of processors inside these two GPUs, besides the number of records processed.

5   Conclusions

In this paper, a training model of neural networks based on LMA and using CUDA architecture was presented to improve the training performance. The use of this algorithm on graphics cards is new and presented excellent results, even with only one part of the training process running on the GPU.

The existing studies are limited to the use of CUDA architecture on the signals propagation through neural networks or training with simple gradient on MLP networks. The model introduced by this paper can train more types of artificial neural networks and in a more efficient way. Another important concern of this paper was the comparative experiments performed. In these experiments, all measures of time made on the CPU were made directly using MKL library from a program written in C language. This library has an exceptional performance and some comparisons made with it showed gains in the order of hundreds of times for some matrix calculations. This further enhances the results achieved since the proposed model was almost 30 times faster than the sequential model using MKL.

In future works, the whole training process will be transferred to the graphics card and the transfers of data made in each epoch will be replaced by an initial transfer added to other smaller one at the end, including the process output that comprises only the network weights vector. Thus, it's possible to run real-time training, which is required in various types of problems, for example, a system for up scaling video that needs to train a network on each frame.

References

1. Sheetal, L., Pinky, A., Narayanan, A.: High performance pattern recognition on gpu (2008)
2. Bakhoda, A., George, L., Fung, W., Wong, H., Aamodt, T.: Analyzing cuda workloads using a detailed gpu simulator. In: IEEE International Symposium on Performance Analysis of Systems and Software (2009)

3. Muniz, C., Figueiredo, K., Vellasco, M., Chavez, G., Pacheco, M.: Irregularity detection on low tension electric installations by neural network ensembles. In: IJCNN 2009, Rio de Janeiro, pp. 2176–2182 (2009)
4. Hagan, M.T., Menhaj, M.B.: Training feedforward networks with the marquardt algorithm. IEEE Transactions on Neural Networks 5(6), 989–993 (1994)
5. Haykin, S.: Neural Networks and Learning Machines, 3rd edn. Prentice-Hall (2008)
6. Intel. Math kernel library from intel
7. Jang, H., Park, A., Jung, K.: Neural network implementation using cuda and openmp. In: DICTA 2008: Proceedings of the 2008 Digital Image Computing: Techniques and Applications, pp. 155–161. IEEE Computer Society, Washington, DC (2008)
8. NVIDIA. CUDA Programming Guide. NVIDIA, Santa Clara, 2.3.1 edition (2009)

On the Uniform Convergence of the Orthogonal Series-Type Kernel Regression Neural Networks in a Time-Varying Environment

Meng Joo Er[1] and Piotr Duda[2]

[1] Nanyang Technological University,
School of Electrical and Electronic Engineering, Singapore
emjer@ntu.edu.sg
[2] Department of Computer Engineering, Czestochowa University of Technology,
Czestochowa, Poland
pduda@kik.pcz.pl

Abstract. Sufficient conditions for uniform convergence of general regression neural networks, based on the orthogonal series-type kernel, are given. The convergence is guarantee even if variance of noise diverges to infinity. Simulation results are presented.

1   Introduction

In literature various, nonparametric techniques have been proposed to solve stationary (see e.g. [3], [5], [6],[8], [10], [12] - [15], [21] - [23], [26] - [29]) and non-stationary problem ([7], [16] -[20], [24], [25]), assuming a stationary noise. In this paper we relax a latter assumption. Let $X_1, \ldots, X_n$ be a sequence of independent random variables with a common density function f. Consider the following model

$$Y_i = \phi(X_i) + Z_i, \qquad i = 1, \ldots, n, \tag{1}$$

where Z_i are random variables such that

$$E(Z_i) = 0, \qquad EZ_i^2 = d_i, \qquad i = 1, \ldots, n, \tag{2}$$

and $\phi(\cdot)$ is an unknown function.

$$f(x) \sim \sum_{j=0}^{\infty} a_j g_j(x), \tag{3}$$

where

$$a_j = \int_A f(x) g_j(x) dx = E g_j(X_j). \tag{4}$$

The estimator of density $f(\cdot)$ takes the form:

$$\hat{f}_n(x) = \sum_{j=0}^{N(n)} \hat{a}_j g_j(x), \tag{5}$$

where $N(n) \xrightarrow{n} \infty$ and

L. Rutkowski et al. (Eds.): ICAISC 2012, Part I, LNCS 7267, pp. 39–46, 2012.

$$\hat{a}_j = \frac{1}{n} \sum_{k=0}^{n} g_j(X_k) \tag{6}$$

Let us define

$$R(x) = f(x)\phi(x). \tag{7}$$

We assume that function $R(\cdot)$ has the representation:

$$R(x) \sim \sum_{j=0}^{\infty} b_j g_j(x), \tag{8}$$

where

$$b_j = \int_A \phi(x)f(x)g_j(x)dx = E(Y_j g_j(X_j)) \tag{9}$$

We estimate function $R(\cdot)$ using

$$\hat{R}_n(x) = \sum_{j=0}^{M(n)} \hat{b}_j g_j(x), \tag{10}$$

where $M(n) \xrightarrow{n} \infty$ and

$$\hat{b}_j = \frac{1}{n} \sum_{k=0}^{n} Y_k g_j(X_k). \tag{11}$$

Then the estimator of the regression function is of the following form:

$$\hat{\phi}_n(x) = \frac{\hat{R}_n(x)}{\hat{f}_n(x)} = \frac{\sum_{i=1}^{n} \sum_{j=0}^{M(n)} Y_i g_j(X_i)g_j(x)}{\sum_{i=1}^{n} \sum_{j=0}^{N(n)} g_j(X_i)g_j(x)} \tag{12}$$

It should be noted that procedure (12) corresponds to the Parzen-type kernel general regression neural network introduced by Specht [35].

2   Main Result

Let us assume that

$$\max_{x} |g_j| < G_j. \tag{13}$$

It should be noted that $d = -\frac{1}{12}$ for the Hermite system, $d = -\frac{1}{4}$ for the Laguerre system, $d = 0$ for the Fourier system, $d = \frac{1}{2}$ for the Legendre and Haar systems (see [33], [38]). Let us denote

$$s_i = d_i + \int_A \phi^2(u)f(u)du \tag{14}$$

Theorem 1. *Let*

$$\xi_1 = \sup_{x \in A} |\phi(x)| < \infty, \qquad \xi_2 = \inf_{x \in A} |f(x)| > 0 \tag{15}$$

and

$$\sup_{x \in A} |\sum_{j=0}^{N(n)} a_j g_j(x) - f(x)| \xrightarrow{n} 0 \tag{16}$$

$$\sup_{x \in A} |\sum_{j=0}^{M(n)} b_j g_j(x) - R(x)| \xrightarrow{n} 0 \tag{17}$$

If the following conditions hold

$$\frac{1}{n^2} (\sum_{j=0}^{M(n)} G_j^2)^2 \sum_{i=1}^{n} s_i \xrightarrow{n} 0, \quad M(n) \xrightarrow{n} \infty \tag{18}$$

$$\frac{1}{n} (\sum_{j=0}^{N(n)} G_j^2)^2 \xrightarrow{n} 0, \quad N(n) \xrightarrow{n} \infty \tag{19}$$

then

$$\sup_{x \in A} |\phi_n(x) - \phi(x)| \xrightarrow{n} 0 \qquad \text{in probability.} \tag{20}$$

Proof. One can see that:

$$\sup_{x \in A} |\phi(x) - \hat{\phi}_n(x)| \leq \frac{\xi_1}{\inf_{x \in A} \hat{f}_n(x)} \sup_{x \in A} |\hat{f}_n(x) - f(x)| + \frac{1}{\inf_{x \in A} \hat{f}_n(x)} \sup_{x \in A} |\hat{R}_n(x) - R(x)| \tag{21}$$

So it is sufficient to show:

$$\sup_{x \in A} |\hat{R}_n(x) - R(x)| \xrightarrow{n} 0 \tag{22}$$

$$\sup_{x \in A} |\hat{f}_n(x) - f(x)| \xrightarrow{n} 0 \tag{23}$$

in probability.
One can see that

$$\sup_{x \in A} |\hat{R}_n(x) - R(x)| \leq \sup_{x \in A} |\sum_{j=0}^{M(n)} b_j g_j(x) - R(x)| + \sup_{x \in A} |\sum_{j=0}^{M(n)} (\hat{b}_j - b_j) g_j(x)| \tag{24}$$

Using Schwartz inequality we get

$$E[\sup_{x \in A} |\sum_{j=0}^{M(n)} (\hat{b}_j - b_j) g_j(x)|] \leq \frac{1}{n} \sum_{j=0}^{M(n)} G_j^2 (\sum_{i=1}^{n} (\int_A \phi^2(u) f(u) du + d_i))^{1/2}. \tag{25}$$

Similarly we can show that

$$E[\sup_{x \in A} | \sum_{j=0}^{N(n)} (\hat{a}_j - a_j) g_j(x)|] \leq \frac{1}{\sqrt{n}} \sum_{j=0}^{N(n)} G_j^2. \tag{26}$$

This concludes the proof.

It should be noted that conditions for uniform convergence of series (16) and (17) can be found in [1], [33], [38], [39].

3   Experimental Results

For computer simulations we will use synthetic data. Distribution of random variables X_i is uniform on the interval $A = [-5; 5]$, for $i = 1, \ldots, n$. Let us assume that:

$$M(n) = [c_1 n^{q_M}], \quad N(n) = [c_2 n^{q_N}], \quad d_n = c_3 n^{\alpha}, \tag{27}$$

where q_M, q_N and α are positive number.

Consider the following model

$$\phi(x) = \frac{2^x}{x^2 + 1}, \tag{28}$$

with noise Z_i taking values from the normal distribution $N(0, d_i)$, $d_i = i^{\alpha}$, $\alpha > 0$. Note that in this case both inequalities (15) hold on A. The constants c_1 and c_2 are equal to 4. Parameters q_M and q_N are both equal to $0, 3$. The constant c_3 is equal to 1. The Hermite orthonormal system is chosen to perform calculations.

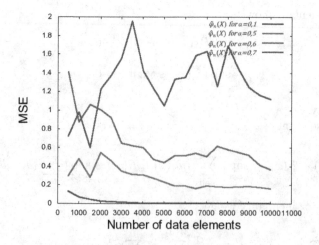

Fig. 1. The MSE as a function of n

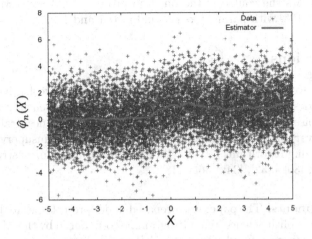

Fig. 2. Training set and obtained estimator

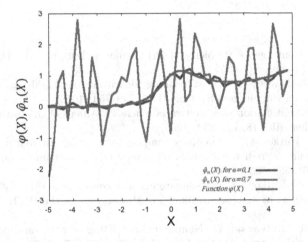

Fig. 3. Function $\phi(\cdot)$ and its estimators for different values of parameter α

Number of data set is taken from the interval $[500; 10000]$ and parameter α is tested in the interval $[\frac{1}{10}, \frac{12}{10}]$.

Figure 1 shows how the MSE (Mean Square Error) changes with number of data elements n for different values of parameter α. For parameter $\alpha \in [0, 1; 0, 6]$ we can see that, when n goes to infinity, the MSE goes to 0. For $\alpha = 0, 7$ this trend is not maintained. Moreover, value of the MSE is much bigger than for lower values of parameter α. Experimental results show that for higher values of α the MSE is growing. For $\alpha = 1, 2$ and $n = 10^5$, the MSE is equal to 117,37.

In Figure 2 input data and the result of estimation for $n = 10^4$ and $\alpha = 0, 1$ is indicated. As we can see the estimator found in the appropriate manner center of data and maintained its trend.

Figure 3 shows the course of the function given by (28) and estimators obtained for $n = 10^4$, with parameters α equal to $0, 1$ and $1, 2$.

4   Conclusions

In this paper we studied the general regression neural networks, based on the orthogonal series-type kernel. We proved the uniform convergence assuming that variance of noise diverges to infinity. Further work can be concentrated on handling of time-varying noise by making use of supervised and unsupervised neural networks learning algorithms [2], [4], [11] and various neurofuzzy structures developed in [9], [30] - [32], [34], [36] - [38].

Acknowledgments. The paper was prepared under project operated within the Foundation for Polish Science Team Programme co-financed by the EU European Regional Development Fund, Operational Program Innovative Economy 2007-2013, and also supported by the National Science Center NCN.

References

1. Alexits, G.: Convergence Problems of Orthogonal Series, pp. 261–264. Academia and Kiado, Budapest (1961)
2. Bilski, J., Rutkowski, L.: A fast training algorithm for neural networks. IEEE Transactions on Circuits and Systems II 45, 749–753 (1998)
3. Cacoullos, P.: Estimation of a multivariate density. Annals of the Institute of Statistical Mathematics 18, 179–190 (1965)
4. Cierniak, R., Rutkowski, L.: On image compression by competitive neural networks and optimal linear predictors. Signal Processing: Image Communication - a Eurasip Journal 15(6), 559–565 (2000)
5. Gałkowski, T., Rutkowski, L.: Nonparametric recovery of multivariate functions with applications to system identification. Proceedings of the IEEE 73, 942–943 (1985)
6. Gałkowski, T., Rutkowski, L.: Nonparametric fitting of multivariable functions. IEEE Transactions on Automatic Control AC-31, 785–787 (1986)
7. Greblicki, W., Rutkowska, D., Rutkowski, L.: An orthogonal series estimate of time-varying regression. Annals of the Institute of Statistical Mathematics 35(Part A), 147–160 (1983)
8. Greblicki, W., Rutkowski, L.: Density-free Bayes risk consistency of nonparametric pattern recognition procedures. Proceedings of the IEEE 69(4), 482–483 (1981)
9. Nowicki, R.: Rough Sets in the Neuro-Fuzzy Architectures Based on Non-monotonic Fuzzy Implications. In: Rutkowski, L., Siekmann, J.H., Tadeusiewicz, R., Zadeh, L.A. (eds.) ICAISC 2004. LNCS (LNAI), vol. 3070, pp. 518–525. Springer, Heidelberg (2004)
10. Parzen, E.: On estimation of a probability density function and mode. Analysis of Mathematical Statistics 33(3), 1065–1076 (1962)
11. Patan, K., Patan, M.: Optimal training strategies for locally recurrent neural networks. Journal of Artificial Intelligence and Soft Computing Research 1(2), 103–114 (2011)

12. Rutkowski, L.: Sequential estimates of probability densities by orthogonal series and their application in pattern classification. IEEE Transactions on Systems, Man, and Cybernetics SMC-10(12), 918–920 (1980)
13. Rutkowski, L.: Sequential estimates of a regression function by orthogonal series with applications in discrimination, New York, Heidelberg, Berlin. Lectures Notes in Statistics, vol. 8, pp. 236–244 (1981)
14. Rutkowski, L.: On system identification by nonparametric function fitting. IEEE Transactions on Automatic Control AC-27, 225–227 (1982)
15. Rutkowski, L.: Orthogonal series estimates of a regression function with applications in system identification. In: Probability and Statistical Inference, pp. 343–347. D. Reidel Publishing Company, Dordrecht (1982)
16. Rutkowski, L.: On Bayes risk consistent pattern recognition procedures in a quasi-stationary environment. IEEE Transactions on Pattern Analysis and Machine Intelligence PAMI-4(1), 84–87 (1982)
17. Rutkowski, L.: On-line identification of time-varying systems by nonparametric techniques. IEEE Transactions on Automatic Control AC-27, 228–230 (1982)
18. Rutkowski, L.: On nonparametric identification with prediction of time-varying systems. IEEE Transactions on Automatic Control AC-29, 58–60 (1984)
19. Rutkowski, L.: Nonparametric identification of quasi-stationary systems. Systems and Control Letters 6, 33–35 (1985)
20. Rutkowski, L.: The real-time identification of time-varying systems by nonparametric algorithms based on the Parzen kernels. International Journal of Systems Science 16, 1123–1130 (1985)
21. Rutkowski, L.: A general approach for nonparametric fitting of functions and their derivatives with applications to linear circuits identification. IEEE Transactions Circuits Systems CAS-33, 812–818 (1986)
22. Rutkowski, L.: Sequential pattern recognition procedures derived from multiple Fourier series. Pattern Recognition Letters 8, 213–216 (1988)
23. Rutkowski, L.: Nonparametric procedures for identification and control of linear dynamic systems. In: Proceedings of 1988 American Control Conference, June 15-17, pp. 1325–1326 (1988)
24. Rutkowski, L.: An application of multiple Fourier series to identification of multivariable nonstationary systems. International Journal of Systems Science 20(10), 1993–2002 (1989)
25. Rutkowski, L.: Nonparametric learning algorithms in the time-varying environments. Signal Processing 18, 129–137 (1989)
26. Rutkowski, L., Rafajłowicz, E.: On global rate of convergence of some nonparametric identification procedures. IEEE Transaction on Automatic Control AC-34(10), 1089–1091 (1989)
27. Rutkowski, L.: Identification of MISO nonlinear regressions in the presence of a wide class of disturbances. IEEE Transactions on Information Theory IT-37, 214–216 (1991)
28. Rutkowski, L.: Multiple Fourier series procedures for extraction of nonlinear regressions from noisy data. IEEE Transactions on Signal Processing 41(10), 3062–3065 (1993)
29. Rutkowski, L., Gałkowski, T.: On pattern classification and system identification by probabilistic neural networks. Applied Mathematics and Computer Science 4(3), 413–422 (1994)
30. Rutkowski, L.: A New Method for System Modelling and Pattern Classification. Bulletin of the Polish Academy of Sciences 52(1), 11–24 (2004)

31. Rutkowski, L., Cpałka, K.: A general approach to neuro - fuzzy systems. In: Proceedings of the 10th IEEE International Conference on Fuzzy Systems, Melbourne, December 2-5, vol. 3, pp. 1428–1431 (2001)
32. Rutkowski, L., Cpałka, K.: A neuro-fuzzy controller with a compromise fuzzy reasoning. Control and Cybernetics 31(2), 297–308 (2002)
33. Sansone, G.: Orthogonal functions, vol. 9. Interscience Publishers In., New York (1959)
34. Scherer, R.: Boosting Ensemble of Relational Neuro-fuzzy Systems. In: Rutkowski, L., Tadeusiewicz, R., Zadeh, L.A., Żurada, J.M. (eds.) ICAISC 2006. LNCS (LNAI), vol. 4029, pp. 306–313. Springer, Heidelberg (2006)
35. Specht, D.F.: Probabilistic neural networks. Neural Networks 3, 109–118 (1990)
36. Starczewski, J., Rutkowski, L.: Interval type 2 neuro-fuzzy systems based on interval consequents. In: Rutkowski, L., Kacprzyk, J. (eds.) Neural Networks and Soft Computing, pp. 570–577. Physica-Verlag, Springer-Verlag Company, Heidelberg, New York (2003)
37. Starczewski, J., Rutkowski, L.: Connectionist Structures of Type 2 Fuzzy Inference Systems. In: Wyrzykowski, R., Dongarra, J., Paprzycki, M., Waśniewski, J. (eds.) PPAM 2001. LNCS, vol. 2328, pp. 634–642. Springer, Heidelberg (2002)
38. Szegö, G.: Orthogonal Polynomials, vol. 23. American Mathematical Society Coll. Publ. (1959)
39. Zygmund, A.: Trigonometric Series. Cambridge University Press, Cambridge (1959)

On the Strong Convergence of the Orthogonal Series-Type Kernel Regression Neural Networks in a Non-stationary Environment

Piotr Duda[1], Yoichi Hayashi[2], and Maciej Jaworski[1]

[1] Department of Computer Engineering, Czestochowa University of Technology, Czestochowa, Poland
[2] Department of Computer Science, Meiji University, Tama-ku, Kawasaki, Japan
{pduda,maciej.jaworski}@kik.pcz.pl, hayashiy@cs.meiji.ac.jp

Abstract. Strong convergence of general regression neural networks is proved assuming non-stationary noise. The network is based on the orthogonal series-type kernel. Simulation results are discussed in details.

1 Introduction

In this paper we consider the following model

$$Y_i = \phi(X_i) + Z_i, \quad i = 1, \ldots, n, \tag{1}$$

where $X_1, \ldots, X_n$ are independent random variables with a probability density $f(\cdot)$, Z_i are random variables such that

$$E(Z_i) = 0, \quad EZ_i^2 = d_i, \quad i = 1, \ldots, n, \tag{2}$$

and $\phi(\cdot)$ is an unknown function. We assume that function $f(\cdot)$ has the representation

$$f(x) \sim \sum_{j=0}^{\infty} a_j g_j(x), \tag{3}$$

where

$$a_j = \int_A f(x)g_j(x)dx = Eg_j(X_i). \tag{4}$$

and $\{g_j(\cdot)\}$, $j = 0, 1, 2, \ldots$ is a complete orthonormal series (see e.g. [1]) defined on $A \subset R^p$. Then the estimator of density $f(x)$ takes the form

$$\hat{f}_n(x) = \sum_{j=0}^{N(n)} \hat{a}_j g_j(x), \tag{5}$$

where $N(n) \xrightarrow{n} \infty$ and

$$\hat{a}_j = \frac{1}{n} \sum_{k=0}^{n} g_j(X_k) \tag{6}$$

L. Rutkowski et al. (Eds.): ICAISC 2012, Part I, LNCS 7267, pp. 47–54, 2012.

Let us define

$$R(x) = f(x)\phi(x). \tag{7}$$

We assume that function $R(\cdot)$ has the representation

$$R(x) \sim \sum_{j=0}^{\infty} b_j g_j(x), \tag{8}$$

where

$$b_j = \int_A \phi(x)f(x)g_j(x)dx = E(Y_k g_j(X_k)) \tag{9}$$

We estimate function $R(\cdot)$ using

$$\hat{R}_n(x) = \sum_{j=0}^{M(n)} \hat{b}_j g_j(x), \tag{10}$$

where $M(n) \xrightarrow{n} \infty$ and

$$\hat{b}_j = \frac{1}{n} \sum_{k=0}^{n} Y_k g_j(X_k). \tag{11}$$

Then the estimator of the regression function is of the following form

$$\hat{\phi}_n(x) = \frac{\hat{R}_n(x)}{\hat{f}_n(x)} = \frac{\sum\limits_{i=1}^{n} \sum\limits_{j=0}^{M(n)} Y_i g_j(X_i)g_j(x)}{\sum\limits_{i=1}^{n} \sum\limits_{j=0}^{N(n)} g_j(X_i)g_j(x)} \tag{12}$$

This algorithm creates a so-called general regression neural network [37]. Figure 1 shows block diagram for $M(n) = N(n)$. There are many papers in literature

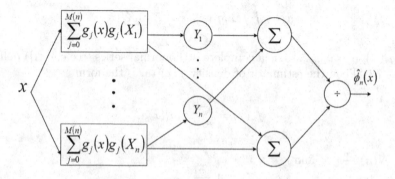

Fig. 1. Regression neural network

where nonparametic regression estimates were studied in a stationary environment e.g. [4], [5],[7], [11], [13] - [17], [23] - [25], [28] - [31] and in a non-stationary environment e.g. [6], [18] -[22], [26], [27]. For excellent overviews on these techniques the reader is referred to [8] and [9].

2 Main Result

Let us assume that

$$\max_x |g_j| < G_j. \tag{13}$$

Theorem 1. *Let us denote:*

$$s_i = d_i + \int_A \phi^2(u)f(u)du. < \infty \tag{14}$$

If the following conditions hold

$$\sum_{n=1}^{\infty} \frac{s_n}{n^2} (\sum_{j=0}^{M(n)} G_j^2)^2 < \infty, \quad M(n) \xrightarrow{n} \infty \tag{15}$$

$$\sum_{n=1}^{\infty} \frac{1}{n^2} (\sum_{j=0}^{N(n)} G_j^2)^2 < \infty, \quad N(n) \xrightarrow{n} \infty \tag{16}$$

then

$$\hat{\phi}_n(x) \xrightarrow{n} \phi(x) \qquad \text{with probability 1,} \tag{17}$$

at every point $x \in A$ at which series (3) and (8) converge to $f(x)$ and $R(x)$ respectively.

Proof. It is sufficient to show that:

$$\hat{R}_n(x) - E[\hat{R}_n(x)] \xrightarrow{n} 0 \tag{18}$$

$$\hat{f}_n(x) - E[\hat{f}_n(x)] \xrightarrow{n} 0, \tag{19}$$

with probability one, at every point $x \in A$, at which series (3) and (8) are convergent to $f(x)$ and $R(x)$ respectively. Denote

$$T_i = \sum_{j=0}^{M(i)} (g_j(X_i)Y_i - b_j)g_j(x) \tag{20}$$

Observe that

$$\hat{R}_n(x) - E\hat{R}_n(x) = \frac{1}{n} \sum_{i=1}^{n} T_i \tag{21}$$

Using Cauchy's inequality:

$$ET_n^2 \leq (\int_A \phi^2(u)f(u)du + d_n)(\sum_{j=0}^{M(n)} G_j^2)^2 \tag{22}$$

Applying Kolmogorov's strong law we obtain

$$\lim_{n\to\infty} \frac{1}{n}\sum_{i=1}^{n}(T_i - ET_i) = 0 \tag{23}$$

with probability one.

Similarly, for $T_i = \sum_{j=0}^{N(n)}(g_j(X_i) - a_j)g_j(x)$

$$\hat{f}_n(x) - E\hat{f}_n(x) = \frac{1}{n}\sum_{i=1}^{n}T_i \tag{24}$$

we obtain

$$ET_n^2 \leq (\sum_{j=0}^{N(n)} G_j^2)^2 \tag{25}$$

which implies that

$$\lim_{n\to\infty} \frac{1}{n}\sum_{i=1}^{n}(T_i - ET_i) = 0 \tag{26}$$

with probability one. This concludes the proof.

Example. Let assume that

$$M(n) = [c_1 n^{q_M}] \quad N(n) = [c_2 n^{q_N}] \quad d_n = c_3 n^{\alpha} \quad G_j = c_4 j^d, \tag{27}$$

where q_m, q_n and α are positive numbers. It is easily seen that if

$$4dq_M + 2q_M + \alpha < 1, \qquad 4dq_N + 2q_N < 1 \tag{28}$$

then Theorem 1 holds. It should be noted that $d = -\frac{1}{12}$ for the Hermite sytem, $d = -\frac{1}{4}$ for the Laguerre system, $d = 0$ for the Fourier system, $d = \frac{1}{2}$ for the Legendre and Haar systems (see [35]).

3   Experimental Results

For computer simulations we will use synthetic data. Distribution of random variables X_i is uniform on interval $[0;3]$, for $i = 1,\ldots,n$. Consider the following model

$$\phi(x) = 8e^{-x^2}, \tag{29}$$

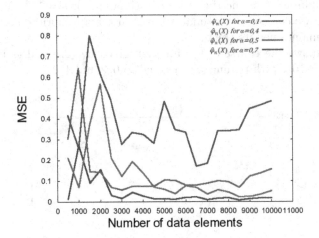

Fig. 2. The MSE as a function of n

with Z_i which are realizations of random variables $N(0, d_i)$, $d_i = i^\alpha$, $\alpha > 0$. Constants c_1, c_2 in (27) are equal to 2 and $c_3 = 1$. Parameters q_M and q_N are both equal to $0, 4$. The Laguerre orthonormal system is chosen to perform calculations. Number of data set is taken from the interval $[500; 10000]$ and parameter α is tested in the interval $[\frac{1}{10}, \frac{12}{10}]$.

Figure 2 shows how the MSE (Mean Square Error) changes with the number of data elements n for different values of parameter α. For parameter $\alpha \in [0, 1; 0, 4]$ we can see that, when n goes to infinity, the MSE goes to 0. For $\alpha = 0, 5$ or $\alpha = 0, 7$ this trend is not maintained. Moreover, for $\alpha = 0, 7$, value of the MSE is much bigger than for lower values of parameter α. Experimental results show that for higher values of α the MSE is growing. For $\alpha = 1, 2$ and $n = 10^4$, the MSE is equal to 19,18.

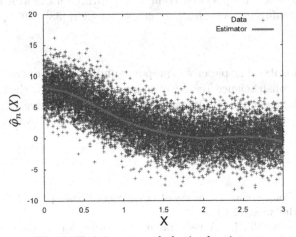

Fig. 3. Training set and obtained estimator

In Figure 3 input data and the result of estimation for $n = 10^4$ and $\alpha = 0,2$ is indicated. As we can see the estimator found in the appropriate manner center of data and maintained its trend.

Figure 4 shows the course of the function given by (29) and estimators obtained for $n = 10^4$, with parameters α equal to $0,2$ and $1,2$.

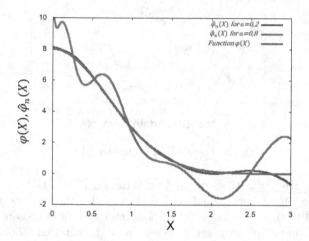

Fig. 4. Function $\phi(\cdot)$ and its estimators for different values of parameter α

4   Conclusions

In this paper we studied general regression neural networks based on the orthogonal series-type kernel. We established the strong convergence assuming non-stationary noise. Further research will focus on how to adopt methods based on unsupervised and unsupervised training algorithms for neural networks [2], [3], [12] and neurofuzzy structures [10], [32] - [34], [36], [38], [39] to handle non-stationary noise.

Acknowledgments. The paper was prepared under project operated within the Foundation for Polish Science Team Programme co-financed by the EU European Regional Development Fund, Operational Program Innovative Economy 2007-2013, and also supported by the National Science Center NCN.

References

1. Alexits, G.: Convergence Problems of Orthogonal Series, pp. 261–264. Academia and Kiado, Budapest (1961)
2. Bilski, J., Rutkowski, L.: A fast training algorithm for neural networks. IEEE Transactions on Circuits and Systems II 45, 749–753 (1998)

3. Cierniak, R., Rutkowski, L.: On image compression by competitive neural networks and optimal linear predictors. Signal Processing: Image Communication - a Eurasip Journal 15(6), 559–565 (2000)

4. Gałkowski, T., Rutkowski, L.: Nonparametric recovery of multivariate functions with applications to system identification. Proceedings of the IEEE 73, 942–943 (1985)

5. Gałkowski, T., Rutkowski, L.: Nonparametric fitting of multivariable functions. IEEE Transactions on Automatic Control AC-31, 785–787 (1986)

6. Greblicki, W., Rutkowska, D., Rutkowski, L.: An orthogonal series estimate of time-varying regression. Annals of the Institute of Statistical Mathematics 35(Part A), 147–160 (1983)

7. Greblicki, W., Rutkowski, L.: Density-free Bayes risk consistency of nonparametric pattern recognition procedures. Proceedings of the IEEE 69(4), 482–483 (1981)

8. Greblicki, W., Pawlak, M.: Nonparametric system indentification. Cambridge University Press (2008)

9. Györfi, L., Kohler, M., Krzyżak, A., Walk, H.: A Distribution-Free Theory of Nonparametric Regression, USA. Springer Series in Statistics (2002)

10. Nowicki, R., Pokropińska, A.: Information Criterions Applied to Neuro-Fuzzy Architectures Design. In: Rutkowski, L., Siekmann, J.H., Tadeusiewicz, R., Zadeh, L.A. (eds.) ICAISC 2004. LNCS (LNAI), vol. 3070, pp. 332–337. Springer, Heidelberg (2004)

11. Parzen, E.: On estimation of a probability density function and mode. Analysis of Mathematical Statistics 33(3), 1065–1076 (1962)

12. Patan, K., Patan, M.: Optimal training strategies for locally recurrent neural networks. Journal of Artificial Intelligence and Soft Computing Research 1(2), 103–114 (2011)

13. Rafajłowicz, E.: Nonparametric orthogonal series estimators of regression: A class attaining the optimal convergence rate in L_2. Statistics and Probability Letters 5, 219–224 (1987)

14. Rutkowski, L.: Sequential estimates of probability densities by orthogonal series and their application in pattern classification. IEEE Transactions on Systems, Man, and Cybernetics SMC-10(12), 918–920 (1980)

15. Rutkowski, L.: Sequential estimates of a regression function by orthogonal series with applications in discrimination, New York, Heidelberg, Berlin. Lectures Notes in Statistics, vol. 8, pp. 236–244 (1981)

16. Rutkowski, L.: On system identification by nonparametric function fitting. IEEE Transactions on Automatic Control AC-27, 225–227 (1982)

17. Rutkowski, L.: Orthogonal series estimates of a regression function with applications in system identification. In: Probability and Statistical Inference, pp. 343–347. D. Reidel Publishing Company, Dordrecht (1982)

18. Rutkowski, L.: On Bayes risk consistent pattern recognition procedures in a quasi-stationary environment. IEEE Transactions on Pattern Analysis and Machine Intelligence PAMI-4(1), 84–87 (1982)

19. Rutkowski, L.: On-line identification of time-varying systems by nonparametric techniques. IEEE Transactions on Automatic Control AC-27, 228–230 (1982)

20. Rutkowski, L.: On nonparametric identification with prediction of time-varying systems. IEEE Transactions on Automatic Control AC-29, 58–60 (1984)

21. Rutkowski, L.: Nonparametric identification of quasi-stationary systems. Systems and Control Letters 6, 33–35 (1985)

22. Rutkowski, L.: The real-time identification of time-varying systems by nonparametric algorithms based on the Parzen kernels. International Journal of Systems Science 16, 1123–1130 (1985)
23. Rutkowski, L.: A general approach for nonparametric fitting of functions and their derivatives with applications to linear circuits identification. IEEE Transactions Circuits Systems CAS-33, 812–818 (1986)
24. Rutkowski, L.: Sequential pattern recognition procedures derived from multiple Fourier series. Pattern Recognition Letters 8, 213–216 (1988)
25. Rutkowski, L.: Nonparametric procedures for identification and control of linear dynamic systems. In: Proceedings of 1988 American Control Conference, June 15-17, pp. 1325–1326 (1988)
26. Rutkowski, L.: An application of multiple Fourier series to identification of multivariable nonstationary systems. International Journal of Systems Science 20(10), 1993–2002 (1989)
27. Rutkowski, L.: Nonparametric learning algorithms in the time-varying environments. Signal Processing 18, 129–137 (1989)
28. Rutkowski, L., Rafajłowicz, E.: On global rate of convergence of some nonparametric identification procedures. IEEE Transaction on Automatic Control AC-34(10), 1089–1091 (1989)
29. Rutkowski, L.: Identification of MISO nonlinear regressions in the presence of a wide class of disturbances. IEEE Transactions on Information Theory IT-37, 214–216 (1991)
30. Rutkowski, L.: Multiple Fourier series procedures for extraction of nonlinear regressions from noisy data. IEEE Transactions on Signal Processing 41(10), 3062–3065 (1993)
31. Rutkowski, L., Gałkowski, T.: On pattern classification and system identification by probabilistic neural networks. Applied Mathematics and Computer Science 4(3), 413–422 (1994)
32. Rutkowski, L.: A New Method for System Modelling and Pattern Classification. Bulletin of the Polish Academy of Sciences 52(1), 11–24 (2004)
33. Rutkowski, L., Cpałka, K.: A general approach to neuro - fuzzy systems. In: Proceedings of the 10th IEEE International Conference on Fuzzy Systems, Melbourne, December 2-5, vol. 3, pp. 1428–1431 (2001)
34. Rutkowski, L., Cpałka, K.: A neuro-fuzzy controller with a compromise fuzzy reasoning. Control and Cybernetics 31(2), 297–308 (2002)
35. Sansone G.: Orthogonal functions, vol. 9. Interscience Publishers In., New York (1959)
36. Scherer, R.: Boosting Ensemble of Relational Neuro-fuzzy Systems. In: Rutkowski, L., Tadeusiewicz, R., Zadeh, L.A., Żurada, J.M. (eds.) ICAISC 2006. LNCS (LNAI), vol. 4029, pp. 306–313. Springer, Heidelberg (2006)
37. Specht, D.F.: Probabilistic neural networks. Neural Networks 3, 109–118 (1990)
38. Starczewski, J., Rutkowski, L.: Interval type 2 neuro-fuzzy systems based on interval consequents. In: Rutkowski, L., Kacprzyk, J. (eds.) Neural Networks and Soft Computing, pp. 570–577. Physica-Verlag, Springer-Verlag Company, Heidelberg, New York (2003)
39. Starczewski, J., Rutkowski, L.: Connectionist Structures of Type 2 Fuzzy Inference Systems. In: Wyrzykowski, R., Dongarra, J., Paprzycki, M., Waśniewski, J. (eds.) PPAM 2001. LNCS, vol. 2328, pp. 634–642. Springer, Heidelberg (2002)

On the Strong Convergence of the Recursive Orthogonal Series-Type Kernel Probabilistic Neural Networks Handling Time-Varying Noise

Piotr Duda and Marcin Korytkowski

Department of Computer Engineering, Czestochowa University of Technology,
Czestochowa, Poland
{pduda,marcin.korytkowski}@kik.pcz.pl

Abstract. Sufficient conditions for strong convergence of recursive general regression neural networks are given assuming nonstationary noise. The orthogonal series-type kernel is applied. Simulation results show convergence even if variance of noise diverges to infinity.

1   Introduction

Let $X_1, \ldots, X_n$ be a sequence of independent random variables with a common desity function f. Consider the following model

$$Y_i = \phi(X_i) + Z_i, \qquad i = 1, \ldots, n, \tag{1}$$

where Z_i are random variables, such that

$$E(Z_i) = 0 \quad E(Z_i^2) = d_i \quad i = 1, \ldots, n. \tag{2}$$

and the input random variables $(X_1, \ldots, X_n)$ have the same probability density function $f(\cdot)$. To estimate function $\phi(\cdot)$ we propose the following formula

$$\hat{\phi}_n(x) = \frac{\hat{R}_n(x)}{\hat{f}_n(x)}, \tag{3}$$

where

$$\hat{R}_n(x) = \frac{1}{n} \sum_{i=1}^{n} \sum_{j=0}^{M(i)} Y_i g_j(X_i) g_j(x), \tag{4}$$

and

$$\hat{f}_n(x) = \frac{1}{n} \sum_{i=1}^{n} \sum_{j=0}^{N(i)} g_j(X_i) g_j(x), \tag{5}$$

where $\{g_j\}$ is a complete orthonormal system and

$$N(i) \xrightarrow{i} \infty \qquad M(i) \xrightarrow{i} \infty. \tag{6}$$

L. Rutkowski et al. (Eds.): ICAISC 2012, Part I, LNCS 7267, pp. 55–62, 2012.

One can see that the estimators $\hat{f}(x)$ and $\hat{R}(x)$ can be expressed as follows:

$$\hat{f}_n(x) = \hat{f}_{n-1}(x) + \frac{1}{n}[\sum_{j=0}^{N(n)} g_j(X_n)g_j(x) - \hat{f}_{n-1}(x)], \tag{7}$$

$$\hat{R}_n(x) = \hat{R}_{n-1}(x) + \frac{1}{n}[\sum_{j=0}^{M(n)} Y_n g_j(X_n)g_j(x) - \hat{R}_{n-1}(x)], \tag{8}$$

where $M(\cdot), N(\cdot)$ are the same as in (6). The above algorithm is so-called prob-abilistic neural network [36], which diagram is depicted in Fig. 1, for $M(n) = N(n)$. It corresponds to nonparametic density and regression estimates

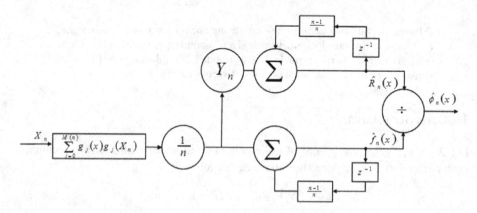

Fig. 1. Recursive probabilistic neural network

developed to solve stationary (e.g. [2], [4], [5],[7], [11], [13] - [17], [23] - [25], [28] - [31]) and non-stationary case (e.g. [6], [18] -[22], [26], [27]). For excellent overviews on these methods the reader is referred to [8] and [9].

2   Main Result

Let us assume that

$$\max_x |g_j| \leq G_j, \tag{9}$$

Theorem 1. *Let us denote*

$$s_i = d_i + \int_A \phi^2(u)f(u)du < \infty \tag{10}$$

If the following conditions hold

$$\sum_{n=1}^{\infty} \frac{s_n}{n^2}(\sum_{j=0}^{M(n)} G_j^2)^2 < \infty, \quad M(n) \xrightarrow{n} \infty \tag{11}$$

$$\sum_{n=1}^{\infty} \frac{1}{n^2} \left(\sum_{j=0}^{N(n)} G_j^2 \right)^2 < \infty, \quad N(n) \xrightarrow{n} \infty \tag{12}$$

then

$$\hat{\phi}_n(x) \xrightarrow{n} \phi(x) \qquad \text{with probability 1}, \tag{13}$$

at every point $x \in A$ at which

$$\sum_{j=0}^{N(n)} a_j g_j(x) \xrightarrow{n} f(x), \tag{14}$$

$$\sum_{j=0}^{M(n)} b_j g_j(x) \xrightarrow{n} R(x) \tag{15}$$

where

$$a_j = \int_A f(x) g_j(x) dx = E g_j(X_i). \tag{16}$$

$$b_j = \int_A \phi(x) f(x) g_j(x) dx = E(Y_i g_j(X_i)) \tag{17}$$

Proof. The proof can be based on the arguments similar to those in [15].

3   Experimental Results

Let us assume that

$$M(n) = [c_1 n^{q_M}], \quad N(n) = [c_2 n^{q_N}], \quad d_n = c_3 n^{\alpha}, \quad G_j = c_4 j^d, \tag{18}$$

where q_M, q_N and α are positive numbers. It should be noted that $d = -\frac{1}{12}$ for the Hermite sytem, $d = -\frac{1}{4}$ for the Laguerre system, $d = 0$ for the Fourier system, $d = \frac{1}{2}$ for the Legendre and Haar systems (see [39]).

We consider the following regression function

$$\phi(x) = x^4 - 5x^2 + 4. \tag{19}$$

Distribution of random variables X_i is uniform on the interval $[-\pi, \pi]$, for $i = 1, \ldots, n$ and Z_i are realizations of random variables $N(0, i^{\alpha})$, where $\alpha > 0$. Parameters q_M and q_N are both equal to $0, 3$. The constants c_1, c_2 are equal to 4 and c_3 is equal to 1. The Fourier orthonormal system is chosen to perform calculations. Number of data set is taken from the interval $[500; 10000]$, and parameter α is tested in the interval $[\frac{1}{10}, \frac{12}{10}]$.

Figure 2 shows how the MSE (Mean Square Error) changes with number of data elements n for different values of parameter α. For parameter $\alpha \in [0, 1; 0, 2]$ we can see that, when n goes to infinity, the MSE goes to 0. For $\alpha \geq 0, 5$ value

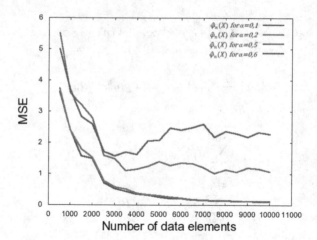

Fig. 2. The MSE as a function of n

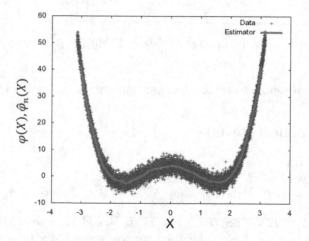

Fig. 3. Training set and obtained estimator

of the MSE is much bigger than for lower values of parameter α. For $\alpha = 1, 2$ and $n = 10^4$, the MSE is equal to 390,66.

In Figure 3 input data and the results of estimation for $n = 10^4$ and $\alpha = 0, 1$ are depicted. As we can see estimator found in the appropriate manner center of data and maintained its trend.

Figure 3 shows the course of the function given by (19) and estimators obtained for $n = 10^4$, with parameters α equal to $0, 1$ and $0, 6$. Figure 4 shows this course on the interval $[-1, 1]$.

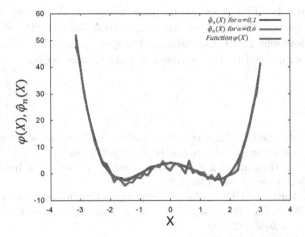

Fig. 4. Function $\phi(\cdot)$ and its estimators for different values of parameter α

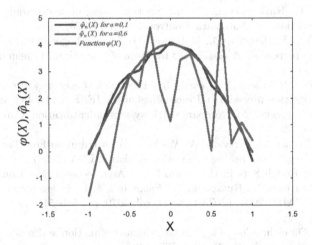

Fig. 5. Function $\phi(\cdot)$ and its estimators for different values of parameter α

4   Conclusions

In this paper we studied a recursive general regression neural network, based on the orthogonal series-type kernels. We established strong convergence assuming nonstationary noise. There are still other interesting problems of handling time varying noise, which include but are not limited to making use of supervised and unsupervised neural networks learning methods [1], [3], [12] or neurofuzzy structures developed in [10], [32] - [34], [35], [37], [38].

Acknowledgments. The paper was prepared under project operated within the Foundation for Polish Science Team Programme co-financed by the EU European Regional Development Fund, Operational Program Innovative Economy 2007-2013, and also supported by the National Science Center NCN.

References

1. Bilski, J., Rutkowski, L.: A fast training algorithm for neural networks. IEEE Transactions on Circuits and Systems II 45, 749–753 (1998)
2. Cacoullos, P.: Estimation of a multivariate density. Annals of the Institute of Statistical Mathematics 18, 179–190 (1965)
3. Cierniak, R., Rutkowski, L.: On image compression by competitive neural networks and optimal linear predictors. Signal Processing: Image Communication - a Eurasip Journal 15(6), 559–565 (2000)
4. Gałkowski, T., Rutkowski, L.: Nonparametric recovery of multivariate functions with applications to system identification. Proceedings of the IEEE 73, 942–943 (1985)
5. Gałkowski, T., Rutkowski, L.: Nonparametric fitting of multivariable functions. IEEE Transactions on Automatic Control AC-31, 785–787 (1986)
6. Greblicki, W., Rutkowska, D., Rutkowski, L.: An orthogonal series estimate of time-varying regression. Annals of the Institute of Statistical Mathematics 35(Part A), 147–160 (1983)
7. Greblicki, W., Rutkowski, L.: Density-free Bayes risk consistency of nonparametric pattern recognition procedures. Proceedings of the IEEE 69(4), 482–483 (1981)
8. Greblicki, W., Pawlak, M.: Nonparametric system indentification. Cambridge University Press (2008)
9. Györfi, L., Kohler, M., Krzyzak, A., Walk, H.: A Distribution-Free Theory of Nonparametric Regression. Springer Series in Statistics, USA (2002)
10. Nowicki, R.: Rough Sets in the Neuro-Fuzzy Architectures Based on Monotonic Fuzzy Implications. In: Rutkowski, L., Siekmann, J.H., Tadeusiewicz, R., Zadeh, L.A. (eds.) ICAISC 2004. LNCS (LNAI), vol. 3070, pp. 510–517. Springer, Heidelberg (2004)
11. Parzen, E.: On estimation of a probability density function and mode. Analysis of Mathematical Statistics 33(3), 1065–1076 (1962)
12. Patan, K., Patan, M.: Optimal training strategies for locally recurrent neural networks. Journal of Artificial Intelligence and Soft Computing Research 1(2), 103–114 (2011)
13. Rafajłowicz, E.: Nonparametric orthogonal series estimators of regression: A class attaining the optimal convergence rate in L_2. Statistics and Probability Letters 5, 219–224 (1987)
14. Rutkowski, L.: Sequential estimates of probability densities by orthogonal series and their application in pattern classification. IEEE Transactions on Systems, Man, and Cybernetics SMC-10(12), 918–920 (1980)
15. Rutkowski, L.: Sequential estimates of a regression function by orthogonal series with applications in discrimination, New York, Heidelberg, Berlin. Lectures Notes in Statistics, vol. 8, pp. 236–244 (1981)
16. Rutkowski, L.: On system identification by nonparametric function fitting. IEEE Transactions on Automatic Control AC-27, 225–227 (1982)

17. Rutkowski, L.: Orthogonal series estimates of a regression function with applications in system identification. In: Probability and Statistical Inference, pp. 343–347. D. Reidel Publishing Company, Dordrecht (1982)

18. Rutkowski, L.: On Bayes risk consistent pattern recognition procedures in a quasi-stationary environment. IEEE Transactions on Pattern Analysis and Machine Intelligence PAMI-4(1), 84–87 (1982)

19. Rutkowski, L.: On-line identification of time-varying systems by nonparametric techniques. IEEE Transactions on Automatic Control AC-27, 228–230 (1982)

20. Rutkowski, L.: On nonparametric identification with prediction of time-varying systems. IEEE Transactions on Automatic Control AC-29, 58–60 (1984)

21. Rutkowski, L.: Nonparametric identification of quasi-stationary systems. Systems and Control Letters 6, 33–35 (1985)

22. Rutkowski, L.: The real-time identification of time-varying systems by nonparametric algorithms based on the Parzen kernels. International Journal of Systems Science 16, 1123–1130 (1985)

23. Rutkowski, L.: A general approach for nonparametric fitting of functions and their derivatives with applications to linear circuits identification. IEEE Transactions Circuits Systems CAS-33, 812–818 (1986)

24. Rutkowski, L.: Sequential pattern recognition procedures derived from multiple Fourier series. Pattern Recognition Letters 8, 213–216 (1988)

25. Rutkowski, L.: Nonparametric procedures for identification and control of linear dynamic systems. In: Proceedings of 1988 American Control Conference, June 15-17, pp. 1325–1326 (1988)

26. Rutkowski, L.: An application of multiple Fourier series to identification of multivariable nonstationary systems. International Journal of Systems Science 20(10), 1993–2002 (1989)

27. Rutkowski, L.: Nonparametric learning algorithms in the time-varying environments. Signal Processing 18, 129–137 (1989)

28. Rutkowski, L., Rafajłowicz, E.: On global rate of convergence of some nonparametric identification procedures. IEEE Transaction on Automatic Control AC-34(10), 1089–1091 (1989)

29. Rutkowski, L.: Identification of MISO nonlinear regressions in the presence of a wide class of disturbances. IEEE Transactions on Information Theory IT-37, 214–216 (1991)

30. Rutkowski, L.: Multiple Fourier series procedures for extraction of nonlinear regressions from noisy data. IEEE Transactions on Signal Processing 41(10), 3062–3065 (1993)

31. Rutkowski, L., Gałkowski, T.: On pattern classification and system identification by probabilistic neural networks. Applied Mathematics and Computer Science 4(3), 413–422 (1994)

32. Rutkowski, L.: A New Method for System Modelling and Pattern Classification. Bulletin of the Polish Academy of Sciences 52(1), 11–24 (2004)

33. Rutkowski, L., Cpałka, K.: A general approach to neuro - fuzzy systems. In: Proceedings of the 10th IEEE International Conference on Fuzzy Systems, Melbourne, December 2-5, vol. 3, pp. 1428–1431 (2001)

34. Rutkowski, L., Cpałka, K.: A neuro-fuzzy controller with a compromise fuzzy reasoning. Control and Cybernetics 31(2), 297–308 (2002)

35. Scherer, R.: Boosting Ensemble of Relational Neuro-fuzzy Systems. In: Rutkowski, L., Tadeusiewicz, R., Zadeh, L.A., Żurada, J.M. (eds.) ICAISC 2006. LNCS (LNAI), vol. 4029, pp. 306–313. Springer, Heidelberg (2006)

36. Specht, D.F.: Probabilistic neural networks. Neural Networks 3, 109–118 (1990)
37. Starczewski, J., Rutkowski, L.: Interval type 2 neuro-fuzzy systems based on interval consequents. In: Rutkowski, L., Kacprzyk, J. (eds.) Neural Networks and Soft Computing, pp. 570–577. Physica-Verlag, Springer-Verlag Company, Heidelberg, New York (2003)
38. Starczewski, J., Rutkowski, L.: Connectionist Structures of Type 2 Fuzzy Inference Systems. In: Wyrzykowski, R., Dongarra, J., Paprzycki, M., Waśniewski, J. (eds.) PPAM 2001. LNCS, vol. 2328, pp. 634–642. Springer, Heidelberg (2002)
39. Szegö, G.: Orthogonal Polynomials, vol. 23. American Mathematical Society Coll. Publ. (1959)

Incidental Neural Networks
as Nomograms Generators

Bogumił Fiksak[1] and Maciej Krawczak[1,2]

[1] Systems Research Institute, Polish Academy of Sciences
Newelska 6, Warsaw, Poland
[2] Warsaw School of Information Technology
Newelska 6, Warsaw, Poland
{fiksak,krawczak}@ibspan.waw.pl

Abstract. In this paper we developed a new architecture of neural networks for generating nomograms based on series of data vectors. The paper was inspired by the XIII Hilbert's problem which was presented 1900 in the context of nomography, for the particular nomographic construction. The problem was solved by V. Arnold (a student of Andrey Kolomogorov) in 1957. For numeric data of unknown functional relation we developed the *incidental neural networks* as nomograms generators – the graphic calculating devices.

Keywords: nomography, feedforward neural networks, function approximation.

1 Introduction

A nomogram is a graphical calculating device developed by Belgian engineer Junius Massau and French mathematician Maurice d'Ocagne in 1884 [20]. The definition of a nomogram can be stated as follows: a nomogram is a function plotted on two-dimensionally space with n parameters, and knowing $n - 1$ parameters, the unknown one can be find in easy way. Generally, nomograms are used in such applications where an approximate answer is appropriated and useful; otherwise, the nomogram may be used to check the answer obtained from an exact calculation method.

One of the best monographs devoted to nomograms was written by Polish mathematician Edward Otto, Professor of Technical University of Warsaw, entitled *Nomography* issued by Oxford Pergamon Press in 1964 [16].

Since the 1970s developments of electronic calculators as well as computers have eliminated out needs of using nomograms for approximated solutions of complex functional relations. However, in spite of the main fault of nomograms, namely limited accuracy of reading, nomograms are still in use e.g. in hydraulic calculations, electrical engineering, in enterprises, banks and so on for estimating considered values. No doubt, there is one extremely important merit of nomograms – they give capability to represent a multidimensional space on a plane.

L. Rutkowski et al. (Eds.): ICAISC 2012, Part I, LNCS 7267, pp. 63–71, 2012.

The simplest nomogram is represented by a plot of a function $y = f(x)$ drown on a plane. In general, it is assumed that nomograms represent the functional relation given in the analytical form ([3], [4], [6], [15], [16], [18], [20]), e.g.

$$F(u, v, w) = 0 \tag{1}$$

In order to find a value of one variable knowing values of the rest often are used nomograms.

There is a very interesting problem to generate nomograms when the analytical form of the functional relations (1) is unknown, and data of some relation are available in a table, e.g.:

No.	u	v	w
1	u_1	v_1	w_1
2	u_2	v_2	w_2
⋮	⋮	⋮	⋮
N	u_n	v_n	w_n

In this paper a novel architecture of artificial neural networks is proposed. For complex process of calculating and drawing of nomograms a new as well as specialized architecture of neural networks was developed – the new architecture of neural networks was named as *incidental neural networks*. The term of *incidence* is known in geometry and is understood in the following way: a point is incidental to a line if and only if the point lies on the line.

The new architecture of neural networks is constructed in the following way, a number of feedforward single input and single output neural networks – called *an elementary neural network*) are joined into one. Each elementary neural network is associated with a single dimension of a considered problem. All the elementary neural networks are merged via their outputs by so called Soreau equation ([4], [15]). The Soreau equation just describes the incidence properties of elementary neural networks outputs.

Such an incidental neural network after learning is able to generate nomograms. An example was performed in order to show proper functioning of the developed incidental neural networks.

2   Nomograms

In the seventeenth century Rene Descartes introduced the coordinate system allowing algebraic equations to be expressed in geometric way and created analytical geometry ([2], [17]), the bridge between algebra and geometry. The next step was the introducing a log-log plane by Leon Lalaane in 1843 [4, 6]. However nomograms developed by Maurice d'Ocagne in the 1880s became groundbreaking in the graphical calculations, and in geometric solutions of algebraic functions. Since that time nomograms have become commonly used as calculating devices by engineers during almost a hundred years.

How important nomograms were it is worth to notice that David Hilbert set out 23 problems during the world congress of mathematicians in Paris in 1900. Hilbert's XIII problem was presented in the context of nomography, for the particular nomographic construction. The problem was solved by 19 year old Vladimir Arnold (a student of Andrey Kolomogorov) in 1957.

It is necessarily to notice that Polish mathematicians were also involved in development of the theory of nomography, e.g. Hugo Steinhaus [18, 19, 20], Edward Otto [15, 16].

There were developed several types of nomograms e.g. [4, 6, 16], but generally we can distinguish two main categories of nomograms: the first are called collinear nomograms and the second – the grid nomograms [6, 15, 16]. In this work we will focus on the collinear nomograms.

2.1   Graphic Interpretation of Multiplication/Division Operation

Let us consider a simple nomogram which can realize the following relations $x_3 = x_1 \, x_2$ shown in Fig. 1

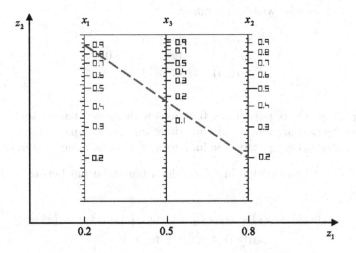

Fig. 1. Nomogram realising multiplication operation

Reading values of variables from the nomogram which consists of three axes is obvious. Connection by a straight line of a chosen point of a functional axis x_1 with a chosen point of a functional axis x_2 one obtains the solution laying on a functional axis x_3. The procedure allows finding a value of any variable under the assumption that two other variable values are known.

3   Collinear Nomograms

Let us consider a three dimensional Euclidean space. Necessary and sufficient condition in order to three points A, B, C lie on one straight line is zeroing the following matrix determinant

$$\begin{vmatrix} z_{11} & z_{12} & 1 \\ z_{21} & z_{22} & 1 \\ z_{31} & z_{32} & 1 \end{vmatrix} = 0 \tag{2}$$

where: (z_{11}, z_{12}) – the coordinates of point A, (z_{21}, z_{22}) – the coordinates of point B, (z_{31}, z_{32}) – the coordinates of point C.

The matrix determinant in (2) describes also the area of the triangle ABC. This area is equal to zero for collinear points. The exemplary matrix in (2) consists of nine entries, where the rows are related to the variables appearing in the functional relation (1); and the first column corresponds to the nomographic coordinate z_1, while the second column corresponds to the nomographic coordinate z_2, the third column consists of 1s. Such determinants are called Soreau ones, and equation (2) – Soreau equation, e.g. [16].

Equation (2) can be written as follows

$$\begin{vmatrix} z_{11}(x_1) & z_{12}(x_1) & 1 \\ z_{21}(x_2) & z_{22}(x_2) & 1 \\ z_{31}(x_3) & z_{32}(x_3) & 1 \end{vmatrix} = 0 \tag{3}$$

where:

$z_{11}(x_1)$, $z_{12}(x_1)$ are parametric functions with x_1 as a parameter,
$z_{21}(x_2)$, $z_{22}(x_2)$ are parametric functions with x_2 as a parameter,
$z_{31}(x_3)$, $z_{32}(x_3)$ are parametric functions with x_3 as a parameter.

Equation (3) can be rewritten in a form describing relations between values x_1, x_2 and x_3:

$$z_{11}(x_1)\left[z_{22}(x_2) - z_{32}(x_3)\right] - z_{21}(x_2)\left[z_{12}(x_1) - z_{32}(x_3)\right]$$
$$+z_{31}(x_3)\left[z_{12}(x_1) - z_{22}(x_2)\right] = 0 \tag{4}$$

For instance, for the case, depictured in Fig. 1, realizing multiplication which has the following general form

$$f_3(x_3) = f_1(x_1)f_2(x_2) \tag{5}$$

and Soreau equation has the form

$$\begin{vmatrix} Z_{11} & z_{12}(x_1) & 1 \\ z_{21}(x_2) & Z_{22} & 1 \\ Z_{31} & z_{32}(x_3) & 1 \end{vmatrix} = 0 \tag{6}$$

where Z_{11}, Z_{22} and Z_{31} are constant numbers.

Up to now in nomographic practice it has been assumed that the functional relation of type (1) was given in an analytic form.

However, nowadays it happens very often in practice, data are available as series of numbers of unknown relations. In such a case following the theory of nomograms we face a problem to construct functional relation of numeric data. Let us assume that data are given as k series, each of N elements, and nothing is assumed about reciprocal relation between data within each series. This way a difficult problem of constructing nomograms for non-monotonic mappings arises. In this paper this problem is solved via introducing additional dimensions. Additionally k-element series of numbers can be represented by k parametric mappings, and these mappings can be always represented just by collinear nomograms.

4   Incidental Neural Networks

The theory of neural networks was described in many papers and books, e.g. [5, 11, 12, 14]. In Fig. 2 there is shown a feedforward neural network with a single input and a single output consisting with an input and output layers, respectively, and two hidden layers. Such a network we will call *an elementary neural network*.

Artificial neural networks can be connected in many various ways. In literature one can find some examples of systems built with simple neural networks [5, 11, 14]. In considered here problem it is required to find some relation between elements of data series. For that it is proposed a new architecture of neural networks which consists of some number of elementary neural network, see Fig. 2.

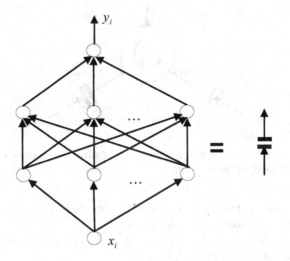

Fig. 2. Elementary neural network and it symbolic representation

It is assumed that a single elementary neural network is related or is responsible to a single dimension of the considered problem. The proposed elementary neural network consists of:

— one input neuron,
— one or two hidden layers (a number of neurons within hidden layers determines level of approximation accuracy),
— one output neuron.

Such an elementary neural network is able to model a single dimensional function, and can be used to approximate a functional axis in nomograms. From the other point of view, each element of Soreau determinant depends on one variable, and can be represented by one elementary neural network [9]. In such an elementary neural network the input is just one variable while the output constitutes a nomographic coordinate.

For instance, for the general multiplication operation (5)

$$f_3(x_3) = f_1(x_1)f_2(x_2)$$

the responsible incidental neural network is shown in Fig. 3. The exemplary new architecture consists of three elementary neural networks, each marked by two parallel thick bars, interfaced through the constraint represented by Soreau determinant depictured by a double circle.

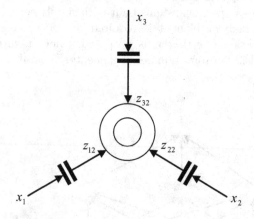

Fig. 3. The incidental neural network – a system of three elementary neural networks interfaced through Soreau determinant

The system of elementary neural networks is interfaced under some constraints as results of expressions of Soreau determinant.

It is worth to emphasise that applied special kind of elementary networks connection does not fulfil Kirchhoff low.

Adjusting Soreau determinant (6) to zero it is guaranteed that values of co-ordinates $z_{12}(x_1)$, $z_{22}(x_2)$ and $z_{32}(x_3)$ are coherent to relationship (3). The corresponding variables values x_1, x_2 and x_3 fulfil equation (4).

5   Illustrative Example

The nomogram presented in Fig. 1 consists of two vertical parallel functional axes and one horizontal. In this section we will solve the same problem as a collinear nomogram under the assumption that the relation $x_3 = x_1 x_2$ is given as several series of numbers data realising this multiplication operation.

For such a case Soreau determinant has the following form

$$\begin{vmatrix} 0.2 & z_{12}(x_1) & 1 \\ 0.5 & z_{22}(x_2) & 1 \\ 0.8 & z_{32}(x_3) & 1 \end{vmatrix} = 0 \qquad (7)$$

The considered problem is three dimensional therefore the incidental neural networks consists of three elementary neural networks interfaced by (7), such incidental network (see Fig. 3) represents the collinear as well as rectilinear nomogram. The collinear nomogram is built of three parallel functional axes. The first column in (7) is related to the first nomographic coordinate z_1, it means that $Z_{11} = 0.2$, $Z_{21} = 0.5$ and $Z_{31} = 0.8$; while the second column in (7) is related to the second nomographic coordinate z_2, and is responsible of changing of each nomographic coordinate, respectively. The values Z_{11}, Z_{21} and Z_{31} were chosen arbitrarily.

The equation (7) can be rewritten as follows

$$z_{12}(0.5 - 0.8) + z_{22}(0.8 - 0.2) + z_{32}(0.2 - 0.5) = 0 \qquad (8)$$

Each particular elementary neural network will be taught according to the following schema

$$z_{12} = \frac{-z_{22}(0.8 - 0.2) - z_{32}(0.2 - 0.5)}{0.5 - 0.8} \qquad (9)$$

$$z_{22} = \frac{-z_{12}(0.8 - 0.2) - z_{32}(0.2 - 0.5)}{0.8 - 0.2} \qquad (10)$$

$$z_{32} = \frac{-z_{12}(0.5 - 0.8) - z_{22}(0.8 - 0.2)}{0.2 - 0.5} \qquad (11)$$

For this numerical example each elementary neural networks consists of one neuron in the input layer, five neurons in the first and second hidden layers and one neuron in the output layer. After choosing constant point along the axis z_1 there is a task to find changeability of nomographic axes z_{12}, z_{22} and z_{32}.

For the learning process of the incidental neural network the backpropagation algorithm with momentum was applied; the parameters were adjusted as follows: the learning coefficient = 0.7, the momentum coefficient =0.3 and the number of steps for each elementary network within each learning sequence =10000.

The algorithm of learning of incidental neural networks can be shortly described as follows:

Step 1

Values of numerical series data are presented to inputs of the incidental neural network.

Step 2

The respective outputs of elementary neural networks are calculated subject to actual weights and neurons activation functions.

Step 3

The values z_{12}, z_{22}, z_{32} are obtained from (9)–(11).

Step 4

Differences between values obtained in Step 2 and in Step 3 are considered as learning errors in learning processes in each elementary neural network. The elementary networks are trained sequentially one network after another; it means the values z_{12}, z_{22}, z_{32} are used in training.

Step 5

If the assumed level of accuracy is not reached then the weights must be changed and algorithm starts from the beginning, otherwise the algorithm is stopped.

This way, the functional axes which are parallel, they are perpendicular to nomographic axis of abscissae z_1; in result the nomogram is developed. In the incidental neural network the inputs are represented by variables x_1, x_2 and x_3, while the outputs of the elementary networks $z_{12}(x_1)$, $z_{22}(x_2)$ and $z_{32}(x_3)$ represent location of x_1, x_2 and x_3 on axis of ordinates z_2 (the coordinates of the functional axes).

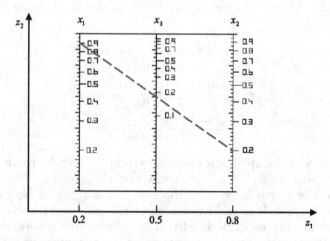

Fig. 4. Collinear nomogram realising multiplication operation

Using of nomograms is very easy, in the case of the example from Fig. 4, one needs to draw a straight line between the axes x_1 and x_2 – the result of the multiplication operation is read as the intersection of this drew line and the axis x_3.

6   Conclusions

In this paper it was shown that using collinear nomograms one can visualise and analyse causes of changeability of functional relation in multidimensional spaces.

In order to generate nomograms for numeric data of unknown relations we developed the new architecture of neural networks, here called the incidental neural networks. For such neural networks we developed the training algorithm based on the well-known backpropagation one.

Solution of many examples, also multidimensional, showed correctness of the assumptions as well as efficiency of the computer implementation.

References

1. Arnold, V.I.: Representation of continuous functions of three variables by the super-position of continuous functions of two variables. Matematicheski Sbornik 48(90) (1959)
2. Borsuk, K.: Analitic multidimensional geometry. PWN, Warsaw (1983)
3. Chen, C.-H., Härdle, W., Unwin, A. (eds.): Handbook of Data Visualization. Springer, Heidelberg (2008)
4. Doerfler, R.: The Lost Art of Nomography (2010),
   http://myreckonings.com/wordpress/wp-content/uploads/nomography.pdf
5. Duch, W., Korbicz, J., Rutkowski, L., Tadeusiewicz, R.: Neural networks, vol. 6. Academic Press Exit, Warsaw (2000)
6. Evesham, H.A.: The History and Development of Nomography. Docent Press (2010)
7. Fiksak, B.: Aplication of Kohonen map for strategic analysis of enterprise. Transition to Advanced Market Institutions and Economies. IBS PAN, Warszawa (1997)
8. Fiksak, B.: Neuron model as a nomogram. In: Hołubiec, J. (ed.) Systems Analysis in Finance and Management. SRI PAS, Warsaw (2010)
9. Fiksak, B.: Nomogram as a graphical calculator in four-dimensional space. In: Hołubiec, J. (ed.) Systems Analysis in Finance and Management. SRI PAS, Warsaw (2011)
10. Hankins, T.L.: Blood, Dirt, and Nomograms: A Particular History of Graphs, vol. 90, pp. 50–80. The University of Chicago Press, Isis (1999)
11. Korbicz, J., Obuchowicz, A., Uciński, D.: Artificial neural networks. Academic Press PLJ, Warsaw (1994)
12. Kurkova, V.: Kolmogorov's Theorem and Multilayer Neural Networks. Neural Networks 5(3), 501–506 (1992)
13. Mihoc, M.: About canonical forms of the nomographic functions. Studia Univ. "Babes-Bolyai" Mathematica, vol. LIV(3) (2009)
14. Ossowski, S.: Neural networks. Academic Press PW, Warsaw (2000)
15. Otto, E.: Nomography. Macmillan, New York (1964)
16. Otto, E.: Nomografia. In: Steinhaus, H. (ed.) Elements of Modern Mathematics for Engineers. PWN, Warsaw–Wroclaw (1971)
17. Sierpiński, W.: Algebra principles. PTM, Warsaw (1951)
18. Steinhaus, H.: On various functional scales and their applications. Parametr. 2 (1931)
19. Steinhaus, H.: One hundred problems in elementary mathematics. PWN, Warsaw (1958)
20. Steinhaus, H.: Mathematical Snapshots. WSiP, Warsaw (1989)

Selection of Activation Functions in the Last Hidden Layer of the Multilayer Perceptron

Krzysztof Halawa

Wrocław University of Technology,
27 Wybrzeże Wyspiańskiego St.,
50-370 Wrocław, Poland
krzysztof.halawa@pwr.wroc.pl

Abstract. The paper presents some novel methods of the activation function selection in the last hidden layer of a multilayer perceptron. For this selection, the least squares method is used. The proposed ways make it possible to decrease the cost function value. They enable achievement of a good compromise between the network complexity and the results being obtained. The methods do not require a start of learning of neural networks from the very beginning. They fit very well for improvement of the action of learnt multilayer perceptrons. They may be particularly useful for construction of the devices under microprocessor control, that have not a big memory nor computing power.

Keywords: neural networks, multilayer perceptron, activation functions, least squares method.

1 Introduction

The multilayer perceptron (MLP) is one of more popular architectures of neural networks. Its significant advantage is the predisposition for processing of multidimensional data. In [2], it was shown that MLPs are very suitable for approximation of multidimensional functions that have a bound on the first moment of the magnitude distribution of the Fourier transform. In [2], it was shown that, in the case of approximation of such functions with the use of MLP with one hidden layer, the integrated squared error does not depend on the problem dimension and is of the $O(1/n)$ order, where n is the neuron number in the hidden layer.

The multilayer perceptron learning produces many difficulties. For the learning, gradient algorithms are used mainly, that may be stuck at many local minima of a cost function. The learning process is often repeated many times, starting at various initial values of the weights. In [8] and [1], the learning methods with the use of recurrent least squares method were shown. MPL learning algorithms that make use of the nonlinear optimisation method and the least squares method (LSM) were published. One of them is the staggered training (ST) of MLP, described in [9]. In the first step, the output layer weights are computed with use of LSM. Next, the weights in the other layers are determined

L. Rutkowski et al. (Eds.): ICAISC 2012, Part I, LNCS 7267, pp. 72–80, 2012.

with use of the nonlinear optimisation methods. The two steps are repeated alternately.

Many works were published wherein perceptrons of various activation functions were applied, e.g. with splines. In the microcontroller-based devices, wherein the low computing capability is very significant, the look-up tables are used, including the values used for fast interpolation of the sigmoidal functions [5]. In [4], the activation functions $f(x) = a(1 - exp(-bx))/(1 + exp(-bx))$ were applied, where a and b were the parameters selected with use of gradient algorithms. The method presented in [7] may be used to improve the action of the MLP trained earlier. This includes the exchange of all activation functions in the last hidden layer into the weighed sums of functions of the series

$$f\left(\frac{x}{2^h}\right), f\left(\frac{x}{2^{h-1}}\right), \ldots, f(x), \ldots, f\left(2^{h-1}x\right), f\left(2^h x\right), \tag{1}$$

where h is a positive integer and f are sigmoid functions. The method proposed in [7] was described in Sect. 2 of this paper. In [7], the computer simulation results were presented, a part of which was done with use of data of the well-known UCI Benchmarks [6]. Due to application of this method for MLPs trained by the Levenberg-Marquardt algorithm, a considerable decrease of the cost function was achieved

$$E = \frac{1}{N} \sum_{i=1}^{N} \left(\hat{y}(\mathbf{u}_i) - d_i\right)^2, \tag{2}$$

where $\hat{y}(\mathbf{u}_i)$ is the MLP output value when the inputs are equal to the elements of the vector $\mathbf{u}_i = [u_{1,i}, u_{2,i}, \ldots, u_{q,i},]^T$, q is the number of the network inputs, d_i is the desired value of the network output, related with $\mathbf{u}_i$, N is the number of pairs $\{\mathbf{u}_i, d_i\}$ in the learning set.

In [7] the method making use of the activation functions created with the use of some elements of the series (1) only is also presented. This method is a crummy one. In the Sect. 3 of this article, much better methods for selecting these elements have been proposed and the results of the simulation experiments carried out have been shown. The methods presented in the Sect. 3 make it possible to achieve a good compromise between the number of the necessary computations and the results being obtained. They may be particularly useful for construction of the devices under microprocessor control, that have not, at their disposal, a big memory nor computing power. The methods may be used also for the network regularisation. Because of the concise notations, in the present study, the formulae for the networks that have only one output have been presented. The proceeding for the networks of a higher number of outputs is analogical.

2 Method for Improvement of the Multilayer Perceptron Action through Application of Various Activation Functions in the Last Hidden Layer

The method described in [7] may be applied with MLP that has, in the output layer, the neurons with linear activation functions, $f_{lin}(x) = x$. In this layer, linear activation functions are applied very often. The method shown in [7] may be used for improvement of the action of MLP trained by an arbitrary algorithm, e.g. by the Levenberg-Marquardt algorithm. In [7], it has been shown that, in some cases, it makes it possible to decrease the cost function value (2) of several orders in a very short time. Let $g(x)$ denote the sigmoid activation function of neurons in the last hidden layer. The method described in [7] may be presented, in short, in the following steps:

◇ **Step 1.** Computation of the cost function value (2).
◇ **Step 2.** A change of the activation functions for all neurons in the last hidden layer to the functions defined by the formula

$$f_k(x) = w_{k,1} g\left(\frac{x}{2^h}\right) + w_{k,2} g\left(\frac{x}{2^{h-1}}\right) + \ldots$$
$$+ w_{k,\lceil m/2 \rceil} g(x) \tag{3}$$
$$+ \ldots + w_{k,m-1} g\left(2^{h-1}x\right) + w_{k,m} g\left(2^h x\right),$$

where $k = 1, \ldots, s$ denotes the number of neuron in the last hidden layer, s is the number of neurons in this layer, $w_{k,1}, \ldots, w_{k,m}$, are real numbers, the selection way of which has been described in step 5.
◇ **Step 3.** A change of the values of all weights in the output layer to one.
◇ **Step 4.** Solving the set of normal equations

$$\mathbf{Zw} = \mathbf{d}, \tag{4}$$

where $\mathbf{w} = [w_{1,1}, w_{1,2}, \ldots, w_{1,m}, w_{2,1}, w_{2,2}, \ldots, w_{2,m}, \ldots, w_{s,1}, w_{s,2}, \ldots, w_{s,m}, b]^T$,
$\mathbf{d} = [d_1, d_2, \ldots, d_N]^T$,

$$\mathbf{Z} = \begin{bmatrix} \mathbf{z}_1(\mathbf{u}_1) & \mathbf{z}_2(\mathbf{u}_1) & \cdots & \mathbf{z}_s(\mathbf{u}_1) & 1 \\ \mathbf{z}_1(\mathbf{u}_2) & \mathbf{z}_2(\mathbf{u}_2) & \cdots & \mathbf{z}_s(\mathbf{u}_2) & 1 \\ \vdots & \vdots & \ddots & \vdots & \vdots \\ \mathbf{z}_1(\mathbf{u}_N) & \mathbf{z}_2(\mathbf{u}_N) & \cdots & \mathbf{z}_s(\mathbf{u}_N) & 1 \end{bmatrix},$$

$$\mathbf{z}_k(\mathbf{u}_i) = \left[g\left(\frac{x_k(\mathbf{u}_i)}{2^h}\right), g\left(\frac{x_k(\mathbf{u}_i)}{2^{h-1}}\right), \ldots, g\left(2^{h-1}x_k(\mathbf{u}_i)\right), g\left(2^h x_k(\mathbf{u}_i)\right) \right],$$

$i = 1, \ldots, N$, $k = 1, \ldots, s$, $x_k(\mathbf{u}_i)$ is the weighted sum of neuron inputs for the k-th neuron in the last hidden layer when network inputs are equal to the elements of the vector $\mathbf{u}_i$, b is the bias of the neuron in the output layer.

The values of parameters of the new activation functions, that minimise the cost function (2) are given by the formula

$$\mathbf{w} = (\mathbf{Z}^T \mathbf{Z})^{-1} \mathbf{Z} \mathbf{d}. \tag{5}$$

Due to the numerical errors, the elements of the vector $\mathbf{w}$ should not be calculated from the equation (5), but determined by solving the normal equation set (4), using the numerical methods [3].

In [7], it was specified that, possibly, the following step 5 may be carried out.

◇ **Optional step 5.** Remove the columns of the matrix $\mathbf{Z}$, corresponding to the least elements of the vector $\mathbf{w}$ and solve the modified least squares problem (MLSP) that will be obtained after the removal of the columns. MLSP may be solved fast by using an appropriate algorithm that make use of the QR distribution [3]. Omit the terms of the activation function (3) with the least elements of the vector $\mathbf{w}$. If the value of the cost function decreased considerably, than step 5 should be repeated; in the other case, the changes input within the last iteration should be cancelled.

Step 5 may be summarized as follows:

− From the vector $\mathbf{w}$, remove the elements much lower than the other ones.
− From the matrix $\mathbf{Z}$, remove the columns related with the removed elements.
− Simplify the activation functions of the neurons in the last hidden layer, by omitting the terms of the formula (3), that are related to the removed elements of the vector $\mathbf{w}$.
− Determine the new values of the elements of the shorted vector $\mathbf{w}$ by solving MLSP achieved from appropriate numerical methods.

In the next section, the proceeding methods that are much better than the procedure specified in step 5 are proposed.

In [7], it was shown that the execution of the steps 1-4 may significantly decrease the cost function value in a time much shorter than one epoch of the Levenberg-Marquardt algorithm training. This procedure is perfectly suited to further improve the operation of the application wherein MLP successfully works for some time. It is not needed to begin the whole process from the very beginning. The hazard of being stuck at a "crummy" local minimum of the cost function does not exist.

The steps 1-4 make it possible to reduce the cost function value though further learning with the gradient-type methods does not result in a noticeable improvement. The application of these steps brought very positive results even for large networks that had several dozens of inputs. The described procedure was tested, among others, on the databases of the UCI benchmarks, that had many inputs and a high number of instances [6].

3 Activation Function Selection Methods for the Last Hidden Layer of a Multilayer Perceptron

Omitting the term $w_{k,\lceil m/2 \rceil} g(x)$ in step 5 may increase the value (2); therefore such a procedure is not advised. In a later part of this study, the results of the computer simulations were presented, where, due to such proceeding, the value (2) was significantly increased.

It is vital that, in the sum (3), the term wherein the function $g(cx)$, where $c = 1$, is not omitted since, after training the network with a gradient algorithm, the neurons weights in the last hidden layer are matched for the neurons with the activation functions $g(cx)$.

In the present study, the application of one of the following methods has been proposed:

Method 1

- From the vector $\mathbf{w}$, remove all elements much lower than the other ones, except of the elements $w_{k,\lceil m/2 \rceil}$, where $k = 1, \ldots, s$. Let us note that, in the formula (3), the functions $g(x)$ are multiplied by the elements $w_{k,\lceil m/2 \rceil}$.
- From the matrix $\mathbf{Z}$, remove the columns related with the removed elements of the vector $\mathbf{w}$.
- Simplify the activation functions for the neurons in the last hidden layer, by omitting the terms on the right hand side of the equation (3), that are related with the removed elements of the vector $\mathbf{w}$.
- Determine the new values of the shortened vector through solving MLSP achieved, with appropriate numerical methods.

Method 2

a) Assume $k = 1$.
b) From between the elements $w_{k,1}, w_{k,2}, \ldots, w_{k,m}$, leave only the biggest element and the element $w_{k,\lceil m/2 \rceil}$.
c) if $k \neq s$, then increase k and go to step b.
d) From the matrix $\mathbf{Z}$, remove the columns related with the removed elements of the vector $\mathbf{w}$.
e) Simplify the activation functions of the neurons in the last hidden layer, through omitting the terms of (3), that are related with the removed elements of the vector $\mathbf{w}$.
f) Determine the new values of the shortened vector elements through solving MLSP achieved, by appropriate numerical methods.

Method 3

Assume $h = 2$. Carry out the steps 1-4 described in the Sect. 2. Till the value of the cost function (2) is too high, increase the value of h and repeat the steps 1-4.

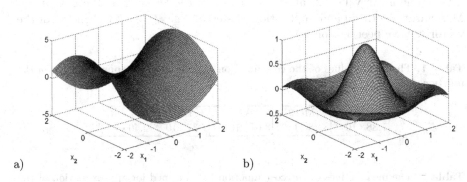

a)   b)

Fig. 1. The plots of the functions a) $f_1(x_1, x_2) = x_1^2 - x_2^2$ b) $f_2(x_1, x_2) =$ sinc $\left(\sqrt{x_1^2 - x_2^2} \right)$

3.1   Computer Simulations

The MLPs were trained to approximate the following functions:

a) $f_1(x_1, x_2) = x_1^2 - x_2^2$,

b) $f_2(x_1, x_2) = $ sinc $\left(\sqrt{x_1^2 - x_2^2} \right)$, where sinc $= \begin{cases} \frac{\sin x}{x} & \text{for } x \neq 0 \\ 1 & \text{for } x = 0 \end{cases}$.

The functions have been presented in Fig. 3.1. MLPs had one hidden layer, each, wherein there were 40 neurons with a bipolar activation function $f_{last}(x) = 2/(1 + \exp(-2x)) - 1$. In the output layer, there was one neuron with a linear activation function. The hidden layer's weights and biases were initialized according to the Nguyen-Widrow algorithm [10]. To initialize the output layer, random values were used. The learning with the Levenberg-Marquardt algorithm was interrupted after 200 epochs since the value of the cost function, (2), was changing very insignificantly only. It was assumed $h = 3$.

In the tables 1 and 2, the mean values of the cost function, that were obtained when applying various proceeding methods. These mean values were computed from 10 simulation results. In the tables 1 and 2, the following denotations have been used:

LM - The mean value (2) after completion of learning with the Levenbeg-Maquardt algorithm. The procedure described in Sect. 2 has not been used.
ALL - The mean value (2) after completion of learning with the Levenberg-Marquardt algorithm and application of the steps 1-4 presented in Sect. 2. No elements were removed from the vector **w**.
Met2 - The mean value (2) after completion of the learning by the Levenberg-Marquardt algorithm and application of the steps 1-4 and method 2.
LSM - The mean value (2) after completion of the learning by the Levenberg-Marquardt algorithm and computing of the weights in the output layer, with the use of LSM.

LAR - The mean value (2) after completion of the learning by the Levenberg-Marquardt algorithm and application of step 5. The 40 biggest elements of the vector **w** have been left only.

Table 1. The mean values of the cost function (2) obtained for approximation of the function f_1

LM	Met2	ALL	LSM	LAR
$7.38 \cdot 10^{-8}$	$8.85 \cdot 10^{-9}$	$3.67 \cdot 10^{-15}$	$7.37 \cdot 10^{-8}$	$2.40 \cdot 10^{-6}$

Table 2. The mean values of the cost function (2) obtained for approximation of the function f_2

LM	Met2	ALL	LSM	LAR
$1.60 \cdot 10^{-6}$	$1.36 \cdot 10^{-6}$	$8.24 \cdot 10^{-8}$	$1.60 \cdot 10^{-6}$	$7.18 \cdot 10^{-4}$

In Tables 3 and 4, there are presented the mean network learning time with the Levenberg-Marquardt algorithm and the step 4 execution time for the functions f_1 and f_2. In these tables, the following denotations have been assumed:
t_{LM} - learning time with the Levenberg-Marquardt algorithm,
t_{LSM} - step 4 execution time,
$t_{LM}/t_{LSM} = \frac{t_{LSM}}{t_{LM}}$.

Table 3. The mean computation time for the f_1 function

$t_{LM}[s]$	$t_{LSM}[s]$	t_{LM}/t_{LSM}
35.19	0.6811	51.67

The values in the columns ALL of Tables 1 and 2 are of several orders of magnitude lower than the values in the columns LM, what proves the effectiveness of the steps 1-4. When comparing the values in the columns denoted by LM and LAR, one with another, it is easy to find that step 5 specified in Sect. 2 should not be applied. If it is desirable that the determination of the output values happens with the use of a low number of arithmetical operations, then one of the methods 1,2,3 specified in this section may be applied. The methods 1 and 3 may be used for conduction of the regularisation. If the data for learning and testing is at our disposal, then - applying the method 3 - it is possible to increase the number of elements of the vector **w** till the instant that the cost function for the test set starts to increase. Repeating the method 1 several times, the number of elements of the vector **w** may be decreased till the cost function starts to increase.

Table 4. The mean computation time for the f_2 function

$t_{LM}[s]$	$t_{LSM}[s]$	t_{LM}/t_{LSM}
41.92	0.4931	85.13

Among the steps 1-4, step 4 is characterised with the highest computational complexity. The information about the number of calculations necessary to solve the normal equation set (4) with various numerical methods is given in [3]. The execution time for the steps 1-4 is more than 50 times less than the learning time with the Levenberg-Marquardt algorithm. The execution time of each of the methods 1,2 and 3 is much less than the execution time for the steps 1-4. On the basis of the data of Tables 3 and 4, it may be easily noticed that the steps 1-4 and the methods 1-3 are executed much faster than learning MLP with the Levenberg-Marquardt algorithm. They feature with a considerably lower computational complexity than 200 epochs of the Levenberg-Marquardt algorithm.

4 Summary

The steps 1-4 of the method described in Sect. 2 make it possible to improve significantly the approximation capability of the network in a short time. The author does not recommend to apply step 5. If it is desirable to accelerate computation of the output values, then it is better to apply the methods proposed in Sect. 3. Due to application of method 2, simple activation functions are obtained, that are the sums of maximally two terms. The methods proposed enable to reach an adequate compromise between the number of computations and the results being obtained. The methods 1 and 3 may be applied to carry out the regularisation. In practical applications, often, MLPs of a very high number of inputs and neurons (several hundred inputs) are often used. The learning of such networks is a long term process. The steps 1-4 complete with the methods proposed in Sect. 3 do not need to begin network learning from the very beginning and may be applied to improve the operation of the networks trained by various algorithms.

The methods presented may be implemented easily, making use of ready-for-use libraries for solving the normal equation sets. There are many open Source libraries licensed under free software licenses e.g. the GNU General Public License.

References

1. Azimi-Sadjadi, M.R., Liou, R.J.: Fast learning process of multilayer neural networks using recursive least squares method. IEEE Transactions on Signal Processing 40(2), 446–450 (1992)
2. Barron, A.: Universal Approximation Bounds for Superpositions of a Sigmoidal Function. IEEE Transactions on Information Theory 39(3), 930–945 (1993)

3. Björck, A.: Numerical Methods for Least Squares Problems. SIAM, Philadelphia (1996)
4. Chyi-Tsong, C., Wei-Der, C.: A Feedforward Neural Network with Function Shape Autotuning. Neural Networks 9(4), 627–641 (1996)
5. Ebert, T., Bänfer, O., Nelles, O.: Multilayer Perceptron Network with Modified Sigmoid Activation Functions. In: Wang, F.L., Deng, H., Gao, Y., Lei, J. (eds.) AICI 2010. LNCS, vol. 6319, pp. 414–421. Springer, Heidelberg (2010)
6. Frank, A., Asuncion, A.: UCI Machine Learning Repository. University of California, School of Information and Computer Science, Irvine, CA (2010), http://archive.ics.uci.edu/ml
7. Halawa, K.: A method to improve the performance of multilayer perceptron by utilizing various activation functions in the last hidden layer and the least squares method. Neural Processing Letters 34(3), 293–303 (2011)
8. Al-Batah, M.S., Isa, N.A.M., Zamli, K.Z., Azizli, K.A.: Modified Recursive Least Squares algorithm to train the Hybrid Multilayered Perceptron (HMLP) network. Applied Soft Computing 10, 236–244 (2010)
9. Nelles, O.: Nonlinear System Identification: From Classical Approaches to Neural Networks and Fuzzy Models, pp. 253–255. Springer, Berlin (2001)
10. Nguyen, D., Widrow, B.: Improving the learning speed of 2-layer neural networks by choosing initial values of the adaptive weights. In: Proceedings of the International Joint Conference on Neural Networks, vol. 3, pp. 21–26 (1990)

Information Freedom
and Associative Artificial Intelligence

Adrian Horzyk

AGH University of Science and Technology,
Automatics Department, 30-059 Cracow, Mickiewicza Av. 30, Poland
horzyk@agh.edu.pl
http://home.agh.edu.pl/~horzyk

Abstract. Today, majority of collected data and information are usually passively stored in data bases and in various kinds of memory cells and storage media that let them do nothing more than waiting for being used by some algorithms that will read, write or modify them. Nowadays, the majority of computational techniques do not allow pieces of information to associate with each other automatically. This paper introduces a novelty theory that lets information be free and active. There is allowed that some pieces of information can automatically and autonomously associate with the other pieces of it after some introduced associative rules characteristic also for biological information systems. As a result of this, each new information has an automatic impact on information processing in a brainlike artificial neural structure that can enable machines to associate various pieces of information automatically and autonomously. It can also enable machines actively perform some cognitive and thinking processes and constitute real artificial intelligence in the future.

Keywords: associative artificial intelligence AAI, associative graph data structure AGDS, actively associated data neural networks AADNN, associative graph neurocomputing AGNC, autonomous association of pieces of information, cognitive science.

1 Introduction

Contemporary computer science is a wide field of knowledge that is focused on searching for even more efficient and optimal algorithms that let people solve many complex problems of our civilization. Nowadays, various algorithms process data that are usually stored in relational data bases and in various collections like tables, lists etc. Almost all today used data structures and computer science methodologies treat data and information like passive objects that are separated from algorithms. Information has neither active nor autonomous influence on a way of data processing except some concepts of the reactive programming [1]. The stored information is usually confined and trapped in such kind of passive memories. Moreover, data base tables define only a few intentionally defined relations between some pieces of information and data. Only sorting, searching or other data mining algorithms can try to arrange many various pieces

L. Rutkowski et al. (Eds.): ICAISC 2012, Part I, LNCS 7267, pp. 81–89, 2012.

of information and get a new converted, transformed or extracted information. The computer science tries to develop sophisticated algorithms that will be able to create new algorithms that will be able to solve even more complex tasks. Such sophisticated algorithms usually use many nested loops that usually lead to high computational complexity and cause many numerical errors and instability. Nowadays, we have to solve the NP-hard and NP-complete tasks using some soft-computing or approximated algorithms that usually supply some suboptimal solutions.

This paper focuses attention on some information associative processes that can autonomously and automatically influence the computational process using natural associations between data and a special active associative graph data structure (AGDS) modeling these associations. Moreover, this paper introduces the additional associative adaptation process that can take place between some pieces of information in order to create new associations and rebuild or supplement the information data structure that can be widespread to solve various complex tasks. Each new piece of information has to be free to rearrange the previously constructed associative information data structure in order to enable it to automatically influence and change next associative processes that can autonomously improve next results of associative computation. Each new piece of information can partially change the way of data processing in the AGDS. Each new piece of information changes the associative algorithms built in the AGDS. The introduced associative rules let many pieces of information create some associative graph structures that are able to solve some computational tasks on the basis of these pieces of information and limited to them and their derivatives. This alternative way to classical computational methodology is called here an associative artificial intelligence (AAI).

At first, there is explained how the pieces of information can be associated in the biological brainlike way. Next, a novelty associative graph data structure (AGDS) will be described, constructed for exemplary data and shown how the pieces of information can be associated to influence each other. Then, the AGDS will be transformed into a novelty actively associated data neural networks (AADNN) that is an active neuronal graph. This graph enables us to activate some pieces of information and compute some derived pieces of information using associative connections. Moreover, the AADNN can develop its graph structure to specialize in solving some computational tasks. This special kind of graph computation is called here an associative graph neurocomputing (AGNC). The AGNC never uses nested loops and usually decreases computational complexity because usually all necessary pieces of information are closely associated (interconnected) to the initializing piece of information. The associations cause that any given data have not to be searched through in many various loops like in the classical computational methodology.

Following the words of prof. Ryszard Tadeusiewicz "it's time to facilitate our everyday life by thinking machines" [6].

This work has been supported and subsidized by the grant "Modeling and algorithms for control and decision making for discrete dynamics processes".

2   Autonomous Associations of Pieces of Information

There are some questions that have to be answered before we start with the brainlike associative neural computing: How to recall some pieces of information from biological associative systems? How some pieces of information can automatically influence the other pieces of it and recall them associatively? How such associative processes are controlled and what rules manage them? How some new pieces of information can influence the thinking and cognition processes? What data structures are needed to represent associated pieces of information and let them activate each other to enable us thinking and cognition?

Brains - biological associative systems - have their own mechanisms to get access to the pieces of information collected in the past. When we ask somebody something we create a context for the associative processes we want to trigger in the brain of the asked person. The asked person adds the question to his context of thinking. Then, the whole context automatically and regardless of ones will recalls the other associated pieces of information that widespread or partially substitutes the previous context. The human conscious will can partially control reactions and decide what to do next with the recalled pieces of information. He can also ask oneself to widespread the context of the next associations after his needs or fears [3]. The asking person also activates his associative processes. If he gets an answer it is automatically associated with the question. The questions are the natural way to recall the other associated pieces of information and widespread the knowledge of associative systems. The questions let us create some new associations and develop our intelligence.

The questions and the following answers to them are a special case of the following pieces of information that are automatically associated and remembered. Also the other following pieces of information in space or in time are automatically associated and remembered even if they could have no special meaning or sense. Even completely pointless pieces of information can be associated and remembered if only they follow in space or in time. Such kind of association is called here an association of sequence (ASEQ) [4]. It lets us learn many necessary rules of action and reactions, examine consequences, develop, specify, clarify, deduct, learn etc. It also causes that we make mistakes and could be wrong.

The questions also recall some similar pieces of information that match these questions. The recalled similar pieces of information activate the other pieces of information partially creating an answer to the question. This process can be gradual and is dependent on a difficulty of the given question. The similarities can activate the associated answer or some pieces of information that can be next associated in the ASEQ way with the other pieces of information and so on. This second important associative mechanism is called here an association of similarity (ASIM). The ASIM recalls some pieces of information if the context contains some subset of the same or close data values. In this way some equivalent, resemble, negative, inverse, included or complementary pieces of information can be automatically activated because there is a subgroup of data values (forming these pieces of information) that is the same or similar.

The ASIM and ASEQ can let natural or artificial associative systems recall some next pieces of information in various configurations and influence the process of thinking. These two fundamental kinds of association let us also be creative because all recalled pieces of information after the ASIM and ASEQ can create many new contexts constructed from the recalled pieces of information. Following the words of Albert Einstein, one of the most important ability is the ability to construct questions and ask. The development of intelligence is not possible without asking, associating, comparing, controlling and gathering well-associated pieces of information that forms our knowledge and enables us intelligent behaviours.

3   Associative Structures, Networks and Computations

The associative graph data structure AGDS is created for the associative representation of many pieces of information. It is a special kind of a graph that consists of nodes and edges. This structure is passive and reflects only the given pieces of information of the data set together with the ASIM and ASEQ that could be found in this data set. The nodes represent separated values of parameters, all pieces of information and some extra information about e.g. classes. The edges interconnect all the nodes of the most closest values separately for each parameter (ASIM), the nodes representing pieces of information that follow one another in space or in time (ASEQ), the nodes representing parameter values with the nodes representing the pieces of information (ADEF) and the nodes representing the other information, e.g. classes, clusters etc. It is able to map all existing ASIM and ASEQ in data set into this structure. In order to start any associative computations all pieces of information gathered in tables or data bases should be converted to the AGDS (fig. 1a). The AGDS rearranges the traditional data structure connecting the most similar data values after the known numerical or lexical orders. It also connects the pieces of information that appear in a chronological sequence or a spatial neighborhood. The AGDS arranges all pieces of information in such a way to be able to perform associative graph neurocomputing (AGNC) using ASIM, ASEQ and ADEF to retrieve the other associated pieces of information from this structure in the constant computational complexity (CCC). Moreover, the same parameter values are never duplicated but represented by the same graph nodes. In such a way the AGDS usually aggregates many same values of various pieces of information. This aggregation creates automatically many dependencies between various pieces of information. Furthermore, the closest parameter values are interconnected, so the similar pieces of information are also automatically partially associated (ASIM) in an appropriate degree to this similarity computing a weight (1) of this connection (fig. 1b). Finally, the pieces of information are connected after their spatial or chronological sequence defining the ASEQ (fig. 1b).

$$w^{VN} = \frac{ParameterRange - |Value - NeighborValue|}{ParameterRange} \tag{1}$$

In order to trigger any piece of information, the AGDS has to be converted into the active neural network called here an actively associated data neural network (AADNN). The AADNN consists of various kinds of neurons that represent parameter values and each piece of information from the data set. The basic AADNN is built from the AGDS. The AGDS nodes are converted into the AADNN neurons and the AGDS edges are converted into the AADNN connections. The similar parameter values are connected and weighted (1) to reflect the influence on other close parameter values that are connected to this neuron. The unordered (e.g. symbolic) parameter values are not directly connected. All defining connections between the neurons representing the pieces of information (SN_k) and the neurons representing parameter values (VN_j) could be weighted to reflect the degree of representativeness of each parameter value (2) or the other associations that define each piece of information. The number of all existing associations between the VN_j neuron and all other connected SN_k neurons is denoted as q_j. The less associations from the VN_j neuron to the other SN_k neurons are there the more associatively defining (ADEF) is this connection and the bigger weight it has. The neurons representing the pieces of information compute simple weighted sum and are chronologically or spatially connected only if they represent some known sequences or spatial arrangements. All defining connections between the neurons representing classes and the neurons representing the samples of these classes are usually not weighted. The class neurons usually compute the maximum of the incoming excitations from all connected sample neurons.

$$w_j^{SN_k} = \frac{1}{q_j \sum_{i \in SN_k} 1/q_i} \tag{2}$$

The AGDS construction is the most favourable if constructing together with the AADNN on parallel and reactive [1] working neurons. Any new piece of information activates the current AADNN and where the excitement is the strongest, there is added this new piece of information. There is even no need to compute the global maximum of all neuron excitations. There is only necessary to define the time in which each neuron will start its parallel process of interconnecting with the new piece of information and its parameter values due to its strength of the excitation by it and its type defining to which part of the new piece of information it can connect. This process reflects the natural plasticity processes known in biological neurons that can put out their dendrites or branch their axonal trees. The stronger excited neuron the earlier it reacts on the new piece of information and starts trying to interconnect with it. When the new piece of information is already interconnected enough then it refuses and rejects interconnecting to the other not so strongly excited neurons they ask it for connecting later. In this way each new piece of information is always connected to the strongest excited neurons in the CCC and is automatically putted in the order. The AGDS together with the AADNN can be constructed in the linear computational complexity (LCC) after any given classical data set. If simulating it on a nonparallel machine it takes pessimistically the square computational

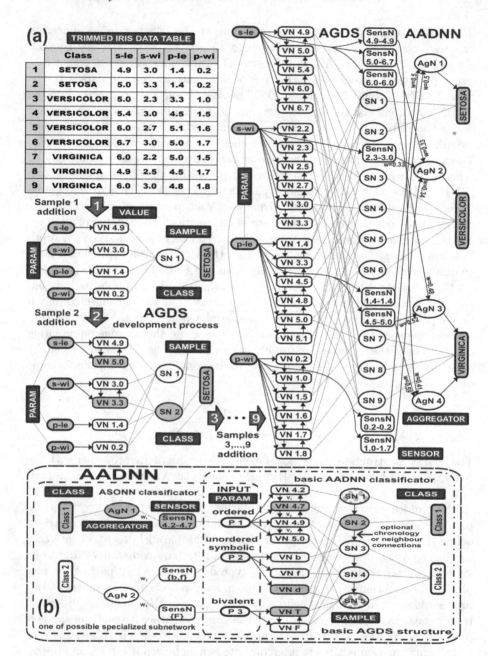

Fig. 1. (a) The conversion from the classical table data structure of trimmed Iris data set into the AGDS and AADNN. The final AADNN is developed into the specialized AADNN containing the extra subnetwork ASONN for classification. Each sensor is sensitive for some given range of the parameter values. Each aggregator computes the weighted sum of some sensors outputs. (b) The AGDS, AADNN, ASONN for the exemplar numerical, symbolic and boolean input value parameters.

complexity (SCC). The neurons of the AADNN are conditionally reactive and there are some similarities to the reactive programming [1].

The AADNN can grow up, develop and create some specialized neuronal substructures (e.g. the sensors and aggregators in the ASONN in fig. 1) dedicated to some kind of computation due to the information that can be gathered from the existing information and the created AADNN associations. In order to start the grown up processes, the AADNN has to be excited by some subgroup of neurons (i.e. the context) representing the goal of the desirable specialization, e.g. the classification to one of the defined classes. In case of classification, the neurons representing classes are separately excited one after the other examining the reactions of the associated neurons and the following associated neurons and so on. The excited class neuron triggers gradually the neurons representing training samples that define this class. The excited sample neuron triggers the value neurons that define this sample. The excited value neurons trigger other close value neurons due to their similarity and also partially trigger the other sample neurons that are defined by these exited value neurons. The other excited sample neurons can be a member of the same class or a member of the other class. The stronger is the excitation of such neurons the more correlated are these neurons with the firstly triggered sample neuron by the class neuron at the beginning of this process. The strongest excited samples of the other classes should be discriminated at first, so the most discriminating are the value neurons that do not excite these samples of the other classes. Such value neurons should be aggregated and they can create together the specialized sensor neurons that will be profitable for the specialized classification subnetwork called here an associative self-optimizing neural network (ASONN) which precise construction will be described in the other paper [5]. This short sample demonstrates only the ability of the AADNN to develop after its intentional excitation. All above presented computations have the CCC for each initially exited neuron or any subgroup of neurons. Such computations based on some subgroups of intentionally excited neurons in the AADNN are called here an associative graph neurocomputing (AGNC). The AGNC does not use any loops because all necessary data are directly or indirectly interconnected to the neurons that need them. The AGNC is always local but can make neurons conditionally react on the other excited neurons and in such a way control the excitation process inside the whole AADNN gathering necessary information for the desired goal. In case of the ASONN, the AGNC is gathering the information about all correlations with the sample neurons representing the other classes and creates some new aggregation neurons that reflect discriminative combinations of the value neurons. The neighbour value neurons are transformed into the sensor neurons shown in figure 1.

In this associative methodology, each new piece of information has an impact and influence on the other pieces of information associatively stored in the AADNN. Each new piece of information can also recall the other associated pieces of information from the AADNN. There is also no separation between data and algorithms because the whole AADNN and its structure store all associated pieces of information and the way of activation of its neurons (the substitution for the algorithms). The more pieces of information are represented in the AGDS or AADNN the more thrifty and efficient are the AGDS and AADNN.

Table 1. The comparisons of average classification results of 10 folds cross-validation

Data set (from ML Repository):	Voting		Ionosphere		Wine		Iris	
Average results for 10 folds Cross Validation results:	TRAIN	VALID	TRAIN	VALID	TRAIN	VALID	TRAIN	VALID
AADNN (simple config. without specialized structures)	100.0	92.6	100.0	91.5	100.0	97.2	100.0	94.0
ASONN (specialized AADNN) (discrimlevel=1; cutlevel=1)	100.0	94.5	98.5	89.7	100.0	96.7	100.0	95.3
ASONN (specialized AADNN) (discrimlevel=1; cutlevel=2)	100.0	95.2	98.5	88.6	100.0	96.1	100.0	95.3
ASONN (specialized AADNN) (discrimlevel=2; cutlevel=1)	100.0	94.7	99.1	90.9	100.0	98.9	100.0	94.0
ASONN (specialized AADNN) (discrimlevel=2; cutlevel=2)	100.0	94.7	99.3	91.7	100.0	99.4	100.0	94.0
ASONN (specialized AADNN) (discrimlevel=3; cutlevel=1)	100.0	94.5	99.2	90.9	100.0	98.9	100.0	94.0
kNN (k=1)	100.0	92.9	100.0	86.9	100.0	77.5	100.0	96.0
kNN (k=3)	92.5	92.4	85.8	83.5	67.5	66.3	94.5	94.0
kNN (k=5)	91.2	91.9	82.4	80.3	66.3	66.2	95.6	94.7
kNN (k=10)	91.2	90.3	78.3	76.9	68.9	64.1	93.9	96.0
kNN (k=15)	89.2	89.2	75.2	74.1	64.8	65.1	92.1	96.0
SVM Multiclass Linear (cost=1; eps=0.1)	97.2	96.1	93.2	87.7	33.1	33.1	94.9	93.3
SVM Multiclass Linear (cost=10; eps=0.1)	97.0	95.9	94.0	90.0	33.1	33.1	95.2	95.3
SVM Multiclass Linear (cost=100; eps=0.1)	96.7	96.1	92.1	87.2	33.1	33.1	94.6	94.0
SVM Multiclass Linear (cost=50; eps=0.1)	96.8	96.5	92.7	89.7	33.1	33.1	94.7	94.0
SVM Multiclass Linear (cost=20; eps=0.1)	97.2	95.9	93.8	88.9	33.1	33.1	94.4	92.0
SVM Multiclass Linear (cost=20; eps=0.01)	97.5	95.8	94.7	88.0	95.5	93.3	95.5	94.7
SVM Multiclass Linear (cost=20; eps=0.001)	97.5	96.1	94.9	88.9	96.4	95.0	95.6	95.3
SVM Multiclass RBF (cost=10; sigma=0.5; eps=0.1)	100.0	78.4	100.0	88.3	100.0	39.9	99.3	96.0
SVM Multiclass RBF (cost=10; sigma=1; eps=0.1)	100.0	86.0	100.0	94.3	100.0	39.9	98.4	96.7
SVM Multiclass RBF (cost=10; sigma=5; eps=0.1)	98.6	96.1	97.1	94.3	100.0	66.3	97.3	94.7
SVM Multiclass RBF (cost=10; sigma=10; eps=0.1)	96.7	95.4	94.1	90.3	100.0	76.9	95.7	95.3
SVM Multiclass Polynom (cost=10; d=3; eps=0.01)	73.7	75.2	97.9	86.0	33.1	33.1	33.3	33.3
SVM Multiclass Polynom (cost=10; d=4; eps=0.01)	55.3	57.4	97.0	90.1	33.1	33.1	33.3	33.3
SVM Multiclass Polynom (cost=10; d=6; eps=0.01)	55.3	57.4	81.2	80.3	33.1	33.1	33.3	33.3
RBFN (k=5; f=multisquare; random centres)	NaN	NaN	80.4	80.3	69.8	66.8	95.4	94.0
RBFN (k=10; f=multisquare; random centres)	93.0	92.9	88.5	86.9	65.0	62.9	97.2	96.0
RBFN (k=15; f=multisquare; random centres)	NaN	NaN	91.0	89.7	69.8	68.0	NaN	NaN
RBFN (k=20; f=multisquare; random centres)	NaN	NaN	91.5	89.7	67.3	66.4	97.1	94.0
RBFN (k=5; f=gaussian; k-means centres)	94.0	93.3	84.3	83.2	86.2	85.5	95.4	94.7
RBFN (k=10; f=gaussian; k-means centres)	95.1	94.9	90.0	88.3	97.2	97.8	97.7	96.0
RBFN (k=15; f=gaussian; k-means centres)	96.0	96.1	90.9	90.3	99.8	98.3	98.4	97.3
RBFN (k=20; f=gaussian; k-means centres)	96.5	95.8	92.1	87.8	99.9	98.3	98.7	98.0
RBFN (k=5; f=multisquare; k-means centres)	91.0	89.9	78.9	79.8	69.8	66.8	95.4	94.7
RBFN (k=10; f=multisquare; k-means centres)	94.2	94.0	87.0	82.9	68.9	70.2	NaN	NaN
RBFN (k=15; f=multisquare; k-means centres)	95.9	95.2	91.0	90.3	NaN	NaN	97.3	94.0
RBFN (k=20; f=multisquare; k-means centres)	NaN	NaN	91.8	89.2	NaN	NaN	97.0	94.7
PNN Simple (sigma=0.1)	100.0	93.1	100.0	78.4	100.0	5.7	100.0	96.0
PNN Simple (sigma=1)	98.7	92.2	94.3	86.3	100.0	75.8	94.6	94.0
PNN Simple (sigma=10)	89.4	89.0	65.5	65.3	90.8	75.8	91.5	90.7
PNN Simple (sigma=100)	89.3	89.0	65.3	65.0	73.9	73.0	91.5	90.7

The basic AADNN can be triggered by any training or test sample. The excitation is forwarded to the other associated neurons: at first, the other value neurons due to their similarity (ASIM) and the sample neurons defining some pieces of information (ADEF) and then to the class neurons defined by some subgroups of the sample neurons (ADEF). The class neurons react on an excitation and produce classification results, so even the basic AADNN can be used as the classificator (fig. 1b) without any training. Such classificator has not the optimized structure. Its structure can be optimized reducing some minor value neurons or it can be developed and specialized into the e.g. ASONN subnetwork (fig. 1) that can classify even separately from the basic part of the AADNN.

The AADNN adapted to classification tasks has shown that AADNN classification results are comparable to the results obtained by computationally much more complex algorithms like SVM, RBFN, PNN, kNN shown in table 1.

4   Summary and Conclusion

In this paper the new associative graph data structure (AGDS) and the actively associated data neural network (AADNN) have been introduced. It has been shown that they can enable us to perform some computations on the associated pieces of information and obtain some results far more quickly than in the traditional computing methodologies. The AADNN stores associated information not only in connection weights but also in neurons as well as in the structure of interconnections. Such associations can substitute many time-consuming nested loops and algorithms used for searching, sorting and examining accordance, conformity, similarity and differences, recognition, classification, clusterization or regression. The associative graph neurocomputing (AGNC) does not use loops at all and performs computation incomparably faster using associative interconnection because it keeps all necessary pieces of information close to the neurons that need them to use. The introduced AADNN and AGNC are very similar to the biological brainlike computing where neurons do not compute complex mathematical equations or expressions even though the biological information systems react very fast on various complex signals and pieces of information.

The classical as well as associative computations have their strong and weak points but together they can improve computational abilities of the future computer systems decreasing computational complexity and reducing numerical errors. Cooperation always brings more benefits than competition.

References

[1] Back, R.J.R.: Refinement Calculus, Parallel and Reactive Programs. In: de Bakker, J.W., de Roever, W.-P., Rozenberg, G. (eds.) REX 1989. LNCS, vol. 430, pp. 42–66. Springer, Heidelberg (1990)

[2] Dudek-Dyduch, E., Tadeusiewicz, R., Horzyk, A.: Neural Network Adaptation Process Effectiveness Dependent of Constant Training Data Availability. Neurocomputing 72, 3138–3149 (2009)

[3] Horzyk, A., Tadeusiewicz, R.: A Psycholinguistic Model of Man-Machine Interactions Based on Needs of Human Personality. Man-Machine Interactions. In: Cyran, K.A. (ed.) Proc. of ICMMI 2009. AISC, vol. 59, pp. 55–67. Springer, Heidelberg (2009)

[4] Horzyk, A.: Awaiting for Artificial Intelligence. Software Developer's Journal 4, 10–17 (2011) ISSN: 1734-3917

[5] Horzyk, A.: Self-Optimizing Neural Network 3. In: Franco, L., Elizondo, D.A., Jerez, J.M. (eds.) Constructive Neural Networks. SCI, vol. 258, pp. 83–101. Springer, Heidelberg (2009)

[6] Tadeusiewicz, R., Rowiński, T.: Computer science and psychology in information society. AGH (2011)

On the Application of the Parzen-Type Kernel Regression Neural Network and Order Statistics for Learning in a Non-stationary Environment

Maciej Jaworski[1], Meng Joo Er[2], and Lena Pietruczuk[1]

[1] Department of Computer Engineering, Czestochowa University of Technology, Armii Krajowej 36, 42-200 Czestochowa, Poland
{maciej.jaworski,lena.pietruczuk}@kik.pcz.pl
[2] School of Electrical & Electronic Engineering, Nanyang Technological University, 50 Nanyang Avenue, Singapore
emjer@ntu.edu.sg

Abstract. A problem of learning in non-stationary environment is solved by making use of order statistics in combination with the Parzen kernel-type regression neural network. Probabilistic properties of the algorithm are investigated and weak convergence is established. Experimental results are presented.

1 Introduction

In this paper a system described by the following equation is considered

$$Y_i = \phi(X_i) + ac_i + Z_i, \ i \in \{1, \ldots, n\}, \tag{1}$$

where $X_i \in A \subset \mathbb{R}^p$ are i.i.d. input random variables with unknown probability distribution $f(x)$, $Y_i \in \mathbb{R}$ are output random variables and c_i are elements of some known sequence, satisfying $\lim_{i \to \infty} |c_i| = \infty$. Random variables $Z_i \in \mathbb{R}$ introduce a noise into the system and satisfy the following assumption

$$E[Z_i] = 0, \ Var(Z_i) = E[Z_i^2], \ i \in \{1, \ldots, n\}. \tag{2}$$

The function $\phi : A \to \mathbb{R}$ and the constant a are not known and can be estimated with the use of some generalized nonlinear regression method. In the paper, the algorithm based on order statistics and Parzen kernels is proposed.

It should be noted that such a problem, i.e. concerning nonstationary noise, was never studied in literature before. The method applied in this paper is based on the nonparametric estimators, which are known, in the area of soft computing, as probabilistic neural networks [36]. For the case of stationary noise, nonparametric regression estimates in stationary environment were considered in [3], [4], [6], [10], [12], [14], [15]-[17], [23]-[25] and [28]-[31] whereas non-stationary environment was studied in [7], [18]-[22], [26] and [27]. For excellent surveys on these algorithms the reader is referred to [8] and [5].

L. Rutkowski et al. (Eds.): ICAISC 2012, Part I, LNCS 7267, pp. 90–98, 2012.
© Springer-Verlag Berlin Heidelberg 2012

2   Algorithm and Main Result

To estimate the value of parameter a in model (1), the order statistics approach can be applied. Let $F(w)$ denote the cumulative distribution function of the random variables $\phi(X_i) + Z_i$, $i \in \{1, \ldots, n\}$

$$F(w) = P(\phi(X_i) + Z_i < w). \tag{3}$$

Then, the sequence of cumulative distribution functions $F_i(y)$ for random variables Y_i, $i \in \{1, \ldots, n\}$ can be introduced

$$F_i(y) = P(Y_i < y) = P(\phi(X_i) + ac_i + Z_i < y) = F(y - ac_i). \tag{4}$$

The probability density function, corresponding to the cumulative distribution function $F(y)$, is further denoted by $p(y)$.

In [13] the following method for estimating the parameter a was proposed for model (4)

$$\hat{a}_n = \text{Med} \left\{ \frac{Y_j - Y_i}{c_j - c_i} : \; i, j \in \{1, \ldots, n\}, \; j < i \right\}. \tag{5}$$

The function $\phi(x)$, according to model (1), represents the relation between the random variables pairs (X_i, V_i) given by

$$(X_i, V_i) = (X_i, Y_i - ac_i), \; i \in \{1, \ldots, n\}. \tag{6}$$

Since the actual value of parameter a is not known, variables V_i have to be estimated with the use of estimator $\hat{a}_n$

$$\hat{V}_{i,n} = Y_i - \hat{a}_n c_i, \; i \in \{1, \ldots, n\}. \tag{7}$$

For the estimation of the function $\phi(x)$ one can apply the nonparametric method based on kernel functions. Denoting $R(x) = \phi(x)f(x)$, in each x such that $f(x) \neq 0$ the function $\phi(x)$ can be expressed by

$$\phi(x) = \frac{R(x)}{f(x)}. \tag{8}$$

For the functions $R(x)$ and $f(x)$ the following estimators can be proposed

$$\hat{R}_n(x, \hat{a}_n) = \frac{1}{n} \sum_{i=1}^{n} \hat{V}_{i,n} K_n(x, X_i), \tag{9}$$

$$\hat{f}_n(x) = \frac{1}{n} \sum_{i=1}^{n} \sum_{i=1}^{n} K'_n(x, X_i), \tag{10}$$

where $K_n : A \times A \to \mathbb{R}$ and $K'_n : A \times A \to \mathbb{R}$ are some known functions given in the form

$$K_n(x, u) = \frac{1}{h_n^p} \prod_{k=1}^{p} K\left(\frac{x - u}{h_n}\right), \tag{11}$$

$$K_n'(x, u) = \frac{1}{h_n'^p} \prod_{k=1}^{p} K\left(\frac{x-u}{h_n'}\right), \tag{12}$$

Sequences h_n and h_n' tend to 0 as n goes to infinity. Function $K : \mathbb{R} \to \mathbb{R}$ is called the Parzen kernel and has to satisfy the following conditions

$$\sup_{w \in \mathbb{R}} |K(w)| < \infty, \tag{13}$$

$$\int_{\mathbb{R}} |K(w)| dw < \infty, \tag{14}$$

$$\lim_{\|w\| \to \infty} \|w\|^p |K(w)| = 0, \tag{15}$$

$$\int_{\mathbb{R}} K(w) dw = 1. \tag{16}$$

Finally, according to expression (8), the estimator $\hat{\phi}_n(x, \hat{a}_n)$ of the regression function $\phi(x)$ is simply given by

$$\hat{\phi}_n(x, \hat{a}_n) = \frac{\hat{R}_n(x, \hat{a}_n)}{\hat{f}_n(x)}. \tag{17}$$

The algorithm presented above is known as a general regression neural network (GRNN) [37]. The scheme of the network is presented in Fig. 1.

To ensure the convergence of the above algorithm, assumptions of the following theorem should be satisfied:

Theorem 1. *If conditions (2), (13), (14), (15) and (16) are satisfied, $F(y)$ and $p(y)$ are absolutely continuous functions, c_i is never decreasing or never increasing and additionally the following conditions hold*

$$\int_{\mathbb{R}} p^2(y) dy < \infty, \tag{18}$$

$$\lim_{n \to \infty} h_n = 0, \quad \lim_{n \to \infty} \frac{1}{n^2 h_n^p} = 0, \tag{19}$$

$$\lim_{n \to \infty} h_n' = 0, \quad \lim_{n \to \infty} \frac{1}{n^2 h_n'^p} = 0, \tag{20}$$

then

$$\hat{a}_n \overset{n \to \infty}{\longrightarrow} a \text{ in probability} \tag{21}$$

and

$$\hat{\phi}_n(x, \hat{a}_n) \overset{n \to \infty}{\longrightarrow} \phi(x) \text{ in probability.} \tag{22}$$

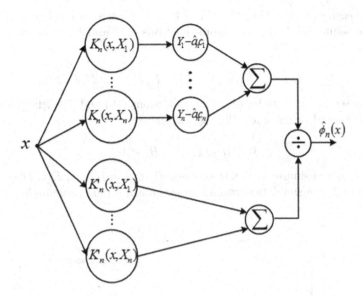

Fig. 1. Scheme of the general regression neural network

Proof. According to Theorem 3 in [13], the estimator $\hat{a}_n$ is asymptothically normal. This is in turn a sufficient condition for convergence (21). Convergence (22) can be proven combining (21), convergence of estimator $\hat{\phi}_n(x, \hat{a}_n)$ [5] and Theorem 4.3.8 in [40].

3   Experimental Results

In the following simulations a one-dimensional case is considered ($p = 1$). The input random variables are taken from the normal distribution $N(0, 2)$ and Z_i are from the standard normal distribution $N(0, 1)$. The following regression function $\phi(x)$ is chosen

$$\phi(x) = 10 \arctan x + 10. \tag{23}$$

For this function, the probability density function $p(y)$ of random variable $\phi(X_i) + Z_i$ satisfies condition (18). The sequence c_i is taken in the form

$$c_i = i^t, \tag{24}$$

which is never decreasing. In simulations the parameter t is set to $0, 5$. The actual value of parameter a is set to 2. To estimate the regression function $\phi(x)$ the rectangular Parzen kernel is proposed

$$K(w) = \begin{cases} 0, 5, & w \in [-1, 1], \\ 0, & w \in (-\infty, -1) \cup (1, \infty). \end{cases} \tag{25}$$

It can be easily checked that the above kernel satisfies all the conditions (13)-(16). The sequences h_n and h'_n from functions (11) and (12) are taken in the form

$$h_n = Dn^{-H}, \quad h'_n = D'n^{-H'}, \quad D, D' > 0, \ H, H' > 0. \tag{26}$$

It is easily seen that, in order to satisfy conditions (19) and (20), the parameters H and H' should satisfy the following inequalities

$$0 < H < 1, \ 0 < H' < 1. \tag{27}$$

In the considered simulations it is assumed that $H = H'$ and $D = D' = 1$.

In Figure 2, the simulation results for estimator $\hat{a}_n$ are presented.

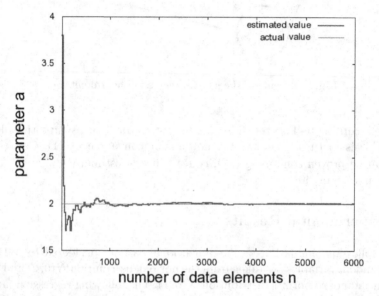

Fig. 2. Estimator $\hat{a}_n$ as a function of number of data elements n and its comparison with the actual value of a

The value of estimator $\hat{a}_n$ converges quite fast to the value $a = 2$. This fact enables an acceptable estimation of random variables V_i and, in consequence, the proper estimation of functions $R(x)$ and $\phi(x)$. To show this, several simulations were performed for different values of parameters $H = H'$. Values of the Mean Squared Error (MSE) of $\hat{\phi}_n(x, \hat{a}_n)$ for different numbers of data elements n are presented in Fig. 3.

For $H = H' = 0,1$ the estimator $\hat{\phi}_n(x, \hat{a}_n)$ converges very fast to the regression function $\phi(x)$. For the higher values of $H = H'$ the convergence is worse, but the trend is still satisfactory. In Figure 4, estimator (17), obtained for $n = 5000$ data elements, is compared with the regression function (23).

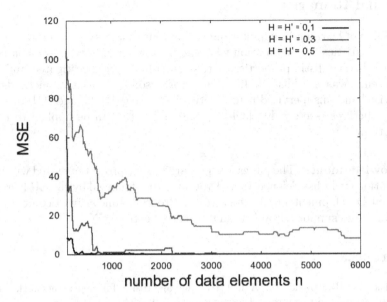

Fig. 3. Mean Squared Error of the estimator $\hat{\phi}_n(x, \hat{a}_n)$ as a function of number of data elements n, for three different values of parameters $H = H'$: $H = H' = 0, 1$, $H = H' = 0, 3$ and $H = H' = 0, 5$

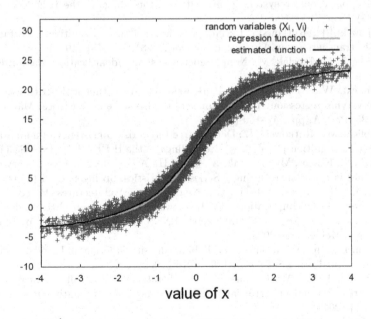

Fig. 4. Estimator $\hat{\phi}_n(x, \hat{a}_n)$, obtained for $n = 5000$ data elements, in comparison with the regression function $\phi(x)$. Data points represent the random variable pairs (X_i, V_i).

4   Final Remarks

A problem of learning in non-stationary environment was solved by making use of order statistics in combination with the Parzen kernel-type regression neural network. Probabilistic properties of the algorithm were investigated and weak convergence was established. In future works some alternative methods, e.g. supervised and unsupervised neural networks (see e.g. [1], [2] and [11]) or neuro-fuzzy structures (see e.g. [9], [32]-[35], [38] and [39]), can be applied to handle nonstationary noise.

Acknowledgments. The paper was prepared under project operated within the Foundation for Polish Science Team Programme co-financed by the EU European Regional Development Fund, Operational Program Innovative Economy 2007-2013, and also supported by National Science Centre NCN.

References

1. Bilski, J., Rutkowski, L.: A fast training algorithm for neural networks. IEEE Transactions on Circuits and Systems II 45, 749–753 (1998)
2. Cierniak, R., Rutkowski, L.: On image compression by competitive neural networks and optimal linear predictors. Signal Processing: Image Communication - a Eurasip Journal 15(6), 559–565 (2000)
3. Gałkowski, T., Rutkowski, L.: Nonparametric recovery of multivariate functions with applications to system identification. Proceedings of the IEEE 73, 942–943 (1985)
4. Gałkowski, T., Rutkowski, L.: Nonparametric fitting of multivariable functions. IEEE Transactions on Automatic Control AC 31, 785–787 (1986)
5. Greblicki, W., Pawlak, M.: Nonparametric system indentification. Cambridge University Press (2008)
6. Greblicki, W., Rutkowska, D., Rutkowski, L.: An orthogonal series estimate of time-varying regression, Tokyo. Annals of the Institute of Statistical Mathematics, vol. 35, Part A, pp. 147–160 (1983)
7. Greblicki, W., Rutkowski, L.: Density-free Bayes risk consistency of nonparametric pattern recognition procedures. Proceedings of the IEEE 69(4), 482–483 (1981)
8. Györfi, L., Kohler, M., Krzyżak, A., Walk, H.: A Distribution-Free Theory of Nonparametric Regression. Springer Series in Statistics. Springer, USA (2002)
9. Nowicki, R.: Rough Sets in the Neuro-Fuzzy Architectures Based on Non-monotonic Fuzzy Implications. In: Rutkowski, L., Siekmann, J.H., Tadeusiewicz, R., Zadeh, L.A. (eds.) ICAISC 2004. LNCS (LNAI), vol. 3070, pp. 518–525. Springer, Heidelberg (2004)
10. Parzen, E.: On estimation of a probability density function and mode. Analysis of Mathematical Statistics 33(3), 1065–1076 (1962)
11. Patan, K., Patan, M.: Optimal Training Strategies for Locally Recurrent Neural Networks. Journal of Artificial Intelligence and Soft Computing Research 1(2), 103–114 (2011)
12. Rafajłowicz, E.: Nonparametric orthogonal series estimators of regression: A class attaining the optimal convergence rate in L_2. Statistics and Probability Letters 5, 219–224 (1987)

13. Rao, P.V., Thornby, J.I.: A robust point estimator in a generalized regression model. Analysis of Mathematical Statistics 40(5), 1784–1790 (1969)
14. Rutkowski, L.: Sequential estimates of probability densities by orthogonal series and their application in pattern classification. IEEE Transactions on Systems, Man, and Cybernetics SMC 10(12), 918–920 (1980)
15. Rutkowski, L.: Sequential estimates of a regression function by orthogonal series with applications in discrimination, New York, Heidelberg, Berlin. Lectures Notes in Statistics, vol. 8, pp. 236–244 (1981)
16. Rutkowski, L.: On system identification by nonparametric function fitting. IEEE Transactions on Automatic Control AC 27, 225–227 (1982)
17. Rutkowski, L.: Orthogonal series estimates of a regression function with applications in system identification. In: Probability and Statistical Inference, pp. 343–347. D. Reidel Publishing Company, Dordrecht (1982)
18. Rutkowski, L.: On Bayes risk consistent pattern recognition procedures in a quasi-stationary environment. IEEE Transactions on Pattern Analysis and Machine Intelligence PAMI 4(1), 84–87 (1982)
19. Rutkowski, L.: On-line identification of time-varying systems by nonparametric techniques. IEEE Transactions on Automatic Control AC 27, 228–230 (1982)
20. Rutkowski, L.: On nonparametric identification with prediction of time-varying systems. IEEE Transactions on Automatic Control AC 29, 58–60 (1984)
21. Rutkowski, L.: Nonparametric identification of quasi-stationary systems. Systems and Control Letters 6, 33–35 (1985)
22. Rutkowski, L.: The real-time identification of time-varying systems by nonparametric algorithms based on the Parzen kernels. International Journal of Systems Science 16, 1123–1130 (1985)
23. Rutkowski, L.: A general approach for nonparametric fitting of functions and their derivatives with applications to linear circuits identification. IEEE Transactions Circuits Systems CAS 33, 812–818 (1986)
24. Rutkowski, L.: Sequential pattern recognition procedures derived from multiple Fourier series. Pattern Recognition Letters 8, 213–216 (1988)
25. Rutkowski, L.: Nonparametric procedures for identification and control of linear dynamic systems. In: Proceedings of 1988 American Control Conference, June 15-17, pp. 1325–1326 (1988)
26. Rutkowski, L.: An application of multiple Fourier series to identification of multivariable nonstationary systems. International Journal of Systems Science 20(10), 1993–2002 (1989)
27. Rutkowski, L.: Nonparametric learning algorithms in the time-varying environments. Signal Processing 18, 129–137 (1989)
28. Rutkowski, L., Rafajłowicz, E.: On global rate of convergence of some nonparametric identification procedures. IEEE Transaction on Automatic Control AC 34(10), 1089–1091 (1989)
29. Rutkowski, L.: Identification of MISO nonlinear regressions in the presence of a wide class of disturbances. IEEE Transactions on Information Theory IT 37, 214–216 (1991)
30. Rutkowski, L.: Multiple Fourier series procedures for extraction of nonlinear regressions from noisy data. IEEE Transactions on Signal Processing 41(10), 3062–3065 (1993)
31. Rutkowski, L., Gałkowski, T.: On pattern classification and system identification by probabilistic neural networks. Applied Mathematics and Computer Science 4(3), 413–422 (1994)

32. Rutkowski, L.: A New Method for System Modelling and Pattern Classification. Bulletin of the Polish Academy of Sciences 52(1), 11–24 (2004)
33. Rutkowski, L., Cpałka, K.: A general approach to neuro - fuzzy systems. In: Proceedings of the 10th IEEE International Conference on Fuzzy Systems, Melbourne, December 2-5, vol. 3, pp. 1428–1431 (2001)
34. Rutkowski, L., Cpałka, K.: A neuro-fuzzy controller with a compromise fuzzy reasoning. Control and Cybernetics 31(2), 297–308 (2002)
35. Scherer, R.: Boosting Ensemble of Relational Neuro-fuzzy Systems. In: Rutkowski, L., Tadeusiewicz, R., Zadeh, L.A., Żurada, J.M. (eds.) ICAISC 2006. LNCS (LNAI), vol. 4029, pp. 306–313. Springer, Heidelberg (2006)
36. Specht, D.F.: Probabilistic neural networks. Neural Networks 3, 109–118 (1990)
37. Specht, D.F.: A general regression neural network. IEEE Transactions on Neural Networks 2, 568–576 (1991)
38. Starczewski, J., Rutkowski, L.: Interval type 2 neuro-fuzzy systems based on interval consequents. In: Rutkowski, L., Kacprzyk, J. (eds.) Neural Networks and Soft Computing, pp. 570–577. Physica-Verlag, Springer-Verlag Company, Heidelberg, New York (2003)
39. Starczewski, J.T., Rutkowski, L.: Connectionist Structures of Type 2 Fuzzy Inference Systems. In: Wyrzykowski, R., Dongarra, J., Paprzycki, M., Waśniewski, J. (eds.) PPAM 2001. LNCS, vol. 2328, pp. 634–642. Springer, Heidelberg (2002)
40. Wilks, S.S.: Mathematical Statistics. John Wiley, New York (1962)

On Learning in a Time-Varying Environment by Using a Probabilistic Neural Network and the Recursive Least Squares Method

Maciej Jaworski and Marcin Gabryel

Department of Computer Engineering, Czestochowa University of Technology,
Armii Krajowej 36, 42-200 Czestochowa, Poland
{maciej.jaworski,marcin.gabryel}@kik.pcz.pl

Abstract. This paper presents the recursive least squares method, combined with the general regression neural networks, applied to solve the problem of learning in time-varying environment. The general regression neural network is based on the orthogonal-type kernel functions. The appropriate algorithm is presented in a recursive form. Sufficient simulations confirm empirically the convergence of the algorithm.

1 Introduction

The idea of probabilistic neural networks and general regression neural networks was first proposed by Specht in [35] and [36], respectively. Such networks are nonparametric tools, designed for estimating probability density and regression functions. In literature, their usability in solving stationary (see e.g. [4], [5], [7], [12]-[16], [22]-[24] and [27]-[30]) and nonstationary problems (see e.g. [8], [17]-[21], [25] and [26]) has been widely studied. It should be emphasized that in both cases the noise was assumed to be stationary. An excellent overwiew of the methods mentioned above can be found in [6] and [9].

Let us consider a system, which processes p-dimensional data elements $X_i \in A \subset \mathbb{R}^p$, $i = 1, \ldots$, with some unknown function $\phi : A \to \mathbb{R}$ ($E[\phi(X_i)] < \infty$). The probability density function of the random variables X_i, described by $f(x)$, is unknown as well. Let us assume that the output $\phi(X_i)$ of the system is accompanied with a noise, consisting of two components

- deterministic part ac_i, where a is some unknown constant, and c_i is an element of known sequence, satisfying $\lim_{i \to \infty} |c_i| = \infty$,
- probabilistic part Z_i, which is a random variable satisfying the following condition

$$E[Z_i] = 0, \ E[Z_i^2] = d_i < \infty. \tag{1}$$

Therefore, the output random variable Y_i, received from the system, is given by the equation

$$Y_i = \phi(X_i) + ac_i + Z_i. \tag{2}$$

L. Rutkowski et al. (Eds.): ICAISC 2012, Part I, LNCS 7267, pp. 99–110, 2012.

The aim of the generalized nonlinear regression is to estimate simultaneously the regression function $\phi(x)$ and the constant a, given n pairs of random variables $(X_1, Y_1), \ldots, (X_n, Y_n)$ and the sequence c_i.

2 Estimation of the Parameter a

For the estimation of the parameter a, the recursive least square method [1] can be applied

$$\hat{a}_n = \hat{a}_{n-1} + \frac{c_n}{\sum_{i=1}^n c_i^2} \left(Y_n - \hat{a}_{n-1} c_n\right). \tag{3}$$

This method can be further generalized into the form

$$\hat{a}_n^{(\omega)} = \hat{a}_{n-1}^{(\omega)} + \frac{c_n^{\omega-1}}{\sum_{i=1}^n c_i^{\omega}} \left(Y_n - \hat{a}_{n-1}^{(\omega)} c_n\right), \tag{4}$$

where ω is a real nonnegative number.

The assumptions of the following theorem ensure the convergence of the estimator $\hat{a}_n^{(\omega)}$ to the actual value of parameter a

Theorem 1. *If conditions (1) holds and additionally the following conditions are satisfied*

$$E[\phi^2(X_i)] = \int_A \phi^2(x) f(x) dx < \infty, \tag{5}$$

$$\lim_{n\to\infty} \left(\frac{\sum_{i=1}^n c_i^{\omega-1}}{\sum_{i=1}^n c_i^{\omega}}\right) = 0, \tag{6}$$

$$\lim_{n\to\infty} \left(\frac{\sum_{i=1}^n c_i^{2\omega-2} s_i}{\left(\sum_{i=1}^n c_i^{\omega}\right)^2}\right) = 0, \tag{7}$$

where s_i is defined as follows

$$s_i = \max\{Var[\phi(X_i)], d_i\}, \tag{8}$$

then

$$\hat{a}_n^{(\omega)} \xrightarrow{n\to\infty} a \text{ in probability.} \tag{9}$$

Proof. The theorem can be proven using simple analysis of the bias and the variance of estimator (4), which leads to the following convergence

$$\lim_{n\to\infty} E\left[(\hat{a}_n^{(\omega)} - a)^2\right] = 0. \tag{10}$$

Convergence (10) is the sufficient condition for convergence (9).

3   Estimation of the Regression Function $\phi(x)$

To find the regression function $\phi(x)$, the nonlinear regression procedures should be applied to the pairs of random variables (X_i, V_i), where

$$V_i = Y_i - ac_i. \tag{11}$$

Since the actual value of the parameter a is not known, the random variables V_i have to be estimated, using some estimator $\bar{a}_i$

$$\hat{V}_i(\bar{a}_i) = Y_i - \bar{a}_i c_i, \ i = 1, \dots, n. \tag{12}$$

It is easily seen that if $\bar{a}_i = a$, then $\hat{V}_i(\bar{a}_i) = \hat{V}_i(a) \equiv V_i$. In this section, for further considerations of the convergence of the regression function estimator, it is assumed that $\bar{a}_i = a$, $i = 1, \dots, n$.

The regression function $\phi(x)$ can be expressed in the following form

$$\phi(x) = \frac{\phi(x) f(x)}{f(x)} \overset{def.}{=} \frac{R(x)}{f(x)}, \tag{13}$$

at each point x, for which $f(x) \neq 0$. The nominator and the denominator of the above expression can be estimated separately. In this paper the nonparametric estimation based on kernel functions is proposed. Given $2n$ kernel functions $\tilde{K}_i, \tilde{K}_i' : A \times A \to \mathbb{R}$, $i = 1, \dots, n$, the estimators $\tilde{R}_n(x, a)$ and $\tilde{f}_n(x)$ can be expressed in the following form

$$\tilde{R}_n(x, a) = \frac{1}{n} \sum_{i=1}^{n} \hat{V}_i(a) \tilde{K}_i(x, X_i), \tag{14}$$

$$\tilde{f}_n(x) = \frac{1}{n} \sum_{i=1}^{n} \tilde{K}_i'(x, X_i), \tag{15}$$

One way of constructing the kernel functions is the application of orthogonal series. Let $g_j : \mathbb{R} \to \mathbb{R}$, $j = 1, \dots$ denote the functions of the complete orthogonal system, satisfying the following condition

$$\forall_{j \in \mathbb{N}} \sup_{w \in \mathbb{R}} |g_j(w)| \leq G_j. \tag{16}$$

Then the kernel functions K, K', for one-dimensional case ($p = 1$), can be defined as follows

$$\tilde{K}_i(x, u) = \sum_{j=0}^{M(i)} g_j(x) g_j(u), \ \tilde{K}_i'(x, u) = \sum_{j=0}^{N(i)} g_j(x) g_j(u), \ i = 1, \dots, n, \tag{17}$$

where $M(i)$ and $N(i)$ are sequences satisfying $\lim_{i \to \infty} M(i) = \infty$ and $\lim_{i \to \infty} N(i) = \infty$, respectively. The convergence of estimators (14) and (15) with kernel functions (16) can be slightly improved by the applicaion of so-called Cesaro means. Let us denote $S_j(x, u)$ as the following partial sums

$$S_j(x, u) = \sum_{k=0}^{j} q_k(x) g_k(u), \ j = 1, \ldots, n. \tag{18}$$

Then, the kernel functions $K, K' : A \times A \to \mathbb{R}$ can be proposed as the Cesaro means of these partial sums

$$K_i(x, u) = \frac{1}{M(i) + 1} \sum_{j=0}^{M(i)} S_j(x, u) = \sum_{j=0}^{M(i)} \left(1 - \frac{j}{M(i) + 1} \right) g_j(x) g_j(u), \ i = 1, \ldots, n, \tag{19}$$

$$K_i'(x, u) = \frac{1}{N(i) + 1} \sum_{j=0}^{N(i)} S_j(x, u) = \sum_{j=0}^{N(i)} \left(1 - \frac{j}{N(i) + 1} \right) g_j(x) g_j(u), \ i = 1, \ldots, n \tag{20}$$

Finally, the estimator for functions $R(x)$ and $f(x)$ can be proposed in the following forms

$$\overline{R}_n(x, a) = \frac{1}{n} \sum_{i=1}^{n} \hat{V}_i(a) K_i(x, X_i) = \frac{1}{n} \sum_{i=1}^{n} \sum_{j=0}^{M(i)} \hat{V}_i(a) \left(1 - \frac{j}{M(i) + 1} \right) g_j(x) g_j(X_i), \tag{21}$$

$$\overline{f}_n(x) = \frac{1}{n} \sum_{i=1}^{n} K_i'(x, X_i) = \frac{1}{n} \sum_{i=1}^{n} \sum_{j=0}^{N(i)} \left(1 - \frac{j}{N(i) + 1} \right) g_j(x) g_j(X_i), \tag{22}$$

Then, in light of formula (13), the estimator of the regression function $\phi(x)$ is given by

$$\overline{\phi}_n(x, a) = \frac{\overline{R}_n(x, a)}{\overline{f}_n(x)}. \tag{23}$$

To ensure the convergence of estimator (23), assumptions of the following theorem have to be satisfied.

Theorem 2. *If conditions (1) and (5) hold and additionally the following conditions are satisfied*

$$\lim_{n \to \infty} N(n) = 0, \quad \lim_{n \to \infty} \left[\frac{1}{n^2} \sum_{i=1}^{n} \left(\sum_{j=1}^{N(i)} G_j^2 \right)^2 \right] = 0, \tag{24}$$

$$\lim_{n\to\infty} M(n) = 0, \quad \lim_{n\to\infty}\left[\frac{1}{n^2}\sum_{i=1}^{n}\left(\sum_{j=1}^{M(i)} G_j^2\right)^2 s_i\right] = 0, \tag{25}$$

where s_i is defined as in (8), then

$$\overline{\phi}_n(x, a) \overset{n\to\infty}{\longrightarrow} \phi(x) \text{ in probability.} \tag{26}$$

Proof. The proof of the theorem can be found in [14].

4   Probabilistic Neural Network

In the real world applications, the value of the parameter a is not known, therefore the random variables V_i have to be estimated, using formula (12). In particular, the estimators $\overline{a}_i$ can be the same for each variable V_i, e.g.

$$\forall_{i\in\{1,\ldots,n\}} \ \overline{a}_i = \hat{a}_n^{(\omega)}. \tag{27}$$

Then, the estimator of the regression function $\phi(x)$ can be proposed as $\overline{\phi}_n(x, \hat{a}_n^{(\omega)})$ (replacing a by $\hat{a}_n^{(\omega)}$ in formulas (21) and (23)). The convergence of this estimator can be proven combining Theorems 1 and 2 and Theorem 4.3.8 in [40]. The estimator $\overline{\phi}_n(x, \hat{a}_n^{(\omega)})$ is calculated in a two-step process. First, given all output variables Y_i, $i = 1, \ldots, n$, the estimator $\hat{a}_n^{(\omega)}$ is computed. Then, after the first step is completed, the estimation of the regression function $\phi(x)$ can be provided.

The main disadvantage of the approach presented above is that the algorithm cannot be performed in a recursive way. To maintain this ability, we propose a slightly modified form of estimator (21) (and in consequence (23)). Let us assume that for each $i = 1, \ldots, n$ an estimator $\overline{a}_n$ is different end equal to $\hat{a}_n^{(\omega)}$. Then, the estimator of function $R(x)$ can be proposed as follows

$$\hat{R}_n(x, \{\hat{a}_i^{(\omega)}\}_n) = \frac{1}{n}\sum_{i=1}^{n}\hat{V}_i(\hat{a}_i^{(\omega)})K_i(x, X_i), \tag{28}$$

where $\{\hat{a}_i^{(\omega)}\}_n$ denotes the subset of estimators $\{\hat{a}_1^{(\omega)}, \ldots, \hat{a}_n^{(\omega)}\}$ and K_i is the kernel function given by (19). Estimator (28) can be easily written in a recursive way

$$\hat{R}_n(x, \{\hat{a}_i^{(\omega)}\}_n) = \frac{n-1}{n}\hat{R}_{n-1}(x, \{\hat{a}_i^{(\omega)}\}_{n-1}) + \frac{1}{n}\hat{V}_n(\hat{a}_n^{(\omega)})K_n(x, X_n), \tag{29}$$

where estimators $\hat{a}_n^{(\omega)}$ are computed using recursive formula (4). Estimator (22) can be expressed in a recursive way without any additional modifications

$$\overline{f}_n(x) = \frac{n-1}{n}\overline{f}_{n-1}(x) + \frac{1}{n}K_n'(x, X_n). \tag{30}$$

Finally, the estimator of the regression function $\phi(x)$ is, analogously to (23), given by

$$\hat{\phi}_n(x, \{\hat{a}_i^{(\omega)}\}_n) = \frac{\hat{R}_n(x, \{\hat{a}_i^{(\omega)}\}_n)}{\overline{f}_n(x)}. \qquad (31)$$

The algorithm presented above can be considered as a general regression neural network [36]. The appropriate scheme of this network is presented in Fig. 1.

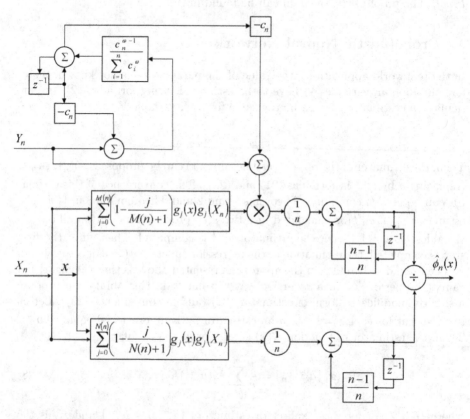

Fig. 1. The block digram of the probabilistic neural network, adopted to performing algorithms presented in sections 2 and 3

We do not present any theorem, which would ensure the convegence of estimator (31). Instead, in the next section the convergence is tested empirically, on a basis of several numerical simulations.

5   Simulations

In the following simulations a system described by equation (2) is considered, with the constant a equal to $2,5$ and the regression function $\phi(x)$ given by

$$\phi(x) = 10\frac{2x^3 - x}{\cosh(2x)}. \tag{32}$$

The random variables X_i are generated from the uniform probability distribution, from the interval $X_i \in [-5,5]$, $i = 1,\ldots,n$. The random variables Z_i come from the normal distribution $N(0, d_i)$, where d_i is given in the form

$$d_i = i^\alpha, \; i = 1,\ldots,n, \; \alpha > 0. \tag{33}$$

The elements of the sequence c_i are taken in a similar form

$$c_i = i^t, \; i = 1,\ldots,n, \; t > 0. \tag{34}$$

In the presented simulations, the parameter t is set to $t = 0,2$. It is easily seen that, in order to obey assumptions 6) and (7) of Theorem 1, the exponent α has to satisfy the following inequality

$$\alpha < 2t + 1. \tag{35}$$

In the estimators of functions $R(x)$ and $f(x)$, the Hermite orthogonal system is proposed

$$g_j(x) = \begin{cases} \dfrac{\exp\left(-x^2/2\right)}{\sqrt[4]{\pi}} & j = 0, \\ -\sqrt{2}x g_0(x) & j = 1, \\ -\sqrt{\dfrac{2}{j}}x g_{j-1}(x) - \sqrt{\dfrac{j-1}{j}}g_{j-2}(x) & j > 0. \end{cases} \tag{36}$$

The functions g_j can be bounded by (see [39])

$$\forall_{j \in \mathbb{N}} \sup_{x \in \mathbb{R}} |g_j(x)| \le G_j = Cj^{-1/12}. \tag{37}$$

Assuming that the sequences $M(n)$ and $N(n)$ are given in the following forms

$$M(n) = \lceil Dn^Q \rceil, \, D > 0, Q > 0, \; N(n) = \lceil D'n^{Q'} \rceil, \, D' > 0, Q' > 0, \tag{38}$$

the assumptions (24) and (25) of Theorem 2 are satisfied if the parameters Q and Q' satisfy the following conditions

$$Q' < \frac{3}{5}, \; Q < \frac{3}{5}(1 - \alpha). \tag{39}$$

In all of the simulations, parameters Q and Q' are kept the same, i.e. $Q = Q'$. Parameters D and D' are set to $D = D' = 1,5$.

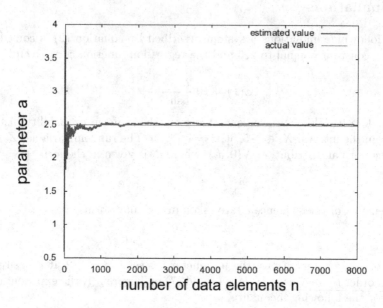

Fig. 2. Convergence of the estimator $\hat{a}_n^{(8)}$ to the actual value of parameter a, for $\alpha = 0,2$

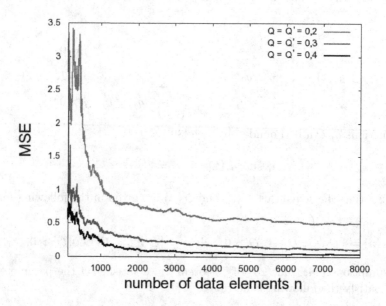

Fig. 3. MSE values for estimator $\hat{\phi}_n(x, \{\hat{a}_i^{(8)}\}_n)$ in a function of number of data elements n, for three different values of parameter $Q = Q'$: $Q = Q' = 0,2$, $Q = Q' = 0,3$ and $Q = Q' = 0,4$ $(alpha = 0,2)$

The constant a is estimated by making use of estimator (4), with parameter $\omega = 8$. The results of the simulation, obtained for $\alpha = 0, 2$, are shown in Fig. 2.

The estimator $\hat{a}_n^{(8)}$ converges to value $2, 5$ quite fast. This satisfactory result should be reflected in the quality of estimation of the regression function $\phi(x)$. To investigate the quality of estimator (31) the Mean Squared Error (MSE) value is calculated for each considered number of data elements n. Simulations are performed for three different values of parameter $Q = Q'$. Parameter α is set to $0, 2$. Results are presented in Fig. 3.

For all considered values of $Q = Q'$ the estimator $\hat{\phi}_n(x, \{\hat{a}_i^{(8)}\}_n)$ seems to converge to the regression function $\phi(x)$ as the number of data elements n increases. It is easily seen that for $\alpha = 0, 2$, inequalities (39) are satisfied. An interesting question arrised how the estimator (31) behaves if inequalities (39) are not held. To answer this question simulations for three different values of α are performed, keeping fixed $Q = Q' = 0, 3$. According to inequalities (39), for $Q = 0, 3$ the parameter α should obey $\alpha < 0, 5$. Obtained results are shown in Fig. 4.

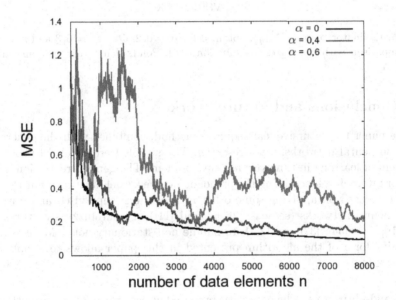

Fig. 4. MSE values for estimator $\hat{\phi}_n(x, \{\hat{a}_i^{(8)}\}_n)$ in a function of number of data elements n, for three different values of α: $\alpha = 0$, $\alpha = 0, 4$ and $\alpha = 0, 6$ ($Q = Q' = 0, 3$)

In Figure 5 an example estimator $\hat{\phi}_n(x, \{\hat{a}_i^{(8)}\}_n)$, obtained for $n = 8000$, $Q = Q = 0, 3$ and $\alpha = 0, 2$ is presented in comparison with the regression function (32).

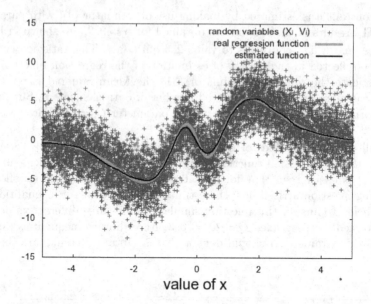

Fig. 5. Estimator $\hat{\phi}_n(x, \{\hat{a}_i^{(\omega)}\}_n)$, obtained for $\alpha = 0, 2$, $Q = Q' = 0, 3$ and $n = 8000$, in comparison with the regression function $\phi(x)$. Points denote the random variable pairs (X_i, V_i).

6   Conclusions and Future Work

In the paper the recursive least squares method, combined with the general regression neural networks, was presented. Thess tools were applied to solve the problem of learning in time-varying environment. The general regression neural network were developed using the orthogonal-type kernel functions. Future work can be focused on applying some other methods, e.g. supervised and unsupervised neural networks (see e.g. [2], [3] and [11]) or neurofuzzy structures (see e.g. [10], [31]-[34], [37] and [38]), to handle non-stationary noise. Moreover, the recursive form of the algorithm presented in this paper allows to adopt it for data streams.

Acknowledgments. The paper was prepared under project operated within the Foundation for Polish Science Team Programme co-financed by the EU European Regional Development Fund, Operational Program Innovative Economy 2007-2013, and also supported by National Science Centre NCN.

References

1. Albert, A.E., Gardner, L.A.: Stochastic Approximation and Nonlinear Regression, No. 42. MIT Press, Cambridge (1967)
2. Bilski, J., Rutkowski, L.: A fast training algorithm for neural networks. IEEE Transactions on Circuits and Systems II 45, 749–753 (1998)

3. Cierniak, R., Rutkowski, L.: On image compression by competitive neural networks and optimal linear predictors. Signal Processing: Image Communication - a Eurasip Journal 15(6), 559–565 (2000)

4. Gałkowski, T., Rutkowski, L.: Nonparametric recovery of multivariate functions with applications to system identification. Proceedings of the IEEE 73, 942–943 (1985)

5. Gałkowski, T., Rutkowski, L.: Nonparametric fitting of multivariable functions. IEEE Transactions on Automatic Control AC 31, 785–787 (1986)

6. Greblicki, W., Pawlak, M.: Nonparametric system indentification. Cambridge University Press (2008)

7. Greblicki, W., Rutkowska, D., Rutkowski, L.: An orthogonal series estimate of time-varying regression, Tokyo. Annals of the Institute of Statistical Mathematics, vol. 35, Part A, pp. 147–160 (1983)

8. Greblicki, W., Rutkowski, L.: Density-free Bayes risk consistency of nonparametric pattern recognition procedures. Proceedings of the IEEE 69(4), 482–483 (1981)

9. Györfi, L., Kohler, M., Krzyżak, A., Walk, H.: A Distribution-Free Theory of Nonparametric Regression. Springer Series in Statistics. Springer, USA (2002)

10. Nowicki, R.: Nonlinear modelling and classification based on the MICOG defuzzifications. Journal of Nonlinear Analysis, Series A: Theory, Methods and Applications 7(12), 1033–1047 (2009)

11. Patan, K., Patan, M.: Optimal Training Strategies for Locally Recurrent Neural Networks. Journal of Artificial Intelligence and Soft Computing Research 1(2), 103–114 (2011)

12. Rafajłowicz, E.: Nonparametric orthogonal series estimators of regression: A class attaining the optimal convergence rate in L_2. Statistics and Probability Letters 5, 219–224 (1987)

13. Rutkowski, L.: Sequential estimates of probability densities by orthogonal series and their application in pattern classification. IEEE Transactions on Systems, Man, and Cybernetics SMC 10(12), 918–920 (1980)

14. Rutkowski, L.: Sequential estimates of a regression function by orthogonal series with applications in discrimination, New York, Heidelberg, Berlin. Lectures Notes in Statistics, vol. 8, pp. 236–244 (1981)

15. Rutkowski, L.: On system identification by nonparametric function fitting. IEEE Transactions on Automatic Control AC 27, 225–227 (1982)

16. Rutkowski, L.: Orthogonal series estimates of a regression function with applications in system identification. In: Probability and Statistical Inference, pp. 343–347. D. Reidel Publishing Company, Dordrecht (1982)

17. Rutkowski, L.: On Bayes risk consistent pattern recognition procedures in a quasi-stationary environment. IEEE Transactions on Pattern Analysis and Machine Intelligence PAMI 4(1), 84–87 (1982)

18. Rutkowski, L.: On-line identification of time-varying systems by nonparametric techniques. IEEE Transactions on Automatic Control AC 27, 228–230 (1982)

19. Rutkowski, L.: On nonparametric identification with prediction of time-varying systems. IEEE Transactions on Automatic Control AC 29, 58–60 (1984)

20. Rutkowski, L.: Nonparametric identification of quasi-stationary systems. Systems and Control Letters 6, 33–35 (1985)

21. Rutkowski, L.: The real-time identification of time-varying systems by nonparametric algorithms based on the Parzen kernels. International Journal of Systems Science 16, 1123–1130 (1985)

22. Rutkowski, L.: A general approach for nonparametric fitting of functions and their derivatives with applications to linear circuits identification. IEEE Transactions Circuits Systems CAS 33, 812–818 (1986)
23. Rutkowski, L.: Sequential pattern recognition procedures derived from multiple Fourier series. Pattern Recognition Letters 8, 213–216 (1988)
24. Rutkowski, L.: Nonparametric procedures for identification and control of linear dynamic systems. In: Proceedings of 1988 American Control Conference, June 15-17, pp. 1325–1326 (1988)
25. Rutkowski, L.: An application of multiple Fourier series to identification of multivariable nonstationary systems. International Journal of Systems Science 20(10), 1993–2002 (1989)
26. Rutkowski, L.: Nonparametric learning algorithms in the time-varying environments. Signal Processing 18, 129–137 (1989)
27. Rutkowski, L., Rafajłowicz, E.: On global rate of convergence of some nonparametric identification procedures. IEEE Transaction on Automatic Control AC 34(10), 1089–1091 (1989)
28. Rutkowski, L.: Identification of MISO nonlinear regressions in the presence of a wide class of disturbances. IEEE Transactions on Information Theory IT 37, 214–216 (1991)
29. Rutkowski, L.: Multiple Fourier series procedures for extraction of nonlinear regressions from noisy data. IEEE Transactions on Signal Processing 41(10), 3062–3065 (1993)
30. Rutkowski, L., Gałkowski, T.: On pattern classification and system identification by probabilistic neural networks. Applied Mathematics and Computer Science 4(3), 413–422 (1994)
31. Rutkowski, L.: A New Method for System Modelling and Pattern Classification. Bulletin of the Polish Academy of Sciences 52(1), 11–24 (2004)
32. Rutkowski, L., Cpałka, K.: A general approach to neuro-fuzzy systems. In: Proceedings of the 10th IEEE International Conference on Fuzzy Systems, Melbourne, December 2-5, vol. 3, pp. 1428–1431 (2001)
33. Rutkowski, L., Cpałka, K.: A neuro-fuzzy controller with a compromise fuzzy reasoning. Control and Cybernetics 31(2), 297–308 (2002)
34. Scherer, R.: Boosting Ensemble of Relational Neuro-fuzzy Systems. In: Rutkowski, L., Tadeusiewicz, R., Zadeh, L.A., Żurada, J.M. (eds.) ICAISC 2006. LNCS (LNAI), vol. 4029, pp. 306–313. Springer, Heidelberg (2006)
35. Specht, D.F.: Probabilistic neural networks. Neural Networks 3, 109–118 (1990)
36. Specht, D.F.: A general regression neural network. IEEE Transactions on Neural Networks 2, 568–576 (1991)
37. Starczewski, J., Rutkowski, L.: Interval type 2 neuro-fuzzy systems based on interval consequents. In: Rutkowski, L., Kacprzyk, J. (eds.) Neural Networks and Soft Computing, pp. 570–577. Physica-Verlag, Springer-Verlag Company, Heidelberg, New York (2003)
38. Starczewski, J.T., Rutkowski, L.: Connectionist Structures of Type 2 Fuzzy Inference Systems. In: Wyrzykowski, R., Dongarra, J., Paprzycki, M., Waśniewski, J. (eds.) PPAM 2001. LNCS, vol. 2328, pp. 634–642. Springer, Heidelberg (2002)
39. Szegö, G.: Orthogonal Polynomials, vol. 23. American Mathematical Society Coll. Publ. (1959)
40. Wilks, S.S.: Mathematical Statistics. John Wiley, New York (1962)

Binary Perceptron Learning Algorithm Using Simplex-Method

Vladimir Kryzhanovsky, Irina Zhelavskaya, and Jakov Karandashev

Center of Optical Neural Technologies,
Scientific Research Institute for System Analysis,
Russian Academy of Sciences,
Vavilova St., 44/2, 119333 Moscow, Russia
Vladimir.Krizhanovsky@gmail.com, winjei@ya.ru,
Yakov.Karandashev@phystech.edu

Abstract. A number of researchers headed by E. Gardner have proved that a maximum achievable memory load of binary perceptron is 2. A learning algorithm allowing reaching and even exceeding the critical load was proposed. The algorithm was reduced to solving the linear programming problem. The proposed algorithm is sequel to Krauth and Mezard ideas. The algorithm makes it possible to construct networks storage capacity and noise stability of which are comparable to those of Krauth and Mezard algorithm. However suggested modification of the algorithm outperforms.

Keywords: Binary neural networks, simplex-method.

1 Introduction

We shall deal with binary perceptron with N inputs and one binary output. A neuron here is a typical adder with $sign(h)$ activation function and zero threshold.

Storage capacity of such perceptron taught by Hebb rule with randomly and independently generated reference patterns reaches the value $M_{max} = 0.14N$. Attempts at training with a larger number of patterns ($M > M_{max}$) results in a complete collapse of associative memory [1]. Hebb rule also proves unequal to its task in case if those patterns are correlated ($M_{max} \ll 0.14N$). On the other hand it was proved [2-3] that maximum storage capacity is comes up to $2N$.

In order to understand why Hebb rule gives us networks with such small storage capacity and high sensitivity of patterns mutual correlations, let us consider energy surface forming in process of training.

Except that perceptron performance cannot be described by energy in contrast to fully connected Hopfield network, the authors took the liberty of doing so.

Given M uncorrelated patterns $\mathbf{X}_m = (x_{m1}, x_{m2}, \ldots, x_{mN})$, where $x_{mi} = \pm 1$ and $m = 1, 2, \ldots, M$, the perceptron should produce a response $y_m = \pm 1$ when noisy pattern $\mathbf{X}_m$ is presented. Then, according to Hebb rule, synaptic weights (of a network) can be described by N-dimensional vector:

L. Rutkowski et al. (Eds.): ICAISC 2012, Part I, LNCS 7267, pp. 111–118, 2012.

$$\mathbf{W} = \sum_{m=1}^{M} y_m \mathbf{X}_m.$$ (1)

Storing some few patterns ($M < M_{max}$) leads to energy surface presented in fig.1.a. Local minima are formed at points of a space corresponding to stored patterns. Depths and basins of attraction of these minima are the same. Spatial distribution of obtained local minima is uniform due to uncorrelatedness of patterns. Attempts to form extra minima with the same depths and basins of attraction result in strong deformation of energy surface: the existing local minima either shift or merge with each other. Because the correlated patterns are more densely placed in the space, memory collapse takes place even in case of fewer stored patterns.

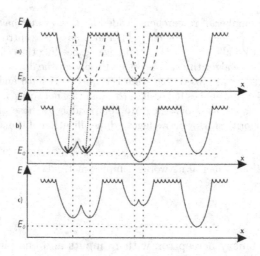

Fig. 1. Stages of energy surface forming: a) memory load $M < M_{max}$ (broken curves denote the extra minima to be added); b) $M > M_{max}$ associative memory collapse; c) $M > M_{max}$ local minima are formed at desired points of the space although their depths and basins of attraction are respectively smaller

From the qualitative situation presented in Fig. 1 it follows that an effort to form local minima of the same depths without taking into account their relative positions is not reasonable. It is intriguing to have local minima of different depths adaptively at desired points. This can be achieved by sacrificing depths and basins of attraction of local minima corresponding to closely adjacent patterns (fig. 1.b).

It was demonstrated [4] that the depth E_0 and the size of basin of attraction n_m of local minimum can be described by one coefficient rm introduced in Hebb rule (1) in this way:

$$\mathbf{W} = \sum_{m=1}^{M} r_m y_m \mathbf{X}_m,$$ (2)

where $r_m \in (0; 1]$. Local minimum energy is estimated by the expression

$$E_m = -r_m N^2,$$

with an accuracy to small fluctuations, and the radius of basin of attraction is determined by this estimate:

$$n_m = \frac{N}{2} \left(1 - \frac{r_0}{r_m} \sqrt{1 - r_m^2} \right), r_0 = \sqrt{2 \ln N / N}.$$

Hence learning task reduces to the problem of finding weight coefficients r_m for given set of pairs $(\mathbf{X}_m; y_m)$. As it will be shown later, this task in its turn reduces to linear programming problem.

The idea of simplex-method approach to learning of perceptron was first put forward by Krauth and Mezard in 1987 [5]. Application of both approaches enables to store up to $2N$ patterns which is equivalent of theoretical memory capacity limit [2].

This paper is constructed in the following way. In section 2 we show how to reduce assigned problem to linear programming problem, discussed Krauth and Mezard algorithm and make a comparison between this and proposed one. Experimental research of properties of suggested algorithm was conducted in section 3. The resume of the work is presented in conclusions.

2   Simplex-Method

Let's assume vector $\mathbf{X}$ obtained as a result of garbling of pattern $\mathbf{X}_m$ is an input vector of the perceptron. Thereafter binary perceptron switches to the true state providing that local field is codirectional with y_m, i.e. on condition of following inequality:

$$y_m \sum_{j=1}^{N} w_j \tilde{x}_{mj} > 0,$$

where $\tilde{x}_{mj}$ is a noisy j-coordinate of pattern number $m - \mathbf{X}_m$.

For better recognition stability parameter $\Delta(\Delta > 0)$ is introduced and training of the perceptron goes on under the condition:

$$y_m \sum_{j=1}^{N} w_j x_{mj} > \Delta,$$ (3)

for the whole of given set of pairs $(\mathbf{X}_m; y_m), m = 1, \ldots, M$.

Parameter Δ is responsible for depth and size of basins of attraction of local minima being formed. The more Δ is in the process of training the more the probability of right recognition of noisy patterns is. Therefore with regard to (2) it is necessary to find such weight coefficients r_m wherein inequality (3) is satisfied for all reference patterns for as large as possible value of Δ. In this case the depth of local minima formed is maximum possible.

Let's formulize the assigned task. It is required to find $(M+1)$ variables $(r_1, r_2, ..., r_M, \Delta)$ which appear to be a solution to the linear programming problem:

$$\begin{cases} \sum_{m=1}^{M} r_m y_m y_\mu(\mathbf{X}_m, \mathbf{X}_\mu) - \Delta \geq 0, \\ 0 < r_m \leq 1, \quad \mu, m = \overline{1, M} \\ \Delta > 0. \end{cases} \tag{4}$$

$$f(r_1, r_2, ..., r_M, \Delta) = \Delta \rightarrow \max$$

The similar idea was formulated by Krauth and Mezard [5]. They took N weight coefficients w_j and stability parameter Δ straight as unknown quantities.

As seen in fig.2, the proposed algorithm and one of Krauth and Mezard produce similar results.

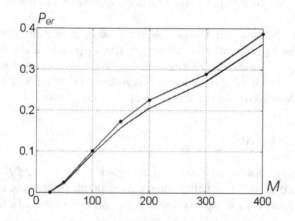

Fig. 2. Probability of incorrect recognition of noisy reference patterns as a function of number of stored patterns M. Results for Krauth and Mezard algorithm are specified by marked curve, ones for proposed algorithm by full curve. Patterns length is $N = 200$, noise level is $a = 0.09$.

Algorithms vary in number of unknown parameters. In the region for $M < N$ the proposed algorithm outperforms. This region is of a great practical interest because in this case minima have non-zero basins of attraction. As is clear from fig.3 proposed algorithm outworks. Running time ratio of algorithms is an inverse function of memory load.

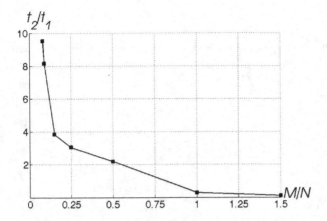

Fig. 3. Ratio of Krauth and Mezard learning time t_2 to proposed algorithm learning time t_1 as a function of memory load M/N. The curve has been plotted experimentally for $N = 1000$.

3   Suggested Learning Rule Analysis

In this section we analyze experimentally properties of the proposed algorithm.

Lets neglect domains of attraction for a while and determine by an experiment the maximum storage capacity of the perceptron being trained by simplex-method.

The experiment is as follows. Lets try to train the network on the set of M patterns by simplex-method. If simplex-method possesses a solution (i.e. all M patterns are fixed points) at the next step we try to train the network on the set of $M + 1$ patterns, otherwise the algorithm should be terminated and running value of M is chosen as a solution. This procedure is repeated 100 times and the average result is calculated.

As can be seen in the fig.4 applying such learning rule makes it possible to reach storage capacity of $2N$. Experimental results for Hebb rule are also presented in the figure for comparison.

Next we show that stability parameter is responsible for the size of basins of attraction of local minima being formed. For this purpose we hold fixed parameter Δ, i.e. we move this one out of unknown quantities of the system (4) and introduce new cost function:

$$f(r_1, r_2, ..., r_M) = \sum_{m=1}^{M} r_m y_m \sum_{\mu=1}^{M} y_\mu(\mathbf{X}_m, \mathbf{X}_\mu) \qquad (5)$$

This linear programming problem is solved for various parameter values $\Delta = 30; 70; 150, N = 200, M = 40$. Fig.5 illustrates the probability of incorrect patterns recognition Per as a function of amount of noise a of input data. It is apparent from the figure that stability parameter increment leads to basins of attraction expansion.

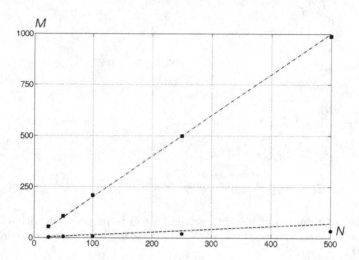

Fig. 4. Storage capacity M as a function of network size N: theoretical capacity for Hebb rule, $M = 0.14N$ (*dashed line*); theoretical value of maximum possible capacity, $M = 2N$ (*dash-dot line*); experimental values of maximum storage capacity for the proposed algorithm and for the Hebb rule (*square and circle markers, respectively*)

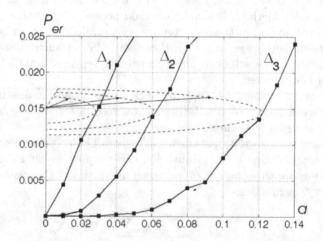

Fig. 5. Probability of incorrect recognition P_{er} as a function of noise level a. Curves are plotted for three values of stability parameter values $\Delta = 30; 70; 150$, $N = 200$, $M = 40$. Borders of basins of attraction of local minima are depicted with dashed curves and their radii - with arrows.

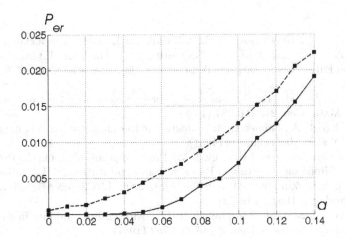

Fig. 6. Probability of incorrect recognition P_{er} as a function of noise level a: for training by Hebb rule (*dashed curve*) and by algorithm using simplex-method (*full curve*) for $N = 200, M = 30, \Delta = 110$

Application of linear programming (4) for training networks is also works very well for $M < 0.14N$. As fig.6 shows, in case of small amount of noise (up to 9%) to input patterns, the probability of incorrect patterns recognition is more than twofold bigger in training by Hebb rule than in training by the proposed method.

4 Conclusions

In this paper the perceptron learning algorithm using simplex-method for weight coefficients setting was proposed. The discussed algorithm is sequel to Krauth and Mezard ideas published in 1987 [5]. The algorithms are different in the number of parameters: M (the number of stored patterns) parameters in the suggested approach and N (the length of pattern vectors) ones in Krauth and Mezard algorithm. In the field of practical interest ($M < N$) the proposed learning algorithm outperforms above-said one, but both methods show similar results for noise stability and storage capacity.

It has been shown that the proposed learning rule make it possible to construct networks with $2N$ storage capacity. This value is a theoretically proved upper limit [2]. Application of this method is also well-proved for loads in the region of $M \approx 0.14N$, since networks trained with this rule appear to be more noise-resistant, as opposed to ones trained with Hebb learning rule.

Acknowledgments. This work is supported by Russian Foundation for Basic Research RFBR, grant 09-07-00159-a.

References

1. Karandashev, I., Kryzhanovsky, B., Litinskii, L.: Hopfield-type memory without catastrophic forgetting. In: Future Computing 2011: The Third International Conference on Future Computational Technologies and Applications, pp. 57–61. IARIA (2011)
2. Gardner, E., Derrida, B.: Optimal storage properties of neural network models. J. Phys. A: Math. Gen. 21, 271–284 (1988)
3. Hertz, J., Krogh, A., Palmer, R.: Introduction to the Theory of Neural Computation. Addison-Wesley, Massachusetts (1991)
4. Kryzhanovsky, B.V., Kryzhanovsky, V.M.: Binary Optimization: On the Probability of a Local Minimum Detection in Random Search. In: Rutkowski, L., Tadeusiewicz, R., Zadeh, L.A., Zurada, J.M. (eds.) ICAISC 2008. LNCS (LNAI), vol. 5097, pp. 89–100. Springer, Heidelberg (2008)
5. Krauth, W., Mezard, M.: Learning algorithms with optimal stability in neural networks. J. Phys. A: Math. Gen. 20, L745–L752 (1987)

Objects Auto-selection from Stereo-Images Realised by Self-Correcting Neural Network

Lukasz Laskowski

Czestochowa University of Technology,
Department of Computer Engineering,
Al, A.K. 36, 42-200 Czestochowa, Poland

Abstract. In the present thesis the author undertakes the problem of the objects selecting on pictures. The novel conception of using depth map as a base to objects marking was proposed here. objects separation can be done on the base of depth (disparity), corresponding to points that should be marked. This allows for elimination of textures, occurring in background and also on objects. The object selection process must be preceded by picture's depth analysis. This can be done by the novel neural structure: Self-Correcting Neural Network. This structure is working point-by-point with no picture's segmentation before.

Keywords: Hopfield, self-correcting neural networks, stereovision, depth analysis, object selection.

1   Introduction

Objects selection refers to the mechanism of extracting objects of interest while ignoring other objects and background in a given visual scene [1]. It is a fundamental issue for many computer vision and image analysis techniques and it is still a challenging task to artificial visual systems. Some further information concerning to techniques of the object selection one can find in [2],[3]. The majority of objects selectors is based on shape recognition, while very often the shape is not known. We deal with this situation e.g. in the photography (e.g. blurring the background on picture with no blurring first plane person) or in the film industry (mainly in the special effects, the background is replaced by some computer generated scene). In mentioned situations, there is no possibility to predict of the object's shape (or shape's predicting is very difficult). In this case the objects detection with no user interference is not possible. In author's conception, the shape of the object needn't to be known. The objects selecting is carried out on the base of distance to point, have to be selected. Thanks to this, the objects selection can be carried out in completely automatic way, with no user interference. To this end, the information about 3rd dimension of each point on the scene (picture) is necessary. The most appropriate way to reach this seems to register the pictures by stereo-cameras system and find each spatial coordinates by the stereo-matching process [4]. Unfortunately most of existing and

L. Rutkowski et al. (Eds.): ICAISC 2012, Part I, LNCS 7267, pp. 119–125, 2012.

well-working algorithms is based on picture segmentation and matching of segments [5], what can caused some inaccuracy. Any minor inaccuracies can not be accepted in the case of application in film and photography. In this instance the extreme accuracy is required.

In the present thesis the author presents novel algorithm of the objects selection. Presented here method is based on the stereo-matching process, carried out by Self Correcting Neural Networks (SCNN). This kind of neural structure is working with extremely high accuracy. Another advantage of this structure is working point-by-point with no earlier picture segmentation. this gives points matching with the accuracy not reachable for any other algorithms known from articles. On the base of information about each spatial coordinates corresponding to picture's points, the objects can be selected in automatic way. Assuming extremely low error, presented here method can be applied in photography and in the film industry.

2   The Self-Correcting Neural Network

the main part of the object's auto-selection algorithm is depth analysis algorithm based on Self-Correcting Neural Network. Some information about depth analysis with the use of Hopfield-like neural network one can find in [6]. The SCNN was introduced by the author in [7]. The architecture of this neural network was depicted in fig. 1.

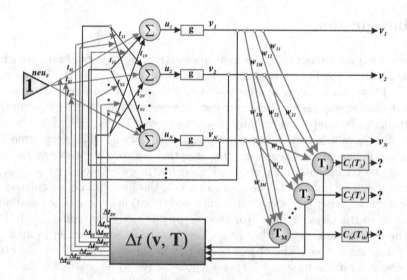

Fig. 1. The architecture of dual mode neural network

As can be seen, this kind of structure consists of two kinds of neurons: neurons in basic layer and neurons in managementing layer. The role of these two kinds of neurons is completely different. The additional neuron neu_{00} is still active (potential equal 1) and its role is to supply external currents to neurons in basic layer. *The basic layer* is realized by continuous Hopfield-like neural network [8],[9]. The proposed network consists of $n \times n$ neurons for one epipolar lines in an image. It is easy to note that the target system will consist of n networks working pararely - each network will realize stereo-matching problem for one epipolar line. n is dimension of images ($width = height = n$). Each neuron neu_{ik} is responsible for fitting i-point in right image to k-point in left image. The higher the external potential of neu_{ik}, the better the fitting of points is. In the final configuration only for corresponding points i in right image to k in left image potential of neu_{ik} will equal 1, for the rest point external potential of neurons will equal 0. It is very convenient to represent neurons an a matrix, named Fitting Matrix (FM), where number of row represent i index, and number of column represents k index. As can be easily concluded, one in FM means fitting of points, values between zero and one (for continuous activation function, used here) can be interpreted as probability of stereo-matching of points. The role of basic layer is to minimize their energy function, defined by weight connections between neurons. Heuristic filling of weight matrix significantly accelerates the algorithm working and makes it more efficient. From this reason the Initial Energy Function (IEF) was introduced (will be clarified below). This layer is working as classical continuous Hopfield-like network. After finding the minimum of IEF (stable state), weights are modified depending on the verification of the result (carried out by managementing neurons).

The managementing layer can be built with different neurons - their type depends on problem specification. Thanks to using managementing neurons the solution reached, obtained by basic layer, is verified. Each neuron is controlling one of the conditions of syntactic correctness of the solution. If the condition a given neuron is responsible for, is not met, the range of weight modification is calculated, and interconnection weights $t_{ik,jl}$ between neurons v_{ik} and v_{jl} in basic layer are modified (which means also modification of energy function) according following equation:

$$\Delta t_{ik,jl} = - \begin{cases} \sum_m \eta_m \frac{\partial C_m}{\partial T_m} w_{m,ik} v_{jl} \\ + \sum_m \eta_m \frac{\partial C_m}{\partial T_m} w_{m,ik} v_{ik} & \text{for jl} \neq 00 \\ \\ \sum_m \eta_m \frac{\partial C_m}{\partial T_m} w_{m,ik} v_{jl} & \text{for jl} = 00 \end{cases} . \tag{1}$$

In the equation (1) η is gradient step, C_m is restriction assigned to managementing neuron T_m, w_{mi} is weight of connection m-neuron in managementing layer and i-neuron in basic layer. After the modification, basic layer is starting minimization procedure once again. This procedure is repeated until the solution is to be perfect, in the meaning of problem expression. This means that objective function is minimized, with keeping all conditions of syntactic correctness of solution.

Detailed information about Self-Correcting Neural Network will be available in [10].

3   Experimental Results

An operational procedure of the objects auto selection is carried out in two stages:

1. depth analysis of picture's with using of stereo-matching (carried out by SCNN),
2. selection of the objects on the base of 3rd dimension of the points.

3.1   Stereo-matching Algorithm

As can be easy noticed, the stereo-matching process plays crucial role in the objects selecting algorithm. The results of stereo matching process carried out by SCNN can be seen in fig. 2.

At figure 2 in the first row stereo pictures, used for stereo matching process was shown. The second row shows neurons activity maps for 80 scanning line (arbitrary assumed) in iterations (number of "n")of basic layer of the SCNN. The neurons activity map is helpful to the analysis of network working. It can be interpreted as a graphical form of fitting matrix to investigated line. In next row obtained (by basic layer of the SCNN) the depth map can be seen. The same sequence (instead of stereo-pictures) was repeated after the modification of connection weights in basic layer.

The analysis of first running of basic layer for simulated pictures (fig. 2), numerous mistakes of fitting can be seen. The relatively high error (29.49%) was obtain. On the basis of output depth map, managementing neurons are calculating the connection weight's corrections and adjust it towards minimization of Dual Function. After the modification, basic layer is activated with new interconnections strengths. In this running the error amounts to 11.45%, which is significantly less then with no connection modification. After the third running the solution obtained is much better, then in the previous running. The relative error amounts only to 4.37%. The stereo matching seems to be unique and disparity is continuous in areas. the sequence of disparity is also kept. The result of stereo-matching can be accepted as a data to the objects selection process.

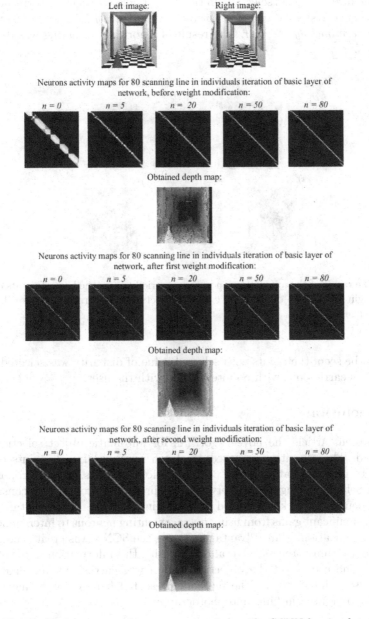

Fig. 2. The result of stereo matching process carried out by SCNN for simulated stereo-images "corridor"

3.2 Objects Selection Algorithm

The procedure of objects selection on the base of points disparity (corresponding to depth) is very simple: *mark each points with disparity belonging to particular range, determined by the user.* The result of algorithm's working was depicted on figure 3.

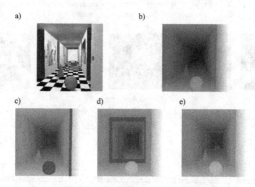

Fig. 3. The result of the auto-selection process carried out on the base of points disparity; a - origin picture, b - depth map, c, d, e - objects selected (red colour) for different depth's range

As can be seen, the points with selected value of disparity was selected. This process was carried out with no interference with the user.

4 Conclusion

In the present article the novel algorithm for automatic object selection was introduced. The algorithm is based on depth analysis of each points on the picture. To get information about 3rd dimension of points, author proposed of using the Self Correcting Neural Network. The promising properties of considered artificial neural network was tested on stereo images. The experimental results indicated significant gains from using managementing neurons to interconnection weights modification. Main advantage of using the SCNN was great accuracy of the stereo matching process, what allows on using this information to the objects selection. The process of the objects selection was carried out automatically, with no user's interference. The method, presented here seems to have great application potential in films and photography.

References

[1] Breve, F., Zhao, L., Quiles, M., Macau, E.: Chaotic phase synchronization and desynchronization in an oscillator network for object selection. Neural Networks 22, 728–737 (2009)

[2]   Dunka, A., Haffegeea, A., Alexandrov, V.: Selection methods for interactive creation and management of objects in 3D immersive environments. Procedia Computer Science 1, 2609–2617 (2010)

[3]   Mokhtarian, F., Abbasi, S.: Robust automatic selection of optimal views in multi-view free-form object recognition. Pattern Recognition 38, 1021–1031 (2005)

[4]   Faugeras, O.: Three-dimensional computer vision. A Geometric Viewpoint. MIT (1993)

[5]   Fua, P.: A parallel stereo algorithm that produces dense depth maps and preserves image features. Mach. Vision Appl. 6, 35–49 (1993)

[6]   Laskowski, L.: Hybrid-Maximum Neural Network for Depth Analysis from Stereo-Image. In: Rutkowski, L., Scherer, R., Tadeusiewicz, R., Zadeh, L.A., Zurada, J.M. (eds.) ICAISC 2010, Part II. LNCS, vol. 6114, pp. 47–55. Springer, Heidelberg (2010)

[7]   Laskowski, L.: A Novel Continuous Dual Mode Neural Network in Stereo-Matching Process. In: Diamantaras, K., Duch, W., Iliadis, L.S. (eds.) ICANN 2010, Part III. LNCS, vol. 6354, pp. 294–297. Springer, Heidelberg (2010)

[8]   Hopfield, J.J., Tank, D.W.: "Neural" computation of decisions in optimization problems. Biological Cybernetics 52, 141–152 (1985)

[9]   Hopfield, J.J., Tank, D.W.: Artificial neural networks. IEEE Circuits and Devices Magazine 8, 3–10 (1988)

[10] Laskowski, L.: A Novel Self-Correcting Neural Network in the Objects Selection Task (publication under redaction)

On-Line Trajectory-Based Linearisation of Neural Models for a Computationally Efficient Predictive Control Algorithm

Maciej Ławryńczuk

Institute of Control and Computation Engineering,
Warsaw University of Technology
ul. Nowowiejska 15/19, 00-665 Warsaw, Poland
M.Lawrynczuk@ia.pw.edu.pl

Abstract. The direct application of a neural model in Model Predictive Control (MPC) algorithms results in a nonlinear, in general non-convex, optimisation problem which must be solved on-line. A linear approximation of the model for the current operating point can be used for prediction in MPC, but for significantly nonlinear processes control accuracy may be not sufficient. MPC algorithm in which the neural model is linearised on-line along a trajectory is discussed. The control policy is calculated from a quadratic programming problem, nonlinear optimisation is not necessary. Accuracy and computational burden of the algorithm are demonstrated for a high-purity high-pressure distillation column.

1 Introduction

A unique feature of Model Predictive Control (MPC) algorithms is the fact that a dynamic model of the process is directly used on-line to predict its behavior over some time horizon and to optimise the future control policy [8,13]. When compared with other control techniques, their advantages are: constraints can be easily imposed on process inputs (manipulated variables) and outputs (controlled variables), they are able to control multivariable processes very efficiently, they can be applied for processes with difficult dynamic properties (e.g. with significant time-delays or the inverse response). In consequence, MPC algorithms have been successfully used for years in thousands of advanced industrial applications, e.g. in refineries, in chemical engineering, in the paper industry, in mining and metallurgy, in food processing, in the automobile industry and even in aerospace [12].

In the simplest case linear models are used for prediction in MPC. Because the majority of technological processes have nonlinear properties, linear MPC techniques may give insufficient control accuracy. Nonlinear MPC algorithms in which nonlinear models are used have been researched over the last years [4,10,13,14]. Different nonlinear models can be used in MPC, e.g. fuzzy structures, polynomials, Volterra series, wavelets. Neural models are particularly interesting, because they offer excellent approximation accuracy, as practical experience clearly indicates, they have a moderate number of parameters and their

L. Rutkowski et al. (Eds.): ICAISC 2012, Part I, LNCS 7267, pp. 126–134, 2012.

structure is not complicated. As a result, neural models can be efficiently used
in different nonlinear MPC algorithms [6,11,13].

When a neural model is directly used for prediction in MPC, a nonlinear, in
general non-convex, optimisation problem must be solved on-line at each sampling instant. Despite significant progress in optimisation algorithms [1,2,9,15],
practical application of on-line nonlinear optimisation is always an issue. Since
the solution must be obtained in real-time, low computational complexity is very
desirable. A straightforward solution is to calculate successively on-line a linear
approximation of the neural model and use the linearised model for prediction
[6]. Unfortunately, for significantly nonlinear processes obtained control accuracy may be not sufficient. This paper discusses an MPC algorithm in which the
neural model is linearised on-line along a trajectory. The control policy is calculated on-line from a quadratic programming problem, nonlinear optimisation
is not necessary. Control accuracy and computational burden of the described
algorithm are demonstrated for a high-purity high-pressure distillation column.

2 Model Predictive Control (MPC) Algorithms

In MPC algorithms at each consecutive sampling instant k, $k = 0, 1, 2, \ldots$, a set
of future control increments

$$\triangle \boldsymbol{u}(k) = [\triangle u(k|k) \; \triangle u(k+1|k) \ldots \triangle u(k + N_{\mathrm{u}} - 1|k)]^{\mathrm{T}} \tag{1}$$

is calculated, where $\triangle u(k + p|k) = u(k + p|k) - u(k + p - 1|k)$. It is assumed
that $\triangle u(k+p|k) = 0$ for $p \geq N_{\mathrm{u}}$, where N_{u} is the control horizon. The objective
is to minimise differences between the reference trajectory $y^{\mathrm{ref}}(k + p|k)$ and
predicted values of the output $\hat{y}(k + p|k)$ over the prediction horizon $N \geq N_{\mathrm{u}}$.
Constraints are usually imposed on input and output variables. Future control
increments (1) are determined from the following MPC optimisation task (hard
output constraints are used for simplicity of presentation)

$$\min_{\triangle \boldsymbol{u}(k)} \left\{ \sum_{p=1}^{N} (y^{\mathrm{ref}}(k + p|k) - \hat{y}(k + p|k))^2 + \lambda \sum_{p=0}^{N_{\mathrm{u}}-1} (\triangle u(k + p|k))^2 \right\}$$

subject to $\tag{2}$

$$u^{\mathrm{min}} \leq u(k + p|k) \leq u^{\mathrm{max}}, \quad p = 0, \ldots, N_{\mathrm{u}} - 1$$
$$- \triangle u^{\mathrm{max}} \leq \triangle u(k + p|k) \leq \triangle u^{\mathrm{max}}, \quad p = 0, \ldots, N_{\mathrm{u}} - 1$$
$$y^{\mathrm{min}} \leq \hat{y}(k + p|k) \leq y^{\mathrm{max}}, \quad p = 1, \ldots, N$$

Only the first element of the determined sequence (1) is applied to the process,
i.e. $u(k) = \triangle u(k|k) + u(k - 1)$. At the next sampling instant, $k + 1$, the output
measurement is updated, and the whole procedure is repeated.

Let the dynamic process under consideration be described by the following
discrete-time Nonlinear Auto Regressive with eXternal input (NARX) model

$$y(k) = f(\boldsymbol{x}(k)) = f(u(k - \tau), \ldots, u(k - n_{\mathrm{B}}), y(k - 1), \ldots, y(k - n_{\mathrm{A}})) \tag{3}$$

As the model a neural network of Multi Layer Perceptron (MLP) or Radial Radial Basis Function (RBF) type [3] can be used. Consecutive output predictions over the prediction horizon ($p = 1, \ldots, N$) are calculated recurrently

$$\hat{y}(k+p|k) = f(\underbrace{u(k-\tau+p|k), \ldots, u(k|k)}_{I_{\mathrm{uf}}(p)}, \underbrace{u(k-1), \ldots, u(k-n_{\mathrm{B}}+p)}_{I_{\mathrm{u}}-I_{\mathrm{uf}}(p)},$$

$$\underbrace{\hat{y}(k-1+p|k), \ldots, \hat{y}(k+1|k)}_{I_{\mathrm{yf}}(p)}, \underbrace{y(k), \ldots, y(k-n_{\mathrm{A}}+p)}_{n_{\mathrm{A}}-I_{\mathrm{yf}}(p)}) + d(k)$$

where $I_{\mathrm{uf}}(p) = \max(\min(p - \tau + 1, I_{\mathrm{u}}), 0)$, $I_{\mathrm{yf}}(p) = \min(p - 1, n_{\mathrm{A}})$ and $d(k)$ is an estimation of the unmeasured disturbance [13]. Since the model is nonlinear, future predictions are nonlinear functions of the calculated control policy (1). As a result, the MPC optimisation problem (2) is in fact a nonlinear, in general non-convex, task which must be solved in real time on-line. Computational complexity of such an approach may be high and the whole algorithm may be unable to find the solution within the required time.

The general idea of reducing computational burden of nonlinear MPC is quite intuitive: at each sampling instant a linear approximation

$$y(k) = \sum_{l=1}^{n_{\mathrm{B}}} b_l(k)u(k-l) - \sum_{l=1}^{n_{\mathrm{A}}} a_l(k)y(k-l)$$

of the nonlinear neural model (3) is obtained on-line for the current operating point, where

$$a_l(k) = -\frac{\partial f(\boldsymbol{x}(k))}{\partial y(k-l)}, \quad b_l(k) = \frac{\partial f(\boldsymbol{x}(k))}{\partial u(k-l)}$$

are coefficients of the linearised model. The linearised model is used for prediction over the whole prediction horizon. Thanks to linearisation, predictions $\hat{y}(k+1|k), \ldots, \hat{y}(k+N|k)$ are linear functions of future control increments (1), i.e. the decision variables of the algorithm. In consequence, the MPC optimisation problem (2) becomes a quadratic programming task. The described linearisation method is used in the MPC algorithm with Nonlinear Prediction and Linearisation (MPC-NPL) [6,7,13]. During calculations the structure of the neural model is exploited.

3   MPC Algorithm with Nonlinear Prediction and Linearisation along the Trajectory (MPC-NPLT)

In the MPC-NPL algorithm linearisation is carried out for the current operating point of the process and the same linearised model is used for prediction over the whole prediction horizon. Intuitively, prediction accuracy of such a model may be insufficient, in particular when the process is significantly nonlinear and changes of the reference trajectory are fast and big. A potentially better method is to linearise the model for an assumed future input trajectory

$$\boldsymbol{u}^{\mathrm{traj}}(k) = \left[u^{\mathrm{traj}}(k|k) \ldots u^{\mathrm{traj}}(k + N_{\mathrm{u}} - 1|k) \right]^{\mathrm{T}}$$

of course remembering that $u^{\text{traj}}(k+p|k) = u^{\text{traj}}(k+N_u-1|k)$ for $p = N_u, \ldots, N$. The input trajectory $\boldsymbol{u}^{\text{traj}}(k)$ corresponds to the future output trajectory

$$\hat{\boldsymbol{y}}^{\text{traj}}(k) = \left[\hat{y}^{\text{traj}}(k+1|k) \ldots \hat{y}^{\text{traj}}(k+N|k)\right]^{\text{T}}$$

Recalling the Taylor series formula for a scalar function $y(x)\colon \mathbb{R} \to \mathbb{R}$

$$y(x) = y(\bar{x}) + \left.\frac{dy(x)}{dx}\right|_{x=\bar{x}} (x - \bar{x}) + \ldots$$

a linear approximation of the nonlinear trajectory $\hat{\boldsymbol{y}}(\boldsymbol{u}(k))\colon \mathbb{R}^{N_u} \to \mathbb{R}^N$ where

$$\hat{\boldsymbol{y}}(k) = \left[\hat{y}(k+1|k) \ldots \hat{y}(k+N|k)\right]^{\text{T}}$$
$$\boldsymbol{u}(k) = \left[u(k|k) \ldots u(k+N_u-1|k)\right]^{\text{T}}$$

along the trajectory $\hat{\boldsymbol{y}}^{\text{traj}}(k)$ is

$$\hat{\boldsymbol{y}}(k) = \hat{\boldsymbol{y}}^{\text{traj}}(k) + \boldsymbol{H}(k)(\boldsymbol{u}(k) - \boldsymbol{u}^{\text{traj}}(k)) \tag{4}$$

where

$$\boldsymbol{H}(k) = \left.\frac{d\hat{\boldsymbol{y}}(k)}{d\boldsymbol{u}(k)}\right|_{\substack{\hat{\boldsymbol{y}}(k)=\hat{\boldsymbol{y}}^{\text{traj}}(k) \\ \boldsymbol{u}(k)=\boldsymbol{u}^{\text{traj}}(k)}} = \begin{bmatrix} \dfrac{\partial \hat{y}^{\text{traj}}(k+1|k)}{\partial u^{\text{traj}}(k|k)} & \cdots & \dfrac{\partial \hat{y}^{\text{traj}}(k+1|k)}{\partial u^{\text{traj}}(k+N_u-1|k)} \\ \vdots & \ddots & \vdots \\ \dfrac{\partial \hat{y}^{\text{traj}}(k+N|k)}{\partial u^{\text{traj}}(k|k)} & \cdots & \dfrac{\partial \hat{y}^{\text{traj}}(k+N|k)}{\partial u^{\text{traj}}(k+N_u-1|k)} \end{bmatrix}$$

is a matrix of dimensionality $N \times N_u$. Thanks to using the prediction equation (4), the optimisation problem (2) becomes the quadratic programming task

$$\min_{\triangle \boldsymbol{u}(k)} \left\{ J(k) = \left\| \boldsymbol{y}^{\text{ref}}(k) - \boldsymbol{H}(k)\boldsymbol{J}\triangle\boldsymbol{u}(k) - \hat{\boldsymbol{y}}^{\text{traj}}(k) \right.\right.$$
$$\left.\left. -\boldsymbol{H}(k)(\boldsymbol{u}(k-1) - \boldsymbol{u}^{\text{traj}}(k)) \right\|^2 + \|\triangle\boldsymbol{u}(k)\|_{\boldsymbol{\Lambda}}^2 \right\}$$

subject to $\tag{5}$

$$\boldsymbol{u}^{\min} \leq \boldsymbol{J}\triangle\boldsymbol{u}(k) + \boldsymbol{u}(k-1) \leq \boldsymbol{u}^{\max}$$
$$-\triangle\boldsymbol{u}^{\max} \leq \triangle\boldsymbol{u}(k) \leq \triangle\boldsymbol{u}^{\max}$$
$$\boldsymbol{y}^{\min} \leq \boldsymbol{H}(k)\boldsymbol{J}\triangle\boldsymbol{u}(k) + \hat{\boldsymbol{y}}^{\text{traj}}(k) + \boldsymbol{H}(k)(\boldsymbol{u}(k-1) - \boldsymbol{u}^{\text{traj}}(k)) \leq \boldsymbol{y}^{\max}$$

where

$$\boldsymbol{y}^{\text{ref}}(k) = \left[y^{\text{ref}}(k+1|k) \ldots y^{\text{ref}}(k+N|k)\right]^{\text{T}}$$
$$\boldsymbol{y}^{\min} = \left[y^{\min} \ldots y^{\min}\right]^{\text{T}}$$
$$\boldsymbol{y}^{\max} = \left[y^{\max} \ldots y^{\max}\right]^{\text{T}}$$

are vectors of length N,

$$\boldsymbol{u}^{\min} = \left[u^{\min} \dots u^{\min}\right]^{\mathrm{T}}$$
$$\boldsymbol{u}^{\max} = \left[u^{\max} \dots u^{\max}\right]^{\mathrm{T}}$$
$$\boldsymbol{u}(k-1) = \left[u(k-1) \dots u(k-1)\right]^{\mathrm{T}}$$
$$\triangle\boldsymbol{u}^{\max} = \left[\triangle u^{\max} \dots \triangle u^{\max}\right]^{\mathrm{T}}$$

are vectors of length N_{u}, $\boldsymbol{\Lambda} = \mathrm{diag}(\lambda, \dots, \lambda)$, $\boldsymbol{J}$ is the all ones lower triangular matrix of dimensionality $N_{\mathrm{u}} \times N_{\mathrm{u}}$.

Steps repeated at each sampling instant k of the MPC-NPLT algorithm are:

1. The neural model is used to find the future output trajectory $\hat{\boldsymbol{y}}^{\mathrm{traj}}(k)$ which corresponds to the assumed input trajectory $\boldsymbol{u}^{\mathrm{traj}}(k)$.
2. The neural model is linearised along the trajectory $\hat{\boldsymbol{y}}^{\mathrm{traj}}(k)$: the matrix $\boldsymbol{H}(k)$ is obtained.
3. The quadratic programming task (5) is solved to find $\triangle\boldsymbol{u}(k)$.
4. The first element of the obtained future control policy is applied to the process: $u(k) = \triangle u(k|k) + u(k-1)$.
5. Set $k := k + 1$, go to step 1.

During calculation of the output trajectory $\hat{\boldsymbol{y}}^{\mathrm{traj}}(k)$ and linearisation along this trajectory (calculation of the matrix $\boldsymbol{H}(k)$) the structure of the neural model is exploited.

Selection of the future input trajectory $\boldsymbol{u}^{\mathrm{traj}}(k)$ affects the linearisation accuracy and, in consequence, quality of control. A straightforward choice is to use the control signal calculated at the previous sampling instant, i.e.

$$\boldsymbol{u}^{\mathrm{traj}}(k) = \left[u(k-1) \dots u(k-1)\right]^{\mathrm{T}}$$

As a result, the neural model is linearised along the free trajectory, the algorithm is denoted by MPC-NPLT$_{\boldsymbol{y}^0(k)}$. The alternative is to use $N_{\mathrm{u}} - 1$ elements of the future control sequence calculated at the previous sampling instant (the quantity $u(k-1|k-1)$ is actually used for control at the sampling instant $k-1$), i.e.

$$\boldsymbol{u}^{\mathrm{traj}}(k) = \left[u(k|k-1) \dots u(k+N_{\mathrm{u}}-3|k-1)\ u(k+N_{\mathrm{u}}-2|k-1)\ u(k+N_{\mathrm{u}}-2|k-1)\right]^{\mathrm{T}}$$

The algorithm is denoted by MPC-NPLT$_{\hat{y}(k-1)}$. It is possible to combine MPC-NPL and MPC-NPLT techniques (the MPC-NPL-NPLT algorithm). In the first phase of the hybrid approach the neural model is linearised for the current operating point, the MPC-NPL quadratic programming task is solved. In the second phase the neural model is linearised once again along the predicted trajectory which corresponds to the obtained input trajectory and the MPC-NPLT quadratic programming task (5) is solved. Furthermore, linearisation along the predicted trajectory can be repeated in an iterative manner [5]: nonlinear prediction, linearisation and quadrating programming are repeated a few times at each sampling instant.

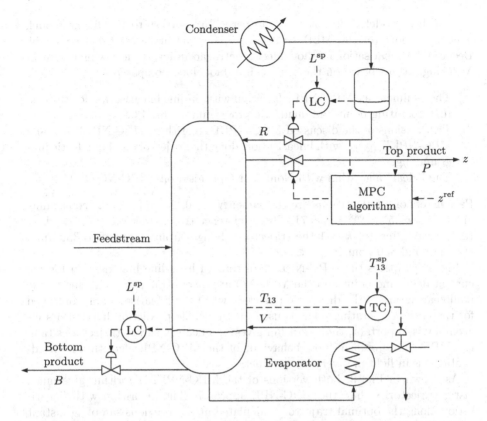

Fig. 1. High-purity ethylene-ethane distillation column control system structure

4   Simulations

The considered process is a high-purity, high-pressure (1.93 MPa) ethylene-ethane distillation column shown in Fig. 1. The feed stream consists of ethylene (approx. 80%), ethane (approx. 20%) and traces of hydrogen, methane and propylene. The distillation product (the top product) is ethylene which can contain up to 1000 ppm (parts per million) of ethane. The MPC algorithm must be able to increase relatively fast the impurity level of the product. Reducing the purity of the product results in decreasing energy consumption. Production scale is very big, nominal value of the product stream flow rate is 43 ton/h.

The supervisory control loop has one manipulated variable r, which is the reflux ratio $r = R/P$, where R and P are reflux and product stream flow rates, respectively, and one controlled variable z, which is the impurity of the product. The column has 121 trays, the feed stream is delivered to the tray number 37. The reflux is delivered to the column by the top tray and the product is taken from the tray number 110.

As shown in [5,7,13,14] the process is significantly nonlinear and difficult to control. A simple linear model is inadequate, hence, the MPC algorithm which uses such a model does not work properly. In contrast to the linear model, a neural model (of the MLP structure) is very accurate as discussed in [5]. Because the linearisation method affects control accuracy, the following nonlinear MPC algorithms based on the same neural model are compared:

a) The rudimentary MPC-NPL algorithm with on-line linearisation for the current operating point and quadratic programming [6,7,13].
b) Two versions of the discussed MPC-NPLT algorithm (MPC-NPLT$_{y^0(k)}$ and MPC-NPLT$_{\hat{y}(k-1)}$) with linearisation along the trajectory and quadratic programming.
c) The "ideal" algorithm with Nonlinear Optimisation (MPC-NO) [6,13].

Parameters of all algorithms are the same: $N = 10$, $N_u = 3$, $\lambda = 2$, constraints are $r^{min} = 4.051$, $r^{max} = 4.4571$. Three reference trajectories are considered: at the sampling instant $k = 1$ the trajectory changes from 100 ppm to 350 ppm, 600 ppm and 850 ppm, respectively.

Fig. 2 compares the MPC-NPL algorithm with on-line linearisation for the current operating point and the MPC-NO approach. Unfortunately, due to the nonlinear nature of the distillation process, when the linearised model obtained for the current operating point is used for the whole prediction horizon, its inaccuracy is important, the algorithm gives significantly slower trajectories than the MPC-NO approach. Slow behaviour of the MPC-NPL algorithm is disadvantageous in light of a very big production scale.

As shown in Fig. 3, both versions of the MPC-NPLT algorithm give much faster trajectories than the MPC-NPL approach. The algorithm with linearisation along the optimal trajectory calculated at the previous sampling instant (MPC-NPLT$_{\hat{y}(k-1)}$) is faster than the algorithm with linearisation along the free trajectory (MPC-NPLT$_{y^0(k)}$). It is not surprising, because in the first approach for linearisation predicted behaviour of the process is taken into account whereas in the second one the influence of the past is only considered.

Table 1 shows accuracy (in terms of Sum of Squared Errors, SSE) and computational load (in terms of floating point operations, MFLOPS) of compared nonlinear algorithms, summarised results for all three reference trajectories are given. Computational burden of the MPC-NPLT algorithm is approximately 6.43 times smaller when compared with that of the MPC-NO approach.

Table 1. Accuracy (SSE) and computational load (MFLOPS) of compared nonlinear MPC algorithms based on the same neural model

Algorithm	Optimisation	SSE	MFLOPS
MPC-NPL	Quadratic	5.3717×10^6	0.1545
MPC-NPLT$_{y^0(k)}$	Quadratic	5.1085×10^6	0.3313
MPC-NPLT$_{\hat{y}(k-1)}$	Quadratic	4.8599×10^6	0.3408
MPC-NO	Nonlinear	4.3869×10^6	2.1299

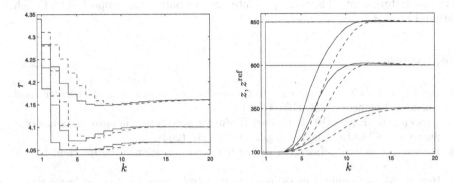

Fig. 2. The MPC-NPL algorithm with linearisation for the current operating point and quadratic programming (*dashed line*) vs. the MPC-NO algorithm with nonlinear optimisation (*solid line*)

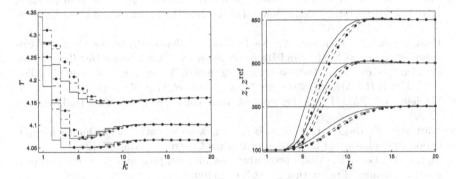

Fig. 3. The MPC-NPLT$_{y^0(k)}$ algorithm (*dash-dotted line*) and the MPC-NPLT$_{\hat{y}(k-1)}$ algorithm (*dashed line*) with linearisation along the trajectory and quadratic programming vs. the MPC-NO algorithm with nonlinear optimisation (*solid line*)

5   Conclusions

For the considered distillation column the MPC-NPLT algorithm in which the neural model is linearised on-line along a trajectory is much faster than the rudimentary MPC-NPL algorithm with linearisation for the current operating point. At each sampling instant of the MPC-NPLT algorithm only one quadratic programming problem is solved, nonlinear optimisation is not necessary. Of course, linearisation along the predicted trajectory and quadratic programming can be repeated a few times at each sampling instant [5], but it increases the computational burden. Although in simulations presented in the paper the MLP neural model is used, the described algorithm is very general, different types of models can be used. The chosen model structure must be taken into account during calculation of the output trajectory $\hat{y}^{\text{traj}}(k)$ and linearisation along this trajectory (calculation of the matrix $H(k)$).

Acknowledgement. The work presented in this paper was supported by Polish national budget funds for science.

References

1. Biegler, L.T., Grossmann, I.E.: Retrospective on optimization. Computers and Chemical Engineering 28, 1169–1192 (2004)
2. Grossmann, I.E., Biegler, L.T.: Part II. Future perspective on optimization. Computers and Chemical Engineering 28, 1193–1218 (2004)
3. Haykin, S.: Neural networks–a comprehensive foundation. Prentice Hall, Englewood Cliffs (1999)
4. Henson, M.A.: Nonlinear model predictive control: current status and future directions. Computers and Chemical Engineering 23, 187–202 (1998)
5. Ławryńczuk, M.: On improving accuracy of computationally efficient nonlinear predictive control based on neural models. Chemical Engineering Science 66, 5253–5267 (2011)
6. Ławryńczuk, M.: A family of model predictive control algorithms with artificial neural networks. International Journal of Applied Mathematics and Computer Science 17, 217–232 (2007)
7. Ławryńczuk, M., Tatjewski, P.: An Efficient Nonlinear Predictive Control Algorithm with Neural Models and Its Application to a High-Purity Distillation Process. In: Rutkowski, L., Tadeusiewicz, R., Zadeh, L.A., Żurada, J.M. (eds.) ICAISC 2006. LNCS (LNAI), vol. 4029, pp. 76–85. Springer, Heidelberg (2006)
8. Maciejowski, J.M.: Predictive control with constraints. Prentice Hall, Harlow (2002)
9. Martinsen, F., Biegler, L.T., Foss, B.A.: A new optimization algorithm with application to nonlinear MPC. Journal of Process Control 14, 853–865 (2004)
10. Morari, M., Lee, J.H.: Model predictive control: past, present and future. Computers and Chemical Engineering 23, 667–682 (1999)
11. Nørgaard, M., Ravn, O., Poulsen, N.K., Hansen, L.K.: Neural networks for modelling and control of dynamic systems. Springer, London (2000)
12. Qin, S.J., Badgwell, T.A.: A survey of industrial model predictive control technology. Control Engineering Practice 11, 733–764 (2003)
13. Tatjewski, P.: Advanced control of industrial processes. Structures and Algorithms. Springer, London (2007)
14. Tatjewski, P., Ławryńczuk, M.: Soft computing in model-based predictive control. International Journal of Applied Mathematics and Computer Science 16, 101–120 (2006)
15. Wächter, A., Biegler, L.T.: On the implementation of a primal-dual interior point filter line search algorithm for large-scale nonlinear programming. Mathematical Programming 106, 25–57 (2006)

Short Time Series of Website Visits Prediction by RBF Neural Networks and Support Vector Machine Regression

Vladimir Olej and Jana Filipova

Institute of System Engineering and Informatics,
Faculty of Economics and Administration, University of Pardubice,
Studentska 84, 532 10 Pardubice, Czech Republic
{vladimir.olej,jana.filipova}@upce.cz

Abstract. The paper presents basic notions of web mining, radial basis function (RBF) neural networks and ε-insensitive support vector machine regression (ε-SVR) for the prediction of a short time series (website of the University of Pardubice, Czech Republic). There are various short time series according to different visitors or interest of visitors (students, employees, documents). Further, a model (including RBF neural networks and ε-SVRs) was developed for short time series prediction. The model includes decomposition of data to training and testing data set using the cluster procedure. The next part of the paper describes the predictions of the web domain visits, which depend on this model, as well as outlines an analysis of the results.

Keywords: Web mining, RBF neural networks, ε-SVR, short time series, data set decomposition, prediction.

1 Introduction

For prediction, classification and optimization of user behavior on the web, web mining can be used [1–4]. Analyzed data represent the results of user-web interactions. The data consist of data obtained from the log files or from cookies and IP address, which represent user behavior on the web, and data characterizing the virtual server, with the help of which the data are obtained. As data are acquired from a web server which represents a complex system (usually a virtual system works with several virtual computes over multiple databases), modelling of the mentioned system is necessary. Particular virtual system is characterized by the parameters of its operations, which keep changing over time, therefore, it is a dynamic system. Data show non-linear character, are heterogeneous, inconsistent, missing and indeterminate. Based on this, prediction of short time series of website visits (by RBF neural networks and ε-SVRs) obtained from the log files by web mining will enable higher quality characteristics of the web space.

The presented paper takes up time series modelling of web domain visit (web upce.cz) with uncertainty [5, 6]. Further, it derives from modelling of short,

L. Rutkowski et al. (Eds.): ICAISC 2012, Part I, LNCS 7267, pp. 135–142, 2012.

intermediate and long time series of documents visits, employees and students visits with RBF neural networks and ε-SVRs [7]. The paper presents the problem formulation with the aim of describing short time series at the web upce.cz (students, employees, documents). Next, basic notions of RBFs [8] neural networks and ε-SVRs [4, 9] for time series prediction are presented. The input to the designed model for time series prediction at web.upce.cz (web site visits), which predicts using RBF neural networks and ε-SVRs, are short time series (students, employees, documents). Training O_{train} and testing O_{test} data sets are defined by the cluster method [10]. The model is characterized (from the view of data division into training O_{train} and testing O_{test} set) with Root Mean Squared Error (RMSE) of predicted visits at web upce.cz. The next part of the paper compares and analysis the results with already designed model.

2   Problem Formulation

The data for prediction of the time series at web upce.cz over a short time period were obtained from Google Analytics. This web mining tool, which makes use of Java-Script code implemented in a web presentation, offers a wide spectrum of operation characteristics (web metrics). In order to predict the visit rate at the University of Pardubice, the Czech Republic, website (web upce.cz), we need to monitor the indicator of the number of visits within a given short time period. One 'visit' here is defined as an unrepeated combination of IP address and cookies. A sub-metrics is absolutely a unique visit defined by unrepeatable IP address and cookies within a given time period. A clear trend is obvious there, with Monday having the highest visit rate, which in turn decreases as the week progresses; Saturday has the lowest visit rate; The average number of pages visited is more than three; A visitor stays on certain page five and half a minutes on average; The bounce rate is approximately 60%; Visitors generally come directly to the website, which is positive; The favourite pages is the main page, followed by the pages of the Faculty of Economics and Administration. The general formulation of the model for prediction time series (TS) web.upce.cz Fig. 1 by time series can be stated in this manner $y' = f(x_1(t), x_2(t), x_3(t))$, where y' is daily web upce.cz visits in time $t + 1$, y is daily web upce.cz visits in time t, $x_1(t)$ is TS_D of documents visits, $x_2(t)$ is TS_E of employees visits, and $x_3(t)$ is TS_{ST} of students visits at time t. Based on the analysis in [7] it is possible to characterize them as short time series.

3   Basic Notions of RBF Neural Networks and ε-SVRs

The term RBF neural network [8] refers to any kind of feed-forward neural networks that use RBF as their activation function. RBF neural networks are based on supervised learning. The output $f(x,H,w)$ RBF of a neural network can be defined this way

$$f(x, H, w) = \sum_{i=1}^{q} w_i \times h_i(x), \tag{1}$$

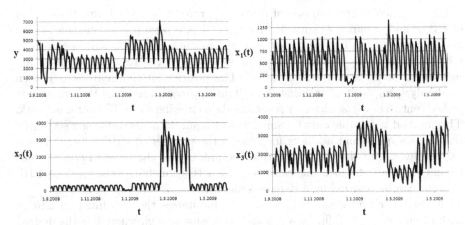

Fig. 1. Time series of web.upce.cz visits (top left), time series TS_D of documents visit (top right), time series TS_E of employees visit (down left), and time series TS_{ST} of students visit (down right)

where $H = \{h_1(x), h_2(x), \ldots, h_i(x), \ldots, h_q(x)\}$ is a set of activation functions RBF of neurons (of RBF functions) in the hidden layer and w_i are synapse weights. Each of the m components of vector $x = (x_1, x_2, \ldots, x_k, \ldots, x_m)$ is an input value for the q activation functions $h_i(x)$ of RBF neurons. The output $f(x, H, w)$ of RBF neural network represents a linear combination of outputs from q RBF neurons and corresponding synapse weights w. The activation function $h_i(x)$ of an RBF neural network in the hidden layer belongs to a special class of mathematical functions whose main characteristic is a monotonous rising or falling at an increasing distance from center c_i of the activation function $h_i(x)$ of an RBF. Neurons in the hidden layer can use one of several activation functions $h_i(x)$ of an RBF neural network, for example a Gaussian activation function (a one-dimensional activation function of RBF), a rotary Gaussian activation function (a two-dimensional RBF activation function), multisquare and inverse multisquare activation functions or Cauchys functions. Results may be presented in this manner

$$h(x, C, R) = \sum_{i=1}^{q} exp(-\frac{\parallel x - c_i \parallel^2}{r_i}), \tag{2}$$

where $x = (x_1, x_2, \ldots, x_k, \ldots, x_m)$ represents the input vector, $C = \{c_1, c_2, \ldots, c_i, \ldots, c_q\}$ are the centres of activation functions $h_i(x)$ of RBF neural network and $R = \{r_1, r_2, \ldots, r_i, \ldots, r_q\}$ are the radiuses of activation functions $h_i(x)$. The neurons in the output layer represent only weighted sum of all inputs coming from the hidden layer. The activation function of neurons in the output layer can be linear, with the unit of the output eventually being converted by jump instruction to binary form. The RBF neural network learning process requires a number of centres c_i of activation function $h_i(x)$ of the RBF neural networks to be set as well as for the most suitable positions for RBF centres c_i to be found.

Other parameters are radiuses of centres c_i, rate of activation functions $h_i(x)$ of RBFs and synapse weights $W(q, n)$. These are set up between the hidden and output layers. The design of an appropriate number of RBF neurons in the hidden layer is presented in [4]. Possibilities of centres recognition c_i are mentioned in [8] as a random choice. The position of the neurons is chosen randomly from a set of training data. This approach presumes that randomly picked centres c_i will sufficiently represent data entering the RBF neural network. This method is suitable only for small sets of input data. Use on larger sets often results in a quick and needless increase in the number of RBF neurons in the hidden layer, and therefore unjustified complexity of the neural network. The second approach to locating centres c_i of activation functions $h_i(x)$ of RBF neurons can be realized by a K-means algorithm.

In nonlinear regression ε-SVR [4, 7, 9] minimizes the loss function $L(d, y)$ with insensitive ε [4, 7, 9]. Loss function $L(d, y) = |d - y|$, where d is the desired response and y is the output estimate. The construction of the ε-SVR for approximating the desired response d can be used for the extension of loss function $L(d, y)$ as follows

$$L_\varepsilon(d, y) = \begin{cases} |d-y|-\varepsilon & for |d-y| \geq \varepsilon \\ 0 & else \end{cases}, \tag{3}$$

where ε is a parameter. Loss function $L_\varepsilon(d, y)$ is called a loss function with insensitive ε. Let the nonlinear regression model in which the dependence of the scalar d vector x expressed by $d = f(x) + n$. Additive noise n is statistically independent on the input vector x. The function $f(.)$ and noise statistics are unknown. Next, let the sample training data $(x_i, d_i), i = 1, 2, ..., N$, where x_i and d_i is the corresponding value of the output model d. The problem is to obtain an estimate of d, depending on x. For further progress it is expected to estimate d, called y, which is widespread in the set of nonlinear basis functions. $\varphi_j(x), j = 0, 1, \ldots, m_1$ this way

$$y = \sum_{j=0}^{m_1} w_j \varphi_j(x) = w^T \varphi(x), \tag{4}$$

where $\varphi(x) = [\varphi_0(x), \varphi_1 x), \ldots, \varphi_{m_1}(x)]^T$ and $w = [w_0, w_1, \ldots, w_{m_1}]$. It is assumed that $\varphi_0(x) = 1$ in order to the weight w_0 represents bias b. The solution to the problem is to minimize the empirical risk

$$R_{emp} = \frac{1}{N} \sum_{i=1}^{N} L_\varepsilon(d_i, y_i), \tag{5}$$

under conditions of inequality $\| w \|^2 \leq c_0$, where c_0 is a constant. The restricted optimization problem can be rephrased using two complementary sets of non-negative variables. Additional variables ξ and ξ' describe loss function $L_\varepsilon(d, y)$ with insensitivity ε. The restricted optimization problem can be written as an equivalent to minimizing the cost function

$$\phi(w, \xi, \xi') = C(\sum_{i=1}^{N} (\xi_i + \xi_i')) + \frac{1}{2} w^T w, \tag{6}$$

under the constraints of two complementary sets of non-negative variables ξ and ξ'. The constant C is a user-specified parameter. Optimization problem [7] can be easily solved in the dual form. The basic idea behind the formulation of the dual-shaped structure is the Lagrangian function [9] from the objective function and restrictions. Then, the Langrangian function can be defined with its multipliers and parameters which ensure optimality of these multipliers. Optimization of the Lagrangian function describes only the original regression problem. To formulate the corresponding dual problem a convex function can be obtained (for shorthand)

$$Q(\alpha_i, \alpha_i') = \sum_{i=1}^{N} d_i(\alpha_i - \alpha_i') - \varepsilon \sum_{i=1}^{N}(\alpha_i + \alpha_i') - \frac{1}{2}\sum_{i=1}^{N}\sum_{j=1}^{N}(\alpha_i - \alpha_i')(\alpha_j - \alpha_j')K(x_i, x_j),$$
(7)

where $K(x_i, x_j)$ is kernel function defined in accordance with Mercer's theorem [4, 8]. Solving optimization problem is obtained by maximizing $Q(\alpha, \alpha')$ with respect to Lagrange multipliers α and α' and provided a new set of constraints, which hereby incorporated constant C contained in the function definition $\phi(w, \xi, \xi')$. Data points covered by the $\alpha \neq \alpha'$ define support vectors [4, 7, 9].

4   Modelling and Analysis of the Results

The input into the model $y' = f(x_1(t), x_2(t), x_3(t))$ for time series at web.upce.cz are short time series of documents $(x_1(t))$, employees $(x_2(t))$, and students $(x_3(t))$. Training O_{train} and testing O_{test} data sets are defined using [10]. Structures of RBF neural networks and ε-SVR with RBF and polynomial kernel functions are designed for the time series prediction at web.upce.cz y'. The analysis in [7] presents recommendations for optimized settings (with 10-fold cross validation) of parameters of RBF neural networks and ε-SVRs structures for short time series.

Let there be an easy method of object set O decomposition to training O_{train} and testing O_{test} sets [10], $O = O_{train} \cup O_{test}$. Further, let there be a cluster method which would decompose object set O to disjunctive subsets (clusters) $O = O_1 \cup O_2 \cup \ldots \cup O_i \cup \ldots \cup O_p$, which contain similar objects from the viewpoint of metrics, used in the cluster method. Then, i-th cluster O_i contains n_i objects from the object set O, $O_i = (o_1^{(i)}, o_2^{(i)}, \ldots, o_{n_i}^{(i)}) \subset O$, while assumption is given that object $o_1^{(i)} \in O_i$ is such an object from i-th cluster O_i which lies the nearest to its center. This object serves as a representative of objects in cluster O_i. The training O_{train} and testing O_{test} sets are defined by objects

$$O_{train} = (o_1^{(1)}, o_1^{(2)}, \ldots, o_1^{(p)}), O_{test} = ((O_1 - o_1^{(1)}) \cup (O_2 - o_1^{(2)}) \cup \ldots \cup (O_p - o_1^{(p)})).$$
(8)

This means that the training set O_{train} is composed of all representatives of objects while testing set O_{test} contains all remaining objects. The number of objects in the training set is equal to the number of clusters $|O_{train}| = p$ and

$|O_{test}| = |O| - p$. Based on decomposition of the object set O, various ratios of $O_{train} : O_{test}$ were generated for modelling of time series prediction at web.upce.cz. Fig. 2 shows the dependencies of RMSE for different ratios $O_{train} : O_{test}$ with optimized parameters of RBF neural network and ε-SVRs.

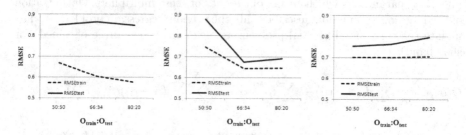

Fig. 2. RMSE dependencies between RBF neural network (left), ε-SVR with RBF kernel function (center) and ε-SVR with polynomial kernel function (right)

It can be implied from Fig. 2 that the smallest RMSE is reached by structure ε-SVR with RBF kernel function, with ratio of $O_{train} : O_{test}$ (66:34). For structure RBF $RMSE_{test}$ does hardly change with different $O_{train} : O_{test}$ ration, $RMSE_{train}$ decreases with increasing ratio of $O_{train} : O_{test}$. Further, in structure ε-SVR with polynomial kernel function $RMSE_{train}$ hardly changes with changing ratio ratio $O_{train} : O_{test}$, however, $RMSE_{test}$ grows slowly with increasing O_{train}.

In Table 1 are shown representative results (for optimized parametres) of the analysis of the experiments of the RBF neural networks (with RBF activation function) and ε-SVRs (with RBF and polynomial kernel functions) with various ratios of $O_{train} : O_{test}$ of data sets and same amount of learning at $m=600$ cycles. Parameter q in Table 1 represents the number of neurons in the hidden

Table 1. RMSE for RBF neural network, $q = 80, \mu = 0.9, \nu = 1$ (left); RMSE for ε-SVR with RBF kernel function, $C = 10, \varepsilon = 0.1, \gamma = 0.4$ (centre); RMSE for ε-SVR with polynomial kernel function, $C = 8, \varepsilon = 0.1, \beta = 1, \gamma = 0.2$ (right)

$RMSE_{train}$	$RMSE_{test}$	$RMSE_{train}$	$RMSE_{test}$	$RMSE_{train}$	$RMSE_{test}$	$O_{train}:O_{test}$
0.668	0.850	0.746	0.879	0.701	0.753	50:50
0.604	0.863	0.644	0.674	0.702	0.764	66:34
0.574	0.848	0.647	0.690	0.706	0.796	80:20

layer. The parameter μ allows for an overrun of the local extreme in the learning process and the following progress of learning. The parameter ν represents the selection of centers of RBFs as well as guarantees the correct allocation of neurons in the hidden layer for the given data entering the RBF neural network. The confirmation of conclusions presented in [7] is verified by the analysis of results (with 10-fold cross validation). The parameters C, ε are functions of kernel functions $K(x, x_i)$ [4, 7, 9] variations. Parameter C controls the trade off between errors of the ε-SVR of training data and margin maximization; ε [4] selects support vectors in the ε-SVRs structures, and β represents the rate of polynomial kernel function $K(x, x_i)$. The coefficient γ characterizes polynomial and RBF kernel function. Table 2 presents a comparison of the $RMSE_{train}$ and $RMSE_{test}$ on the training and testing set to other designed and analyzed structures. Concretely, fuzzy inference system (FIS) Takagi-Sugeno [5, 6], intuitionistic fuzzy inference system (IFIS) Takagi-Sugeno [5, 6], feed-forward neural networks (FFNNs), time delay neural networks (TDNNs), RBF[1] neural networks and ε-SVR[1] with RBF and ε-SVR[2] with polynomial kernel function were used [7]. The inputs to the listed systems are defined by time series of web domain visits. The inputs to the modeled system with structures RBF[2] neural networks and ε-SVR[3] with RBF and ε-SVR[4] with polynomial kernel function are short time series TS_D, TS_E and TS_{ST}. As presented in Table 2, FIS and IFIS are suitable for the prediction of web domain visits as they show the lowest values of RMSE [5, 6]. The model based on FIS Takagi-Sugeno and IFIS Takagi-Sugeno allows processing uncertainty and expert knowledge. Intuitionistic fuzzy sets can be viewed in the context as a proper tool for representing hesitancy concerning both membership and non-membership of an element to a set. IFIS defined works more effective than the standard FIS of Takagi-Sugeno type as it provides stronger possibility to accommodate imprecise information and better model imperfect fact and imprecise knowledge. FFNN and TDNN show significantly higher $RMSE_{test}$. In the case of structures RBF[1], ε-SVR[1] and ε-SVR[2] are visible lower $RMSE_{test}$, when the modeled time series of web domains visits is with pre-processes mathematical-statistical methods [7], than RBF[2], ε-SVR[3] and ε-SVR[4], when the modeled time series of domains visits uses short time series TS_D, TS_E and TS_{ST}.

Table 2. Comparison of the $RMSE_{train}$ and $RMSE_{test}$ on the training and testing data to other designed and analyzed structures of fuzzy inference systems and neural networks

	FIS	IFIS	FFNN	TDNN	RBF[1]	ε-SVR[1]	ε-SVR[2]	RBF[2]	ε-SVR[3]	ε-SVR[4]
$RMSE_{train}$	0.221	0.224	0.236	0.286	0.311	0.343	0.411	0.574	0.644	0.701
$RMSE_{test}$	0.237	0.239	0.587	0.839	0.408	0.414	0.419	0.848	0.674	0.753

5   Conclusion

The paper presents results of modelling of time series prediction at web.upce.cz (web presentations visits) based on short time series TS_D, TS_E and TS_{ST} using RBF neural networks and ε-SVRs with different ratios $O_{train} : O_{test}$. The designed model includes data generation by the cluster method. The analysis of the results shows that RMSE acquired by the RBF[2] neural networks and ε-SVR[3] with RBF and ε-SVR[4] with polynomial kernel function shows higher values as visible in Table 2. It is necessary to state that there is a significant difference between $RMSE_{test}$ and $RMSE_{train}$ for RBF^2 which demonstrates that the mentioned neural network is not suitable for prediction of short time series. From the complex modelling of data from the log files which represent user behavior on the web and characteristics of the virtual server, result recommendations to the ways of generating data for consequent web mining and also a set of recommendations how to increase the quality of the activity of the complex virtual system which generates the data. Listed recommendations will represent a methodological lead for system engineers who maintain the complex virtual system. Based on the provided facts, the system engineers can characterize the load on the complex virtual system and its dynamics.

Acknowledgments. This work was supported by the scientific research projects sponsored by the Ministry of Education, Youth and Sports, Czech Republic under Grant No: CZ.1.07/2.2.00/28.0327.

References

1. Cooley, R., Mobasher, B., Srivistava, J.: Web Mining: Information and Pattern Discovery on the World Wide Web. In: 9th IEEE Int. Conf. on Tools with Artificial Intelligence, ICTAI 1997, Newport Beach, CA (1997)
2. Krishnapuram, R., Joshi, A., Yi, L.: A Fuzzy Relative of the K-medoids Algorithm with Application to Document and Snippet Clustering. In: IEEE Int. Conf. on Fuzzy Systems, Korea, pp. 1281–1286 (1999)
3. Pedrycz, W.: Conditional Fuzzy C-means. Pattern Recognition Letters 17, 625–632 (1996)
4. Haykin, S.: Neural Networks: A Comprehensive Foundation. Prentice-Hall Inc., New Jersey (1999)
5. Olej, V., Hajek, P., Filipova, J.: Modelling of Web Domain Visits by IF-Inference System. WSEAS Transactions on Computers 9(10), 1170–1180 (2010)
6. Olej, V., Filipova, J., Hajek, P.: Time Series Prediction of Web Domain Visits by IF-Inference System. In: Mastorakis, N., et al. (eds.) 14th WSEAS Int. Conf. on Systems, Latest Trends on Computers, Greece, vol. 1, pp. 156–161 (2010)
7. Olej, V., Filipová, J.: Modelling of Web Domain Visits by Radial Basis Function Neural Networks and Support Vector Machine Regression. In: Iliadis, L., Maglogiannis, I., Papadopoulos, H., et al. (eds.) EANN/AIAI 2011, Part II. IFIP AICT, vol. 364, pp. 229–239. Springer, Heidelberg (2011)
8. Broomhead, D.S., Lowe, D.: Multivariate Functional Interpolation and Adaptive Networks. Complex Systems 2, 321–355 (1988)
9. Smola, A., Scholkopf, J.: A Tutorial on Support Vector Regression. Statistics and Computing 14, 199–222 (2004)
10. Kvasnicka, V., et al.: Introduction to Neural Networks, Iris, Bratislava (1997) (in Slovak)

Spectra of the Spike-Flow Graphs
in Geometrically Embedded Neural Networks

Jarosław Piersa and Tomasz Schreiber*

Faculty of Mathematics and Computer Science,
Nicolaus Copernicus University, Poland
piersaj@mat.umk.pl

Abstract. In this work we study a simplified model of a neural activity flow in networks, whose connectivity is based on geometrical embedding, rather than being lattices or fully ,connected graphs. We present numerical results showing that as the spectrum (set of eigenvalues of adjacency matrix) of the resulting activity-based network develops a scale-free dependency. Moreover it strengthens and becomes valid for a wider segment along with the simulation progress, which implies a highly organised structure of the analysed graph.

Keywords: geometric neural networks, graph spectrum, scale-freeness.

1 Introduction

The spectrum of the graph is considered as an important characteristic of the graph. A set of graph features can be easily obtained from the sole spectrum analysis, for instance bi-partitioning, connectivity, a clustering coefficient [6] etc. While the spectrum does not provide a unique description of the graph up to the isomorphism [6] it is graph-invariant.

Throughout this paper, by *graph spectrum* we understand a set of eigenvalues of the graph adjacency matrix A, namely set of $\lambda \in \mathbb{C}$ such that $A \cdot x = \lambda \cdot x$ for some vector x . Since A is symmetric, all eigenvalues are strictly real [6].

In this work we set out to analyse activity graphs of the geometrically embedded neural networks. Clearly, one can distinguish between the *structural* (i.e. underlying) and the *functional* or *spike-flow graphs* (evolved during the dynamics) of the network [3]. Since the structural graph is strictly dependent on selected network model, we shall focus on the latter case, namely a spontaneously emerged subgraph. As it was presented in [10,11], the resulting graph has a significantly different input degree distribution. Here we provide more insight into differences between predefined and resulting networks.

The rest paper is organized as follows: we present the simplified activity flow model and the formal definition of the spike-flow graph in Sec. 2. Then we discuss the results concerning an emergence of *power-law* or *scale-free* dependency

---

* 1975-2010, Associate Professor at Faculty of Mathematics and Computer Science, NCU, researcher on the fields of probability, artificial intelligence and physics.

L. Rutkowski et al. (Eds.): ICAISC 2012, Part I, LNCS 7267, pp. 143–151, 2012.

(scaling as $\mathbb{P}(X = x) \propto \frac{1}{x^k}$, where X is measured value and $k > 1$ is fixed parameter) in the spectrum of the obtained network in Sec. 3. Finally the work is concluded and potential aims of a future work are pointed in Sec. 4.

2   Simulation Model

We adopt the simplified model of neural activity coined in [10]. We argue, that it is valid for a modelling of activity in neurons and groups of neurons on cortical level. The model might seem to have an abundance of degrees of freedom, but they are mandatory, if the model is to exhibit an energy-driven self-organisation which is a feature of complex systems such as brain, see [5].

Given a two-dimensional sphere S_2 and expected density $\rho \gg 1$ of neurons in a square unit of the surface, we pick neurons from Poisson process on the sphere with intensity $\lambda = |S_2|\rho$. Each neuron is given its Euclidean coordinates $(x_v, y_v, z_v) \in \mathbb{R}^3$ accordingly to the process as well as an *initial activity* or charge σ_v, which is stored in the unit. It should be interpreted as an abstract activity level of the neuron. In the model only non-negative integer values for charge are allowed $\sigma_v \in \mathbb{N}_{\geq 0}$. Starting configuration can be seen in Fig. 1.

For every pair of neurons $\{u, v\}$ a *synaptic connection* $e = \{u, v\}$ is added to the set of network's edges $\mathcal{E}$ independently with probability $\mathbb{P}(e \in \mathcal{E}) = g(e)$, where $g()$ is a connectivity function

$$g(\{u, v\}) = \begin{cases} d(u, v)^{-\alpha} & d(u, v) \geq 1 \\ 1 & \text{otherwise,} \end{cases} \tag{1}$$

where $d()$ is euclidean distance and α is the *decay exponent* approximately equal to the dimension of the embedding space (2 in our case), the formula of the connectivity function was put forward in [7]. The synapse denotes a possibility of direct interaction between connected units. Note, that formula (1) admits self-loops. Since the expected density of neurons ρ is large, with huge probability we obtain a connected network. The geometrical embedding of the network along with formula of $g()$ result in varying lengths of the synapses. The number of short or local ones is much greater, than of the long ones, which provide a connection between the distant areas of the network. On the other hand a scale-free formula of Eq. (1) ensures, that long synapses do not vanish too fast when the radius of the sphere increases, which would result in lattice-like structural network. Such system seems to be more feasible to modelling of a real neural networks, than built on all-to-all connected graphs or regular grids.

Each synapse, which was added to the graph, receives a gaussian *weight* w_{uv}, which indicates its excitatory or inhibitory nature. The weight can be read as an averaging over a number of factors, thus a gaussian distribution seems adequate. Positive weight indicates a tendency favour equal activity levels for connected neurons, while inhibitory synapse results in large differences (activity in first unit keeps the second silent).

Given a network activity configuration $\bar{\sigma} = [\sigma_1, ..., \sigma_N]$ we define an *energy* of the system as follows:

$$E(\bar{\sigma}) = \sum_{(u,v)\in\mathcal{E}} w_{u,v}|\sigma_v - \sigma_u| \tag{2}$$

The formula (2) bears similarity to the stochastic Boltzmann machine [1], although has been adjusted in order to account for any nonnegative value of the σ_v. Nonetheless, it still has the same interpretation of summarized interaction cost in the network and it still can be negative.

The network undergoes its evolution according to the following dynamics:

1. iterate many times:
   (a) randomly pick a pair of units $u, v \in \mathcal{V}$, such that
      − $\{u, v\} \in \mathcal{E}$,
      − $\sigma_u \geq 1$,
   (b) try to transfer one unit of charge from u to v (i.e. $\sigma_u := \sigma_u - 1$; $\sigma_v := \sigma_v + 1$;),
   (c) if this reduces network energy, then accept the transfer,
   (d) otherwise accept it with probability

   $$\mathbb{P}(u \to v) = \exp(-\beta\Delta E), \tag{3}$$

   where ΔE is an energy increase, which would be caused by the transfer, $\beta > 0$ is an inverse temperature and is assumed to be high ($\beta \gg 1$), which results in rejecting most of jumps towards higher energy states.

The transfer from u to v can be interpreted as spending some activity by u in order to cause an excitation in v or (in the case of inhibitory synapse) inhibiting u by increasing activity in v. Note, that this activity-conserving dynamics mimics a *criticality* state of the dynamics, i.e. the total activity in the network neither vanishes nor explodes. As Chialvo suggests, the emergence of scale-freeness is typical for such critical systems [5].

The stop condition can be either fixed number of iterations or the moment, when the network reaches its steady state i.e. when most of charge is stored in small number of neurons and the dynamics freezes, such situation will be referred as a *ground state* and the neurons with remaining charge as an *elite*. Both starting and ending phases are presented in Fig. 1.

During the evolution the amount of activity flowing through an edge $e = (u, v)$ (in both ways) is recorded, we will adopt the notation d_e for this value. We define a *spike-flow graph* $\mathcal{G}' = (\mathcal{V}', \mathcal{E}')$ as a multi-graph, consisting of all neurons $\mathcal{V}' = \mathcal{V}$ and all the synapses, which are present in $\mathcal{E}$ and the flow through them exceeded the threshold value $\mathcal{E}' = \{e \in \mathcal{E} : d_e \geq \theta\}$, with their multiplicities equal to the charge flowed ($M(e) = d_e$ if $d_e \geq \theta$ and $M(e) = 0$ otherwise), see Fig. 2.

Unless stated otherwise in our simulations θ is assumed to be one. In such case every accepted transfer adds an edge into $\mathcal{E}'$.

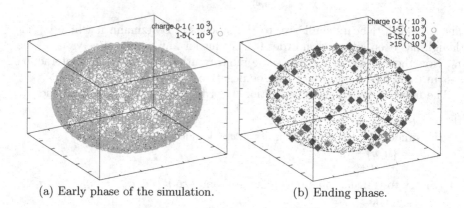

(a) Early phase of the simulation.   (b) Ending phase.

Fig. 1. A plot of the network of $5k = 5 \cdot 10^3$ neurons at early and late states of the simulation. Left — starting, roughly uniform setup. Right — ending phase, all the charge has stuck in the small number of *elite* units.

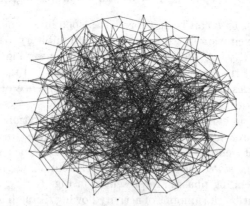

Fig. 2. A plot of resulting spike flow sub-graph obtained at the end phase of the simulation. The resulting graph was limited to around 700 vertices out of over 12000 and was remapped onto a plane.

3   Results

The simulations were carried on networks counting up to 35000 neurons. Figure 3 presents obtained plot of i-th eigenvalue vs index i. The eigenvalues of the resulting spike-flow graph were sorted decreasingly and for log-plot issues negative ones were removed. An interesting feature is the middle part, where locally the plot behaves like a straight line for quite a long segment.

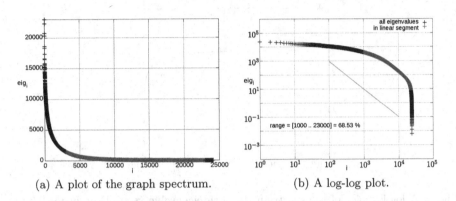

(a) A plot of the graph spectrum.   (b) A log-log plot.

Fig. 3. A plot of the spectrum of the spike-flow graph obtained throughout the dynamics of around 30k neurons. The plots present the i-th eigenvalue vs i, eigenvalues are sorted decreasingly. Middle part of the plot covers around 60% of the whole dataset. For reference — a line segment has a slope -2 (a function x^{-2} in log-log plot).

Note, that such behaviour in fully connected networks with winner-takes-all rule dynamics was theoretically predicted in [12] and confirmed in [9]. Despite the facts, that in our model WTA dynamics is only approximated by an inverse temperature β and the structural network is no longer fully connected (actually it is quite sparse), the model produces strikingly similar feature.

The plot failed to indicate clear scale-free dependence for top eigenvalues, see [9]. Instead this dependency arises in its mid-part and covers about 60% of the whole data. We argue, that this feature might be rooted in lack of direct synaptic connections between the elite neurons, so it is not always possible to transfer large amounts of charge directly between them. Somehow reiterated from [10] is an observable exponential truncation of this scale-free dependency, however without rigorous analysis one cannot state whether it is due to finite simulation sample.

Additionally, there is no sign of first outlying eigenvalue, which is typical for Erdős-Réyni random graph [2], recall that Erdős-Réyni random graph with n vertices and $p \in (0,1)$ is generated by including every edge of the full graph independently with uniform probability p [8]. For comparison, a plot of eigenvalues of the ER model is presented in Fig. 4.

While Fig. 3 presents a spectrum obtained once the simulation was terminated, it turns out even more interesting to see it in various steps of the dynamics. Fig. 5 presents a log-plot of the eigenvalues after computing 2, 10, 30, 50, 70 and 100% of the iterations. It clearly indicates, that the spike-flow graph only begins its self-organization process as a ER random graph. This seems quite natural, as in the dynamics we pick a synaptic edge randomly with uniform distribution and at start its probable that the connected neurons have not been drained from their charge yet. Then, as the dynamics continues, a linear segment emerges and increases in length.

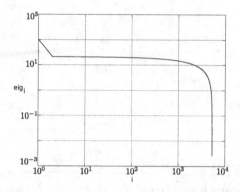

Fig. 4. A log-log plot of the spectrum (the i-th eigenvalue vs i) of the Erdős-Réyni, random graph model with 10k neurons and its average connectivity is the same as in the obtained spike-flow network for the same size. Note the first outlying eigenvalue.

We have adopted following way to estimate the linear segment on the plot. A pair of indices (i_1, i_2) is referred as its borders if:

- $i_1 < i_2$,
- $|\bar{a} - a_1| < E_1$,
- $\frac{1}{(i_2 - i_1)} \sum_{i=i_1}^{i_2} (e_i - a_1 \cdot i - a_0)^2 < E_2$,
- $i_2 - i_1$ is maximal of all satisfying above points,

where $y = a_1 x + a_0$ stands for a formula of line approximating the data set $\{(\log i_1, \log e_{i_1})...(\log i_2, \log e_{i_2})\}$, the formula can be obtained using linear regression for instance; e_j is a j-th largest eigenvalue; thresholds E_1 and E_2 were picked arbitrarily depending on the number of neurons in the simulation and desired accuracy and the $\bar{a}$ is an expected slope. If no such pair exists, we conclude that the spectrum does not have any linear segment (such situation did not occurred, until the threshold values were ridiculously strict).

Evolution of both indices i_1, i_2 defined as above and length of the segment $(i_2 - i_1)$ is presented in Fig. 6. Somehow unsettling, the growth depends mainly on reducing the beginning index i_1, we also observe fluctuations of the upper bound i_2. This seems be related to the vulnerability linear regression on non-uniformly distributed data. Nevertheless, the $i_2 - i_1$ clearly grows as the network undergoes its dynamics suggesting that i-th eigenvalue of the final spike-flow graph decays as $\frac{c}{i^2}$, even if the structural network was not fully connected.

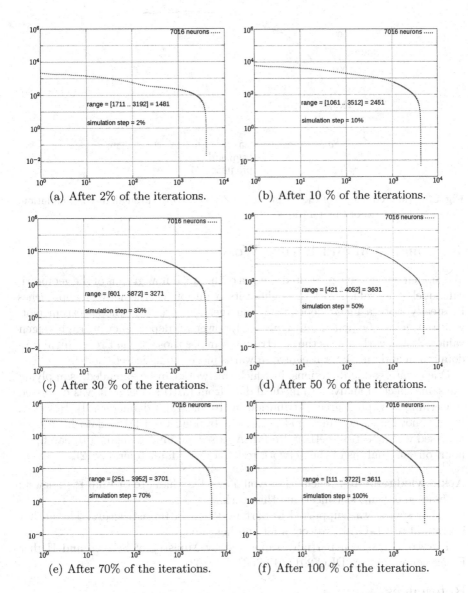

Fig. 5. Log-log plots of the spectrum of the spike-flow graph obtained in various steps of the dynamics. Dotted line denotes whole spectrum, solid line — the estimated linear segment. Simulation was carried on about $7 \cdot 10^3$ neurons and $2 \cdot 10^9$ iterations.

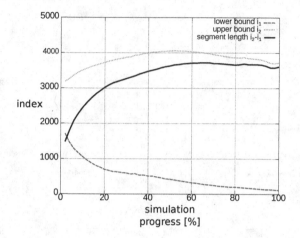

Fig. 6. Estimated length of the linear part of the spectrum throughout the simulation, measured every 2% of the iterations

4   Conclusion and Future Work

To summarize, we have presented spectra of the spike-flow graphs of the geometrical model of neural network throughout its evolution. As the network approaches its steady state a linear dependency emerges and grows in the spectrum plot, which suggests a (exponentially truncated) power law dependency in graph's eigenvalues. At the early stages the spectrum resembles those of the Erdős-Réyni random graph and only later it evolves towards more sophisticated model.

One of interesting directions, in which this work can be extended, is applying the same spectral analysis to medical data from fMRI scans, as it was discussed concerning a graph degree distribution in [10] or graph diameter [11]. However, to our knowledge, no functional networks obtained from fMRI data have been analysed with spectral methods so far. As a second aim of ongoing research, we point out an analysis of the network resiliency and fault tolerance [2].

Acknowledgements. The author would also like thank to dr Filip Piękniewski for hints and remarks concerning this work.

This research was supported in part by PL-Grid Infrastructure. The author is grateful to PL-Grid Project[1] staff and help-line.

The work has been partially supported by Ministry of Science and Higher Education and grant DEC-2011/01/N/ST6/01931.

References

1. Ackley, D.H., Hinton, G.E., Sejnowski, T.J.: A Learning Algorithm for Boltzmann Machines. Cognitive Science 9(1), 147–169 (1985)
2. Albert, R., Barabasi, A.L.: Statistical mechanics of complex networks. Reviews of Modern Physics 74 (January 2002)

---

[1] http://www.plgrid.pl

3. Bullmore, E., Sporns, O.: Complex brain networks: graph theoretical analysis of structural and functional systems. Nature Reviews, Neuroscience 10 (March 2009)
4. Chung, F., Lu, L.: Complex graphs and networks. American Mathematical Society (2006)
5. Chialvo, D.: Critical brain networks. Physica A: Statistical Mechanics and its Applications 340(4) (September 2004)
6. Cvetković, D., Rowlingson, P., Simić, S.: Eigenspaces of graphs. Cambridge University Press (1997)
7. Eguiluz, V., Chialvo, D., Cecchi, G., Baliki, M., Apkarian, V.: Scale-Free Brain Functional Networks, Physical Review Letters, PRL 94 018102 (January 2005)
8. Erdős, P., Réyni, A.: On random graphs I. Publ. Math. Debrecen 6, 290–297 (1959)
9. Piekniewski, F.: Spectra of the Spike Flow Graphs of Recurrent Neural Networks. In: Alippi, C., Polycarpou, M., Panayiotou, C., Ellinas, G. (eds.) ICANN 2009, Part II. LNCS, vol. 5769, pp. 603–612. Springer, Heidelberg (2009)
10. Piersa, J., Piekniewski, F., Schreiber, T.: Theoretical model for mesoscopic-level scale-free self-organization of functional brain networks. IEEE Transactions on Neural Networks 21(11) (November 2010)
11. Piersa, J.: Diameter of the spike-flow graphs of geometrical neural networks. In: 9th International Conference on Parallel Processing and Applied Mathematics (September 2011) (in print)
12. Schreiber, T.: Spectra of winner-take-all stochastic neural networks, 3193(0810), pp. 1–21 (October 2008), arXiv http://arxiv.org/PS_cache/arxiv/pdf/0810/0810.3193v2.pdf

Weak Convergence of the Parzen-Type Probabilistic Neural Network Handling Time-Varying Noise

Lena Pietruczuk[1] and Meng Joo Er[2]

[1] Department of·Computer Engineering, Czestochowa University of Technology,
ul. Armii Krajowej 36, 42-200 Czestochowa, Poland
lena.pietruczuk@kik.pcz.pl
[2] School of Electrical & Electronic Engineering, Nanyang Technological University,
50 Nanyang Avenue, Singapore 639798
emjer@ntu.edu.sg

Abstract. In this paper we study probabilistic neural networks based on the Parzen kernels. Weak convergence is established assuming time-varying noise. Simulation results are discussed in details.

1 Introduction

Let us consider the following system

$$Y_i = \phi(X_i) + Z_i, \ i = 1, \ldots, n \tag{1}$$

where $X_1, \ldots, X_n$ is a sequence of independent and identically distributed variables in R^p with probability density function f, ϕ is an unknown function and $Z_1, \ldots, Z_n$ are independent random variables with unknown distributions such that

$$E[Z_i] = 0, \qquad Var[Z_i] = d_i, \qquad \text{for } i = 1\ldots, n. \tag{2}$$

It should be noted that the variance of Z_i is not equal for all i. The problem is to estimate function ϕ, in the case of time varying (non-stationary) noise Z_i.

It should be emphasized that such problem was never solved in literature. The method applied in this paper is based on the nonparametric estimates, named in the area of soft computing, probabilistic neural networks [40]. Nonparametric regression estimates in a stationary environment were studied in [4], [5], [6], [9], [17]-[21], [27]-[29], [32]-[35], whereas non-stationary environment was considered in [8], [22]-[26], [30] and [31], assuming stationary noise. For excellent surveys on these methods the reader is referred to [7] and [10].

2 Algorithm

Let

$$\hat{\phi}_n(x) = \frac{\hat{R}_n(x)}{\hat{f}_n(x)} \tag{3}$$

L. Rutkowski et al. (Eds.): ICAISC 2012, Part I, LNCS 7267, pp. 152–159, 2012.

be the estimator of regression function ϕ, where $\hat{f}_n$ is the estimator of a density function f in the form

$$\hat{f}_n(x) = \frac{1}{n} \sum_{i=1}^{n} K'_n(x, X_i) \tag{4}$$

and

$$\hat{R}_n(x) = \frac{1}{n} \sum_{i=1}^{n} Y_i K_n(x, X_i) \tag{5}$$

is the estimator of function

$$R(x) = \phi(x)f(x). \tag{6}$$

To estimate the regression function $\phi(x)$ we propose to use the Parzen kernels

$$K'_n(x, u) = h_n'^{-p} K(\frac{x-u}{h'_n}), \quad K_n(x, u) = h_n^{-p} K(\frac{x-u}{h_n}), \tag{7}$$

where K is an appropriately selected function such that

$$\|K\|_\infty < \infty \tag{8}$$

and h_n, h'_n are certain sequences of numbers. Now estimator (3) takes the form

$$\hat{\phi}_n(x) = \frac{\sum_{i=1}^{n} Y_i K(\frac{x-X_i}{h_n})}{\sum_{i=1}^{n} K(\frac{x-X_i}{h'_n})} \tag{9}$$

which is known in the literature under the name probabilistic neural network [40]. The scheme of generalized regression neural network is presented in Fig. 1.

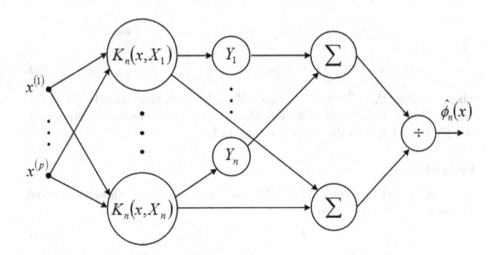

Fig. 1. Generalized regression neural network

Theorem 1. *If*

$$s_i = \sup_x \{(\sigma_i^2 + \phi^2(x))f(x)\} < \infty, \quad i = 1, \ldots, n \tag{10}$$

$$||x||^p K(x) \longrightarrow 0, \qquad ||x|| \longrightarrow \infty, \tag{11}$$

$$n^{-1}h_n'^{-p} \to 0, \tag{12}$$

$$n^{-2}h_n^{-p} \sum_{i=1}^{n} s_i \to 0, \tag{13}$$

$$h_n' \to 0, \qquad h_n \to 0, \tag{14}$$

then $\phi_n(x) \xrightarrow{n} \phi(x)$ *in probability for each* x *where* $\phi(x)$ *is continuous.*

Proof. It is sufficient to show that

$$\hat{f}_n(x) \longrightarrow f(x) \quad \text{in probability for each x where } f(x) \text{ is continuous} \tag{15}$$

and

$$\hat{R}_n(x) \longrightarrow R(x) \quad \text{in probability for each x where } R(x) \text{ is continuous.} \tag{16}$$

Convergence of (15) under condition (12) was proved in [7]. Therefore it is enough to show that (16) is true. Obviously

$$\left| \hat{R}_n(x) - R(x) \right| \le \left| \hat{R}_n(x) - E\left[\hat{R}_n(x)\right] \right| + \left| E\left[\hat{R}_n(x)\right] - R(x) \right|. \tag{17}$$

Observe that

$$Var(\hat{R}_n(x)) = Var(\frac{1}{n}\sum_{i=1}^{n} Y_i K_n(x, X_i)) = \left(\frac{1}{n}h_n^{-p}\right)^2 \sum_{i=1}^{n} \left(Var\left[Y_i K\left(\frac{x - X_i}{h_n}\right)\right]\right) = \tag{18}$$

$$\le \left(\frac{1}{n}h_n^{-p}\right)^2 \sum_{i=1}^{n} \int_{R^p} E\left[Y_i^2 | X_i = u\right] f(u) K^2\left(\frac{x - u}{h_n}\right) du \le \tag{19}$$

$$\le \left(\frac{1}{n}h_n^{-p}\right)^2 \sum_{i=1}^{n} \int_{R^p} (\sigma_n^2 + \phi^2(x)) f(u) ||K||_\infty\left(\frac{x - u}{h_n}\right) du \le \tag{20}$$

$$\le \left(\frac{1}{n}\right)^2 h_n^{-p} \sum_{i=1}^{n} 2s_i ||K||_\infty. \tag{21}$$

Therefore $Var(\hat{R}_n) \xrightarrow{n} 0$ if condition (13) holds and, consequently, $|\hat{R}_n(x) - ER_n(x)| \xrightarrow{n} 0$ in probability. Since $|E\hat{R}_n(x) - R(x)| \xrightarrow{n} 0$ under condition (11) (see [7] and [11]), then the result is established.

Example

We consider the case when $d_n = O(n^\alpha)$ for $\alpha > 0$ and $p = 1$. We choose sequences h_n' and h_n to be in the form

$$h_n' = D'n^{-H'}, \qquad h_n = Dn^{-H} \tag{22}$$

where D, D', H and H' are constants. Then conditions (12)-(14) are satisfied if

$$0 < H' < 1 \text{ and } 0 < H + \alpha < 1. \tag{23}$$

3   Experimental Results

In the following simulations we estimate the function

$$\phi(x) = 5x^2 \sin(x). \tag{24}$$

Let us assume that input data come from the normal distribution with the mean equal to 0 and the standard deviation equal to 4. First we select the kernel function. For the purpose of this paper we choose triangular kernel and assume that $h'_n = h_n$.

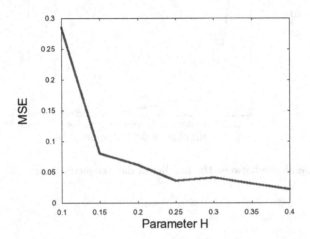

Fig. 2. The dependence between the value of parameter H and the value of the MSE

By examining the relationship between the value of the mean square error and the value of the parameter H we obtained the results illustrated in Fig. 1 for $D = D' = 0.5$ and $\alpha = 0.3$. The experiment was performed on the set of 5000 data. As we can see with increasing value of H the error of the algorithm decreases. For $H = 0.1$ the mean square error is equal to 0.1929 and for $H = 0.4$ the value of this error is equal to 0.0194.

In Figure 2 we show the dependence between the number of elements and the value of the mean square error. We assume that $H = H' = 0.4$, $D = D' = 1$ and $\alpha = 0.3$. Even with increasing variance of Z_n, corresponding to the increasing number of elements, the accuracy of the algorithm improves. For $n = 2000$ the MSE is equal to 0.0334 and for $n = 50000$ it decreases to 0.00027.

In Figure 3 we show the dependence between the value of parameter α and the MSE of the algorithm. In this case $n = 5000$, $D = D' = 1$ and $H = H' = 0.4$. From conditions (23) we can see, that for this value of H and H', value of α should be not bigger than 0.6. For small α the error is small and for α outside the permissible range the error increases very fast.

In Fig. 4 we can see input-output data with $\alpha = 0.3$ and obtained estimator values. In this experiment $H = H' = 0.2$, $D = D' = 1$ and $N = 5000$.

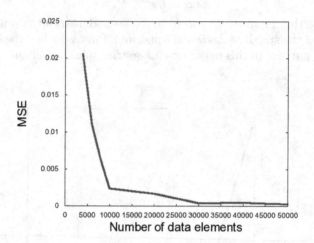

Fig. 3. The dependence between the number of data elements N and the value of the MSE

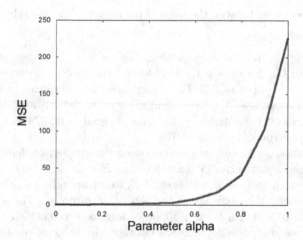

Fig. 4. The dependence between the value of parameter α and the value of the MSE

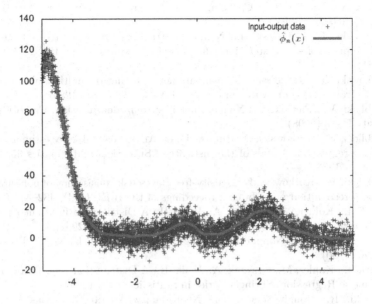

Fig. 5. The input-output data and the obtained estimator values

4   Conclusion and Future Work

In this paper we studied the probabilistic neural networks based on Parzen kernels and we established the weak convergence assuming time-varying noise. In future work it would be interesting to apply supervised and unsupervised neural networks [1], [3], [16] or neuro-fuzzy structures [13], [36]-[39], [41], [42] for learning in time-varying environment.

Acknowledgments. This paper was prepared under project operated within the Foundation for Polish Science Team Programme co-financed by the EU European Regional Development Fund, Operational Program Innovative Economy 2007-2013, and also supported by the National Science Center NCN.

References

1. Bilski, J., Rutkowski, L.: A fast training algorithm for neural networks. IEEE Transactions on Circuits and Systems II 45, 749–753 (1998)
2. Cacoullos, P.: Estimation of a multivariate density. Annals of the Institute of Statistical Mathematics 18, 179–190 (1965)
3. Cierniak, R., Rutkowski, L.: On image compression by competitive neural networks and optimal linear predictors. Signal Processing: Image Communication - a Eurasip Journal 15(6), 559–565 (2000)

4. Chu, C.K., Marron, J.S.: Choosing a kernel regression estimator. Statistical Science 6, 404–436 (1991)
5. Gałkowski, T., Rutkowski, L.: Nonparametric recovery of multivariate functions with applications to system identification. Proceedings of the IEEE 73, 942–943 (1985)
6. Gałkowski, T., Rutkowski, L.: Nonparametric fitting of multivariable functions. IEEE Transactions on Automatic Control AC-31, 785–787 (1986)
7. Greblicki, W., Pawlak, M.: Nonparametric system identification. Cambridge University Press (2008)
8. Greblicki, W., Rutkowska, D., Rutkowski, L.: An orthogonal series estimate of time-varying regression. Annals of the Institute of Statistical Mathematics 35, Part A, 147–160 (1983)
9. Greblicki, W., Rutkowski, L.: Density-free Bayes risk consistency of nonparametric pattern recognition procedures. Proceedings of the IEEE 69(4), 482–483 (1981)
10. Györfi, L., Kohler, M., Krzyżak, A., Walk, H.: A Distribution-Free Theory of Nonparametric Regression. Springer Series in Statistics, USA (2002)
11. Härdle, W.: Applied Nonparametric Regression. Cambridge University Press, Cambridge (1990)
12. Györfi, L., Kohler, M., Krzyżak, A., Walk, H.: A Distribution-Free Theory of Nonparameric Regression. Springer Series in Statistics, USA (2002)
13. Nowicki, R.: Rough Sets in the Neuro-Fuzzy Architectures Based on Non-monotonic Fuzzy Implications. In: Rutkowski, L., Siekmann, J.H., Tadeusiewicz, R., Zadeh, L.A. (eds.) ICAISC 2004. LNCS (LNAI), vol. 3070, pp. 518–525. Springer, Heidelberg (2004)
14. Ozden, M., Polat, E.: A color image segmentation approach for content-based image retrieval. Pattern Recognition 40, 1318–1325 (2007)
15. Parzen, E.: On estimation of a probability density function and mode. Analysis of Mathematical Statistics 33(3), 1065–1076 (1962)
16. Patan, K., Patan, M.: Optimal training strategies for locally recurrent neural networks. Journal of Artificial Intelligence and Soft Computing Research 1(2), 103–114 (2011)
17. Rafajłowicz, E.: Nonparametric orthogonal series estimators of regression: A class attaining the optimal convergence rate in L_2. Statistics and Probability Letters 5, 219–224 (1987)
18. Rutkowski, L.: Sequential estimates of probability densities by orthogonal series and their application in pattern classification. IEEE Transactions on Systems, Man, and Cybernetics SMC-10(12), 918–920 (1980)
19. Rutkowski, L.: Sequential estimates of a regression function by orthogonal series with applications in discrimination, New York-Heidelberg-Berlin. Lectures Notes in Statistics, vol. 8, pp. 236–244 (1981)
20. Rutkowski, L.: On system identification by nonparametric function fitting. IEEE Transactions on Automatic Control AC-27, 225–227 (1982)
21. Rutkowski, L.: Orthogonal series estimates of a regression function with applications in system identification. In: Probability and Statistical Inference, pp. 343–347. D. Reidel Publishing Company, Dordrecht (1982)
22. Rutkowski, L.: On Bayes risk consistent pattern recognition procedures in a quasi-stationary environment. IEEE Transactions on Pattern Analysis and Machine Intelligence PAMI-4(1), 84–87 (1982)
23. Rutkowski, L.: On-line identification of time-varying systems by nonparametric techniques. IEEE Transactions on Automatic Control AC-27, 228–230 (1982)

24. Rutkowski, L.: On nonparametric identification with prediction of time-varying systems. IEEE Transactions on Automatic Control AC-29, 58–60 (1984)
25. Rutkowski, L.: Nonparametric identification of quasi-stationary systems. Systems and Control Letters 6, 33–35 (1985)
26. Rutkowski, L.: The real-time identification of time-varying systems by nonparametric algorithms based on the Parzen kernels. International Journal of Systems Science 16, 1123–1130 (1985)
27. Rutkowski, L.: A general approach for nonparametric fitting of functions and their derivatives with applications to linear circuits identification. IEEE Transactions Circuits Systems CAS-33, 812–818 (1986)
28. Rutkowski, L.: Sequential pattern recognition procedures derived from multiple Fourier series. Pattern Recognition Letters 8, 213–216 (1988)
29. Rutkowski, L.: Nonparametric procedures for identification and control of linear dynamic systems. In: Proceedings of 1988 American Control Conference, June 15-17, pp. 1325–1326 (1988)
30. Rutkowski, L.: An application of multiple Fourier series to identification of multivariable nonstationary systems. International Journal of Systems Science 20(10), 1993–2002 (1989)
31. Rutkowski, L.: Nonparametric learning algorithms in the time-varying environments. Signal Processing 18, 129–137 (1989)
32. Rutkowski, L., Rafajłowicz, E.: On global rate of convergence of some nonparametric identification procedures. IEEE Transaction on Automatic Control AC-34(10), 1089–1091 (1989)
33. Rutkowski, L.: Identification of MISO nonlinear regressions in the presence of a wide class of disturbances. IEEE Transactions on Information Theory IT-37, 214–216 (1991)
34. Rutkowski, L.: Multiple Fourier series procedures for extraction of nonlinear regressions from noisy data. IEEE Transactions on Signal Processing 41(10), 3062–3065 (1993)
35. Rutkowski, L., Gałkowski, T.: On pattern classification and system identification by probabilistic neural networks. Applied Mathematics and Computer Science 4(3), 413–422 (1994)
36. Rutkowski, L.: A New Method for System Modelling and Pattern Classification. Bulletin of the Polish Academy of Sciences 52(1), 11–24 (2004)
37. Rutkowski, L., Cpałka, K.: A general approach to neuro - fuzzy systems. In: Proceedings of the 10th IEEE International Conference on Fuzzy Systems, Melbourne, December 2-5, vol. 3, pp. 1428–1431 (2001)
38. Rutkowski, L., Cpałka, K.: A neuro-fuzzy controller with a compromise fuzzy reasoning. Control and Cybernetics 31(2), 297–308 (2002)
39. Scherer, R.: Boosting Ensemble of Relational Neuro-fuzzy Systems. In: Rutkowski, L., Tadeusiewicz, R., Zadeh, L.A., Żurada, J.M. (eds.) ICAISC 2006. LNCS (LNAI), vol. 4029, pp. 306–313. Springer, Heidelberg (2006)
40. Specht, D.F.: Probabilistic neural networks. Neural Networks 3, 109–118 (1990)
41. Starczewski, L., Rutkowski, L.: Interval type 2 neuro-fuzzy systems based on interval consequents. In: Rutkowski, L., Kacprzyk, J. (eds.) Neural Networks and Soft Computing, pp. 570–577. Physica-Verlag, Springer-Verlag Company, Heidelberg, New York (2003)
42. Starczewski, J.T., Rutkowski, L.: Connectionist Structures of Type 2 Fuzzy Inference Systems. In: Wyrzykowski, R., Dongarra, J., Paprzycki, M., Waśniewski, J. (eds.) PPAM 2001. LNCS, vol. 2328, pp. 634–642. Springer, Heidelberg (2002)

Strong Convergence of the Recursive Parzen-Type Probabilistic Neural Network Handling Nonstationary Noise

Lena Pietruczuk[1] and Yoichi Hayashi[2]

[1] Department of Computer Engineering, Czestochowa University of Technology,
ul. Armii Krajowej 36, 42-200 Czestochowa, Poland
lena.pietruczuk@kik.pcz.pl
[2] Department of Computer Science, Meiji University,
Tama-ku, Kawasaki 214-8571, Japan
hayashiy@cs.meiji.ac.jp

Abstract. A recursive version of the Parzen-type general regression neural network is studied. Strong convergence is established assuming time-varying noise. Experimental results are discussed in details.

1 Introduction

Probabilistic neural networks developed by Specht [39] are net structures corresponding to nonparametric density and regression estimates developed to solve stationary (see e.g. [2], [8], [9], [11], [16]-[20], [26]-[28], [31]-[34], [43] and [46]) and nonstationary problems (see e.g. [10], [21]-[25], [29] and [30]). In a letter case it was assumed in literature that noise was stationary.

In this paper we will consider the problem of estimation of the regression function in the following system

$$Y_i = \phi(X_i) + Z_i, \tag{1}$$

where $X_1, \ldots, X_n$ is a sequence of some independent and equally distributed random variables with the same probability density function f, ϕ is an unknown function and $Z_1, \ldots, Z_n$ are an independent random variables with unknown distribution. The expected values and variances of Z_n have the following property:

$$E[Z_i] = 0, \quad Var[Z_i] = d_i, \quad \text{for } i = 1 \ldots n. \tag{2}$$

It should be emphasized that the variance of Z_i is changing with time. The problem is to estimate the unknown function ϕ.

2 General Regression Neural Network in Non-stationary Environment

In the non-stationary environment we use the recursive version of the Parzen kernel procedure to estimate the regression function $\phi(x)$. Let us define

L. Rutkowski et al. (Eds.): ICAISC 2012, Part I, LNCS 7267, pp. 160–168, 2012.

$$K_n(x, u) = h_n^{-p} K(\frac{x - u}{h_n}), \quad K'_n(x, u) = h_n'^{-p} K(\frac{x - u}{h'_n}) \tag{3}$$

where K is an appropriately selected and h_n, h'_n are certain sequences of numbers. Let

$$\hat{\phi}_n(x) = \frac{\hat{R}_n(x)}{\hat{f}_n(x)} \tag{4}$$

be an estimate of the regression function

$$\phi(x) = \frac{R(x)}{f(x)} \tag{5}$$

where $R(x) = f(x)\phi(x)$. The estimators $\hat{R}_n$ and $\hat{f}_n$ are in the form

$$\hat{R}_n(x) = \frac{1}{n} \sum_{i=1}^{n} Y_i K_i(x, X_i) \tag{6}$$

and

$$\hat{f}_n(x) = \frac{1}{n} \sum_{i=1}^{n} K'_i(x, X_i). \tag{7}$$

In (7) $f_n(x)$ is an estimator of a density function of random variables $X_1, \ldots, X_n$. Therefore $\hat{\phi}_n$ takes the form

$$\hat{\phi}_n(x) = \frac{\sum_{i=1}^{n} Y_i h_i^{-p} K(\frac{x-X_i}{h_i})}{\sum_{i=1}^{n} h_i^{-p} K(\frac{x-X_i}{h'_i})}. \tag{8}$$

Note that estimates (6) and (7) can be rewritten as follows

$$\hat{R}_i(x) = \frac{1}{n} \sum_{i=1}^{n} Y_i h_i^{-p} K\left(\frac{x - X_i}{h_i}\right) \tag{9}$$

and

$$\hat{f}_i(x) = \frac{1}{n} \sum_{i=1}^{n} h_i^{-p} K\left(\frac{x - X_i}{h_i}\right) \tag{10}$$

The algorithm of recursive generalized regression neural network is shown in Fig. 1.

Theorem 1. *If*

$$s_i = \sup_x \{(\sigma_i^2 + \phi^2(x))f(x)\} < \infty, \ i = 1, \ldots, n \tag{11}$$

$$||x||^p K(x) \longrightarrow 0 \quad ||x||^p < \infty, \tag{12}$$

$$\sum_{i=1}^{\infty} i^{-2} h_i'^{-d} < \infty, \tag{13}$$

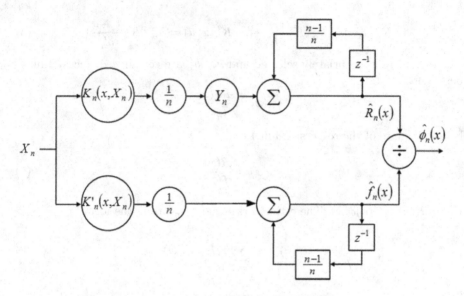

Fig. 1. Scheme of recursive generalized regression neural network

$$\sum_{i=1}^{\infty} i^{-2} h_i^{-d} s_i < \infty, \tag{14}$$

$$h_i' \to 0, \qquad h_i \to 0, \tag{15}$$

then $\phi_n(x) \xrightarrow{n} \phi(x)$ with probability one at each x where $\phi(x)$ is continuous.

Proof. It is sufficient to show that

$$\hat{f}_n(x) \longrightarrow f(x) \quad \text{with probability one at each x where } f(x) \text{ is continuous} \tag{16}$$

and

$$\hat{R}_n(x) \longrightarrow R(x) \quad \text{with probability one at each } x \text{ where } R(x) \text{ is continuous.} \tag{17}$$

Convergence of (16) under condition (13) was proved in [46]. Therefore it is enough to show that (17) it true. Obviously

$$\left| \hat{R}_n(x) - R(x) \right| \leq \left| \hat{R}_n(x) - E\left[\hat{R}_n(x) \right] \right| + \left| E\left[\hat{R}_n(x) \right] - R(x) \right|. \tag{18}$$

Observe that

$$\left| \hat{R}_n(x) - E\left[\hat{R}_n(x) \right] \right| = \left| \frac{1}{n} \sum_{i=1}^{n} Y_i K_i(x, X_i) - E\left[\frac{1}{n} \sum_{i=1}^{n} Y_i K_i(x, X_i) \right] \right| = \tag{19}$$

$$= \frac{1}{n} \sum_{i=1}^{n} \left[Y_i K_i(x, X_i) - E\left[Y_i K_i(x, X_i) \right] \right] \tag{20}$$

and

$$\sum_{i=1}^{\infty} \frac{1}{i^2} Var\left(Y_i K_i\left(x, X_i\right)\right) = \sum_{i=1}^{\infty} \frac{1}{i^2} Var\left(Y_i h_i^{-P} K\left(\frac{x - X_i}{h_i}\right)\right) \leq \qquad (21)$$

$$\leq \sum_{i=1}^{\infty} \frac{1}{i^2} E\left[Y_i^2 h_i^{-2P} K^2\left(\frac{x - X_i}{h_i}\right)\right] = \sum_{i=1}^{\infty} \frac{1}{i^2} \int_{R^P} E\left[Y_i^2 | X_i = u\right] f(u) ||K||_\infty h_i^{-2P} K\left(\frac{x - X_i}{h_i}\right) du \leq \qquad (22)$$

$$\sum_{i=1}^{\infty} \frac{1}{i^2} \int_{R^P} 2(\sigma_i^2 + \phi^2(x)) f(u) ||K||_\infty h_i^{-2P} K\left(\frac{x - X_i}{h_i}\right) du \leq \sum_{i=1}^{\infty} \frac{1}{i^2} 2 s_i ||K||_\infty h_i^{-2P} \int_{R^P} K\left(\frac{x - X_i}{h_i}\right) du = \qquad (23)$$

$$= 2||K||_\infty \sum_{i=1}^{\infty} \frac{1}{i^2} s_i h_i^{-P} \qquad (24)$$

Therefore $\sum_{i=1}^{\infty} i^{-2} Var(Y_i K_i(x, X_i)) \leq \infty$ if condition (14) holds and, by using the strong law of big numbers [...], $|\hat{R}_n(x) - E\hat{R}_n(x)| \xrightarrow{n} 0$ with probability one. Since $|E\hat{R}_n(x) - R(x)| \xrightarrow{n} 0$ under condition (12) (see [2]), then the result is established.

2.1   Example

We consider the case when $d_n = O(n^\alpha)$ for $\alpha > 0$. We propose the sequences h_n' and h_n to be in the form

$$h_n' = D'n^{-H'}, \qquad h_n = Dn^{-H}. \qquad (25)$$

Then conditions (13)-(15) are satisfied if

$$H' < 1 \text{ and } H + \alpha < 1. \qquad (26)$$

3   Experimental Results

In the following simulations we will test the algorithm on data from the normal distribution with the mean 0 and the standard deviation 4.9. The function ϕ is of the form

$$\phi(x) = (x^3 + 3x^2 + 16x - 2) \cos(x). \qquad (27)$$

First we selected the kernel function. For the purpose of this article we choose triangular kernel and $h_n' = h_n$ to be in the form (25). By examining the relationship between the value of the mean square error and the value of the parameters $H = H'$ we obtained the results illustrated in Fig. 1. The experiment was obtained on the set of 7000 data, $\alpha = 0.38$ and $D = D' = 5.5$. As we can see with increasing value of H the mean square error (MSE) of the algorithm decreases. For $H = 0$ the MSE was equal to 8988.1349 and for $H = 0.5$ the value of the MSE decreased to 0.6837.

In Figure 2 we show the dependence between the number of samples and the MSE. The value of $H = H'$ was equal to 0.28, $D = D' = 5.8$ and $\alpha = 0.33$. Observe that even with increasing variance of Z_n, for increasing number of elements n, the accuracy of the algorithm is improved. For $n = 4000$ it is equal to 58.7501 and for $n = 50000$ it decreases to 3.7163.

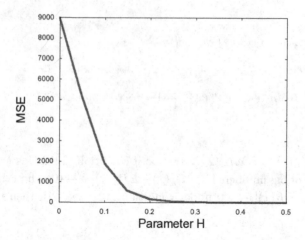

Fig. 2. The dependence between the value of parameter H and the value of the MSE

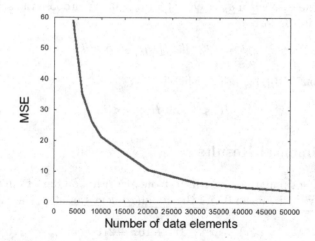

Fig. 3. The dependence between the number of data elements n and the value of the MSE

In Figure 3 we show the dependence between the parameter α and the MSE of the algorithm. In this case $n = 6000$, $D = D' = 6$ and $H = H' = 0.29$. From the conditions (26) we can see, that for this value of H, the value of α should be not bigger than 0.71. For small value of α the MSE is small, however for α outside the permissible range the MSE begins to increase.

In the next experiment we examine the difference between the value of function $\phi(x)$ and the value of estimator in point $x = 1$. The parameters are as follows

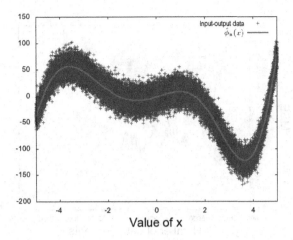

Fig. 4. The dependence between the value of parameter α and the value of the MSE

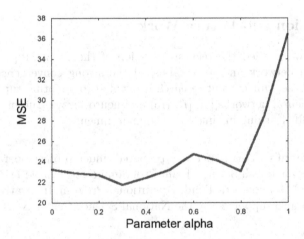

Fig. 5. The dependence between the number of elements and the value of the MSE for $x = 1$

$\alpha = 0.36$, $H = H' = 0.28$, $D = D' = 5.7$ and input data are from the normal distribution $\mathcal{N}(0, (3.6)^2)$. In Figure (5) we can see the dependence between the number of data elements and the value of the MSE. It shows that the MSE decreases with the growth of the number of input data.

In Figure 4 we can see the tested data with $\alpha = 0.47$ and estimator obtained for these data. For this experiment $H = H' = 0.3$, $D = D' = 5.9$ and $n = 8500$.

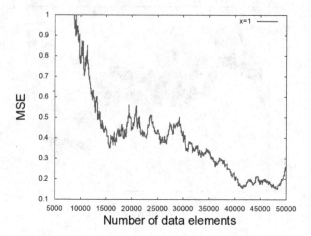

Fig. 6. The input-output data and the obtained estimator values

4   Conclusion and Future Work

In this paper we studied the recursive version of the Parzen-type general regression neural network and we established the strong convergence assuming time-varying noise. Our current research is devoted to adapting supervised and unsupervised neural networks [5], [7], [15] and neuro-fuzzy structures [12], [35]-[38], [41], [42] for learning in time-varying environment.

Acknowledgments. This paper was prepared under project operated within the Foundation for Polish Science Team Programme co-financed by the EU European Regional Development Fund, Operational Program Innovative Economy 2007-2013, and also supported by the National Science Center NCN.

References

1. Aggarwal, C.: Data Streams. Models and Algorithms. Springer, New York (2007)
2. Ahmad, I.A., Lin, P.E.: Nonparametric sequential estimation of multiple regression function. Bulletin of Mathematical Statistics 17, 63–75 (1976)
3. Apostol, M.: Mathematical Analysis. Addison Wesaley (1974)
4. Benedetti, J.: On the nonparametric estimation of regression function. Journal of Royal Statistical Society B 39, 248–253 (1977)
5. Bilski, J., Rutkowski, L.: A fast training algorithm for neural networks. IEEE Transactions on Circuits and Systems II 45, 749–753 (1998)
6. Cacoullos, P.: Estimation of a multivariate density. Annals of the Institute of Statistical Mathematics 18, 179–190 (1965)
7. Cierniak, R., Rutkowski, L.: On image compression by competitive neural networks and optimal linear predictors. Signal Processing: Image Communication - a Eurasip Journal 15(6), 559–565 (2000)

8. Gałkowski, T., Rutkowski, L.: Nonparametric recovery of multivariate functions with applications to system identification. Proceedings of the IEEE 73, 942–943 (1985)

9. Gałkowski, T., Rutkowski, L.: Nonparametric fitting of multivariable functions. IEEE Transactions on Automatic Control AC-31, 785–787 (1986)

10. Greblicki, W., Rutkowska, D., Rutkowski, L.: An orthogonal series estimate of time-varying regression. Annals of the Institute of Statistical Mathematics 35, Part A, 147–160 (1983)

11. Greblicki, W., Rutkowski, L.: Density-free Bayes risk consistency of nonparametric pattern recognition procedures. Proceedings of the IEEE 69(4), 482–483 (1981)

12. Nowicki, R.: Rough Sets in the Neuro-Fuzzy Architectures Based on Non-monotonic Fuzzy Implications. In: Rutkowski, L., Siekmann, J.H., Tadeusiewicz, R., Zadeh, L.A. (eds.) ICAISC 2004. LNCS (LNAI), vol. 3070, pp. 518–525. Springer, Heidelberg (2004)

13. Ozden, M., Polat, E.: A color image segmentation approach for content-based image retrieval. Pattern Recognition 40, 1318–1325 (2007)

14. Parzen, E.: On estimation of a probability density function and mode. Analysis of Mathematical Statistics 33(3), 1065–1076 (1962)

15. Patan, K., Patan, M.: Optimal training strategies for locally recurrent neural networks. Journal of Artificial Intelligence and Soft Computing Research 1(2), 103–114 (2011)

16. Rafajłowicz, E.: Nonparametric orthogonal series estimators of regression: A class attaining the optimal convergence rate in L_2. Statistics and Probability Letters 5, 219–224 (1987)

17. Rutkowski, L.: Sequential estimates of probability densities by orthogonal series and their application in pattern classification. IEEE Transactions on Systems, Man, and Cybernetics SMC-10(12), 918–920 (1980)

18. Rutkowski, L.: Sequential estimates of a regression function by orthogonal series with applications in discrimination, New York-Heidelberg-Berlin. Lectures Notes in Statistics, vol. 8, pp. 236–244 (1981)

19. Rutkowski, L.: On system identification by nonparametric function fitting. IEEE Transactions on Automatic Control AC-27, 225–227 (1982)

20. Rutkowski, L.: Orthogonal series estimates of a regression function with applications in system identification. In: Probability and Statistical Inference, pp. 343–347. D. Reidel Publishing Company, Dordrecht (1982)

21. Rutkowski, L.: On Bayes risk consistent pattern recognition procedures in a quasi-stationary environment. IEEE Transactions on Pattern Analysis and Machine Intelligence PAMI-4(1), 84–87 (1982)

22. Rutkowski, L.: On-line identification of time-varying systems by nonparametric techniques. IEEE Transactions on Automatic Control AC-27, 228–230 (1982)

23. Rutkowski, L.: On nonparametric identification with prediction of time-varying systems. IEEE Transactions on Automatic Control AC-29, 58–60 (1984)

24. Rutkowski, L.: Nonparametric identification of quasi-stationary systems. Systems and Control Letters 6, 33–35 (1985)

25. Rutkowski, L.: The real-time identification of time-varying systems by nonparametric algorithms based on the Parzen kernels. International Journal of Systems Science 16, 1123–1130 (1985)

26. Rutkowski, L.: A general approach for nonparametric fitting of functions and their derivatives with applications to linear circuits identification. IEEE Transactions Circuits Systems CAS-33, 812–818 (1986)

27. Rutkowski, L.: Sequential pattern recognition procedures derived from multiple Fourier series. Pattern Recognition Letters 8, 213–216 (1988)
28. Rutkowski, L.: Nonparametric procedures for identification and control of linear dynamic systems. In: Proceedings of 1988 American Control Conference, June 15-17, pp. 1325–1326 (1988)
29. Rutkowski, L.: An application of multiple Fourier series to identification of multivariable nonstationary systems. International Journal of Systems Science 20(10), 1993–2002 (1989)
30. Rutkowski, L.: Nonparametric learning algorithms in the time-varying environments. Signal Processing 18, 129–137 (1989)
31. Rutkowski, L., Rafajłowicz, E.: On global rate of convergence of some nonparametric identification procedures. IEEE Transaction on Automatic Control AC-34(10), 1089–1091 (1989)
32. Rutkowski, L.: Identification of MISO nonlinear regressions in the presence of a wide class of disturbances. IEEE Transactions on Information Theory IT-37, 214–216 (1991)
33. Rutkowski, L.: Multiple Fourier series procedures for extraction of nonlinear regressions from noisy data. IEEE Transactions on Signal Processing 41(10), 3062–3065 (1993)
34. Rutkowski, L., Gałkowski, T.: On pattern classification and system identification by probabilistic neural networks. Applied Mathematics and Computer Science 4(3), 413–422 (1994)
35. Rutkowski, L.: A New Method for System Modelling and Pattern Classification. Bulletin of the Polish Academy of Sciences 52(1), 11–24 (2004)
36. Rutkowski, L., Cpałka, K.: A general approach to neuro - fuzzy systems. In: Proceedings of the 10th IEEE International Conference on Fuzzy Systems, Melbourne, December 2-5, vol. 3, pp. 1428–1431 (2001)
37. Rutkowski, L., Cpałka, K.: A neuro-fuzzy controller with a compromise fuzzy reasoning. Control and Cybernetics 31(2), 297–308 (2002)
38. Scherer, R.: Boosting Ensemble of Relational Neuro-fuzzy Systems. In: Rutkowski, L., Tadeusiewicz, R., Zadeh, L.A., Żurada, J.M. (eds.) ICAISC 2006. LNCS (LNAI), vol. 4029, pp. 306–313. Springer, Heidelberg (2006)
39. Specht, D.F.: A general regression neural network. IEEE Transactions Neural Networks 2, 568–576 (1991)
40. Specht, D.F.: Probabilistic neural networks. Neural Networks 3, 109–118 (1990)
41. Starczewski, L., Rutkowski, L.: Interval type 2 neuro-fuzzy systems based on interval consequents. In: Rutkowski, L., Kacprzyk, J. (eds.) Neural Networks and Soft Computing, pp. 570–577. Physica-Verlag, Springer-Verlag Company, Heidelberg, New York (2003)
42. Starczewski, J.T., Rutkowski, L.: Connectionist Structures of Type 2 Fuzzy Inference Systems. In: Wyrzykowski, R., Dongarra, J., Paprzycki, M., Waśniewski, J. (eds.) PPAM 2001. LNCS, vol. 2328, pp. 634–642. Springer, Heidelberg (2002)
43. Wegman, E.J., Davies, H.I.: Remarks on some recursive estimators of a probability density. Annals of Statistics 7, 316–327 (1979)
44. Wilks, S.S.: Mathematical Statistics. Wiley, New York (1962)
45. Wolverton, C.T., Wagner, T.J.: Recursive estimates of probability density. IEEE Transactions on Systems Science and Cybernetics 5, 307 (1969)
46. Yamato, H.: Sequential estimation of a continuous probability density function and the mode. Bulletin of Mathematical Statistics 14, 1–12 (1971)

Improving Performance of Self-Organising Maps with Distance Metric Learning Method

Piotr Płoński and Krzysztof Zaremba

Institute of Radioelectronics, Warsaw University of Technology,
Nowowiejska 15/19, 00-665 Warsaw, Poland
{pplonski,zaremba}@ire.pw.edu.pl

Abstract. Self-Organising Maps (SOM) are Artificial Neural Networks used in Pattern Recognition tasks. Their major advantage over other architectures is human readability of a model. However, they often gain poorer accuracy. Mostly used metric in SOM is the Euclidean distance, which is not the best approach to some problems. In this paper, we study an impact of the metric change on the SOM's performance in classification problems. In order to change the metric of the SOM we applied a distance metric learning method, so-called 'Large Margin Nearest Neighbour'. It computes the Mahalanobis matrix, which assures small distance between nearest neighbour points from the same class and separation of points belonging to different classes by large margin. Results are presented on several real data sets, containing for example recognition of written digits, spoken letters or faces.

Keywords: Self-Organising Maps, Distance Metric Learning, LMNN, Mahalanobis distance, Classification.

1 Introduction

Some real-world problems do not have an exact algorithmic solution. Currently, there is a vast number of Artificial Intelligence(AI) methods which can be used to solve them. One of the branches of AI are Artificial Neural Networks. They are mathematical models inspired by biology. In 1982 T.Kohonen presented architecture called Self-Organising Maps (SOM) [10], which provides a method of feature mapping from multi-dimensional space to usually a two-dimensional grid of neurons in an unspervised way. This way of data analysis was proved as an efficient tool in many applications, both in academic and industrial solutions [11]. For example in character recognition tasks, image recognition tasks, face recognition [2], analysis of words[12], grouping of documents [9], visualisation [5], and even bioinformatics (for example phylogenetic tree reconstruction [4]).

There exists a huge number of methods for improving SOM's performance. Some of them concentrated on finding an optimal size of a network[1], faster learning [14] or applying different neighbourhood functions [8]. In this paper we investigate two additional improvements. The first one [6], [2] uses Mahalanobis metric instead of the Euclidean one. The second improvement [13] shows how to use SOM in a supervised manner.

L. Rutkowski et al. (Eds.): ICAISC 2012, Part I, LNCS 7267, pp. 169–177, 2012.

In our approach, contrary to [6], [2], [3], instead of computing the Mahalanobis matrix as an inverse of covariance matrix, it is learned in a way assuring the smallest distance between points from the same class and large margin separation of points from different classes. Several algorithms exist for distance metric learning (DML) [17], [7]. In this paper we use so-called Large Margin Nearest Neighbour (LMNN) method [16]. It introduces the distance metric learning problem as a convex optimization, which assures that the global minimum can be efficiently computed. First, we shortly describe SOM model used in supervised manner and LMNN method. Then we show how we combine these two approaches into our SOM+DML model. Finally we present results on real data sets.

2   Methods

Let's denote data set as $D = \{(\boldsymbol{x_i}, \boldsymbol{y_i})\}$, where $\boldsymbol{x_i}$ is an attribute vector of i-th sample, and $\boldsymbol{y_i}$ is a class vector, where $\boldsymbol{y_{ij}} = 0$ for $j \neq class_i$ and $\boldsymbol{y_{ij}} = 1$ for $j = class_i$, where $class_i$ is class number for i-th sample.

2.1   SOM Model

In this paper, we used the SOM architecture in a supervised manner so-called 'Learning Associations by Self-Organisation' (LASSO), first described in [13]. The main difference between this SOM architecture and the original Kohonen's SOM architecture [10] is that during the learning phase the LASSO method takes into consideration class vector, additionally to attributes. Herein, we used two-dimensional grid of neurons. Each neuron is represented by a weight vector W_{pq}, consisting of a vector corresponding to attributes A_{pq}, and to a class C_{pq} ($W_{pq} = [A_{pq}; C_{pq}]$), where (p, q) are indexes of the neuron in the grid. In a learning phase all samples are shown to the network in one epoch. For each sample we search for a neuron which is closest to the i-th sample. The distance is computed by:

$$Dist_{train}(D_i, W_{pq}) = (\boldsymbol{x_i} - A_{pq})^T(\boldsymbol{x_i} - A_{pq}) + (\boldsymbol{y_i} - C_{pq})^T(\boldsymbol{y_i} - C_{pq}). \quad (1)$$

The neuron (p, q) with the smallest distance to i-th sample is called the Best Matching Unit (BMU), we note its indexes as (B_i, B_j). Once the BMU is found, the weight update step is executed. The weights of each neuron are updated with following formulas:

$$A_{pq} = A_{pq} + \eta(A_{pq} - \boldsymbol{x_i}), \quad (2)$$

$$C_{pq} = C_{pq} + \eta(C_{pq} - \boldsymbol{y_i}), \quad (3)$$

where η is a learning coefficient, consisting of a learning step size parameter μ and a neighbourhood function τ, so $\eta = \mu\tau$. Learning speed parameter is decreased between consecutive epochs, so that network's ability to remember patterns is improved. It is described by $\mu = \mu_0 exp(-t\lambda)$, where μ_0 is a starting value of the learning speed, t is the current epoch and λ is responsible for regulating the speed of the decrease. Neighbourhood function controls changing the weights with respect to the distance to the BMU. It is noted as $\tau = exp(-\alpha S(B_i, B_j, p, q))$, where α describes the neighbourhood function width and $S(B_i, B_j, p, q)$ is the distance in the grid between the neuron and the BMU, computed by the following formula:

$$S(B_i, B_j, p, q) = (B_i - p)^2 + (B_j - q)^2. \tag{4}$$

We assumed a cost function as a sum of distances between samples and corresponding BMUs:

$$F = \sum_l Dist_{train}(D_l, W_{B_i, B_j}). \tag{5}$$

We train network till the cost function stops decreasing or a selected number of learning procedure iterations is exceed.

The exploitation phase is performed after the learning phase. New samples, which do not take part in the training, are shown to the network in order to designate their class. It should be noted that only the part with attributes is presented to the network. The BMU is found by computing a distance between an attribute input vector and an attribute part of the weights using the following formula:

$$Dist_{test}(D_i, W_{pq}) = (\boldsymbol{x_i} - A_{pq})^T(\boldsymbol{x_i} - A_{pq}). \tag{6}$$

For the tested sample, the designated class corresponds to position of maximum value in the part which code class information C_{pq} in BMU weights.

2.2   LMNN Method

In many cases the mostly used metric is an Euclidean one. It often gives poor accuracy, because it takes all dimensions with equal contribution and assumes no correlations between the dimensions. Mahalanobis distance seems a better metric choice, because it is scale-invariant and takes into account input dimensions correlations. It is defined by:

$$Dist_M(\boldsymbol{x_i}, \boldsymbol{x_j}) = (\boldsymbol{x_i} - \boldsymbol{x_j})^T M(\boldsymbol{x_i} - \boldsymbol{x_j}), \tag{7}$$

where M is usually an inverse of a covariance matrix. In case where M is an identity matrix, the distance (7) is equal to the Euclidean distance.

In this paper, we learned Mahalanobis matrix using the method described in [16]. Matrix coefficients are computed in a way assuring large margin separation of points from different classes and a small distance between the points of the same class. Before starting the matrix learning for each point, k nearest neighbours with the same class are found. They are called target neighbours, denoted by $\theta_{ij} = \{0, 1\}$, where $\theta_{i,j} = 1$ means that x_j is the target neighbour of x_i, and $\theta_{i,j} = 0$ means otherwise. With no prior knowledge, the Euclidean distance can be used to point the target neighbours. Target neighbours are unchanged during the whole learning. Let's add a variable to indicate when the two samples have the same class, denoted as $y_{il} = \{0, 1\}$, where $y_{il} = 1$ when i-th and l-th samples are from the same class, zero when they are from different classes.

Finding an optimal matrix M can be expressed as a semidefinite programming (SDP) optimization problem with the following cost function (8) and constrains (9), (10), (11):

$$minimize \sum_{ij} \theta_{i,j} Dist_M(\boldsymbol{x_i}, \boldsymbol{x_j}) + c \sum_{i,j,l} \theta_{i,j}(1 - y_{il})\xi_{ijl}, \tag{8}$$

$$Dist_M(\boldsymbol{x_i}, \boldsymbol{x_l}) - Dist_M(\boldsymbol{x_i}, \boldsymbol{x_j}) \geq 1 - \xi_{ijl}, \tag{9}$$

$$\xi_{ijl} \geq 0, \tag{10}$$

$$M \succeq 0. \tag{11}$$

The first term in the minimization function penalizes a large distance between the samples and their target neighbours. The second term penalizes a small distance between the samples from different classes - it is expressed as slack variables ξ_{ijl}. The c parameter balances the influence between these two terms. In this paper it is set to 0.5, which gives equal strength to each term. The constraint given in (11) requires the M matrix to be positive semidefinite - all its eigenvalues should be nonnegative. Semidefinite programming is a convex optimization problem, so a global minimum can be efficiently computed. SPD can be solved using general purpose solvers, however in our approach we used Matalb implementation code[1] described in [16], which is finely tuned to efficiently solve this kind of problems. Here most of slack variables are not used because samples are well separated.

2.3   SOM+DML Model

We are interested in a such linear transformation of sample attributes that will assure that the Euclidean distance computed on the transformed attributes will be equal to the Mahalanobis distance computed on the original attributes. Mahalanobis matrix M can be written as $M = L^T L$, where L is the searched transformation. Lets denote $\boldsymbol{u_i}$ as the transformed attributes of i-th sample and $\boldsymbol{u_j}$ as the transformed attributes of j-th sample:

$$\boldsymbol{u_i} = L\boldsymbol{x_i}, \tag{12}$$

$$\boldsymbol{u_j} = L\boldsymbol{x_j}. \tag{13}$$

The distance between the transformed attributes in Euclidean distance should be equal to Mahalanobis distance between the original attributes:

$$Dist_M(\boldsymbol{x_i}, \boldsymbol{x_j}) = Dist_E(\boldsymbol{u_i}, \boldsymbol{u_j}). \tag{14}$$

---

[1] Matalb impementation of LMNN algorithm available from
http://www.cse.wustl.edu/~kilian/code/code.html

We will now search for L. Now for matrix M we will find eigenvectors Φ and a matrix with eigenvalues on diagonal Λ:

$$M\Phi = \Phi\Lambda. \tag{15}$$

Matrix Λ can be expressed as:

$$\Phi^T M\Phi = \Lambda. \tag{16}$$

Since matrix M found by the LMNN algorithm is positive semidefine, diagonal elements in matrix Λ are nonnegative. Thus, we can write:

$$\Lambda^{-\frac{1}{2}}\Lambda\Lambda^{-\frac{1}{2}} = I. \tag{17}$$

Substituting (16) into (17), we obtain:

$$\Lambda^{-\frac{1}{2}}\Phi^T M\Phi\Lambda^{-\frac{1}{2}} = I. \tag{18}$$

Now we can note L as:

$$L = \Lambda^{-\frac{1}{2}}\Phi^T. \tag{19}$$

Using (19) we can write (18) as:

$$LML^T = I. \tag{20}$$

We see that $M = L^T L$ and hence we can write:

$$(x_i - x_j)^T M(x_i - x_j) = (Lx_i - Lx_j)^T(Lx_i - Lx_j) \tag{21}$$

From (21) we see that (14) is true. This transformation of input attributes is also known as *whitening transform*. It is worth mentioning that, in a transformation phase, only attributes x are transformed, the class part of input vector y is unchanged. Therefore, even though the data were pre-processed using the L transformation, we still can use the original SOM algorithm.

3 Results

Performance of the SOM+DML method was compared to the SOM model on six real data sets. As an accuracy measure we take the percentage of incorrect classifications. It is worth mentioning that getting the highest number of correct classifications is not the goal of this paper. Data sets are described in Table 1. Sets 'Wine', 'Ionosphere', 'Iris', 'Isolet', 'Digits' are sets from the 'UCI Machine Learing Repository' [2], set 'Faces' are from the 'The ORL Database of Faces'[3].

Now we briefly introduce the origin of the sets. Data sets 'Wine', 'Ionosphere', 'Iris' are classic benchmark sets, often used in testing newly developed classification algorithms. 'Isolet' data set represents a spoken letter recognition task.

---

[2] http://archive.ics.uci.edu/ml/

[3] http://www.cl.cam.ac.uk/research/dtg/attarchive/facedatabase.html

Its samples correspond to 26 letters of the alphabet. The original number of attributes (617) was projected by PCA to 100 principal components, which covers 93% of its variance. 'Digits' data set represents a handwritten digit recognition problem. The samples are from 10 classes obtained from 43 people. Original images were 32x32 bitmaps downsampled to 64 attributes by creators. The face recognition task is presented by data set 'Faces'. It contains images of faces obtained from 40 people (40 classes). For each person 10 images were taken in different times, varying lightening, changing facial expressions and details. The original data - 92x112 pixels images in 256 gray levels was projected by PCA to 50 leading components (83% of variance), the so-called egienfaces method[15]. Each data set, if not originally divided to train/test subsets, was randomly divided by us - 70% of data to training subset and 30% to testing subset.

Table 1. Description of data sets used to test performance of the LASSO+DML method and parameters of networks. The number of nearest neighbour in the LMNN was set by cross validation. (*) In 'Isolet' and 'Faces' data sets, the number of attributes was reduced with PCA.

	Wine	Ionosphere	Iris	Isolet	Digits	Faces
Train examples	126	246	105	6238	3823	280
Test examples	52	105	45	1559	1797	120
Attributes	13	34	4	100*	64	50*
Classes	3	2	3	26	10	40
Runs	100	100	100	20	20	20
Net size	4x4	6x6	6x6	20x20	20x20	20x20
k in LMNN	2	5	1	4	3	3

For each data set, we arbitrarily chose the network size (selecting optimal network size is not in the scope of this paper). The network size for the SOM and the SOM+DML models was equal. For all data sets, the following values of the learning parameters were used: $\mu_0 = 0.01$, $\lambda = 0.005$, $\alpha = 0.1$. For each data set a number of k target neighbours in the LMNN algorithm was selected using cross validation with ten times repetition. Fig.1 presents results of a selecting the target neighbours parameter (k) for all sets. Resulting k values are shown in Table 1. SOM weights were initialized with random numbers drawn from a normal distribution with mean 0 and standard deviation 0.5. Several runs were performed for each data set (see Table 1), so that local minimums were avoided. The final result is a mean over runs. The SOM and the SOM+DML models were trained with identical number of iterations.

The comparison of results obtained by the SOM and the SOM+DML method is presented in Table 2. With one exception the SOM+DML method achieves lower error rates in both training and testing subsets. On the 'Iris' data set the LMNN algorithm seems to cause the overfitting effect. It is clearly visible in Fig.1 during search for the k parameter. The greatest improvement was achieved on

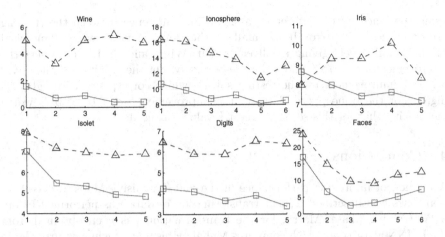

Fig. 1. Searching for optimal number of target neighbours in the LMNN method for all data set. On the x-axis there is k number of target neighbours, on the y-axis is percent of incorrect classification. Triangles with dashed lines represent test error and squares with solid lines illustrate a train error.

Table 2. Percent of incorrect classification on training and testing subsets for the SOM and the SOM+DML method. Results are means over all runs.

	Wine		Ionosphere		Iris		Isolet		Digits		Faces	
	Train	Test	Train	Test	Train	Test	Train	Test	Train	Test	Train	Test
SOM	4.66	5.31	16.26	18.10	9.14	**7.78**	7.90	9.20	6.89	8.84	26.84	32.75
SOM+DML	**1.05**	**3.56**	**8.13**	**11.43**	8.76	8.44	**5.32**	**7.31**	**3.86**	**6.16**	**4.52**	**11.88**

Fig. 2. Example of pictures from the 'Faces' data set classified as the same person by (a) the SOM model and by (b) the SOM+DML model

the 'Faces' set (20.87% over the SOM model). The comparison of example face pictures classified as belonging to the same class by the SOM method and the SOM+DML method is presented in the Fig.2. For the SOM+DML method, when using the 'Faces' set we observed a significant difference between the training error and the testing error. It is a small set, therefore the metric was well matched to the training set, giving small error. On 'Wine' and 'Isolet' data sets the improvement was 1.75% and 1.89% respectively. On the 'Digits' set there was a 2.68% improvement on the testing subset, which corresponds to roughly 50 digits. For the 'Ionosphere' data set the improvement was 6.67%. It is worth mentioning that for this set the largest k value was used.

4   Conclusions

A method of improving performance of the Self-Organising Maps in classification tasks was described. Linear transformation of data was performed before SOM training phase. Matrix for the transformation has been obtained from the LMNN algorithm, which computes Mahalanobis matrix while assuring large margin separation between the points of different classes. We called our method SOM+DML. Testing of the method was demonstrated on several data sets, focused on recognition of: faces, handwritten digits and spoken letters. Test results confirm that the distance metric learning method improves the performance of the SOM network. Finding the optimal matrix for linear transformation plays a crucial role in obtaining improved results. Matlab implementation of the SOM+DML model is available from http://home.elka.pw.edu.pl/ pplonski/ som_dml .

References

1. Alahakoon, D., Halgamuge, S.K., Sirinivasan, B.: Dynamic Self Organizing Maps With Controlled Growth for Knowledge Discovery. IEEE Transactions on Neural Networks 11, 601–614 (2000)
2. Aly, S., Tsuruta, N., Taniguchi, R.: Face Recognition under Varying Illumination Using Mahalanobis Self-organizing Map. Artificial Life and Robotics 13(1), 298–301 (2008)
3. Bobrowski, L., Topczewska, M.: Improving the K-NN Classification with the Euclidean Distance Through Linear Data Transformations. In: Industrial Conference on Data Mining, pp. 23–32 (2004)
4. Dopazo, J., Carazo, J.M.: Phylogenetic reconstruction using an unsupervised growing neural network that adopts the topology of a phylogenetic tree. Journal of Molecular Evolution 44(2), 226–233 (1997)
5. Duch, W., Naud, A.: On Global Self-Organizing Maps. In: ESANN, pp. 91–96 (1996)
6. Fessant, F., Aknin, P., Oukhellou, L., Midenet, S.: Comparison of Supervised Self-Organizing Maps Using Euclidian or Mahalanobis Distance in Classification Context. In: Mira, J., Prieto, A.G. (eds.) IWANN 2001. LNCS, vol. 2084, pp. 637–644. Springer, Heidelberg (2001)
7. Goldberger, J., Roweis, S., Hinton, G., Salakhutdinov, R.: Neighbourhood components analysis. In: NIPS, pp. 513–520 (2005)
8. Jiang, F., Berry, H., Schoenauer, M.: The impact of network topology on self-organizing maps. In: GEC Summit, pp. 247–254 (2009)

9. Kłopotek, M.A., Pachecki, T.: Create Self-organizing Maps of Documents in a Distributed System. In: Intelligent Information Systems, Siedlce, pp. 315–320 (2010)
10. Kohonen, T.: Self-organized formation of topologically correct feature maps. Biological Cybernetics 43, 59–69 (1982)
11. Kohonen, T., Oja, E., Simula, O., Visa, A., Kangas, J.: Engineering applications of the self-organizing map. Proceedings of the IEEE 84(10), 1358–1384 (2002)
12. Kohonen, T., Xing, H.: Contextually Self-Organized Maps of Chinese Words. In: Laaksonen, J., Honkela, T. (eds.) WSOM 2011. LNCS, vol. 6731, pp. 16–29. Springer, Heidelberg (2011)
13. Midenet, S., Grumbach, A.: Learning Associations by Self-Organization: The LASSO model. Neurocomputing 6(3), 343–361 (1994)
14. Rauber, A., Tomsich, P., Merkl, D.: parSOM: A Parallel Implementation of the Self-Organizing Map Exploiting Cache Effects: Making the SOM Fit for Interactive High-Performance Data Analysis. In: International Joint Conference on Neural Networks, pp. 177–182 (2000)
15. Turk, M., Pentland, A.: Eigenfaces for recognition. Journal of Cognitive Neuroscience 3(1), 71–86 (1991)
16. Weinberger, K.Q., Blitzer, J., Saul, L.K.: Distance Metric Learning for Large Margin Nearest Neighbor Classification. In: NIPS, pp. 1473–1480 (2006)
17. Xing, E.P., Ng, A.Y., Jordan, M.I., Russell, S.J.: Distance Metric Learning with Application to Clustering with Side-Information. In: NIPS, pp. 505–512 (2002)

Robust Neural Network
for Novelty Detection on Data Streams

Andrzej Rusiecki

Wroclaw University of Technology, Wroclaw, Poland
andrzej.rusiecki@pwr.wroc.pl

Abstract. In the on-line data processing it is important to detect a
novelty as soon as it appears, because it may be a consequence of gross
errors or sudden change in the analysed system. In this paper we present
a framework of novelty detection, based on the robust neural network.
To detect novel patterns we compare responses of two autoregressive
neural networks. One of them is trained with a robust learning algorithm designed to remove the influence of outliers, while the other uses
simple training, based on the least squares error criterion. We present
also a simple and easy to use approach that adapts this technique to
data streams. Experiments conducted on data containing novelty and
outliers have shown promising performance of the new method, applied
to analyse temporal sequences.

1 Introduction

In a data stream, data points are observed sequentially, one by one. Novelty
and outlier detection may be considered as identification of unforeseen or ab-
normal phenomena embedded in a temporal sequence. Because such sequence
is increasing in time, the changes that might be detected may be the result of
model drift, as well as of gross errors. One of the approaches to outlier detection
is modelling data normality or, in a very few cases, abnormality. Such approach
is often known as novelty detection or novelty recognition [10]. In this paper we
present a method of novelty detection based on the neural network approach.
Our algorithm involves two types of neural networks: regular feedforward network and robust neural network, trained to minimise a non-quadratic criterion
function. The second type of network is designed to remove the influence that
outliers may have on a training process. Comparing the responses of such networks allows us to decide whether given observation is a novelty. Such models
has to be created on-line, based on the accumulated knowledge, brought by the
analysed time series.

Applying artificial neural networks to the problem of outlier detection is not
a new approach. Feedforward neural networks were proposed as a tool to detect
outliers in [8,13], and feedforward auto-associative networks were used in [20].
There are also approaches based on Hopfield networks [6], and RBF networks
[2]. Currently, the most common type of neural networks applied in the field
of outlier or novelty detection are self organising maps (SOM) [1,21,9,15]. Our

L. Rutkowski et al. (Eds.): ICAISC 2012, Part I, LNCS 7267, pp. 178–186, 2012.

approach is different because it involves a feedforward neural network trained with a method robust to outliers in a data set. This is why it may help not only in detecting changes but also in identifying outliers in data streams.

2   Algorithm Based on the Robust Neural Network

The idea of our algorithm is, in its basis, rather simple. We propose to apply two feedforward neural networks: one trained with a robust learning algorithm and one with the traditional backpropagation algorithm (preferably with one of its faster, second-order modifications such as conjugated gradients or Levenberg-Marquardt method). In the first case we minimise a robust error measure decreasing the influence of outliers to the training process. The second network builds a model based on the least squares method, and typical quadratic error criterion. One can assume that the network outputs should differ significantly for outlying input patterns. After a comparison is made, and the difference between two network responses is larger than a certain threshold, we can suspect that a given element is an outlier.

To make the network training process as fast as possible, we chose the simplest of the robust learning algorithms, so-called robust LMLS (*Least Mean Log Squares*) learning algorithm proposed by Liano in [12]. There are many other, more sophisticated robust learning methods, such as based on the Hampel's hyperbolic tangent as a new error criterion used by Chen and Jain [3], combined idea of the M-estimator with the annealing concept applying the annealing scheme [5], an error function based on robust tau-estimates [16], or an approach based on the MCD estimator [17].

2.1   Robust LMLS Learning Algorithm

The basic idea of this algorithm [12] is to replace the mean squared error with a new loss function, called Least Mean Log Squares (LMLS), to introduce a robust error measure. The LMLS function was given as:

$$\rho(r_i) = \log(1 + \frac{1}{2}r_i{}^2), \tag{1}$$

where r_i is an error for the i-th training pattern. For the loss function, the influence function is bounded and can be written as:

$$\psi(r_i) = \frac{r_i}{1 + \frac{1}{2}r_i{}^2}. \tag{2}$$

The influence function describes the influence that outliers can potentially have on the network training. One might say that the LMLS algorithm cuts off the training patterns with largest errors, so they are not taken into account during the training. Though, the method was originally proposed for the on-line learning type, it can be easily generalized to the batch learning, where the weights are updated after presentation of all training vectors. In this case, the network error in a certain epoch can be written as:

$$E(\boldsymbol{w}) = \sum_{k=1}^{N} \sum_{i=1}^{m} \log(1 + \frac{1}{2}r_{ki}^{2}(\boldsymbol{w})), \tag{3}$$

where $r_{ki} = (y_{ki}(\boldsymbol{w}) - t_{ki})$ is the error of i-th output for the k-th training set element, $\boldsymbol{w}$ is the vector of network weights and m is the number of network outputs. The network error criterion function defined by (3) can be easily used with one of the gradient learning algorithms. Similarly to other robust learning methods, we can apply a simple (and slow) gradient-descent learning algorithm or more sophisticated conjugate-gradient algorithm. A dedicated method similar to the Levenberg-Marquardt algorithm [7] was also proposed [18].

2.2   Novelty Detection Algorithm

We propose to create a novelty detection method based on two feedforward neural networks. Usually the feedforward networks applied to the problems of novelty detection are autoassociative neural trained to form an implicit model of the data. For such a network, the input variables are simultaneously the output variables, so the network builds a compressed model of the training data. Unlike the typical use of the autoassociative networks [8], where the data are stationary, for a data stream, the concept generating the data drifts with the time, due to changes in the environment [4]. This is why the simple strategy of identifying outliers as patterns that are poorly reconstructed by the network cannot be applied. Our approach then is to use two autoregressive networks (ANN) that are potentially able to capture also time dependencies.

Moreover, the problem of outliers is even more complicated for the data streams, because the new outlying observations may be the result of unwanted noise as well as the concept drift. In the first case they should be removed from the data, in the latter case they can inform about important changes in the system. This is why we propose the method that allows us identify data suspected to be novel in a data stream, without determining whether they are caused by gross errors or not. In our method, as mentioned above, two ANNs are used. One of them is the typical ANN trained to minimise the error given as:

$$E(\boldsymbol{w}) = \sum_{k=1}^{N} \sum_{i=1}^{m} r_{ki}^{2}(\boldsymbol{w}). \tag{4}$$

For this network, residua generated by each training pattern have proportional influence on the model built by the network. The second one is the network trained to minimise the LMLS-based error function, defined by (3). In this case the impact of the largest residua on the training process is reduced or even removed. After the ANNs were trained on a packet of data, they can be simulated to determine if we find some observations, for which the difference between networks outputs is above certain threshold. Such observations are signed as novel, in the sense that they deviate from the bulk of data used to form the model.

Certainly, this idea must be adopted to the streaming data type. Having limited resources, we'd like to make the method fast enough to assure on-line responses for a data stream. Besides, we assume, that the memory is also limited, so we cannot store all the growing data. Feedforward neural networks usually need much time to learn but the computation of their outputs is not very time-consuming. We've applied the Levenberg-Marquardt learning algorithm [7] to train the traditional network and the LMLS-dedicated algorithm [18] to train the network with robust LMLS criterion. These algorithms are considered to be the most effective in their class. Their memory requirements are larger than for the modifications of the steepest gradient algorithm but they are still limited and affordable.

Because the data are observed one by one in a data stream, it is impossible to use all of them as the training set. Besides, this would not address the issue of adaptation. This is why we need to use another strategy. Adapting the network weights after presentation of each pattern would be computationally expensive, so it should be better to train the networks once for a given period of time cycles, after gathering certain amount of new data. Our approach uses a time window of predefined length, which moves not continuously but rather with a discrete step, jumping from one position to another, to represent recently obtained data. The network weights are then updated only based on the observations from the time window, and they become still until we are ready to present a new window.

2.3 Algorithm Details

To define basic parameters of such approach, first of all we need to set a proper window length. If it is too short, we cannot teach the network properly and we do not incorporate in our model information of what is common and what might be a novelty in the data set. From the other side, when we set the length too large, the time for networks training may become too long. The second parameter to be predefined is the distance between the time windows. Since they do not have to cover all the incoming data, the new window can start a while after the last window passed. To take into account each incoming observation, we need to set the distance to zero. In such case every training pattern belongs to one and only one window and the network weights are updated after we accumulate an amount of data for a new window. This assumption was also made for our simulations.

When the networks weights are frozen, we can simulate both networks for the incoming patterns. If the output of the traditional ANN is significantly different from the output of the robust network, we can suspect the pattern to be a novelty. So, for each pattern we can calculate simple absolute difference given by:

$$D(x_i) = |y_{mse}(x_i) - y_{lmls}(x_i)|, \tag{5}$$

where $y_{mse}(x_i)$ is the output of the traditional ANN and $y_{lmls}(x_i)$ the output of the robust network for the i-th training pattern. If $D(x_i)$ is above a preset threshold, the novelty is detected. Finding a proper threshold parameter value seems to be rather difficult. We propose one approach, which is based on the standard deviation of differences between networks outputs. Hence, for a given time window size, we calculate cumulative standard deviation of the differences between network responses for each pattern. Then the threshold may be written as:

$$Tr = k * \text{Std}(|y_{mse}(x_i) - y_{lmls}(x_i)|), \qquad (6)$$

where constant k may be chosen in the wide range. The ROC curve presented in the next section may help in setting this parameter.

Then the whole algorithm may be written as follows:

1. Accumulate a training set from the data stream. The size of the set depends on the parameter *window length*.
2. Train the ANNs on the gathered data and simultaneously start accumulating a new training set .
3. For each incoming element of the data stream, calculate networks responses and the difference between networks outputs given by (5). If the distance is higher than a given threshold, sign the pattern as a novelty. When the training set is fully collected, go to step 2.

3   Simulation Results

In this short article we present only exemplary results of our experiments, demonstrating general performance of the proposed method. All the experiments were conducted for the simple autoregressive network structure with one input, one hidden layer of 15 neurons, and one output. The hidden neurons had sigmoid activation function, whereas the output neuron was linear. The network had a tap delay line of predefined length $l = 2$ on its input. This means that each network output value was predicted based on the 2 past values. We've examined also the algorithm behaviour for the different lengths of the delay line but the resulting ROC curves for $l = 5$ and $l = 10$ were very similar (even better) to that shown in the Figure 1, so the simplest solution with $l = 2$ was chosen. The window length was set to 400, and $k = 3$ for all the simulations. To train the networks, two learning algorithms were involved: the Levenberg-Marquardt method for the MSE network, and the dedicated algorithm [18] for the LMLS network.

3.1   Novelty Detection

The proposed algorithm was tested on the task of detecting novelty in a data stream generated from the following stochastic processes, proposed in [14]:

$$X_0(t) = \sin(\frac{40 * \pi}{N} * t) + \epsilon(t) \qquad (7)$$

$$X_1(t) = \sin(\frac{40 * \pi}{N} * t) + \epsilon(t) + e_1(t) \qquad (8)$$

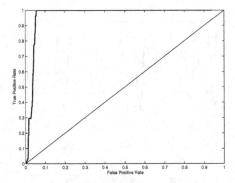

Fig. 1. The ROC curve generated for different thresholds Tr for the CSTR data set

$$X_2(t) = \sin(\frac{40 * \pi}{N} * t) + \epsilon(t) + e_1(t) + e_2(t), \tag{9}$$

where $t = 1 \ldots 1200$, $\epsilon(t)$ is an additive Gaussian noise $N(0,0.1)$, $e_1(t)$ and $e_2(t)$ are novel events simulated as:

$$e_1(t) = \begin{cases} n_1(t) & t \in [600, 620] \\ 0 & \text{otherwise} \end{cases} \tag{10}$$

where $n_1(t)$ has normal distribution $N(0, 0.5)$, and:

$$e_2(t) = \begin{cases} 0.4 * \sin(\frac{40\pi}{N}t) & t \in [820, 870] \\ 0 & \text{otherwise} \end{cases}. \tag{11}$$

Results of our experiments were presented in the figures. The upper curves are the signals X_0, X_1, and X_2, when the lower curves show results of novelty detection. Peaks on these curves correspond with positive detections.

In the Figure 2 we may observe how the method behaves for the signal X_0. We assumed that the signal didn't contain any novel points but for this case two randomly generated patterns were detected as novelty. In general case, this might be result of improper setting of the method sensitivity (in the term of threshold Tr) but here it illustrates that the noise $\epsilon(t)$ may also generate outlying points. For the signal given by (8) one may notice novelty detection peaks only in the region of interest (Figure 3). Unfortunately, the detection is not positive for each point in the novel region. However, in this region we have many patterns detected as novel, so the method works properly. In the case of signal X_2, containing two novel events (Figure 4) in both regions where novelty appear, our methods finds novelty. It is possible then to determine the beginning of the special event but it is not so easy to guess when it ends. This is because our algorithm is designed as an on-line method. If the method could analyse data also after some following patterns appear, it could potentially detect also the duration time of the novel event.

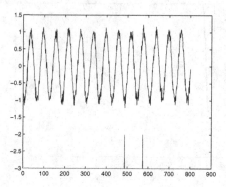

Fig. 2. Experimental results for the signal X0: false detection

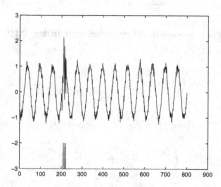

Fig. 3. Experimental results for the signal X1

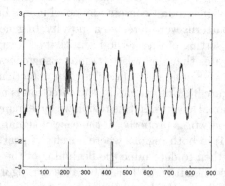

Fig. 4. Experimental results for the signal X2

3.2   Outlier Detection

To study the algorithm ability to detect single outliers in the data stream, we used high value outliers artificially injected into the data with error distribution $F N(0,10)$. The data was the Continuous Stirred Tank Reactor (CSTR) data set [19].

For the outlier detection task the situation is much better than for the novelty detection. As may be noticed in the Figure 5, almost each outlying point was properly identified. Only one false alarm was set for the point of sudden change in the temporal sequence, which might be actually considered as novelty.

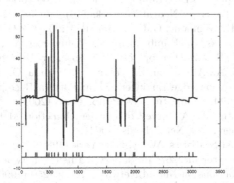

Fig. 5. Experimental results of outlier detection for the CSTR data set

4   Conclusion

In this paper we presented a new method of detecting novelty in data streams. The algorithm based on comparison of responses of two neural networks acts relatively well. As it was expected, it can detect some elements of the intervals, in which novelty appear. Moreover, it is able to detect single outliers that might appear in a data stream.

It can be successfully applied to the on-line data processing because it doesn't need information of the whole data to build a proper model. The main problem to be solved is the issue of setting proper algorithm parameters, such as time-window size, or a threshold of output differences. Future work should focus on building adaptive strategies to set these parameters. However, this method may be considered as simple, effective and easy to use approach to novelty detection.

References

1. Barreto, G.A., Aguayo, L.: Time Series Clustering for Anomaly Detection Using Competitive Neural Networks. In: Príncipe, J.C., Miikkulainen, R. (eds.) WSOM 2009. LNCS, vol. 5629, pp. 28–36. Springer, Heidelberg (2009)

2. Brotherton, T., Johnson, T., Chadderdon, G.: Classification and Novelty Detection using Linear Models and a Class Dependent - Elliptical Bassi Function Neural Network. In: Proc. of the International Conference on Neural Networks, Anchorage (1998)
3. Chen, D.S., Jain, R.C.: A robust back propagation learning algorithm for function approximation. IEEE Trans. on Neural Networks 5, 467–479 (1994)
4. Chu, F., Wang, Y., Zaniolo, C.: An Adaptive Learning Approach for Noisy Data Streams. In: Proc. of the 4th IEEE Int. Conf. on Data Mining, pp. 351–354 (2004)
5. Chuang, C., Su, S., Hsiao, C.: The Annealing Robust Backpropagation (ARBP) Learning Algorithm. IEEE Trans. on Neural Networks 11, 1067–1076 (2000)
6. Crook, P., Hayes, G.: A Robot Implementation of a Biologically Inspired Method for Novelty Detection. In: Proceedings of TIMR 2001, Manchester (2001)
7. Hagan, M.T., Menhaj, M.B.: Training Feedforward Networks with the Marquardt Algorithm. IEEE Trans. on Neural Networks 5(6), 989–993 (1994)
8. Hawkins, S., He, H., Williams, G.J., Baxter, R.A.: Outlier Detection Using Replicator Neural Networks. In: Kambayashi, Y., Winiwarter, W., Arikawa, M. (eds.) DaWaK 2002. LNCS, vol. 2454, pp. 170–180. Springer, Heidelberg (2002)
9. Himberg, J., Jussi, A., Alhoniemi, E., Vesanto, J., Simula, O.: The Self-Organizing Map as a Tool in Knowledge Engineering. In: Pattern Recognition in Soft Computing Paradigm, Soft Computing, WSP, pp. 38–65 (2001)
10. Hodge, V.J., Austin, J.: A Survey of Outlier Detection Methodologies. Kluwer Academic Publishers, The Netherlands (2004)
11. Huber, P.J.: Robust Statistics. Wiley, New York (1981)
12. Liano, K.: Robust error measure for supervised neural network learning with outliers. IEEE Transactions on Neural Networks 7, 246–250 (1996)
13. Liu, J., Gader, P.: Neural Networks with Enhanced Outlier Rejection Ability for Off-line Handwritten Word Recognition. Pattern Recognition 35(10), 2061–2071 (2002)
14. Ma, J., Perkins, S.: Online Novelty Detection on Temporal Sequences. In: Proc. of 9th ACM SIGKDD International Conference on Knowledge Discovery and Data Mining, Washington, D.C, pp. 613–618 (2003)
15. Marsland, S.: On-Line Novelty Detection Through Self-Organisation, with Application to Inspection Robotics, Ph.D. thesis, Faculty of Science and Engineering, University of Manchester, UK (2001)
16. Pernia-Espinoza, A.V., Ordieres-Mere, J.B., Martinez-de-Pison, F.J., Gonzalez-Marcos, A.: TAO-robust backpropagation learning algorithm. Neural Networks 18, 191–204 (2005)
17. Rusiecki, A.: Robust MCD-Based Backpropagation Learning Algorithm. In: Rutkowski, L., Tadeusiewicz, R., Zadeh, L.A., Zurada, J.M. (eds.) ICAISC 2008. LNCS (LNAI), vol. 5097, pp. 154–163. Springer, Heidelberg (2008)
18. Rusiecki, A.: Fast Robust Learning Algorithm Dedicated to LMLS Criterion. In: Rutkowski, L., Scherer, R., Tadeusiewicz, R., Zadeh, L.A., Zurada, J.M. (eds.) ICAISC 2010, Part II. LNCS, vol. 6114, pp. 96–103. Springer, Heidelberg (2010)
19. Seborg, D.E., et al.: WIE Process Dynamics and Control, 2nd edn. Wiley (2004)
20. Taylor, O., Addison, D.: Novelty Detection Using Neural Network Technology. In: Proceedings of the COMADEN Conference (2000)
21. Weekley, R.A., Goodrich, R.K., Cornman, L.B.: An Algorithm for Classification and Outlier Detection of Time-Series Data. Journal of Atmospheric and Oceanic Technology 27(1), 94–107 (2010)

Solving Differential Equations by Means of Feed-Forward Artificial Neural Networks

Marek Wojciechowski

Chair of Geotechnics and Engineering Structures,
Technical University of Łódź,
Al. Politechniki 6, Łódź, Poland
mwojc@p.lodz.pl

Abstract. A method for solving both, ordinary and partial, non-linear differential equations (DE) by means of the feed-forward artificial neural networks (ANN) is presented in this paper. Proposed approach consist in training ANN in such a way, that it approximates a function being a particular solution of DE and all its derivatives, up to the order of the equation. This is achieved by special construction of the cost function which contains informations about derivatives of the network. ANNs with sigmoidal activation functions in hidden nodes, thus infinitely differentiable, are considered in this paper. Illustrative examples of the solution of a non-linear DE are also presented.

Keywords: feed-forward neural networks, derivatives, differential equations.

1 Introduction

A significant effort in using feed-forward artificial neural networks (ANN) for solving both, ordinary and partial, differential equations (DE) has been made in recent years. Fundamental works in this area are those by Milligen [1] and Lagaris [2]. The common point of these works is the idea that ANN can approximate efficiently a solution of the DE subject to the given initial/boundary conditions (BCs), i.e. the problem of DE integration can be transformed to the ANN weights optimization problem. However there is an essential difference in the definition of the cost function being minimized during training in these works. In [1] the cost function is proposed to be a weighted sum of the errors generated by conditions describing DE and its BCs. This approach is followed in (just to mention recent works) [3–5]. The main advantage of this method is its generality - it is applicable in a straightforward way to almost any DE or system of DEs defined on arbitrarily shaped domain, subject to arbitrary set of initial/boundary conditions. However the BCs are never fulfilled exactly with this method (but the error magnitude at boundaries can be controlled). On the other hand in [2] the error function is constructed in such a way that BCs are always fulfilled

L. Rutkowski et al. (Eds.): ICAISC 2012, Part I, LNCS 7267, pp. 187–195, 2012.

exactly. This idea is extensively exploited in [6–8]. However the exactness of the BCs calculation is achieved at cost of loss of generality, i.e. the final shape of error function depends strongly on the domain dimension, boundary shape and DE and BCs formulation.

Though both approaches are showed to produce solutions of good quality (see introduction in [7]), the generality of the first method makes it much more promising (according to author's opinion). In this method, the quality of the solution depends on the following factors:

- number of hidden neurons in the artificial neural network,
- number and distribution of ANN training samples, i.e. collocation points representing the solution domain,
- weighting coefficients which are assigned to each component of the error function (DE and BCs),

The number of hidden neurons and the distribution of collocation points have to assure acceptable balance between the CPU time needed to train the model and the approximation quality. The proper choices generally are not known á priori. The similar problem appear however in other, say, hard computing DE solution methods. For example in finite element method we have to choose á priori the domain discretization density and shape functions degree. Then special, computationally intensive, techniques are used to refine meshes and/or increase the elements degree if necessary (method known as h-p refinement). When using ANN as the DE solver, the "refinement" is as easy as adding new neurons to the network and/or sampling new points from the domain and adding them to the training set. However, the proper choices for number of nodes and collocation points can be often reliably estimated also á priori (it depends on the problem being solved). Such assumption is present in most aforementioned papers. In [4] a stochastic (evolutionary programming) method is proposed to specify the number of neurons, and [5] presents a training algorithm which includes also number of nodes determination. The third factor influencing the quality of DE solution by ANN training are the weighting coefficients in cost function. They are responsible for keeping the balance between the errors generated by DE equation in the solution domain and errors in fulfilling boundary conditions.

In the following we present the formulas describing the layered neural network and its partial derivatives up to k-th order. We constrain ourselves to the case of three-layered neural network, but equivalent formulation is possible also for general feed-forward architectures (though this extension is far from trivial). In order to exploit gradient methods in neural network training the gradient of the ANN and also its derivatives with respect to the parameters (weights and biases) is needed. The necessary formulas are also provided. Then the general rules for the construction of cost function to be minimized in order to solve the given DE are showed. Finally two illustrative examples of solving second order nonlinear equation of cantilever beam are presented.

2   Neural Network and Its Derivatives

A special case of three-layered neural network with nonlinear activation functions in hidden nodes, identity inputs and single identity output can be represented by the following closed formula (following notation from [2]):

$$y = f(x_1, \ldots, x_n) = \sum_{j=1}^{m} v_j g_j \left(\sum_{i=1}^{n} w_{ji} x_i + b_j \right) \tag{1}$$

k-th partial derivative of the function realized by the network f can be computed also by means of the closed equation:

$$\frac{\partial^{k_1}}{\partial x_1^{k_1}} \frac{\partial^{k_2}}{\partial x_2^{k_2}} \cdots \frac{\partial^{k_n}}{\partial x_n^{k_n}} f = D f^{(k)} = \sum_{j=1}^{m} \left(v_j g_j^{(k)} P_j \right) \tag{2}$$

where $g_j^{(k)}$ is k-th derivative of g_j and:

$$k = \sum_{i=1}^{n} k_i, \qquad P_j = \prod_{l=1}^{n} w_{jl}^{k_l} \tag{3}$$

In [9] it is shown that this kind of networks can approximate simultaneously any continuous function f_0 and its derivatives. This approximation is arbitrarily well in the supremum norm, i.e.:

$$\left| \frac{\partial^{k_1}}{\partial x_1^{k_1}} \frac{\partial^{k_2}}{\partial x_2^{k_2}} \cdots \frac{\partial^{k_n}}{\partial x_n^{k_n}} f_0 - \sum_{j=1}^{m} \left(v_j g_j^{(k)} P_j \right) \right| < \varepsilon \tag{4}$$

if only the number of hidden units m is arbitrarily large. These approximation capabilities has been also proved for networks with two hidden layers [10] and can be extended to the general case of the feed-forward networks with nonlinear activation functions. The results are applicable for any finite input domain (not only for unitary hypercube).

In order to exploit Newton methods in ANN training a gradient of the function f and its derivatives with respect to weights and biases is needed. Let's represent the formula for network derivatives (2) in the following way:

$$h(v_j, b_j, w_{ji}) = \sum_{j=1}^{m} \left(v_j g_j^{(k)} P_j \right) \tag{5}$$

Then, gradient of h with respect to output weights v_j, biases b_j and input weights w_{ij} is given by formulas:

$$\frac{\partial h}{\partial v_j} = g_j^{(k)} P_j$$

$$\frac{\partial h}{\partial b_j} = v_j g_j^{(k+1)} P_j$$

$$\frac{\partial h}{\partial w_{ji}} = x_i v_j g_j^{(k+1)} P_j + v_j k_i w_{ji}^{k_i - 1} g_j^{(k)} Q_j \tag{6}$$

where:

$$Q_j = \prod_{l=1, l \neq i}^{n} w_{jl}^{k_l} \tag{7}$$

It's easy to observe that if $k = 0$ then $h \equiv f$ and the above equations represent the usual gradient of the network output with respect to network parameters. Thus the presented formulas can be viewed as a generalization of the standard three layer feed-forward neural network definition.

3   Cost Function

Let's take: $\mathbf{x} = [x_1, \ldots, x_n] \in \mathbb{D}^n$ as input vector of the network, $\mathbf{w} = [w_1, \ldots, w_p]$ - network parameters (weights and biases) and $f(\mathbf{x}, \mathbf{w}) : \mathbb{R}^n \to \mathbb{R}$ - function realized by neural network. The quality of ANN approximation is measured by the condition L which represents distance between f and the function being approximated f_0. This can be written as:

$$L = L(\mathbf{x}, f(\mathbf{x}, \mathbf{w})) = f(\mathbf{x}, \mathbf{w}) - f_0(\mathbf{x}) \tag{8}$$

Then, the most commonly used cost function in training feed forward neural networks is the integral of squared errors:

$$E = \frac{1}{2} \int_{\mathbb{D}^n} L^2 dx \tag{9}$$

Obviously, only discreet number of realizations of f_0 in domain $\mathbb{D}^n$ is usually available and the integral in the above equation becomes a sum over the known points.

For solving differential equations, a generalization of quality measurement is needed. Firstly we assume that the condition L can include also the derivatives of f. Secondly, a number of conditions is assumed to be satisfied simultaneously. This can be written as the following set of conditions:

$$L(\mathbf{x}, f(\mathbf{x}, \mathbf{w}), Df^{(1)}(\mathbf{x}, \mathbf{w}), \ldots, Df^{(k)}(\mathbf{x}, \mathbf{w})) = 0$$

$$B_1(\mathbf{x}, f(\mathbf{x}, \mathbf{w}), Df^{(1)}(\mathbf{x}, \mathbf{w}), \ldots, Df^{(k)}(\mathbf{x}, \mathbf{w})) = 0$$

$$\ldots$$

$$B_r(\mathbf{x}, f(\mathbf{x}, \mathbf{w}), Df^{(1)}(\mathbf{x}, \mathbf{w}), \ldots, Df^{(k)}(\mathbf{x}, \mathbf{w})) = 0 \tag{10}$$

where L can be viewed a partial differential equation and B can be interpreted as the initial/boundary conditions. Then the cost function to be minimized is written as:

$$E = \frac{1}{2} \left[\lambda_L \int_{\mathbb{D}^n} L^2 dx + \sum_{s=1}^{r} \left(\lambda_s \int_{\mathbb{C}_s^n} B_s^2 dx \right) \right] \tag{11}$$

where $\mathbb{D}^n$, $\mathbb{C}_s^n$ are domains of the DE and its BCs respectively and λ_L, λ_s are the given coefficients. This way we defined a problem of multi-objective optimization for training ANN. It is to note, that determination of parameters λ is beyond the scope of the paper. However, for the example presented below we have taken values which are inversely proportional to the number of points representing domains of the conditions involved in discreet version of (11). This choice seems to be reasonable for most applications.

It should be also noted that minimization of (11) can be performed by means of fast gradient optimization methods as we can calculate gradients of f and all its derivatives with respect to $\mathbf{w}$ components from equations (6).

4   Numerical Examples

4.1   Cantilever Beam 1D

Let's consider a cantilever beam of the length l and cross section characterized by stiffness EJ. Beam is fixed at one end and loaded by vertical force P at the second tip. Differential equation of such a beam, where the unknown function is the rotation angle of the section θ, is given by:

$$\theta'' + \alpha \cos(\theta) = 0, \quad \theta(0) = 0, \quad \theta(1)' = 0 \tag{12}$$

Function θ depends on the non-dimensional length variable $\xi \in \langle 0, 1 \rangle$, i.e. $\theta = \theta(\xi)$, and the coefficient $\alpha = \frac{Pl^2}{EJ}$. For large values of α this equation is highly nonlinear.

In our approach, the unknown θ is represented by artificial neural network. Let's write then the conditions for training ANN:

$$\begin{aligned}
L(\xi, \mathbf{w}) &= D\theta^{(2)}(\xi, \mathbf{w}) + \alpha \cos(\theta(\xi, \mathbf{w})) = 0, \quad \xi \in \langle 0, 1 \rangle \\
B_1(\xi, \mathbf{w}) &= \theta(\xi, \mathbf{w}) = 0, \quad \xi \in \{0\} \\
B_2(\xi, \mathbf{w}) &= D\theta^{(1)}(\xi, \mathbf{w}) = 0, \quad \xi \in \{1\}
\end{aligned} \tag{13}$$

In order to train the network we have chosen 10 regularly distributed points in $\xi \in \langle 0, 1 \rangle$. Condition L have to be satisfied at all points, B_1 and B_2 at single points $\xi = 0$ and $\xi = 1$ respectively. Coefficients λ in (11) were chosen as $\lambda_L = 0.1$ and $\lambda_1 = \lambda_2 = 1$.

Network training was performed by means of the open source **ffnet** software [11] with use of the truncated Newton method ([12]). Standard sigmoid activation function was used at hidden nodes of the network. It's worth to cite here the training script used for the considered example:

```
from deffnet.desolver import DESolver
from numpy import linspace

class Cantilever(DESolver):
    functions = 'F'
    variables = 'x'
    equations = \
```

```
"""
dFxx + 3.*cos(F) = 0 : domain
F = 0                : bcdomain1
dFx = 0              : bcdomain2
"""
domain = linspace(0, 1, 10)
bcdomain1 = [0]
bcdomain2 = [1]

cantilever = Cantilever(6)
cantilever.train(maxfun = 5000)
```

After running this script circa 300-500 calls of cost function (and gradient evaluations with respect to weights) is needed to reach the value of the error at the level 10^{-6}. In this example a network of architecture 1-6-1 was used. The results generated for $\alpha = 3$ are shown on Figure 1. It is to note that derivatives of this solution can be also easily provided by the network.

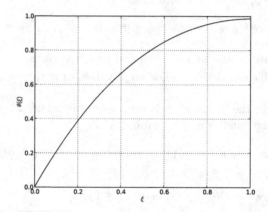

Fig. 1. Solution of equation (12) for $\alpha = 3$ obtained with ANN of the architecture 1-6-1. This result is in exact agreement with solutions found in literature (for example [13]).

4.2   Cantilever Beam 2D

Problem (12) can be easily extended to 2D case if we assume α is the additional variable in the differential equation. In the following we assumed $\alpha \in \langle 0, 10 \rangle$ and the solution domain (ξ, α) was represented by 200 regularly spaced points. The training script used here is very similar to the previous one and has the form:

```
from deffnet.desolver import DESolver
from deffnet.domains import Rectangular
from numpy linspace

R = Rectangular(p1=(0, 0), p2=(1, 10), \
                n1 = 10, n2 = 20)
```

```
class Cantilever(DESolver):
    functions = 'F'
    variables = 'xa'
    equations = \
    """
    dFxx + a*cos(F) = 0        : domain
    F = 0                      : bcdomain1
    dFx = 0                    : bcdomain2
    """
    domain = R.body()
    bcdomain1 = R.left()
    bcdomain2 = R.right()

cantilever = Cantilever(20)
cantilever.train(maxfun = 5000)
```

Solution for this 2-dimensional problem is obtained after c.a. 5000 calls of cost function and the final error value is of order 10^{-4}. Neural network of the architecture 2-20-1 was used in this example. The solution $\theta(\xi, \alpha)$ and its first derivative $\theta' = \frac{\partial \theta}{\partial \xi}$ are shown on Figures 2

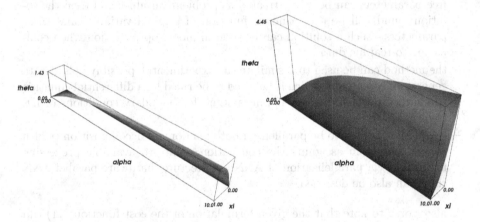

Fig. 2. Solution of the equation (12) for $\alpha \in \langle 0, 10 \rangle$ obtained with neural network of the architecture 2-20-1 (left) and its first derivative (right). Cross section of the solution at $\alpha = 3$ is shown on Figure 1.

5   Conclusions

Presented method allows to solve general ordinary and partial differential equations taking advantage of the approximation capabilities of feed-forward neural networks. Numerical examples indicate, that it is possible to obtain solutions of high accuracy with this approach. Dimension of the problem is handled simply by adjusting the number of input nodes of the neural network. The training scripts show practical flexibility of the method.

The main advantages which motivate further development in this area are:

- no mesh over domain is needed nor even the regularly spaced collocation points are necessary to look for the DE solution; moreover representation of the domain can vary during ANN training - this is as easy as adding/removing samples from training set;
- increasing the number of sampling points does not increase significantly the complexity of the solution;
- once network is trained it constitutes a *continuous*, differentiable approximation of the DE solution; this means that solution values can be accessed instantaneously at any point of the domain (in contrast to other commonly used methods where solution is known only at finite number of points and additional interpolation, post-processing techniques have to be used to cover the whole domain);
- increasing the problem dimensionality is as easy as adding new input neurons to the ANN - training procedures does not depend on the domain dimension;
- solution of the same DE problem, but with changed free parameters can be performed just by retraining the existing network - this saves computational time needed to find new solution;
- free parameters can be easily treated as problem variables and then the solution found will be a continuous function of original variables and these parameters - such a solution can be used in model optimization when comparing to real life data;
- the method can be used to assimilate the experimental, possibly noised data generated by a system which is believed to be ruled by a differential equation - in such a problem measured values stand for boundary conditions of DE (see e.g. [14]);
- the method is easy to be parallelized both via domain decomposition (which consist simply in assigning the collocation points to available processing units) and via parallelization of ANN architecture; hardware parallel ANN chips can also be designed.

It's also worth to note that the given formulation of the cost function (11) can be viewed as a generalization of the standard supervised NN learning. One can incorporate during training knowledge about derivatives of the dependence being trained (if known obviously). Moreover some components of (11) can serve as specialized *regularization terms* in training process. "Regularity" of the network derivatives (see Figure 2) indicates possible effectiveness of such approach.

Acknowledgments. The scientific research reported here has been carried out as a part of the Project "Innovative recourses and effective methods of safety improvement and durability of buildings and transport infrastructure in the sustainable development" at the Technical University of Łódź, Poland, financed by the European Union from the European Fund of Regional Development based on the Operational Program of the Innovative Economy.

References

1. van Milligen, B., Tribaldos, V., Jimnez, J.: Neural network differential equation and plasma equilibrium solver. Physical Review Letters 75(20), 3594–3597 (1995)
2. Lagaris, I.E., Likas, A., Fotiadis, D.I.: Artificial neural networks for solving ordinary and partial differential equations. Technical Report CS-UOI-GR 15-96 (May 1997)
3. Parisi, D., Mariani, M., Laborde, M.: Solving differential equations with unsupervised neural networks. Chemical Engineering and Processing 42(8-9), 715–721 (2003)
4. Tsoulos, I.G., Gavrilis, D., Glavas, E.: Solving differential equations with constructed neural networks. Neurocomputing 72(10-12), 2385–2391 (2009)
5. Shirvany, Y., Hayati, M., Moradian, R.: Multilayer perceptron neural networks with novel unsupervised training method for numerical solution of the partial differential equations. Applied Soft Computing 9(1), 20–29 (2009)
6. Malek, A., Beidokhti, R.S.: Numerical solution for high order differential equations using a hybrid neural networkoptimization method. Applied Mathematics and Computation 183(1), 260–271 (2006)
7. Beidokhti, R.S., Malek, A.: Solving initial-boundary value problems for systems of partial differential equations using neural networks and optimization techniques. Journal of the Franklin Institute 346(9), 898–913 (2009)
8. Effati, S., Pakdaman, M.: Artificial neural network approach for solving fuzzy differential equations. Information Sciences 180(8), 1434–1457 (2010)
9. Hornik, K., Stinchcombe, M., White, H.: Universal approximation of an unknown mapping and its derivatives using multilayer feedforward networks. Neural Networks 3, 551–560 (1990)
10. Blum, E., Li, L.: Approximation theory and feedforward networks. Neural Networks 4(4), 511–515 (1991)
11. Wojciechowski, M.: Feed-forward neural network for python (2007), http://ffnet.sourceforge.net
12. Nash, S.: A survey of truncated-Newton methods. Journal of Computational and Applied Mathematics 124(1-2), 45–59 (2000)
13. Wang, J., Chen, J., Liao, S.: An explicit solution of the large deformation of a cantilever beam under point load at the free tip. J. Comput. Appl. Math. 212(2), 320–330 (2008)
14. Liaqat, A., Fukuhara, M., Takeda, T.: Application of neural network collocation method to data assimilation. Computer Physics Communications 141(3), 350–364 (2001)

Practical Application of Artificial Neural Networks in Designing Parameters of Steel Heat Treatment Processes

Emilia Wołowiec and Piotr Kula

Technical University of Lodz,
Institute of Materials Science and Engineering,
Stefanowski St. 1/15, 90-924 Lodz, Poland
emilia.wolowiec@p.lodz.pl
http://iim.p.lodz.pl

Abstract. The article is dedicated to the possibilities of practical application of artificial neural networks in designing parameters of steel vacuum carburization processes and preparing for cooling in high-pressure gas. In the following sections, the nature of vacuum carburization technology, the course of research on the precipitation phenomena, the construction of an artificial neural network and the algorithm of searching process parameters have been presented.

Keywords: prediction model, neural network, vacuum carburizing.

1 Introduction

Vacuum carburization differs from conventional carburization in its high coal-bearing potential, which gives actual opportunities of shortening the duration and reducing costs of the entire process. However, as opposed to gas carburization, vacuum carburization is a much more complex process, which makes treatment with the use of this method more difficult to control, and hence, enforces more intensified control over the whole technological process. For this reason, conducting processes in the atmosphere carbon potential similar to maximum concentration of carbon in austenite is connected with the necessity of using tools to control the course of the process.

Effective vacuum carburization processes and obtaining repetitive carburized layers require maintaining constant control over the process and the possibilities of assessing output parameters of processed steel elements as early as during the stage of carburization process designing. Therefore, the tools for designing and simulation of thermal processing are becoming increasingly popular.

2 Current Model of Vacuum Carburizing of Steel

The effect of researches described in papers [5], [3] was a development of a mathematical model that supports vacuum carburizing technology. A computer

L. Rutkowski et al. (Eds.): ICAISC 2012, Part I, LNCS 7267, pp. 196–203, 2012.

program which based on the model allows designing carburization processes and hardening in high-pressure gas, as well as analyzing and optimization of processes without the necessity of conducting expensive test processes on real details. The development of the model and its capabilities have been described in articles [8], [9]. The algorithm of program is a combination of a mathematical and heuristic model based on gradual layer building with simultaneous preventing from the formation of carbides in the thermally improved material. An important assumption of the algorithm is the condition that carbon concentration in austenite during the process cannot exceed the value of marginal concentration.

Still, it needs to be remembered that its operation is limited by the complexity level of physical and chemical relations occurring in the material during processing. In other words, creating a mathematical model of the precipitation phenomena takes place with carbon levels exceeding the maximum value of carbon solubility in austenite is a difficult issue to be executed and hence enforces the use of far-reaching simplifications.

Applying the artificial intelligence method, in particular artificial neural networks, provides a real chance to by-pass this stage. The main objective of this method is prediction, i.e. forecasting results for the data included in the problem domain, but outside the set of learning cases. Artificial neural networks do not require any mathematical and physical equations, because during the learning process, based on empirical cases, they formulate the relations between phenomenon parameters independently. A correctly built network can map even very complex functions [7] and is easy to use (in practice, it builds the necessary model according to the examples presented) [1], [11]. Therefore, such a network can be used wherever there are problems connected with working out mathematical models, which provides an opportunity to construct models for barely known and examined phenomena and processes [2], [4], [10], [12].

3   Neural Model for Prediction of Heat Treating of Steel

The primary objective of the research was to create a model that would support vacuum carburization process designing. It was also important to include that in many cases, a user has very concrete and specific expectations concerning the carburized layer and needs parameters of the process that will result in the creation of the desired carbon profile in the surface layer of a detail. Therefore, creating a network which, based on the carburized layer criteria, would calculate the time of boost and diffusion segments of the process, necessary to obtain the expected material parameters, was another very important stage of the research.

It was assumed that a new network would be a part of the already existing application for simulation of vacuum carburization processes. The algorithm based on a neural network was worked out as an alternative method of process execution. The main concept principles were as follows:

1. The network-based algorithm creates a process comprised of one boost segment and one diffusion segment (heuristic algorithm calculates a process composed of many boost and diffusion segments).

2. The method allows for the occurrence carbide-forming phenomena during the process; however, provided that all carbides have dissolved by the time the process ends (so far, various methods have been based on conducting the process below the maximum solubility level of carbon in austenite, which somehow restricts such methods).

3.1   Building a Neural Network Structure

By analyzing experimental processes of vacuum carburization, the following parameters were considered significant: process temperature [K], boost segment time [s], diffusion segment time [s], chemical composition of the material, in particular percentage contents of alloy elements: C, Si, Mn, Cr, Ni, Mo, Al, V and Cu.

In order to prepare learning templates for the network, besides the said parameters, carbon boost on sample's surface [%], carbon content at the examined depth from sample's surface [%], content of carbides at the examined depth from sample's surface [%] and distance of the examined place from sample's surface [μm] were additionally archived.

Based on the research on carbon and carbide decomposition in the samples' carburized layer, 5500 templates were designed. Next, the templates were divided at random into learning, testing and validating sets in the following proportions: 70% learning templates, 15% testing templates, 15% validating templates.

When devising the neural network, it was noticed that the network should have extrapolating properties, i.e. it should correctly predict cases that are not contained in the learning set. The aforementioned assumption prevailed in support of MLP (Multi Layer Perceptron) because of its capabilities in this field (RBF type network did not cope well with data extrapolation).

Carburization process parameters and chemical composition of a thermally improved detail were set as input signals of the network: percentage concentration of carbon in the core (C), percentage concentration of: silicon (Si), manganese (Mn), chromium (Cr), nickel (Ni) and molybdenum (Mo) in the core, carburization process temperature [K] (Temp), distance from the surface of a spot, which is to be described by network output values, in μm (X), percentage concentration of carbon on the surface (Cp), percentage concentration of carbon in point X from the surface (Cx), percentage concentration of carbides in point X from the surface (MeC). Information describing percentage contents of aluminum, vanadium and copper were rejected due to a narrow scope of such data.

Output signals of the network represented segment times of the carburization process necessary for the material to obtain the desired parameters: boost segment time in seconds (Carb) and diffusion segment time in seconds (Diff). By creating training templates for the network, boost and diffusion segment times were given in seconds to ensure higher algorithm precision.

The next stage in the process of network construction was to determine the correct number of layers and neurons in the layers, as well as to choose correct activation functions. Based on the Kolmogorov and Cybenko theorems, it was assumed that one hidden layer would suffice to solve the problem.

Several dozens architectures with varied number of hidden neurons (it was arbitrarily assumed that there should be at least 10 and not more than 30 neurons) and characterized by different activation functions (linear, sigmoid, tangential and exponential functions) were tested.

Eventually, MLP type network was selected based on which provided the best responses. The network possessed 11 input neurons and 2 output neurons, and 22 hidden neurons (the network was called MLP 11-22-2). The figure (Fig. 1) presents a diagram of the above-presented neural networks that were examined. The network training stage was a very important element of building the neural

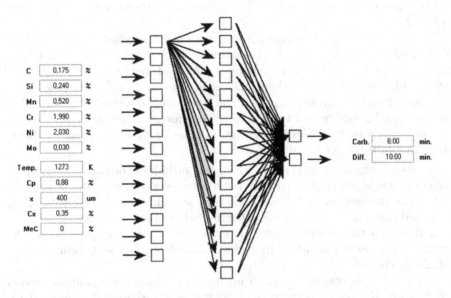

Fig. 1. Diagram of artificial neural network

network. It was extremely significant for the method and precision of network operation [6]. At the beginning of the training process, the neurons between individual layers were connected with one another.

Network weights were initialized with random values and later taught with the method of steepest ascent, BFGS (Broyden-Fletcher-Goldfarb-Shanno method) and conjugate gradients to determine the best method of learning for each network.

The BFGS algorithm turned out to be the best training method for the network selected. Detailed training parameters are presented in the table (Tab. 1).

Table 1. Summary of the neural network training process

Parameter	MLP 11-22-2
Input layer neurons count	11
Hidden layer neurons count	22
Output layer neurons count	2
Training method	BFGS
Training epochs count	850
Error function	Sum squares of differences function
Activation function (hidden layer)	Sigmoid function
Activation function (output layer)	Linear function

4   The Algorithm of Searching Process Parameters

A diagram of process searching based on the carburized layer criteria is presented in Fig. 2.

The first step of the algorithm is to answer a question whether a technologist plans a subcooling stage during the entire process. If yes, it means that after diffusion segment completion, carbon profile in the element will still be modified (by the subcooling segment), whereas the layer criteria entered are not the values after the diffusion segment completion, but final values obtained after the end of the entire cycle, together with subcooling. Therefore, it is necessary to calculate carbon profile after the diffusion segment. In order to do so, the already existing program tool is initiated, which:

1. Sets a multi-segment process, which also includes subcooling, after which carbon profile is compatible with the criteria set by a technologist.

2. Performs simulation of "boost/diffusion" segments omitting the subcooling stage and calculates carbon profile after the last segment of diffusion.

3. Based on the received profile, it measures carbon concentration on the surface (Cp) and in distance x from the surface (Cx), and sets them as input signals for the network.

4. The following values are given for network inputs: carburization process temperature [K] (Temp), percentage concentration of carbon on the surface (Cp), percentage concentration of carbon in point X (Cx), percentage concentration of carbides in point X (MeC), distance from detail's surface [μm] (X), percentage concentration of carbon in steel before carburization (C), percentage concentration of silicon in steel (Si), percentage concentration of manganese in steel (Mn), percentage concentration of chromium in steel (Cr), percentage concentration of nickel in steel (Ni), percentage concentration of molybdenum in steel (Mo).

5. After calculations, the network provides output times of the boost segment (marked as Carb [s]) and the diffusion segment (marked as Diff [s]).

If a technologist does not plan a subcooling stage during the process, it means that the layer criteria set in the program are the values after the diffusion segment completion. If such is the case, these values are given directly to network's inputs.

The last step of the algorithm is to visually present calculation results.

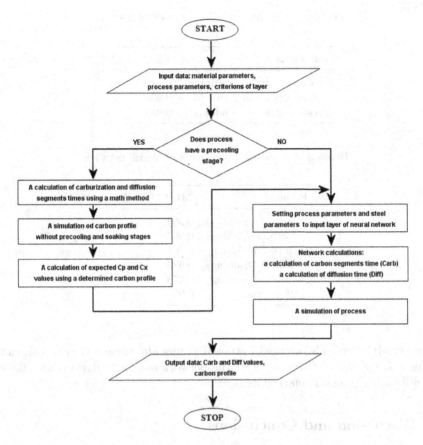

Fig. 2. The algorithm used to search vacuum carburization process parameters

5   The Analysis of Neural Networks Operation

The assessment of correct operation of neural network was based on quality and correlation coefficients, and on network prediction graphs.

Network quality is a linear correlation coefficient between actual theoretical values (calculated with the use of a model) and its value is presented in an interval [0,1]. In other words, the closer the network quality is to 1, the more the network's answers are closer to the answers expected.

Validation quality (Tab. 2) is usually lower than learning quality, because in this case the network answers to questions which it has not encountered before. Therefore, a greater validation mistake should not be worrying. In the table (Tab. 3), correlation coefficients for MLP 11-22-2 networks are presented. These coefficients are close to 1, hence we can draw a conclusion that there is a strong connection between the output values generated by the network and the

Table 2. Quality coefficients of neural network

Parameter	MLP 11-22-2
Network quality (training)	0.940
Network quality (testing)	0.939
Network quality (validation)	0.939

Table 3. Correlation coefficients of neural network

Parameter	MLP 11-22-2
Carb [s] (training)	0.904
Carb [s] (testing)	0.903
Carb [s] (validation)	0.901
Diff [s] (training)	0.980
Diff [s] (testing)	0.975
Diff [s] (validation)	0.977

actual (real) values. The network output that provides time of the carburization segment is marked as Carb, whereas the network output that provides time of the diffusion segment is marked as Diff.

6   Discussion and Conclusions

It needs to be underlined that the method of vacuum carburization by carbides and their dissolving makes it possible to obtain a carburized layer structure that is identical as in the case of the traditional method of carburization, i.e. the so-called multi-segment method performed in the atmosphere potential below the threshold of carbides precipitation. This conclusion is the reason and justification for further experiments over the method of shortening the time of the process by conducting it with potential above the margin of maximum solubility of carbon in austenite.

As a result of the experimental processes of vacuum carburization and material tests, the course of precipitation and dissolution of carbides in austenite (which take place during the process of vacuum carburization) and the influence of carburization process parameters on this phenomenon were analyzed. Moreover, an example of artificial neural network application in designing vacuum carburization processes in a practical aspect was presented.

With the help of a neural network, we can imitate the course of the vacuum carburization process taking into account the kinetics of forming and dissolving carbides without knowing the analytical equations of this phenomenon. Collecting a sufficient number of carbide layer measurements allows designing and training a one-direction MLP network capable of mapping the dynamics of carbide phenomena with arbitrary precision. However, it needs to be remembered that an application based on a set of neural networks provides greater certainty of receiving a correct result than an application based on a single neural network.

The method of vacuum carburization by carbides and their dissolving makes it possible to obtain a carburized layer structure that is identical as in the case of the traditional method of carburization, i.e. the so-called multi-segment method performed in the atmosphere potential below the threshold of carbides precipitation. At the moment, further tests and experiments are conducted with the aim of finding practical applications for this method.

Acknowledgment. The paper is issued in range of the project no 5216/B/T02/2010/39 financed by the Ministry of Science and Higher Education and Sciences.

References

1. Cader, L., Rutkowski, L.: Artificial Intelligence and Soft Computing. EXIT Academic Publishing House, Warsaw (2006) (in Polish)
2. Dobrzański, L., Trzaska, J.: Application of Neural Networks for Prediction of Critical Values of Temperatures and Time of the Supercooled Austenite Transformations. J. of Materials Processing Technology (155-156), 1950–1955 (2004)
3. Dybowski, K.: The Computing of Effective Carbon Diffusion Coefficient in Steels to a Process of Vacuum Carburizing Control. Ph.D. thesis, Technical University of Lodz (2005)
4. El-Kassas, E., Mackie, R., El-Sheikh, A.: Using Neural Networks in Cold-formed Steel Design. Computers and Structures 79, 1687–1696 (2001)
5. Górecki, M.: The Study of Deep Holes Surface Hardness using Vacuum Carburizing Method. Ph.D. thesis, Technical University of Lodz (2003)
6. Hagan, M., Demuth, H., Beale, M.: Neural Networks Design. PWS Publishing Company, Boston (1996)
7. Hornik, K., Stinchcombe, M., White, H.: Multi-layer Feed Forward Networks are Universal Approximations. Neural Networks 2(115), 359–366 (1989)
8. Kula, P., Olejnik, J., Kowalewski, J.: Smart Control System Optimizes Vacuum Carburizing Process. Industrial Heating 03, 99–102 (2003)
9. Kula, P., Pietrasik, R., Dybowski, K.: Vacuum Carburizing – Process Optimization. J. Mater. Process. Tech. (164-165), 876–881 (2005)
10. Rafiq, M., Bugmann, G., Easterbrook, D.: Neural Network Design for Engineering Applications. Computers and Structures 79, 1541–1552 (2001)
11. Tadeusiewicz, R.: Neural Networks. RM Academic Publishing House, Warsaw (1993) (in Polish)
12. Wang, S.: Neural Networks in Generalizing Expert Knowledge. Computers Ind. Engineering 32(1), 67–76 (1997)

Part II

Fuzzy Systems and Their Applications

A New Method for Dealing
with Unbalanced Linguistic Term Set

Łukasz Bartczuk, Piotr Dziwiński, and Janusz T. Starczewski

Department of Computer Engineering, Czestochowa University of Technology,
al. Armii Krajowej 36, 42-200 Czestochowa, Poland
{lukasz.bartczuk,piotr.dziwinski,janusz.starczewski}@kik.pcz.pl

Abstract. In this paper, a new method for dealing with an unbalanced linguistic term set is introduced. The proposed method is a modification of the 2-tuple linguistic model, in which we use a set of extended linguistic terms. The extended linguistic term is a pair that consists a linguistic label and a value of correction factor which describes the term shift relative to its position in an equidistant term set. This modification allows us to obtain the method that is computationally less expensive and give simpler semantics than method based on linguistic hierarchies.

1 Introduction

Modeling and solving of many real world problems may require processing of knowledge that often cannot be characterized in an exact and precise way because the available data are imprecise in nature, for example presented in a linguistic form. In order to process such data, we can use the computing with words methodology which has been a topic of many research during last years. It has its origin in Zadeh's papers [11–13] that presents concept of a linguistic variable.

The linguistic variable is a quadruple $<L, S, \Omega, M>$ in which L is a name of variable, S is a countable term set, Ω is an universe of discourse and M is a semantic rule. The semantic rule M is a function that associates each label in set S with its meaning which can be defined as a type 1 fuzzy set [7, 11–13], a type 2 fuzzy set[8–10], symbolic[1], 2-tuple[2–5]. The 2-tuple linguistic model proposed by Herrera and Martinez[2, 4, 5] is very interesting, but it can be used only when the linguistic terms are symmetrically and uniformly distributed. This kind of model is very simple to define; however, it may not be appropriate in some real world applications. For that reason, Herrera and Martinez extended their method to deal with unbalanced linguistic terms[3]. This algorithm, which is based on linguistic hierarchy [6], solves the mentioned problem but it is still a computationally expensive method that requires additional linguistic term sets.

In this paper, we would like to propose a new method to deal with an unbalanced linguistic term set. Our method is based on the 2-tuple model but we assume that linguistic term is represented as a pair that contains a linguistic label and a value of a correction factor which describes term shift relative to its

L. Rutkowski et al. (Eds.): ICAISC 2012, Part I, LNCS 7267, pp. 207–212, 2012.

position in an equidistant term set. The paper is organized as follows: the next section briefly describes the 2-tuple linguistic model, section 3. depicts proposed method for dealing with unbalanced linguistic term set, section 4. presents an illustrative example and the last section draws final conclusions.

2   A 2-Tuple Fuzzy Linguistic Representation Model

In the paper [4], Herrera and Martinez propose a simple but powerful and accurate linguistic representation model. In their model, linguistic information is represented by a pair (s, α) where $s \in S$ is a linguistic label and $\alpha \in [-0.5, 0.5)$ is a linguistic translation.

Definition 1 ([4]). *Let $S = \{s_0, \ldots, s_g\}$ be a linguistic term set and $\beta \in [0, g]$ a value representing the result of a symbolic aggregation, then the 2-tuple that expresses the equivalent information to β is obtained with following function:*

$$\Delta(\beta) = \begin{cases} s_i, & i = round(\beta) \\ \alpha = \beta - i, & \alpha \in [-0.5, 0.5) \end{cases} \tag{1}$$

where round($\cdot$) is the usual round operation, s_i has closest index label to "β", and "α" is the value of symbolic translation.

Proposition 1 ([4]). *Let $S = \{s_0, \ldots, s_g\}$ be a linguistic term set and (s_i, α) be a 2-tuple. There is always a Δ^{-1} function such that from a 2-tuple it returns its equivalent numerical value $\beta \in [0, g] \subset R$:*

$$\Delta^{-1}(s_i, \alpha) = i + \alpha = \beta \tag{2}$$

Herrera and Martinez also propose a basic set of operations on 2-tuples like negation, comparison and aggregation. The great advantage of their model is that linguistic information can be processed without loss of information. However, this is the case only when the linguistic terms meet condition described in [5] especially they must be symmetrically and uniformly distributed.

To deal with an unbalanced linguistic term set, they propose a method based on linguistic hierarchies (LH)[3, 6]. Linguistic hierachies method was originally developed to deal with multigranular linguistic term sets. In papers [2, 3], authors describe how to use LH to provide semantics to the terms in unbalanced term set. This method assigns the meaning to terms based on the meaning of corresponding terms included in additional equidistant term sets with the same or different granulation. The main disadvantage of the proposed method is its complexity and a high computational cost.

3   A New Method to Deal with an Unbalanced Linguistic Term Set

In this section we propose a new simple method for dealing with an unbalanced linguistic term set. We assume that every term in linguistic term set $\hat{S}$ is represented as a pair $\hat{s}_i = \{s_i, \gamma_i\}$ where s_i is a label for i^{th} linguistic term and γ_i is a correction factor $\gamma_i \in [-i, g] \subset R$. The correction factor describes term shift relative to its position in an equidistant term set with the same granularity. The linguistic term with the correction factor will be called an extended linguistic term. In order to preserve interpretability of the set of the extended terms every term must meet the following condition:

$$(i - 1) + \gamma_{i+1} < i + \gamma_i < (i + 1) + \gamma_{i+1} \tag{3}$$

which means that the correction factor cannot change the order of the terms. Graphically, the extended terms are represented in Fig. 1

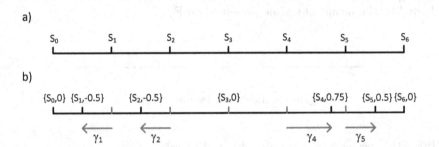

Fig. 1. Graphical presentation of the correction factor: a) an equidistant term set b) an unbalanced linguistic term set with marked shifts of terms in relation to their position in the equidistant term set

With the term set defined as above, the 2-tuple can be obtained from a numerical value by the following function:

$$\hat{\Delta}(\beta) = \begin{cases} \hat{s}_i, & i = \arg\min_i \left(|(\hat{s}_i + \gamma_i) - \beta| \right) \\ \alpha = \frac{\beta - (i + \gamma_i)}{d}, & \alpha \in [-0.5, 0.5) \end{cases} \tag{4}$$

where $\beta \in [0, g]$ is a value representing the result of a symbolic aggregation, $\hat{s}_i$ is an extended term, $\hat{s}_i \in \hat{S}$ and d is a distance between adjacent terms:

$$d = \begin{cases} (i + 1 + \gamma_{i+1}) - (i + \gamma_i) = 1 + \gamma_{i+1} - \gamma_i, & \text{when } \beta - i \geq 0 \\ (i + \gamma_i) - ((i - 1) + \gamma_{i-1}) = 1 + \gamma_i - \gamma_{i-1}, & \text{when } \beta - i < 0 \end{cases} \tag{5}$$

The inversion function can be defined as follows:

$$\hat{\Delta}^{-1}(\hat{s}_i, \alpha) = (i + \gamma_i) + d * \alpha \tag{6}$$

It should be noticed that when we have an equidistant term set then $\gamma = 0$ for all terms and our model reduces to 2-tuple model proposed by Herrera and Martinez. Because of the fact that all operators that operate on 2-tuples in fact are based on numerical values they can also be used with our model. For example, the arithmetic mean of 2-tuples is computed by the following function:

$$\overline{x}^e = \hat{\Delta}\left(\frac{1}{n}\sum_{i=1}^{n}\beta_i\right) = \hat{\Delta}\left(\frac{1}{n}\sum_{i=1}^{n}\hat{\Delta}^{-1}(\hat{s}_i, \alpha_i)\right) \tag{7}$$

4   An Illustrative Example

In order to illustrate the proposed method we use the same example like Herrera et al. [3]. Suppose a teacher wants to obtain a global evaluation of his students by taking into account the grades they received on different tests. Every test is evaluated by the means of a scale presented on Fig. 2.

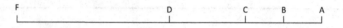

Fig. 2. Grading scale used in example

Table 1 shows exemplary results obtained by two students.

Table 1. Examplary results for two students

John Smith	D	C	B	C	C	C
Martina Johnson	A	D	D	C	B	A

In order to obtain global evaluation Herrera et al. define three additional equidistant term sets with 3, 5 and 9 terms respectively (Fig. 3(a)).

As the result of their algorithm, they obtain the following global evaluations:

$$\overline{x}^{JS} = (s_2, -0.08) \qquad \overline{x}^{MJ} = (s_2, 0.16)$$

The detailed description of this example and required computations is presented in paper [3].

Now, we solve the same task with our method. First, we have to define the set of the extended linguistic terms:

$$\hat{S} = \left\{F = \{s_0, 0\}, D = \{s_1, 1\}, C = \{s_2, 1\}, B = \{s_3, 0.5\}, A = \{s_4, 0\}\right\}$$

Graphical representations of this set of the extended terms and the corresponding equidistant term set are presented in Fig. 2(b).

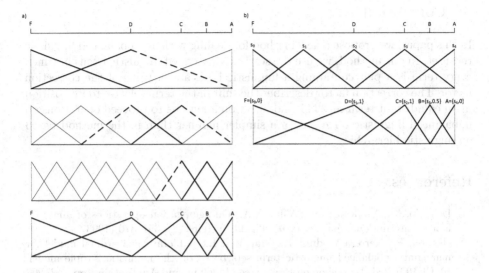

Fig. 3. The definition of semantic representation of terms in example a) based on linguistic hierarchies [3] b) based on the method proposed in this paper

Next we can compute global evaluations by applying the arithmetic mean operator (7) to data presented in Table 1, in the following manner:

$$\overline{x}^{JS} = \hat{\Delta}\left(\frac{1}{6}\left(\hat{\Delta}^{-1}(D) + 4 \cdot \hat{\Delta}^{-1}(C) + \hat{\Delta}^{-1}(B)\right)\right)$$

$$= \hat{\Delta}\left(\frac{1}{6}\left(2 + 3 + 3.5 + 3 + 3 + 3\right)\right) = \hat{\Delta}(2.92)$$

$$= \begin{cases} \arg\min_i\{2.92, 0.92, 0.08, 0.58, 1.08\} \\ (2.92 - 3)/1 \end{cases} = (\{\hat{s}_2, 1\}, -0.08)$$

$$= (C, -0.08)$$

$$\overline{x}^{MJ} = \hat{\Delta}\left(\frac{1}{6}\left(2 \cdot \hat{\Delta}^{-1}(A) + 2 \cdot \hat{\Delta}^{-1}(D) + \hat{\Delta}^{-1}(C) + \hat{\Delta}^{-1}(B)\right)\right)$$

$$= \hat{\Delta}\left(\frac{1}{6}\left(4 + 2 + 2 + 3 + 3.5 + 4\right)\right) = \hat{\Delta}(3.08)$$

$$= \begin{cases} \arg\min_i\{3.08, 1.08, 0.08, 0.42, 0.92\} \\ (3.08 - 3)/0.5 \end{cases} = (\{\hat{s}_2, 1\}, 0.16)$$

$$= (C, 0.16)$$

5   Conclusion

In this paper, we propose a new method for dealing with an unbalanced linguistic term set. In our method, we use the set of the extended linguistic terms in which every term is a pair containing a linguistic label and a value of the correction factor. The correction factor describes the shift of the term relative to its position in an equidistant term set. This modification allows us to proceed operations on unbalanced linguistic term sets in a simpler manner than in the method based on linguistic hierarchies.

References

1. Delgado, M., Verdegay, J.L., Vila, M.A.: On aggregation operations of linguistic labels. International Journal of Intelligent Systems (8), 351–370 (1993)
2. Herrera, F., Herrera-Viedma, E., Martinez, L.: A hierarchical ordinal model for managing unbalanced linguistic term sets based on the linguistic 2-tuple model. In: EUROFUSE Workshop on Preference Modelling and Applications, pp. 201–206 (2001)
3. Herrera, F., Herrera-Viedma, E., Martinez, L.: A fuzzy linguistic methodology to deal with unbalanced linguistic term set. IEEE Transactions on Fuzzy Systems 16(2), 354–370 (2008)
4. Herrera, F., Martinez, L.: A 2-tuple fuzzy linguistic representation model for computing with words. IEEE Transactions on Fuzzy Systems 8(6), 746–752 (2000)
5. Herrera, F., Martinez, L.: An approach for combining linguistic and numerical information based on 2-tuple fuzzy representation model in decision making. International Journal of Uncertainty, Fuzziness and Knowledge-Based Systems 8(5), 539–562 (2000)
6. Herrera, F., Martinez, L.: A model based on linguistic 2-tuples for dealing with multigranularity hierarchical linguistic contexts in multiexpert decision making. IEEE Transactions on Systems, Man and Cybernetics. Part B: Cybernetics 31(2), 227–234 (2001)
7. Klir, G.J., Yuan, B.: Fuzzy Sets and fuzzy logic: Theory and Applications. Prentice-Hall PTR (1995)
8. Mendel, J.M.: An architecture for making judgement using computing with words. International Journal of Applied Mathematics and Computer Science 12(3), 325–335 (2002)
9. Mendel, J.M.: Computing with words and its relationships with fuzzistics. Information Sciences 177(4), 988–1006 (2007)
10. Mendel, J.M., Wu, D.: Perceptual Computing: Aiding People in Making Subjective Judgments. IEEE Press Series on Computational Intelligence. John Wiley & Sons (2010)
11. Zadeh, L.A.: The concept of a linguistic variable and its applications to approximate reasoning. part I. Information Sciences (8), 199–249 (1975)
12. Zadeh, L.A.: The concept of a linguistic variable and its applications to approximate reasoning. part II. Information Sciences (8), 301–357 (1975)
13. Zadeh, L.A.: The concept of a linguistic variable and its applications to approximate reasoning, part III. Information Sciences (8), 43–80 (1975)

Fuzzy Clustering of Intuitionistic Fuzzy Data

Bohdan S. Butkiewicz

Warsaw University of Technology,
Nowowiejska 15/19, 00-665 Warsaw, Poland
B.Butkiewicz@ii.pw.edu.pl
http://www.ii.pw.edu.pl/english/index.html

Abstract. In the paper a new method of fuzzy clustering basing on fuzzy features is presented. Objects are described by set of features with intuitionistic fuzzy values. Generally, the method uses the concept of modified fuzzy c-means procedure applied to intuitionistic fuzzy data which describes the features. New distance measure between data and cluster centers is suggested. Some examples of clustering results are presented. The method is efficient and very fast.

Keywords: fuzzy c-means clustering, fuzzy intuitionistic data.

1 Introduction

In fuzzy clustering the limits between clusters are fuzzy and input data can belong to different clusters partially with different levels of membership. However, in many practical clustering problems the input data must be treated as fuzzy sets. Thus, in the paper, an approach to fuzzy clustering basing on intuitionistic fuzzy features is presented. Objects are described by set of features with intuitionistic fuzzy values. Generally, the method uses modified c-means procedure applied to such feature's data.

The applications of intuitionistic fuzzy sets in clustering problems begin for year 2004. Hung, Lee and Fuh [4], proposed the fuzzy clustering algorithm based on intuitionistic fuzzy relations. In years 2007-2008 were published some papers on fuzzy clustering of intuitionistic fuzzy data [5] [8] [9]. In [8] the novel variant of the FCM algorithm uses a distance metric based on a similarity measure to RGB color image clustering. In the paper [5] the clustering is based on intuitionistic fuzzy intersection is applied to computer vision problem. The paper [9] concerns application of intuitionistic fuzzy clustering to information retrieval from cultural databases. In the paper [13] the clustering algorithm is based on definition of association coefficients of intuitionistic fuzzy sets. Also interval-valued intuitionistic fuzzy sets were considered. The intuitionistic fuzzy hierarchical clustering algorithm was presented in [14]. In [15] Xu and Wu proposed intuitionistic fuzzy C-means clustering algorithms for intuitionistic fuzzy set and interval-valued intuitionistic fuzzy set, respectively. A novel intuitionistic fuzzy c-means color clustering on human cell images is proposed by Chaira [2]. The non-membership values are calculated from Sugeno's type intuitionistic

L. Rutkowski et al. (Eds.): ICAISC 2012, Part I, LNCS 7267, pp. 213–220, 2012.

fuzzy complement. In [12] identical similarity measure as in [8] was used as distance measure in cluster membership matrix. In [11] the concept of the α-level fuzzy relation was extended introducing the definition of (α, β)-level intuitionistic fuzzy relation. Next, the idea of intuitionistic fuzzy tolerance matrix was described and clustering algorithm based on this matrix was proposed.

In [1] the author suggested a modification of fuzzy c-means algorithm and applied this modification to clustering of fuzzy data. The idea is developed here for intuitionistic fuzzy data.

2   Fuzzy C-Means with Intuitionistic Fuzzy Data

Consider input data set $X = (x_1, ..., x_N)$ where any data x_i is described by a vector $F_i = (f_{i1}, ..., f_{iL})$ of fuzzy features f_{il}. Any feature f_{il} represents a linguistic variable. Let any linguistic variable be real numeric values. Thus, any feature is described by set of intuitionistic fuzzy sets with membership functions μ_{lk} and non-membership ν_{lk}. Let denote vector of membership by μ_l and non-membership by ν_l. In practical situations triangular or trapezoidal shapes of membership and non-membership functions are useful. Consider now a set $V = (V_1, ..., V_c)$ of fuzzy clusters. Let unknown centers of clusters be denoted by $v_1, ..., v_c$. Any data x_i can belong to any cluster V_j with unknown membership u_{ij}. The goal of the robust fuzzy c-means algorithm is to find optimal number of clusters and centers of clusters to minimize objective function $J(U, V)$.

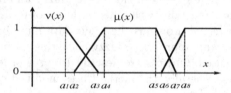

Fig. 1. Membership and non-membership functions for data

In the paper the following procedure, called IFCM, is proposed. Firstly, centers of intuitionistic fuzzy sets are found. Many methods are proposed in literature to find centers: association coefficients [13], maximum and minimum values of each feature [12], tolerance value [10][11], Sugeno type intuitionistic fuzzy complement [2], etc. Here some solutions were considered but very simple and reasonable procedure is applied for finding centers $x_{il} = (a_{1il} + a_{2il} + a_{3il} + a_{4il} + a_{5il} + a_{6il} + a_{7il} + a_{8il})/8$, where $a_{1il}..a_{8il}$ denote the characteristic values of l feature for element i.

Next, optimal positions of the centers of clusters are looking for. In FCM procedure the objective function is equal

$$J(U, V) = \sum_{i=1}^{N} \sum_{j=1}^{c} u_{ij}^m \, \rho[d(x_i, v_j)/\gamma] \qquad (1)$$

where $d(x_i, v_j)$ is the distance measure between data x_i and center v_j of the cluster V_j, γ is a scaling constant, and u_{ij} is the membership value of x_i in the cluster V_j. The function $\rho(x)$ is introduced in order to reduce the impact of outliers, placed very far away from the cluster centers. The procedure proposed by Kersten [6] [7] who modified RFCM algorithm of Choi and Krishnapuram [3] is considered here to apply. They proposed reduction of outliers using Huber function

$$\rho(x) = \begin{cases} x^2/2 & \text{if } |x| \le 1 \\ 1/|x| & \text{if } |x| > 1 \end{cases} \tag{2}$$

However, in the paper the author suggests a new, not conventional, form of function $\rho(x)$

$$\rho(x) = \begin{cases} x^2/2 & \text{if } |x| \le 1 \\ |x| - 1/2 & \text{if } |x| > 1 \end{cases} \tag{3}$$

The definition also reduce influence of outliers, but it seems more reasonable. The value of constant γ can be found experimentally or by calculating standard deviation or median. The choice of γ was not very critical. Next, the distance between center of any data and center of any cluster were calculated using definition of ρ

$$D(x_i, v_j) = \begin{cases} d_m^2(x_i, v_j)/2 & \text{if } d_m^2(x_i, v_j) \le 1 \quad \text{else} \\ d_m(x_i, v_j) - 1/2 \end{cases} \tag{4}$$

Thus, the value $D(x_i, v_j)$ divided by constant γ is put in (1). Now, the matrix of membership $[u_{ij}]$ of data x_i in the cluster c_j is updated in the following way

$$u_{ij} = \Big[\sum_{k=1}^{c} \Big(\frac{D(x_i, v_j)}{D(x_i, v_k)} \Big)^{1/(m-1)} \Big]^{-1} \tag{5}$$

New values of u_{ij} are normalized in all clusters to 1

$$u'_{ij} = \frac{u_{ij}}{\sum_{j=1}^{c} u_{ij}} \tag{6}$$

In the next step, using weighting function

$$w[d_m(x_i, v_j)] = \begin{cases} 1 & \text{if } 1/d_m(x_i, v_j) \le 1 \quad \text{else} \\ 1/d_m^2(x_i, v_j) \end{cases} \tag{7}$$

new centers of clusters are calculated as follows

$$v_j = \frac{\sum_{i=1}^{N} u_{ij}^m \, w[d_m(x_i, v_j)] x_i}{\sum_{i=1}^{N} u_{ij}^m \, w[d_m(x_i, v_j)]} \tag{8}$$

The center of cluster can be crisp or intuitionistic fuzzy. Fuzzy center is more interesting, because it may represent fuzziness of data belonging to the cluster.

All membership functions of the data have trapezoidal shape; therefore, new intuitionistic center is calculated as weighted mean

$$a_{2jl} = \frac{\sum_{i=1}^{N} u_{ij}\, a_{2il}}{\sum_{i=1}^{N} u_{ij}} \qquad a_{7jl} = \frac{\sum_{i=1}^{N} u_{ij}\, a_{7il}}{\sum_{i=1}^{N} u_{ij}} \tag{9}$$

The points a_{4jl}, a_{5jl}, where alpha-cut is equal to 1, are calculated in similar way. As a result it obtains trapezoidal shape of membership for cluster centers. Similar procedure is used for non-membership function

$$a_{1jl} = \frac{\sum_{i=1}^{N} u_{ij}\, a_{1il}}{\sum_{i=1}^{N} u_{ij}} \qquad a_{8jl} = \frac{\sum_{i=1}^{N} u_{ij}\, a_{0il}}{\sum_{i=1}^{N} u_{ij}} \tag{10}$$

and analogically for points a_{3jl}, a_{6jl}. It is not necessary to execute this procedure in every step. It will be sufficient to calculate intuitionistic centers at the end of clustering procedure.

FCM algorithm requires declaring maximal number of clusters c_{max}. During any iteration merging procedure can diminish the number of clusters if the distance between their centers is small. Several methods for merging procedure are proposed in literature. Here, merging criterion is based on concepts of variation, cardinality, and compactness. Variation σ_j of the cluster c_j is defined as weighted mean function of distance

$$\sigma_j = \sum_{i=1}^{N'} u_{ij} D(x_i, v_j) \tag{11}$$

Fuzzy cardinality is a measure of the cluster size and is equal

$$n_j = \sum_{i=1}^{N} u_{ij} \tag{12}$$

Compactness of the cluster is a ratio

$$\pi_j = \frac{\sum_{i=1}^{N} u_{ij}^{m} D(x_i, v_j)}{\sum_{i=1}^{N} u_{ij}^{m}} \tag{13}$$

Separation between two clusters c_j and c_k can be calculated using modified distance $d_m(x_i, v_j)$ between cluster centers v_j and v_k. Decision about merging two clusters is taken with help of validity index. Validity index is defined in [1] as ratio

$$\omega_{jk} = \frac{D(v_j, v_k)}{\sqrt{\pi_j \pi_k}} \tag{14}$$

During every iteration the validity index is calculated for any pair of clusters c_j, c_k and if $\omega_{jk} < \alpha$ then merging procedure is initiated. The value $\alpha = 1$

corresponds to situation when distance between clusters is equal to geometric mean of the cluster compactness. In practice the values in the range $[0.1, 0.35]$ work well. The center v_l of new cluster c_l is located in the weighted middle

$$v_l = \frac{v_j n_j + v_k n_k}{n_j + n_k} \tag{15}$$

Two old clusters are eliminated after merging and replaced by new cluster. After merging, the membership values are recalculated and the IFCM procedure repeats. Stop criterion is based on the change of membership values u_{ij} after each iteration. If maximal change is lower than threshold ϵ then procedure is stopped.

3   Simulation Experiments

In the paper input data have probabilistic nature. Every datum x_i is generated as two-dimensional vector of intuitionistic fuzzy trapezoidal sets (Fig. 1) $x_{il} = (a_{1il}..a_{8il})$ and $y_{il} = (b_{1il}..b_{8il})$ on the plain $(x, y) = 640 \times 480$ pixels. Probabilistic distributions for fuzzy parameters were used: triangular and trapezoidal. As a result we obtain a fuzzy value with two-dimensional membership function in the form of pyramid with top cut off.

First, the values a, b were generated with uniform $[0, 1]$ distribution. The values a_{i1}, b_{i1} with triangle density functions were generated using formula of the type:

if number of clusters $2 \le c \le 5$ then for $j := 1$ to c do begin
$a_2 := 10 + (j - 1)600/c + (300/c)(1 + sign\ sqr(a))$;
$b_2 := 10 + 220(1 + sign1\ sqr(b))$; end.

The values $sign$ and $sign1$ are equal to 1 or -1 and they were changed during generation to obtain axial symmetry of probability density. For circular distribution

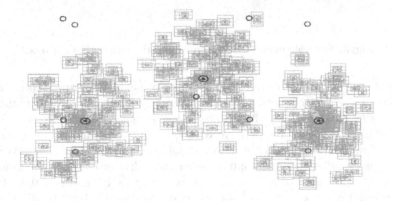

Fig. 2. Example of clustering of intuitionistic data with 3 clusters

uniform density was used for radius and angle. Other parameters of fuzzy numbers were obtained using formula

$$a_4 := a_2 + 4 + Random(5); \; a_5 := a_4 + 4 + Random(5); \; a_7 := a_5 + 4 + Random(5);$$
$$b_4 := b_2 + 3 + Random(5); \; b_5 := b_4 + 3 + Random(5); \; b_7 := a_5 + 3 + Random(5);$$
$$a_1 := a_2 - 4 - Random(5); \; a_3 := a_4 - 1 - Random(5); \; a_6 := a_5 + 1 + Random(5);$$
$$a_8 := a_7 + 1 + Random(5);$$
$$b_1 := b_2 - 3 - Random(5); \; b_3 := b_4 - 1 - Random(5); \; b_6 := b_5 + 1 + Random(5);$$
$$b_8 := b_7 + 1 + Random(5);$$

Every time 2% or 5% of data was generated as outliers with uniform distribution on the whole plain. Following values were used: number of data $N=300$, 500 or 1000, real number of clusters $c=1$, 2, 3, 4, maximal (start) value $c_{max}=4$, 5 or 6, $m=1.5$, $\gamma=0.1...1000$, $\alpha=0.2..0.3$, $\epsilon=0.005..0.01$. The size of clusters was identical. Some examples of results are presented. In Fig. 2 the holes represent successive centers of clusters during clustering and merging procedure. The initial number of clusters was chosen to 6. The starting points had random repartition on whole plane. Big circles with point in the center mark final position of cluster centers. The algorithm works very well and fast. In Fig. 4 an example of N=1000

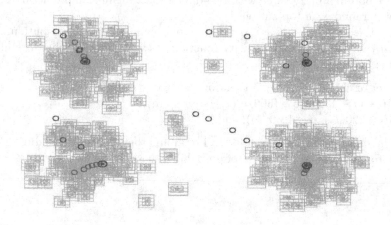

Fig. 3. Example of clustering of intuitionistic data with 4 clusters

data is shown. It can be seen, following circles presented in figure, representing successive centers of clusters, that after about 11 iterations initial number of 6 clusters are diminished to 3 clusters and centers are found correctly. More than 500 investigations were performed. The results were almost always correct despite of random repartition of data and initial cluster centers. The choice of parameters α and γ had some influence on the behavior of the procedure but not critical. The value of parameter m was chosen as 1.5 and $\epsilon = 0.01$. Only for very small values of $\epsilon < 0.001$ the procedure works long, but visualization of centers in any step permits to stop procedure and to find optimal value of ϵ in any conditions.

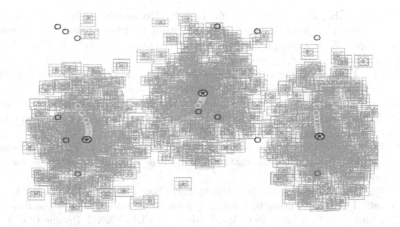

Fig. 4. Example of clustering of intuitionistic data with 4 clusters and N=1000

4 Conclusion

In the paper is presented a modification of conventional c-means clustering algorithm. New weighted distance measure is suggested. The method is applied to fuzzy intuitionistic input data. First, the data are defuzzified in order to calculate centers of data. During clustering procedure, crisp centers of the clusters are used. It facilitates and reduces time of the calculations. When final positions of the centers are found, the mean membership and non-membership are calculated for cluster centers. The method works well and fast. Moreover, many known modifications and improvements of conventional FCM algorithm can be applied to presented method. Existence of outliers does not disturb calculation and the results, because the weighted distance is used in the procedure. In the paper trapezoidal membership were chosen, but it can be replaced by other shapes as bell or Gaussian functions. In such case other procedure for defuzzification must be used. However, assumption about infinite support of membership functions are not realistic.

References

1. Butkiewicz, B.S.: Robust Fuzzy Clustering with Fuzzy Data. In: Szczepaniak, P.S., Kacprzyk, J., Niewiadomski, A. (eds.) AWIC 2005. LNCS (LNAI), vol. 3528, pp. 76–82. Springer, Heidelberg (2005)
2. Chaira, T.: A novel intuitionistic fuzzy c means color clustering on human cell images. IEEE (2009) 978-1-4244-5612-3/09/$26.00 ©2009
3. Choi, Y.: Kirishnapuram: Fuzzy and robust formulations of maximum-likelihood-based Gaussian mixture decomposition. In: Proc. Fifth IEEE Int. Conf. on Fuzzy Systems, New Orleans, LA, pp. 1899–1905 (1996)
4. Hung, W.-L., Lee, J.-S., Fuh, C.-D.: Fuzzy clustering based on intuitionistic fuzzy relations. Intern. Journal of Uncertainty, Fuzziness and Knowledge-Based Systems 12, 513–529 (2004)

5. Iakovidis, D.K., Pelekis, N., Kotsifakos, E.E., Kopanakis, I.: Intuitionistic Fuzzy Clustering with Applications in Computer Vision. In: Blanc-Talon, J., Bourennane, S., Philips, W., Popescu, D., Scheunders, P. (eds.) ACIVS 2008. LNCS, vol. 5259, pp. 764–774. Springer, Heidelberg (2008)
6. Kersten, P.: Fuzzy order statistics and their application to fuzzy clustering. IEEE Trans. Fuzzy Systems 7(6), 708–712 (1999)
7. Kersten, P., Lee, R., Verdi, J., Carvalho, R., Yankovich, S.: Segmenting SAR images using fuzzy clustering. In: Proc. 19th Int. Conf. of the North American Fuzzy Information Processing Society, pp. 105–108 (2000)
8. Pelekis, N., Iakovidis, D.K., Kotsifakos, E.E., Kopanakis, I.: Fuzzy clustering of intuitionistic fuzzy data. International Journal of Business Intelligence and Data Mining 3(1), 45–65 (2008)
9. Pelekis, N., Iakovidis, D.K., Kotsifakos, E.E., Karanikas, U., Kopanakis, I.: Intuitionistic Fuzzy Clustering to Information Retrieval from Cultural Databases. In: 22nd European Conf. on Operational Research, EURO XXII, Prague (2007)
10. Torra, V., Myamoto, S., Endo, Y., Ferrer, J.D.: On intuitionistic fuzzy clustering for its application to privacy. In: 2008 IEEE Int. Conf. on Fuzzy Systems, pp. 1042–1048 (2008)
11. Viattchenin, D.A.: An Outline for a New Approach to Clustering Based on Intuitionistic Fuzzy Relations. NIFS 16, 40–60 (2010)
12. Visalakshi, N.K., Thangavel, K., Parvathi, R.: An Intuitionistic Fuzzy Approach to Distributed Fuzzy Clustering. Int. Journ. of Computer Theory and Engineering 2(2), 1793–8201 (2010)
13. Xu, Z., Chen, J., Wu, J.: Clustering algorithm for intuitionistic fuzzy sets. Journal Information Sciences 178(19), 3775–3790 (2008)
14. Xu, Z.: Intuitionistic fuzzy hierarchical clustering algorithms. Journal of Systems Engineering and Electronics 20(1), 90–97 (2009)
15. Xu, Z., Wu, J.: Intuitionistic fuzzy C-means clustering algorithms. Journ. of Systems Engineering and Electronics 21(4), 580–590 (2010)

A New Method for Comparing Interval-Valued Intuitionistic Fuzzy Values

Ludmila Dymova, Pavel Sevastjanov, and Anna Tikhonenko

Institute of Comp. & Information Sci., Czestochowa University of Technology,
Dabrowskiego 73, 42-200 Czestochowa, Poland
sevast@icis.pcz.pl

Abstract. This paper presents a new approach to comparing interval-valued intuitionistic fuzzy values. The interval score and accuracy functions are used to build the "net profit" and "risk" local criteria. These criteria are aggregated in a generalized criterion taking into account their weights, which depend on the risk aversion of a decision maker. As opposed to the known methods, a new approach makes it possible to estimate the strength of relations between interval-valued intuitionistic fuzzy values. Using some numerical examples, it is shown that the proposed approach provides intuitively clear results.

Keywords: Interval-valued intuitionistic fuzzy value, Two-criteria method for comparison.

1 Introduction

Intuitionistic fuzzy set proposed by Atanassov [1], abbreviated here as $A - IFS$ (the reasons for this are presented in [6]), is one of the possible generalizations of Fuzzy Sets Theory and appears to be relevant and useful in some applications. The concept of $A - IFS$ is based on the simultaneous consideration of membership μ and non-membership ν of an element of a set to the set itself [1]. By definition $0 \leq \mu + \nu \leq 1$.

The most important applications of $A - IFS$ are the multiple criteria decision making ($MCDM$) problem [5,7] and group decision making problem [3,4] when the values of local criteria (attributes) of alternatives and/or their weights are intuitionistic fuzzy values ($IFVs$).

It seems quite natural that if local criteria used in the formulation of $MCDM$ problem are $IFVs$, then the resulting alternative's evaluation should be an IFV too. Therefore, there are many methods for aggregating of local criteria in $A - IFS$ setting proposed in the literature (see, e.g., [13,16,17]) which provide the final scores of alternatives in the form of $IFVs$. If the final scores of alternatives are presented by $IFVs$, the problem of comparison of such values arises. Therefore, the specific methods were developed to compare $IFVs$.

For this purpose, Chen and Tan [5] proposed to use the so-called score function $S(x) = \mu(x) - \nu(x)$, where x is IFV. Let a and b be $IFVs$. It is intuitively appealing that if $S(a) > S(b)$ then a should be greater (better) than b, but if $S(a) = S(b)$

L. Rutkowski et al. (Eds.): ICAISC 2012, Part I, LNCS 7267, pp. 221–228, 2012.

this does not always mean that a is equal to b. Therefore, Hong and Choi [7] introduced the so-called accuracy function $H(x) = \mu(x) + \nu(x)$ and showed that the relation between functions S and H is similar to the relation between mean and variance in statistics. Xu [14] used the functions S and H to construct order relations between any pair of intuitionistic fuzzy values as follows:

$$
\begin{aligned}
&If \, (\text{S(a)} > \text{S(b)}), \, then \, \text{b} \, is \, smaller \, than \, \text{a}; \\
&If \, (\text{S(a)} = \text{S(b)}), \, then \\
&(1) \, If \, (\, \text{H(a)=H(b)}), \, then \, \text{a=b}; \\
&(2) \, If \, (\text{H(a)} < \text{H(b)}) \, then \, \text{a} \, is \, smaller \, than \, \text{b}.
\end{aligned}
\tag{1}
$$

The method for $IFVs$ comparison based on the functions S and H seems to be intuitively obvious and this is its undeniable merit. On the other hand, as two different functions S and H are needed to compare $IFVs$, this method generally does not provide an appropriate technique for the estimation of an extent to which an IFV is greater/lesser than another one, whereas such information is usually important for a decision maker.

A more complicated problem is the comparison of interval-valued intuitionistic fuzzy values ($IVIFVs$). In this case, a similar (as in (1)) line of thinking can be adopted. For instance, Xu and Cai [15] proposed the score and the accuracy functions for $IVIFVs$ and applied them to compare two $IVIFVs$. Wang at al. [10] showed that due to the specific characteristics of intervals, the score and accuracy functions together sometimes cannot indicate the difference between two $IVIFVs$. In this case, it is necessary to examine the difference between two $IVIFVs$ using two additional functions.

The common limitation of these methods is that they are based on real-valued representations of the score, accuracy and hesitation degree functions of $IVIFVs$. Obviously, such a type reduction (from intervals to real values) leads inevitable to the loss of important information.

Therefore, in this paper, we propose a new two-criteria approach based on the interval-valued score and accuracy functions which is free of above mentioned limitations of known methods for $IVIFVs$ comparison.

For these reasons the rest of paper is set out as follows. In Section 2, we analyze the limitations of known approaches to $IFVs$ comparison based on the method (1) and describe our approach to comparing $IFVs$, which is free of these limitations. Section 3 is devoted to the presentation of two-criteria method to $IVIFVs$ comparison based on the interval-valued score and accuracy functions. Finally, the concluding section summarizes the paper.

2   Preliminaries

Let us start from analyzing the limitations of the known methods for $IFVs$ comparison based on the reasoning (1).

Let $A = \langle \mu_A, \nu_A \rangle$, $B = \langle \mu_B, \nu_B \rangle$ be $IFVs$. Then the score and accuracy functions for A and B are calculated as follows: $S_A = \mu_A - \nu_A$, $H_A = \mu_A + \nu_A$, $S_B = \mu_B - \nu_B$, $H_B = \mu_B + \nu_B$. A score function is usually treated as the "net membership". Therefore if A is a local criterion in a decision making problem, then S_A may be treated as the "net profit" providing by A. An accuracy function $H_A = \mu_A + \nu_A$ may be presented in its equivalent form $H_A = 1 - \pi_A$ where π_A is the hesitation degree or degree of uncertainty. Hence π_A may be treated as the degree of risk associated with the "net profit" S_A. Therefore the following thinking may be justified: the smaller is H_A, the greater is the hesitation π_A and, as a consequence, the smaller is A.

There are three important limitations of the method (1):

1). This method generally does not provide a technique for estimation of a degree to which an IFV is greater/lesser than another one, whereas such information is usually important for a decision maker.

2). The lack of continuity in comparison of $IFVs$ by this method.

Let us consider the following critical example. For two $IFVs$ $A = \langle 0.5, 0.3 \rangle$ and $B = \langle 0.4, 0.2 \rangle$ we obtain $S_A = 0.2$, $S_B = 0.2$, $H_A = 0.8$, $H_B = 0.6$. Since $S_A = S_B$ and $H_A > H_B$, using (1) we get $A > B$. Let us introduce a bit modification of B in this example: $B' = \langle 0.4, 0.1999 \rangle$. Then we obtain $S_A = 0.2$, $S_{B'} = 0.2001$. Since $S_A < S_{B'}$, taking into account (1) we are forced to conclude that $A < B'$, although the difference $S_{B'} - S_A = 0.0001$ which can serve as an argument in favor of $A < B'$ is negligible in comparison with the difference $H_A - H_{B'} = 0.2001$ which is the evidence for $A > B'$. Obviously, in the last case, it should be acknowledged that $A > B'$ if the accuracy function is not completely negligible local criterion for comparison of $IFVs$.

In our opinion, the shown problems with the method (1) are caused by the fact that when comparing $IFVs$, we deal with two local criteria: the "net profit" represented by the score function S and the "risk" criterion represented by the accuracy function H. From this point of view, we can see that in the method (1), the "risk" criterion is implicitly assumed to be of negligible importance, whereas the weight of this criterion depends on the risk aversion of a decision maker. Therefore, when comparing two alternatives represented by $IFVs$ A with $S_A = 0.2$, $H_A = 0.6$ and B with $S_B = 0.21$, $H_A = 0.39$, a decision maker may prefer an alternative A though it provides a bit lesser "net profit" than B, but with the considerably greater accuracy, i.e., with the considerably lesser "risk".

3). In the method (1), the implicitly introduced local "net profit" and "risk" criteria are not taken into account simultaneously, although in the decision making practice, a small value of "net profit" criterion may be compensated by the small value of "risk" criterion and so on.

Therefore, to avoid the above mentioned limitations of the known methods, we propose to formulate the problem of $IFVs$ comparison directly as a two-criteria task.

In a new method, the possibilities $P(A > B)$ and $P(A < B)$ are calculated to indicate what IFV is greater and to get a strength of inequality.

For two $IFVs$ A and B we denote $\Delta S = S_A - S_B$ and $\Delta H = H_A - H_B$ and introduce two functions $\mu_{\Delta S}(\Delta S)$ and $\mu_{\Delta H}(\Delta H)$ representing the local "net profit" and "risk" criteria, respectively.

These functions

$$\mu_{\Delta S}(\Delta S) = \frac{\Delta S + 2}{4}, \ \mu_{\Delta H}(\Delta H) = \frac{\Delta H + 2}{4} \tag{2}$$

are defined on the intervals $-2 \leq \Delta S \leq 2$ and $-2 \leq \Delta H \leq 2$.

There are many approaches to the aggregation of local criteria proposed in the literature. Since in our case we assume that a small value of local criterion based on $\Delta S = S_A - S_B$ may be partially compensated by a big value of the criterion based on $\Delta H = H_A - H_B$, the weighted sum seems to be the most suitable aggregating mode.

Then the possibilities $P(A > B)$ and $P(A < B)$ can be presented as aggregations of introduced local criteria:

$$P(A > B) = \alpha\mu_{\Delta S}(S_A - S_B) + (1 - \alpha)\mu_{\Delta H}(H_A - H_B),$$
$$P(B > A) = \alpha\mu_{\Delta S}(S_B - S_A) + (1 - \alpha)\mu_{\Delta H}(H_B - H_A), \tag{3}$$

where $0 \leq \alpha \leq 1$ is the weight which depends on the risk aversion of a decision maker.

The functions (2) and possibilities (3) are constructed in such a way that if $P(A > B) > P(B > A)$ then $A > B$ and

$$ST(A > B) = P(A > B) - P(B > A) \tag{4}$$

is the strength of this inequality.

It is easy to prove that the proposed approach to $IFVs$ comparison is free of limitations of known method (1) and provides the transitive quantitative assessments of a degree to which an IFV is greater/lesser than another one.

3   Two-Criteria Method for Comparing Interval-Valued Intuitionistic Fuzzy Values

In real-world applications, it may not be easy to identify exact values for membership and non-membership degrees of an element to a set. In such cases, a range of value may be a more appropriate measurement to present the vagueness. As such, Atanassov and Gargov [2] introduced the notion of interval-valued intuitionistic fuzzy set ($IVIFS$).

Definition 1 [2]. Let X be a non-empty set of universe. Then interval-valued intuitionistic fuzzy set $\tilde{A}$ in X is defined by the expression
$\tilde{A} = \left\{ \left\langle x, [\mu_{\tilde{A}}^L, \mu_{\tilde{A}}^U], [\nu_{\tilde{A}}^L, \nu_{\tilde{A}}^U] \right\rangle \right\}$, where $\mu_{\tilde{A}}^L, \mu_{\tilde{A}}^U$ and $\nu_{\tilde{A}}^L, \nu_{\tilde{A}}^U$ are the lower and upper bounds of interval membership and non-membership degrees, respectively, such that
$\mu_{\tilde{A}}^U + \nu_{\tilde{A}}^U \leq 1, \ 0 \leq \mu_{\tilde{A}}^L \leq \mu_{\tilde{A}}^U \leq 1, \ 0 \leq \nu_{\tilde{A}}^L \leq \nu_{\tilde{A}}^U \leq 1$. As it was shown in Introduction, to compare $IVIFVs$, the real valued representations of the score, accuracy and some other functions are usually used. Since such approaches are based on the type reduction from intervals to real values, they can lead to the loss of important information.

Therefore, to avoid a type reduction, here we shall use directly the interval arithmetic rules [8]. As the result, the interval-valued score and accuracy function are obtained as follows:

$$[S]_{\tilde{A}} = [\mu_{\tilde{A}}^L - \nu_{\tilde{A}}^U, \mu_{\tilde{A}}^U - \nu_{\tilde{A}}^L], \quad [H]_{\tilde{A}} = [\mu_{\tilde{A}}^L + \nu_{\tilde{A}}^L, \mu_{\tilde{A}}^U + \nu_{\tilde{A}}^U]. \tag{5}$$

As we deal with the interval-valued functions $[S]_{\tilde{A}}$ and $[H]_{\tilde{A}}$, the operation of interval comparison and the distance between intervals should be defined.

3.1 Interval Comparison

There are many methods for interval comparison proposed in the literature (see reviews in [9,11]). Generally, they provide similar results. This is not a surprising conclusion as Wang at al. [12] noted that "most of the proposed interval comparison methods are totally based on the midpoints of interval numbers".
Therefore, here we propose to use directly the operation of interval subtraction [8] to define the operation of interval comparison. So for intervals $A = [a^L, a^U]$ and $B = [b^L, b^U]$, the result of subtraction is the interval $C = A - B = [c^L, c^U]$; $c^L = a^L - b^U$, $c^U = a^U - b^L$. It is easy to see that in the case of overlapping intervals A and B, we always obtain a negative left bound of interval C and a positive right bound.
Therefore, to get a measure of distance between intervals which additionally indicates which interval is greater/lesser than another one, we propose here to use the following value:

$$\Delta_{A-B} = \frac{1}{2}\left((a^L - b^U) + (a^U - b^L)\right). \tag{6}$$

It is easy to prove that for intervals with common center, Δ_{A-B} is always equal to 0. Really, expression (6) may be rewritten as follows:

$$\Delta_{A-B} = \left(\frac{1}{2}(a^L + a^U) - \frac{1}{2}(b^U + b^L)\right). \tag{7}$$

The sign of Δ_{A-B} indicates which interval is greater/lesser and the values of $abs(\Delta_{A-B})$ may be treated as the distances between intervals.
It easy to see that the result of subtraction of intervals with common centers is an interval centered around 0. In the framework of interval analysis, such interval is treated as the interval 0. More strictly, if a is a real value, then 0 can be defined as $a - a$. Similarly, if A is an interval, then interval zero may be defined as the interval $A - A = [a^L - a^U, a^U - a^L]$ which is centered around 0. Therefore, the value of Δ_{A-B} equal to 0 for A and B having a common center may be treated as a real valued representation of interval zero.
Hence, we can say that the equality of intervals with a common center is an inherent property of interval arithmetic.
The reason for this is that such intervals may be linguistically interpreted as "near common center", i.e., they are equal ones at least in linguistic sense.

In addition, if we compare two $IVIFVs$ $\tilde{A}$ and $\tilde{B}$, then the interval score functions $[S]_{\tilde{A}}$, $[S]_{\tilde{B}}$ and the interval accuracy functions $[H]_{\tilde{A}}$, $[H]_{\tilde{B}}$ should be compared. Suppose $[H]_{\tilde{A}}$, $[H]_{\tilde{B}}$ are completely equal interval values, i.e., they have a common center and equal width, and $[S]_{\tilde{A}}$, $[S]_{\tilde{B}}$ have a common center and different widths. Therefore, we should compare only $[S]_{\tilde{A}}$ and $[S]_{\tilde{B}}$, and as they are "near common center", finally their widths should be compared. Suppose that the width of $[S]_{\tilde{A}}$ is greater that the width of $[S]_{\tilde{B}}$. Then only what we can say in this case, is that $[S]_{\tilde{A}}$ is a more uncertain representation of the common center than $[S]_{\tilde{B}}$. But we can not say that $\tilde{A} > \tilde{B}$ or $\tilde{A} < \tilde{B}$. Therefore, the proposition $\tilde{A} = \tilde{B}$ seems to be justified enough in such situations.

3.2   Comparing Interval-Valued Intuitionistic Fuzzy Values

Using described above methods for interval comparison and estimation of distance between intervals, we can obtain the method for comparing $IVIFVs$ as a direct interval extension of the method presented in the previous section.

Then for two $IVIFVs$ $\tilde{A}$ and $\tilde{B}$ we can obtain the interval-valued "net profit" and "risk" criteria as follows:

As the intervals $[S]_{\tilde{A}}$ and $[H]_{\tilde{A}}$ are defined by expressions (5), we get the interval "net profit" and "risk" criteria using the direct interval extension of expressions (2):

$$\mu_{\Delta S}\left([S]_{\tilde{A}} - [S_{\tilde{B}}]\right) = \frac{([S]_{\tilde{A}} - [S_{\tilde{B}}]) + 2}{4},$$

$$\mu_{\Delta H}\left([H]_{\tilde{A}} - [H_{\tilde{B}}]\right) = \frac{([H]_{\tilde{A}} - [H_{\tilde{B}}]) + 2}{4}. \tag{8}$$

Then for interval possibilities $[P(\tilde{A} > \tilde{B})]$ and $[P(\tilde{B} > \tilde{A})]$ from (3) we obtain:

$$[P(\tilde{A} > \tilde{B})] = \alpha\mu_{\Delta S}([S]_{\tilde{A}} - [S]_{\tilde{B}}) + (1 - \alpha)\mu_{\Delta H}([H]_{\tilde{A}} - [H]_{\tilde{B}}), \tag{9}$$

$$[P(\tilde{B} > \tilde{A})] = \alpha\mu_{\Delta S}([S]_{\tilde{B}} - [S]_{\tilde{A}}) + (1 - \alpha)\mu_{\Delta H}([H]_{\tilde{B}} - [H]_{\tilde{A}}). \tag{10}$$

The functions (8) and possibilities (9) and (10) are constructed in such a way that if $[P(\tilde{A} > \tilde{B})] > [P(\tilde{B} > \tilde{A})]$ in the interval sense, then $\tilde{A} > \tilde{B}$ and

$$[ST(\tilde{A} > \tilde{B})] = [P(\tilde{A} > \tilde{B})] - [P(\tilde{B} < \tilde{A})] \tag{11}$$

is the interval-valued strength of this relation.

The real-valued strength of relation can be obtained from (6) and (11) as follows:

$$ST_{\tilde{A} - \tilde{B}} = \frac{1}{2}\left((P(\tilde{A} > \tilde{B})^L - P(\tilde{B} > \tilde{A})^U) + (P(\tilde{A} < \tilde{B})^U - P(\tilde{B} < \tilde{A})^L)\right). \tag{12}$$

Let us consider some illustrative critical examples.

Example 1. Consider $\tilde{A} = \langle[0.1, 0.3], [0.2, 0.6]\rangle$ and $\tilde{B} = \langle[0.2, 0.3], [0.2, 0.4]\rangle$. To obtain an approximate real-valued estimation of the result of these $IVIFVs$

comparison we can use the centers of intervals. Then we obtain S_A=-0.2 and S_B=-0.05. Therefore, according to (1) we have (approximately) $\tilde{B} > \tilde{A}$. Using the rules of interval arithmetic, we get $[S]_{\tilde{A}}$ =[-0.5,0.1], $[S]_{\tilde{B}}$ =[-0.2,0.1], $[H]_{\tilde{A}}$ =[0.3,0.9], $[H]_{\tilde{B}}$ =[0.4,0.7] and $[\Delta S] = [S]_{\tilde{A}} - [S]_{\tilde{B}}$=[-0.6,0.3], $[\Delta H] = [H]_{\tilde{A}} - [H]_{\tilde{B}}$=[-0.4,0.5]. Substituting obtained $[\Delta S]$ and $[\Delta H]$ into (8) we have the result:

$\mu_{\Delta S} ([S]_{\tilde{A}} - [S_{\tilde{B}}])$=[0.35,0.575], $\mu_{\Delta H} ([H]_{\tilde{A}} - [H_{\tilde{B}}])$=[0.4,0.625] which is illustrated in Fig.1. Then assuming α=0.98, from (9) we obtain $[P(\tilde{A} > \tilde{B})]$=[0.351,

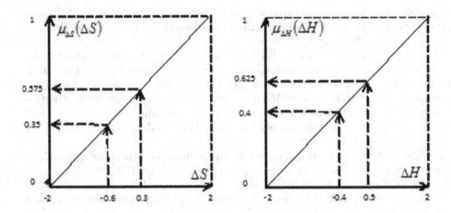

Fig. 1. Interval values of local criteria

0.576]. Similarly, from (10) we get $[P(\tilde{B} > \tilde{A})]$=[0.424,0.649]. Comparing these intervals using the method for interval comparison based on the difference Δ_{A-B}, presented in previous subsection, we obtain $\tilde{B} > \tilde{A}$.

Example 2. Consider $\tilde{A} = \langle [0.1, 0.3], [0.2, 0.6] \rangle$ and $\tilde{B} = \langle [0, 0.3], [0.2, 0.5] \rangle$. In this example, $[S]_{\tilde{A}} = [S]_{\tilde{B}}$=[-0.5,0.1], $[H]_{\tilde{A}}$=[0.3,0.9], $[H]_{\tilde{B}}$=[0.2,0.8]. Using the method for interval comparison described in the previous subsection, we obtain $[H]_{\tilde{A}} > [H]_{\tilde{B}}$ and therefore $\tilde{A} > \tilde{B}$. Finally, for α=0.98 we obtain $[P(\tilde{A} > \tilde{B})]$=[0.3505,0.6015], $[P(\tilde{B} > \tilde{A})]$=[0.3495,0.6005]. Then using the method for interval comparison based on the difference Δ_{A-B}, we get $\tilde{A} > \tilde{B}$ with strength of this relation $\tilde{A} > \tilde{B}$ equal to 0.002.

Summarizing, we can say that the proposed approach to $IVIFVs$ comparison provides intuitively clear results (see examples 1-2) and as opposed to the known methods, makes it possible to estimate the strength of relations between considered $IFVs$ and $IVIFVs$.

4   Conclusion

Two-criteria approach to comparing interval-valued intuitionistic fuzzy values is developed. The first local criterion named "net profit" is based on the interval-valued score function. The second local criterion named "risk" is based on the interval-valued accuracy function. These local criteria are aggregated into the generalized one taking into account the weights of considered local criteria dependent on the risk aversion of a decision maker. As opposed to the known methods, the developed approach makes it possible to estimate the strength of relations between compared interval-valued intuitionistic fuzzy values. Using some illustrative examples, it is shown that the proposed approach provides intuitively clear results.

References

1. Atanassov, K.: Intuitionistic fuzzy sets. Fuzzy Sets and Systems 20, 87–96 (1986)
2. Atanassov, K., Gargov, G.: Interval-valued intuitionistic fuzzy sets. Fuzzy Sets and Systems 31, 343–349 (1989)
3. Atanassov, K., Pasi, G., Yager, R.: Intuitionistic fuzzy interpretations of multi-person multicriteria decision making. In: Proc. of 2002 First International IEEE Symposium Intelligent Systems, vol. 1, pp. 115–119 (2002)
4. Atanassov, K., Pasi, G., Yager, R., Atanassova, V.: Intuitionistic fuzzy group interpretations of multi-person multi-criteria decision making. In: Proc. of the Third Conference of the European Society for Fuzzy Logic and Technology EUSFLAT 2003, Zittau, pp. 177–182 (2003)
5. Chen, S.M., Tan, J.M.: Handling multicriteria fuzzy decision-making problems based on vague set theory. Fuzzy Sets and Systems 67, 163–172 (1994)
6. Dubois, D., Gottwald, S., Hajek, P., Kacprzyk, J., Prade, H.: Terminological difficulties in fuzzy set theory-The case of "Intuitionistic Fuzzy Sets". Fuzzy Sets and Systems 156, 485–491 (2005)
7. Hong, D.H., Choi, C.-H.: Multicriteria fuzzy decision-making problems based on vague set theory. Fuzzy Sets and Systems 114, 103–113 (2000)
8. Moore, R.E.: Interval analysis. Prentice-Hall, Englewood Cliffs (1966)
9. Sevastjanov, P.: Numerical methods for interval and fuzzy number comparison based on the probabilistic approach and Dempster–Shafer theory. Information Sciences 177, 4645–4661 (2007)
10. Wang, Z., Li, K.W., Wang, W.: An approach to multiatribute decision making with interval valued intuitionistic fuzzy assessment and incomplete weights. Information Sciences 179, 3026–3040 (2009)
11. Wang, X., Kerre, E.E.: Reasonable properties for the ordering of fuzzy quantities (I) (II). Fuzzy Sets and Systems 112, 387–405 (2001)
12. Wang, Y.M., Yang, J.B., Xu, D.L.: A two-stage logarithmic goal programming method for generating weights from interval comparison matrices. Fuzzy Sets and Systems 152, 475–498 (2005)
13. Xu, Z.S.: Intuitionistic fuzzy aggregation operators. IEEE Transactions on Fuzzy Systems 15, 1179–1187 (2007)
14. Xu, Z.S.: Intuitionistic preference relations and their application in group decision making. Information Sciences 177, 2363–2379 (2007)
15. Xu, Z.S., Cai, X.Q.: Incomplete interval-valued intuitionistic preference relations. International Journal of General Systems 38, 871–886 (2009)
16. Xu, Z.S., Yager, R.R.: Some geometric aggregation operators based on intuitionistic fuzzy sets. International Journal of General Systems 35, 417–433 (2006)
17. Xu, Z.S., Yager, R.R.: Dynamic intuitionistic fuzzy multi-attribute decision making. International Journal of Approximate Reasoning 48, 246–262 (2008)

The Use of Belief Intervals in Operations on Intuitionistic Fuzzy Values

Ludmila Dymova, Pavel Sevastjanov, and Kamil Tkacz

Institute of Comp. & Information Sci., Czestochowa University of Technology,
Dabrowskiego 73, 42-200 Czestochowa, Poland
sevast@icis.pcz.pl

Abstract. This paper presents a critical analysis of conventional operations on intuitionistic fuzzy values ($IFVs$) and their applicability to the solution of multiple criteria decision making ($MCDM$) problems in the intuitionistic fuzzy setting. A set of operations on $IFVs$ based on the interpretation of intuitionistic fuzzy sets in the framework of the Dempster-Shafer theory of evidence (DST) is proposed and analyzed. This interpretation makes it possible to represent mathematical operations on $IFVs$ as operations on belief intervals. The corresponding method for aggregation of local criteria presented by $IFVs$ in the framework of DST is proposed and analyzed. The proposed approach allows us to solve $MCDM$ problems without intermediate defuzzification when not only criteria, but their weights are $IFVs$. The advantages of the proposed approach are illustrated by numerical examples.

Keywords: Intuitionistic fuzzy values, Belief intervals, Operations.

1 Introduction

Intuitionistic Fuzzy Set (A-IFS) proposed by Atanassov [1], is one of the possible generalizations of fuzzy sets theory and appears to be relevant and useful in some applications. The concept of A-IFS is based on the simultaneous consideration of membership μ and non-membership ν of an element of a set to the set itself [1]. By definition $0 \leq \mu + \nu \leq 1$. The most important applications of A-IFS is the decision making problem [4].

In [7], it is shown that there exists a strong link between A-IFS and the Dempster-Shafer Theory of evidence (DST). This link makes it possible to use directly the Dempster's rule of combination to aggregate local criteria presented by $IFVs$ in the $MCDM$ problem. The usefulness of the developed method was illustrated using the known example of $MCDM$ problem.

As the most important applications of A-IFS are $MCDM$ problems when the values of local criteria (attributes) of alternatives and/or their weights are $IFVs$, it seems quite natural that the resulting alternative's evaluation should be IFV too. Therefore, appropriate operations on $IFVs$ used for aggregation of local criteria should be properly defined. Obviously, if the final scores of alternatives are $IFVs$, then appropriate methods for their comparison are needed to select the best alternative.

L. Rutkowski et al. (Eds.): ICAISC 2012, Part I, LNCS 7267, pp. 229–236, 2012.

In [1], Atanassov defined A-IFS as follows.

Definition 1. Let $X = \{x_1, x_2, ..., x_n\}$ be a finite universal set. An intuitionistic fuzzy set A in X is an object having the following form:
$A = \{< x_j, \mu_A(x_j), \nu_A(x_j) > | x_j \in X\}$, where the functions $\mu_A : X \to [0, 1]$, $x_j \in X \to \mu_A(x_j) \in [0, 1]$ and $\nu_A : X \to [0, 1]$, $x_j \in X \to \nu_A(x_j) \in [0, 1]$ define the degree of membership and degree of non-membership of the element $x_j \in X$ to the set $A \subseteq X$, respectively, and for every $x_j \in X$, $0 \le \mu_A(x_j) + \nu_A(x_j) \le 1$. Following to [1], we call $\pi_A(x_j) = 1 - \mu_A(x_j) - \nu_A(x_j)$ the intuitionistic index (or the hesitation degree) of the element x_j in the set A. It is obvious that for every $x_j \in X$ we have $0 \le \pi_A(x_j) \le 1$.

In [7], this definition is reformulated in terms of DST. The origins of the Dempster-Shafer theory go back to the work by A.P. Dempster [5,6] who developed a system of upper and lower probabilities. Following this work his student G. Shafer proposed a more thorough explanation of belief functions [10].

Assume A is a subsets of X. A DS belief structure has associated with it a mapping m, called basic assignment function, from subsets of X into a unit interval, $m : 2^X \to [0, 1]$ such that $m(\emptyset) = 0$, $\sum_{A \subseteq X} m(A) = 1$. The subsets of X for which the mapping does not assume a zero value are called focal elements. The null set is never a focal element. In [10], Shafer introduced a number of measures associated with this structure. The measure of belief is a mapping $Bel : 2^X \to [0, 1]$ such that for any subset B of X

$$Bel(B) = \sum_{\emptyset \ne A \subseteq B} m(A). \tag{1}$$

A second measure introduced by Shafer [10] is a measure of plausibility which is a mapping $Pl : 2^X \to [0, 1]$ such that for any subset B of X

$$Pl(B) = \sum_{A \cap B \ne \emptyset} m(A). \tag{2}$$

It is easy to see that $Bel(B) \le Pl(B)$. An interval $[Bel(B), Pl(B)]$ is called the belief interval (BI).

It is shown in [7] that in the framework of DST the triplet $\mu_A(x)$, $\nu_A(x)$, $\pi_A(x)$ represents the basic assignment function. Really, when analyzing any situation in context of A-IFS, we implicitly deal with the following three hypotheses: $x \in A$, $x \notin A$ and the situation when both the hypotheses $x \in A$, $x \notin A$ can not be rejected (the case of hesitation). In the spirit of DST, we can denote these hypotheses as Yes ($x \in A$), No ($x \notin A$) and (Yes, No) (the case of hesitation when both the hypotheses $x \in A$ and $x \notin A$ can not be rejected).

In this context, $\mu_A(x)$ may be treated as the probability or evidence of $x \in A$, i.e., as the focal element of the basic assignment function: $m(Yes) = \mu_A(x)$. Similarly, we can assume that $m(No) = \nu_A(x)$. Since $\pi_A(x)$ is usually treated as a hesitation degree, a natural assumption is $m(Yes, No) = \pi_A(x)$. Taking into account that $\mu_A(x) + \nu_A(x) + \pi_A(x) = 1$ we come to the conclusion that triplet $\mu_A(x)$, $\nu_A(x)$, $\pi_A(x)$ represents a correct basic assignment function.

According to the DST formalism we get $Bel_A(x)=m(Yes)=\mu_A(x)$ and $Pl_A(x)=m(Yes)+m(Yes,No)=\mu_A(x)+\pi_A(x)=1-\nu_A(x)$.

Therefore, in [7] the following definition was introduced:

Definition 2. Let $X = \{x_1, x_2, ..., x_n\}$ be a finite universal set and x_j is an object in X presented by the functions $\mu_A(x_j), \nu_A(x_j)$ which represent the degree of membership and degree of non-membership of $x_j \in X$ to the set $A \subseteq X$ such that $\mu_A : X \to [0,1]$, $x_j \in X \to \mu_A(x_j) \in [0,1]$ and $\nu_A : X \to [0,1]$, $x_j \in X \to \nu_A(x_j) \in [0,1]$ and for every $x_j \in X$, $0 \le \mu_A(x_j) + \nu_A(x_j) \le 1$. An intuitionistic fuzzy set A in X is an object having the following form: $A = \{< x_j, BI_A(x_j) > | x_j \in X\}$, where $BI_A(x_j) = [Bel_A(x_j), Pl_A(x_j)]$ is the belief interval, $Bel_A(x_j) = \mu_A(x_j)$ and $Pl_A(x_j) = 1-\nu_A(x_j)$ are the measures of belief and plausibility that $x_j \in X$ belongs to the set $A \subseteq X$.

At first glance, the Definition 2 seems as a simple redefinition of A-IFS in terms of Interval Valued Fuzzy Sets, but here we show that using the DST semantics it is possible to enhance the performance of A-IFS when dealing with the operations on $IFVs$ and $MCDM$ problems.

As the most important applications of A-IFS are $MCDM$ problems when the values of local criteria (attributes) of alternatives and/or their weights are $IFVs$, it seems quite natural that the resulting alternative's evaluation should be IFV too. Therefore, appropriate operations on $IFVs$ used for aggregation of local criteria should be properly defined. Obviously, if the final scores of alternatives are $IFVs$, then appropriate methods for their comparison are needed to select the best alternative.

The rest of the paper is set out as follows. In Section 2, we provide a critical analysis of the commonly used operations on $IFVs$ to elicit their disadvantages. In Section 3, we introduce a set of operations on $IFVs$ represented in the form of belief intervals. The corresponding method for aggregation of local criteria presented by $IFVs$ in the framework of DST is proposed and analyzed. The advantages of the proposed approach are illustrated by numerical examples. Finally, the concluding section summarizes the paper.

2   Operations on $IFVs$ and Some of Their Limitations

The operations of addition $\oplus$ and multiplication $\otimes$ on $IFVs$ were defined by Atanassov [2] as follows. Let $A = \langle \mu_A, \nu_A \rangle$ and $B = \langle \mu_B, \nu_B \rangle$ be $IFVs$. Then

$$A \oplus B = \langle \mu_A + \mu_B - \mu_A\mu_B, \nu_A\nu_B \rangle, \tag{3}$$

$$A \otimes B = \langle \mu_A\mu_B, \nu_A + \nu_B - \nu_A\nu_B \rangle. \tag{4}$$

The following operations were later for all real values $\lambda > 0$:

$$\lambda A = \langle 1 - (1 - \mu_A)^\lambda, \nu_A^\lambda \rangle, \tag{5}$$

$$A^\lambda = \langle \mu_A^\lambda, 1 - (1 - \nu_A)^\lambda \rangle. \tag{6}$$

The operations (3)-(6) have the following algebraic properties:

Theorem 1. [12]. Let $A = \langle \mu_A, \nu_A \rangle$ and $B = \langle \mu_B, \nu_B \rangle$ be $IFVs$. Then
$A \oplus B = B \oplus A$, $A \otimes B = B \otimes A$, $\lambda(A \oplus B) = \lambda A \oplus \lambda B$, $(A \otimes B)^\lambda = A^\lambda \otimes B^\lambda$,
$\lambda_1 A \oplus \lambda_2 A = (\lambda_1 + \lambda_2)A$, $A^{\lambda_1} \otimes A^{\lambda_2} = A^{\lambda_1 + \lambda_2}$, ($\lambda_1, \lambda_2 > 0$).

The operations (3)-(6) are used to aggregate local criteria for solving $MCDM$ problems in the intuitionistic fuzzy setting.

Let $A_1, ..., A_n$ be $IFVs$ representing the values of local criteria and $w_1, ..., w_n$, $\sum_{i=1}^{n} w_i = 1$, be their weights. Then Intuitionistic Weighted Arithmetic Mean $(IWAM)$ can be obtained using operations (3) and (5) as follows:

$$IWAM = w_1 A_1 \oplus w_2 A_2 \oplus ... \oplus w_n A_n = \left\langle 1 - \prod_{i=1}^{n} (1 - \mu_{A_i})^{w_i}, \prod_{i=1}^{n} \nu_{A_i}^{w_i} \right\rangle. \quad (7)$$

This aggregation operator provides $IFVs$, is idempotent and currently is most popular in the solution of $MCDM$ problems in the intuitionistic fuzzy setting.

An important problem is the comparison of $IFVs$. This problem arises, e.g., if we have to choose the best alternative when the final scores of alternatives are presented by $IFVs$, e.g., by $IWAM$. Chen and Tan [4] proposed to use the so-called score function (or net membership) $S(x) = \mu(x) - \nu(x)$. Let a and b be $IFVs$. It is intuitively appealing that if $S(a) > S(b)$ then a should be greater (better) than b, but if $S(a) = S(b)$ this does not always mean that a is equal to b. Therefore, Hong and Choi [8] in addition to the above score function introduced the so-called accuracy function $H(x) = \mu(x) + \nu(x)$ and showed that the relation between functions S and H is similar to the relation between mean and variance in statistics. Xu [12] used the functions S and H to construct order relations between any pair of intuitionistic fuzzy values a and b as follows:

$$\begin{aligned} &If\,(\text{S(a)} > \text{S(b)}),\ then\,\text{b}\,is\,smaller\,than\,\text{a}; \\ &If\,(\text{S(a)} = \text{S(b)}),\ then \\ &(1)\,If\,(\text{ H(a)=H(b)}),\ then\,\text{a=b}; \\ &(2)\,If\,(\text{H(a)} < \text{H(b)})\,then\,\text{a}\,is\,smaller\,than\,\text{b}. \end{aligned} \quad (8)$$

Some limitations of conventional operations on $IFVs$ were analyzed in [3]. Here we contribute to this study considering additional limitations which we have found and present persuasive critical examples.

The addition (3) is not an addition invariant operation. To show this, consider the following example:

Example 1. Let $A = \langle 0.5, 0.3 \rangle$, $B = \langle 0.4, 0.1 \rangle$, and $C = \langle 0.1, 0.1 \rangle$. Since $S(A) = 0.2$ and $S(B) = 0.3$ then according to (8) we have $A < B$. On the other hand, $A \oplus C = \langle 0.55, 0.03 \rangle$, $B \oplus C = \langle 0.46, 0.01 \rangle$, $S(A \oplus C)=0.52$, $S(B \oplus C)=0.45$ and from $S(A \oplus C) > S(B \oplus C)$ be get $(A \oplus C) > (B \oplus C)$.

The undesirable property of multiplication (5) is that it is not preserved under multiplication by a scalar: $A < B$ does not necessarily imply $\lambda A < \lambda B$, $\lambda > 0$. To illustrate this, consider the following example.

Example 2. Let $A = \langle 0.5, 0.4 \rangle$, $B = \langle 0.4, 0.3 \rangle$, and $\lambda = 0.5$. Then $S(A) = S(B) = 0.1$, $H(A) = 0.9$, $H(B) = 0.7$ and from (8) we get $A > B$. Using (5) we obtain $\lambda A = \langle 0.2928, 0.632 \rangle$, $\lambda B = \langle 0.225, 0.5477 \rangle$, $S(\lambda A) = -0.3396$, $S(\lambda B) = -0.3227$. Since $S(\lambda A) < S(\lambda B)$ we get $\lambda A < \lambda B$.

3   Operations on Belief Intervals Representing *IFVs*

Let $X = \{x_1, x_2, ..., x_n\}$ be a finite universal set. Assume A are subsets of X. It is important to note that in the framework of DST a subset A may be treated also as a question or proposition and X as a set of propositions or mutually exclusive hypotheses or answers.

In such a context, a belief interval $BI(A) = [Bel(A), Pl(A)]$ may be treated as an interval enclosing a true power of statement (argument, proposition, hypothesis, *ets*) that $x_j \in X$ belongs to the set $A \subseteq X$. Obviously, the value of such a power lies in interval $[0,1]$.

Therefore, a belief interval $BI(A) = [Bel(A), Pl(A)]$ as a whole may be treated as a not exact (interval valued) statement (argument, proposition, hypothesis, *ets*) that $x_j \in X$ belongs to the set $A \subseteq X$.

Based on this reasoning, we can say that if we pronounce this statement, we can obtain some result, e.g., as a reaction on this statement or as the answer to the some question, and if we repeat this statement twice, the result does not change.

Such a reasoning implies the following property of addition operator: $BI(A) = BI(A) + BI(A) + ... + BI(A)$. This is possible only if we define the addition $\oplus$ of belief intervals as follows: $BI(A) \oplus BI(A) = \left[\frac{Bel(A) + Bel(A)}{2}, \frac{Pl(A) + Pl(A)}{2} \right]$. So the addition of belief intervals is represented by their averaging.

Therefore, if we have n different statements represented by belief intervals $BI(A_i)$ then their sum $\oplus$ can be defined as follows:

$$ BI(A_1) \oplus BI(A_2) \oplus .... \oplus BI(A_n) = \left[\frac{1}{n} \sum_{i=1}^{n} Bel(A_i), \frac{1}{n} \sum_{i=1}^{n} Pl(A_i) \right]. \qquad (9) $$

To obtain a complete set of operations, we propose to use the addition operator (9), the multiplication operators

$$ BI(A) \otimes BI(A) = [Bel(A)Bel(B), Pl(A)Pl(B)] \qquad (10) $$

and

$$ \lambda BI(A) = [\lambda Bel(A), \lambda Pl(A)], \qquad (11) $$

where λ is a real value. This operator is defined only for $\lambda \in [0, 1]$ as for $\lambda > 1$ this operation does not always provide a true belief interval. This restriction is justified enough since we define operations on belief intervals to deal with $MCDM$ problems, where λ usually represents the weight of local criterion, which is lesser than 1.

The power operation is defined as follows

$$BI(A)^{\lambda} = [Bel(A)^{\lambda}, Pl(A)^{\lambda}] \tag{12}$$

and provides true belief intervals for all $\lambda \geq 0$.

The formalism of DST makes it possible to define a new operation $BI(A)^{BI(B)}$, which does not exist in the body of conventional A-IFS theory. This operation is needed to define the geometric aggregation operator, when both the local criteria and their weights are $IFVs$ represented by belief intervals.

Using conventional interval arithmetic rule [9] we get: $BI(A)^{BI(B)} =$

$[\min \left\{ Bel(A)^{Bel(B)}, Pl(A)^{Bel(B)}, Bel(A)^{Pl(B)}, Pl(A)^{Pl(B)} \right\},$
$\max \left\{ Bel(A)^{Bel(B)}, Pl(A)^{Bel(B)}, Bel(A)^{Pl(B)}, Pl(A)^{Pl(B)} \right\}].$

Taking into account the properties of BIs this expression may be reduced to

$$BI(A)^{BI(B)} = [Bel(A)^{Pl(B)}, Pl(A)^{Bel(B)}]. \tag{13}$$

The IF representation of this expression is as follows: $A^{B} = \left\langle \mu_A^{1-\nu_B}, (1-\nu_A)^{\mu_B} \right\rangle$.

The defined set of operations have the good algebraic properties (the same as in the case of conventional A-IFS, see Section 2)):
$BI(A) \oplus BI(B) = BI(B) \oplus BI(A),\ BI(A) \otimes BI(B) = BI(B) \otimes BI(A),\ (BI(A) \otimes BI(B))^{\lambda} = BI(A)^{\lambda} \otimes BI(B)^{\lambda},\ BI(A)^{\lambda_1} \otimes BI(A)^{\lambda_1} = BI(A)^{\lambda_1+\lambda_2},\ \lambda BI(A) \oplus \lambda BI(B) = \lambda(BI(A) \oplus BI(B)),\ \lambda_1 BI(A) \oplus \lambda_2 BI(A) = (\lambda_1 + \lambda_2)BI(A).$

Using expressions (9) and (11) we obtain the following Intuitionistic Weighted Arithmetic Mean:

$$IWAM_{DST} = \left[\frac{1}{n} \sum_{i=1}^{n} w_i Bel_i, \frac{1}{n} \sum_{i=1}^{n} w_i Pl_i \right]. \tag{14}$$

This aggregation operator is not idempotent. Nevertheless, the small modification of (14) (multiplying by n) provides the idempotent operator

$$IWAM_{DST} = \left[\sum_{i=1}^{n} w_i Bel_i, \sum_{i=1}^{n} w_i Pl_i \right]. \tag{15}$$

It is easy to see that operators (14) and (15) in practice will produce equivalent orderings of compared alternatives.

Taking into account that " most of the proposed methods for interval comparison are totally based on the midpoints of interval numbers" [11], we can conclude that the belief interval $BI(A)$ is greater than $BI(B)$ if $(Bel(A) + Pl(A)) > (Bel(B) + Pl(B))$. It is easy to see that this inequality is equivalent to the inequality $(1 + S(A)) > (1 + S(B))$ which obviously may be reduced to $S(A) > S(B)$, where $S(A)$ and $S(B)$ are the score functions.

In the case of $(Bel(A) + Pl(A)) = (Bel(B) + Pl(B))$, in the spirit of A-IFS, we propose to compare additionally the values of $Pl(A) - Bel(A)$ and $Pl(B) - Bel(B)$. It is easy to show that $Pl(A) - Bel(A) = \pi(A)$ and $Pl(B) - Bel(B) = \pi(B)$. Therefore, finally we obtain the following rule

$$if\ (Bel(A) + Pl(A)) > (Bel(B) + Pl(B))\ then\ BI(B) < BI(A);$$
$$if\ (Bel(A) + Pl(A)) = (Bel(B) + Pl(B))\ then$$
$$(if\ (Pl(A) - Bel(A)) > (Pl(B) - Bel(B))\ then\ BI(B) > BI(A);$$
$$if\ (Pl(A) - Bel(A)) = (Pl(B) - Bel(B))\ then\ BI(B) = BI(A)). \tag{16}$$

To study the properties of introduced operations on belief intervals, we shall use the data from the Examples 1-2.

Opposite to the case of conventional A-IFS theory, the addition (9) is an addition invariant operation:

Example 3. Let $A = \langle 0.5, 0.3 \rangle$, $B = \langle 0.4, 0.1 \rangle$ and $C = \langle 0.1, 0.1 \rangle$ as in Example 1 . Since $BI(A) = [0.5, 0.7]$, $BI(B) = [0.4, 0.9]$ and $BI(C) = [0.1, 0.9]$, from (16) we get $BI(B) > BI(A)$. Then from (9) we get $BI(A \oplus C) = BI(A) \oplus BI(C) = [0.3, 0.8]$ and $BI(B \oplus C) = BI(B) \oplus BI(C) = [0.25, 0.9]$. From (16) we get $BI(B \oplus C) > BI(A \oplus C)$.

It has been shown in Section 2 that conventional multiplication (5) is not preserved under multiplication by a scalar, i.e., $A < B$ does not necessarily imply $\lambda A < \lambda B$, $\lambda > 0$.

The use of (11) with (16) is free of this undesirable property:

Example 4. Let $A = \langle 0.5, 0.4 \rangle$, $B = \langle 0.4, 0.3 \rangle$, and $\lambda = 0.5$. In the Example 2, we have shown that $A > B$, but using (5) we obtain $\lambda A < \lambda B$.

In the framework of our approach, we get $BI(A) = [0.5, 0.6]$, $BI(B) = [0.4, 0.7]$. From (16) we obtain $BI(A) > BI(B)$.

Denoting $\lambda BI(A)$ as $BI(\lambda A) = [Bel(\lambda A), Pl(\lambda A)]$ and $\lambda BI(B)$ as $BI(\lambda B) = [Bel(\lambda B), Pl(\lambda B)]$, from (16) we get $\lambda BI(A) > \lambda BI(B)$.

4   Conclusion

It is shown that DST may serve as a good methodological base for interpretation of A-IFS. This interpretation makes it possible to represent mathematical operations on $IFVs$ as operations on belief intervals. The use of the semantics of DST makes it possible to enhance the performance of A-IFS when dealing with the operations on $IFVs$ and $MCDM$ problems. The critical analysis of conventional operations on intuitionistic fuzzy values is presented.

A set of operations on $IFVs$ based on the interpretation of intuitionistic fuzzy sets in the framework of the DST is proposed and analyzed. It is shown, that operations based on belief intervals perform better than operations on $IFVs$ defined in the framework of conventional A-IFS.

The corresponding method for aggregation of local criteria presented by $IFVs$ in the framework of DST is proposed and analyzed. Particularly, when solving $MCDM$ problems, the proposed approach allows us to aggregate the local criteria presented by $IFVs$ when their weights are $IFVs$ too, without intermediate defuzzification.

References

1. Atanassov, K.T.: Intuitionistic fuzzy sets. Fuzzy Sets and Systems 20, 87–96 (1986)
2. Atanassov, K.T.: New operations defined over the intuitionistic fuzzy sets. Fuzzy Sets and Systems 61, 137–142 (1994)
3. Beliakov, G., Bustince, H., Goswami, D.P., Mukherjee, U.K., Pal, N.R.: On averaging operators for Atanassov's intuitionistic fuzzy sets. Information Sciences 182, 1116–1124 (2011)
4. Chen, S.M., Tan, J.M.: Handling multicriteria fuzzy decision-making problems based on vague set theory. Fuzzy Sets and Systems 67, 163–172 (1994)
5. Dempster, A.P.: Upper and lower probabilities induced by a muilti-valued mapping. Ann. Math. Stat. 38, 325–339 (1967)
6. Dempster, A.P.: A generalization of Bayesian inference (with discussion). J. Roy. Stat. Soc., Series B. 30, 208–247 (1968)
7. Dymova, L., Sevastjanov, P.: An interpretation of intuitionistic fuzzy sets in terms of evidence theory. Decision Making Aspect. Knowledge-Based Systems 23, 772–782 (2010)
8. Hong, D.H., Choi, C.-H.: Multicriteria fuzzy decision-making problems based on vague set theory. Fuzzy Sets and Systems 114, 103–113 (2000)
9. Moore, R.E.: Interval analysis. Prentice-Hall, Englewood Cliffs (1966)
10. Shafer, G.: A mathematical theory of evidence. Princeton University Press, Princeton (1976)
11. Wang, Y.M., Yang, J.B., Xu, D.L.: A preference aggregation method through the estimation of utility intervals. Computers and Operations Research 32, 2027–2049 (2005)
12. Xu, Z.: Intuitionistic preference relations and their application in group decision making. Information Sciences 177, 2363–2379 (2007)

A Method of Fast Application of the Fuzzy PID Algorithm Using Industrial Control Device

Sławomir Jaszczak and Joanna Kołodziejczyk

Westpomeranian University of Technology in Szczecin,
Department of Computer Science
{sjaszczak,jkolodziejczyk}@wi.zut.edu.pl

Abstract. Linear PID algorithms commonly used in industry might perform insufficiently when controlling nonlinear operating systems. Solutions such as the fuzzy PID controller can exchange the linear PID controller because it develops a nonlinear control surface. The main advantage of the fuzzy PID controller is the ability to adjust to a controlled plant by the rule based modification, nonlinear membership function application and inference rule selection. However, the tuning process is one of the most difficult steps in the fuzzy PID controller designing and therefore discourages most practical applications.

A simplification of the fuzzy PID controller tuning process is described in this article. The presented methodology allows fast transformation from a classic PID algorithm into a fuzzy PID algorithm. A proposed algorithm is tested on a programmable PLC which is a typical industrial implementation platform. A temperature stabilization is chosen as the controlled plant and some experimental results are then described. In conclusion authors suggest directions for similar real time fuzzy PID algorithm implementations.

Keywords: Rapid Prototyping, Control Systems, Fuzzy Control, PID Algorithm, Embedded Input/Output Functions.

1 Introduction

A PID algorithm is still the main solution to control analog processes and plants in industry. This situation will not change in the near future [8]. The PID algorithm with a feedback provides relatively high resistance to the non-stationarity, the non-linearity and the random noise. Nonetheless, practical obstacles such as a time consuming tuning and a retuning when regimes in motion are changing force PID controller designers to look for alternative control methods or quality improvements in systems with PID algorithms. In last two decades fuzzy logic based algorithms e.g. Mamdani, Takagi-Sugeno, fuzzy adaptive controllers, fuzzy supervisory controllers, hybrid fuzzy algorithms (artificial neural networks, genetic algorithms, machine learning, etc.), working on the superior control level became increasingly popular.

L. Rutkowski et al. (Eds.): ICAISC 2012, Part I, LNCS 7267, pp. 237–246, 2012.

Fuzzy logic (FL) employs a control strategy of an experienced engineer described as a mathematical formula. Expert knowledge about the controlled system is given in a form of linguistic rules. Therefore the mathematical model essential in classical approaches is unnecessary to control dynamic plants when using FL. Fuzzy systems are composed of fuzzification, inference and defuzzification modules. The fuzzy algorithm synthesis requires many experiments based on trial by error to find an acceptable set of parameters [3], [4], [5]. The number of adjustable parameters and therefore many degrees of freedom prevent FL from practical implementation. There is no methodology for tuning fuzzy parameters in contrast to tuning PID algorithms. A solution to those problems is a novel approach to fuzzy PID algorithm design [4], [7] leading to a reduction in degrees of freedom and a linkage of fuzzy and classic PID algorithm designing methodology.

Alternative solutions to a classic PID algorithm are expected to be easily applicable, simply tunable, maintainable and of high operation quality [6]. Moreover, an industrial control application is limited by the target hardware which is usually the programmable PLC controller.

This paper describes a fast transformation procedure from the classic PID algorithm into the non-linear fuzzy PID algorithm. The procedure employs a methodology from [4] modified by adding a rapid prototyping [5] step. Authors assume that the fuzzy PID algorithm replace the classic PID algorithm if only coherent prototyping procedure is able to build fuzzy PID algorithm based on a working classic PID algorithm. The proposed method might lead to overcoming the reluctance to substitute classic controllers with fuzzy ones.

The presented solution is not recommended in systems with the perfectly working and rarely tuned classic PID algorithm. However, systems that often tune parameters and employ expert knowledge to change them by trial and error method might benefit from the proposed methodology. In the proposed method expert knowledge is used but even in more convenient for the expert way i.e. in natural language. It is unique for fuzzy systems that the rule base is filled with expertises given in comprehensive verbal form.

2   The Fast Transformation from the PID Algorithm into the Fuzzy PID Algorithm

To perform a fast transformation procedure the classic PID algorithm working for a real process is required. A Matlab-Simulink algorithm is modeled based on the PID algorithm. Additionally, the working algorithm is the source of initial values of all adjustable parameters (Fig. 1 - step 0).

Next (Fig. 1 - step 1) a Fuzzy Logic Toolbox is applied to build a corresponding linear fuzzy algorithm. In the next step (Fig. 1 - step 2) the linear model is transformed into a nonlinear one. The non-linearity is obtained by nonlinear membership functions employed either in fuzzification and defuzification blocks and nonlinear inference and defuzification methods. The fuzzy algorithm is expanded by embedded functions (Fig. 1 - step 3). Then an executive code that

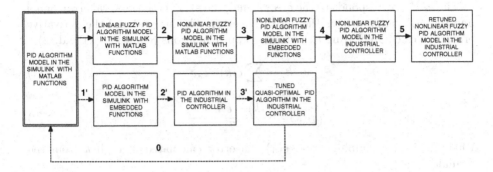

Fig. 1. A procedure of rapid prototyping of the fuzzy PID algorithm

includes the architecture of an industrial controller is generated (Fig. 1 - step 4). The following step (Fig. 1 - step 5) tunes the algorithm in real time. The presented procedure provides a model in the loop simulation.

Let consider the procedure of a totally new control system synthesis. It begins the same: by modeling the algorithm in Matlab-Simulink. However, the initial tuning based on real data is impossible. In such case the classic PID algorithm is prototyped (Fig. 1 - steps 1' and 2') and tuned using e.g. the Ziegler-Nichols method.

The main idea in the proposed procedure is the integration of the fuzzy system methodology with the classic PID optimization methodology. Authors claim that this approach should simplify implementation and service process of fuzzy algorithms in industrial practice.

Step 1 — Design of the Linear Fuzzy PID

The fuzzy PID algorithm is developed based on the working classic PID algorithm. The general diagram of the fuzzy PID algorithm is shown in Fig. 2.

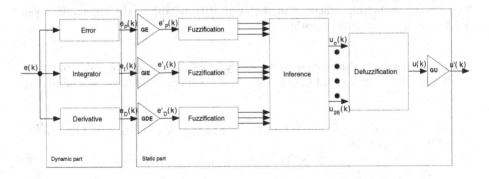

Fig. 2. A general structure of the fuzzy PID algorithm

The $e_P(k)$ corresponds to the error signal, the $e_I(k)$ is the integral error signal and the e_Dk signal defines the derivative error. The integral and the derivative errors are calculated using the simplest approximations (equation (1) and (2)):

$$e_I(k) = \sum e(k) \cdot T_s, \tag{1}$$

$$e_D(k) = \frac{e(k) - e(k-1)}{T_s}, \tag{2}$$

where T_s is the sampling rate, $e(k)$ the error calculated in each k from the formula:

$$e_(k) = SP(k) - PV(k). \tag{3}$$

$SP(k)$ is a reference value and $PV(k)$ is a value of the controlled signal.

First $e_P(k), e_I(k), e_D(k)$. signals are scaled by GE, GIE and GDE factors respectively. Then a fuzzification using the triangular membership function is performed on them. The main advantage of scaling factors is fast correlation of signal range and required signal range (Fig. 3 (a)) that is range without membership functions saturation. Unfortunately, factor values must be chosen experimentally likewise the determination of signal domains. This significantly impedes the algorithm pre-tuning process in slowly changing plants.

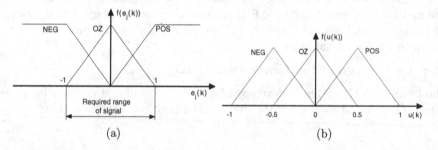

Fig. 3. (a) Membership functions in the fuzzy PID algorithm, (b) a defuzzification function in the fuzzy PID algorithm

Three linguistic values are used for every input. Therefore from combination of all fuzzified inputs 27 inference rules R_i are generated. They are formulated as follows:

R_1: IF $[e_P(k) = e_{PNEG}(k)]$ AND $[e_I(k) = e_{INEG}(k)]$ AND $[e_D(k) = e_{DNEG}(k)]$
    THEN $[U(k) = U_{26}(k)]$
R_{14}: IF $[e_P(k) = e_{POZ}(k)]$ AND $[e_I(k) = e_{IOZ}(k)]$ AND $[e_D(k) = e_{DOZ}(k)]$
    THEN $[U(k) = U_{13}(k)]$
R_{27}: IF $[e_P(k) = e_{PPOS}(k)]$ AND $[e_I(k) = e_{IPOZ}(k)]$ AND $[e_D(k) = e_{DPOZ}(k)]$
    THEN $[U(k) = U_0(k)]$

A membership of premise of each rule R_i is computated using the AND operator.

A COG (center of gravity) defuzzification is applied in the algorithm using a triangular membership function (Fig. 3 (b)) and is calculated as follows:

$$U(k) = \frac{\sum_i f(u_i(k)) \cdot u_i(k)}{\sum_i f(u_i(k))} \qquad (4)$$

The classic PID algorithm can be very accurately reconstructed by the designed fuzzy PID algorithm with triangular membership functions intersecting in the 0.5 point, the linear inference and the COG defuzzification method. An incomplete rule base not covering all possible combinations of linguistic labels is one of the main source of nonlinearity. Some tests on the influence of the rule base completeness are presented in the experimental results section.

The control surface of the proportional-integral fuzzy PID algorithm is presented in the Fig. 4. Diagrams shows that fuzzy PID algorithm works exactly as classic linear PID algorithm in the assumed ranges of $e_P(k)$ and $e_I(k)$ signals.

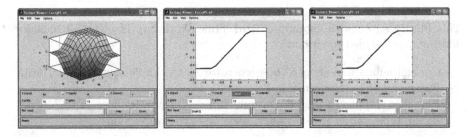

Fig. 4. A control surface of the proportional-integral part of the fuzzy PID algorithm with sections for $e_I(k) = 0$ and $e_P(k) = 0$

Step 2 — Making the Linear Fuzzy PID Algorithm Nonlinear

A nonlinearity in the fuzzy PID algorithm is obtained either by:

1. some rules removal from the rule base
2. nonlinear membership functions employment
3. application of nonlinear inference operators
4. using nonlinear defuzzification methods.

An application any of the modification produce the control surface that is no longer a plane within a given range of signal variation.

Step 3 — Embeded Functions Introduction

A prototype of a fuzzy PID algorithm is developed with the use of the Fuzzy Logic Toolbox, Simulink and B&R Automation Studio Toolbox (Fig 5).

The algorithm modeled in Simulink is connected with the Bernecker&Reiner hardware by using B&R Automation Studio Target Library for Simulink [1].

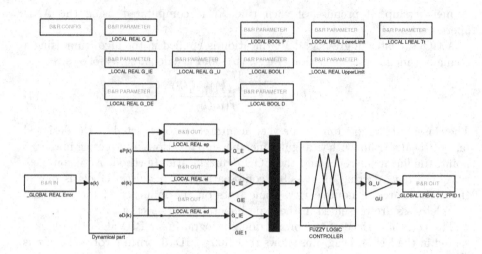

Fig. 5. A prototype of the fuzzy PID algorithm with embedded functions in Simulink

This library extends the standard Real TIme Workshop library and includes additional embedded functions:

- Config (defines a mode of a code generator for the implementation platform)
- Parameter (model parameters)
- Extended Input, Extended Output, Input, Output (defines input/output signal, type, range, initial values, scale and type conversion).

Step 4 — Executive Code for the Nonlinear Fuzzy PID Algorithm

A control algorithm is implemented in the Matlab/Simulink environment which corresponds to the Model In The Loop procedure. Afterwards, embedded I/O functions are included and a sampling rate is determined. At that point a specific task class is assigned to B&R control devices. Next, the Ansi C code is automatically generated. A resultant model of the algorithm is attached to a project in Automation Studio. Such software is sent to the target implementation platform.

Step 5 — Tuning the Nonlinear Fuzzy PID Algorithm

A process of tuning the fuzzy PID algorithm is done by GE, GIE, GDE, GU factors modification. This is comparable to tuning a classic PID algorithm. However some inequalities must be satisfied:

$$1 \leq GE \cdot A(e_P(k)) \leq 1$$

$$-1 \leq G_I E \cdot A(e_I(k)) \leq 1$$

$$-1 \leq G_D E \cdot A(e_D(k)) \leq 1,$$

where $A(*)$ is the amplitude.

Exceeding the limits results in transitioning into a state of saturation which is a logical ON-OFF control state. In that case the fuzzy PID algorithm is ineffective. The influence of scaling factors on static and dynamic integral performance indices is presented in section 3. Conclusions will help the designer in tuning the fuzzy PID algorithm analogously to a classic PID algorithm. Additionally, the rule base can be modified. However this manipulation distorts the control surface and changes the control system response.

3   Experimental Results

The fuzzy PID algorithm presented in the paper is tested on a temperature control system (Fig. 6). The Power Panel PP45 by Bernecker&Reiner uses a X2X network to communicate with Input/Output modules (AC/CA CM8281 modules and AT2222 temperature module). The plant is a thermal chamber with implementing systems (a heater and a fan) and the measuring system (PT1000 probe) [2]. The voltage $U_3(t)$ representing the temperature $T_{PV}(t)$ is the controlled signal. The voltage $U_1(t)$ corresponding to the heat stream generated by the heater is the controlling signal. The voltage $U_2(t)$ controls the fan rotational speed and is considered as a source of disturbance.

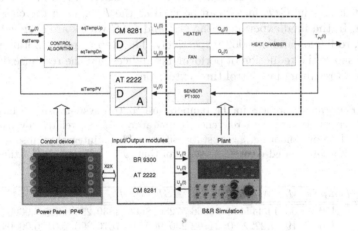

Fig. 6. A temperature control system with the developed fuzzy PID algorithm

Experiments on the fuzzy PID algorithm have been conducted with similar initial conditions (initial temperature) and resulted in step responses. A 5% tolerance around the reference point is established (a red line on Fig. 7). Static and dynamic, as well as integral performance indices are used for comparative analysis. Simple tuning rules for fuzzy PID algorithm are formulated as a conclusion. All analysis are presented in the table 1.

The GE factor increased from 0.005 to 0.01 results in sufficient control improvement: the static and dynamic performance indices are decreased 300% and

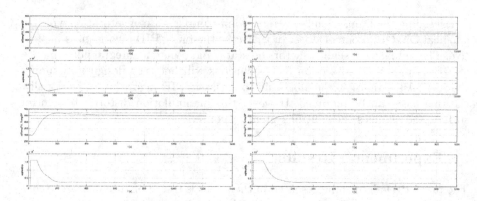

Fig. 7. Step response data temperature control system, where $aqHeatUp$ - controlling signal, $aiTempPV$ - measured signal, $TempSP$ - reference temperature

integral performance indices are decreased 200%. The GE factor should be tuned opposite to the Kp factor in the classic PID algorithm. The influence of the GIE factor (increased from 0.00004 to 0.00008) on the control performance is tested. The effect of such increase was a deterioration in the quality control, which manifested itself in the extension of regulation time by nearly 80% and overshooting rise about 40%. The GIE factor can be used as the K_i gain in the classic PID algorithm. In the final experiment the GE and GIE values are changed simultaneously, to 0.0005 and 0.00002 respectively. The step response obtained from the study shows the reduction of performance indices and the response dynamic deterioration resulting in control time extension.

Table 1. Performance indices in the temperature control system using a fuzzy PID algorithm, where: $TempSP$ — reference temperature, M_p — relative overshooting, M_{pp} — absolute overshooting, e_u — static offset, IAE — integral of absolute error, ISE — integral of squared error, T_r — control time, FP — first point of the output curve

Lp.	$TempSP$	M_p	M_{pp}	e_u	IAE	ISE	T_r	FP	GE	GIE
1	450	65	14.4444	0	60866	5728618	435.4839	250	0.005	0.00004
2	450	19	4.2222	0	31162	2305902	109.7670	290	0.01	0.00004
3	450	102	22.6667	0	82484	6175124	729.0323	282	0.005	0.00008
4	450	7	1.5556	0	29029	2602305	102.5986	280	0.01	0.00002

One of the source of nonlinearity is an incomplete rule base. The effect of a such modification is also tested. The Fig. 8 shows the original rule base for fuzzy PID algorithm, modified rule base and corresponding control surfaces.

After the rule base modification the fuzzy PID algorithm became more similar to proportional algorithm and the static offset reached value of 29.

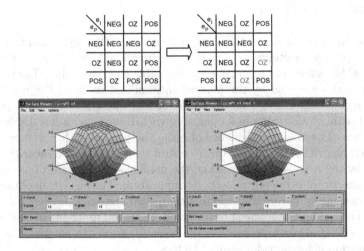

Fig. 8. Rule base modification in fuzzy PID algorithm

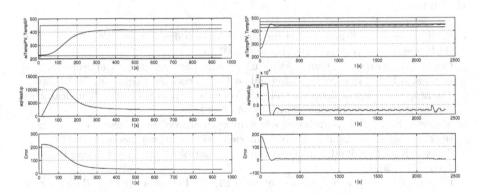

Fig. 9. Step response data in the temperature control system, where $Error = TempSP - aiTempPV$ — control error, $aqHeatUp$ — controlling signal, $aiTempPV$ — measured signal, $TempSP$ — reference temperature

Table 2. Performance indices in the temperature control system using a fuzzy PID algorithm, where: $TempSP$ — reference temperature, M_p — relative overshooting, M_{pp} — absolute overshooting, e_u — static offset, IAE — integral of absolute error, ISE — integral of squared error, T_r — control time, FP — first point of the output curve

Lp.	TempSP	M_p	M_{pp}	e_u	IAE	ISE	T_r	FP	GE	GIE
1	450	0	0	29	1.1186e+005	1.2504e+007	423.3871	250	0.005	0.00004
2	450	4	0.8889	4	57260	3565682	106.4068	260	0.04	0.00004

4 Conclusions

The proposed in the paper methodology for the fuzzy PID algorithm fast implementation gives a possibility to obtain a fully functional algorithm implemented on a typical industrial platform i.e. programmable PLC controller. The resulting control quality expressed by the performance indices confirms the usability of the implemented algorithm. Noteworthy is the fact that the fuzzy PID algorithm generated with Matlab/Simulink operating with 100ms cycles has 0.883% time consumption. The main consequence of using the proposed improvement of the classic PID algorithm is the nonlinear control surface. The nonlinearity can be obtained by the rule base modification, the nonlinear membership functions application and suitable inference methods application. The algorithm obtained by such changes can be better adjusted to a controlled system. However there is one difficulty i.e. scaling factors need to be tuned. Potential problems in tuning nonlinear fuzzy PID algorithms, provide the basis for trying to use the self-tuning and adaptation algorithms for scaling factors.

References

1. B&R Automation Studio Target for Simulink, Technical Manual TM140
2. B&R Simulation Technical Description (2007)
3. Chopra, S., Mitra, R., Kumar, V.: Fuzzy controller. choosing an appropriate and smallest rule set. International Journal on Computational Cognition, 73–79 (2005)
4. Jantzen, J.: Design of fuzzy controllers. Technical Report 98-E-864, Technical. University of Denmark: Dept. of Automation (1998)
5. Jaszczak, S.: Szybkie prototypowanie cyfrowych algorytmw sterowania z wykorzystaniem programu simulink. Metody Informatyki Stosowanej (accepted 2011)
6. Astrom, K.J., Hagglund, T.: The future of pid control. Control Engineering Practice, 1163–1175 (2001)
7. Pivonka, P.: Comparative analysis of fuzzy PI/PD/PID controller based on classical PID controller approach. Fuzzy Systems, 541–546 (2002)
8. Ross, T., Parkinson, W., Booker, J.: Fuzzy Logic and Probability Applications-Bridging the Gap. SIAM Publishers, Philadelphia (2002)

Implications on Ordered Fuzzy Numbers and Fuzzy Sets of Type Two

Magdalena Kacprzak[1], Witold Kosiński[1,2], and Piotr Prokopowicz[2]

[1] Polish-Japanese Institute of Information Technology, Warsaw, Poland
[2] Kazimierz-Wielki University, Bydgoszcz, Poland
{kacprzak,wkos}@pjwstk.edu.pl, piotrekp@ukw.edu.pl

Abstract. Ordered fuzzy numbers (OFN) as generalization of convex fuzzy numbers represented in parametric form and invented by the second and the third authors and their coworker in 2002, make possible to utilize the fuzzy arithmetic and to construct the lattice structure on them. Fuzzy inference mechanism and implications are proposed together with step fuzzy numbers that may be used for approximations as well as for constructing new fuzzy sets of type two.

1 Introduction

The fuzzy sets were presented by L.A. Zadeh in 1965 to process and then to manipulate data and information affected by unprobabilistic imprecision (uncertainty). These were designed to mathematically represent the vagueness and uncertainty of linguistic problems; thereby obtaining formal tools to work with intrinsic imprecision in different type of problems. The construction can be considered as a generalization of the classic set theory.

The type-2 fuzzy sets were invented and used for modelling uncertainty and imprecision in a better way. These type-2 fuzzy sets were fuzzy since the fuzzy degree of membership is a type-1 fuzzy set [18]. The new concepts were introduced by Mendel and Liang [11] allowing the characterization of a type-2 fuzzy set with a superior membership function and an inferior membership function; these two functions can be represented each one by a type-1 fuzzy set membership function. The interval between these two functions represent the footprint of uncertainty (FOU), which is used to characterize a type-2 fuzzy set.

We know that the classical fuzzy set theory and its restriction to fuzzy numbers, better to say - to convex fuzzy numbers of Nguyen [15] leads to several inconvenience and drawbacks, especially when the operations on them are concerned. Hence some generalization of the convex fuzzy numbers (CFN), known in their parametric form, has been recently proposed by two of us (W.K.& P.P.) and our coworker D. Ślęzak [8] in the form of ordered fuzzy numbers (OFN) and new operations defined on them. Then the original continuity of members of functions appearing in representation of OFN has been dropped in the paper [7]. Thanks to them step ordered fuzzy numbers could be introduced [9,17].

Classical two-valued logic copes with propositions and claims about which we can say that are *"black"* or *"white"*, i.e. formally *"true"* or *"false"*. To capture

L. Rutkowski et al. (Eds.): ICAISC 2012, Part I, LNCS 7267, pp. 247–255, 2012.
© Springer-Verlag Berlin Heidelberg 2012

diversity of approaches concerning expressions like "obesity", in literature are considered multi-valued logics or fuzzy logics. The fuzzy logics has its functional counterpart in the form of the fuzzy set theory. It gives effective tools to model the satisfaction of decision made by an agent or the level of truth of a statement. In particular, each decision objective can be described with a fuzzy membership function where degree zero (one) expresses the minimum (maximum) satisfaction of the objective, while all the intermediate values represent degrees of partial satisfaction.

A fuzzy implication (FI), commonly defined as a two-place operation on the unit interval, is an extension of the classical binary implication. It plays important roles in both mathematical and applied sides of fuzzy set theory. The importance of fuzzy implications in applications of fuzzy logic (FL) to approximate reasoning (AR), decision support systems (DSS), fuzzy control (FC), etc., is hard to exaggerate. Many different fuzzy implication operators have been proposed; most of them fit into one of the two classes: implication operations that are based on an explicit representation of implication $A \implies B$ in terms of alternative, conjunction and negation and R-implications that are based on an implicit representation of implication $A \implies B$ as the weakest C for which $C \wedge B$ implies A. However, some fuzzy implication operations cannot be naturally represented in this form [1].

For example, to the first class belong the Kleene–Dienes operation, called a binary implication, which is a fuzzy counterpart of the RHS of the binary logic tautology $a \implies b \equiv b \vee \neg a$. To have it one has to invent the negation operator $\neg$ to the membership function μ_A of a fuzzy set A and to define a membership function of $\neg A$ as $\mu_{\neg A} := 1 - \mu_A$, and the alternative of two fuzzy sets $C = A \vee B$, and its membership function μ_C as $\mu_C := \max\{\mu_A, \mu_B\}$. Then the Kleene–Dienes implication $A \implies B$ will be $\max\{1 - \mu_A, \mu_B\}$. The simple generalization of the last implication is the so-called S-implication $I_s(A, B)$ defined by the formula

$$I_s(A, B) = S(1 - \mu_A, \mu_B), \tag{1}$$

where S is any S-norm. This generalization is obvious in view of the fact that any S-norm is a generalization of the sum (alternative) of two fuzzy sets. Implication invented by Łukasiewicz [12] which takes the form $\min\{1, 1 - \mu_A + \mu_B\}$ together with the Reichenbach and Fodor implications serve as examples of $I_s(A, B)$ implication [1]. What is unpleasant with all those implications: they do not lead to convex fuzzy numbers, they have, in general, unbounded supports.

2   Ordered Fuzzy Numbers

Proposed recently by the second author and his two coworkers: P.Prokopowicz and D. Ślęzak [8] an extended model of convex fuzzy numbers [15] (CFN), called ordered fuzzy numbers (OFN), does not require any existence of membership functions. In this model an ordered fuzzy number is a pair of continuous functions defined on the interval $[0, 1]$ with values in $\mathbf{R}$. To see OFN as an extension of CFN - model, take a look on a parametric representation know since 1986, [3] of convex fuzzy numbers.

Then four algebraic operations have been proposed between fuzzy numbers and crisp (real) numbers, in which componentwise operations are present. In particular if $A = (f_A, g_A), B = (f_B, g_B)$ and $C = (f_C, g_C)$ are mathematical objects called ordered fuzzy numbers, then the sum $C = A + B$, product $C = A \cdot B$, division $C = A \div B$ and scalar multiplication by real $r \in \mathbf{R}$, are defined in natural way:

$$r \cdot A = (r f_A, r g_A),$$

and

$$f_C(y) = f_A(y) \star f_B(y), \qquad g_C(y) = g_A(y) \star g_B(y), \tag{2}$$

where "$\star$" works for "$+$", "$\cdot$", and "$\div$", respectively, and where $A \div B$ is defined, if the functions $|f_B|$ and $|g_B|$ are bigger than zero. Notice that the subtraction of B is the same as the addition of the opposite of B, i.e. the number $(-1) \cdot B$, and consequently $B - B = 0$. From this follows that any fuzzy algebraic equation $A + X = C$ with given A and C as OFN possesses a solution, that is OFN, as well. Moreover, to any convex and continuous[1] fuzzy number correspond two OFNs, they differ by the orientation: one has positive, say (f, g), another (g, f) has negative.

A relation of partial ordering in the space of all OFN, denoted by $\mathcal{R}$, can be introduced by defining the subset of 'positive' ordered fuzzy numbers: a number $A = (f, g)$ is not less than zero, and by writing

$$A \geq 0 \quad \text{iff} \quad f \geq 0, g \geq 0. \tag{3}$$

In this way the set $\mathcal{R}$ becomes a partially ordered ring. Notice, that for each two fuzzy numbers $A = (f_A, g_A), B = (f_B, g_B)$ as above, we may define $\inf(A, B) =: F$ and $\sup(A, B) =: G$, both from $\mathcal{R}$, by the relations:

$$F = (f_F, g_F), \text{if} f_F = \inf\{f_A, f_B\}, g_F = \inf\{g_A, g_B\}. \tag{4}$$

Similarly, we define $G = \sup(A, B)$.

Notice that in the definition of OFN it is not required that two continuous functions f and g are (partial) inverses of some membership function. Moreover, it may happen that the membership function corresponding to A does not exist; such numbers are called improper.

In this new framework new fuzzy implications have been invented. One of the most promising implications is that suggested by P.Prokopowicz in his Ph.D. thesis and called implication with multiplication, in which the algebraic structure of operations on OFN has been used. Before its formula will be given we have to repeat after its author [16] the corresponding membership function $\tilde{\mu}_A$, which can be defined for any improper ordered fuzzy number [2] as

$$\tilde{\mu}_A(x) = \max \arg\{f(s) = x, g(y) = x\}, \tag{5}$$

---

[1] However, the recent extension presented in [7] includes all convex fuzzy numbers.
[2] If f is strictly increasing and g decreasing, and $f(s) \leq g(s)$, for $s \in [0, 1]$, then A is called proper and possesses the classical membership function, moreover it represents a CFN.

if $x \in \text{Range}(f) \cup \text{Range}(g)$ and

$$\tilde{\mu}_A(x) = 1 \ , \ \text{if } x \in [f(1), g(1)] \cup [g(1), f(1)] \ , \tag{6}$$
$$\text{and } \tilde{\mu}_A(x) = 0$$

where one of the intervals $[f(1), g(1)]$ or $[g(1), f(1)]$ may be empty, depending on the sign of $f(1) - g(1)$, (i.e., if the sign is -1 then the second interval is empty). Notice that $\tilde{\mu}$ in (5) is defined by the inverse functions of f and g is the both are strictly monotonous, particularly, if A is proper.

Then the Prokopowicz's implication $A \Rightarrow B$ has value $v(A \Rightarrow B)$ given by

$$v(A \Rightarrow B) = \tilde{\mu}_A B \ , \tag{7}$$

where $\tilde{\mu}_A$ is defined by (5),(6) in the case when A is improper. However, when A is proper it possesses the classical membership function. The result of this implication is an ordered fuzzy number and is close to the engineering implication of Mamdani type, rather.

2.1   Defuzzification Functional

In dealing with applications of fuzzy numbers we need set of functionals that map each fuzzy number into real, and in such a way that is consistent with operations on reals. Those operations are called defuzzifications. To be more strict we introduce.

Definition 1. A map ϕ from the space $\mathcal{R}$ of all OFN's to reals is called a defuzzification functional if it satisfies:

1. $\phi(c^{\ddagger}) = c$,
2. $\phi(A + c^{\ddagger}) = \phi(A) + c$,
3. $\phi(cA) = c\phi(A)$, for any $c \in \mathbf{R}$ and $A \in \mathcal{R}$.

where $c^{\ddagger}(s) = (c, c)$, $s \in [0, 1]$, represents crisp number (a real) $c \in \mathbf{R}$.

¿From this follow that each defuzzification functional must be homogeneous of order one, restrictive additive, and some how normalized.

2.2   Lattice Structure on OFN

Let us consider the set $\mathcal{R}$ with operations $\vee$ and $\wedge$ such that for $A = (f_A, g_A)$ and $B = (f_B, g_B)$,

$$A \vee B = (sup\{f_A, f_B\}, sup\{g_A, g_B\})$$

and

$$A \wedge B = (inf\{f_A, f_B\}, inf\{g_A, g_B\}).$$

Observe that $\vee$ and $\wedge$ are operations in $\mathcal{R}_K$ which are idempotent, commutative and associative. Moreover, these two operations are connected by the absorption laws which ensure that the set $\mathcal{R}$ with an order $\leq$ defined as $A \leq B$ iff $B = A \vee B$ is a partial ordering within which meets and joins are given through the operations $\vee$ and $\wedge$. The following theorem holds:

Theorem 1. The algebra $(\mathcal{R}, \vee, \wedge)$ is a lattice.

3 Step Ordered Fuzzy Numbers

To include all CFN in OFN the second author in [7] assumed functions of bounded variation ($\mathcal{R}_{BV}$). Then operations are defined in the similar way, the norm, however, will change into the norm of the cartesian product of the space of functions of bounded variations (BV). Then all convex fuzzy numbers are contained in this new space $\mathcal{R}_{BV}$ of OFN. Notice that functions from BV are continuous except for a countable number of points.

If we fix a natural number K and split $[0,1)$ into $K-1$ subintervals $[a_i, a_{i+1})$, i.e. $\bigcup_{i=1}^{K-1} [a_i, a_{i+1}) = [0,1)$, where $0 = a_1 < a_2 < ... < a_K = 1$, and define a step function f of resolution K by putting u_i on each subinterval $[a_i, a_{i+1})$, then each such function f is identified with a K-dimensional vector $f \sim u = (u_1, u_2 ... u_K) \in \mathbf{R}^K$, the K-th value u_K corresponds to $s = 1$, i.e. $f(1) = u_K$. Taking a pair of such functions we have an ordered fuzzy number from $\mathcal{R}_{BV}$. Now we introduce.

Definition 2. By a step ordered fuzzy number A of resolution K we mean an ordered pair (f, g) of functions such that $f, g : [0,1] \rightarrow \mathbf{R}$ are K-step functions.

We use $\mathcal{R}_K$ for denotation the set of elements satisfying Def. 2. The set $\mathcal{R}_K \subset \mathcal{R}_{BV}$ has been extensively elaborated by our students in [4] and [9]. We can identify $\mathcal{R}_K$ with the Cartesian product of $\mathbf{R}^K \times \mathbf{R}^K$ since each K-step function is represented by its K values. It is obvious that each element of the space $\mathcal{R}_K$ may be regarded as an approximation of elements from $\mathcal{R}_{BV}$, by increasing the number K of steps we are getting the better approximation. The norm of $\mathcal{R}_K$ is assumed to be the Euclidean one of $\mathbf{R}^{2K}$, then we have a inner-product structure for our disposal.

Due to the fact that $\mathcal{R}_K$ is isomorphic to $\mathbf{R}^K \times \mathbf{R}^K$ we conclude, from the Riesz theorem and the condition 1 that a general linear defuzzification functional on $\mathcal{R}_K$ has the representation $H(\underline{u}, \underline{v}) = \underline{u} \cdot \underline{b} + \underline{v} \cdot \underline{d}$, with arbitrary $\underline{b}, \underline{d} \in \mathbf{R}^K$, such that $\underline{1} \cdot \underline{b} + \underline{1} \cdot \underline{d} = 1$, where $\cdot$ denotes the inner (scalar) product in $\mathbf{R}^K$ and $\underline{1} = (1, 1, ..., 1) \in \mathbf{R}^K$ is the unit vector in $\mathbf{R}^K$, while the pair $(\underline{1}, \underline{1})$ represents a crisp one in $\mathcal{R}_K$. It means that such a functional is represented by the vector $(\underline{b}, \underline{d}) \in \mathbf{R}^{2K}$. Notice that all functionals of the type $\phi_j = \underline{e}_j, j = 1, 2, ..., 2K$, where $\underline{e}_j \in \mathbf{R}^{2K}$ has all zero component except for 1 on the j-th position, form a basis of $\mathcal{R}_K{}^*$ - the space adjoint to $\mathcal{R}_K$, they are called *fundamental functionals*

Let us take $\underline{b} = \underline{c}$ and such, that all their components are equal to $1/2K$, and denote such defuzzification functional by ψ_K.

Now let us introduce the particular subset $\mathcal{N}$ of $\mathcal{R}_K$, with $\underline{u}, \underline{v} \in \mathcal{N}$ such that each component of the vector $\underline{u}$ as well as of $\underline{v}$ has value 1 or 0. Since each element of $\mathcal{N}$ is represented by a $2K$-dimensional binary vector binary the cardinality of the set $\mathcal{N}$ is 2^{2K}. Then if we apply the functional ψ_K to elements of $\mathcal{N}$ we may obtain all possible fractional numbers $i/2K$, with $i = 0, 1, ..., 2K$, as the values of defuzzification functional ψ_K on $\mathcal{N}$. The set $\mathcal{N}$ and the functional ψ_K will play fundamental roles in the next section.

3.1 Fuzzy Implication on $\mathcal{R}_K$

It is easy to observe that all subsets of $\mathcal{N}$ have both a join and a meet in $\mathcal{N}$. Therefore $\mathcal{N}$ creates a *complete lattice*. In such a lattice we can distinguish the greatest element $\underline{1}$ represented by the vector $= (1, 1, ..., 1)$ and the least element $\underline{0}$ represented by the vector $(0, 0, ..., 0)$.

Theorem 2. The algebra $(\mathcal{N}, \vee, \wedge)$ is a complete lattice.

In a lattice in which the greatest and the least elements exist it is possible to define compliments. The compliment of a number A will be marked with $\neg A$ and is defined as follows. Let $A \in \mathcal{N}$ be a step ordered fuzzy number represented by a binary vector $(a_1, a_2, \ldots, a_K)$. Then the compliment of A equals

$$A = (1 - a_1, 1 - a_2, \ldots, 1 - a_K).$$

On the set $\mathcal{N}$ new operation equivalent to classical binary implication is introduced, which provides a new method of approximate reasoning. We introduce

Definition 4. For $A, B \in \mathcal{N}$ the operation of fuzzy implication $\rightarrow$ is defined as

$$A \rightarrow B := \neg A \vee B.$$

This operation satisfies the basic property of the logical implication, i.e., it returns *false* if and only if the first term is *true*, and the second term is *false*. In fact, since $\neg\underline{0} = \underline{1}$ and $\neg\underline{1} = \underline{0}$ it holds that: $\underline{1} \rightarrow \underline{0} = \underline{0}$ and $\underline{0} \rightarrow \underline{0} = \underline{0} \rightarrow \underline{1} = \underline{1} \rightarrow \underline{1} = \underline{1}$.

3.2 Łukasiewicz Implication of SOFN

Let us introduce another subset of SOFN, called $\mathcal{M}$ which contains as a proper subset $\mathcal{N}$. We assume, as previously, the fixed resolution K and assume now that each element of $\mathcal{M}$ is $2K$ dimensional vector from $\mathbf{R}^{2K}$ and such that each its component is rational (or real, in general) number from $[0, M]$. Then on $\mathcal{M}$ we may introduce another implication. Let us introduce two other operations of conjunction $\sqcap$ on disjunction $\sqcup$. Take $A, B \in \mathcal{M}$, we define

$$A \sqcup B = C, \text{with } C = (c_1, c_2, \ldots, c_{2K}) \text{ and } c_i = \min\{M, a_i + b_i\} \qquad (8)$$

$$A \sqcap B = C, \text{with } C = (c_1, c_2, \ldots, c_{2K}) \text{ and } c_i = \frac{1}{M}(a_i \cdot b_i).$$

Notice that we have the following properties for any pair A, B:

$$A \leq A \sqcup B \text{ and } B \leq A \sqcup B, \text{ and } A \sqcap B \leq A \text{ and } A \sqcap B \leq B. \qquad (9)$$

It is evident that taking $M = 1$ we may regard the space $\mathcal{M}$ as a simple extension of $\mathcal{N}$, since values of each fundamental defuzzification functional lays in $I = [0, 1]$. Let us stay in this space, and denote it by $\mathcal{M}_1$ and define the negation of A as previously by $\neg A = (1 - a_1, 1 - a_c, \ldots, 1 - a_{2K})$. Now implementing the classical definition of the binary negation, however with the new sup - operator $\sqcup$,

$$A \to B := \neg A \sqcup B,$$

we obtain

$$\text{if } C := A \to B, \text{ then } C = (c_1, c_2, \ldots, c_{2K}) \text{ with } c_i = \min\{1, 1 - a_i + b_i\}, \qquad (10)$$

which is nothing else than the Łukasiewicz type implication. It is evident that in the general case, i.e. in the space $\mathcal{M}$ we may introduce the counterpart of the last implication.

Theorem 1. *On the space $\mathcal{M}_1$ the implication $A \to B := \neg A \sqcup B$, is a generalization of the Łukasiewicz implication to step ordered fuzzy numbers.*

4   New Fuzzy Sets of Type 2

In this subsection we extend the application of the ordered fuzzy numbers and their particular subset $\mathcal{N}$ of SOFN to define fuzzy sets of type two.

Consider a classical (convex) fuzzy number $Z \in$ CFN with its membership function μ_Z. Let us recall that for Z we may define for each $s \in (0, 1]$ the s-cut (or s-section) of the number (of the membership function) Z as the classical set Z_s by

$$Z_s = \{x \in \mathbf{R} : \mu_Z(x) \geq s\}. \qquad (11)$$

For each convex fuzzy number Z and two numbers $s_1 \leq s_s$ the following relation $Z_{s_2} \subset Z_{s_1}$ between the corresponding s-sections holds.

Now let us fix the resolution K of step functions defining the $\mathcal{R}_K$ and take the partition of the unit interval into $K-1$ subintervals $\bigcup\limits_{i=1}^{K-1} [a_i, a_{i+1}) \cup \{a_K\} = [0, 1]$, with $0 = a_1 < a_2 < \ldots < a_K = 1$.

Then we may define a mapping

$$val_K : \mathbf{R} \times \text{CFN} \to \mathcal{N} \qquad (12)$$

which for given Z and each $x \in Z_{a_i} - Z_{a_{i+1}}$ attaches an element of the set $\mathcal{N}$, a step ordered fuzzy number, in such a way that $\psi_K(val_K(x, Z)) = a_i$, i.e. after defuzzifying the value of $val_K(x, Z)$ we get the value of the membership function of Z at the lower end of the s-section to which x belongs. In this way the one-variable function $val_K(\cdot, Z) : \mathbf{R} \to \mathcal{N}$ is piecewise constant: it is constant on each subinterval $Z_{a_i} - Z_{a_{i+1}}$. It means that after defuzzification the correspondence given by the function $val_K(\cdot, Z)$ is in agreement with the value of the membership function attached to x by μ_Z, module the assumed finite step-wise approximation of values of the membership function.

If we use the so-called parametric representation of convex fuzzy numbers [3] in terms of two left-continuous functions α_1, α_2, the both defined on the interval $[0,1]$ with values in $\mathbf{R}$, and denote by x_{1-} and x_{1+} the points from the support of μ_Z, such that $\mu_Z(x_{1-}) = \mu_Z(x_{1+}) = 1$, and at the point x_{1-} the membership function attains for the first time the value 1, and the point x_{1+} is the last point with this property [3], then the condition $x \in Z_{a_i} - Z_{a_{i+1}}$, may be written as $\alpha_1(a_i) \leq x \leq \alpha_2(a_{i+1})$ if $x \leq x_{1-}$ and $\alpha_1(a_{i+1}) \leq x \leq \alpha_2(a_i)$ if $x \geq x_{1+}$. This is so, because the function α_1 is non-decreasing and the function α_2 is non-increasing.

Notice that for a classical fuzzy rule [2]: If 'a condition is satisfied' Then 'a consequence follows' , where both parts: premise and consequent are fuzzy, the mapping val_K may be applied to the both and then our new fuzzy inference given previously.

5   Conclusion

Ordered fuzzy numbers was applied to deal with optimization problems when data are fuzzy. In this paper a new fuzzy implication on step ordered fuzzy numbers is introduced. It can be used for approximate *reasoning*. In classical two-valued logics only two logical values are applied: 0 or 1. In fuzzy logics it is extended to the values from the interval $[0,1]$. Our contribution is to enrich these formal systems and use for logical justification step ordered fuzzy numbers. This approach is very innovative and allows for including in logical value more information than that something is true, true with some degree or false. In future work we are going to show application and usefulness of this new reasoning on diverse examples, especially for modelling uncertain beliefs of agents in multi-agent systems.

References

1. Baczyński, M., Jayaram, B.: Fuzzy Implications. Studies in Fuzziness and Soft Computing, vol. 231. Springer, Berlin (2008) ISBN: 978-3-540-69080-1
2. Buckley James, J.: Solving fuzzy equations in economics and finance. Fuzzy Sets and Systems 48, 289–296 (1992)
3. Goetschel Jr., R., Voxman, W.: Elementary fuzzy calculus. Fuzzy Sets and Systems 18(1), 31–43 (1986)
4. Gruszczyńska, A., Krajewska, I.: Fuzzy calculator on step ordered fuzzy numbers, UKW, Bydgoszcz (2008) (in Polish)
5. Karnik, N.N., Mendel, J.M.: An Introduction to Type-2 Fuzzy Logic Systems. Univ. of Southern Calif., Los Angeles (1998)

---

[3] It means that $x_{1-} = \alpha_1(1)$ and $x_{1+} = \alpha_2(1)$.

6. Kosiński, W.: On Defuzzyfication of Ordered Fuzzy Numbers. In: Rutkowski, L., Siekmann, J.H., Tadeusiewicz, R., Zadeh, L.A. (eds.) ICAISC 2004. LNCS (LNAI), vol. 3070, pp. 326–331. Springer, Heidelberg (2004)
7. Kosiński, W.: On fuzzy number calculus. Int. J. Appl. Math. Comput. Sci. 16(1), 51–57 (2006)
8. Kosiński, W., Prokopowicz, P., Ślęzak, D.: Fuzzy numbers with algebraic operations: algorithmic approach. In: Klopotek, M., Wierzchoń, S.T., Michalewicz, M. (eds.) Proc. Intelligent Information Systems, IIS 2002, Poland, June 3-6, pp. 311–320. Physica Verlag, Heidelberg (2002)
9. Kościeński, K.: Module of step fuzzy numbers in motion control. PJIIT, Warsaw (2010) (in Polish)
10. Larsen, P.M.: Industrial applications of fuzzy logic controler. Intern. J. Man-Machine Studies 12(1), 3–10 (1980)
11. Liang, Q., Mendel, J.: Interval type-2 fuzzy logic systems: Theory and design. IEEE Transactions Fuzzy Systems 8, 535–550 (2000)
12. Łukasiewicz, J.: Elements of the Mathematical Logic. PWN, Warszawa (1958) (in Polish)
13. Mamdani, E.H.: Advances in the linguistic synthesis of fuzzy controllers. Intern. J. Man-Machine Studies 8, 669–678 (1976)
14. Mendel, J.: Uncertain Rule-Based Fuzzy Logic Systems: Introduction and New Directions. Prentice-Hall, NJ (2001)
15. Nguyen, H.T.: A note on the extension principle for fuzzy sets. J. Math. Anal. Appl. 64, 369–380 (1978)
16. Prokopowicz, P.: Algorithmization of Operations on Fuzzy Numbers and its Applications, Ph. D. Thesis, IPPT PAN (2005)
17. Kosiński, W., Węgrzyn-Wolska, K., Borzymek, P.: Evolutionary algorithm in fuzzy data problem. In: Kita, E. (ed.) Evolutionary Algorithms, pp. 201–218. InTech (April 2011) ISBN 978-953-307-171-8
18. Zadeh, L.A.: Fuzzy Logic. Computer 1(4), 83–93 (1988)

Fuzzy Supervised Self-Organizing Map
for Semi-supervised Vector Quantization

Marika Kästner and Thomas Villmann

Computational Intelligence group at the Department
for Mathematics/Natural & Computer Sciences,
University of Applied Sciences Mittweida, Mittweida, Germany
{kaestner,villmann}@hs-mittweida.de

Abstract. In this paper we propose a new approach to combine unsupervised and supervised vector quantization for clustering and fuzzy
classification using the framework of neural vector quantizers like self-
organizing maps or neural gas. For this purpose the original cost functions are modified in such a way that both aspects, unsupervised vector
quantization and supervised classification, are incorporated. The theoretical justification of the convergence of the new algorithm is given by
an adequate redefinition of the underlying dissimilarity measure now interpreted as a dissimilarity in the data space combined with the class
label space. This allows a gradient descent learning as known for the
original algorithms. Thus a semi-supervised learning scheme is achieved.
We apply this method for a spectra image cube of remote sensing data
for landtype classification. The obtained fuzzy class visualizations allow
a better understanding and interpretation of the spectra.

1 Introduction

Unsupervised and supervised vector quantization by neural maps is still an important issue. Neural maps are prototype based algorithms inspired by biological
neural systems. Prominent models are the self-organizing map (SOM) and the
neural gas network (NG) [7],[9]. These approaches are designed for unsupervised data clustering (NG) and visualization (SOM). Supervised learning vector
quantization follows the idea of prototype based representaion of classes. Well
known such models are the family of learning vector quantizers (LVQ) based on a
heuristic adaptation scheme [7], or their cost function based counterpart named
generalized LVQ (GLVQ) [12]. These algorithms represent the classes by class
typical prototypes in contrast to support vector machines, which emphasize the
class borders to describe data classes.

There exist only a few methods to combine unsupervised and supervised learning in SOM or NG. The most intuitive one is simple post labeling after unsupervised training. In the approach Learning Association by Self-Organization
(LASSO) fuzzy labels are concatenated to the data and prototype vectors by
means of unary coding [10]. These new vectors are treated as usual in SOM and
NG during learning. Resepective variants of the usual NG and SOM (in the HES-
KES variant, [4]) are Fuzzy Labeled NG (FLNG) and the Fuzzy Labeled SOM

L. Rutkowski et al. (Eds.): ICAISC 2012, Part I, LNCS 7267, pp. 256–265, 2012.

(FLSOM) use modifications of the cost function incorporating the supervised information in an additive manner [17,20]. Yet, their theoretical justifications are tricky and partially unsatisfactory.

In this paper we propose a modification applying a new dissimilarity measure, which merges both unsupervised and supervised data information into a quasi metric [11]. Thereby the combination is multiplicative with an offset to prevent trivial solutions. Thus, it turns out that the structural framework of standard vector quantizer SOM and NG is preserved and their convergence properties are transferred. The new approach can be seen as a kind of semi-supervised learning in case of mixed labeled and unlabeled data. Moreover, the model can be applied to both crisp and fuzzy labeled data.

In the following we introduce the methodology for the Heskes-SOM. Subsequent transfer to NG is obviously. In the experimental section we present the results for an artificial data set and a real world classification problem in satellite remote sensing data analysis.

2 The Fuzzy Supervised SOM Model

2.1 The SOM for Unsupervised Vector Quantization

The usual SOM model assumes data points $\mathbf{v} \in V \subset \mathbb{R}^n$ with the data density $P(\mathbf{v})$. The prototypes $\mathbf{w_r}$ are assigned to an external lattice A with $\mathbf{r} \in A$, whereby A is equipped with an underlying topological structure usually chosen as a regular grid [7]. We denote the grid distance between nodes $\mathbf{r}$ and $\mathbf{r}'$ by $d_A(\mathbf{r}, \mathbf{r}')$, and $d(\mathbf{v}, \mathbf{w_r})$ denotes the differentiable dissimilarity in the data space as above, frequently chosen to be the squared Euclidean metric. In the Heskes-variant the mapping (winner determination) rule is given by

$$\mathbf{s}(\mathbf{v}) = \operatorname{argmin}_{\mathbf{r} \in A} \left(\sum_{\mathbf{r}' \in A} h_\sigma^{SOM}(\mathbf{r}, \mathbf{r}') d(\mathbf{v}, \mathbf{w_{r'}}) \right) \tag{1}$$

with

$$h_\sigma^{SOM}(\mathbf{r}, \mathbf{r}') = \exp\left(-\frac{d_A(\mathbf{r}, \mathbf{r}')}{2\sigma^2}\right) \tag{2}$$

as neighborhood function [4]. Following this ansatz we denote

$$e_\mathbf{r}(\mathbf{v}) = \sum_{\mathbf{r}' \in A} h_\sigma^{SOM}(\mathbf{r}, \mathbf{r}') d(\mathbf{v}, \mathbf{w_{r'}}) \tag{3}$$

as local costs for neuron $\mathbf{r}$ given the input $\mathbf{v}$ such that (1) can be rewritten as

$$\mathbf{s}(\mathbf{v}) = \operatorname{argmin}_{\mathbf{r} \in A}(e_\mathbf{r}(\mathbf{v})). \tag{4}$$

Then a cost function for SOM can be defined by

$$E_{\text{SOM}} = \int P(\mathbf{v}) e_{\mathbf{s}(\mathbf{v})}(\mathbf{v}) d\mathbf{v} \tag{5}$$

which leads to the stochastic gradient learning rule

$$\triangle \mathbf{w_r} = -h_\sigma^{SOM} \left(\mathbf{r}, \mathbf{s}\left(\mathbf{v}\right)\right) \frac{\partial d\left(\mathbf{v}, \mathbf{w_r}\right)}{\partial \mathbf{w_r}}. \tag{6}$$

We remark that this derivation of the gradient descent learning is only valid iff the local costs $e_\mathbf{r}\left(\mathbf{v}\right)$ in the cost function (5) are exactly the same as those used for the mapping in (1).

In the following we develop a new variant, which integrates the additional class information for (semi-)supervised learning into the standard model, which is also applicable to fuzzy classification problems and therefore denoted as Fuzzy Supervised SOM – (FSSOM).

2.2   The FSSOM-Model

First in this section, we shortly review the LASSO approach [10] to deal with fuzzy labeled data learning and point out its difficulties. Second, we turn to the new FSSOM model, which overcome some of these problems.

LASSO. For LASSO [10], we suppose C data classes. Each data vector $\mathbf{v}$ is accompanied by a data assignment vectors $\mathbf{c_v} = \left(c_\mathbf{v}^1, \ldots, c_\mathbf{v}^C \right)^T \in [0,1]^C$ with vector entries taken as class probability or possibility assignments. Crisp classification is obtained by the additional requirement of $c_\mathbf{v}^j \in \{0,1\}$. Analogously, we also equip the prototypes $\mathbf{w_r}$ with class labels $\mathbf{y_r}$. In the LASSO approach new data points are generated by concatenation of the data vectors and their class label vectors yielding new data vectors $\tilde{\mathbf{v}}$ and analogously prototypes $\tilde{\mathbf{w}}_\mathbf{r}$. Then during the learning phase, the usual SOM model is applied with the dissimilarity

$$D_{LASSO}\left(\tilde{\mathbf{v}}, \tilde{\mathbf{w}}_\mathbf{r} \right) = \left[d\left(\mathbf{v}, \mathbf{w_r}\right) + d\left(\mathbf{c_v}, \mathbf{y_r}\right) \right] \tag{7}$$

in the local costs $e_\mathbf{r}\left(\mathbf{v}\right)$ from (3) replacing the squared Euclidean distance $d\left(\mathbf{v}, \mathbf{w_r}\right)$ by this combined measure, where $d\left(\mathbf{c_v}, \mathbf{y_r}\right)$ is also the squared Euclidean distance. In that way both, the prototypes $\mathbf{w_r}$ and their labels $\mathbf{y_r}$ are adapted using $\tilde{\mathbf{v}}$ and $\tilde{\mathbf{w}}_\mathbf{r}$ in (1) and (6). In the recall phase, however, the labels are unknown. Therefore, the mapping rule (1) is applied using the prototypes $\mathbf{w_r}$ and the data point $\mathbf{v}$ with $d\left(\mathbf{v}, \mathbf{w_r}\right)$, only. The class association for that data vector is taken as $\mathbf{y}_{\mathbf{s}(\mathbf{v})}$. This model was generalized by means of separated dissimilarity measures for both, the data space and the label space

$$\widetilde{D}\left(\tilde{\mathbf{v}}, \tilde{\mathbf{w}}_\mathbf{r} \right) = \left[\left(1 - \gamma\right) d\left(\mathbf{v}, \mathbf{w_r}\right) + \gamma \delta\left(\mathbf{c_v}, \mathbf{y_r}\right) \right] \tag{8}$$

with the balancing parameter $\gamma \in [0,1]$ determining the influence of the class information. The resulting SOM model is called Fuzzy Labeled SOM (FLSOM,[21]) and can be easily transferred to the NG [17]. Yet, the FLSOM using this *additive* distortion measure is reported to be unstable and sensitive to the choice of the balancing parameter γ [20]. Moreover, for NG there are further difficulties concerning the neighborhood cooperativeness to assure a valid convergence proof [17]. We will see in the following that the new FSSOM and FSNG proposed here, are less affected by such difficulties.

The New Fuzzy Supervised SOM Model – FSSOM. For the FSSOM model, we now consider the new *multiplicative* deviation measure

$$D_\varepsilon\left(\mathbf{v}, \mathbf{w_r}, \gamma\right) = D_\varepsilon^\delta\left(\mathbf{c_v}, \mathbf{y_r}, \gamma\right) \cdot D_\varepsilon^d\left(\mathbf{v}, \mathbf{w_r}, \gamma\right) - \varepsilon_\delta \varepsilon_d \tag{9}$$

with

$$D_\varepsilon^\delta\left(\mathbf{c_v}, \mathbf{y_r}, \gamma\right) = \left(\gamma \cdot \delta\left(\mathbf{c_v}, \mathbf{y_r}\right) + \varepsilon_\delta\right) \tag{10}$$

and

$$D_\varepsilon^d\left(\mathbf{v}, \mathbf{w_r}, \gamma\right) = \left((1 - \gamma) \cdot d\left(\mathbf{v}, \mathbf{w_r}\right) + \varepsilon_d\right) \tag{11}$$

where the parameter vector $\varepsilon = (\varepsilon_\delta, \varepsilon_d)$ determines an offset term. This offset is necessary for D_ε to prevent unexpected behavior of the FSSOM under certain conditions, which are discussed more detailed later. It turns out that $D_\varepsilon\left(\mathbf{v}, \mathbf{w_r}, \gamma\right)$ is a quasi metric [11], which takes into account both the usual dissimilarity $d\left(\mathbf{v}, \mathbf{w_r}\right)$ between data and prototypes as well as their dissimilarity $\delta\left(\mathbf{c_v}, \mathbf{y_r}\right)$ for the class information as before for FLSOM. Again, the parameter $\gamma \in [0, 1]$ determines the influence of the class information with $\gamma = 0$ yielding the standard Heskes-SOM.

In the easiest case, both measures, $d\left(\mathbf{v}, \mathbf{w_r}\right)$ and $\delta\left(\mathbf{c_v}, \mathbf{y_r}\right)$, could be chosen as the (quadratic) Euclidean distance. Yet, the mapping rule (1) of the original SOM remains structurally unchanged in this FSSOM model, but replacing the original distances $d\left(\mathbf{v}, \mathbf{w_r}\right)$ by the combination measure in the local costs (3).

Finally, the FSSOM model leads to a prototype adaptation influenced by the class agreement $\delta\left(\mathbf{c_v}, \mathbf{y_r}\right)$:

$$\triangle\mathbf{w_r} = -\left(1 - \gamma\right) \cdot D_\varepsilon^\delta\left(\mathbf{c_v}, \mathbf{y_r}, \gamma\right) \cdot h_\sigma^{SOM}\left(\mathbf{r}, \mathbf{s}\left(\mathbf{v}\right)\right) \cdot \frac{\partial d\left(\mathbf{v}, \mathbf{w_r}\right)}{\partial \mathbf{w_r}} \tag{12}$$

and accompanied by the label adaptation

$$\triangle\mathbf{y_r} = -\gamma \cdot D_\varepsilon^d\left(\mathbf{v}, \mathbf{w_r}, \gamma\right) \cdot h_\sigma^{SOM}\left(\mathbf{r}, \mathbf{s}\left(\mathbf{v}\right)\right) \cdot \frac{\partial \delta\left(\mathbf{c_v}, \mathbf{y_r}\right)}{\partial \mathbf{y_r}} \tag{13}$$

such that both, prototype vectors and their class assignment vectors, are parallely adjusted.

The visualization of the fuzzy class label vectors $\mathbf{y_r}$ of the neuron $\mathbf{r}$ assigned to prototype $\mathbf{w_r}$ according to the grid structure of the neuron lattice A may provide information of class overlaps, if the underlying substructure of usual Heskes-SOM is at least roughly topology preserving [1,15]. From this overlap information knowledge about class similarities may be extracted.

Obviously, the transfer to the NG algorithm is straightforward. It can be shown that for the resulting FSNG the difficulties concerning the neighborhood cooperativeness known from FLNG vanish [6].

2.3 Properties of the Dissimilarity Measure $D_\varepsilon\left(\mathbf{v}, \mathbf{w_r}, \gamma\right)$

The stochastic gradient descent with respect to the prototypes $\mathbf{w_r}$ and their class label vectors $\mathbf{y_r}$ is carried out for a given data vector $\mathbf{v}$ and its class assignment $\mathbf{c_v}$ proportionally to the partial derivatives

$$\frac{\partial E_{\text{FSSOM}}}{\partial \mathbf{w_r}} = \frac{\partial E_{\text{FSSOM}}}{\partial D_\varepsilon (\mathbf{v}, \mathbf{w_r}, \gamma)} \frac{\partial D_\varepsilon (\mathbf{v}, \mathbf{w_r}, \gamma)}{\partial \mathbf{w_r}} \tag{14}$$

and

$$\frac{\partial E_{\text{FSSOM}}}{\partial \mathbf{y_r}} = \frac{\partial E_{\text{FSSOM}}}{\partial D_\varepsilon (\mathbf{v}, \mathbf{w_r}, \gamma)} \frac{\partial D_\varepsilon (\mathbf{v}, \mathbf{w_r}, \gamma)}{\partial \mathbf{y_r}}. \tag{15}$$

Therefore, we have to investigate the partial derivatives of $D_\varepsilon (\mathbf{v}, \mathbf{w_r}, \gamma)$ with respect to $\mathbf{w_r}$ and $\mathbf{y_r}$:

$$\frac{\partial D_\varepsilon (\mathbf{v}, \mathbf{w_r}, \gamma)}{\partial \mathbf{w_r}} = (1 - \gamma) \cdot D_\varepsilon^\delta (\mathbf{c_v}, \mathbf{y_r}, \gamma) \cdot \frac{\partial d (\mathbf{v}, \mathbf{w_r})}{\partial \mathbf{w_r}} \tag{16}$$

and

$$\frac{\partial D_\varepsilon (\mathbf{v}, \mathbf{w_r}, \gamma)}{\partial \mathbf{y_r}} = \gamma \cdot D_\varepsilon^d (\mathbf{v}, \mathbf{w_r}, \gamma) \cdot \frac{\partial \delta (\mathbf{c_v}, \mathbf{y_r})}{\partial \mathbf{y_r}} \tag{17}$$

determining the update formula (12) and (13). If the quadratic Euclidean distance is used for $d (\mathbf{v}, \mathbf{w_r})$ and $\delta (\mathbf{c_v}, \mathbf{y_r})$, we immediately find

$$\frac{\partial d (\mathbf{v}, \mathbf{w_r})}{\partial \mathbf{w_r}} = -2 (\mathbf{v} - \mathbf{w_r}) \tag{18}$$

and

$$\frac{\partial \delta (\mathbf{c_v}, \mathbf{y_r})}{\partial \mathbf{y_r}} = -2 (\mathbf{c_v} - \mathbf{y_r}) \tag{19}$$

for prototype and class assignment adaptation, respectively. However, other choices are possible [16].

It should be mentioned that $D_\varepsilon (\mathbf{v}, \mathbf{w_r}, \gamma)$ is not a standard (mathematical) metric since it violates the triangle inequality. However, $D_\varepsilon (\mathbf{v}, \mathbf{w_r}, \gamma)$ fulfills the requirements of a quasi-metric [11]. In particular, we have $D_\varepsilon (\mathbf{v}, \mathbf{w_r}, \gamma) = 0$ for a perfect match of the prototype as well as its labels.

For learning in FSSOM we have to distinguish the following extreme cases, which should be of special interest:

1. $d (\mathbf{v}, \mathbf{w_r}) = 0$ and $\delta (\mathbf{c_v}, \mathbf{y_r}) \neq 0$, i.e. the prototype is perfectly placed but its label is not adequate: In that case a non-vanishing term

$$\frac{\partial D_\varepsilon (\mathbf{v}, \mathbf{w_r}, \gamma)}{\partial \mathbf{y_r}}\Big|_{d(\mathbf{v}, \mathbf{w_r})=0} = (1 - \gamma) \cdot \varepsilon_d \cdot \frac{\partial \delta (\mathbf{c_v}, \mathbf{y_r})}{\partial \mathbf{y_r}} \tag{20}$$

remains, which guarantees the label adaptation.

2. $d (\mathbf{v}, \mathbf{w_r}) \neq 0$ and $\delta (\mathbf{c_v}, \mathbf{y_r}) = 0$, i.e. the prototype label perfectly matches but the prototype itself is not optimally adjusted: In that case

$$\frac{\partial D_\varepsilon (\mathbf{v}, \mathbf{w_r}, \gamma)}{\partial \mathbf{w_r}}\Big|_{\delta(\mathbf{c_v}, \mathbf{y_r})=0} = \gamma \cdot \varepsilon_\delta \cdot \frac{\partial d (\mathbf{v}, \mathbf{w_r})}{\partial \mathbf{w_r}} \tag{21}$$

is non-vanishing such that prototype learning is still possible.

2.4 Semi-supervised Learning – Balancing between Unsupervised and Supervised Learning by the Parameter γ

The quasi-metric $D_\varepsilon (\mathbf{v}, \mathbf{w_r}, \gamma)$ depends on the balancing parameter γ weighting the unsupervised and supervised aspects. Experiences from earlier models (Fuzzy Label NG – FLNG, [17]) suggest a careful control of this parameter beginning with $\gamma(0) = 0$ and later (adiabatic) increase up to a final value γ_{max}, which should be chosen as $\gamma_{max} < 1$ to avoid instabilities and should be taken into account also for FSSOM. This can be interpreted as a remaining influence of unsupervised learning in the supervised learning phase. Moreover, if for a data vector $\mathbf{v}$ no class label is available at least standard SOM learning is applicable. In this manner the information provided by this data vector is not lost realizing a semi-supervised learning.

3 Experimental Results

3.1 Artificial Data Set

We start with an artificial data set of two two-dimensional isotropic separated Gaussians in $\mathbb{R}^2$. We distinguish two cases: In the first case, the class labels are in agreement with the Gaussians, whereas in the second case the classes are again exactly separated but diametric, see Fig. 1. Both situations are perfectly separable. However, the second case is much more complicate because prototypes have to balance between data density and class distribution. As we can observe, standard GLVQ classifier is able to distinguish the classes in the first case. After switch of the labels the prototypes (triangles) shift into a new position but with bad classification accuracy of only 52%. FSSOM places the prototypes (stars) nearby the class borders, which leads after the switch to a better accuracy of 76%. Thereby, the balancing parameter was set to $\gamma = 0.7$.

3.2 LANDSAT TM- Colorado

The second example is a real world data set: the multi-spectral LANDSAT TM satellite image of the Colorado area previously used in [3,18]. LANDSAT TM satellites create pictures with pixel resolution of $30m \times 30m$ in seven different spectral bands in the range of $0.45\mu m - 2.35\mu m$ and $10.4\mu m - 12.5\mu m$, whereby the last (thermal) band is dropped because of lower resolution. These bands are designed for detect and distinction of different vegetation, cultural features, rock formations, and water. The size of the Colorado-image is 1907×1784 pixels with ground truth labels, whereby there are 14 different types of vegetation or geological formations [18]. The spectral vectors roughly span a two-dimensional manifold in $\mathbb{R}^6$ such that a two-dimensional 7×6 FSSOM-lattice can be used to obtain a topology preserving mapping [15], i.e. $N = 42$. Thereby, the number of lattice nodes is also chosen in agreement with earlier investigations using 3 prototypes per class [3]. For the training only 0.5% of the data set were used, testing is done for the whole image cube. We compare the results with standard

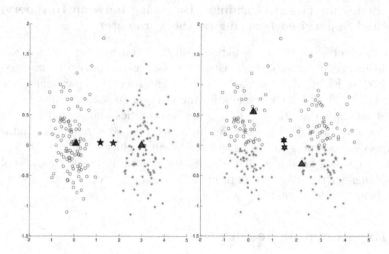

Fig. 1. Visualization artificial data set with different labeling: according to the cluster densities (left) and diametric (right). The result of the FSSOM ($\star$) and GLVQ ($\triangle$).

LASSO of same lattice size and GLVQ with 3 prototypes for each class. Because the class labels are crisp, we calculate accuracy based on the maximum class assignments $y_{\mathbf{s}(\mathbf{v})}^{max} = \max_{j=1\ldots C}\left(y_{\mathbf{s}(\mathbf{v})}^{j}\right)$ for a given data sample $\mathbf{v}$ for FSSOM and LASSO. Further, we computed the fuzzyκ-index for class agreement [2]. As it is depicted in Tab.1, GLVQ generates best results where LASSO shows the worst result. FSSOM with optimal choice of the balancing paramter γ achieves better accuracy and κ-values than LASSO but not as good as GLVQ. Thereby, a wide stability range of γ delivers high accuracy performance. Further, the fuzzy labels of FSSOM provide additional details, if the class assignments are visualized according to the topological structure of the neuron lattice A, see Fig.2. Using the topology preservation property of the underlying SOM, class similarities can be easily detected, which cannot be observed from pure classifier systems like GLVQ.

Table 1. Accuracies and κ-values for the Colorado data set for LASSO, GLVQ and FSSOM with different balancing values γ

		LASSO	GLVQ	FSSOM					
				$\gamma=0.1$	$\gamma=0.2$	$\gamma=0.45$	$\gamma=0.7$	$\gamma=0.9$	$\gamma=0.95$
accuracy	train	74.4%	86.6%	78.5%	80.5%	83.1%	81.4%	80.5%	77.6%
	test	74.3%	86.3%	78.9%	80.8%	83.4%	81.5%	80.6%	77.7%
Fuzzyκ-index	train	0.611	0.848	0.590	0.661	0.719	0.710	0.687	0.700
	test	0.613	0.830	0.591	0.663	0.710	0.687	0.688	0.700

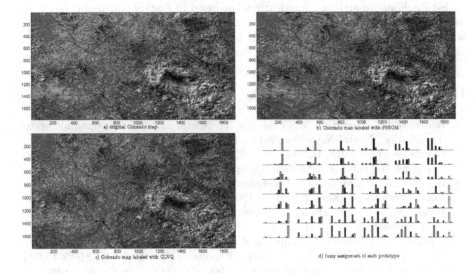

Fig. 2. False color composite of the Colorado-LANDSAT TM-image: pixels are colored according to their class labels. top-left: original image; bottom-left: GLVQ-result (misclassified pixels are colored black); top-right: FSSOM-result; bottom-right: barplots of class labels according to the FSSOM-lattice (colors correspond to those in the image). Class similarities can easily be detected using the topology preservation property of the underlying SOM. A color version of this figure can be obtained from the authors on request.

4   Conclusion

We provide in this paper a new approach for semi-supervised learning self-organizing maps. The new approach combines in a dissimilarity measure both, the dissimilarity between data and prototypes as well as their class dissimilarity in a *multiplicative* manner, the balancing of which is controlled by the balancing parameter γ. We show that the mathematical structure of the underlying cost function is the same than for the original Heskes-variant of SOMs based on local costs such that the respective theoretical framework also justifies the new approach. The transfer to neural gas algorithm is straightforward.

We demonstrated the abilities and properties of the new scheme for an artificial data set as well as LANDSAT TM image data set. Here we get comparable results but providing additional information about class similarities. Further, we demonstrated the robustness according to the choice of γ.

Obviously, the new approach allows a broad variability of dissimilarity measures d in the data space and δ for the fuzzy labels. Surely, the Euclidean distance is a good choice. However, interesting alternatives are under discussion for different data types at least for the data dissimilarity measures. Prominent examples are the scaled Euclidean metric for relevance learning [3] and their functional counterpart [5], or the Sobolev distance [19] and other functional norms [8], if the data are supposed to be representations of functions. Generalization of the scaled Euclidean metric are quadratic forms used in matrix learning [14]. Divergences are proposed for spectral data as suitable data dissimilarity measures [16], whereas the utilization of differentiable kernel also seems to be a new promising alternative for data dissimilarity judgment [13].

References

1. Bauer, H.-U., Herrmann, M., Villmann, T.: Neural maps and topographic vector quantization. Neural Networks 12(4-5), 659–676 (1999)
2. Geweniger, T., Zühlke, D., Hammer, B., Villmann, T.: Median fuzzy c-means for clustering dissimilarity data. Neurocomputing 73(7-9), 1109–1116 (2010)
3. Hammer, B., Villmann, T.: Generalized relevance learning vector quantization. Neural Networks 15(8-9), 1059–1068 (2002)
4. Heskes, T.: Energy functions for self-organizing maps. In: Oja, E., Kaski, S. (eds.) Kohonen Maps, pp. 303–316. Elsevier, Amsterdam (1999)
5. Kästner, M., Villmann, T.: Functional relevance learning in generalized learning vector quantization. Machine Learning Reports 5(MLR-01-2011), 81–89 (2011), http://www.techfak.uni-bielefeld.de/~fschleif/mlr/mlr_01_2011.pdf ISSN:1865-3960
6. Kästner, M., Villmann, T.: Fuzzy supervised neural gas for semi-supervised vector quantization – theoretical aspects. Machine Learning Reports 5(MLR-02-2011), 1–16 (2011), http://www.techfak.uni-bielefeld.de/~fschleif/mlr/mlr$_$_011.pdf ISSN:1865-3960
7. Kohonen, T.: Self-Organizing Maps. Springer Series in Information Sciences, vol. 30. Springer, Heidelberg (1995) (Second Extended Edition 1997)
8. Lee, J., Verleysen, M.: Generalization of the l_p norm for time series and its application to self-organizing maps. In: Cottrell, M. (ed.) Proc. of Workshop on Self-Organizing Maps, WSOM 2005, Paris, Sorbonne, pp. 733–740 (2005)
9. Martinetz, T.M., Berkovich, S.G., Schulten, K.J.: 'Neural-gas' network for vector quantization and its application to time-series prediction. IEEE Trans. on Neural Networks 4(4), 558–569 (1993)
10. Midenet, S., Grumbach, A.: Learning associations by self-organizatiom: the LASSO model. Neurocomputing 6, 343–361 (1994)
11. Pekalska, E., Duin, R.: The Dissimilarity Representation for Pattern Recognition: Foundations and Applications. World Scientific (2006)
12. Sato, A., Yamada, K.: Generalized learning vector quantization. In: Touretzky, D.S., Mozer, M.C., Hasselmo, M.E. (eds.) Proceedings of the 1995 Conference on Advances in Neural Information Processing Systems, vol. 8, pp. 423–429. MIT Press, Cambridge (1996)
13. Schleif, F.-M., Villmann, T., Hammer, B., Schneider, P., Biehl, M.: Generalized Derivative Based Kernelized Learning Vector Quantization. In: Fyfe, C., Tino, P., Charles, D., Garcia-Osorio, C., Yin, H. (eds.) IDEAL 2010. LNCS, vol. 6283, pp. 21–28. Springer, Heidelberg (2010)
14. Schneider, P., Hammer, B., Biehl, M.: Adaptive relevance matrices in learning vector quantization. Neural Computation 21, 3532–3561 (2009)
15. Villmann, T., Der, R., Herrmann, M., Martinetz, T.: Topology Preservation in Self-Organizing Feature Maps: Exact Definition and Measurement. IEEE Transactions on Neural Networks 8(2), 256–266 (1997)

16. Villmann, T., Haase, S.: Divergence based vector quantization. Neural Computation 23(5), 1343–1392 (2011)
17. Villmann, T., Hammer, B., Schleif, F.-M., Geweniger, T., Herrmann, W.: Fuzzy classification by fuzzy labeled neural gas. Neural Networks 19, 772–779 (2006)
18. Villmann, T., Merényi, E., Hammer, B.: Neural maps in remote sensing image analysis. Neural Networks 16(3-4), 389–403 (2003)
19. Villmann, T., Schleif, F.-M.: Functional vector quantization by neural maps. In: Chanussot, J. (ed.) Proceedings of First Workshop on Hyperspectral Image and Signal Processing: Evolution in Remote Sensing (WHISPERS 2009), pp. 1–4. IEEE Press (2009) ISBN: 978-1-4244-4948-4
20. Villmann, T., Schleif, F.-M., Merenyi, E., Hammer, B.: Fuzzy Labeled Self-Organizing Map for Classification of Spectra. In: Sandoval, F., Prieto, A.G., Cabestany, J., Graña, M. (eds.) IWANN 2007. LNCS, vol. 4507, pp. 556–563. Springer, Heidelberg (2007)
21. Villmann, T., Seiffert, U., Schleif, F.-M., Brüß, C., Geweniger, T., Hammer, B.: Fuzzy Labeled Self-Organizing Map with Label-Adjusted Prototypes. In: Schwenker, F., Marinai, S. (eds.) ANNPR 2006. LNCS (LNAI), vol. 4087, pp. 46–56. Springer, Heidelberg (2006)

Fuzzy Inference-Based Reliable Fall Detection Using Kinect and Accelerometer

Michal Kepski[1,*], Bogdan Kwolek[1], and Ivar Austvoll[2]

[1] Rzeszów University of Technology, 35-959 Rzeszów, Poland
bkwolek@prz.edu.pl
[2] University of Stavanger, N-4036 Stavanger, Norway
ivar.austvoll@uis.no

Abstract. Falls are major causes of mortality and morbidity in the elderly. However, prevalent methods only utilize accelerometers or both accelerometers and gyroscopes to separate falls from activities of daily living. This makes it not easy to distinguish real falls from fall-like activities. The existing CCD-camera based solutions require time for installation, camera calibration and are not generally cheap. In this paper we show how to achieve reliable fall detection. The detection is done by a fuzzy inference system using low-cost Kinect and a device consisting of an accelerometer and a gyroscope. The experimental results indicate high accuracy of the detection and effectiveness of the system.

1 Introduction

In developed countries the segment of the elderly population over 65 years of age is growing quickly. About one third of people aged over 65 years are failing once a year at least. This rate increases to one half for the segment of people aged over 80 years. 20 up to 30% of 65+ adults who fall suffer moderate to severe injuries, and 2% of such falls result in broken hips [4]. Approximately 30% of people older than 60 years live alone. Considerable portion of the elderly population is also willing to accept new technologies to increase safety and the quality of life. The above mentioned issues stimulated a great interest in fall detection systems.

Most proposed systems to fall detection are based on a wearable device that monitor the movements of an individual, recognize a fall and trigger an alarm. Body attached accelerometers [2][5] and gyroscopes [8] are widely used in monitoring human movement and detecting falls. Fall detection methods can be divided into two groups of methods in relation to how kinetic data is utilized to distinguish activities of daily living (ADLs) from falls. To the first group belong methods that are based on a fixed threshold. In [2] a system based on magnitude of acceleration values has been proposed, whereas in [1] an algorithm using measures of angular velocity obtained from gyroscopes has been presented. The critical issue in such algorithms is to determine proper threshold. However, several ADLs like fast sitting have similar kinematic motion patterns to those of

---

* M. Kepski is currently a student, doing his MSc thesis on fall detection.

L. Rutkowski et al. (Eds.): ICAISC 2012, Part I, LNCS 7267, pp. 266–273, 2012.

real falls and in consequence the methods belonging to this group might trigger many false alarms. In the second group of approaches are methods that combine kinematic thresholds with posture. The method proposed in [8] assumes that a fall always ends in a lying position. The assumption that a fall always ends in a lying pose permits to separate out some fall-like ADLs like sitting, running and jumps. However, such an assumption might also lead to both false positive alarms when a person lies quickly on a bed or false negatives in case of remaining in a sitting position after a harmless fall. According to the experimental evaluation of the method its sensitivity is 91%, while specificity is 92%. In general, the solutions mentioned above are somehow intrusive for people as they require wearing continuously at least one device or smart sensor.

Several attempts were made to amend the limitations mentioned above. Some of them propose the use of two or more wearable devices [10]. However, such methods can be uncomfortable for elderly people. Moreover, body attached devices might be uncomfortable when sleeping, during change of clothes, wash, etc. Some approaches focus on ambient devices, which are installed in the places to be monitored. Common examples of such sensors are pressure sensors on the floor, bed exit detectors, etc. However, pressure sensitive mats have unavoidable edges that can cause falls. In addition, the installation of such multiple sensors is time consuming and monitoring is strictly limited to the places with the sensors.

There have also been several attempts to achieve reliable human fall detection using single CCD cameras [11], multiple cameras [3] or specialized omnidirectional ones [9]. A vision system [7], which uses a camera mounted on the ceiling was tested on 21 volunteers who carried out simulated falls. The fall detection ratio was 77%. There are several advantages of using video cameras, among others the ability to detect various events. Another advantage is low intrusiveness. In some circumstances, the possibility of remote verification of fall events might be very important. Internet network IP cameras, including GigE vision cameras can be used to achieve such capability easily. However, the existing solutions require time for installation and/or camera calibration and are not generally cheap. Moreover, in monocular camera based approaches the lack of depth information may lead to false alarms. The shortcomings mentioned above motivated us to develop a low-cost and reliable system to trigger a fall alarm.

Our system employs both an accelerometer and a video camera, which complement each other. The system is based on expert knowledge and demonstrates high generalization abilities. The main part of the algorithm is based on a fuzzy inference system (FIS). We show that low-cost Kinect contribute toward reliable fall detections. The disadvantage of Kinect is that it only can monitor restricted areas. In such areas we utilized an accelerometer. On the other hand, in some ADLs during which the use of this wearable sensor might not be comfortable, for instance during changing clothes, wash, etc., the system relies on Kinect camera only. An advantage of Kinect is that it can be put in certain places according to the user requirements. Moreover, the system operates on depth images and thus preserves privacy for people being monitored. In this context, it is worth noting that Kinect uses infrared light and therefore it is able to extract depth images in a room that is dark to our eyes. Using both devices, our system can reliably distinguish the falls from activities of daily living, and thus the number of false alarms is reduced.

2   The System

Our fall detection system uses both data from Kinect and motion data from a wearable smart device containing accelerometer and gyroscope sensors. Data from the smart device (Sony PlayStation Move) are transmitted wirelessly via Bluetooth to a notebook computer on which the signal processing is done, whereas Kinect is connected via USB, see Fig. 1. The device contains one tri-axial accelerometer and a tri-axial gyroscope consisting of a dual-axis gyroscope and a Z-axis gyroscope. The fall alarm is triggered by a fuzzy inference engine based on expert knowledge, which is declared explicitly by fuzzy rules and sets. As inputs the engine takes the acceleration, the angular velocity and the distance of the person's gravity center to the altitude at which the Kinect is placed. The acceleration's vector length is calculated using data provided by the tri-axial accelerometer, whereas the angular velocity is provided by the gyroscope.

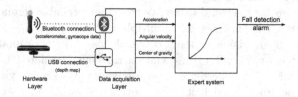

Fig. 1. The system architecture

A tri-axial accelerometer is a sensor that returns a real valued estimate of acceleration along x, y and z axes. Data from an accelerometer contains time and acceleration along three axes. Figure 2 depicts the plots of acceleration and angular velocities readings vs. time for walking and simulated falling. The sampling rate of both sensors is equal to 60 Hz. The measured acceleration signals were median filtered with a window length of three samples to suppress the noise and then used to calculate the acceleration's vector length. When people fall, acceleration and angular velocity are rapidly changed, as demonstrated at right plots at Fig. 2. A lot of attention to the optimal sensor placement on the body has been done until now [5]. The attachment of the sensor to trunk or lower back is recommended because such body parts represent the major component of body mass and move with most activities. The depicted plots were obtained for the device that was worn at the waist or near the pelvis region.

Kinect is a motion sensing input device for the Xbox 360 video game console. The Kinect device has two cameras and one laser-based IR projector. The IR camera and the IR projector form a stereo pair with a baseline of approximately 75 mm. The IR projector sends out a fixed pattern and dark speckles. The

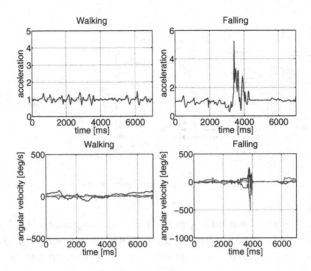

Fig. 2. Acceleration and angular velocity for walking and a real fall

depth is determined by triangulation against a known pattern. Then the pattern is remembered at known depth. Given the known depth of such a plane and the disparity, the depth for each pixel is calculated by the triangulation. In Fig. 3 color and depth images that were acquired by Kinect are depicted. The depth image was then segmented using OpenNI library. Finally, on the basis of the segmented objects the center of gravity of the object of interest was calculated.

Color Image | Depth Image

Fig. 3. Color and depth images provided by Kinect

Figure 4 illustrates the architecture of the fall detection system. A fuzzy inference system proposed by Takagi and Sugeno (TS) [12] is used to generate the fall alarm. It expresses human expert knowledge and experience by using fuzzy inference rules represented in $if - then$ statements. In such an inference system the linear submodels associated with TS rules are combined to describe the global behavior of the nonlinear system.

When input data is fed into the TS type fuzzy inference system, each feature value of the unknown input vector is fuzzified, i.e., converted to a fuzzy number, through their membership functions (MFs), see Fig. 4. The common types of membership functions are singletons, triangles, trapezoids, Gaussians, etc. Every kind of membership function has its advantages and disadvantages. For example, triangular membership function is very easy to implement and it can be calculated fast. Figure 5 shows the membership functions (MFs), which were designed

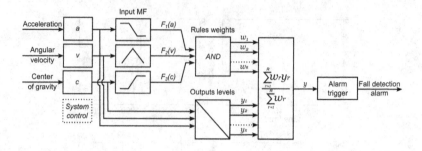

Fig. 4. The fuzzy inference system

by an expert. The acceleration is proportional to the gravitational acceleration g, angular velocity is expressed in degrees, whereas the center of gravity is the difference between the estimated persons gravity center to the floor level and the Kinect altitude.

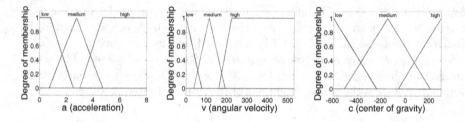

Fig. 5. Membership functions

The inference is done by the TS fuzzy system consisting of R rules of the following form: *if x_1 is A_{1r} and ... and x_i is A_{ir} and ... and x_N is A_{Nr} then $y_r = p_{0r} + p_{1r}x_1 + \cdots + p_{Nr}x_N$* , where A_{ir} denotes the linguistic labels of the ith input variable ($i = 1, \ldots, N$), associated with the rth rule ($r = 1, \ldots, R$), p_{0r}, p_{ir} are the parameters of the rth rule, whereas x_i stands for the numerical value of the ith input variable. The inference function is given by the following expression:

$$y = \frac{\sum_{r=1}^{R} w_r y_r}{\sum_{r=1}^{R} w_r} \tag{1}$$

The twenty seven rules in the system produce a decision surface. The decision surfaces of our fall detection system for the two inputs are illustrated in Fig. 6. The filtered data from the accelerometer and the gyroscope were interpolated and decimated as well as synchronized with the data from Kinect, i.e. the center of gravity of the moving person. The output y that is generated with 30 Hz is fed into the alarm trigger module, see also Fig. 4, which makes the final decision. The alarm is triggered if a specified number of samples in a predefined period of time is above a predefined value.

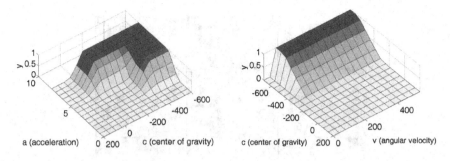

Fig. 6. Decision surfaces of the fuzzy inference engine

3   Experimental Results

Three volunteers with age over 26 years attended in evaluation of our developed algorithm and system. Intentional falls were performed towards carpets of various thicknesses ranging from 2 cm to 5 cm. During the simulation of falls, it was paid attention to falling not too heavily. The accelerometer was worn near the pelvis. Each individual performed three types of falls, namely forward, backward and lateral at least three times. Each individual performed also ADLs like walking, sitting, crouching down, leaning down/picking up objects from the floor, lying on a bed. Figure 7 depicts some example images with selected ADLs.

Fig. 7. Images with activities of daily living: walking, crouching down, lying on a bed, leaning down/picking up objects from the floor, sitting and falling (from left to right and from top to bottom), which were shot by Kinect

The corresponding depth images, which were extracted by Kinect, are depicted in Fig. 8. As we can observe, one of the disadvantages of Kinect is a blind spot that cannot be directly observed. Kinect's field of view is fifty-seven degrees horizontally and forty-three degrees vertically and in consequence some areas at the floor close to Kinect are not observable, see also the right-down image at Fig. 8. The minimum range for the Kinect is about 0.6 m and the maximum range is somewhere between 4-5 m.

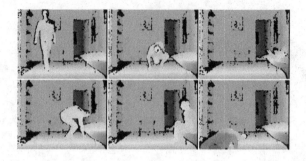

Fig. 8. Depth images corresponding to images from Fig. 7, extracted by Kinect

Figure 9 demonstrates some example outputs of our fall detection system, that were generated during performing some ADLs, including a fall simulated by a volunteer. These plots show that a single accelerometer with gyroscope and Kinect are completely sufficient to implement a reliable fall detection system. All intentional falls performed by three volunteers were detected correctly. In particular, sitting down fast, which is not easily distinguishable from a typical fall when only accelerometer or even accelerometer and gyroscope are used, was detected reliably by our system. One activity consisting in seating on a sofa was wrongly classified as a fall using only Kinect. The false alarm was altered because on the depth image acquired by Kinect the legs were merged with the sofa bottom part. In consequence, the gravity center extracted by the OpenNI library was situated at a relatively small distance to the floor. It is worth noting that in the near future the modern mobile devices will be equipped with some fall detection capabilities, but in some daily activities their helpfulness can still

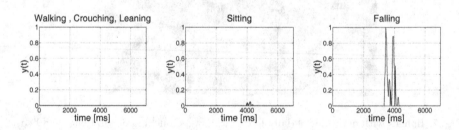

Fig. 9. FIS output smoothed with a moving average filter. Person fall is easily recognizable.

be reduced. Our results demonstrate that the use of low-cost Kinect will make it possible to construct unobtrusive and reliable fall detection systems. Moreover, using Kinect it will be possible to recognize simultaneously some daily activities, which is an important and challenging problem [6].

4   Conclusions

In this paper we demonstrate how to achieve reliable fall detection. The detection was done by fuzzy inference system using Kinect, accelerometer and gyroscope. The results show that a single accelerometer with gyroscope and Kinect are completely sufficient to implement a reliable fall detection system.

Acknowledgment. This work has been partially supported by the Norwegian Financial Mechanism and the National Science Centre (NCN) within the project N N516 483240.

References

1. Bourke, A., Lyons, G.: A threshold-based fall-detection algorithm using a bi-axial gyroscope sensor. Medical Engineering & Physics 30(1), 84–90 (2008)
2. Bourke, A., O'Brien, J., Lyons, G.: Evaluation of a threshold-based tri-axial accelerometer fall detection algorithm. Gait & Posture 26(2), 194–199 (2007)
3. Cucchiara, R., Prati, A., Vezzani, R.: A multi-camera vision system for fall detection and alarm generation. Expert Systems 24(5), 334–345 (2007)
4. Heinrich, S., Rapp, K., Rissmann, U., Becker, C., König, H.H.: Cost of falls in old age: a systematic review. Osteoporosis International 21, 891–902 (2010)
5. Kangas, M., Konttila, A., Lindgren, P., Winblad, I., Jamsa, T.: Comparison of low-complexity fall detection algorithms for body attached accelerometers. Gait & Posture 28(2), 285–291 (2008)
6. Kwolek, B.: Visual system for tracking and interpreting selected human actions. Journal of WSCG 11(2), 274–281 (2003)
7. Lee, T., Mihailidis, A.: An intelligent emergency response system: preliminary development and testing of automated fall detection. Journal of Telemedicine and Telecare, 194–198 (2005)
8. Li, Q., Stankovic, J., Hanson, M., Barth, A., Lach, J., Zhou, G.: Accurate, fast fall detection using gyroscopes and accelerometer-derived posture information. In: Int. Wksp. on Wearable and Implantable Body Sensor Networks, pp. 138–143 (2009)
9. Miaou, S.G., Sung, P.-H., Huang, C.-Y.: A customized human fall detection system using omni-camera images and personal information. Distributed Diagnosis and Home Healthcare, 39–42 (2006)
10. Noury, N., Fleury, A., Rumeau, P., Bourke, A., Laighin, G., Rialle, V., Lundy, J.: Fall detection - principles and methods. In: Annual Int. Conf. of the IEEE Engineering in Medicine and Biology Society, pp. 1663–1666 (2007)
11. Rougier, C., Meunier, J., St-Arnaud, A., Rousseau, J.: Monocular 3D head tracking to detect falls of elderly people. In: Annual Int. Conf. of the IEEE Engineering in Medicine and Biology Society, pp. 6384–6387 (2006)
12. Takagi, T., Sugeno, M.: Fuzzy Identification of Systems and its Applications to Modeling and Control. IEEE Trans. on SMC 15(1), 116–132 (1985)

Defuzzification Functionals Are Homogeneous, Restrictive Additive and Normalized Functions

Witold Kosiński[1], Agnieszka Rosa[2],
Dorota Cendrowska[1], and Katarzyna Węgrzyn-Wolska[3]

[1] Polish-Japanese Institute of Information Technology, Warsaw, Poland
{wkos,dc}@pjwstk.edu.pl
[2] Kazimierz-Wielki University, Bydgoszcz, Poland
agnieszka.rosa@hotmail.com
[3] École Supérieure d'Ingénieurs en Informatique et Génie de
Télécommunication (ESIGETEL), France
katarzyna.wegrzyn@esigetel.fr

Abstract. Defuzzification operators, that play the main role when dealing with fuzzy controllers and fuzzy inference systems, are discussed for convex as well for ordered fuzzy numbers. Three characteristic conditions are formulated for them. It is shown that most of known defuzzification functionals meet these requirements. Some approximation methods for determining of the functionals are given and then applied.

1 Fuzzy Numbers

Convex fuzzy numbers (CFN) of [23] form a general and well developed class of fuzzy sets defined on the real line. When operating on convex fuzzy numbers we have the interval arithmetic for our disposal. As long as one works with fuzzy numbers that possess continuous membership functions, the two procedures: the extension principle of Zadeh and the α-cut and the interval arithmetic method, give the same results (cf. [2]). Since results of multiple operations on convex fuzzy numbers are leading to a large growth of the fuzziness, and depend on the order of the operations due to the lack of the distributive law, new approaches could be required as well as more general definitions. It has been done recently by the first author and his co-workers in a number of publications [15], [16], [17] where they have introduced and then developed main concepts of the space of ordered fuzzy numbers (OFNs).

To be more specific, let us recall the definitions of a convex fuzzy number and an ordered fuzzy number. A convex fuzzy number is a particular case of a fuzzy set, for which its membership function is defined on the real line $\mathbf{R}$ and possesses some properties [3], [23].

Definition 1. *By a convex fuzzy number A we understand a fuzzy set defined on the real line $\mathbf{R}$ with the membership function $\mu_A : \mathbf{R} \to [0,1]$ which is convex and achieves the maximum value 1 with a convex subset, i.e. if its each α-cut $A[\alpha]$, with $0 < \alpha \leq 1$, of the membership function μ_A*

L. Rutkowski et al. (Eds.): ICAISC 2012, Part I, LNCS 7267, pp. 274–282, 2012.

$$A[\alpha] = \{x : \mu_A(x) \geq \alpha\}$$

is closed interval.

Sometimes one adds to this an extra condition on left-continuity of the membership function (cf. [2], [4]). Let us denote the space of all CFN by $\mathcal{F}$.

In the approach developed for OFN the concept of membership functions has been weakened by requiring a mere *membership relation* .

Definition 2. *Pair (f,g) of continuous functions such that $f, g : [0,1] \rightarrow \mathbf{R}$ is called an ordered fuzzy number A.*

Notice that f and g need not be inverse functions of some membership function. If, however, f is increasing and g – decreasing, both on the unit interval $I = [0,1]$, and $f \leq g$, then one can attach to this pair a continuous function μ and regard it as a membership function a convex fuzzy number with an extra feature, namely the orientation of the number. This attachment can be done by the formula $f^{-1} = \mu|_{incr}$ and $g^{-1} = \mu|_{decr}$. Notice that pairs (f,g) and (g,f) represent two different ordered fuzzy numbers, unless $f = g$. They differ by their orientations. It is worthwhile to point out that the class of ordered fuzzy numbers (OFNs) represents the whole class of convex fuzzy numbers with continuous membership functions. To include all CFN with piecewise continuous membership functions more general class of functions f and g in Def.2 is needed. This has been already done by the first author who in [7] assumed they are functions of bounded variation. The new space is denoted by $\mathcal{R}_{BV}$. Then operations on elements of $\mathcal{R}_{BV}$ are defined in the similar way- the norm, however, changes into the norm of the Cartesian product of the space of functions of bounded variations (BV). Then all convex fuzzy numbers are contained in this new space $\mathcal{R}_{BV}$ of OFN. Notice that functions from BV are continuous except for a countable numbers of points.

All arithmetic operations on OFN are defined on pairs of functions, . e.g. the sum of $A = (f_A, g_A)$ and $B = (f_B, g_B)$ is defined as $C = (f_C, g_C) = (f_A + f_B, g_A + g_B)$. Similarly we define the multiplication and division. Scalar multiplication by real $r \in \mathbf{R}$ is defined as $r \cdot A = (rf_A, rg_A)$. The subtraction of B is the same as the addition of the opposite of B, and consequently $B - B = 0$, where $0 \in \mathbf{R}$ is the crisp zero. It means that subtraction is not compatible with the extension principle of Zadeh, if we confine OFNs to CFN. However, the addition operation is compatible, if its components have the same orientations. Notice, however, that addition, as well as the subtraction, of two OFNs that are represented by affine functions and possess classical membership functions, may lead to a result which may not possess its membership functions (in general $f(1)$ needs not be less than $g(1)$). Notice that to any convex fuzzy number correspond two OFNs, they differ by the orientation: one has positive, say (f,g) , another (g,f) has negative. Let us denote the space of all OFN by $\mathcal{R}$.

2   Defuzzification Functionals

Dealing with applications of fuzzy numbers some functionals are required to map each fuzzy number into a real one. Those operations are called defuzzifications.

They cannot be quite arbitrary, they should be defined in such a way that is consistent with operations on reals. To be more strict an introduction of three obvious conditions in our definition is brought in.

Definition 3. *A map ϕ from the space $\mathcal{R}$ of all OFN's (equivalently from $\mathcal{F}$) to reals is called a **defuzzification functional** if is satisfies:*

1. $\phi(c^{\ddagger}) = c$,
2. $\phi(A + c^{\ddagger}) = \phi(A) + c$,
3. $\phi(cA) = c\phi(A)$, *for any $c \in \mathbf{R}$ and $A \in \mathcal{R}$.*

Here by writing $\phi(c^{\ddagger})$ we understand the action of the functional ϕ on the crisp number $c^{\ddagger}$, which in $\mathcal{R}$ is represented by the pair of constant functions $(c^{\dagger}, c^{\dagger})$, with $c^{\dagger}(s) = c, s \in [0,1]$, while in $\mathcal{F}$ is represented by the membership function $\chi_{\{1\}}$ equals to the characteristic function of the one-element set $\{1\}$. The condition 2. is a *restricted additivity*, since the second component is a crisp number. The condition 3. requires from ϕ to be *homogeneous of order one*, while the condition 1. is most obvious and consistent with the operations on reals, since $\mathbf{R}$ forms a subspace in each of the spaces $\mathcal{R}$ and $\mathcal{F}$. It requires from defuzzification functional to be *normalized*.

2.1 Defuzzification of Ordered Fuzzy Numbers

In this subsection, we will consider the case of Def. 3 with ϕ defined on $\mathcal{R}$. First, let us take into consideration linear and continuous functionals on the space $\mathcal{R}$, which can be identified with the Cartesian product of $C(0,1)$ - the space of continuous functions on $[0,1]$ (then $\mathcal{R}$ becomes a Banach space). Due to the Riesz-Banach-Saks-Kakutami representation theorem each continuous, linear functionals on $\mathcal{R}$, say ϕ, has the representation by the sum of two Stieltjes integrals with respect to two functions h_1, h_2 of bounded variation[1]

$$\phi(f,g) = \int_0^1 f(s)dh_1(s) + \int_0^1 g(s)dh_2(s) . \tag{1}$$

It is obvious that ϕ satisfies the conditions 2. and 3. of Def.3. To satisfy the condition 1. we need the equality $\int_0^1 dh_1(s) + \int_0^1 dh_2(s) = 1$.

Notice that if for $h_1(s)$ and $h_2(s)$ we put $\lambda H(s)$ and $(1-\lambda)H(s)$, respectively, with $0 \leq \lambda \leq 1$ and $H(s)$ as the Heaviside function with the unit jump at $s = 1$, then the defuzzification functional in (1) will lead to the classical MOM – middle of maximum, FOM (first of maximum), LOM (last of maximum) and RCOM (random choice of maximum), with an appropriate choice of λ. For example if for $h_1(s)$ and $h_2(s)$ we put $1/2\, H(s)$ then the defuzzification functional in (1) will represent the classical MOM – middle of maximum

$$\phi(f,g) = 1/2(f(1) + g(1)) . \tag{2}$$

---

[1] Those functions are uniquely determined [1] if they vanish at $s = 0$, and $s = 1$.

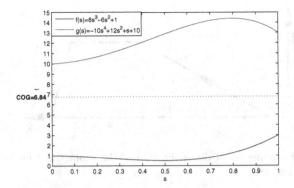

Fig. 1. Example of an ordered fuzzy number of polynomial type and its center of gravity defuzzification value COG

This new model gives the continuum number of defuzzification operators both linear and nonlinear, which map ordered fuzzy numbers into reals. Nonlinear functional can be defined, see [12,21], for example, a center of gravity defuzzification functional (COG) calculated at OFN (f, g) is (cf. Fig. 1.)

$$\phi_{COG}(f,g) = \frac{\int_0^1 \frac{f(s)+g(s)}{2}|f(s)-g(s)|ds}{\int_0^1 |f(s)-g(s)|ds}. \tag{3}$$

If $A = c^\ddagger$ then we put $\phi_{COG}(c^\ddagger) = c$. When $\int_0^1 |f(s)-g(s)|ds = 0$ in (3) we write

$$\phi_{COG}(f,f) = \int_0^1 f(s)ds / \int_0^1 ds.$$

It is rather easy to show [26] that ϕ_{COG} possesses all properties formulated in Def. 3. Other nonlinear functional was originally proposed by [28] in her Master Thesis, and called a defuzzification by the geometrical mean, and defined by the formula (cf. Fig. 2.)

$$\phi_{GM}(f,g) = \frac{g(1)g(0) - f(0)f(1)}{g(1) + g(0) - (f(0) + f(1))} \tag{4}$$

in which the denotation used are obvious. In this case we can show [26] that ϕ_{GM} possesses all properties formulated in Def. 3.

2.2   Defuzification of Convex Fuzzy Numbers

In this subsection, we will consider the case of Def. 3 with ϕ defined on $\mathcal{F}$. Then we have, similar to the case of ordered fuzzy numbers, the list of known linear

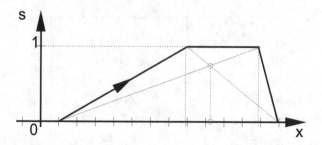

Fig. 2. Example of calculation of defuzzification of the geometrical mean of a trapezoidal ordered fuzzy number

functionals: MOM, FOM, LOM, RCOM. Their linearity gives the fulfilment of all three conditions of Def. 3.

Let us consider the nonlinear case and the center of gravity functional defined on a membership function μ_A by

$$\psi_{COG}(\mu_A) = \frac{\int_{-\infty}^{\infty} x \cdot \mu_A(x)dx}{\int_{-\infty}^{\infty} \mu_A(x)dx},$$

and if A represents a crisp number c, i.e. its membership function μ_A is the characteristic function of the one-element set $\{c\}$ equals to $\chi_{\{c\}}$, where

$$\chi_{\{c\}}(x) = \begin{cases} 1 \text{ for } x = c \\ 0 \text{ for } x \neq c, \end{cases}$$

then we put $\psi_{COG}(\mu_A) = c$.

Now we show that ψ_{COG} defined on $\mathcal{F}$ satisfies the conditions of Def.3. The first condition is satisfied from the definition.

Let us pass to the restricted additivity in condition 2. of Def.3, and define $C = A + c^{\ddagger}$ and use the denotation $\oplus$ for the operation on the membership function, then $\mu_C = c \oplus \mu_A$. Applying the extension principle we obtain

$$\mu_C(x) = \mu_A(x) \oplus c^{\ddagger} = \mu_A(x - c).$$

Proposition 1. $\boxed{\psi_{COG}(\mu_A \oplus c^{\ddagger}) = \psi_{COG}(\mu_A) + c}$

Proof

$$\psi_{COG}(\mu_A \oplus c^{\ddagger}) = \frac{\int_{-\infty}^{\infty} x \cdot (\mu_A \oplus c^{\ddagger})(x)dx}{\int_{-\infty}^{\infty} (\mu_A \oplus c^{\ddagger})(x)dx} = \frac{\int_{-\infty}^{\infty} x \cdot \mu_A(x - c)dx}{\int_{-\infty}^{\infty} \mu_A(x - c)dx} =$$

$$= \left\{ x - c =: y \Rightarrow x = y + c \right\} = \frac{\int_{-\infty}^{\infty} (y + c) \cdot \mu_A(y) \, d(y + c)}{\int_{-\infty}^{\infty} \mu_A(y) \, d(y + c)} =$$

$$= \frac{\int_{-\infty}^{\infty} y \cdot \mu_A(y) dy + c \cdot \int_{-\infty}^{\infty} \mu_A(y) dy}{\int_{-\infty}^{\infty} \mu_A(y) dy} =$$

$$= \frac{\int_{-\infty}^{\infty} y \cdot \mu_A(y) dy}{\int_{-\infty}^{\infty} \mu_A(y) dy} + \frac{c \cdot \int_{-\infty}^{\infty} \mu_A(y) dy}{\int_{-\infty}^{\infty} \mu_A(y) dy} = \psi_{COG}(\mu_A) + c .$$

To show the third condition let us take $c \neq 0$ and $A \in \mathcal{F}$. According to the Zadeh extension principle the number $C = cA$ will have its membership function

$$\mu_C(x) = c \odot \mu_A(x) := \mu_A\left(\frac{x}{c}\right),$$

where by $\odot$ we have denoted the operation on membership function corresponding to the scalar multiplication.

Proposition 2. $\boxed{\psi_{COG}(c \odot \mu_A) = c \cdot \psi_{COG}(\mu_A)}$

Proof

$$\psi_{COG}(c \odot \mu_A) = \frac{\int_{-\infty}^{\infty} x \cdot c \odot \mu_A(x) dx}{\int_{-\infty}^{\infty} c \odot \mu_A(x) dx} = \frac{\int_{-\infty}^{\infty} x \cdot \mu_A\left(\frac{x}{c}\right) dx}{\int_{-\infty}^{\infty} \mu_A\left(\frac{x}{c}\right) dx} =$$

$$= \left\{ \frac{x}{c} =: y \Rightarrow x = c \cdot y \right\} = \frac{\int_{-\infty}^{\infty} c \cdot y \cdot \mu_A(y) d(c \cdot y)}{\int_{-\infty}^{\infty} \mu_A(y) d(c \cdot y)} =$$

$$= c \cdot \frac{\int_{-\infty}^{\infty} y \cdot \mu_A(y) \cdot c \cdot dy}{\int_{-\infty}^{\infty} \mu_A(y) \cdot c \cdot dy} = c \cdot \psi_{COG}(\mu_A) .$$

In this way we show that the classical defuzzification functionals known in the theory of CFN are homogeneous functions of order one, restrictive additive and normalized. In her Engineering Thesis Agnieszka Rosa showed more, that discussed in [29] the so-called BADD - basic defuzzifcation distribution

$$\psi_{BADD}(\mu_A; \lambda) = \frac{\int_{-\infty}^{\infty} x \cdot [\mu_A(x)]^\lambda \, dx}{\int_{-\infty}^{\infty} [\mu_A(x)]^\lambda \, dx} , \tag{5}$$

where $\lambda \in [0, \infty)$ satisfies all 3 conditions. Moreover, she has derived its counterpart for OFN in the space $\mathcal{R}$.

3   Approximation of Defuzzification Functional

An ultimate goal of fuzzy logic is to provide foundations for approximate reasoning. It uses imprecise propositions based on a fuzzy set theory developed by L.Zadeh, in a way similar to the classical reasoning using precise propositions based on the classical set theory. Defuzzification is the main operation which appears in fuzzy controllers and fuzzy inference systems where fuzzy rules are present. It was extensively discussed by the authors of [27]. They have classified the most widely used defuzzification techniques into different groups, and examined the prototypes of each group with respect to the defuzzification criteria.

The problem arises when membership functions are not continuous or do not exist at all. In our recent paper [10] we have that on particular subsets of fuzzy sets, namely *step ordered fuzzy numbers* approximation formula of a defuzzification functionals can be searched based on some number of training data. This was a quite new problem never investigated within (step ordered) fuzzy numbers. Let finite set of training data be given in the form of N pairs: ordered fuzzy number and value (of action) of a defuzzification functional on it, i.e.

$$\mathsf{TRE} = \{(A_1, r_1), (A_2, r_2), ..., (A_N, r_N)\}.$$

For a given small ϵ find a continuous functional $H : \mathcal{R}_K \to \mathbf{R}$ which approximates the values of the set TRE within the error smaller than ϵ, i.e. $\max\limits_{1 \le p \le N} |H(A_p) - r_p| \le \epsilon$, where $(A_p, r_p) \in$ TRE . The problem mentioned may possess several solution methods, e.g. a dedicated evolutionary algorithm [8], [11] or an artificial neural network. Thanks to the results of [9] we could use a particular representation of the searched defuzzification functional in which a homogeneous, of order one, function appears. We have shown that feedforward neural network with a bipolar sigmoidal activation function can be used to this aim. It is obvious that more investigations must be done in this field and different computational intelligence tools can be used there. It will be the subject of our further research.

References

1. Alexiewicz, A.: Functional Analysis. PWN, Warszawa (1969) (in Polish)
2. Buckley, J.J., Eslami, E.: An Introduction to Fuzzy Logic and Fuzzy Sets. Physica-Verlag, Heidelberg (2005)
3. Chen, G., Pham, T.T.: Introduction to Fuzzy Sets, Fuzzy Logic, and Fuzzy Control Systems. CRS Press LLC, Washington (2001)
4. Drewniak, J.: Fuzzy numbers. In: Chojcan, J., Łęski, J. (eds.) Fuzzy Sets and Their Applications, pp. 103–129. Silesian Technical University Publishers, Gliwice (2001) (in polish)
5. Koleśnik, R., Kosiński, W., Prokopowicz, P., Frischmuth, K.: On algebra of ordered fuzzy numbers. In: Atanassov, K.T., Hryniewicz, O., Kacprzyk, J. (eds.) Soft Computing – Foundations and Theoretical Aspects, pp. 291–302. Academic Press House EXIT, Warszawa (2004)

6. Kosiński, W.: On Defuzzyfication of Ordered Fuzzy Numbers. In: Rutkowski, L., Siekmann, J.H., Tadeusiewicz, R., Zadeh, L.A. (eds.) ICAISC 2004. LNCS (LNAI), vol. 3070, pp. 326–331. Springer, Heidelberg (2004)
7. Kosiński, W.: On fuzzy number calculus. Int. J. Appl. Math. Comput. Sci. 16(1), 51–57 (2006)
8. Kosiński, W.: Evolutionary algorithm determining defuzzyfication operators. Engineering Applications of Artificial Intelligence 20(5), 619–627 (2007), http://dx.doi.org/10.1016/j.engappai.2007.03.003
9. Kosiński, W.: Optimization with fuzzy data via evolutionary algorithms. In: International Conference on Numerical Analysis and Applied Mathematics, ICNAAM 2010, September 19-25. American Institute of Physics, Rhodes Greece (2010)
10. Kosiński, W., Kacprzak, M.: Fuzzy implications on lattice of ordered fuzzy numbers. In: Atanssov, K.T., Baczyński, M., Drewniak, J., Kacprzyk, J., Krawczyk, M., Szmidt, E., Wygralek, M., Zadrożny, S. (eds.) Recent Advances in Fuzzy Sets, Intuitionistic Fuzzy sets, Generalized Nets and Related Topics. Foundations, vol. I, pp. 95–110. IBS PAN - SRI PAS, Warszawa (2010)
11. Kosiński, W., Markowska-Kaczmar, U.: An evolutionary algorithm determining a defuzzyfication functional. Task Quarterly 11(1-2), 47–58 (2007)
12. Kosiński, W., Piasecki, W., Wilczyńska-Sztyma, D.: On Fuzzy Rules and Defuzzification Functionals for Ordered Fuzzy Numbers. In: Burczyński, T., Cholewa, W., Moczulski, W. (eds.) Proc. of AI-Meth 2009 Conference, Gliwice. AI-METH Series, pp. 161–178 (November 2009)
13. Kosiński, W., Prokopowicz, P.: Algebra of fuzzy numbers. Applied Mathematics. Mathematics for the Society 5/46, 37–63 (2004) (in Polish)
14. Kosiński, W., Prokopowicz, P., Kacprzak, D.: Fuzziness – Representation of Dynamic Changes by Ordered Fuzzy Numbers. In: Seising, R. (ed.) Views on Fuzzy Sets and Systems from Different Perspectives. STUDFUZZ, vol. 243, pp. 485–508. Springer, Heidelberg (2009)
15. Kosiński, W., Prokopowicz, P., Ślęzak, D.: Fuzzy numbers with algebraic operations: algorithmic approach. In: Kłopotek, M., Wierzchoń, S.T., Michalewicz, M. (eds.) Proc. of Intelligent Information Systems, IIS 2002, Sopot, June 3-6, pp. 311–320. Physica Verlag, Heidelberg (2002)
16. Kosiński, W., Prokopowicz, P., Ślęzak, D.: On algebraic operations on fuzzy reals. In: Rutkowski, L., Kacprzyk, J. (eds.) Proc. of the Sixth Int. Conference on Neural Network and Soft Computing, Advances in Soft Computing, Zakopane, Poland, June 11-15, pp. 54–61. Physica-Verlag, Heidelberg (2003)
17. Kosiński, W., Prokopowicz, P., Ślęzak, D.: Ordered fuzzy numbers. Bulletin of the Polish Academy of Sciences 51(3), 327–338 (2003)
18. Kosiński, W., Prokopowicz, P., Ślęzak, D.: On algebraic operations on fuzzy numbers. In: Kłopotek, M., Wierzchoń, S.T., Trojanowski, K. (eds.) Intelligent Information Processing and Web Mining, Proc. of Int. IIS: IIPWM 2003, Conference held in Zakopane, Poland, June 2-5, pp. 353–362. Physica-Verlag, Heidelberg (2003)
19. Kosiński, W., Prokopowicz, P., Ślęzak, D.: Calculus with Fuzzy Numbers. In: Bolc, L., Michalewicz, Z., Nishida, T. (eds.) IMTCI 2004. LNCS (LNAI), vol. 3490, pp. 21–28. Springer, Heidelberg (2005)
20. Kosiński, W., Węgrzyn - Wolska, K., Borzymek, P.: Evolutionary algorithm in fuzzy data problem. In: Kita, E. (ed.) Evolutionary Algorithms, pp. 201–218. InTech (2011)
21. Kosiński, W., Wilczyńska-Sztyma, D.: Defuzzification and implication within ordered fuzzy numbers. In: IEEE World Congress on Computational Intelligence, WCCI 2010, CCIB, Barcelona, July 18-23, pp. 1073–1079 (2010)

22. Kościeński, K.: Modul of step ordered fuzzy numbers in control of material point motion. Engineering Thesis, PJWSTK, Warszawa (2010) (in Polish)
23. Nguyen, H.T.: A note on the extension principle for fuzzy sets. J. Math. Anal. Appl. 64, 369–380 (1978)
24. Prokopowicz, P.: Algorithmisation of operations on fuzzy numbers and its applications. Ph.D. Thesis, IPPT PAN, Warszawa (2005) (in Polish)
25. Prokopowicz, P.: Using ordered fuzzy numbers arithmetic. In: Cader, A., Rutkowski, L., Tadeusiewicz, R., Zurada, J. (eds.) Proc. of the 8th International Conference on Artificial Intelligence and Soft Computing, Fuzzy Control in Artificial Intelligence and Soft Computing, June 25-29, pp. 156–162. Academic Publishing House EXIT, Warszawa (2006)
26. Rosa, A.: Modelling using orderd fuzzy numbers. Engineering Thesis, WMFiT, Kazimierz-Wielki University, Bydgoszcz (2011) (in Polish)
27. Van Leekwijck, W., Kerre, E.E.: Defuzzification: criteria and classification. Fuzzy Sets and Systems 108, 159–178 (1999)
28. Wilczyńska, D.: On control aspects within ordered fuzzy numbers in MATLAB environment. Master Thesis, WMFiT, Kazimierz-Wielki University, Bydgoszcz (2007) (in Polish)
29. Yager, R.R., Filev, D.P.: Essentials of Fuzzy Modeling and Control. John Wiley & Sons, New York (1994)
30. Zadeh, L.A.: Fuzzy sets. Information and Control 8, 338–353 (1965)
31. Z.L.A.: The concept of a linguistic variable and its application to approximate reasoning. Part I. Information Sciences 8, 199–249 (1975)

Determining OWA Operator Weights
by Mean Absolute Deviation Minimization

Michał Majdan[1,2] and Włodzimierz Ogryczak[1]

[1] Institute of Control and Computation Engineering,
Warsaw University of Technology, Warsaw, Poland
[2] National Institute of Telecommunications, Warsaw, Poland
{m.majdan,w.ogryczak}@gmail.com

Abstract. The ordered weighted averaging (OWA) operator uses the weights assigned to the ordered values rather than to the specific criteria. This allows one to model various aggregation preferences, preserving simultaneously the impartiality (neutrality) with respect to the individual attributes. The determination of ordered weighted averaging (OWA) operator weights is a crucial issue of applying the OWA operator for decision making. This paper considers determining monotonic weights of the OWA operator by minimization the mean absolute deviation inequality measure. This leads to a linear programming model which can also be solved analytically.

1 Introduction

The problem of aggregating multiple numerical criteria to form overall objective functions is of considerable importance in many disciplines. The most commonly used aggregation is based on the weighted sum. The preference weights can be effectively introduced with the so-called Ordered Weighted Averaging (OWA) aggregation developed by Yager [17]. In the OWA aggregation the weights are assigned to the ordered values (i.e. to the smallest value, the second smallest and so on) rather than to the specific criteria. Since its introduction, the OWA aggregation has been successfully applied to many fields of decision making [8,12,21]. The OWA operator allows us to model various aggregation functions from the maximum through the arithmetic mean to the minimum. Thus, it enables modeling of various preferences from the optimistic to the pessimistic one.

Several approaches has been introduced for obtaining the OWA weights with a predefined degree of orness [2,16]. O'Hagan [7] proposed a maximum entropy approach, which involved a constrained nonlinear optimization problem with a predefined degree of orness as its constraint and the entropy as the objective function. Actually, the maximum entropy model can be transformed into a polynomial equation and then solved analytically [3]. A minimum variance approach to obtain the minimal variability OWA operator weights was also considered [4]. The minimax disparity approach proposed by Wang and Parkan [14] was the first method of finding OWA operator using Linear Programming (LP) This

L. Rutkowski et al. (Eds.): ICAISC 2012, Part I, LNCS 7267, pp. 283–291, 2012.

method determines the OWA operator weights by minimizing the maximum difference between two adjacent weights under a given level of orness. The minimax disparity approach was further extended [1,13] and related to the minimum variance approaches [6]. The maximum entropy approach was generalized for various Minkowski metrics [19,20] and in some cases expressed with LP models [15]. In this paper we analyze a possibility to use another LP solvable models. In particular, we develop the LP model to determine the OWA operator weights by minimizing the Mean Absolute Deviation (MAD) inequality measure. In addition to the LP model an analytical formula is also derived.

2   Orness and Inequality Measures

Let $\mathbf{w} = (w_1, \ldots, w_m)$ be a weighting vector of dimension m such that $w_i \geq 0$ for $i = 1, \ldots, m$ and $\sum_{i=1}^{m} w_i = 1$. The corresponding OWA aggregation of outcomes $\mathbf{y} = (y_1, \ldots, y_m)$ can be mathematically formalized as follows [17]. First, we introduce the ordering map $\Theta : R^m \to R^m$ such that $\Theta(\mathbf{y}) = (\theta_1(\mathbf{y}), \theta_2(\mathbf{y}), \ldots, \theta_m(\mathbf{y}))$, where $\theta_1(\mathbf{y}) \geq \theta_2(\mathbf{y}) \geq \cdots \geq \theta_m(\mathbf{y})$ and there exists a permutation τ of set I such that $\theta_i(\mathbf{y}) = y_{\tau(i)}$ for $i = 1, \ldots, m$. Further, we apply the weighted sum aggregation to ordered achievement vectors $\Theta(\mathbf{y})$, i.e. the OWA aggregation has the following form:

$$A_{\mathbf{w}}(\mathbf{y}) = \sum_{i=1}^{m} w_i \theta_i(\mathbf{y}) \tag{1}$$

The OWA aggregation may model various preferences from the optimistic (max) to the pessimistic (min). Yager [17] introduced a well appealing concept of the orness measure to characterize the OWA operators. The degree of orness associated with the OWA operator $A_{\mathbf{w}}(\mathbf{y})$ is defined as

$$\text{orness}(\mathbf{w}) = \sum_{i=1}^{m} \frac{m-i}{m-1} w_i \tag{2}$$

For the max aggregation representing the fuzzy 'or' operator with weights $\mathbf{w} = (1, 0, \ldots, 0)$ one gets orness$(\mathbf{w}) = 1$ while for the min aggregation representing the fuzzy 'and' operator with weights $\mathbf{w} = (0, \ldots, 0, 1)$ one has orness$(\mathbf{w}) = 0$. For the average (arithmetic mean) one gets orness$((1/m, 1/m, \ldots, 1/m)) = 1/2$. Actually, one may consider a complementary measure of andness defined as andness$(\mathbf{w}) = 1 - \text{orness}(\mathbf{w})$. OWA aggregations with orness greater or equal $1/2$ are considered or-like whereas the aggregations with orness smaller or equal $1/2$ are treated as and-like. The former corresponds to rather optimistic preferences while the latter represents rather pessimistic preferences.

The OWA aggregations with monotonic weights are either or-like or and-like. Exactly, decreasing weights $w_1 \geq w_2 \geq \ldots \geq w_m$ define an or-like OWA operator, while increasing weights $w_1 \leq w_2 \leq \ldots \leq w_m$ define an and-like OWA operator. Actually, the orness and the andness properties of the OWA operators with monotonic weights are total in the sense that they remain valid for any subaggregations defined by subsequences of their weights.

Yager [18] proposed to define the OWA weighting vectors via the regular increasing monotone (RIM) quantifiers, which provide a dimension independent description of the aggregation. A fuzzy subset Q of the real line is called a RIM quantifier if Q is (weakly) increasing with $Q(0) = 0$ and $Q(1) = 1$. The OWA weights can be defined with a RIM quantifier Q as $w_i = Q(i/m) - Q((i-1)/m)$. and the orness measure can be extended to a RIM quantifier (according to $m \to \infty$) as follows [18]

$$\text{orness}(Q) = \int_0^1 Q(\alpha)\, d\alpha \tag{3}$$

Thus, the orness of a RIM quantifier is equal to the area under it.

Monotonic weights can be uniquely defined by their distribution. First, we introduce the right-continuous cumulative distribution function (cdf):

$$F_\mathbf{w}(d) = \sum_{i=1}^m \frac{1}{m} \delta_i(d) \quad \text{where} \quad \delta_i(d) = \begin{cases} 1 & \text{if } w_i \leq d \\ 0 & \text{otherwise} \end{cases} \tag{4}$$

which for any real value d provides the measure of weights smaller or equal to d. Alternatively one may use the left-continuous right tail cumulative distribution function $\overline{F}_\mathbf{w}(d) = 1 - F_\mathbf{w}(d)$ which for any real value d provides the measure of weights greater or equal to d.

Next, we introduce the quantile function $F_\mathbf{w}^{(-1)} = \inf\{\eta : F_\mathbf{y}(\eta) \geq \xi\}$ for $0 < \xi \leq 1$ as the left-continuous inverse of the cumulative distribution function $F_\mathbf{w}$, ie., $F_\mathbf{w}^{(-1)}(\xi) = \inf\{\eta : F_\mathbf{w}(\eta) \geq \xi\}$ for $0 < \xi \leq 1$. Similarly, we introduce the right tail quantile function $\overline{F}_\mathbf{w}^{(-1)}$ as the right-continuous inverse of the cumulative distribution function $\overline{F}_\mathbf{w}$, i.e., $\overline{F}_\mathbf{w}^{(-1)}(\xi) = \sup\{\eta : \overline{F}_\mathbf{w}(\eta) \geq \xi\}$ for $0 < \xi \leq 1$. Actually, $\overline{F}_\mathbf{w}^{(-1)}(\xi) = F_\mathbf{w}^{(-1)}(1 - \xi)$. It is the stepwise function $\overline{F}_\mathbf{w}^{(-1)}(\xi) = \theta_i(\mathbf{w})$ for $\frac{i-1}{m} < \xi \leq \frac{i}{m}$.

Dispersion of the weights distribution can be described with the Lorenz curves and related inequality measures. Classical Lorenz curve used in income economics as a cumulative population versus income curve to compare equity of income distributions. Although, the Lorenz curve for any distribution may be viewed [5] as a normalized integrated quantile function. In particular, for distribution of weights $\mathbf{w}$ one gets

$$L_\mathbf{w}(\xi) = \frac{1}{\mu(\mathbf{w})} \int_0^\xi F_\mathbf{w}^{(-1)}(\alpha)d\alpha = m \int_0^\xi F_\mathbf{w}^{(-1)}(\alpha) \tag{5}$$

where while dealing with normalized weights w_i we have always $\mu(\mathbf{w}) = 1/m$. Graphs of functions $L_\mathbf{w}(\xi)$ take the form of piecewise linear convex curves. They are also nondecreasing, due to nonnegative weights w_i. Any perfectly equal distribution of income has the diagonal line as the Lorenz curve (the same independently from the income value).

Alternatively, the upper Lorenz curve may be used which integrates the right tail quantile function. For distribution of weights $\mathbf{w}$ one gets

$$\overline{L}_{\mathbf{w}}(\xi) = \frac{1}{\mu(\mathbf{w})} \int_0^\xi \overline{F}_{\mathbf{w}}^{(-1)}(\alpha) d\alpha = m \int_0^\xi \overline{F}_{\mathbf{w}}^{(-1)}(\alpha) \tag{6}$$

Graphs of functions $\overline{L}_{\mathbf{w}}(\xi)$ take the form of piecewise linear concave curves. They are also nondecreasing, due to nonnegative weights w_i. Similar to $L_{\mathbf{w}}$, the vector of perfectly equal weights has the diagonal line as the upper Lorenz curve. Actually, both the classical (lower) and the upper Lorenz curves are symmetric with respect to the diagonal line in the sense that the differences

$$\bar{d}_{\mathbf{w}}(\xi) = \overline{L}_{\mathbf{w}}(\xi) - \xi \quad \text{and} \quad d_{\mathbf{w}}(\xi) = \xi - L_{\mathbf{w}}(\xi) \tag{7}$$

are equal for symmetric arguments $\bar{d}_{\mathbf{w}}(\xi) = d_{\mathbf{w}}(1 - \xi)$. Hence,

$$\overline{L}_{\mathbf{w}}(\xi) + L_{\mathbf{w}}(1 - \xi) = 1 \quad \text{for any } 0 \le \xi \le 1 \tag{8}$$

Note that in the case of nondecreasing OWA weights $0 \le w_1 \le \ldots \le w_m \le 1$ the corresponding Lorenz curve $L_{\mathbf{w}}(\xi)$ is (weakly) increasing with $L_{\mathbf{w}}(0) = 0$ and $L_{\mathbf{w}}(1) = 1$ as well as the OWA weights can be defined with L as $w_i = L_{\mathbf{w}}(i/m) - L_{\mathbf{w}}((i-1)/m)$. Hence, $L_{\mathbf{w}}$ may be considered then as a RIM quantifier generating weights $\mathbf{w}$ [10]. Following (3), the orness measure of RIM quantifier is given as $\text{orness}(L) = \int_0^1 L(\alpha)\, d\alpha$, thus equal to the area under $L_{\mathbf{w}}$. Certainly, for any finite m the RIM orness $\text{orness}(L_{\mathbf{w}})$ differs form the orness, but the difference depends only on the value of m, exactly,

$$\text{orness}(L_{\mathbf{w}}) = \sum_{i=1}^m \frac{m-i}{m} w_i + \sum_{i=1}^m \frac{1}{2m} w_i = \frac{m-1}{m} \text{orness}(\mathbf{w}) + \frac{1}{2m} \tag{9}$$

In the case of nonincreasing OWA weights $1 \ge w_1 \ge \ldots \ge w_m \ge 0$ the corresponding upper Lorenz curve $\overline{L}_{\mathbf{w}}(\xi)$ is (weakly) increasing with $\overline{L}_{\mathbf{w}}(0) = 0$ and $\overline{L}_{\mathbf{w}}(1) = 1$ as well as the OWA weights can be defined with $\overline{L}$ as $w_i = \overline{L}_{\mathbf{w}}(i/m) - \overline{L}_{\mathbf{w}}((i-1)/m)$. Hence, $\overline{L}_{\mathbf{w}}$ may be considered then as a RIM quantifier generating weights $\mathbf{w}$. Similar to (9), the difference between the RIM orness $\text{orness}(\overline{L}_{\mathbf{w}})$ and $\text{orness}(\mathbf{w})$ depends only on the value of m.

Typical inequality measures are some deviation type dispersion characteristics. They are *inequality relevant* which means that they are equal to 0 in the case of perfectly equal outcomes while taking positive values for unequal ones.

The simplest inequality measures are based on the absolute measurement of the spread of outcomes, like the *(Gini's) mean absolute difference*

$$\Gamma(\mathbf{w}) = \frac{1}{2m^2} \sum_{i=1}^m \sum_{j=1}^m |w_i - w_j| \tag{10}$$

In most application frameworks a better intuitive appeal may have inequality measures related to deviations from the mean value like the Mean Absolute Deviation (MAD) from the mean

$$\delta(\mathbf{w}) = \frac{1}{m} \sum_{i=1}^{m} |w_i - \mu(\mathbf{w})| \tag{11}$$

In economics one usually considers relative inequality measures normalized by the mean. Among many inequality measures perhaps the most commonly accepted by economists is the *Gini index*, which is the relative mean difference.

$$G(\mathbf{w}) = \Gamma(\mathbf{w})/\mu(\mathbf{w}) = m\Gamma(\mathbf{w}) \tag{12}$$

Similar, one may consider the relative mean deviation which is known as the *Schutz index*

$$S(\mathbf{w}) = \delta(\mathbf{w})/\mu(\mathbf{w}) = m\delta(\mathbf{w}) \tag{13}$$

Note that due to $\mu(\mathbf{w}) = 1/m$, the relative inequality measures are proportional to their absolute counterparts and any comparison of the relative measures is equivalent to comparison of the corresponding absolute measures.

The above inequality measures are closely related to the Lorenz curve [8] and its differences from the diagonal (equity) line (7). First of all

$$G(\mathbf{w}) = 2 \int_0^1 \bar{d}_\mathbf{w}(\alpha)d\alpha = 2 \int_0^1 d_\mathbf{w}(\alpha)d\alpha \tag{14}$$

thus

$$G(\mathbf{w}) = 2 \int_0^1 \overline{L}_\mathbf{w}(\alpha)d\alpha - 1 = 1 - 2 \int_0^1 L_\mathbf{w}(\alpha)d\alpha \tag{15}$$

Recall that in the case of nondecreasing OWA weights $0 \le w_1 \le \ldots \le w_m \le 1$ the corresponding Lorenz curve $L_\mathbf{w}(\xi)$ may be considered as a RIM quantifier generating weights $\mathbf{w}$. Following (9), one gets

$$G(\mathbf{w}) = 1 - 2\text{orness}(L_\mathbf{w}) = \frac{m-1}{m}(1 - 2\text{orness}(\mathbf{w})) \tag{16}$$

enabling easy recalculation of the orness measure into the Gini index and vice versa. Similarly, in the case of nonincreasing OWA weights $1 \ge w_1 \ge \ldots \ge w_m \ge 0$, one gets

$$G(\mathbf{w}) = 2\text{orness}(\overline{L}_\mathbf{w}) - 1 = \frac{m-1}{m}(2\text{orness}(\mathbf{w}) - 1) \tag{17}$$

3   Mean Absolute Deviation Minimization

We focus on the case of monotonic weights. Following (16) and (17), the Gini index is then uniquely defined by a given orness value. Nevertheless, one may still select various weights by minimization the MAD measure. Although related to the Lorenz curve it is not uniquely defined by the Gini index and the orness measure. Actually, the MAD minimization approach may be viewed as the generalized entropy maximization based on the first Minkowski metric [15].

Let us define differences

$$\bar{d}_i(\mathbf{w}) = \overline{L}_\mathbf{w}\left(\frac{i}{m}\right) - \frac{i}{m} \quad \text{and} \quad d_i(\mathbf{w}) = \frac{i}{m} - L_\mathbf{w}\left(\frac{i}{m}\right) \qquad \text{for } i = 1, \ldots, m \quad (18)$$

where due to nonnegativity of weights, for all $i = 1, \ldots, m - 1$

$$\bar{d}_i(\mathbf{w}) \leq \frac{1}{m} + \bar{d}_{i+1}(\mathbf{w}) \quad \text{and} \quad d_i(\mathbf{w}) \leq \frac{1}{m} + d_{i-1}(\mathbf{w}) \qquad (19)$$

with $d_0(\mathbf{w}) = \bar{d}_0(\mathbf{w}) = 0$ and $d_m(\mathbf{w}) = \bar{d}_m(\mathbf{w}) = 0$. Thus

$$\bar{d}_{m-i}(\mathbf{w}) \leq \frac{i}{m} \quad \text{and} \quad d_i(\mathbf{w}) \leq \frac{i}{m} \qquad \text{for } i = 1, \ldots, m - 1 \quad (20)$$

The Gini index represents the area defined by $\bar{d}_i(\mathbf{w})$ or $d_i(\mathbf{w})$, respectively,

$$G(\mathbf{w}) = \frac{2}{m} \sum_{i=1}^{m-1} \bar{d}_i(\mathbf{w}) = \frac{2}{m} \sum_{i=1}^{m-1} d_i(\mathbf{w}) \qquad (21)$$

while the relative MAD (Schutz index) may be represented [8] as

$$S(\mathbf{w}) = m\delta(\mathbf{w}) = \max_{i=1,\ldots,m-1} \bar{d}_i(\mathbf{w}) = \max_{i=1,\ldots,m-1} d_i(\mathbf{w}) \qquad (22)$$

Assume there is given some orness value $0.5 \leq \alpha \leq 1$ and we are looking for monotonic weights $1 \geq w_1 \geq \ldots \geq w_m \geq 0$ such that $\text{orness}(\mathbf{w}) = \alpha$ and $S(\mathbf{w})$ is minimal. Following (17), (21) and (22) it leads us to the problem

$$\min \max_{i=1,\ldots,m-1} m\bar{d}_i(\mathbf{w})$$
$$\text{s.t. } \frac{2}{m} \sum_{i=1}^{m-1} \bar{d}_i(\mathbf{w}) = \frac{m-1}{m}(2\alpha - 1) \qquad (23)$$

with additional constraints (19). This allows us to form the following LP model

$$\min \quad md \qquad (24)$$
$$\text{s.t. } \bar{d}_i \leq d \qquad\qquad\qquad\qquad \text{for } i = 1, \ldots, m - 1 \quad (25)$$
$$\bar{d}_1 + \ldots + \bar{d}_{m-1} = (m-1)(\alpha - 0.5) \qquad\qquad (26)$$
$$0 \leq \bar{d}_i \leq \frac{1}{m} + \bar{d}_{i+1} \qquad\qquad\quad \text{for } i = 1, \ldots, m - 1 \quad (27)$$

with variables $\bar{d}_i$ for $i = 1, \ldots, m - 1$, auxiliary variable d and constant $\bar{d}_m = 0$. Having solved the above LP problem, the corresponding weights can be simply calculated according to the following formula (with $\bar{d}_0 = \bar{d}_m = 0$):

$$w_i = \bar{d}_i - \bar{d}_{i-1} + \frac{1}{m} \qquad \text{for } i = 1, \ldots, m \qquad (28)$$

Symmetrically, having given an orness value $0 \le \alpha \le 0.5$ and looking for monotonic weights $0 \le w_1 \le \ldots \le w_m \le 1$ such that orness($\mathbf{w}$) $= \alpha$ and $S(\mathbf{w})$ is minimal, following (16), (21) and (22), one gets the problem

$$\min \max_{i=1,\ldots,m-1} md_i(\mathbf{w})$$
$$\text{s.t.} \ \frac{2}{m} \sum_{i=1}^{m-1} d_i(\mathbf{w}) = \frac{m-1}{m}(1-2\alpha) \tag{29}$$

with additional constraints (19). Thus leading to the LP problem

$$\begin{aligned}
\min \ &md \\
\text{s.t.} \ &d_i \le d & \text{for } i = 1,\ldots,m-1 \\
&d_1 + \ldots + d_{m-1} = (m-1)(0.5 - \alpha) \\
&0 \le d_i \le \tfrac{1}{m} + d_{i-1} & \text{for } i = 1,\ldots,m-1
\end{aligned} \tag{30}$$

with variables d_i for $i = 1,\ldots,m-1$, auxiliary variable d and constant $d_0 = 0$. The corresponding weights can be found according to the formula

$$w_i = d_{i-1} - d_i + \frac{1}{m} \qquad \text{for } i = 1,\ldots,m \tag{31}$$

where $d_0 = d_m = 0$.

(a) (b)

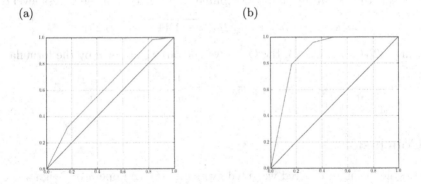

Fig. 1. Lorenz curve for MAD minimization: (a) $0.5 \le \alpha \le 0.5 + 1/m$, (b) $\alpha > 0.5 + 1/m$

LP models (24)–(27) and (30) allow for application standard optimization techniques to solve them. However, their structure is so simple that the problem of MAD minimization can also be solved analytically. We will show this in details for the case of $0.5 \le$ orness($\mathbf{w}$) ≤ 1 and the corresponding model (24)–(27).

One may take advantage of the fact that an optimal solution to the minimax problem $\min\{\max_{i\in I} y_i : \sum_{i\in I} y_i = b\}$ are perfectly equal values $y_i = b/|I|$ for all $i \in I$. Hence, when the required orness level is small enough (still not below 0.5), then the optimal solution is defined by

$$\bar{d}_1 = \ldots = \bar{d}_{m-1} = \Delta$$

where $\Delta = \alpha - 0.5$ is defined by the orness equation (26) while leaving inequalities (27) inactive. Exactly, this is a case when $0.5 \leq \alpha \leq 0.5 + 1/m$ as illustrated in Fig. 1(a). Note that such a solution is generated by weights:

$$w_1 = \frac{1}{m} + \Delta, \quad w_2 = \ldots = w_{m-1} = \frac{1}{m}, \quad w_m = \frac{1}{m} - \Delta$$

When the required orness level is larger then some constraints (27) become active thus setting some κ tail differences on their upper limits: $\bar{d}_{m-k} = \frac{k}{m}$ for $k = 1, \ldots, \kappa$, as illustrated in Fig. 1(b). This leads us to the solution

$$\bar{d}_1 = \ldots = \bar{d}_{m-\kappa-1} = \Delta, \quad \bar{d}_{m-k} = \frac{k}{m} \quad \text{for } k = 1, \ldots, \kappa \tag{32}$$

where, following the orness equation (26),

$$\Delta = \frac{m-1}{m-\kappa-1}(\alpha - 0.5) - \frac{\kappa(\kappa+1)}{2m(m-\kappa-1)} \tag{33}$$

Exactly, formulas (32)-(33) are valid when

$$\frac{(2m-1-\kappa)\kappa}{2m(m-1)} \leq \alpha - 0.5 \leq \frac{(2m-1-(\kappa+1))(\kappa+1)}{2m(m-1)}$$

which means that κ can be simply computed as a function of the orness level α

$$\kappa = \kappa(\alpha) = \lfloor m - 1 - \sqrt{2m(m-1)(1-\alpha) + 0.25} \rfloor$$

Following (32)-(33) and (28), the OWA weights are then given by the formula

$$w_1 = \frac{1}{m} + \Delta, \quad w_2 = \ldots = w_{m-\kappa-1} = \frac{1}{m}, \quad w_{m-\kappa} = \frac{\kappa+1}{m} - \Delta$$
$$w_{m-k} = 0 \quad \text{for } k = 1, \ldots, \kappa - 1$$

4   Conclusion

The determination of ordered weighted averaging (OWA) operator weights is a crucial issue of applying the OWA operator for decision making. We have considered determining monotonic weights of the OWA operator by minimization of the mean absolute deviation inequality measure. This leads us to a linear programming model which can also be solved analytically. The analytic approach results in simple direct formulas. The LP models allow us to find weights by the use of efficient LP optimization techniques and they enable easy enhancement of the preference model with additional requirements on the weights properties. The latter is the main advantage over the standard method of entropy maximization. Both the standard method and the proposed one do have their analytical solutions. However, if we try to elaborate them further by adding some auxiliary (linear) constraints on the OWA weights, then the entropy minimization model forms a difficult nonlinear optimization task while the MAD minimization is still easily LP-solvable.

Acknowledgements. The research was partially supported by the Polish National Budget Funds 2010–2013 for science under the grant N N514 044438.

References

1. Amin, G.R., Emrouznejad, A.: An extended minimax disparity to determine the OWA operator weights. Comput. Ind. Eng. 50, 312–316 (2006)
2. Fuller, R.: On obtaining OWA operator weights: a short survey of recent developments. In: Proc. 5th IEEE Int. Conf. Comput. Cybernetics, Gammarth, Tunisia, pp. 241–244 (2007)
3. Fuller, R., Majlender, P.: An analytic approach for obtaining maximal entropy OWA operator weights. Fuzzy Sets and Systems 124, 53–57 (2001)
4. Fuller, R., Majlender, P.: On obtaining minimal variability OWA operator weights. Fuzzy Sets and Systems 136, 203–215 (2003)
5. Gastwirth, J.L.: A general definition of the Lorenz curve. Econometrica 39, 1037–1039 (1971)
6. Liu, X.: The solution equivalence of minimax disparity and minimum variance problems for OWA operators. Int. J. Approx. Reasoning 45, 68–81 (2007)
7. O'Hagan, M.: Aggregating template or rule antecedents in real-time expert systems with fuzzy set logic. In: Proc. 22nd Annu. IEEE Asilomar Conf. Signals, Syst., Comput., Pacific Grove, CA, pp. 681–689 (1988)
8. Ogryczak, W.: Inequality measures and equitable approaches to location problems. Eur. J. Opnl. Res. 122, 374–391 (2000)
9. Ogryczak, W., Śliwiński, T.: On solving linear programs with the ordered weighted averaging objective. Eur. J. Opnl. Res. 148, 80–91 (2003)
10. Ogryczak, W., Śliwiński, T.: On efficient WOWA optimization for decision support under risk. Int. J. Approx. Reason. 50, 915–928 (2009)
11. Sen, A.: On Economic Inequality. Clarendon Press, Oxford (1973)
12. Torra, V., Narukawa, Y.: Modeling Decisions Information Fusion and Aggregation Operators. Springer, Berlin (2007)
13. Wang, Y.-M., Luo, Y., Liu, X.: Two new models for determining OWA operator weights. Comput. Ind. Eng. 52, 203–209 (2007)
14. Wang, Y.-M., Parkan, C.: A minimax disparity approach for obtaining OWA operator weights. Information Sciences 175, 20–29 (2005)
15. Wu, J., Sun, B.-L., Liang, C.-Y., Yang, S.-L.: A linear programming model for determining ordered weighted averaging operator weights with maximal Yager's entropy. Comput. Ind. Eng. 57, 742–747 (2009)
16. Xu, Z.: An overview of methods for determining OWA weights. Int. J. Intell. Syst. 20, 843–865 (2005)
17. Yager, R.R.: On ordered weighted averaging aggregation operators in multicriteria decision making. IEEE Trans. Systems, Man and Cyber. 18, 183–190 (1988)
18. Yager, R.R.: Quantifier guided aggregation using OWA operators. Int. J. Intell. Syst. 11, 49–73 (1996)
19. Yager, R.R.: Measures of entropy and fuzziness related to aggregation operators. Information Sciences 82, 147–166 (1995)
20. Yager, R.R.: On the dispersion measure of OWA operators. Information Sciences 179, 3908–3919 (2009)
21. Yager, R.R., Kacprzyk, J.: The Ordered Weighted Averaging Operators: Theory and Applications. Kluwer AP, Dordrecht (1997)

Efficient MPC Algorithms Based on Fuzzy Wiener Models and Advanced Methods of Prediction Generation

Piotr M. Marusak

Institute of Control and Computation Engineering,
Warsaw University of Technology,
ul. Nowowiejska 15/19, 00-665 Warszawa, Poland
P.Marusak@ia.pw.edu.pl

Abstract. Efficient Model Predictive Control (MPC) algorithms based on fuzzy Wiener models with advanced methods of prediction are proposed in the paper. The methods of prediction use values of future control changes which were derived by the MPC algorithm in the last iteration. Such an approach results in excellent control performance offered by the proposed algorithms. Moreover, they are formulated as numerically efficient quadratic optimization problems. Advantages of the proposed fuzzy MPC algorithms are demonstrated in the control systems of a nonlinear plant.

Keywords: fuzzy systems, fuzzy control, predictive control, nonlinear control, constrained control.

1 Introduction

MPC algorithms generate control signals using prediction of the process behavior in the future. Such an approach is the source of advantages of the MPC algorithms and very good control performance offered by them [4, 8, 17, 20]. Prediction is derived using a model of the control plant. In standard MPC algorithms linear models are used. In such a case, the MPC algorithm can be formulated as an easy to solve, quadratic optimization problem. Unfortunately, if the control plant is nonlinear, application of such an algorithm may bring unsatisfactory results.

If a nonlinear process model is used directly in the MPC algorithm, it leads to its formulation as a nonlinear, nonquadratic, in general nonconvex optimization problem which must be solved in each iteration of the algorithm. The obtained problem is however difficult to solve and computationally demanding. Time needed to find the solution is hard to predict, numerical problems may occur and there is also a problem of local minima. MPC algorithms which are based on linear approximations of the nonlinear models obtained in each iteration of the algorithm do not have these drawbacks; see e.g. [10–13, 15, 20].

Wiener models have an interesting structure. In these models a linear dynamic part precedes a nonlinear static part [7]. Many processes can be successfully

L. Rutkowski et al. (Eds.): ICAISC 2012, Part I, LNCS 7267, pp. 292–300, 2012.

modeled using the Wiener models (see e.g. [2, 9]) and thanks to the structure of these models, controllers can be designed relatively easy. The proposed methods of prediction are based on fuzzy Wiener models in which the fuzzy Takagi–Sugeno (TS) model is used as the static part of the Wiener model. The methods are better than the one proposed in [12] because they use values of the future control changes, derived by the MPC algorithm in the previous iteration, to improve the prediction. At the same time, they remain relatively simple not affecting control performance in a negative way.

In the next section the standard MPC algorithms are reminded. In Sect. 3 the MPC algorithms based on fuzzy Wiener models and the advanced methods of prediction are proposed. Results obtained in the control system of a nonlinear plant, illustrating efficacy of the proposed fuzzy MPC algorithms are presented in Sect. 4. The paper is summarized in the last section.

2   Model Predictive Control Algorithms

In the Model Predictive Control (MPC) algorithms future behavior of the control plant many sampling instants ahead is predicted using a process model. The control signal is derived in such a way that the prediction fulfills assumed criteria. Usually, the following optimization problem is solved at each iteration of the algorithm [4, 8, 17, 20]:

$$\arg\min_{\Delta u}\left\{ J_{\mathrm{MPC}} = \sum_{i=1}^{p}\left(\overline{y}_k - y_{k+i|k}\right)^2 + \sum_{i=0}^{s-1}\lambda\left(\Delta u_{k+i|k}\right)^2 \right\} \tag{1}$$

subject to:

$$\Delta u_{\min} \leq \Delta u \leq \Delta u_{\max} , \tag{2}$$

$$u_{\min} \leq u \leq u_{\max} , \tag{3}$$

$$y_{\min} \leq y \leq y_{\max} , \tag{4}$$

where $\overline{y}_k$ is a set–point value, $y_{k+i|k}$ is a value of the output for the $(k + i)^{\mathrm{th}}$ sampling instant, predicted at the kth sampling instant, $\Delta u_{k+i|k}$ are future changes of the control signal, $\lambda \geq 0$ is a tuning parameter, p and s denote prediction and control horizons, respectively; $\Delta u = \left[\Delta u_{k+1|k}, \ldots, \Delta u_{k+s-1|k}\right]$, $u = \left[u_{k+1|k}, \ldots, u_{k+s-1|k}\right]$, $y = \left[y_{k+1|k}, \ldots, y_{k+p|k}\right]$; $\Delta u_{\min}, \Delta u_{\max}, u_{\min}, u_{\max}, y_{\min}, y_{\max}$ are vectors of lower and upper limits of changes and values of the control signal and of the values of the output signal, respectively. The solution of the optimization problem (1–4) is the optimal vector of changes of the control signal. From this vector, the first element is applied to the control plant and then the optimization problem is solved again in the next iteration of the MPC algorithm.

The predicted output variables $y_{k+i|k}$ are calculated using a dynamic model of the control plant. If the model used for prediction is nonlinear then the optimization problem (1–4) is nonlinear, nonquadratic and, in general, nonconvex. Algorithms of this kind will be referred to as NMPC. Examples of such algorithms based on fuzzy models can be found e.g. in [3, 5] and those utilizing Wiener models – e.g. in [2, 9]. Unfortunately, the optimization problem in the NMPC algorithm is hard to solve and the control signal must be calculated at each iteration of the algorithm.

If the model used in the MPC algorithm is linear then the superposition principle can be applied and the vector of predicted output values y is given by the following formula:

$$y = \widetilde{y} + A \cdot \Delta u , \qquad (5)$$

where $\widetilde{y} = \left[\widetilde{y}_{k+1|k}, \ldots, \widetilde{y}_{k+p|k}\right]$ is a free response (it contains future values of the output signal calculated assuming that the control signal does not change in the prediction horizon); $A \cdot \Delta u$ is the forced response which depends only on future changes of the control signal (decision variables);

$$A = \begin{bmatrix} a_1 & 0 & \cdots & 0 & 0 \\ a_2 & a_1 & \cdots & 0 & 0 \\ \vdots & \vdots & \ddots & \vdots & \vdots \\ a_p & a_{p-1} & \cdots & a_{p-s+2} & a_{p-s+1} \end{bmatrix} \qquad (6)$$

is the dynamic matrix composed of coefficients of the control plant step response [4, 8, 17, 20].

Thus, if a linear process model is used then the optimization problem (1–4) becomes a standard quadratic programming problem. Let us introduce the vector $\overline{y} = [\overline{y}_k, \ldots, \overline{y}_k]$ of length p. The performance function from (1), after utilization of the prediction (5), can be rewritten in the matrix–vector form as:

$$J_{\text{LMPC}} = (\overline{y} - \widetilde{y} - A \cdot \Delta u)^T \cdot (\overline{y} - \widetilde{y} - A \cdot \Delta u) + \Delta u^T \cdot \Lambda \cdot \Delta u , \qquad (7)$$

where $\Lambda = \lambda \cdot I$ is the $s \times s$ matrix. The performance function (7) depends quadratically on future control increments (decision variables) Δu.

Note that if the constraints need not be taken into consideration, the vector minimizing the performance function (7) is given by the following formula:

$$\Delta u = \left(A^T \cdot A + \Lambda\right)^{-1} \cdot A^T \cdot (\overline{y} - \widetilde{y}) . \qquad (8)$$

As the quadratic optimization problems can be easily solved using well known, numerically robust methods, MPC algorithms based on linear approximations of the nonlinear process models obtained at each iteration were designed [15, 20]. The algorithms of this type based on fuzzy process models one can find e.g. in [10–13].

3   MPC Algorithms Based on Fuzzy Wiener Models

It is assumed that the static part of the Wiener process model is a fuzzy Takagi–Sugeno model which consists of the following rules:

Rule j: if v_k is M_j, then

$$y_k^j = g_j \cdot v_k + h_j,   \tag{9}$$

where g_j, h_j are coefficients of the model, M_j are fuzzy sets, $j = 1, \ldots, l$, l is the number of fuzzy rules (local models). The output of the static part of the model is thus described by the following formula:

$$\widehat{y}_k = \sum_{j=1}^{l} w_j(v_k) \cdot y_k^j = \widetilde{g}_k \cdot v_k + \widetilde{h}_k ,   \tag{10}$$

where v_k is the input to the static block and the output of the dynamic block, $w_j(v_k)$ are weights obtained using fuzzy reasoning (see e.g. [16, 19]),

$$\widetilde{g}_k = \sum_{j=1}^{l} w_j(v_k) \cdot g_j, \ \widetilde{h}_k = \sum_{j=1}^{l} w_j(v_k) \cdot h_j.$$

It is assumed that the dynamic part of the model is a difference equation:

$$v_k = b_1 \cdot v_{k-1} + \ldots + b_n \cdot v_{k-n} + c_1 \cdot u_{k-1} + \ldots + c_m \cdot u_{k-m} ,   \tag{11}$$

where b_j, c_j are parameters of the model. Thus, the output of the Wiener model is given by the following formula:

$$\widehat{y}_k = \widetilde{g}_k \cdot \left(\sum_{j=1}^{n} b_j \cdot v_{k-j} + \sum_{j=1}^{m} c_j \cdot u_{k-j} \right) + \widetilde{h}_k ,   \tag{12}$$

In the algorithms proposed in [12] the fuzzy (nonlinear) Wiener model (12) is used to obtain the free response of the plant, assuming that the control signal is constant on the whole prediction horizon. In the approach proposed in the current paper future control increments derived by the MPC algorithm in the last sampling instant are used during calculation of the free response. It is thus assumed that future control values can be decomposed as follows:

$$u_{k+i|k} = \breve{u}_{k+i|k} + u_{k+i|k-1} ,   \tag{13}$$

where $\breve{u}_{k+i|k}$ can be interpreted as the correction of the control signal $u_{k+i|k-1}$ which was obtained in the last $(k-1)^{\text{st}}$ iteration of the MPC algorithm.

The output of the linear part of the model in the $(k+i)^{\text{th}}$ sampling instant is described by the following formula:

$$\widehat{v}_{k+i} = \sum_{j=1}^{i} c_j \cdot u_{k-j+i|k} + \sum_{j=i+1}^{m} c_j \cdot u_{k-j+i} + \sum_{j=1}^{n} b_j \cdot \widehat{v}_{k-j+i} ,   \tag{14}$$

where $\widehat{v}_{k+i}$ are values of the internal signal of the fuzzy Wiener model, calculated recursively. After using (13), one can rewrite (14) as:

$$\widehat{v}_{k+i} = \sum_{j=1}^{i} c_j \cdot \breve{u}_{k-j+i|k} + \sum_{j=1}^{i} c_j \cdot u_{k-j+i|k-1} + \sum_{j=i+1}^{m} c_j \cdot u_{k-j+i} + \sum_{j=1}^{n} b_j \cdot \widehat{v}_{k-j+i} .$$

$$\tag{15}$$

In (15) only the first component is unknown whereas the second one is known and can be included in the free response of the control plant. Therefore, the free response is given by the following formula:

$$\widetilde{y}_{k+i|k} = \widetilde{g}_k \cdot \left(\sum_{j=1}^{i} c_j \cdot u_{k-j+i|k-1} + \sum_{j=i+1}^{m} c_j \cdot u_{k-j+i} + \sum_{j=1}^{n} b_j \cdot \widehat{v}_{k-j+i} \right) + \widetilde{h}_k + d_k ,$$

$$(16)$$

where $d_k = y_k - \widehat{y}_k$ is the DMC–type disturbance model (assumed the same on the whole prediction horizon). Note that thanks to the structure of the utilized fuzzy Wiener model the analytical equations describing the free response were obtained.

The dynamic matrix, needed to predict the influence of the corrections of the control signal can be obtained in two ways. The first one is the same as described in [12], i.e. the step response coefficients of the dynamic part of the Wiener model a_n ($n = 1, \ldots, p_d$) are obtained and the following linear approximation of the fuzzy Wiener model (12) is used at each iteration of the algorithm:

$$\widehat{y}_k = dy \cdot \left(\sum_{n=1}^{p_d-1} a_n \cdot \Delta u_{k-n} + a_{p_d} \cdot u_{k-p_d} \right) .$$

$$(17)$$

where p_d is the dynamics horizon equal to the number of sampling instants after which the step response can be assumed as settled, dy is the slope of the static characteristic near the current value v_k which can be approximated by:

$$dy = \frac{\left(\left(\sum_{j=1}^{l} w_j(v_k) \cdot (g_j \cdot v_k + h_j) \right) - \left(\sum_{j=1}^{l} w_j(v_{k-}) \cdot (g_j \cdot (v_{k-}) + h_j) \right) \right)}{dv} ,$$

$$(18)$$

where $v_{k-} = v_k - dv$, dv is a small number. The dynamic matrix is therefore described by:

$$\boldsymbol{A}_k = dy \cdot \boldsymbol{A} .$$

$$(19)$$

The second, more advanced method uses the trajectory of future values of the input to the static part of the Wiener model (15). The dynamic matrix is constructed in such a way that changes of the $\widehat{v}_{k+i}$ values are taken into consideration. It can be done by calculating the slope of the static characteristic dy_{k+i} near each of the values $\widehat{v}_{k+i}$. Then, the dynamic matrix is described by the following formula:

$$\boldsymbol{A}_k = \begin{bmatrix} a_1^{k+1} & 0 & \cdots & 0 & 0 \\ a_2^{k+2} & a_1^{k+2} & \cdots & 0 & 0 \\ \vdots & \vdots & \ddots & \vdots & \vdots \\ a_p^{k+p} & a_{p-1}^{k+p} & \cdots & a_{p-s+2}^{k+p} & a_{p-s+1}^{k+p} \end{bmatrix} ,$$

$$(20)$$

where $a_n^{k+i} = a_n \cdot dy_{k+i}$.

The free response (16) and the dynamic matrix (19) or (20) are then used to obtain the prediction:

$$y = \widetilde{y} + A_k \cdot \Delta\breve{u} \ . \tag{21}$$

where $\Delta\breve{u} = \left[\Delta\breve{u}_{k+1|k}, \ldots, \Delta\breve{u}_{k+s-1|k}\right]^T$ is the vector of the correction of the control signal trajectory. After application of prediction (21) to the performance function from (1), one obtains:

$$J_{\mathrm{FMPC}} = (\overline{y} - \widetilde{y} - A_k \cdot \Delta\breve{u})^T \cdot (\overline{y} - \widetilde{y} - A_k \cdot \Delta\breve{u}) + (\Delta\breve{u} + \Delta u^p)^T \cdot \Lambda \cdot (\Delta\breve{u} + \Delta u^p) \ . \tag{22}$$

where $\Delta u^p = \left[\Delta u_{k|k-1}, \ldots, \Delta u_{k+s-2|k-1}, 0\right]^T$. Thus, as in the case of the MPC algorithm based on a linear model, a quadratic optimization problem is obtained.

Remark. Versions of the proposed algorithms guaranteeing stability of the control system can be relatively easily obtained by adapting the dual–mode approach proposed for fuzzy predictive controllers in [13]. In short, the approach is based on the idea described in [14] and developed in [18], and consists in application of two controllers. The first one, a constrained MPC controller, should bring the trajectory of the control system into a (convex) target set W, which contains the equilibrium point in its interior and is inside the admissible set. The second, stabilizing, unconstrained feedback controller is used if the state of the process is inside the set W. It is designed in such a way that the control system with the stabilizing controller is asymptotically stable in the set W, and any trajectory of the control system which starts in the set W remains there. More details about the dual–mode approach for predictive algorithms based on fuzzy models one can find in [13].

4 Testing of the Proposed Approach

The control plant under consideration is a valve for control of fluid flow, often used in tests of the control algorithms (see e.g. [1, 6]). It is described by the following Wiener model:

$$v_k = 1.4138 \cdot v_{k-1} - 0.6065 \cdot v_{k-2} + 0.1044 \cdot u_{k-1} + 0.0883 \cdot u_{k-2} \ , \tag{23}$$

$$y_k = \frac{0.3163 \cdot v_k}{\sqrt{0.1 + 0.9 \cdot (v_k)^2}} \ , \tag{24}$$

where u_k is the pneumatic control signal applied to the stem, v_k is the stem position (it is the output signal of the linear dynamic block and the input signal of the nonlinear static block), y_k is flow through the valve (it is the output of the plant). The static part of the model was approximated using the following fuzzy model which consists of two rules [12]:

Rule 1: if v_k is M_1, then

$$y_{k+1}^1 = 0.3289 \;, \tag{25}$$

Rule 2: if v_k is M_2, then

$$y_{k+1}^2 = -0.3289 \;. \tag{26}$$

The assumed membership functions are given by:

$$\mu_{M_1}(v_k) = \frac{1}{1 + e^{-5 \cdot v_k}}, \; \mu_{M_2}(v_k) = 1 - \mu_{M_1}(v_k) \;. \tag{27}$$

The operation of the proposed fuzzy MPC (FMPC) algorithms was compared with other approaches; four MPC algorithms were designed (prediction horizon $p = 30$, control horizon $s = 15$ and weighting coefficient $\lambda = 5$ were assumed):

1. LMPC – with a linear model,
2. NMPC – with nonlinear optimization,
3. FMPC1 – with the advanced prediction based on fuzzy Wiener model and the first version of the dynamic matrix,
4. FMPC2 – with the advanced prediction based on fuzzy Wiener model and the second, advanced version of the dynamic matrix.

The responses obtained after changes of the set–point value are shown in Fig. 1. The slowest among the tested algorithms is LMPC algorithm. It generated the worst responses (much slower than other algorithms). In the case of set–point change from 0 to 0.3, the FMPC1 and FMPC2 algorithms are faster than the NMPC one. Both fuzzy algorithms give very similar responses. The situation is different in the case of the set–point change from 0.3 to 0. Though all three algorithms based on nonlinear models give similar responses, FMPC1 is slightly slower than NMPC. The fastest is the FMPC2 algorithm.

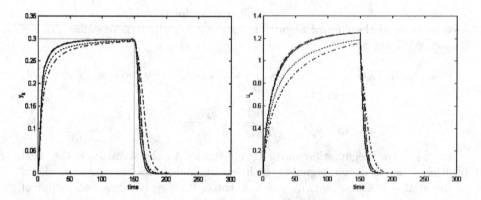

Fig. 1. Responses of the control systems to the changes of the set–point value to $\overline{y}_1 = 0.3$ and $\overline{y}_2 = 0$; FMPC1 (dashed lines), FMPC2 (solid lines), NMPC (dotted lines), LMPC (dash–dotted lines); grey line – set–point signal; left – output signal, right – control signal

5   Summary

The fuzzy MPC algorithms utilizing the advanced methods of prediction based on fuzzy Wiener models are proposed in the paper. In the advanced methods of prediction the values of the future changes of the control signal, calculated in the last iteration of the FMPC algorithm, are used to derive the free response of the control plant. In the proposed two algorithms the dynamic matrix is constructed in two different ways. In the first one, elements of the dynamic matrix are calculated using a single linearization of the process model in each iteration of the algorithm. In the second algorithm, elements of the dynamic matrix are calculated using a few linear models obtained after linearization performed alongside the free response trajectory. The proposed FMPC algorithms generate much better responses than the LMPC algorithm and also better than the NMPC algorithm. The best among the algorithms tested in the example control system is the FMPC2 algorithm with the advanced method of the dynamic matrix construction.

Acknowledgment. This work was supported by the Polish national budget funds for science 2009–2011.

References

1. Al–Duwaish, H., Karim, M.N., Chandrasekar, V.: Use of multilayer feedforward neural networks in identification and control of Wiener model. IEE Proceedings on Control Theory and Applications 143, 255–258 (1996)
2. Arefi, M.M., Montazeri, A., Poshtan, J., Jahed–Motlagh, M.R.: Wiener–neural identification and predictive control of a more realistic plug-flow tubular reactor. Chemical Engineering Journal 138, 274–282 (2008)
3. Babuska, R., te Braake, H.A.B., van Can, H.J.L., Krijgsman, A.J., Verbruggen, H.B.: Comparison of intelligent control schemes for real–time pressure control. Control Engineering Practice 4, 1585–1592 (1996)
4. Camacho, E.F., Bordons, C.: Model Predictive Control. Springer, Heidelberg (1999)
5. Fink, A., Fischer, M., Nelles, O., Isermann, R.: Supervision of nonlinear adaptive controllers based on fuzzy models. Control Engineering Practice 8, 1093–1105 (2000)
6. Hsu, Y.-L., Wang, J.-S.: A Wiener–type recurrent neural network and its control strategy for nonlinear dynamic applications. Journal of Process Control 19, 942–953 (2009)
7. Janczak, A.: Identification of nonlinear systems using neural networks and polynomial models: a block–oriented approach. Springer, Heidelberg (2005)
8. Maciejowski, J.M.: Predictive control with constraints. Prentice Hall, Harlow (2002)
9. Mahmoodi, S., Poshtan, J., Jahed–Motlagh, M.R., Montazeri, A.: Nonlinear model predictive control of a pH neutralization process based on Wiener-Laguerre model. Chemical Engineering Journal 146, 328–337 (2009)

10. Marusak, P.: Advantages of an easy to design fuzzy predictive algorithm in control systems of nonlinear chemical reactors. Applied Soft Computing 9, 1111–1125 (2009)
11. Marusak, P.: Efficient Model Predictive Control Algorithm with Fuzzy Approximations of Nonlinear Models. In: Kolehmainen, M., Toivanen, P., Beliczynski, B. (eds.) ICANNGA 2009. LNCS, vol. 5495, pp. 448–457. Springer, Heidelberg (2009)
12. Marusak, P.: Application of Fuzzy Wiener Models in Efficient MPC Algorithms. In: Szczuka, M., Kryszkiewicz, M., Ramanna, S., Jensen, R., Hu, Q. (eds.) RSCTC 2010. LNCS (LNAI), vol. 6086, pp. 669–677. Springer, Heidelberg (2010)
13. Marusak, P., Tatjewski, P.: Effective dual–mode fuzzy DMC algorithms with on–line quadratic optimization and guaranteed stability. International Journal of Applied Mathematics and Computer Science 19, 127–141 (2009)
14. Michalska, H., Mayne, D.: Robust receding horizon control of constrained nonlinear systems. IEEE Trans. Automatic Control 38, 1623–1632 (1993)
15. Morari, M., Lee, J.H.: Model predictive control: past, present and future. Computers and Chemical Engineering 23, 667–682 (1999)
16. Piegat, A.: Fuzzy Modeling and Control. Physica-Verlag, Berlin (2001)
17. Rossiter, J.A.: Model-Based Predictive Control. CRC Press, Boca Raton (2003)
18. Scokaert, P., Mayne, D., Rawlings, J.: Suboptimal model predictive control (feasibility implies stability). IEEE Trans. Automatic Control 44, 648–654 (1999)
19. Takagi, T., Sugeno, M.: Fuzzy identification of systems and its application to modeling and control. IEEE Trans. Systems, Man and Cybernetics 15, 116–132 (1985)
20. Tatjewski, P.: Advanced Control of Industrial Processes; Structures and Algorithms. Springer, London (2007)

Evaluation of Health-Related Fitness
Using Fuzzy Inference Elements

Tadeusz Nawarycz[1], Krzysztof Pytel[2], and Lidia Ostrowska-Nawarycz[1]

[1] Department of Biophysics, Medical University of Lodz, Poland
[2] Department of Theoretical Physics and Computer Science,
University of Lodz, Poland
tadeusz.nawarycz@umed.lodz.pl, kpytel@uni.lodz.pl

Abstract. Low physical activity (PA), and often concomitant over-
weight in the developmental age are well documented risk factors for
cardiovascular diseases (CVD) and many other chronic civilization diseases. Regular monitoring of health related physical fitness (H-RF) is
an important part of early prevention and school health education. An
assessment of components of H-RF is complex and controversial. In the
assessment of H-RF components, systems of fuzzy inference based on
simple linguistic variables can be used. The paper presents a system intended to support the evaluation of the H-RF components based on the
EUROFIT battery tests and the anthropometric measurements. A basis
of the system is the EUROFIT calculator which converts absolute results
of individual trials to standarized values and the fuzzy inference system
for four H-RF components (Morphological, Cardiorespiratory, Musculoskeletal and Motor Fitness). The system is implemented in MS Visual
Studio in C# and has a friendly graphical interface for archiving test
results. An application of fuzzy inference elements in the evaluation of
the H-RF components is a new approach that can be used in monitoring
and rational planning of PA dosing in prophylaxis and therapy.

Keywords: Health Related Fitness, children and youth, EUROFIT,
Fuzzy inference.

1 Introduction

A reduced overall physical activity (PA) and an excessive body weight are well
known risk factors for cardiovascular diseases (CVD) and many other civilization diseases [1]. Epidemiological data indicate that negative trends are observed
both in adults as well as in the pediatric population [2]. Low PA has been often associated with osteoporosis, spinal pain, impaired carbohydrate and lipid
metabolism, diabetes, asthma and other health problems [3]. Regular PA is required for proper development of the child and should be an essential element
in early prevention of civilization diseases [4].

Physical fitness (PF) usually means the ability to perform various forms of
movement, associated with a particular level of development of motor characteristics, and morphological, physiological as well as mental functions. PF depends

L. Rutkowski et al. (Eds.): ICAISC 2012, Part I, LNCS 7267, pp. 301–309, 2012.

on many overlapping factors of both genetic and environmental origin. PF tests are divided into laboratory tests and simple field tests. They involve an execution of complex motor actions or sets of activities (battery of tests). The most popular fitness tests are the International Physical Fitness Test and EUROFIT test. Health-Related Fitness (H-RF) is a relatively new concept of the PF.

1.1   Health-Related Fitness – The Basic Concepts

In the recently promoted concept of H-RF, the results of individual fitness tests should primarily support changes in health-related behavior patterns, create a healthy lifestyle and not solely concentrate on their numerical figures. The physiological and medical components of H-RF and the system energy efficiency are both of great importance.

According to Bouchard and Shephard [5], the essential components of H-RF are as follows: a) Morphological Component (Body Mass Index, body composition, subcutaneous fat distribution, abdominal visceral fat, bone density), b) Musculoskeletal Component (power, strength, endurance, flexibility), c) Motor Component (agility, balance, coordination, speed of movement), d) Cardiorespiratory Component (submaximal exercise capacity, maxima aerobic power, heart functions, lung functions, blood pressure), e), Metabolic Component (glucose tolerance, insulin sensitivity, lipid and lipoprotein metabolism, oxidation of substrates).

Skinner and Oja emphasize that the H-RF includes those components that have a positive impact on health, and those that can be improved by regular PA [6]. Sharkey, in turn, specifically highlights the importance of energy efficiency (aerobic and anaerobic capacity - energetic fitness). In practice, the H-RF components are evaluated using various tests which sometimes hinder comparative analysis. For example, cardiorespiratory fitness (CRF) is usually assessed on the basis of: 20 m endurance shuttle run test (ESR) [7], the maximal treadmill test [8], submaximal cycle ergometer test [9], and others.

CRF is considered to be the most important component of the H-RF. Submaximal exercise capacity and endurance are referred to as tolerance to prolonged exercise with relatively low power. A person with low submaximal exercise capacity quickly gets tired and may have a problem while making normal daily activities. Results of the test depend on the efficiency of the systems responsible for providing oxygen efficiency, thermoregulatory processes and other physiological and metabolic factors. It is emphasized that the efforts of aerobic and cardiorespiratory fitness have a positive impact on the cardiovascular system.

Currently, there are many tests based on the concept of H-RF. The more popular tests include: the YMCA test developed by Franks and tests and tools developed at the Cooper Institute [10].

2   The H-RF System Based on the EUROFIT Tests

PF tests have a long history and are constantly improved. They constitute the basis for an assessment of exercise capacity and health status. In 1964, the

International Committee for Standardization of Physical Fitness Test was established in Tokyo, which has since developed a battery of 8 tests known as the "International Physical Fitness Test" [11].

2.1 Characteristics of the EUROFIT Battery of Tests

Unification work carried out in Europe by the European Committee for Sport led to the development of a uniform methodology for estimating motor efficiency in the form of " EUROFIT Test" (European Test of Physical Fitness) [12]. The EUROFIT is a battery of nine PF tests:

- 20 m endurance shuttle run test (ESR) as a measure of cardio-respiratory fitness (CRF),
- hand grip test (HGR) and standing broad jump (SBJ) as a static and explosive strength measure respectively,
- bent arm hang (BAH) and sit-ups (SUP) as a muscle fitness measure,
- 10x5 m shuttle run (SHR) and plate tapping (PLT) as a measure of speed,
- sit and test reach (SAR) as a measure of flexibility,
- flamingo balance (FLB) as a measure of total body balance.

The standardized test battery has been recommended by the Council of Europe for school age children and has been used in many European schools since 1988. The series of tests are designed in such a way that they can be performed within 35 to 40 minutes, using very simple equipment. In several countries, the results of EUROFIT tests in the form of representative reference systems have been designed.

2.2 The Percentile Distributions of the PF for Polish Children

PF references for Polish school age children and youth (7-19), according to EUROFIT test battery, were developed in 2003 at the University of Physical Education in Warsaw [20].

Percentile charts of reference of nine EUROFIT tests for Polish children and youth are presented in a graphic form (for 3rd, 10th, 25th, 50th, 75th, 90th and 97th percentiles) with regard to sex, calendar age (7-20 years) and the so called height age. Nawarycz et al. developed an electronic version of the reference system in the form of a calculator, which greatly facilitates the individual PF assessment [14]. An example of the percentile distributions (for 25th, 50th and 75th percentiles) for the ESR and SHR tests is shown in Fig.1.

2.3 H-RF System Based on EUROFIT Test Battery and Elements of Fuzzy Inference

The evaluated system is based on the results of 9 EUROFIT tests, and 3 anthropometric measurements (Fig.1). According to the H-RF concept, all the input data are grouped into four blocks - components of fitness: Morphological

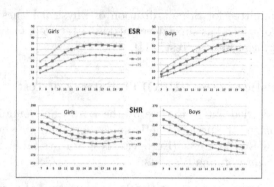

Fig. 1. Smoothed percentile curves of some EUROFIT features for Polish girls and boys. ESR - 20 m Endurance Shuttle Run; SHR - 10 x 5 meter Shuttle Run.

(MorphF: BMI, Ht and WC), Cardiorespiratory (CRF: ESR), Musculoskeletal (MuskF: BAH, HGR, SBJ, SUP, SAR) and Motor Fitness (MoF: SUR, PLT, FLB). The basis of the developed system is the Eurofit calculator that converts the absolute values of all H-RF components into the standardized features (e.g. marked as zESR, zBAH, etc.) or percentile values. The system also uses a simple fuzzy inference module (Fig. 2) that enables the classification of both the indi-vidual tests, the H-RF components and the overall physical fitness (GPF) using linguistic variables: Very Low (VL), Low (L), Median (M), High (H), Very High. (VL, L, M, H, VH).

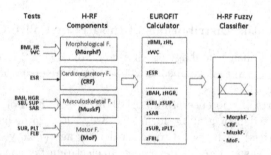

Fig. 2. The H-RF system based on EUROFIT test battery (description in the text)

2.4   The EUROFIT Calculator

The EUROFIT calculator converts the absolute values of the individual measurements into standardized values (z-scores) based on the appropriate reference system. The percentile distributions of the anthropometric parameters for the children from the city of Lodz for the morphological component and the results of the EUROFIT tests, for Polish youth with our own modification were used

Table 1. An example of the LMS parameters of the ESR test distribution for Polish boys and girls [22]

Age	Boys			Girls		
	L	M	S	L	M	S
7	0,350	21,0	0,539	0,316	17,0	0,540
8	0,475	26,0	0,519	0,309	20,0	0,535
9	0,531	31,0	0,482	0,415	24,0	0,513
10	0,642	36,0	0,464	0,491	27,5	0,492
11	0,716	41,0	0,434	0,494	30,0	0,483
12	0,791	46,0	0,410	0,511	32,0	0,466
13	0,828	52,0	0,388	0,467	33,0	0,457
14	0,820	57,0	0,363	0,512	34,0	0,443

as reference data (knowledge base) [14, 15] (Fig. 2). The calculations of standardized values of all analyzed tests in conjunction with morphological fitness component were made by the LMS method using a Box-Cox transformation [16]:

$$zX = \frac{(X/M)^L - 1}{L * S} \; for \; L \neq 0 \tag{1}$$

$$zX = ln\frac{(X/M)}{S} \; for \; L = 0 \tag{2}$$

where:

- X, zX - the absolute and standardized value respectively of the analyzed features ,
- L - exponent for Box-Cox transform, M - median, S - variance index.

The part of knowledge base in the form of the characteristic L, M, S parameters for ESR test is presented in Table 1.

Example: A 14-year-old boys obtained result of n=73 in ESR test.
Using the formulas (1) and (2) and appropriate parameters of the LMS (Table 1), zESR was calculated on the basis of absolute value of the test results, ie ESR = 73:

$$ESR = \frac{(73/57)^{0,82} - 1}{0,82 * 0,363} = 0,7565 \tag{3}$$

Value of zESR = 0.7565 corresponds to the normal distribution probability of 77.5% indicating an adequate percentile position. The EUROFIT calculator calculates the standardized values (zX) for all nine tests (zESR, zBAH, zHGR, zSBJ, zSUP, zSAR, zSUR, zPLT, zFBL) and 4 anthropometric features (zHt, zBM, zBMI and zWC) (Fig. 2).

2.5 H-RF Fuzzy Classifier

The elements of fuzzy clustering were used to assess the individual H-RF components. An equal form of the membership function (MF) for all the analyzed features, based on the classification used in auxology, was assumed (Fig. 3).

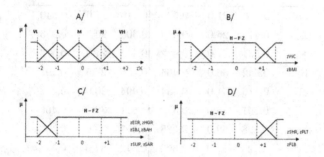

Fig. 3. Forms of the MF adopted in the evaluation of the test results. A) linguistic variables determining the results of individual tests (VL: very low, L: low, M: medium, H: high, VH: very high), B-D) linguistic variables determining the results of individual tests according to the concept of H-RF (H-F Z : Healthy-Fitness Zone)

Based on the data obtained from the measurements, the degrees of different rules were established. The inference block pooled these values, allowing the inclusion of all premises regardless of the degree of their fulfillment.

The fuzzy classifier evaluates the performance of individual components using fuzzy evaluation of range: very low (VL), low (L), normal (NOR), high (H) and very high (VH). Furthermore, the degree of efficiency is presented in the calculator by using color.

Red color indicates a definitely negative result of the efficiency of health, orange - unfavorable performance, green - a positive result of the health efficiency. The method of gravity center is used in the defuzzyfication block. As a result of defuzzyfication, shaped value of the performance assessment is obtained. This assessment may take values from 0 to 100 and increase with increasing efficiency.

2.6 Implementation of the System

The computer system (EUROFIT Calculator) was implemented in MS Visual Studio in C#. It is designed to work on systems with the Windows 9x/2000/XP family. The program requires a working installed .NET Framework runtime environment. The classifier is equipped with an easy to use graphical interface for entering data obtained during the tests, and displays the results of the calculation.

Input data

The following input data should be introduced to the system:

- Personal data: name, first name, personal identification number PESEL, sex and date of birth

- Basic anthropometric data (Ht, BM, and WC)
- Results of 9 EUROFIT tests grouped into components in accordance with the H-RF idea (Fig 4)

Output data

The system enables the presentation of test results in the different forms (Fig. 4): a) graphically - color lines (red color - health definitely unfavorable; orange - the result is health unfavorable, green - the result is health-positive) b) numerical as a standardized form (z -score) and percentile values.

With regard to the assessment of individual components of the H-RF (MorphF, CRF, MuskF and MoF) as well as the overall efficiency (GPF), fuzzy clustering components were used (Fig.4). An important practical convenience of the presented system is its ability to evaluate the results of individual tests in terms of the age of development (biological age) on the basis of an analysis of the child's body height in relation to the reference group [14].

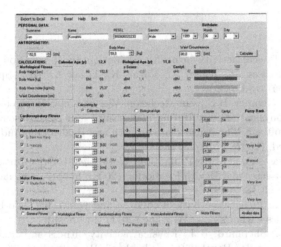

Fig. 4. A view of the main window of the calculator

3   Discussion and Final Report

Proper PF profile is considered one of the most important factors of healthy lifestyle. Effective programs to fight the obesity epidemic and decreasing PA among adults, children and adolescents constitute an important task and a real challenge for a wide range of public health institutions. This is a reason why evaluation of an individual level of physical fitness raised an increasing interest in recent years.

According to the new education reform introduced in Poland, the physical education has a leading role in health education of young people [17]. The purpose of H-RF testing is to better understand the student's own health needs in relation to individual components of their physical fitness and to keep them at the "healthy level" [10].

The presented system, in the form of the extended calculator, is a tool intended to sup-port the assessment of PF of children and adolescents based on the EUROFIT test battery. It may be useful for physical education teachers, pediatricians, health educators and medical school personnel. The system allows one to assess the results of Eurofit tests in relation to the national reference systems as well as enables their linguistic classification based on the concept of H-RF. Optimum selection of personalized exercise using fuzzy logic is being increasingly used in the rehabilitation of certain metabolic diseases such as diabetes in children [18], metabolic syndrome [19] and cardiac problems [20]. The presented tool is based on the EUROFIT test results, but it can be easily redesigned for a different structure of the H-RF components based on the latest research on human motor efficiency and auxology. The system may be helpful in shaping the H-RF components for children and adolescents (especially for children) at risk of developing obesity.

References

[1] Jegier, A.: Physical activity in health promotion and prevention and treatment of chronic diseases. In: Jegier, A., Nazar, K., Dziak A. (eds.) Sports Medicine, Warsaw (2005) (in Polish)

[2] Twisk, J.W., Kemper, H.C., van Mechelen, W.: The relationship between physical fitness and physical activity during adolescence and cardiovascular disease risk factors at adult age. The Amsterdam Growth and Health Longitudinal Study. Int. J. Sports Med. (2002)

[3] Chronic Diseases and Health Promotion. World Health Organization Department of Chronic Diseases and Health Promotion (2008), http://www.who.int/chp/en/ (accessed March 18, 2008)

[4] Zebrowska, A.: Physical activity of children and youth. In: Otto-Buczkowska, E. (ed.) Pediatrics - what's new, Wroclaw (2011) (in Polish)

[5] Bouchard, C., Shephard, R.J.: Physical activity, fitness and health: the model and key concepts. In: Bouchard, C., Shephard, R.J., Stephens, T. (eds.) Physical activity, fitness and health. Human Kinetics Publishers (1994)

[6] Skinner, J.S., Oja, P.: Laboratory and field tests for assessing health- related fitness. In: Bouchard, C., Shephard, R.J., Stephens, T. (eds.) Physical activity, fitness and health. Human Kinetics Publishers (1994)

[7] Boreham, C., Twisk, J., Neville, C., Savage, M., Murray, L., Gallagher, A.: Associations between physical fitness and activity patterns during adolescence and cardiovascular risk factors in young adulthood: the Northern Ireland Young Hearts Project. Int. J. Sports Med. (2002)

[8] Carnethon, M.R., Gidding, S.S., Nehgme, R., Sidney, S., Jacobs, D.R., Liu, K.: Cardiorespiratory fitness in young adulthood and the development of cardiovascular disease risk factors. JAMA (2003)

[9] Andersen, L.B., Hasselstrom, H., Gronfeldt, V., Hansen, S.E., Karsten, F.: The relationship between physical fitness and clustered risk, and tracking of clustered risk from adolescence to young adulthood: eight years follow-up in the Danish Youth and Sport Study. Int. J. Behav. Nutr. Phys. Act. (2004)

[10] Cooper Institute for Aerobics Research FITNESSGRAM test administration manual. Human Kinetics, Champaign (1999)

[11] Pilicz, S., Przeweda, R., Dobosz, J., Nowacka-Dobosz, S.: Physical fitness score tables of polish youth. Criteria for measuring aerobic capacity by the Cooper test. Studies and Monographs Warsaw (2005)

[12] Committee of Experts on Sports Research EUROFIT: Handbook for the EUROFIT Tests of Physical Fitness. Council of Europe, Strasburg, GE (1993)

[13] Stupnicki, R., Przeweda, R., Milde, K.: Percentile reference curves for physical fitness measured by eurofit tests in polish youths, AWF Warszawa (2003)

[14] Nawarycz, T., Pytel, K., Makuch, J., Ostrowska-Nawarycz, L.: Physical fitness calculator for polish children and youth based on Eurofit test battery, XXVIII Congress of Polish Society of Sports Medicine: Physical activity in health and diseases, Lodz (2009)

[15] Ostrowska - Nawarycz, L., Nawarycz, T.: Arterial blood pressure and nutritional indices in children and adolescents from the city of Lodz aged 3-19 years. Medical University of Lodz (2008)

[16] Cole, T.J., Green, P.J.: Smoothing reference centile curves - the LMS method and penalized likelihood. Statistics in medicine (1992)

[17] Woynarowska, B., Makowska-Szkutnik, A., Mazur, J.: Subjective health of adolescents aged 11-15 years in Poland and other countries of the European Union, Developmental Period Medicine (2008)

[18] Novotny, J., Babinec, F.: Simple expert system for exercise therapy in diabetics. In: Szczepaniak, P., Lisboa, P., Kacprzyk, J. (eds.) Fuzzy System in Medicine. Physica - Verlag, Heidelberg (2000)

[19] Nawarycz, T., Pytel, K., Rutkowska, D.: Ostrowska - Nawarycz, L.: Diagnosis of the methabolic syndrome in children - a fuzzy clustering approach. In: 5th Polish and Int PD Forum Conf. on Computer Science, Lodz (2011)

[20] Rutkowska, D., Starczewski, A.: Fuzzy Inference Neural Network and Their Applications to Medical Diagnosis. In: Szczepaniak, P., Lisboa, P., Kacprzyk, J. (eds.) Fuzzy System in Medicine. Physica - Verlag, Heidelberg (2000)

Fuzzy Regression Compared
to Classical Experimental Design
in the Case of Flywheel Assembly

Jacek Pietraszek

Cracow University of Technology
Al. Jana Pawla II 37, 31-864 Krakow, Poland
pmpietra@mech.pk.edu.pl

Abstract. This paper presents the fuzzy regression approach to the automotive industry optimization problem. The flywheel assembly process is subject to investigation, as its parameters require optimization. The paper contains: problem definition, presentation of the measured data and the final analysis with two alternative approaches: the fuzzy regression and the classical regression. The benefits of the fuzzy regression approach are shown in the case of small size samples.

Keywords: design of experiment, fuzzy regression.

1 Introduction

Currently used methods for the design of experiments (DOE) [1] are based on probabilistic uncertainties and simple additive, usually polynomial, models. This means that uncertainties are bound with hidden random mechanisms of observed phenomena. Such an approach necessitates the implementation of experiment replications, what imposes carrying out measurement of the output with the same settings of input (controlled) variables. This increases both the direct and indirect costs of the research, because the need for a randomization is often associated with retooling costs of experimental units (exchange of hardware, cooling or heating devices, material replacement etc.). However, there are cases where this approach cannot be implemented because of:

- limited resources (a limited budget, a completion date, availability of an equipment) preventing the implementation of a repetition,
- a small batch or an unique production preventing appropriate measures of a probabilistic uncertainty,
- imprecise or linguistically defined measurement input variables preventing proper use of methods proposed by the classical theory of the experiment.

In view of these limitations, it is desirable to implement alternative methods of the analysis designed just for such cases. In considering these options for the various stages of DOE, one can take into account the different methods appropriate for the weak artificial intelligence, which seem to be very promising.

L. Rutkowski et al. (Eds.): ICAISC 2012, Part I, LNCS 7267, pp. 310–317, 2012.

The fundamental issue remains the question of the implementation of uncertainty measures being alternative to the classic probabilistic measure [2]. The fuzzy real algebra [3] appears to have the greatest usefulness for this purpose. It has a complete formalism that allows to describe the uncertainty of non-random mechanisms. It also allows to perform rather complex calculations using a fuzzy measure and to create forecasting models.

2   Investigated Object

The investigated object was a flywheel, whose elements were tightened during assembly with the eight screws driven to the cast iron body.

The tightening was carried out with a multiple-spindle machine. Firstly, four screws were tightened. Next, the head was rotated by 45 degrees and next four screws were tightened. The couple of four screws were tightened in four steps. In the beginning step screws were tightened with a rotation velocity of 60 rpm until a torque of 7 Nm was reached. In the second step, screws were tightened with a rotation velocity of 150 rpm until a torque of 8 Nm was reached. In the third step, screws were tightened with a rotation velocity of 60 rpm until a torque of 15 Nm was reached, then the process was suspended for 2 seconds. In the fourth step, screws were tightened with a limited rotation of 35 degrees and the final torque was automatically measured for each screw. The allowable torque range was defined for the assembly process from 35 Nm to 60 Nm.

Originally, the flywheel was mounted using screws with washers. A drastic form of an economic adjustment, induced by the economic crisis has arrived in the form of extreme cutbacks of costs imposed by the design department. The cost reduction was manifested - among others - in the removal of steel screw washers. This led to an instability of the process of tightening the steel screws into cast iron body. The measured torque values were very often located far beyond the allowable range and the production process was blocked due to the necessity of a manual correction. At the current average daily production of 2000 gasoline and diesel engines, it caused a big loss. The direct observation has revealed a significant notch in the screw head in the cast iron body and this phenomenon is the physical cause of instability. Restoring the use of screw washers proved economically impossible. Factory managers decided to implement a recovery program including, among others, a number of DOE-based improvements. Basing on Ishikawa's method, the brainstorming was conducted among managers of production involved in the manufacturing process, resulting in determination of the research object and its factors. The following set of input variables and their ranges was established:

- a torque during the step 2 - T_2 with a variability range $8 \div 12$ Nm,
- a rotation velocity during the step 2 - R_2 with a variability range $150 \div 290$ rpm,
- a rotation velocity during the step 3 - R_3 with a variability range $30 \div 60$ Nm.

The final torque of the cinematically controlled rotation (35 degrees in the fourth step of assembly) was automatically measured by the equipment of the multiple-spindle machine and assumed to be raw output data. For the purpose of DOE analysis, a new output variable T_{out} was defined as a deviation of the average of the final tightening torque from the center of the allowable range, i.e. the value of 47.5 Nm.

The two-level full factorial design for three factors i.e. 2^3 was selected as the most appropriate experimental design. The fundamental utilitarian aim of the investigation was to optimize manufacturing process parameters. The scientific aim was to compare the obtained results with two different approaches used to the same data of the small amount sample. The first analysis approach was provided according to the classic DOE methods i.e. the probability approach. The second approach was provided according to the fuzzy description of uncertainty.

3   Measurements

The measurements were carried out according to the selected design of experiment for two replicates and an appropriate randomization. Finally, the total of 16 measurements were obtained for 8 different cases (Table 1). The torque values were measured automatically by the equipment of the multiple-spindle machine and then transformed into deviation T_{out}.

Measurements have shown that the removal of screw washers had caused a shift of the torque value above the center of the permissible range. Originally it was feared that exceeding the permissible scope may appear, both as undervaluation and overvaluation. During the study, it was found that the obtained values were only too high and therefore the output variable could be directly defined as the deviation T_{out} from the center value of the permissible range and it was not necessary to involve square deviation. Therefore the goal was set to minimize this deviation.

Table 1. Obtained measurements

Case	Input variables			Replication of T_{out}	
	T_2 (Nm)	R_2 (rpm)	R_3 (rpm)	1 (Nm)	2 (Nm)
1	8	150	60	7.87	6.55
2	8	290	60	10.87	8.97
3	8	150	30	7.22	7.52
4	8	290	30	12.35	12.50
5	12	150	60	8.39	8.38
6	12	290	60	11.64	10.18
7	12	150	30	7.12	7.79
8	12	290	30	6.86	6.17

4 Fuzzy Regression Model

On the basis of fuzzy sets, Dubois [3] introduced the concept of fuzzy numbers: a specially-defined fuzzy sets in the space of real numbers. The original definition proposed by Dubois, in which the kernel with a membership equal to 1 is a point, proved to be too narrowly defined for most practical applications. The concept of fuzzy numbers has been expanded and now the following models of fuzzy numbers are applied: the fuzzy numbers of S-type proposed by Zadeh [4], the fuzzy number of type LR proposed by Dubois and Prade [5], the trapezoidal fuzzy numbers [6], triangular fuzzy numbers, rectangular fuzzy numbers (the same as the so-called interval numbers), even verbal fuzzy numbers [7].

The result provided by the fuzzy regression model is a fuzzy number. Fuzzy numbers are modeled in different ways: from accurate descriptions (although, in relation to fuzzy numbers, it sounds like an oxymoron), through the LR description to the most simplified triangular description. The selected type of fuzzy numbers determines, which variant of the regression model will be most convenient:

- regression model with fuzzy parameters and crisp independent variables,
- spread model with three coupled polynomials [8], where the left and the right spread models are linearly dependent on the kernel model,
- the most general model with fuzzy independent variables and fuzzy parameters.

The spread model [8] was selected for further works (eqs.1):

$$
\begin{cases}
z = \sum_{k=1}^{n_b} b_k \cdot f_k(x_1, \ldots, x_i), \\
p = d + c \cdot z, \\
q = h + g \cdot z.
\end{cases} \tag{1}
$$

This model appears to be the most useful in the case of triangular fuzzy number approach. Its identification is provided according to the slightly modified least squares criterion:

$$
\begin{cases}
L = \sum_{k=1}^{u} \left[w_1 \cdot (z_k - \hat{z}_k)^2 + w_2 \cdot (p_k - \hat{p}_k)^2 + w_3 \cdot (q_k - \hat{q}_k)^2 \right], \\
\hat{p}_k \geq 0 \quad k = 1, \ldots, u, \\
\hat{q}_k \geq 0 \quad k = 1, \ldots, u.
\end{cases} \tag{2}
$$

Efficient determination of the fuzzy model parameters is difficult due to the difference between classical arithmetic and fuzzy numbers arithmetic. Some guidance on this issue is provided by theoretical works focused on the constructive solving of fuzzy equations [9]. Minimization of the criterion with the additional conditions is possible by using a generalized form of the Lagrange multipliers known as the Kuhn-Tucker conditions [10]. The smallest obtained value of L criterion is known as the fuzzy least squares distance. The solution may be found exclusively by iterative numerical procedure because of non-linearity appearing in the optimization problem.

There appeared a problem of conversion of two crisp measurements into a fuzzy measure. A symmetrical triangular pattern forming a fuzzy number has been chosen. Two measured repetitions were used to convert the measurements to form a symmetrical triangular fuzzy numbers (eq.3). The following conversion scheme was used:

$$\left(z_{i/1}, z_{i/2}\right) \rightarrow \left(\min(z_{i/1}, z_{i/2}), \frac{z_{i/1} + z_{i/2}}{2}, \max(z_{i/1}, z_{i/2})\right), \qquad (3)$$

where: $z_{i/1}$ – the first repetition of measurement, $z_{i/2}$ – the second repetition of measurement. In this way, the table containing the measurement values of two replicates (Table 1) was converted to a form containing the values in the form of triangular fuzzy numbers (Table 2).

Table 2. Fuzzy measurements for the study of the flywheel tightening

Case	Triangular fuzzy value		
	Left	Central	Right
1	6.55	7.21	7.87
2	8.97	9.92	10.87
3	7.22	7.37	7.52
4	12.35	12.43	12.50
5	8.38	8.385	8.39
6	10.18	10.91	11.64
7	7.12	7.46	7.79
8	6.17	6.52	6.86

The selected model, proposed in 2002 by D'Urso and Gastaldi [8], consists of three coupled polynomials. The main polynomial describes the center of the fuzzy response. The other two polynomials, coupled with the main one, describe the left and the right spread. This model has been modified by introducing, as the central polynomial, the model of main effects with two-way interactions and a three-way interaction. The form of the central polynomial (eq.1) is the same as in the case of classical DOE model i.e.:

$$T_{central} = b_0 + b_1 T_2 + b_2 R_2 + b_3 R_3 + b_{12} T_2 R_2 + \\ b_{13} T_2 R_3 + b_{23} R_2 R_3 + b_{123} T_2 R_2 R_3. \qquad (4)$$

The two spreads p (5) and q (6) are described by polynomials coupled with the central polynomial (4):

$$p(T_2, R_2, R_3) = d + c \cdot T_{central}(T_2, R_2, R_3), \qquad (5)$$

$$q(T_2, R_2, R_3) = h + g \cdot T_{central}(T_2, R_2, R_3). \qquad (6)$$

The coupled polynomials are nonlinear functions of parameters. It was the reason to use Levenberg-Marquardt method to minimize the weighted least-squares criterion (eq.2). In the case of uncoded values of input variables, the obtained parameters of coupled polynomials are given in table 5. It should be strongly emphasized that polynomials (eqs.4-6) may be used for forecasting output values only and they should not be utilized - for example - to evaluate symmetry of the model. Identified parameters are presented in Table 3. The resulting forecasts T_{out} (Table 4) are triangular fuzzy numbers of the form:

$$T_{out} = (T_{central} - p, T_{central}, T_{central} + q) \qquad (7)$$

Table 3. Parameters of coupled polynomials

Polynomial	Coefficient	Value
Central	b_0	-23.569
	b_1	2.89282
	b_2	0.21847
	b_3	0.41012
	b_{12}	$-2.07623 \cdot 10^{-2}$
	b_{13}	$-4.16359 \cdot 10^{-2}$
	b_{23}	$-3.22478 \cdot 10^{-3}$
	b_{123}	$3.35686 \cdot 10^{-4}$
Left spread	d	0.2617
	c	$1.64943 \cdot 10^{-2}$
Right spread	h	0.2617
	g	$1.64943 \cdot 10^{-2}$

Table 4. Fuzzy forecasting T_{out} for the study of the flywheel tightening

Case	Fuzzy forecast of T_{out}		
	Left	Central	Right
1	6.82	7.20	7.58
2	9.57	10.00	10.43
3	6.93	7.31	7.70
4	11.92	12.38	12.85
5	8.00	8.40	8.80
6	10.42	10.86	11.30
7	7.09	7.47	7.86
8	6.19	6.55	6.92

Finally, the smallest value of deviation is predicted for the following values of input variables: $T_2 = 12$ Nm, $R_2 = 290$ rpm, $R_3 = 30$ rpm (case no 8, Table 4). The symmetric triangular fuzzy value $T_{out} = (6.19, 6.55, 6.92)$ Nm is value of the forecast.

5   Classical DOE Regression

The structure of the selected complete factorial experimental design and informational needs related to the investigation process determined the form of the regression model [1]:

$$T_{out} = b_0 + b_1 T_2 + b_2 R_2 + b_3 R_3 + b_{12} T_2 R_2 + \\ b_{13} T_2 R_3 + b_{23} R_2 R_3 + b_{123} T_2 R_2 R_3. \tag{8}$$

where: b_0 – interception (average output); b_1, b_2, b_3 – parameters of main effects; b_{12}, b_{23}, b_{13} – parameters of two-way interactions; b_{123} – parameter of three-way interaction.

The parameter values were obtained for coded input variables and were determined using the least squares criterion: $b_0 = -23.685$; $b_1 = 2.9108$; $b_2 = 0.2215$; $b_3 = 0.4208$; $b_{12} = -2.1080 \cdot 10^{-2}$; $b_{23} = -4.2792 \cdot 10^{-2}$; $b_{13} = -3.3250 \cdot 10^{-2}$; $b_{123} = 3.4583 \cdot 10^{-4}$. The calculations has been provided in Minitab environment [11]. Detailed calculations are not cited because of lack of space. Analysis of variance has shown that one of main effects (R_3) and one of two-way interactions (R_2 vs R_3) are not statistically significant for the coded model at a typical level of 5%. However, they were left in the model to ensure compatibility with the subsequent fuzzy analysis. It seems that the adopted model can be considered correct: the distribution of model residuals was not negated by the test of normality (Shapiro Wilk SW-W = 0.98; p = 0.96). With these results, the calculations have been performed, which allowed to forecast T_{out}, i.e. the torque tightening the screws in the flywheel (Table 5).

Table 5. DOE forecasting T_{out} for the study of the flywheel tightening

Case	DOE-based forecast of T_{out}		
	−95%	Mean	+95%
1	5,15	7,21	9,27
2	7,86	9,92	11,98
3	5,31	7,37	9,43
4	10,36	12,43	14,49
5	6,32	8,37	10,45
6	8,85	10,91	12,97
7	5,39	7,46	9,52
8	4,45	6,52	8,58

Finally, the smallest value of T_{out} is predicted for the following values of input variables: $T_2 = 12$ Nm, $R_2 = 290$ rpm, $R_3 = 30$ rpm (case no 8, Tab.5) and forecasted value is $T_{out} = 6.52$ Nm. For this case 95% confidence interval of predicted T_{out} is determined by the scope from 4.45 Nm to 8.58 Nm.

6 Conclusions

The results obtained from the DOE procedures identified as the best set of values: $T_2 = 12$ Nm, $R_2 = 290$ rpm, $R_3 = 30$ rpm and they are related to forecasted output $T_{out} = 6.52$ Nm. The 95% confidence interval of forecasted single observed output is from 4.45 Nm to 8,58 Nm. The real observations were 6.86 Nm and 6.17 Nm. Due to the low amount of sample the classically calculated confidence interval for a single observation based on raw data is extremely large. The same set of input values: $T_2 = 12$ Nm, $R_2 = 290$ rpm, $R_3 = 30$ rpm are identified as the best set by the fuzzy regression. The central value of forecasted output Tout = 6.55 Nm is slightly different in comparison to probability forecasted mean. The support of forecasted output is from 6.19 Nm to 6.92 Nm which is narrower range than calculated from probabilistic approach but the systematic approach to compare the fuzzy and DOE-based calculations remains an open question. Some hope may be associated with the results of J. Buckley [2]. The classical DOE approach to the problem of industry forecasting is appropriate for large samples. If the size of available samples is small or even unique, then the traditional probabilistic approach results in extremely large confidence interval or it is inapplicable. In the case of small samples or unique measurements, the choice remains between extremely large confidence intervals, or an arbitrary assignment of uncertainties on the basis of fuzzy sets. The results presented in this article show that this approach is effective and consistent with the results obtained by the traditional DOE approach.

References

1. Montgomery, D.C.: Introduction to Statistical Quality Control. Wiley, New York (2009)
2. Buckley, J.J.: Fuzzy Probability and Statistics. Springer, Heidelberg (2006)
3. Dubois, D., Prade, H.: Fuzzy real algebra: some results. Fuzzy Sets and Systems 2, 327–348 (1979)
4. Kacprzyk, J.: Fuzzy sets in system analysis. PWN, Warszawa (1986) (in Polish)
5. Dubois, D.: Rough fuzzy sets and fuzzy rough sets. Int. J. of Gen. Syst. 17, 191–209 (1990)
6. Grzegorzewski, P., Mrówka, E.: Trapezoidal Approximation of Fuzzy Sets. In: De Baets, B., Kaynak, O., Bilgiç, T. (eds.) IFSA 2003. LNCS (LNAI), vol. 2715, pp. 237–244. Springer, Heidelberg (2003)
7. Rakus-Andersson, E.: Factor analysis with Qualitative Factors and Yager's Probability in the Lattice of Verbal Fuzzy Numbers. In: Grzegorzewski, P., Krawczak, M., Zadrozny, S. (eds.) Issues in Soft Computing. Theory and Applications, pp. 241–260. AOW EXIT, Warszawa (2005)
8. D'Urso, P., Gastaldi, T.: An 'orderwise' polynomial regression procedure for fuzzy data. Fuzzy Sets and Systems 130, 1–19 (2002)
9. Tyrala, R.: Linear Systems with Fuzzy Solution. In: Grzegorzewski, P., et al. (eds.) Issues in Soft Computing. Theory and Applications, pp. 277–288. AOW Exit, Warszawa (2005)
10. Kuhn, H.W., Tucker, A.W.: Nonlinear programming. In: Neyman, J. (ed.) Proc. of 2nd Berkeley Symposium, pp. 481–492. Univ. of California Press, Berkeley (1950)
11. Minitab Inc. Minitab 16 (2010), http://www.minitab.com

A New Fuzzy Classifier for Data Streams

Lena Pietruczuk, Piotr Duda, and Maciej Jaworski

Department of Computer Engineering, Czestochowa University of Technology,
ul. Armii Krajowej 36, 42-200 Czestochowa, Poland
{lena.pietruczuk,pduda,maciej.jaworski}@kik.pcz.pl

Abstract. Along with technological developments we observe an increasing amount of stored and processed data. It is not possible to store all incoming data and analyze it on the fly. Therefore many researchers are working on new algorithms for data stream mining. New algorithm should be fast and should use a small amount of memory. We will consider the problem of data stream classification. To increase the accuracy we propose to use an ensemble of classifiers based on a modified FID3 algorithm. The experimental results show that this algorithm is fast and accurate. Therefore it is adequate tool for data stream classification.

Keywords: classification, ensemble algorithm, FID3, data stream, decision tree, fuzzy logic.

1 Introduction

In the rapidly developing world the amount of processed and stored data is growing very fast. This is the reason of creation of a new field called data stream mining. Nowadays many researchers are interested in developing more efficient methods of data stream classification [1], [2], [8]-[10], [20], [21], [26]-[29]. The problem is to create fast and accurate algorithm with limited memory and CPU resources.

In literature there are many algorithms for data classification. The most known method is classification using Hoeffdings decision tree [6] and its modification in algorithms like VFDT [6]. However the mathematical foundations of this algorithm were incorrect and they have been revised in [20]. Well known algorithms based on the modification of k-nearest neighbor algorithm are ANNCAD [11] and LWClass algorithm [7]. The example of algorithm applying the fuzzy logic is FlexDT [8]. However, all these algorithms in the basic form are not suitable for classification of stream data.

In this paper we will introduce new algorithm for data stream classification. It is based on FID3 algorithm [28] however it works on chunks of data instead of all stored data. To reduce the time and memory consumption a new parameter δ is introduced, and to improve the accuracy of the algorithm we propose to build an ensemble algorithm. If the accuracy of single classifier is better than random choice then ensemble of those classifiers improves the accuracy. This property was used by many researchers [2]-[5], [13], [21].

L. Rutkowski et al. (Eds.): ICAISC 2012, Part I, LNCS 7267, pp. 318–324, 2012.

This paper is organized as follows. In section 2 the ensemble modified FID3 algorithm is described and in section 3 the experimental results are presented.

2   FID3 Algorithm

Let us consider the case where for every path of a tree there exists a membership function. Therefore the outcome of a tree for each data element is a vector of values of membership function for every class. Let q be the number of classes. Then the outcome of a tree is vector $(c_1, c_2, \ldots, c_q)$. Let S be the fuzzy set of all elements. To calculate the membership value there must be defined m fuzzy subsets F_v for all attributes a_j, $j \in 1, \ldots, p$. Then the best attribute for split is chosen according to the value of Information Gain $G(a_j, S)$ which is defined as follows

$$G(a_j, S) = I(S) - E(a_j, S), \tag{1}$$

where

$$I(S) = -\sum_{k=1}^{q} \frac{|S^{c_k}|}{|S|} \log_2 \frac{|S^{c_k}|}{|S|}, \tag{2}$$

$$E(a_j, S) = \sum_{v=1}^{m} \frac{|S_{jF_v}|}{\sum_{v=1}^{m} |S_{jF_v}|} I(S_{jF_v}), \tag{3}$$

S^{c_k} is the fuzzy subset in S whose class is c_k, $|S|$ denotes the sum of the membership degrees and S_{jF_v} is fuzzy subset corresponding to the fuzzy set F_v for the j-th attribute. The split does not occur if one of three conditions is satisfied:

1. there are no attributes left to split,
2. the proportion of instances of one class is greater than or equal to predefined threshold τ_1,
3. or the number of instances is less than predefined threshold τ_2.

The membership degree $\beta_k l$ of an element for class k in leaf l is defined as

$$\beta_{kl} = \frac{\sum_{i=1}^{n} \prod_{j \in path_l} \mu_{jl}(x_i) \mu_{kl}(y^i)}{\sum_{i=1}^{n} \prod_{j \in path_l} \mu_{jl}(x_i)}, \tag{4}$$

where $\mu_{jl}(x_i)$ is the membership degree of element x_i for attribute j at leaf l. It is obvious that $\mu_{kl}(y^i)$ equals one when class of x_i is k and zero otherwise. Let splitting attribute be an attribute for which we make a split. Then in formula 4 $path_l$ denotes the vector of all splitting attributes on the path from root to leaf l.

We classify an element x according to the class $(k = 1, \ldots, q)$ for which the value of d_k is the biggest. We calculate the value of d_k from the formula

$$d_k = \sum_{l=1}^{\eta} \mu_{path_l}(x) \cdot \beta_{kl}, \tag{5}$$

where η is the number of leafs.

3   Ensemble Modified FID3 Algorithm

The modification of FID3 algorithm is the parameter δ which limits the depth of the tree. Therefore split is not made if the path from the root to the node is longer than value of δ and this node become a leaf.

The algorithm works as follows. First user has to specify values of parameters τ_1, τ_2, δ, size of ensemble and the size of data chunks. Then it takes the first data chunk and builds on it a new temporary classifier based on the modified FID3. This classifier is then added to the ensemble. The algorithm continues to build new temporary trees on next data chunks and adds them to the ensemble until it reaches the defined size. Then, after creating new temporary tree, it measures the accuracy of all trees in ensemble and the last temporary tree based on new data chunk. If the accuracy of the last temporary tree is better than the weakest tree in the ensemble, it will replace the weakest tree. Every element without a class is classified according to the number of votes that trees in ensemble gives for each class. For this element is assigned a class with the most votes.

Algorithm 1. Ensemble modified FID3

---

01. **while** it is not the end of data stream **do**
02.   take new data chunk of a fix size
03.   make new temporary tree
04.   **if** ensemble is not full **do**
05.   add temporary tree to the ensemble
06.   **end if**
07.   **else**
08.   calculate the accuracy of all trees in ensemble and the last
09.   temporary tree on the current data chunk
10.   **if** the accuracy of the last temporary classifier is higher than the
11.   accuracy of the weakest tree of ensemble **do**
12.   replace the weakest classifier with the last temporary tree
13.   **end if**
14.   **end else**
15. **end while**

---

4   Experimental Results

In the following simulation we used synthetic data of size 300000. Each data is described by values of 20 attributes and one of 15 classes. Fuzzy subsets are defined as follows

$$F^1(x) = \begin{cases} 1 & \text{if } x \leq MEAN - SD \\ \frac{MEAN+SD-x}{2 \cdot SD} & \text{if } MEAN - SD < x \leq MEAN + SD \\ 0 & \text{if } x > MEAN + SD \end{cases}$$

$$F^2(x) = \begin{cases} 0 & \text{if } x \leq MEAN - SD \\ 1 - \frac{MEAN + SD - x}{2 \cdot SD} & \text{if } MEAN - SD < x \leq MEAN + SD \\ 1 & \text{if } x > MEAN + SD \end{cases}$$

where SD and $MEAN$ denotes the standard deviation and the mean of data from data chunk, respectively.

In the first experiment we compare the accuracy of the algorithm with the value of parameter δ. As we can see in Fig. 1 the accuracy improves with increasing value of δ. However with delta greater than 10 the accuracy does not improve as fast as for smaller values. Therefore the size of a tree can be set to value less than 20 to save time and memory.

In the second experiment we examined the influence of the size of ensemble on the accuracy and running time of the algorithm. As we can see in Fig. 2 a) the accuracy improves fast with growing size of the ensemble. However, the running time of the algorithm is growing with increasing value of ensemble (see Fig. 2 b)). Therefore the size of ensemble should be set wisely taking into account the speed of incoming data.

In the third experiment we compare the running time and accuracy of the algorithm with the size of data chunks. For this data the accuracy increases very fast with growing size of data chunk from 50 to 1500 (see Fig. 3 a)). For bigger size of data chunk the accuracy does not increase as fast. In Figure 3 b) we can see how the increasing size of data chunk extends the running time. For data chunk size 3000 the running time was about 429 minutes with the accuracy 91% and for data chunk size 200 the running time decreased to 278 minutes with a decrease in accuracy of 2, 3%.

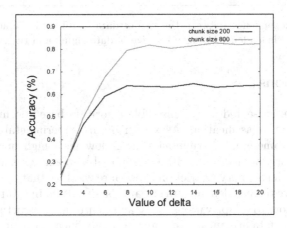

Fig. 1. The dependence between the value of parameter δ and the accuracy of the algorithm

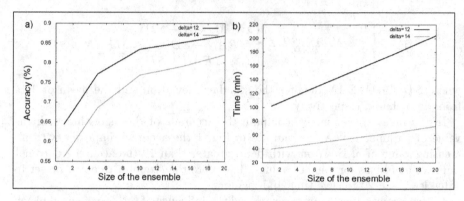

Fig. 2. a) The dependence between the size of the ensemble and the accuracy of the algorithm b) The dependence between the size of ensemble and the running time of the algorithm

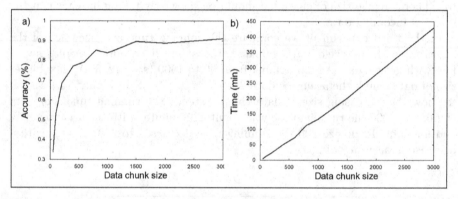

Fig. 3. a) The dependence between the size of data chunk and the accuracy of the algorithm b) The dependence between the size of data chunk and the running time

5   Conclusions

In this paper we presented a new ensemble algorithm based on modified FID3 algorithm for data classification. As shown in the experimental results, with properly set parameters, the running time is low with high accuracy of the algorithm. The original FID3 algorithm was not able to analyze such a big set of data because of the memory restriction. Therefore we show that this algorithm is good tool to solve the problem of data stream classification. In future research we will make an effort to adapt various fuzzy and neuro-fuzzy structures [12], [18], [19], [22]-[25] for data stream mining, and to adapt ideas presented in [14]-[17] to deal with concept drift.

Acknowledgments. This paper was prepared under project operated within the Foundation for Polish Science Team Programme co-financed by the EU

European Regional Development Fund, Operational Program Innovative Economy 2007-2013, and also supported by National Science Center NCN.

References

1. Aggarwal, C.: Data Streams: Models and Algorithms. Springer, New York (2007)
2. Barandela, R., Sánchez, J., Valdovinos, R.: New Applications of Ensembles of Classifiers. Pattern Analysis & Applications 6(3), 245–256 (2003)
3. Bifet, A., Frank, E., Holmes, G., Pfahringer, B.: Accurate Ensembles for Data Streams: Combining Restricted Hoeffding Trees using Stacking. In: 2nd Asian Conference on Machine Learning (ACML 2010), Tokyo, Japan, November 8-10, pp. 225–240 (2010)
4. Bifet, A., Holmes, G., Pfahringer, B., Kirkby, R., Gavalda, R.: New Ensemble Methods For Evolving Data Streams. In: KDD 2009, Paris France, pp. 139–148 (2009)
5. Chu, F., Zaniolo, C.: Fast and Light Boosting for Adaptive Mining of Data Streams. Springer, Heidelberg (2004)
6. Domingos, P., Hulten, G.: Mining High-Speed Data Streams. In: Proceedings of the Association for Computing Machinery Sixth International Conference on Knowledge Discovery and Data Mining, pp. 71–80 (2000)
7. Gaber, M., Krishnaswamy, S., Zaslavsky, A.: Advanced Methods of Knoweldge Discovery from Complex Data. In: Badhyopadhyay, S., Maulik, U., Holder, L., Cook, D. (eds.) On-board Mining of Data Streams in Sensor Networks, Springer, Heidelberg (2005)
8. Hashemi, S., Yang, Y.: Flexible decision tree for data stream classification in the presence fo concept change, noise and missing values. Data Mining and Knowledge Discovery 19(1), 95–131 (2009)
9. Khan, M., Ding, Q., Perrizo, W.: k-nearest Neighbor Classification on Spatial Data Streams Using P-trees. In: Chen, M.-S., Yu, P.S., Liu, B. (eds.) PAKDD 2002. LNCS (LNAI), vol. 2336, pp. 517–518. Springer, Heidelberg (2002)
10. Kirkby, R.: Improving Hoeffding Trees, PhD Thesis, University of Waikato, Department of Computer Science (2007)
11. Law, Y.-N., Zaniolo, C.: An Adaptive Nearest Neighbor Classification Algorithm for Data Streams. In: Jorge, A.M., Torgo, L., Brazdil, P.B., Camacho, R., Gama, J. (eds.) PKDD 2005. LNCS (LNAI), vol. 3721, pp. 108–120. Springer, Heidelberg (2005)
12. Nowicki, R.: Nonlinear modelling and classification based on the MICOG defuzzifications. Journal of Nonlinear Analysis, Series A: Theory, Methods and Applications 7(12), 1033–1047 (2009)
13. Polikar, R.: Ensemble Based Systems in Decision Making. IEEE Circuits and Systems Magazine 6(3), 21–45 (2006)
14. Rutkowski, L.: The real-time identification of time-varying systems by nonparametric algorithms based on the Parzen kernels. International Journal of Systems Science 16, 1123–1130 (1985)
15. Rutkowski, L.: Sequential pattern recognition procedures derived from multiple Fourier series. Pattern Recognition Letters 8, 213–216 (1988)
16. Rutkowski, L.: An application of multiple Fourier series to identification of multivariable nonstationary systems. International Journal of Systems Science 20(10), 1993–2002 (1989)

17. Rutkowski, L.: Nonparametric learning algorithms in the time-varying environments. Signal Processing 18, 129–137 (1989)
18. Rutkowski, L., Cpałka, K.: A general approach to neuro - fuzzy systems. In: Proceedings of the 10th IEEE International Conference on Fuzzy Systems, Melbourne, December 2-5, vol. 3, pp. 1428–1431 (2001)
19. Rutkowski, L., Cpałka, K.: A neuro-fuzzy controller with a compromise fuzzy reasoning. Control and Cybernetics 31(2), 297–308 (2002)
20. Rutkowski, L., Pietruczuk, L., Duda, P., Jaworski, M.: Decision trees for mining data streams based on the McDiarmids bound. IEEE Transactions on Knowledge and Data Engineering 24 (2012)
21. Street, W., Kim, Y.: A Streaming Ensemble Algorithm (SEA) for Large-Scale Classification. In: KDD 2001, San Francisco, pp. 377–382 (2001)
22. Scherer, R.: Boosting Ensemble of Relational Neuro-fuzzy Systems. In: Rutkowski, L., Tadeusiewicz, R., Zadeh, L.A., Żurada, J.M. (eds.) ICAISC 2006. LNCS (LNAI), vol. 4029, pp. 306–313. Springer, Heidelberg (2006)
23. Scherer, R.: Neuro-fuzzy Systems with Relation Matrix. In: Rutkowski, L., Scherer, R., Tadeusiewicz, R., Zadeh, L.A., Zurada, J.M. (eds.) ICAISC 2010. LNCS (LNAI), vol. 6113, pp. 210–215. Springer, Heidelberg (2010)
24. Starczewski, J., Rutkowski, L.: Interval type 2 neuro-fuzzy systems based on interval consequents. In: Rutkowski, L., Kacprzyk, J. (eds.) Neural Networks and Soft Computing, pp. 570–577. Physica-Verlag, Springer-Verlag Company, Heidelberg, New York (2003)
25. Starczewski, J.T., Rutkowski, L.: Connectionist Structures of Type 2 Fuzzy Inference Systems. In: Wyrzykowski, R., Dongarra, J., Paprzycki, M., Waśniewski, J. (eds.) PPAM 2001. LNCS, vol. 2328, pp. 634–642. Springer, Heidelberg (2002)
26. Umanol, M., Okamoto, H., Hatono, I., Tamura, H., Kawachi, F., Umedzu, S., Kinoshita, J.: Fuzzy decision trees by fuzzy ID3 algorithm and its application to diagnosis systems. In: Proceedings of The Third IEEE Conference on Fuzzy Systems, Orlando, FL, June 26-29, vol. 3, pp. 2113–2118 (1994)
27. Vivekanandan, P., Nedunchezhian, R.: Mining Rules of Concept Drift Using Genetic Algorithm. Journal of Artificial Inteligence and Soft Computing Research 1(2), 135–145 (2011)
28. Wang, T., Li, Z.-J., Hu, X., Yan, Y., Chen, H.-W.: A New Decision Tree Classification Method for Mining High-Speed Data Streams Based on Threaded Binary Search Trees. In: Washio, T., Zhou, Z.-H., Huang, J.Z., Hu, X., Li, J., Xie, C., He, J., Zou, D., Li, K.-C., Freire, M.M. (eds.) PAKDD 2007. LNCS (LNAI), vol. 4819, pp. 256–267. Springer, Heidelberg (2007)
29. Wang, T., Li, Z.-J., Yan, Y., Chen, H.-W.: An Incremental Fuzzy Decision Tree Classification Method for Mining Data Streams. In: Perner, P. (ed.) MLDM 2007. LNCS (LNAI), vol. 4571, pp. 91–103. Springer, Heidelberg (2007)

Metasets:
A New Approach to Partial Membership

Bartłomiej Starosta

Polish-Japanese Institute of Information Technology,
ul. Koszykowa 86,
02-008 Warsaw, Poland
barstar@pjwstk.edu.pl

Abstract. Metaset is a new concept of set with partial membership relation. It is designed to represent and process vague, imprecise data – similarly to fuzzy sets. Metasets are based on the classical set theory primitive notions. At the same time they are directed towards efficient computer implementations and applications. The degrees of membership for metasets are expressed as finite binary sequences, they form a Boolean algebra and they may be evaluated as real numbers too. Besides partial membership, equality and their negations, metasets allow for expressing a hesitancy degree of membership – similarly to intuitionistic fuzzy sets. The algebraic operations for metasets satisfy axioms of Boolean algebra.

Keywords: metaset, partial membership, set theory, fuzzy set.

1 Introduction

The paper gives a short overview of metaset theory – a new concept of set with fractional members. Contrary to classical sets and similarly to fuzzy sets [14] or rough sets [6], metasets are sets where an element may be a member of another to a variety of degrees, besides the full membership or non-membership. The mentioned above, traditional approaches to partial membership find broad applications nowadays in science and above all in industry. Unfortunately, they are not well suited for computer implementations. They also have other drawbacks, like the growth of fuzziness by multiple algebraic operations on fuzzy sets. Therefore, we tried to develop another idea of set with fractional members, which would be closer to classical Zermelo-Fraenkel Set Theory (ZFC) [5] and which would allow for efficient computer implementations. Another significant goal was to enable natural and straightforward modeling of vague terms as they are perceived and interpreted by a human. Thus, metasets are targeted at similar scope of applications as other traditional approaches. The theory of metasets is under development, however the results obtained so far indicate success. We point out the most significant of them.

L. Rutkowski et al. (Eds.): ICAISC 2012, Part I, LNCS 7267, pp. 325–333, 2012.
© Springer-Verlag Berlin Heidelberg 2012

2   Metasets

Informally, a metaset is a classical set whose elements are labeled with nodes of the binary tree. The nodes determine the membership degrees of elements in the metaset.

This point of view makes a metaset something similar to a fuzzy set, where the membership function assigns membership degrees to elements of its domain. The most noticeable difference at this point is that elements of a metaset are other metasets, like in the classical set theory, where elements of sets are other sets.

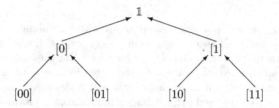

Fig. 1. Initial levels of the binary tree $\mathbb{T}$ and the ordering of nodes. Arrows point at the larger element.

The binary tree used in the definition of the metaset and throughout the paper is the full and infinite one and it is denoted with the symbol $\mathbb{T}$. Its elements are finite binary sequences denoted using square brackets, the root is the empty sequence denoted by $\mathbb{1}$ (see Fig. 1). They are ordered by reverse inclusion, so the root $\mathbb{1}$ is the largest element in $\mathbb{T}$. The nodes [0] and [1], which are direct descendants of the root form the first level of the tree, and so on.

Definition 1. *A set which is either the empty set $\emptyset$ or which has the form:*

$$\tau = \{\, \langle \sigma, p \rangle : \sigma \text{ is a metaset}, \ p \in \mathbb{T} \,\}$$

is called metaset. The $\langle \cdot, \cdot \rangle$ denotes an ordered pair.

The definition of metaset is recursive, however, the Axiom of Foundation (Regularity) in ZFC guarantees that there are no infinite branches in the recursion tree – it is founded by the empty set, which is a metaset too.[1]

From the point of view of classical set theory a metaset is a relation, i.e., a set of ordered pairs. The first element of each pair is another metaset – a member, also called a *potential element*, and the second element is a node of the binary tree. A metaset σ which is a potential element of the metaset τ may be paired with several different nodes simultaneously, e.g. $\tau = \{\, \langle \emptyset, p \rangle, \langle \emptyset, q \rangle \,\}$, for $p \neq q$ (cf. the example 1). Thus, a metaset is usually not a function.

---

[1] Formally, this is a definition by induction on the well founded membership relation $\in$, see [5, Ch. VII, §2] for a justification of such type of definitions.

Since a metaset is a relation, we may adopt some terms and notation connected to relations. For the given metaset τ, the set of its potential elements: $\mathrm{dom}(\tau) = \{\sigma\colon \langle\sigma,p\rangle \in \tau\}$ is called the *domain* of the metaset τ and the set $\mathrm{ran}(\tau) = \{p\colon \langle\sigma,p\rangle \in \tau\}$ is called the *range* of the metaset τ. For arbitrary metasets τ and σ the set $\tau[\sigma] = \{p \in \mathbb{T}\colon \langle\sigma,p\rangle \in \tau\}$ is called the *image* of the metaset τ at the metaset σ. The image $\tau[\sigma]$ is the empty set $\emptyset$, whenever σ is not a potential element of τ.

Example 1. The simplest metaset is the empty set $\emptyset$. It may be a potential element of other metasets:

$$\tau = \{\langle\emptyset,p\rangle\}\,, \qquad \tau[\emptyset] = \{p\}\,, \qquad \mathrm{dom}(\tau) = \{\emptyset\}\,, \qquad \mathrm{ran}(\tau) = \{p\}\,,$$
$$\sigma = \{\langle\emptyset,p\rangle,\langle\emptyset,q\rangle\}\,, \quad \sigma[\emptyset] = \{p,q\}\,, \quad \mathrm{dom}(\sigma) = \{\emptyset\}\,, \quad \mathrm{ran}(\sigma) = \{p,q\}\,.$$
$$\eta = \{\langle\tau,p\rangle,\langle\sigma,q\rangle\}\,, \quad \eta[\emptyset] = \emptyset\,, \qquad \mathrm{dom}(\eta) = \{\tau,\sigma\}\,, \quad \mathrm{ran}(\eta) = \{p,q\}\,.$$

Clearly, $\eta[\tau] = p$, $\eta[\sigma] = q$ and since $\emptyset \notin \mathrm{dom}(\eta)$, then $\eta[\emptyset] = \emptyset$.

A classical, crisp set is called hereditarily finite when it is a finite set and all its members are hereditarily finite sets.

Definition 2. *A metaset τ is called a hereditarily finite metaset, if its domain and range are finite sets, and each potential element is also a hereditarily finite metaset.*

Hereditarily finite metasets are particularly important in computer applications, where representable entities are naturally finite. They also have some interesting properties indicated in section 5.

3   Interpretations

An interpretation of a metaset is a crisp set. It represents one of several possible crisp views on the metaset. An interpretation is determined by a branch in the tree $\mathbb{T}$. A branch in $\mathbb{T}$ is a maximal (with respect to inclusion) set of pairwise comparable nodes. Note, that p is comparable to q only, if there exists a branch containing p and q simultaneously. Similarly, p is incomparable to q whenever no branch contains both p and q.

Definition 3. *Let τ be a metaset and let $\mathcal{C} \subset \mathbb{T}$ be a branch. The set*

$$\tau_\mathcal{C} = \{\sigma_\mathcal{C}\colon \langle\sigma,p\rangle \in \tau \wedge p \in \mathcal{C}\}$$

is called the interpretation of the metaset τ given by the branch $\mathcal{C}$.

Any interpretation of the empty metaset is the empty set, independently of the branch: $\emptyset_\mathcal{C} = \emptyset$, for each $\mathcal{C} \subset \mathbb{T}$. The process of producing the interpretation of a metaset consists in two stages. In the first stage we remove all the ordered pairs whose second elements are nodes which do not belong to the branch $\mathcal{C}$. The second stage replaces the remaining pairs – whose second elements lie on the branch $\mathcal{C}$ – with interpretations of their first elements, which are other metasets. This two-stage process is repeated recursively on all the levels of the membership hierarchy. As the result we obtain a crisp set.

Example 2. Let $p \in \mathbb{T}$, and let $\tau = \{\langle \emptyset, p \rangle\}$. If $\mathcal{C}$ is a branch, then

$$p \in \mathcal{C} \to \tau_\mathcal{C} = \{\emptyset_\mathcal{C}\} = \{\emptyset\},$$
$$p \notin \mathcal{C} \to \tau_\mathcal{C} = \emptyset.$$

Depending on the branch the metaset τ acquires different interpretations.

Each branch in the binary tree determines an interpretation of a metaset, so there may be infinitely many of them in general. Hereditarily finite metasets always have a finite number of different interpretations. There are metasets whose interpretations are all equal, even when they are not hereditarily finite.

When a metaset represents some vague, imprecise term, then its interpretations represent definite, precise approaches to the term. For instance, if we represent the term "warm temperature" as metaset, then its interpretations might be particular ranges of temperatures. Taken together they form the compound concept of "warm temperature".

The technique of interpretation introduces another point of view on metasets. A metaset may be perceived as a "fuzzy" family of crisp sets which are interpretations of the metaset. Here, the word "fuzzy" means that some of the members of the family – i.e., some interpretations of the metaset – occur more frequently than others. Those which appear frequently are better crisp approaches to metaset.

Properties of crisp sets which are interpretations of the given metaset determine its properties. Basic set-theoretic relations for metasets are defined by referring to the relations among interpretations of the metaset. When thinking about a metaset one has to bear in mind its interpretations.

4   Relations for Metasets

The membership relation for metasets is defined by referring to interpretations. In fact, we define an infinite number of relations, each specifying membership satisfied to another degree. The infinite number of relations allows for expressing a variety of different degrees to which membership may hold using classical two-valued logic.

Definition 4. *Let μ, τ be arbitrary metasets. We say that μ belongs to τ under the condition $p \in \mathbb{T}$, whenever for each branch $\mathcal{C} \subset \mathbb{T}$ containing p holds $\mu_\mathcal{C} \in \tau_\mathcal{C}$. We use the notation $\mu \,\epsilon_p\, \tau$.*

Thus, for each $p \in \mathbb{T}$ we define a separate relation ϵ_p. The root $\mathbb{1}$ specifies the highest possible membership degree. Since two metasets may be simultaneously in multiple membership relations specified by different nodes, then the overall membership degree is determined by a set of nodes of $\mathbb{T}$.

The conditional membership reflects the idea that a metaset μ belongs to a metaset τ whenever some conditions are fulfilled. Conditions correspond to nodes of the binary tree. In applications, they designate various circumstances affecting the degrees to which relations hold. For instance, consider the sentence: *John is happy when it is hot and when it is very cold.* In other words: *John* is a member of the metaset of happy people under the conditions *hot* and *very cold*.

Example 3. Let $\sigma = \emptyset$ and $\tau = \{\,\langle\sigma, \mathbb{1}\rangle, \langle\sigma, [0]\rangle\,\}$. If $\mathcal{C}$ is any branch in $\mathbb{T}$, then $\sigma_{\mathcal{C}} = \emptyset$ and $\tau_{\mathcal{C}} = \{\,\sigma_{\mathcal{C}}\,\} = \{\,\emptyset\,\}$, so $\sigma_{\mathcal{C}} \in \tau_{\mathcal{C}}$. Therefore, $\sigma \in_{\mathbb{1}} \tau$. Note, that the ordered pair $\langle\sigma, [0]\rangle$ is redundant in τ; it does not supply any additional membership information above the pair $\langle\sigma, \mathbb{1}\rangle$.

Besides the membership we define separate set of non-membership relations.

Definition 5. *We say that the metaset μ does not belong to the metaset τ under the condition $p \in \mathbb{T}$, whenever for each branch $\mathcal{C} \subset \mathbb{T}$ containing p holds $\mu_{\mathcal{C}} \notin \tau_{\mathcal{C}}$. We use the notation $\mu \notin_p \tau$.*

The reason for introducing independent non-membership relation follows from the fact that negation of conditional membership is not equivalent to conditional non-membership: $\neg\, \mu \in_p \tau$ is not equivalent to $\mu \notin_p \tau$. Indeed, the former – by the definition – means that not for each branch $\mathcal{C}$ containing p holds $\mu_{\mathcal{C}} \in \tau_{\mathcal{C}}$. However, such branches may exist, so we cannot conclude that $\mu_{\mathcal{C}} \notin \tau_{\mathcal{C}}$ for each $\mathcal{C} \ni p$, i.e., $\mu \notin_p \tau$. Because of this $\neg\, \mu \in_p \tau$ cannot be denoted with $\mu \notin_p \tau$, as it is in the classical case. Moreover, even though $\neg\, \mu \in_p \tau$ holds, there still may exist $q \leq p$ such, that for each branch $\mathcal{C}' \ni q$ holds $\mu_{\mathcal{C}'} \in \tau_{\mathcal{C}'}$, so $\mu \in_q \tau$.

Example 4. Let $\tau = \{\,\langle\emptyset, [0]\rangle\,\}$. We check that $\emptyset \in_{[0]} \tau \wedge \emptyset \notin_{[1]} \tau$. Indeed, if $\mathcal{C}^0$ is a branch containing $[0]$, then $\emptyset_{\mathcal{C}^0} = \emptyset \in \{\,\emptyset\,\} = \tau_{\mathcal{C}^0}$. Similarly, if $\mathcal{C}^1$ is a branch containing $[1]$, then $\emptyset_{\mathcal{C}^1} = \emptyset \notin \emptyset = \tau_{\mathcal{C}^1}$. Also, $\neg\, \emptyset \in_{\mathbb{1}} \tau \wedge \neg\, \emptyset \notin_{\mathbb{1}} \tau$, since it is not true, that for each branch $\mathcal{C}$ containing $\mathbb{1}$ holds $\emptyset_{\mathcal{C}} \in \tau_{\mathcal{C}}$ or $\emptyset_{\mathcal{C}} \notin \tau_{\mathcal{C}}$.

When $\sigma \in_{\mathbb{1}} \tau$ (or $\sigma \notin_{\mathbb{1}} \tau$), then for any branch $\mathcal{C}$ holds $\mu_{\mathcal{C}} \in \tau_{\mathcal{C}}$ (or $\mu_{\mathcal{C}} \notin \tau_{\mathcal{C}}$). Since the membership here is independent of the branch and it holds always, then it naturally reflects the crisp, unconditional membership (or non-membership).

The two sets of conditional relations: membership and non-membership taken together realize fully the idea of "partial" membership; they enable formalization of simultaneous being a member and being not a member. Informally speaking, if some part of μ is outside of τ then – at the same time – another part of μ may be inside of τ. Formally we would write in such case $\mu \in_p \tau \wedge \mu \notin_q \tau$, where p and q are some nodes. The above example shows that $\emptyset \in_{[0]} \tau \wedge \emptyset \notin_{[1]} \tau$. Note, that $\mu \notin_p \tau \wedge \mu \in_p \tau$ is false for any p.

The following two lemmas establish the relationships between different conditional membership (and non-membership) relations. They also enable evaluation of membership and non-membership degrees as real numbers. We must introduce some technical terms before.

A set $A \subset \mathbb{T}$ is called antichain in $\mathbb{T}$, if it consists of mutually incomparable elements: $\forall p, q \in A\ (p \neq q \rightarrow \neg\,(p \leq q) \wedge \neg\,(p \geq q))$. On the Fig. 1, the elements $\{\,[00], [01], [10]\,\}$ form a sample antichain. A maximal antichain is an antichain which cannot be extended by adding new elements – it is a maximal element with respect to inclusion of antichains. Examples of maximal antichains on the Fig. 1 are $\{\,[0], [1]\,\}$ or $\{\,[00], [01], [1]\,\}$ or even $\{\,\mathbb{1}\,\}$. Let $R \subset \mathbb{T}$ and $p \in \mathbb{T}$. If R is an antichain A such that $\forall_{q \in A}\,(q \leq p)$, then we say, that R is an antichain below p.

Lemma 1. *Let σ, τ be arbitrary metasets and let $p, q \in \mathbb{T}$. If $p \leq q$ and $\sigma \, \epsilon_q \, \tau$ ($\sigma \, \notin_q \tau$), then $\sigma \, \epsilon_p \, \tau$ ($\sigma \, \notin_p \tau$).*

Lemma 2. *Let σ, τ be arbitrary metasets and let $p, q \in \mathbb{T}$. If $R \subset \mathbb{T}$ is a finite maximal antichain below p such, that for each $q \in R$ holds $\sigma \, \epsilon_q \, \tau$ ($\sigma \, \notin_q \tau$), then also $\sigma \, \epsilon_p \, \tau$ ($\sigma \, \notin_p \tau$).*

The lemmas follow directly from the definition of interpretation and membership. For the detailed proofs the reader is referred to [13].

We now show how to evaluate membership and non-membership degrees as numbers from the unit interval. Let σ, τ be metasets. The sets

$$M(\sigma, \tau) = \max \{ p \in \mathbb{T} : \sigma \, \epsilon_p \, \tau \} , \tag{1}$$

$$N(\sigma, \tau) = \max \{ p \in \mathbb{T} : \sigma \, \notin_p \tau \} . \tag{2}$$

are called membership and non-membership set, respectively. One may easily see that both M and N are antichains. By the above lemmas, the whole membership (non-membership) information for any two metasets is contained in these sets. Therefore, we may use them to evaluate relations numerically as follows:

$$m(\sigma, \tau) = \sum_{p \in M(\sigma, \tau)} \frac{1}{2^{|p|}} , \tag{3}$$

$$n(\sigma, \tau) = \sum_{p \in N(\sigma, \tau)} \frac{1}{2^{|p|}} , \tag{4}$$

where $|p|$ denotes the length of the binary sequence p. The value $m(\sigma, \tau)$ ($n(\sigma, \tau)$) is called the membership (non-membership) value for σ in τ. Clearly, the values fit into the unit interval.

Strangely enough, there exist metasets σ, τ such, that $m(\sigma, \tau) + n(\sigma, \tau) < 1$. The remaining difference $1 - m(\sigma, \tau) - n(\sigma, \tau)$ is interpreted as hesitancy degree of membership for metasets (cf. Th. 2). Such behavior resembles intuitionistic fuzzy sets, where besides membership and non-membership degrees we also have a hesitancy degree [1]. Also, this property allows for representing intuitionistic fuzzy sets as metasets [10].

Although a metaset is not a function, it determines a function which assigns membership degrees to elements of its domain, similarly to fuzzy sets. The range of this membership function is the Boolean algebra of closed-open sets in Cantor space 2^ω. Indeed, each node $p \in \mathbb{T}$ determines a set of branches containing it, which is a closed-open set in this Cantor space. For the given metasets τ and $\sigma \in \mathrm{dom}(\tau)$ the value of this membership function is the clopen set in 2^ω which is the union of the sets determined by elements of $\tau[\sigma]$ or – equivalently – by elements of the membership set $M(\sigma, \tau)$. This function makes metasets similar to L-fuzzy sets whose membership functions are valued in lattices [3].

Analogously to membership and non-membership we define sets of conditional equality, unequality (i.e., negation of equality) and subset relations. They are consistent with partial membership and have similar properties to their classical counterparts (e.g., extensionality). They are investigated in [8].

5 Metasets and Computers

The concept of metaset is directed towards computer implementations and applications. The definitions of set-theoretic relations for computer representable metasets may be reformulated so that they are easily and efficiently implementable in computer languages. We now give an example of reformulation of the membership relation.

A metaset σ is called a *canonical* metaset if $\mathrm{ran}(\sigma) = \{\mathbb{1}\}$ and its domain includes canonical metasets only. In other words, its range and the ranges of its members on all the levels of membership hierarchy contain at most the root $\mathbb{1}$. Such metasets correspond to crisp sets, since the membership relation is two-valued for them. Metasets, whose domains are comprised of canonical metasets only, but their ranges are arbitrary are called *first order* metasets. They correspond to fuzzy sets, where the structure of elements is irrelevant and only the membership of elements matters. Canonical metasets are members of first order metasets, to various degrees.

Theorem 1. *Let σ be a hereditarily finite canonical metaset and let τ be a hereditarily finite first order metaset. For any $p \in \mathbb{T}$, the following are equivalent:*

a) σ belongs to τ under the condition p ($\sigma \in_p \tau$),
b) $\tau[\sigma]$ contains a finite maximal antichain below p, or it contains a node $q \geq p$.

Applying the above theorem we do not have to investigate all possible interpretations to verify the membership. The number of such interpretations may be infinite, what makes the process inapplicable for machines. The theorem delegates the membership problem to relationships between finite subsets of $\mathbb{T}$. Similarly, we may reformulate other relations. For the details, as well as the proof of the theorem, the reader is referred to [13].

It turns out, that metasets representable in machines have many additional interesting properties [12]. One of the most significant says that the membership degree complements the non-membership degree. In terms of real values it may be expressed as follows.

Theorem 2. *If σ and τ are hereditarily finite metasets, then*

$$\mathrm{m}(\sigma, \tau) + \mathrm{n}(\sigma, \tau) = 1 \,.$$

This means, that for such metasets the hesitancy degree disappears. In general, it is possible to construct metasets σ, τ such, that for all $p \in \mathbb{T}$ neither $\sigma \in_p \tau$ nor $\sigma \notin_q \tau$ holds. In such case $\mathrm{m}(\sigma, \tau) + \mathrm{n}(\sigma, \tau) = 0$ and the hesitancy degree is equal to 1. Similarly, one may construct σ, τ such, that $\mathrm{m}(\sigma, \tau) + \mathrm{n}(\sigma, \tau)$ is equal to some arbitrary given value from the unit interval [10].

For the class of hereditarily finite first order metasets – the ones which are represented in computers and are sufficient for most applications – it is possible to define algebraic operations. The definitions rely on relationships between various subsets of $\mathbb{T}$ and they do not involve interpretations, like in Theorem 1. Therefore, they are easy to implement. Algebraic operations for the first order metasets satisfy axioms of Boolean algebra [13]. Contrary to algebraic operations for fuzzy sets, repeatedly applied operations do not increase fuzziness and their ordering does not matter.

The experimental implementation of relations and algebraic operations for metasets was carried out in Java programming language. It was then used in an application for character recognition which is available on-line as Java applet [7]. The mechanism used to match character samples against a defined character pattern is entirely based on metasets. It utilizes the concept of interpretation for representing several character samples as a single entity – a metaset. Membership relation is interpreted as similarity of characters. The application seems to reflect the human perception of similar characters. This construction may be further developed to recognition of arbitrary data with graphical representation [11], [9].

6   Summary

The paper presents the current state of development of the metaset theory. Metasets enable expressing satisfaction of basic set-theoretic relations to a variety of degrees which form a Boolean algebra. Even though the theory of metasets may seem a purely abstract mathematical construction resembling its basis – the Zermelo-Fraenkel Set Theory – it is aimed at practical applications and particularly at computer implementations. It is a tool for modeling imprecise real life phenomena which are hardly representable using classical, crisp techniques. One of its advantages in this respect is the non-linear ordering of membership and equality degrees which facilitates better, more accurate representation of modeled reality and which is closer to human perception and evaluation of most vague terms.

It is worth stressing that besides the results mentioned here the notions of cardinality and equinumerosity for metasets are defined in the form allowing for straightforward algorithmization and they will be published soon. Future works on metasets focus on fast computer implementation of metasets relations and operations using the CUDA technology [4]. Another goal is defining a many-valued logic [2] for metasets based on the technique of metaset forcing [8,12]. It would allow for expressing partial membership using the language similar to the classical set theory using single relational symbol for membership.

References

1. Atanassov, K.T.: Intuitionistic Fuzzy Sets. Fuzzy Sets and Systems 20, 87–96 (1986)
2. Bolc, L., Borowik, P.: Many-valued Logics 1: Theoretical Foundations. Springer, Heidelberg (1992)
3. Goguen, J.: L-fuzzy Sets. Journal of Mathematical Analysis and Applications 18, 145–174 (1967)
4. Hwu, W.W.: GPU Computing Gems Emerald Edition. Applications of GPU Computing. Morgan Kaufmann (2011)

5. Kunen, K.: Set Theory, An Introduction to Independence Proofs. No. 102 in Studies in Logic and Foundations of Mathematics. North-Holland Publishing Company (1980)
6. Pawlak, Z.: Rough Sets. International Journal of Computer and Information Sciences 11, 341–356 (1982)
7. Starosta, B.: Character Recognition Java Applet, http://www.pjwstk.edu.pl/~barstar/Research/MSOCR/index.html
8. Starosta, B.: Partial Membership and Equality for Metasets. Fundamenta Informaticae, in review
9. Starosta, B.: Application of Meta Sets to Character Recognition. In: Rauch, J., Raś, Z.W., Berka, P., Elomaa, T. (eds.) ISMIS 2009. LNCS (LNAI), vol. 5722, pp. 602–611. Springer, Heidelberg (2009)
10. Starosta, B.: Representing Intuitionistic Fuzzy Sets as Metasets. In: Developments in Fuzzy Sets, Intuitionistic Fuzzy Sets, Generalized Nets and Related Topics. Volume I: Foundations. pp. 185–208 (2010)
11. Starosta, B.: Character Recognition with Metasets. In: Document Recognition and Understanding, pp. 15–34. INTECH (2011), http://www.intechopen.com/articles/show/title/character-recognition-with-metasets
12. Starosta, B., Kosiński, W.: Forcing for Computer Representable Metasets, under preparation
13. Starosta, B., Kosiński, W.: Meta Sets. Another Approach to Fuzziness. In: Views on Fuzzy Sets and Systems from Different Perspectives. Philosophy and Logic, Criticisms and Applications. STUDFUZZ, vol. 243, pp. 509–522. Springer, Heidelberg (2009)
14. Zadeh, L.A.: Fuzzy Sets. Information and Control 8, 338–353 (1965)

On an Enhanced Method for a More Meaningful Pearson's Correlation Coefficient between Intuitionistic Fuzzy Sets

Eulalia Szmidt[1,2] and Janusz Kacprzyk[1,2]

[1] Systems Research Institute, Polish Academy of Sciences,
ul. Newelska 6, 01–447 Warsaw, Poland
[2] Warsaw School of Information Technology, ul. Newelska 6, 01-447 Warsaw, Poland
{szmidt,kacprzyk}@ibspan.waw.pl

Abstract. This paper is a continuation of our previous works on correlation coefficients of Atanassov's intuitionistic fuzzy sets (A-IFSs). The Pearson's coefficient we discuss here yields the strength of relationship between the A-IFSs and also indicates the direction of correlation (positive or negative). The proposed correlation coefficient takes into account all three terms describing an A-IFS (membership values, non-membership values, and the hesitation margins).

1 Introduction

The correlation coefficient r proposed by Karl Pearson in 1895 (the so called Pearson's coefficient – the most often applied indices in statistics [15]), indicates how well two variables move together in an linear fashion (reflects their linear relationship). Some extensions to the case of fuzzy data have been proposed by, e.g., Chiang and Lin [7], Hong and Hwang [10], Liu and Kao [13].

Relationships between A-IFSs representing, e.g., preferences, attributes, are of a vital importance in theory and practice, and hence there are many papers discussing the correlation of A-IFSs: Bustince and Burillo [4], Gersternkorn and Mańko [8], Hong and Hwang [9], Hung [11], Hung and Wu [12], Zeng and Li [40]. In some of those papers only the strength of relationship is evaluated (cf. Gersternkorn and Mańko [8], Hong and Hwang [9], Zeng and Li [40]). In other papers (cf. Hung [11], Hung and Wu [12]), a positive and negative type of a relationship is reflected but the third term describing an A-IFS, which is important from the point of view of all similarity, distance or entropy measures (cf. Szmidt and Kacprzyk, e.g., [18], [20], [27], [22], [29]), [30]) is not accounted for.

In this paper we continue our previous works (Szmidt and Kacprzyk [35]) and discuss the concept of correlation for data represented as the A-IFSs adopting concepts from statistics. We calculate the correlation between the A-IFSs by showing both a positive and negative relationship between them, and emphasize the relevance of all three terms describing A-IFSs count.

We illustrate our considerations on the examples (e.g. benchmark data from [14]).

L. Rutkowski et al. (Eds.): ICAISC 2012, Part I, LNCS 7267, pp. 334–341, 2012.
© Springer-Verlag Berlin Heidelberg 2012

2   A Brief Introduction to A-IFSs

One of the possible generalizations of a fuzzy set in X (Zadeh [39]) given by

$$A' = \{< x, \mu_{A'}(x) > | x \in X\} \tag{1}$$

where $\mu_{A'}(x) \in [0, 1]$ is the membership function of the fuzzy set A', is an A-IFS (Atanassov [1], [2], [3]) A is given by

$$A = \{< x, \mu_A(x), \nu_A(x) > | x \in X\} \tag{2}$$

where: $\mu_A : X \to [0, 1]$ and $\nu_A : X \to [0, 1]$ such that

$$0 \leq \mu_A(x) + \nu_A(x) \leq 1 \tag{3}$$

and $\mu_A(x)$, $\nu_A(x) \in [0, 1]$ denote a degree of membership and a degree of non-membership of $x \in A$, respectively. (An approach to the assigning memberships and non-memberships for A-IFSs from data is proposed by Szmidt and Baldwin [16]).

Obviously, each fuzzy set may be represented by the following A-IFS:

$$A = \{< x, \mu_{A'}(x), 1 - \mu_{A'}(x) > | x \in X\}.$$

An additional concept for each A-IFS in X, that is not only an obvious result of (2) and (3) but which is also relevant for applications, we will call (Atanasov [3])

$$\pi_A(x) = 1 - \mu_A(x) - \nu_A(x) \tag{4}$$

a *hesitation margin* of $x \in A$ which expresses a lack of knowledge of whether x belongs to A or not (cf. Atanassov [3]). It is obvious that $0 \leq \pi_A(x) \leq 1$, for each $x \in X$.

The hesitation margin turns out to be important while considering the distances (Szmidt and Kacprzyk [18], [20], [27], entropy (Szmidt and Kacprzyk [22], [29]), similarity (Szmidt and Kacprzyk [30]) for the A-IFSs, etc. i.e., the measures that play a crucial role in virtually all information processing tasks.

Hesitation margins turn out to be relevant for applications - in image processing (cf. Bustince et al. [6], [5]) and classification of imbalanced and overlapping classes (cf. Szmidt and Kukier [36], [37], [38]), group decision making, negotiations, voting and other situations (cf. Szmidt and Kacprzyk [17], [23], [24], [25], [26], [28], [31], [32], [33]).

2.1   Correlation between the A-IFSs

In our previous papers we have proposed a correlation coefficient for two A-IFSs, A and B, so that we could express not only a relative strength but also a positive or negative relationship between A and B. We take into account all three terms describing an A-IFSs (membership, non-membership values and the hesitation margins) as each of them influences the results.

Suppose that we have a random sample $x_1, x_2, \ldots, x_n \in X$ with a sequence of paired data $[(\mu_A(x_1), \nu_A(x_1), \pi_A(x_1)), (\mu_B(x_1), \nu_B(x_1), \pi_B(x_1))], [(\mu_A(x_2), \nu_A(x_2), \pi_A(x_2)), (\mu_B(x_2), \nu_B(x_2), \pi_B(x_2))], \ldots, [(\mu_A(x_n), \nu_A(x_n), \pi_A(x_n)), (\mu_B(x_n), \nu_B(x_n), \pi_B(x_n))]$ which correspond to the membership values, non-memberships values and hesitation margins of A-IFSs A and B defined on X, then the correlation coefficient $r_{A-IFS}(A, B)$ is given by Definition 1.

Definition 1. The correlation coefficient $r_{A-IFS}(A, B)$ between two A-IFSs, A and B in X, is:

$$r_{A-IFS}(A, B) = \frac{1}{3}(r_1(A, B) + r_2(A, B) + r_3(A, B)) \tag{5}$$

where

$$r_1(A, B) = \frac{\sum_{i=1}^{n}(\mu_A(x_i) - \overline{\mu_A})(\mu_B(x_i) - \overline{\mu_B})}{(\sum_{i=1}^{n}(\mu_A(x_i) - \overline{\mu_A})^2)^{0.5}(\sum_{i=1}^{n}(\mu_B(x_i) - \overline{\mu_B})^2)^{0.5}} \tag{6}$$

$$r_2(A, B) = \frac{\sum_{i=1}^{n}(\nu_A(x_i) - \overline{\nu_A})(\nu_B(x_i) - \overline{\nu_B})}{(\sum_{i=1}^{n}(\nu_A(x_i) - \overline{\nu_A})^2)^{0.5}(\sum_{i=1}^{n}(\nu_B(x_i) - \overline{\nu_B})^2)^{0.5}} \tag{7}$$

$$r_3(A, B) = \frac{\sum_{i=1}^{n}(\pi_A(x_i) - \overline{\pi_A})(\pi_B(x_i) - \overline{\pi_B})}{(\sum_{i=1}^{n}(\pi_A(x_i) - \overline{\pi_A})^2)^{0.5}(\sum_{i=1}^{n}(\pi_B(x_i) - \overline{\pi_B})^2)^{0.5}} \tag{8}$$

where: $\overline{\mu_A} = \frac{1}{n}\sum_{i=1}^{n}\mu_A(x_i)$, $\overline{\mu_B} = \frac{1}{n}\sum_{i=1}^{n}\mu_B(x_i)$, $\overline{\nu_A} = \frac{1}{n}\sum_{i=1}^{n}\nu_A(x_i)$,

$\overline{\nu_B} = \frac{1}{n}\sum_{i=1}^{n}\nu_B(x_i)$, $\overline{\pi_A} = \frac{1}{n}\sum_{i=1}^{n}\pi_A(x_i)$, $\overline{\pi_B} = \frac{1}{n}\sum_{i=1}^{n}\pi_B(x_i)$,

The proposed correlation coefficient (5) depends on the amount of information expressed by the membership and non-membership degrees (6)–(7), and the reliability of information expressed by the hesitation margins (8).

Remark: $r_{A-IFS}(A, B)$ makes sense, analogously as for the crisp and fuzzy data, for A-IFS variables whose values vary. If, for instance, the temperature is constant and the amount of ice cream sold is the same, then it is impossible to conclude about their relationship due to 0 in the denominator.

The correlation coefficient $r_{A-IFS}(A, B)$ (5) fulfills the following properties:

1. $r_{A-IFS}(A, B) = r_{A-IFS}(B, A)$
2. If $A = B$ then $r_{A-IFS}(A, B) = 1$
3. $|r_{A-IFS}(A, B)| = \leq 1$

The above properties are fulfilled both by the correlation coefficient $r_{A-IFS}(A, B)$ (5) and by its every component (6)–(8).

Remark: $r_{A-IFS}(A, B) = 1$ occurs not only for $A = B$ but also in the cases of a perfect linear correlation of the data (the same concerns each component (6)–(8)).

We will show now an illustrative example. The size of the data set is too small to be meant as a significant sample but serve the purpose of illustrativeness.

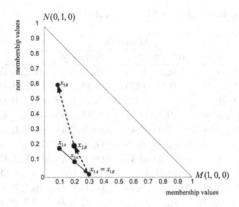

Fig. 1. Visualization of the data from Example 1: it is easy to notice that there is no perfect linear relationship among elements from A and B

Example 1. Let A and B be A-IFSs in $X = \{x_1, x_2, x_3\}$:

$$A = \{(x_1, 0.1, 0.2, 0.7), (x_2, 0.2, 0.09, 0.71), (x_3, 0.3, 0.01, 0.69)\}$$

$$B = \{(x_1, 0.3, 0, 0.7), (x_2, 0.2, 0.2, 0.6), (x_3, 0.1, 0.6, 0.3)\}$$

It is easy to notice that:

– the membership values of the elements in A (i.e.: $0.1, 0.2, 0.3$) increase whereas the membership values of the elements in B (i.e.: $0.3, 0.2, 0.1$) decrease. In the result (6) we have $r_1(A, B) = -1$.
– the non-membership values of the elements in A (i.e.: $0.2, 0.09, 0.01$) decrease whereas the non-membership values of the elements in B (i.e.: $0.0, 0.2, 0.6$) increase. In the result (7) we have $r_2(A, B) = -0.96$.
– the hesitation margins of the elements in A (i.e.: $(0.7, 0.71, 0.69)$ and the hesitation margins of the elements in B (i.e.: $0.7, 0.6, 0.2$) give in the result (8) $r_3(A, B) = 0.73$. Therefore, finally, from (5) we obtain $r_{A-IFS}(A, B) = \frac{1}{3}(-1 - 0.96 + 0.73) = -0.41$.

If we exclude from considerations the hesitation margins, and take into account two components (6) and (7) only, we obtain $r_{A-IFS}(A, B) = \frac{1}{2}(-1 - 0.96) = -0.98$ which means that there is a substantial negative linear relationship between A and B (which is difficult to agree).

In Figure 1 there is a geometrical interpretation of the data from Example 1.

From the point of view of practical problems, the third component (8) of the correlation coefficient (5), related to the lack of knowledge represented by the variables considered, may be important. For example, if the data represent reactions of patients to a new medicine, it seems necessary to carefully examine just the part (8) of the correlation coefficient (5) as it may occur that a new medicine/treatment increases unforeseen reactions. In such situations it may be important not only to examine all the components of (5) separately but even to give them different weights in (5).

We will verify if all the three parts of (5) count for a well known benchmark - "Saturday Morning" [14]. The data set is small and hence illustrative. Next, we know which

Table 1. The "Saturday Morning" data [14] in terms of A-IFSs

No.	Attributes				Class
	Outlook	Temperature	Humidity	Windy	
1	$(0, 0.33, 0.67)$	$(0, 0.33, 0.67)$	$(0, 0.33, 0.67)$	$(0.2, 0, 0.8)$	N
2	$(0, 0.33, 0.67)$	$(0, 0.33, 0.67)$	$(0, 0.33, 0.67)$	$(0, 0.33, 0.67)$	N
3	$(1, 0, 0)$	$(0, 0.33, 0.67)$	$(0, 0.33, 0.67)$	$(0.2, 0, 0.8)$	P
4	$(0.2, 0.11, 0.69)$	$(0, 0, 1)$	$(0, 0.33, 0.67)$	$(0.2, 0, 0.8)$	P
5	$(0.2, 0.11, 0.69)$	$(0.4, 0.11, 0.49)$	$(0.6, 0, 0.4)$	$(0.2, 0, 0.8)$	P
6	$(0.2, 0.11, 0.69)$	$(0.4, 0.11, 0.49)$	$(0.6, 0, 0.4)$	$(0, 0.33, 0.67)$	N
7	$(1, 0, 0)$	$(0.4, 0.11, 0.49)$	$(0.6, 0, 0.4)$	$(0, 0.33, 0.67)$	P
8	$(0, 0.33, 0.67)$	$(0, 0, 1)$	$(0, 0.33, 0.67)$	$(0.2, 0, 0.8)$	N
9	$(0, 0.33, 0.67)$	$(0.4, 0.11, 0.49)$	$(0.6, 0, 0.4)$	$(0.2, 0, 0.8)$	P
10	$(0.2, 0.11, 0.69)$	$(0, 0, 1)$	$(0.6, 0, 0.4)$	$(0.2, 0, 0.8)$	P
11	$(0, 0.33, 0.67)$	$(0, 0, 1)$	$(0.6, 0, 0.4)$	$(0, 0.33, 0.67)$	P
12	$(1, 0, 0)$	$(0, 0, 1)$	$(0, 0.33, 0.67)$	$(0, 0.33, 0.67)$	P
13	$(1, 0, 0)$	$(0, 0.33, 0.67)$	$(0.6, 0, 0.4)$	$(0.2, 0, 0.8)$	P
14	$(0.2, 0.11, 0.69)$	$(0, 0, 1)$	$(0, 0.33, 0.67)$	$(0, 0.33, 0.67)$	N

Table 2. Values of the correlation component (6) between each pair of the attributes for the "Saturday Morning" data from [14]

Attr	Outlook	Temperature	Humidity	Windy
Outlook	1	0.01	0.03	-0.01
Temperature	0.01	1	0.63	-0.1
Humidity	0.03	0.63	1	0
Windy	-0.01	- 0.1	0	1

relationships to expect – three attributes are not strongly related (as each is important from the point of view of classification), the fourth one is not very important from the point of view of classification (more correlated with the others).

The data set consists of 14 examples, 4 nominal attributes, and the target attribute with two classes. The nominal attributes are: **outlook**, with values {sunny, overcast, rain}, **temperature**, with values {cold, mild, hot}, **humidity**, with values {high, normal}, and **windy**, with values {true, false}.

Following the idea presented in Szmidt and Kacprzyk [34], and by Szmidt and Baldwin [16], we have obtained a description of "Saturday Morning" data [14] in terms of A-IFSs (Table 1), i.e., have expressed each attribute in terms of the membership values, non-membership values, and hesitation margin values. Next, we have calculated the three components of (5) for each pair of the attributes. The results are in Tables 2–4.

It is easy to notice that the correlation components (6) resulting from the correlation stemming from the membership values of attributes is significant only in one case (just as we have expected) – between Humidity and Temperature. The second component of (5), i.e., (7) practically in all cases produces the values which are not significant in terms of correlation. Next, the third component of (5), i.e., (8) confirms the conclusions we have drawn from (6). In other words, the values of the correlation expressed in terms

Table 3. Values of the correlation component (7) between each pair of the attributes for the "Saturday Morning" data from [14]

Attr	Outlook	Temperature	Humidity	Windy
Outlook	1	0.01	0.12	-0.07
Temperature	0.01	1	0.12	-0.22
Humidity	0.12	0.12	1	0
Windy	-0.07	-0.22	0	1

Table 4. Values of the correlation component (8) between each pair of the attributes for the "Saturday Morning" from [14]

Attr	Outlook	Temperature	Humidity	Windy
Outlook	1	0.15	-0.005	0.09
Temperature	0.15	1	0.45	-0.1
Humidity	-0.005	0.45	1	0
Windy	0.09	-0.1	0	1

Table 5. Values of the correlation (5) between each pair of the attributes for the "Saturday Morning" data from [14]

Attr	Outlook	Temperature	Humidity	Windy
Outlook	1	0.06	0.05	0.003
Temperature	0.06	1	0.4	-0.14
Humidity	0.05	0.4	1	0
Windy	0.003	-0.14	0	1

of lack of knowledge (8) count, and should not be excluded from considerations when examining the correlation between the attributes. We have obtained similar results for Pima Indians Diabetes Database [41].

3   Conclusion

A new concept of the *Spearman correlation coefficient* for the A-IFSs is discussed and illustrated, extending our previous work [35]. It is a generalization of the *Spearman correlation coefficient* for the crisp sets. The coefficient takes into account all three terms describing an A-IFS (the membership values, non-membership values and hesitation margins) as each term plays an important role in data analysis and decision making, so that each of them should be reflected while assessing the relationship between the A-IFSs.

Acknowledgment. Partially supported by the Ministry of Science and Higher Education Grant Nr N N519 384936.

References

1. Atanassov, K.: Intuitionistic Fuzzy Sets. VII ITKR Session. Sofia (Centr. Sci.-Techn. Libr. of Bulg. Acad. of Sci., 1697/84) (1983) (in Bulgarian)
2. Atanassov, K.: Intuitionistic Fuzzy Sets. Fuzzy Sets and Systems 20, 87–96 (1986)
3. Atanassov, K.: Intuitionistic Fuzzy Sets: Theory and Applications. Springer, Heidelberg (1999)
4. Bustince, H., Burillo, P.: Correlation of interval-valued intuitionistic fuzzy sets. Fuzzy Sets and Systems 74, 237–244 (1995)
5. Bustince, H., Mohedano, V., Barrenechea, E., Pagola, M.: Image thresholding using intuitionistic fuzzy sets. In: Issues in the Representation and Processing of Uncertain and Imprecise Information. In: Atanassov, K., Kacprzyk, J., Krawczak, M., Szmidt, E. (eds.) Fuzzy Sets, Intuitionistic Fuzzy Sets, Generalized Nets, and Related Topics. EXIT, Warsaw (2005)
6. Bustince, H., Mohedano, V., Barrenechea, E., Pagola, M.: An algorithm for calculating the threshold of an image representing uncertainty through A-IFSs. In: IPMU 2006, pp. 2383–2390 (2006)
7. Chiang, D.-A., Lin, N.P.: Correlation of fuzzy sets. Fuzzy Sets and Systems 102, 221–226 (1999)
8. Gersternkorn, T., Manko, J.: Correlation of intuitionistic fuzzy sets. Fuzzy Sets and Systems 44, 39–43 (1991)
9. Hong, D.H., Hwang, S.Y.: Correlation of intuitionistic fuzzy sets in probability spaces. Fuzzy Sets and Systems 75, 77–81 (1995)
10. Hong, D.H., Hwang, S.Y.: A note on the correlation of fuzzy numbers. Fuzzy Sets and Systems 79, 401–402 (1996)
11. Hung, W.L.: Using statistical viewpoint in developing correlation of intuitionistic fuzzy sets. Int. J. of Uncertainty, Fuzziness and Knowledge-Based Systems 9(4), 509–516 (2001)
12. Hung, W.L., Wu, J.W.: Correlation of intuitionistic fuzzy sets by centroid method. Information Sciences 144, 219–225 (2002)
13. Liu, S.-T., Kao, C.: Fuzzy measures for correlation coefficient of fuzzy numbers. Fuzzy Sets and Systems 128, 267–275 (2002)
14. Quinlan, J.R.: Induction of decision trees. Machine Learning 1, 81–106 (1986)
15. Rodgers, J.L., Alan Nicewander, W.A.: Thirteen Ways to Look at the Correlation Coefficient. The American Statistician 42(1), 59–66 (1988)
16. Szmidt, E., Baldwin, J.: Intuitionistic Fuzzy Set Functions, Mass Assignment Theory, Possibility Theory and Histograms. In: 2006 IEEE World Congress on Computational Intelligence, pp. 237–243 (2006)
17. Szmidt, E., Kacprzyk, J.: Remarks on some applications of intuitionistic fuzzy sets in decision making. Notes on IFS 2(3), 22–31 (1996c)
18. Szmidt, E., Kacprzyk, J.: On measuring distances between intuitionistic fuzzy sets. Notes on IFS 3(4), 1–13 (1997)
19. Szmidt, E., Kacprzyk, J.: Group Decision Making under Intuitionistic Fuzzy Preference Relations. In: IPMU 1998, pp. 172–178 (1998)
20. Szmidt, E., Kacprzyk, J.: Distances between intuitionistic fuzzy sets. Fuzzy Sets and Systems 114(3), 505–518 (2000)
21. Szmidt, E., Kacprzyk, J.: On Measures on Consensus Under Intuitionistic Fuzzy Relations. In: IPMU 2000, pp. 1454–1461 (2000)
22. Szmidt, E., Kacprzyk, J.: Entropy for intuitionistic fuzzy sets. Fuzzy Sets and Systems 118(3), 467–477 (2001)
23. Szmidt, E., Kacprzyk, J.: Analysis of Consensus under Intuitionistic Fuzzy Preferences. In: Int. Conf. in Fuzzy Logic and Technology. De Montfort Univ. Leicester, UK, pp. 79–82 (2001)

24. Szmidt, E., Kacprzyk, J.: Analysis of Agreement in a Group of Experts via Distances Between Intuitionistic Fuzzy Preferences. In: 9th Int. Conf. IPMU 2002, pp. 1859–1865 (2002a)
25. Szmidt, E., Kacprzyk, J.: An Intuitionistic Fuzzy Set Based Approach to Intelligent Data Analysis (an application to medical diagnosis). In: Abraham, A., Jain, L., Kacprzyk, J. (eds.) Recent Advances in Intelligent Paradigms and Applications, pp. 57–70. Springer, Heidelberg (2002b)
26. Szmidt, E., Kacprzyk, J.: An Intuitionistic Fuzzy Set Based Approach to Intelligent Data Analysis (an application to medical diagnosis). In: Abraham, A., Jain, L., Kacprzyk, J. (eds.) Recent Advances in Intelligent Paradigms and Applications, pp. 57–70. Springer, Heidelberg (2002c)
27. Szmidt, E., Kacprzyk, J.: Distances Between Intuitionistic Fuzzy Sets: Straightforward Approaches may not work. In: IEEE IS 2006, pp. 716–721 (2006)
28. Szmidt, E., Kacprzyk, J.: An Application of Intuitionistic Fuzzy Set Similarity Measures to a Multi-criteria Decision Making Problem. In: Rutkowski, L., Tadeusiewicz, R., Zadeh, L.A., Żurada, J.M. (eds.) ICAISC 2006. LNCS (LNAI), vol. 4029, pp. 314–323. Springer, Heidelberg (2006)
29. Szmidt, E., Kacprzyk, J.: Some Problems with Entropy Measures for the Atanassov Intuitionistic Fuzzy Sets. In: Masulli, F., Mitra, S., Pasi, G. (eds.) WILF 2007. LNCS (LNAI), vol. 4578, pp. 291–297. Springer, Heidelberg (2007)
30. Szmidt, E., Kacprzyk, J.: A New Similarity Measure for Intuitionistic Fuzzy Sets: Straightforward Approaches may not work. In: 2007 IEEE Conf. on Fuzzy Systems, pp. 481–486 (2007a)
31. Szmidt, E., Kacprzyk, J.: A new approach to ranking alternatives expressed via intuitionistic fuzzy sets. In: Ruan, D., et al. (eds.) Computational Intelligence in Decision and Control, pp. 265–270. World Scientific (2008)
32. Szmidt, E., Kacprzyk, J.: Amount of Information and Its Reliability in the Ranking of Atanassov's Intuitionistic Fuzzy Alternatives. In: Rakus-Andersson, E., Yager, R.R., Ichalkaranje, N., Jain, L.C. (eds.) Recent Advances in Decision Making. SCI, vol. 222, pp. 7–19. Springer, Heidelberg (2009)
33. Szmidt, E., Kacprzyk, J.: Ranking of Intuitionistic Fuzzy Alternatives in a Multi-criteria Decision Making Problem. In: Proceedings of the Conference: NAFIPS 2009, Cincinnati, USA, June 14-17. IEEE (2009) ISBN: 978-1-4244-4577-6
34. Szmidt, E., Kacprzyk, J.: Dealing with typical values via Atanassov's intuitionistic fuzzy sets. International Journal of General Systems 39(5), 489–596 (2010)
35. Szmidt, E., Kacprzyk, J.: Correlation of Intuitionistic Fuzzy Sets. In: Hüllermeier, E., Kruse, R., Hoffmann, F. (eds.) IPMU 2010. LNCS, vol. 6178, pp. 169–177. Springer, Heidelberg (2010)
36. Szmidt, E., Kukier, M.: Classification of Imbalanced and Overlapping Classes using Intuitionistic Fuzzy Sets. In: IEEE IS 2006, London, pp. 722–727 (2006)
37. Szmidt, E., Kukier, M.: A New Approach to Classification of Imbalanced Classes via Atanassov's Intuitionistic Fuzzy Sets. In: Wang, H.-F. (ed.) Intelligent Data Analysis: Developing New Methodologies Through Pattern Discovery and Recovery, pp. 85–101. Idea Group (2008)
38. Szmidt, E., Kukier, M.: Atanassov's intuitionistic fuzzy sets in classification of imbalanced and overlapping classes. In: Chountas, P., Petrounias, I., Kacprzyk, J. (eds.) Intelligent Techniques and Tools for Novel System Architectures. SCI, pp. 455–471. Springer, Heidelberg (2008)
39. Zadeh, L.A.: Fuzzy sets. Information and Control 8, 338–353 (1965)
40. Zeng, W., Li, H.: Correlation coefficient of intuitionistic fuzzy sets. Journal of Industrial Engineering International 3(5), 33–40 (2007)
41. http://archive.ics.uci.edu/ml/datasets/Diabetes

Surface Area of Level-2 Fuzzy Regions

Unifying Possibilistic and Versitic Interpretations of Regions

Jörg Verstraete[1,2]

[1] Systems Research Institute - Polish Academy of Sciences
Newelska 6, 01-447 Warsaw, Poland
jorg.verstraete@ibspan.waw.pl
http://www.ibspan.waw.pl
[2] DDCM - TELIN - Ghent University
Sint Pietersnieuwstraat 41, 9000 Gent, Belgium
jorg.verstraete@telin.ugent.be
http://telin.ugent.be/ddcm

Abstract. In many applications, spatial data is often prone to uncertainty and imprecision. To model this, fuzzy regions have been developed. Our initial model was a fuzzy set over a two dimensional domain, allowing for fuzzy regions and fuzzy points to be modelled. The model had some limitations: all points where treated independently, and it was not possible to group points together. Furthermore, the model depended on meta-information to specify the interpretation. The model was extended to a level-2 fuzzy region to overcome these limitations; here the calculation and interpretation of the surface area will be considered.

1 Introduction

When working with geographic data, one often has to deal with large amounts of data, and this data usually contains some form of uncertainty or imprecision. This can have a number of causes; the uncertainty or imprecision can be inherent to the data (so it is an intrinsic part of the features that are modelled), it can be introduced due to limitations in measurements (the features that are modelled are not uncertain or imprecise, but we cannot assess them exactly) or it can result from combining data from different sources (the sources can contradict or be incompatible). In this work, we consider an entity based approach for modelling data and features: real-world objects and features are represented using basic elements (in the crisp sense these are points, lines and polygons). To represent geographic entities containing uncertainty or imprecision, several approaches have been developed; these usually involve modelling a number of candidate boundaries ([1], [2]); such models mainly served for conceptual purposes and were only developed to a limited extent, lacking many operators.

In our concept of fuzzy regions, a region was considered to be a set of points and a fuzzy region essentially fuzzy set over a two dimensional domain ([3]). It was introduced to overcome the limitations of spatial information systems in

L. Rutkowski et al. (Eds.): ICAISC 2012, Part I, LNCS 7267, pp. 342–349, 2012.

modelling uncertain or imprecise spatial features. The traditional feature based models define features (real world objects or entities) by means of polygons; this representation does not allow for elements of the region to only have a partial membership or for the region to have undetermined boundaries. The fuzzy region model allows for the representation of fuzzy regions (i.e. regions with partial membership), or fuzzy points (i.e. points at an imprecise or uncertain location). From the theoretical model, a number of implementable models have been derived (e.g. [3]) and they have been applied in both querying spatial data as well as image segmentation.

To overcome some shortcomings of this model, an extension has been developed and presented in [4]; it defines a level-2 fuzzy region as a level-2 fuzzy region, thus allowing for both interpretations. This extension yields some changes to operations; in this contribution we consider calculating the surface area of level-2 fuzzy regions. After introducing and defining the fuzzy regions and the first extension in section 2, the level-2 fuzzy regions will be defined in 2.2. Section 3 concerns the surface area of level-2 fuzzy region. A conclusion summarizes the findings.

2   Preliminaries

2.1   Fuzzy Regions

The concept of the original fuzzy regions is simple, but requires a different view of regions. Traditionally, a region is defined by means of its outline (commonly represented by a polygon). A region can however also be seen as a set of points belonging together and delimited by the outline; from this point of view, it is a small step to augment the definition to a fuzzy set ([5]) of points. In [3], a fuzzy region is defined over $\mathbb{R}^2$, thus with each element (point) a membership grade was associated.

Definitions. A fuzzy region essentially is a fuzzy set defined over a two dimensional domain; the concept is illustrated on figure 1. The definition is given below:

$$\tilde{R} = \{(p, \mu_{\tilde{R}}(p)) | p \in \mathbb{R}^2\} \tag{1}$$

With the membership function is defined as:

$$\mu_{\tilde{R}} : \mathbb{R}^2 \mapsto [0, 1]$$
$$p \to \mu_{\tilde{R}}(p)$$

A fuzzy set can have three different interpretations ([6]): veristic, possibilistic and as degrees of truth. In the fuzzy region model, only the first two have been considered so far. A veristic interpretation means that the membership grades express a *degree of beloning to*, thus indicating a partial membership. In the fuzzy region model, this means that all points belong to the set to some specific

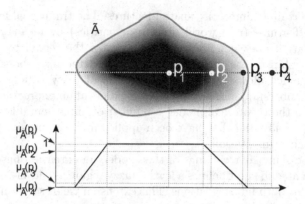

Fig. 1. The concept of a fuzzy region $\tilde{A}$; a fuzzy set over a two dimensional domain. All points belong to some extent to the region; indicated by means of the membership grade. The lower half of the figure shows a cross section. The shades of grey relate to the membership grades: darker shades match higher membership grades (the region has a dark outline to indicate its maximal outline).

extent. As such, this interpretation is used to represent fuzzy regions where some points are considered to belong to a lesser extent to the region. A possibilistic interpretation on the other hand means that the membership grades express the possibility of each element of the domain. Applied in the fuzzy region model, this implies that the fuzzy region is a representation for a single point whose location is not precisely known; all the points of the fuzzy region now are possible candidates for this one specific point. In this interpretation, the region can be seen as a representation of a fuzzy location. While the representation is exactly the same, the difference in interpretation also impacts the operations.

The above definition was extended to allow for grouping of points with the same membership grade ([7]). For this purpose, the domain was altered from $\mathbb{R}^2$ to $\wp(\mathbb{R}^2)$; the powerset of $\mathbb{R}^2$. The powerset $\wp$ of a set A is defined as the set of all possible subsets of that set, including the empty set and the set itself. An example is given below. Using this concept, the fuzzy region can be defined with $\wp(\mathbb{R}^2)$ as the domain. This makes the basic elements of the fuzzy region subregions ([7]).

$$\tilde{R} = \{(P, \mu_{\tilde{R}}(P)) | P \in \wp(\mathbb{R}^2) \wedge \forall P_1, P_2 \in \tilde{R} : P_1 \cap P_2 = \emptyset\} \tag{2}$$

With the membership function is defined as:

$$\mu_{\tilde{R}} : \wp(\mathbb{R}^2) \mapsto [0, 1]$$
$$P \to \mu_{\tilde{R}}(P)$$

Note that in this definition the intersection between any two elements should be empty: it is required that no two elements of the fuzzy region share points. A point can only be considered to belong to the region once, even if it is to a membership grade less than 1. The reason for imposing this restriction is that intersecting subregions would yield unexpected behaviour in the different operations; the basic elements in the original regions are single points and also don't intersect.

2.2 Level-2 Fuzzy Regions

Concept. The level-2 fuzzy region is an extension to the traditional fuzzy regions. It if a further refinement of the extension defined above. In the previous extension, a fuzzy regions was defined as a fuzzy set of non-overlapping crisp regions ([7]). While it solved some initial issues, it had limitations among which the fact that there still was the need for additional metadata to carry the interpretation. In order to overcome this, a level-2 fuzzy region will be model a number of possible candidate regions, which are fuzzy regions themselves. To achieve this, the concept of the fuzzy powerset is used. The fuzzy powerset, denoted $\tilde{\wp}$, of a set A is defined as the set containing all possible fuzzy subsets of A. Using the fuzzy powerset, it is possible to define a fuzzy region similarly as has been done with the powerset in [7]. An example of a level-2 fuzzy region is shown on figure 2.

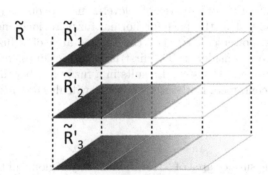

Fig. 2. The concept of a fuzzy region defined over the fuzzy powerset of the two dimensional domain. The region $\tilde{R}$ represents three possible candidates: the regions $\tilde{R}'_1$, $\tilde{R}'_2$ and $\tilde{R}'_3$). These are fuzzy regions that are given a membership grade with a possibilistic interpretation; they are candidates or possibilities.

Definition

$$\tilde{R} = \{(\tilde{R}', \mu_{\tilde{R}}(\tilde{R}'))|\tilde{R}' \in \tilde{\wp}(\mathbb{R}^2)\} \tag{3}$$

with the membership function is defined as:

$$\mu_{\tilde{R}} : \tilde{\wp}(\mathbb{R}^2) \mapsto [0,1]$$
$$\tilde{R}' \to \mu_{\tilde{R}}(\tilde{R}')$$

The elements of the fuzzy region are fuzzy regions as in the original definition. An important difference with the previous definition is that it is now possible that different possible regions share elements: regions are no longer considered as subregions, but rather as candidate regions.

This new definition is what is referred to as a level-2 fuzzy set: a fuzzy set defined over a fuzzy domain ([8], [9]). Most commonly, the interpretation at the second level is possibilistic. It is used to express the possibility of a number of fuzzy candidate elements. This concept is not to be confused with a type-2 fuzzy set ([10]), which is a fuzzy set defined over a crisp domain but with fuzzy membership grades. In type-2 fuzzy sets, uncertainty concerning the membership grades is expressed. While it is possible to use type-2 fuzzy sets to combine both interpretations for fuzzy regions, the level-2 permits us to consider fuzzy regions as candidates (and thus have spatial operations at this lower level). The use of type-2 fuzzy sets would only allow to express different possibilities for different degrees of membership for each point of the universe; it would not allow us to consider regions at a lower level. In [4], it is shown that any statements regarding individual points of the level-2 fuzzy region will result in a type-2 fuzzy set. The model now allows for a region to be represented by a number of fuzzy regions, each with a possibility degree.

3   Surface Area of a Level-2 Fuzzy Region

In this contribution, the surface area of a level-2 fuzzy region will be considered. This has been defined in the past for normal fuzzy regions and fuzzy regions defined using the powerset ([7]). For the surface area of a fuzzy region, two interpretations were considered. The first is an extension of fuzzy cardinality, yielding a crisp number; the second results in a fuzzy number in which possible surface areas are contained. Both interpretations will also be considered for level-2 fuzzy regions.

3.1   Concept

The concept of the surface area of a traditional fuzzy region will be extend to the level-2 fuzzy regions by applying the original definition on the different elements of the level-2 fuzzy region. The surface area for each element (so for each possible region) will be determined and all these areas are then combined to yield a single result. This is illustrated on 3. The approach for the different definitions of the surface area is the same: they will be combined in a fuzzy set; for the above example this will yield as follows:

$$\tilde{S}(\tilde{R}) = \{(\tilde{S}(\tilde{R}'_1), \mu_{\tilde{R}}(\tilde{R}'_1)), (\tilde{S}(\tilde{R}'_2), \mu_{\tilde{R}}(\tilde{R}'_2)), (\tilde{S}(\tilde{R}'_3), \mu_{\tilde{R}}(\tilde{R}'_3))\}$$

In the subsequent sections, the detailed formulas for the surface area calculations are considered.

3.2   Extension of Fuzzy Cardinality

Before we look at the level-2 fuzzy regions, let us first consider the surface area of a fuzzy region. In this interpretation of the surface area, that every element

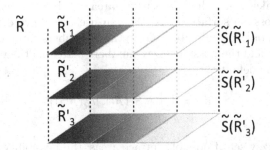

Fig. 3. The surface area of a level-2 fuzzy region. Each candidate region yields a possible surface area.

of the region contributes its membership grade; just like it is the case with fuzzy cardinality. The benefit of this approach is that it allows a single crisp number to give a measurement for the region, while still containing some aspects of the fuzziness.

For a single region candidate region defined using definition 1, the surface area is defined as:

$$\tilde{S}^c(\tilde{R}) = \int_{p(x,y)\in U} \mu_{\tilde{A}}(p(x,y))d(x,y) \tag{4}$$

This has been modified to the extended definition of fuzzy regions (definition 2), in which basic elements themselves can have a surface area:

$$\tilde{S}^c(\tilde{R}) = \int_{X\in\wp(U)} \mu_{\tilde{A}}(X) \int_{p(x,y)\in X} d(x,y)dX \tag{5}$$

While the number gives an indication of the area of the region, the distribution of the fuzziness is lost; this is illustrated on figure 4. A crisp region $\tilde{R}_1$ that covers an area with size x^2, will have the same surface area as a fuzzy region $\tilde{R}_2$ that covers an area of $x/2$ with membership grade 1 and an area of x with membership grade 0.5. Both will result in a surface area of x^2.

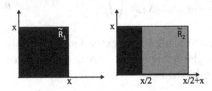

Fig. 4. Two fuzzy regions that yield the same surface area defined as cardinality

To define the surface area for a level-2 fuzzy region, we consider the concept of the level-2 fuzzy region: a fuzzy set containing possible fuzzy regions. This is illustrated on Figure 3, where the surface area for a number of candidate regions is displayed.

As such, it makes sense that the surface area will be represented by a fuzzy set containing possible surface areas. We can use the above definition for the surface area each of the candidate regions; these numbers can then be combined in a fuzzy set to yield the possible fuzzy numbers matching the possible regions. This results in the definition:

$$\tilde{S}^c(\tilde{R}) = \bigcup_{\tilde{R}' \in \tilde{R}} \{(\tilde{S}^c(\tilde{R}'), \mu_{\tilde{R}}(\tilde{R}'))\} \tag{6}$$

The result is a fuzzy set of possible surface areas; the possibility of each surface area matches the possibility of the related candidate fuzzy region. Note that while the fuzzy set representing the possible surface areas is a fuzzy set of the real numeric domain and has a possibilistic interpretation, it is not necessarily a fuzzy number (according to the definition in [9]): not every alpha cut is guaranteed to yield a closed interval.

The compatibility with previous model is obvious from the definition: the previous model for fuzzy regions can be represented using only one level of uncertainty and the compatibility of the surface area for fuzzy regions in defined using definition 2 was already proven in [7].

3.3 Fuzzy Result

In this concept, the surface area of a fuzzy region will be represented by a fuzzy set that reflects the fuzziness of the region. It results in a fuzzy set that contains the surface areas of all alpha-levels. The set is not a fuzzy number, as it carries a veristic interpretation. For a single candidate region defined by definition 1 this was defined in [11], yielding:

$$\tilde{S}^f(\tilde{A}) = \{(x, \mu_{\tilde{S}^f(\tilde{A})}(x)), x \in U\} \tag{7}$$

This was extended in [7] to accommodate definition 2:

$$\tilde{S}^f(\tilde{R}) = \sum_{X | \mu_{\tilde{R}}(X) > 0} \left(\int_{p(x,y) \in X} d(x,y), \mu_{\tilde{R}}(X) \right) \tag{8}$$

Similarly to how the surface area was extended to suit the level-2 fuzzy region in the previous section, the fuzzy surface areas as fuzzy results for each possible region can again be combined here.

$$\tilde{S}^f(\tilde{R}) = \bigcup_{\tilde{R}' \in \tilde{R}} \{(\tilde{S}^f(\tilde{R}'), \mu_{\tilde{R}}(\tilde{R}'))\} \tag{9}$$

Unlike in definition 6 in the previous section, the result now is a level-2 fuzzy set. From its definition, it complies with the previous definition for the fuzzy surface area.

4   Conclusion

In this contribution, the concept of level-2 fuzzy sets was considered; this concept was first defined in [4]. It provides for a unified representation of fuzzy regions, combining both a veristic and a possibilistic interpretation. The model was developed to properly represent regions for which there is knowledge on how the boundaries can change and to allow for more elegant unified definitions. The calculation of the surface area of level-2 fuzzy regions results in two definitions, one considering a surface area as a measure for cardinality; the other maintaining the fuzziness. The definitions for the surface area are still compatible with the original models and with crisp models.

References

1. Clementini, E., Di Felice, P.: An algebraic model for spatial objects with undetermined boundaries. GISDATA Specialist Meeting - revised version (1994)
2. Cohn, A., Gotts, N.M.: Spatial regions with undetermined boundaries. In: Proceedings of the Second ACM Workshop on Advances in GIS, pp. 52–59 (1994)
3. Verstraete, J., De Tré, G., De Caluwe, R., Hallez, A.: Field based methods for the modelling of fuzzy spatial data. In: Fred, P., Vince, R., Maria, C. (eds.) Fuzzy Modeling with Spatial Information for Geographic Problems, pp. 41–69. Springer, Heidelberg (2005)
4. Verstraete, J.: Using Level-2 Fuzzy Sets to Combine Uncertainty and Imprecision in Fuzzy Regions. In: Mugellini, E., Szczepaniak, P.S., Pettenati, M.C., Sokhn, M. (eds.) AWIC 2011. AISC, vol. 86, pp. 163–172. Springer, Heidelberg (2011)
5. Zadeh, L.A.: Fuzzy sets. Information and Control 8, 338–353 (1965)
6. Dubois, D., Prade, H.: The three semantics of fuzzy sets. Fuzzy Sets and Systems 90, 141–150 (1999)
7. Verstraete, J.: Fuzzy Regions: Adding Subregions and the Impact on Surface and Distance Calculation. In: Hüllermeier, E., Kruse, R., Hoffmann, F. (eds.) IPMU 2010. CCIS, vol. 80, pp. 561–570. Springer, Heidelberg (2010)
8. Gottwald, S.: Set theory for fuzzy sets of higher level. Fuzzy sets and systems 2(2), 125–151 (1979)
9. Klir, G.J., Yuan, B.: Fuzzy sets and fuzzy logic: theory and applications. Prentice Hall, New Jersey (1995)
10. Mendel, J.M.: Uncertain rule-based fuzzy logic systems, Introduction and new directions. Prentice Hall (2001)
11. Verstraete, J.: Fuzzy regions: interpretations of surface area and distance. Control & Cybernetics 38(2), 509–526 (2009)

Fuzzy Neural Gas for Unsupervised Vector Quantization

Thomas Villmann, Tina Geweniger, Marika Kästner, and Mandy Lange

Computational Intelligence Group at the Department for Mathematics/Natural &
Computer Sciences,
University of Applied Sciences Mittweida, Mittweida, Germany

Abstract. In this paper we propose the combination of fuzzy c-means
for clustering with neighborhood cooperativeness from the neural gas vector quantizer. The new approach avoids the sensitivity of fuzzy c-means
with respect to initialization as it is known from neural gas compared
to crisp c-means. Thereby, the neural gas paradigm of neighborhood offers a greater flexibility than those of the self-organizing map, which was
combined with fuzzy c-means before. However, a careful reformulation
of neighborhood has to be done to keep the validity of the convergence
proof of this previous approach. We demonstrate the properties for an
artificial as well as for real world data.

1 Introduction

The fuzzy c-means algorithm is one of the most prominent fuzzy clustering algorithms [3,9]. It is a generalization of the classic crisp c-means but inherit-
ing the sensitivity according to initialization. For crisp c-means this problem
was overcome by incorporation of neighborhood cooperativeness as known from
cortical maps in brains. The most famous model for this paradigm is the self-
organizing map (SOM) introduced by T. KOHONEN [17], assuming an external
grid structure between the prototypes, usually a regular hypercubical structure
A. However, other lattice structures are possible with a respective grid distance
measures. For example, general graphs would require the distance taken as
shortest paths [28].

Generally, neighborhood cooperativeness improves vector quantization performance and convergence speed as well as stability of the vector quantization
solution. This SOM concept was also adopted for FCM yielding fuzzy SOM
(FSOM,[6,5,7,23,24,27]). A similar algorithm for fuzzy clustering combined with
topographic learning based on SOMs was also suggested for the soft-topographic
vector quantization based on statistical physics (STVQ,[12]).

Otherwise, for crisp vector quantization, the neural gas algorithm (NG) using
a dynamic prototype based neighborhood generally shows better performance
than SOM [20]. This is mainly dedicated to the flexible neighborhood relations
between the prototypes. Therefore, we propose in this paper the combination
of FCM with neighborhood cooperativeness adopted from NG. The resulting

L. Rutkowski et al. (Eds.): ICAISC 2012, Part I, LNCS 7267, pp. 350–358, 2012.

fuzzy neural gas (FNG) shows stable behavior and good performance as we demonstrate for artificial and real world data.

The paper is organized as follows: First we briefly review FCM and NG to clarify notations and give some details about the underlying theory. Thereafter, we present the new FNG and give suggestions for extensions and variants. The experimental section shows exemplary applications to emphasize the advantages of the new algorithm.

2 Fuzzy c-Means and Neural Gas

In this section we briefly introduce the two basic vector quantizers needed for definition of FNG. The first is the classic fuzzy c-means (FCM) as the fuzzy vector quantization scheme based on an alternating optimization scheme. The other one is the neural gas algorithm as generalization of c-means, which incorporates neighborhood cooperativeness for robust vector quantization.

In the following we assume a data set $V = \{\mathbf{v}_i\}_{i=1}^N \subseteq \mathbb{R}^n$ and a set $W = \{\mathbf{w}_k\}_{k=1}^C \subset \mathbb{R}^n$ of prototypes. Further, we suppose an inner product norm $d_{i,k} = d(\mathbf{v}_i, \mathbf{w}_k)$ between data and prototypes, frequently the Euclidean distance.

2.1 The Fuzzy c-Means Algorithm

For the FCM many variants are proposed such as for relational data [4] or median clustering [10] or using several kinds of dissimilarities like divergences [16,30] or kernels [15]. The original FCM model determines for each data point $\mathbf{v}_i \in V$ and prototype $\mathbf{w}_k \in W$ an assignment $u_{i,k} \in [0,1]$, which is interpreted as the possibility that this data vector is associated with this particular prototype. In FCM the assignments are restricted according to

$$\sum_k u_{i,k} = 1 \tag{1}$$

Thus, FCM is probabilistic and the crisp c-means model is obtained for the additional conditions $u_{i,k} \in \{0,1\}$ [8,19]. The FCM minimizes the cost function

$$E_{FCM}(\mathbf{U}, V, W) = \sum_{k=1}^C \sum_{i=1}^N (u_{i,k})^m (d_{i,k})^2 \tag{2}$$

where $m > 1$ is the fuzziness parameter usually chosen as $m = 2$ [3,9]. The iterated optimization scheme consists of the alternating optimization of the prototypes

$$\mathbf{w}_k = \frac{\sum_{i=1}^N (u_{i,k})^m \mathbf{v}_i}{\sum_{i=1}^N (u_{i,k})^m} \tag{3}$$

accompanied by the optimization of the fuzzy assignments

$$u_{i,k} = \frac{1}{\sum_{l=1}^C \left(\frac{d_{i,k}}{d_{i,l}}\right)^{\frac{2}{m-1}}} \tag{4}$$

derived as the solution of the Lagrange-minimization problem

$$J(\mathbf{U}, V, W, \lambda) = E_{FCM}(\mathbf{U}, V, W) - \sum_{i=1}^{N} \left(\lambda_i \left(\sum_{k=1}^{C} u_{i,k} - 1 \right) \right) \tag{5}$$

with Lagrange multipliers $\lambda = (\lambda_1, \ldots, \lambda_N)$. Here in (3) the assumption of the Euclidean distance for $d_{i,k}$ was made. Variants relax the condition (1) or/and avoid the collapsing of the algorithm for vanishing distances $d_{i,k}$ in (4) [18,22].

2.2   The Neural Gas Vector Quantizer

An alternative to the external grid enforced neighborhood cooperativeness between prototypes used in SOMs is provided for the neural gas (NG) vector quantizer [20]. This approach uses a dynamic neighborhood between the prototypes determined in the data space V. This flexible neighborhood leads to the fact that NG usually outperforms SOM in crisp vector quantization. In NG the neighborhood between prototypes for a given data vector $\mathbf{v}_i \in V$ is based on the winning rank of each prototype $\mathbf{w}_k$

$$rk_k(\mathbf{v}_i, W) = \sum_{l=1}^{N} \Theta(d(\mathbf{v}_i, \mathbf{w}_k) - d(\mathbf{v}_i, \mathbf{w}_l)) \tag{6}$$

where

$$\Theta(x) = \begin{cases} 0 \ \ if \ x \leq 0 \\ 1 \ else \end{cases} \tag{7}$$

is the Heaviside function [20]. The NG neighborhood function includes the ranks according to

$$\hat{h}_\sigma^{NG}(k|\mathbf{v}_i) = c_\sigma^{NG} \cdot \exp\left(-\frac{(rk_k(\mathbf{v}_i, W))^2}{2\sigma^2} \right) \tag{8}$$

with neighborhood range σ with an arbitrary constant $c_\sigma^{NG} > 0$. Then, NG minimizes the cost function

$$E_{NG} = \frac{1}{2K(\sigma)} \sum_{j=1}^{C} \int P(\mathbf{v}) \hat{h}_\sigma^{NG}(j|\mathbf{v}) (d(\mathbf{v}, \mathbf{w}_j))^2 \, d\mathbf{v} \tag{9}$$

with the winner-take-all mapping rule

$$s(\mathbf{v}_i) = \operatorname{argmin}_j (d(\mathbf{v}_i, \mathbf{w}_j)) \tag{10}$$

determining the best matching prototype $\mathbf{w}_s$. The constant $K(\sigma)$ depends on the choice of c_σ^{NG} and could be combined. However, we explicitly need c_σ^{NG} later to be defined appropriately in FNG.

3   The Fuzzy Neural Gas

We now integrate the NG into FCM. Thereby, the aim is to use the theory of FSOM provided in [6,5,7,23,24,27]. For this purpose, we have to verify a fixed graph structure between the prototypes while incorporating the neighborhood cooperativeness. Originally, there is no neighborhood between the prototypes in NG but this information is implicitly given by the winner ranks $rk_k\left(\mathbf{v}_i, W\right)$ defined in (6). We now redefine the neighborhood function of NG and introduce a gradual neighborhood relation between prototypes $\mathbf{w}_k$ and $\mathbf{w}_l$ by

$$h_\sigma^{NG}\left(k|\mathbf{w}_l\right) = c_\sigma^{NG} \cdot \exp\left(-\frac{\left(rk_k\left(\mathbf{w}_l, W\right)\right)^2}{2\sigma^2}\right) \tag{11}$$

for a given neighborhood range σ with the normalization constant c_σ^{NG} such that $\sum_l h_\sigma^{NG}\left(k|\mathbf{w}_l\right) = 1$. It can be shown that this redefinition leads to a NG variant structurally equivalent to the original NG [29]. Moreover, in the convergence phase in the vicinity of the equilibrium the respective neighborhood structure becomes stable due to the stability of optimal packing by $\mathbb{R}^n$-balls with respect to small distortions. Thus, we can interpret the resulting structure as an (irregular) external grid A equipped with the graph distance of shortest paths.

Under these assumptions we define the local cost

$$lc_\sigma^{NG}\left(i, k\right) = \sum_{l=1}^{C} h_\sigma^{NG}\left(k|\mathbf{w}_l\right) \cdot \left(d_{i,l}\right)^2, \tag{12}$$

which can be immediately plugged into FCM instead of the quadratic dissimilarities $\left(d_{i,k}\right)^2$. In this way we obtain a FCM variant with neighborhood cooperativeness denoted as Fuzzy Neural Gas (FNG). The cost function of FNG is

$$E_{FNG}\left(\mathbf{U}, V, W, \sigma\right) = \sum_{k=1}^{C} \sum_{i=1}^{N} \left(u_{i,k}\right)^m lc_\sigma^{NG}\left(i, k\right) \tag{13}$$

and the prototype adaptation is obtained by the Lagrange formalism as proposed for the FSOM:

$$\mathbf{w}_k = \frac{\sum_{i=1}^{N} \sum_{l=1}^{C} \left(u_{i,k}\right)^m \cdot h_\sigma^{NG}\left(k, l\right) \cdot \mathbf{v}_i}{\sum_{i=1}^{N} \sum_{l=1}^{C} \left(u_{i,k}\right)^m \cdot h_\sigma^{NG}\left(k, l\right)} \tag{14}$$

if the Euclidean distance is used for $d_{i,k}$ (or equivalently for inner product based metrics). Analogously, the adaptation of the fuzzy assignments $\left(u_{i,l}\right)^m$ in the FNG are as before defined for FCM in (4) but replacing there the dissimilarity measure $\left(d_{i,k}\right)^2$ by the local costs $lc_\sigma^{NG}\left(i, k\right)$ as in FSOM

$$u_{i,k} = \frac{1}{\sum_{l=1}^{C} \left(\frac{lc_\sigma^{NG}(i,k)}{lc_\sigma^{NG}(i,l)}\right)^{\frac{1}{m-1}}}. \tag{15}$$

As usual, the neighborhood range σ should be decreased adiabatically in an outer loop for optimum performance. However, it has to be mentioned here that this adiabatic decreasing of the neighborhood range σ is not equivalent to an annealing approach based on a free energy depending on this parameter σ [31].

Finally, it should be noticed at this point that the FNG is not restricted to the Euclidean distance for the inner product norms $d_{i,k}$. More general dissimilarity measures are obviously applicable like, for example, the scaled Euclidean distance [14] or generalizations thereof, (kernelized) divergences [30] or other generalized dissimilarity measures [25]. Further, the transfer to the other variants like probabilistic approaches [18,22] or entropy based fuzzy c-means [21,33,11] is obviously straightforward.

4 Experiments

For the verification of the FNG we have chosen two examples: The first one is a multimodal two-dimensional artificial data set, also known as checkerboard, with 4×4 Gausssian squares each consisting of 50 data points (see Fig.1). This experiment shows the ability of FNG to handle multimodal data sets. Accordingly, we run the FNG with 16 prototypes. The positions of the learned prototypes are shown in Fig.1 together with prototype distributiones obtained from standard NG and standard FCM. The FNG as well as standard NG provide a good distribution of the prototypes, one prototype per cluster. The FCM highly depends on the initialization of the prototypes due to the missing neighborhood and, hence, frequently fails the optimal solution.

The second data set, a real world example, consists of hyperspectral vectors of different coffee type samples. Hyperspectral processing along with an appropriate analysis of the acquired high-dimensional spectra has proven to be a suitable and very powerful method to quantitatively assess the biochemical composition of a wide range of biological samples [13,26,2]. By utilizing a hyperspectral camera (HySpex SWIR-320m-e, Norsk Elektro Optikk A/S) we obtained a rather extensive data base of spectra of the different coffee samples (green beans, roasted beans, ground powder). The acquired spectra are in the short-wave infrared range between 970 nm and 2,500 nm at 6 nm resolution yielding 256 bands per spectrum. Proper image calibration was done by using a standard reflection pad (polytetrafluoroethylene, PTFE) [1]. After appropriate image segmentation the obtained spectra were normalized according to the l_2-norm.

The database used in this experiment contains spectra of overall 5 roasted, ground powder, untreated coffee types. In particular, these coffee samples are verified to be not treated chemically before roasting. They all were roasted in the same small exclusive roasting facility using a more or less similar processing scheme. The overall number of spectra is 5000, whereby each coffee type is represented by 1000 samples. Representitives are depicted in Fig.2. We applied FNG and again, for comparison, NG and FCM with $C = 5$ prototypes.

The agreement of the different cluster solutions is judged by two cluster validity measures, to reflect different aspects of cluster quality. We used the XB-index [32].

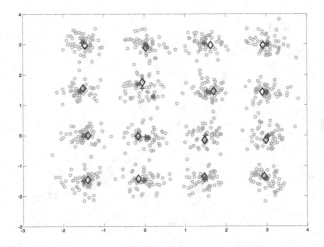

Fig. 1. Checkerboard data set of the size 4×4 with the learned prototypes of NG ($+$), FCM ($\star$) and FNG ($\Diamond$)

$$XB(W,V,\mathbf{U}) = \frac{\sum_{k=1}^{C} \sum_{i=1}^{N} (u_{i,k})^m \cdot (d(\mathbf{v}_i, \mathbf{w}_k))^2}{\frac{1}{C} \sum_{i=1}^{C} \min_{j \in \mathcal{C}, j \neq i} (d(\mathbf{w}_i, \mathbf{w}_j))^2}$$

as the ratio between compactness and seperation. Here the compactness in counter is measured as the *weighted mean* of the distances with assignments as weighting factors. A small XB value means high separation and good compactness. The SVF-index [34] is defined as

$$SVF(W,V,\mathbf{U}) = \frac{\sum_{i=1}^{C} \min_{j \in \mathcal{C}, j \neq i} (d(\mathbf{w}_i, \mathbf{w}_j))^2}{\sum_{k=1}^{C} \max_{\mathbf{v}_j \in V} \; u_{j,k}^m \cdot (d(\mathbf{v}_j, \mathbf{w}_k))^2}$$

whereby the compactnes in the denominator is estimated as the *maximum* of all weighted distance. Hence, a high SVF-value means here a good cluster solution.

For the crisp results of NG we simply set:

$$u_{i,k} = \begin{cases} 1 & if \quad s(\mathbf{v}_i) = k \\ 0 & otherwise \end{cases}$$

using the mapping rule (10).

The results for the different algorithms and validity measures are depicted in Table 1 obtained from 10 runs of each. Obviously, the FNG provides good cluster results for the artificial and the real world data set. For the multimodal checkerboard problem FNG clearly outperforms both, NG and FCM. The variance of the FCM is comparatively high indicating high sensitivity with respect to the initialization of the prototypes. Yet, in case of the real world coffee data set the judgements of the XB and SVF disagree with respect to FNG and FCM

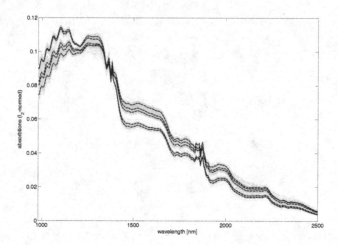

Fig. 2. Spectra of untreated coffee sorts with the learned prototypes of FNG (dashed)

but both are better than crisp NG. This disagreement maybe dedicated to the diffferent aspects emphasized by the respective measures.

Table 1. Clustering results for the checkerboard data set and the coffeee data set

Checkerboard	NG	FCM	FNG	Coffee	NG	FCM	FNG
SVF (10^{-2})	5.40	7.31	7.53	SVF (10^{-3})	2.15	3.26	3.11
variance (10^{-7})	0.004	1.392	0.865	variance (10^{-8})	0.21	2.3	3.3
XB	0.234	0.264	0.183	XB	0.565	0.522	0.467
variance	$8.49 \cdot 10^{-6}$	0.022	0.013	variance (10^{-3})	0.15	3.4	5.1

5   Conclusion

We proposed in this contribution a new variant of FCM using the concept of neighborhood cooperativeness. This paradigm is well-suited in robust neural maps for crisp vector quantization. Here, the dynamic neighborhood scheme of NG is used instead of a neighborhood defined by an external grid as known from SOMs and already earlier transferred to FCM. The resulting FNG shows good performance compared to standard FCM and crisp NG. Further, due to the neighborhood cooperativeness, a robust stability with respect to initialization of the prototypes is achieved while keeping the high quality. It is straightforward, to apply this scheme to other fuzzy variants of c-means (PCM, FPCM,...) as well as utilization of other distance measures [30].

Acknowledgement. We would like to thank Prof. Udo Seiffert from Fraunhofer-Institute Magdeburg (IFF), Biosystems and Engineering Group, for carrying out the spectral measurements for the coffee samples and the *Ganos Kaffeerösterei Leipzig* for providing the coffee.

References

1. Backhaus, A., Bollenbeck, F., Seiffert, U.: High-throughput quality control of coffee varieties and blends by artificial neural networks and hyperspectral imaging. In: Proceedings of the 1st International Congress on Cocoa, Coffee and Tea, CoCoTea 2011, accepted for publication (2011)
2. Backhaus, A., Bollenbeck, F., Seiffert, U.: Robust classification of the nutrition state in crop plants by hyperspectral imaging and artificial neural networks. In: Proceedings of the 3rd IEEE Workshop on Hyperspectral Imaging and Signal Processing: Evolution in Remote Sensing WHISPERS 2011, p. 9. IEEE Press (2011)
3. Bezdek, J.: Pattern Recognition with Fuzzy Objective Function Algorithms. Plenum, New York (1981)
4. Bezdek, J., Hathaway, R., Windham, M.: Numerical comparison of RFCM and AP algorithms for clustering relational data. Pattern Recognition 24, 783–791 (1991)
5. Bezdek, J.C., Pal, N.R.: A note on self-organizing semantic maps. IEEE Transactions on Neural Networks 6(5), 1029–1036 (1995)
6. Bezdek, J.C., Pal, N.R.: Two soft relatives of learning vector quantization. Neural Networks 8(5), 729–743 (1995)
7. Bezdek, J.C., Tsao, E.C.K., Pal, N.R.: Fuzzy Kohonen clustering networks. In: Proc. IEEE International Conference on Fuzzy Systems, pp. 1035–1043. IEEE Service Center, Piscataway (1992)
8. Duda, R., Hart, P.: Pattern Classification and Scene Analysis. Wiley, New York (1973)
9. Dunn, J.: A fuzzy relative of the ISODATA process and its use in detecting compact well-separated clusters. Journal of Cybernetics 3, 32–57 (1973)
10. Geweniger, T., Zühlke, D., Hammer, B., Villmann, T.: Median fuzzy c-means for clustering dissimilarity data. Neurocomputing 73(7-9), 1109–1116 (2010)
11. Ghorbani, M.: Maximum entropy-based fuzzy clustering by using L_1 norm space. Turkish Journal of Mathematics 29(4), 431–438 (2005)
12. Graepel, T., Burger, M., Obermayer, K.: Self-organizing maps: generalizations and new optimization techniques. Neurocomputing 21(1-3), 173–190 (1998)
13. Grahn, H., Geladi, P. (eds.): Techniques and Applications of Hyperspectral Image Analysis. Wiley (2007)
14. Hammer, B., Villmann, T.: Generalized relevance learning vector quantization. Neural Networks 15(8-9), 1059–1068 (2002)
15. Ichihashi, H., Honda, K.: Application of kernel trick to fuzzy c-means with regularization by K-L information. Journal of Advanced Computational Intelligence and Intelligent Informatics 8(6), 566–572 (2004)
16. Inokuchi, R., Miyamoto, S.: Fuzzy c-means algorithms using Kullback-Leibler divergence and Hellinger distance based on multinomial manifold. Journal of Advanced Computational Intelligence and Intelligent Informatics 12(5), 443–447 (2008)
17. Kohonen, T.: Self-Organizing Maps. Springer Series in Information Sciences, vol. 30. Springer, Heidelberg (1995) (Second Extended Edition 1997)
18. Krishnapuram, R., Keller, J.: A possibilistic approach to clustering. IEEE Transactions on Fuzzy Systems 1(4), 98–110 (1993)
19. Linde, Y., Buzo, A., Gray, R.: An algorithm for vector quantizer design. IEEE Transactions on Communications 28, 84–95 (1980)
20. Martinetz, T.M., Berkovich, S.G., Schulten, K.J.: 'Neural-gas' network for vector quantization and its application to time-series prediction. IEEE Trans. on Neural Networks 4(4), 558–569 (1993)

21. Miyamoto, S., Ichihashi, H., Honda, K.: Algorithms for Fuzzy Clustering. Studies in Fuzziness and Soft Computing, vol. 229. Springer, Heidelberg (2008)
22. Pal, N., Pal, K., Keller, J., Bezdek, J.: A possibilistic fuzzy c-means clustering algorithm. IEEE Transactions on Fuzzy Systems 13(4), 517–530 (2005)
23. Pal, N.R., Bezdek, J.C., Tsao, E.C.K.: Generalized clustering networks and Kohonen's self-organizing scheme. IEEE Transactions on Neural Networks 4(4), 549–557 (1993)
24. Pal, N.R., Bezdek, J.C., Tsao, E.C.K.: Errata to Generalized clustering networks and Kohonen's self-organizing scheme. IEEE Transactions on Neural Networks 6(2), 521–521 (1995)
25. Pekalska, E., Duin, R.: The Dissimilarity Representation for Pattern Recognition: Foundations and Applications. World Scientific (2006)
26. Seiffert, U., Bollenbeck, F., Mock, H.-P., Matros, A.: Clustering of crop phenotypes by means of hyperspectral signatures using artificial neural networks. In: Proceedings of the 2nd IEEE Workshop on Hyperspectral Imaging and Signal Processing: Evolution in Remote Sensing WHISPERS 2010, pp. 31–34. IEEE Press (2010)
27. Tsao, E., Bezdek, J., Pal, N.: Fuzzy Kohonen clustering networks. Pattern Recognition 27(5), 757–764 (1994)
28. Villmann, T., Der, R., Herrmann, M., Martinetz, T.: Topology Preservation in Self–Organizing Feature Maps: Exact Definition and Measurement. IEEE Transactions on Neural Networks 8(2), 256–266 (1997)
29. Villmann, T., Geweniger, T., Kästner, M., Lange, M.: Theory of fuzzy neural gas for unsupervised vector quantization. Machine Learning Reports 5(MLR-06-2011), 27–46 (2011),
http://www.techfak.uni-bielefeld.de/~fschleif/mlr/mlr_06_2011.pdf
ISSN:1865-3960
30. Villmann, T., Haase, S.: Divergence based vector quantization. Neural Computation 23(5), 1343–1392 (2011)
31. Villmann, T., Hammer, B., Biehl, M.: Some Theoretical Aspects of the Neural Gas Vector Quantizer. In: Biehl, M., Hammer, B., Verleysen, M., Villmann, T. (eds.) Similarity-Based Clustering. LNCS (LNAI), vol. 5400, pp. 23–34. Springer, Heidelberg (2009)
32. Xie, X., Beni, G.: A validity measure for fuzzy clustering. IEEE Transactions on Pat 13(8), 841–847 (1991)
33. Yasuda, M., Furuhashi, T.: Fuzzy entropy based fuzzy-c-means clustering with deterministic and simulated annealing methods. IEICE Transactions on Information and Systems E92-D, 1232–1239 (2009)
34. Zalik, K., Zalik, B.: Validity index for clusters of different sizes and densities. Pattern Recognition Letters 32, 221–2234 (2011)

Fuzzy Epoch-Incremental Reinforcement Learning Algorithm

Roman Zajdel

Faculty of Electrical and Computer Engineering,
Rzeszow University of Technology, W. Pola 2, 35-959 Rzeszow, Poland
rzajdel@prz.edu.pl

Abstract. The new epoch-incremental reinforcement learning algorithm with fuzzy approximation of action-value function is developed. This algorithm is practically tested in the control of the mobile robot which realizes goal seeking behavior. The obtained results are compared with results of fuzzy version of reinforcement learning algorithms, such as Q(0)-learning, Q(λ)-learning, Dyna-learning and prioritized sweeping. The adaptation of the fuzzy approximator to the model based reinforcement learning algorithms is also proposed.

Keywords: reinforcement learning, fuzzy approximation, epoch-incremental algorithm.

1 Introduction

Reinforcement learning addresses the problem of the agent that must learn to perform a task through trial and error interaction with an unknown environment [11]. There has been a lot of algorithms proposed that successfully implemented the above idea. The fundamental reinforcement algorithms, e.g. Q-learning [13], AHC [2], or Sarsa [9] are characterized by a high simplicity which leads to low computational complexity. However, their efficiency measured by the number of trials necessary to achieve stable optimal strategy is low. The significant improvement in reinforcement learning algorithms' performance is obtained by the use of the eligibility traces. The next stage within development of the algorithms resulting in the achievement of stable strategy after smaller number of trials is the implementation of environment model. Two algorithms are worth paying attention here, i.e. Dyna-learning [10] and prioritized sweeping [7], [8]. The main idea behind these algorithms is the computation, in each iteration, an additional number of assumed number of action-value function actualizations not on the basis of interactions with a real environment, but its model.

The first reinforcement learning algorithms were implemented in the environment of continuous state variables [2]. They used table representation of action-value function which was not adequate for continuous state variables. A better solution would be to apply a continuous function approximator. A lot of attention has been paid to fuzzy approximator [3], in particular Takagi-Sugeno system [4], [5], [15]. The Takagi-Sugeno system adaptation was applied to model based reinforcement learning algorithm i.e. prioritized sweeping [1], but this solution is not widely used. In this work the new adaptation of fuzzy approximation to model based reinforcement learning system will be proposed.

The another approach which allows to decrease the number of trials necessary to determine stable strategy consists in the use of the environment model in epoch mode, i.e. after completion of single trial [14]. In [14] the epoch–incremental algorithm with table representation of action-value function was described. In this work the adaptation of action-value function fuzzy approximator to the algorithm in [14] will be provided. The proposed algorithm is applied to the control of Khepera mobile robot [6].

2   Fuzzy Epoch-Incremental Reinforcement Learning Algorithm

The main idea behind the model based algorithms is to use the environment model in the incremental mode, which leads to significant increase of single iteration time. In case of the stationary environment it is possible to regard the use of the environment model in epoch mode. It makes single iteration time similar to the time of fundamental reinforcement learning algorithms. The modification of the action-value function on basis of the distance of the past active states from the terminal state should impose the optimal strategy.

The epoch-incremental reinforcement learning algorithm is performed in two stages. The first, incremental stage, is realized until the terminal stage is achieved. Then the epoch stage begins, whose task is to modify the agent strategy by using the distances between all visited stages and the terminal one [14]. The following section presents the adaptation of action-value function fuzzy approximator to this algorithm. Such an epoch-incremental reinforcement learning algorithm is denoted from now on as EIFQ(0)-learning.

2.1   Incremental Part

In the incremental part of the method the fuzzy Q(0)-learning algorithm (in short: FQ(0)-learning) is performed and the environment model is created.

FQ(0)-Learning. The goal of a fuzzy approximator is to transform N-dimensional state space $\mathbf{s}$ to a real-valued action function a_i and its corresponding action-value function q_i. Each n-th ($n = 1, .., N$) input state domain is covered by fuzzy sets denoted by A_{ni}, where $i = 1, .., I$ is the rule index. Each fuzzy set is characterised by the membership function $\mu_{A_{ni}}$. In order to fuzzy-approximate the action-value function $Q(\mathbf{s}, a)$, the Takagi-Sugeno fuzzy inference system is used with $if \ ... \ then \ ...$ rule base. For the system with N input states the rule base consisted of I rules can be written as follows:

$$R_i: \text{If } s_1 \text{ is } A_{1i} \text{ and } ... \ s_N \text{ is } A_{Ni} \text{ then } a \text{ is } a_i \text{ with } q_i,$$

where a is the output of the fuzzy system and q_i is the discrete action-value associated to the action value a_i. Thus, the action-value prediction is an output of the Takagi-Sugeno inference system and it is given by [4]:

$$Q\left(\mathbf{s}, a\right) = \sum_{i=1}^{I} \left[\bar{\beta}_i\left(\mathbf{s}\right) \cdot q_i\left(\mathbf{s}, a\right)\right], \tag{1}$$

where

$$\bar{\beta}_i\left(\mathbf{s}\right) = \frac{\beta_i\left(\mathbf{s}\right)}{\sum_{i=1}^{I} \beta_i\left(\mathbf{s}\right)} \tag{2}$$

is the normalized activation of the i-th premise (or simple fuzzy rule) where:

$$\beta_i\left(\mathbf{s}\right) = \mu_{A_{1i}}\left(s_1\right) \cdot \mu_{A_{2i}}\left(s_2\right) \cdot \ldots \cdot \mu_{A_{Ni}}\left(s_N\right). \tag{3}$$

The update of q_i function for all active states is computed as:

$$q_i\left(\mathbf{s}, a\right) \leftarrow q_i\left(\mathbf{s}, a\right) + \alpha \bar{\beta}_i\left(\mathbf{s}\right) \Delta Q\left(\mathbf{s}, a\right), \tag{4}$$

where

$$\Delta Q\left(\mathbf{s}, a\right) = r + \gamma \max_{a'} Q\left(\mathbf{s}', a'\right) - Q\left(\mathbf{s}, a\right). \tag{5}$$

is the temporal differences error [11]. In (5) $\gamma \in [0, 1]$ is a discount rate constant, and $\beta \in (0, 1]$ is the learning rate. The maximization operator refers to the action value a' which may be performed in next state $\mathbf{s}'$. The next stage of the incremental part is the construction of the environment model, which is presented below.

Environment Model for Fuzzy Aproximation of Action-Value Function. The EIFQ(0)-learning algorithm, Dyna-learning and prioritized sweeping use the model of the environment. In the case of a discreet environment this model is a probability of execution of an action a in state $\mathbf{s}$ and a transition to $\mathbf{s}'$ what usually is formalized by the equation $p\left(\mathbf{s}, a, \mathbf{s}'\right) = N\left(\mathbf{s}, a, \mathbf{s}'\right) / N\left(\mathbf{s}, a\right)$ where $N\left(\mathbf{s}, a\right)$ denotes the number of times in which action a is executed in state $\mathbf{s}$, and $N\left(\mathbf{s}, a, \mathbf{s}'\right)$ is the number of times resulting in transition to state $\mathbf{s}'$ [7].

In case of the fuzzy approximation a state is represented by means of degree of activation vector of all fuzzy rules $\beta\left(\mathbf{s}\right) = [\beta_1(\mathbf{s}), .., \beta_i(\mathbf{s}), .., \beta_I(\mathbf{s})]$. The algorithms which use the environment model require unambiguous numerical representation of each state in order to perform sorting of the visited states or to assess their distances from terminal stat. If the shapes of fuzzy sets are assumed in the way that their supports are not identical with a domain of a state variable, then not all the elements of β vector are greater than zero. For example, the triangular or trapezoidal fuzzy sets, in contrast to the Gaussian ones, fulfill this requirement. On the basis of this observation the new numerical representation of fuzzy state is proposed:

$$\tilde{s} = \beta\left(\mathbf{s}\right) \cdot \mathbf{c}^T, \tag{6}$$

where $\mathbf{c} = \begin{bmatrix} c^1, .., c^i, .., c^I \end{bmatrix}$ is a vector of powers of some small real number. Then the probability that, after the execution of the action a in state $\tilde{s}$, the system transits to state $\tilde{s}'$ can be defined as:

$$p(\tilde{s}, a, \tilde{s}') = \frac{N(\tilde{s}, a, \tilde{s}')}{N(\tilde{s}, a)}. \tag{7}$$

The numbers $N(\tilde{s}, a, \tilde{s}')$ and $N(\tilde{s}, a)$ are actualized in each iteration according to the rules: $N(\tilde{s}, a, \tilde{s}') \leftarrow N(\tilde{s}, a, \tilde{s}') + 1$ and $N(\tilde{s}, a) \leftarrow N(\tilde{s}, a) + 1$.

2.2   Epoch Part

The epoch part of the algorithm begins after the terminal stage of the agent is achieved $\tilde{s}' = TERMINAL$. Thereafter, starting form the terminal stage for $p(\tilde{s}, a, TERMINAL) > 0$, one computes these actions a, which provide the transition from the state $\tilde{s}$ to the next, $TERMINAL$ state, and then only for $(\tilde{s}, a)$ pairs one assigns the distance from the terminal state. This procedure repeats for the states preceding the states computed previously until for each visited state, the action a and the distance d are assigned. In this way for all visited states s the suboptimal strategy is calculated [14]. Next, the actualization of these elements of fuzzy approximation of action-value function is performed for which the distance d is assigned according to formula:

$$q(\mathbf{s}, a) \leftarrow q(\mathbf{s}, a) + \alpha \cdot \beta(\mathbf{s}) \cdot \left(r \cdot (\gamma\lambda)^d + \gamma \max_{a'} Q'(a') - Q(a) \right), \tag{8}$$

where r is the reinforcement signal received after the terminal state, and $\lambda \in (0, 1]$ is - by analogy with TD(λ) algorithm - the recency factor. The inspiration of the multiplication of the reinforcement signal by $\gamma\lambda$ coefficient was the observation of the TD(λ) algorithm performance, in which the eligibility trace of state-action pairs was decreased by this factor in each iteration. It is worth noticing that in TD(λ) method, all the elements of the action-value function were actualized in the degree which depends on the distance from the actual state. In case of epoch-incremental algorithm, the actualizations are performed only for these elements of action-value function Q which are responsible for suboptimal strategy determined on the basis of the shorted distance to the absorbing state.

3   Empirical Results

In this work the comparison experiments were carried out on Khepera III mobile robot (Fig. 1). Khepera III is the cylindrical mobile robot equipped with two driving wheels mounted $2R = 88mm$ from each other. In Fig. 2 the sizes of the robot in the start position are doubled. The goal of the tested algorithms was to navigate the robot from the starting point with $(0, 0)$ coordinates to eight points placed in the environment of the robot. The coordinates of the goal points are the following: $(7R, 7R)$, $(-7R, -7R)$, $(-7R, 0)$, $(-7R, 7R)$, $(0, -7R)$, $(7R, -7R)$, $(0, 7R)$, $(7R, 0)$. The goal points are marked in Fig. 2 by means of the circles (of radius R) with the numbers inside which denoted the order of robot arrival. It was assumed that the goal point was reached by the robot when the distance from the robot to this point was less than R. The robot was moved to the staring point after each of the goal points was visited. The goal seeking task, illustrated in Fig. 2, amounts to turning the robot into the goal point (minimization of the turning angle ψ) and then moving forward (minimization of the robot-goal point distance z). The state variables z and ψ were covered by two and three triangle fuzzy sets, respectively [12]. In all the algorithms the value of the actualization coefficient of the fuzzy approximator α was set to 0.1, discount rate γ to 0.995 and in FQ(λ)-learning algorithm the recency factor $\lambda = 0.1$. Additionally, in fuzzy Dyna-learning and fuzzy prioritized sweeping, the number of actualizations performed by using the environment model took the value of 6. In order to choose the action the ϵ-greedy strategy was applied in which $\epsilon = 0.1$. The reinforcement signal was defined as follows:

$$r = \begin{cases} -\frac{|\psi|}{\pi} - \frac{z}{10R}, & \text{for } z > R \\ 0, & \text{for } z \leqslant R. \end{cases} \qquad (9)$$

The reinforcement signal decreased its value along with both the increase of the distance and the turning away from the goal point. Because of the similar shape of the trajectory of the robot movement for all tested algorithms, in Fig. 3 the trajectories only for EIFQ(λ)-learning algorithm are presented. As shown, all eight goal points are reached. In case of the remaining algorithms the goal was also realized, but the robot trajectories were longer.

Fig. 1. Khepera III mobile robot

As the measure of the efficiency of the reinforcement learning algorithms, the number of iterations necessary to visit all eight points was assumed (second column in Table 1). One can observe that FQ(0)-learning algorithm needs the greatest number of the iterations. FQ(λ)-learning performance is slightly better (5%

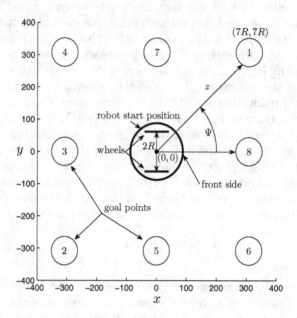

Fig. 2. Two wheel Khepera III mobile robot in the environment of eight goal points

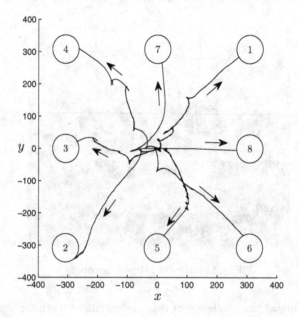

Fig. 3. Robot trajectories obtained by means of reinforcement EIFQ(0)-learning algorithm

Table 1. Comparison of the efficiency of the reinforcement learning algorithms

Algorithm	$Iterations$	t_{inc} [ms]	t_{epoch} [ms]	t_{total} [ms]
FQ(0)-learning	21697	0.21	.-	4556.37
FQ(λ)-learning	20578	0.24	-	4938.72
fuzzy Dyna-learning	17756	0.39	-	6924.84
fuzzy prioritized sweeping	19031	0.38	-	7231.78
EIFQ(0)-learning	14314	0.27	8.63	3933.82

less iterations). The use of the environment model in fuzzy Dyna-learning and fuzzy prioritized sweeping allowed for relatively small decrease of the number of iterations required to achieve the absorbing states (18% and 12%, respectively). The best result was obtained when applying the epoch-incremental algorithm (EIFQ(0)-learning) since the reduction of the number of iterations equalled 34% in relation to FQ(0)-learning algorithm. The third column in Table 1 presents run-time of the incremental part of the algorithms (denoted as t_{inc}). Fuzzy Dyna-learning and fuzzy prioritized sweeping are also worth paying attention because their run-time is by a margin of $0.1ms$ longer than the one measured in case of remaining algorithms. It is influenced by the necessity of computation of some number of actualizations of action-value function represented by fuzzy approximator on the basis of environment model. The fourth column of Table 1 contains the epoch time of the EIFQ(0)-learning algorithm. It is almost 32 times longer than the incremental time. One needs to note that epoch mode was performed only eight times (after each of eight goal points was reached). The last column of Table 1 presents the total time measure (t_{total}) which was calculated according to formula:

$$t_{total} = Iterations \cdot t_{inc} + 8 \cdot t_{epoch}, \qquad (10)$$

where 8 numeral is a consequence of the number of goal points. For epoch-incremental algorithm this time is the shortest.

4   Conclusions

In this contribution the new epoch-incremental reinforcement learning algorithm was proposed. It was applied to Khepera mobile robot control. The reinforcement fuzzy Q(0)-learning algorithm was performed in the incremental mode and the environment model was created. In the epoch mode, on the basis of the environment model, the distances of the fuzzy states representations from absorbing state were determined. This distances were used to compute the actualizations of fuzzy approximator of action-value function. The efficiency of proposed algorithm and fuzzy versions of reinforcement learning algorithms: Q(0)-learning, Q(λ)-learning, Dyna-learning and prioritized sweeping was analyzed. This was performed by comparing of the number of the iterations and the total run-time of the algorithms. The adaptation of fuzzy approximator of action-value function to Dyna-learning and prioritized sweeping algorithms was proposed. The results confirmed validity of assumed solution.

Acknowledgments. This work was supported by Polish Ministry of Science and Higher Education under the grant 3745/B/T02/2009/36.

References

1. Appl, M., Brauer, W.: Fuzzy Mode-Based Reinforcement Learning. In: Proc. of the European Symposium on Intelligent Techniques, pp. 212–218 (2000)
2. Barto, A.G., Sutton, R.S., Anderson, C.W.: Neuronlike adaptive elements that can solve difficult learning problem. IEEE Trans. SMC 13, 834–847 (1983)
3. Berenji, H.R.: Fuzzy Reinforcement Learning and Dynamic Programming. In: L. Ralescu, A. (ed.) IJCAI-WS 1993. LNCS, vol. 847, pp. 1–9. Springer, Heidelberg (1994)
4. Bonarini, A., Lazaric, A., Montrone, F., Restelli, M.: Reinforcement distribution in Fuzzy Q-learning. Fuzzy Sets and Systems 160, 1420–1443 (2009)
5. Deng, C., Er, M.J.: Real-Time Dynamic Fuzzy Q-Learning abd Control of Mobile Robots. In: Proc. of 5th Asian Control Conference, vol. 3, pp. 1568–1576 (2004)
6. Lambercy, F., Caprari, G.: Khepera III manual ver. 2.2, K-Team (2008)
7. Moore, A., Atkeson, C.: Prioritized sweeping: Reinforcement learning with less data and less time. Machine Learning 13, 103–130 (1993)
8. Peng, J., Williams, R.: Efficient learning and planning within the Dyna framework. In: Proc. of the 2nd International Conference on Simulation of Adaptive Behavior, pp. 281–290 (1993)
9. Rummery, G., Niranjan, M.: On line q-learning using connectionist systems. Technical Report CUED/F-INFENG/TR 166, Cambridge University Engineering Department (1994)
10. Sutton, R.: Integrated Architectures for Learning, Planning, and Reacting Based on Approximating Dynamic Programming. In: Proc. of Seventh Int. Conf. on Machine Learning, pp. 216–224 (1990)
11. Sutton, R.S., Barto, A.G.: Reinforcement learning: An Introduction. MIT Press, Cambridge (1998)
12. Wiktorowicz, K., Zajdel, R.: A Fuzzy Navigation of a Mobile Robot. Systems Science 23(4), 87–100 (1997)
13. Watkins, C.J.C.H.: Learning from delayed Rewards. PhD thesis, Cambridge University, Cambridge, England (1989)
14. Zajdel, R.: Epoch-Incremental Queue-Dyna Algorithm. In: Rutkowski, L., Tadeusiewicz, R., Zadeh, L.A., Zurada, J.M. (eds.) ICAISC 2008. LNCS (LNAI), vol. 5097, pp. 1160–1170. Springer, Heidelberg (2008)
15. Zajdel, R.: Fuzzy Q(λ)-Learning Algorithm. In: Rutkowski, L., Scherer, R., Tadeusiewicz, R., Zadeh, L.A., Zurada, J.M. (eds.) ICAISC 2010, Part I. LNCS (LNAI), vol. 6113, pp. 256–263. Springer, Heidelberg (2010)

Part III

Pattern Classification

Part III

Pattern Classification

Statistically–Induced Kernel Function for Support Vector Machine Classifier

Cezary Dendek and Jacek Mańdziuk

Warsaw University of Technology,
Faculty of Mathematics and Information Science,
Plac Politechniki 1, 00-661 Warsaw, Poland
{c.dendek,mandziuk}@mini.pw.edu.pl
http://www.mini.pw.edu.pl/~mandziuk/

Abstract. In this paper a new family of kernel functions for SVM classifiers, based on a statistically–induced measure of distance between observations in the pattern space, is proposed and experimentally evaluated in the context of binary classification problems. The application of the proposed approach improves the accuracy of results compared to the case of training without postulated enhancements.

Numerical results outperform those of the SVM with Gaussian and Laplace kernels.

1 Introduction

The problem of defining an appropriate distance function to be used for measuring distance between observations, or calculating observations proximity, is frequently encountered in numerous application fields, and – in particular – is an important component of many classification algorithms.

The usual approach to the problem of defining a distance function is based on a construction performed in the space observed in experiment, usually modeled by $\mathbb{R}^n$, either directly, or with the use of space transformation, effectively not preserving the structure of a probability space of the modeled phenomena. In order to address this issue the idea of statistically–induced distance measures, built using *p–values* of the arguments equality hypothesis, has been proposed in [1,2] and experimentally evaluated in the context of *k–NN* classifier.

In this paper a generalization of the concept and its application to the field of Support Vector Machines classifiers is presented.

The statistically–induced distance measures are expressed as the *fuzzy equivalence relations* (Sect. 2.3). Since fuzzy equivalences, that can be practically used in the context of distance classification, are typically the kernel functions (please refer to [3,4] for a detailed discussion on this issue), the introduced equivalences are checked for kernel properties. Because of a relative complexity of the functions, which makes a theoretical proof of a semi-positive definition a complicated task, and due to the compactness of kernel domain the verification procedure is performed in a numerical way.

L. Rutkowski et al. (Eds.): ICAISC 2012, Part I, LNCS 7267, pp. 369–377, 2012.

The kernels, introduced individually in each data dimension (Sect. 3.4), are combined using the linking functions (Sect. 3.5). The results of the combination are proven to be the kernels (Sect. 3.5).

The reminder of the paper is organized as follows: Section 2 provides some necessary definitions and describes the idea of observations' proximity measurement expressed as the fuzzy equivalence relation and its relation to kernel functions.

Section 3 describes how this framework is used to build the probability–based equivalences and kernels. The benchmark data sets and results of numerical evaluation of proposed kernels are presented in sections 4 and 5, respectively. Conclusions and directions for future research are placed in the last section.

This piece of work is a direct continuation and generalization of authors' previous works [1,2] introducing probability–related distance measures and works [2,5] related to properties of metrical structure of pattern space.

2 Fuzzy Equivalence and Kernel Functions

2.1 Triangular Norm

A *triangular norm* (*t–norm*) ([6]) is a function $T : [0,1]^2 \to [0,1]$ fulfilling:

- $\forall_{x,y \in [0,1]} T(x,y) = T(y,x)$,
- $\forall_{x,y,z,v \in [0,1]} x \leq z \wedge y \leq v \Rightarrow T(x,y) \leq T(z,v)$,
- $\forall_{x,y,z \in [0,1]} T(T(x,y),z) = T(x,T(y,z))$,
- $\forall_{x \in [0,1]} T(x,1) = x$.

A t–norm particularly noteworthy from the perspective of a relationship between fuzzy equivalences and kernels ([4]) is

$$T_{\cos}(x,y) = \max(xy - \sqrt{1-x^2}\sqrt{1-y^2}, 0).$$

2.2 Kernel

A *kernel* is a real-valued function $K : X^2 \to \mathbb{R}$ that is symmetric and positive semi-defined.

2.3 Fuzzy Equivalence

A *T–fuzzy equivalence* ([6]) is a function E fulfilling following conditions:

1. $E : X^2 \to [0,1]$,
2. $\forall_{x,y \in X} E(x,y) = E(y,x)$,
3. $\forall_{x \in X} E(x,x) = 1$,
4. $\forall_{x,y,z \in X} T(E(x,z), E(z,y)) \leq E(x,y)$.

2.4 Relation between Kernel Functions and Fuzzy Equivalences

The result provided in [4] stating that every kernel function $K : X^2 \to [0,1]$ fulfilling $\forall_{x \in X} K(x,x) = 1$ is a $T_{\cos}$–equivalence, leads to the following procedure:

Function E, fulfilling conditions (1) – (3) of the fuzzy equivalence definition (Sect. 2.3), is a kernel and a fuzzy equivallence if:

1. E is $T_{\cos}$–equivalence,
2. E is positive semi-defined function.

3   Probability–Based Kernels and Equivalences in the Training Patterns Space

3.1   Introduction

The space of observations has a naturally defined structure of metrical space given by its immersion into $\mathbb{R}^n$ with natural (Euclidean) distance function. In the context of kernel functions this approach to distance measurement has been addressed by RBF kernels, e.g. Gaussian:

$$K(x,y) = \exp(-\sigma||x - y||^2),$$

or Laplace:

$$K(x,y) = \exp(-\sigma||x - y||).$$

Despite the fact, that RBF kernels are fuzzy equivalences, this approach does not preserve a structure of probability space, in particular an information about the distribution of the data, which otherwise could have been used to improve accuracy of classifiers, is lost.

Improved immersion can be obtained with the use of *Cumulative Density Functions* (CDF) by transformation of pattern space, as described in [1,2], which preserves the information of marginal distributions.

Let $(\text{CDF})_i$ denote CDF of i-th dimension of observation space, x_i – a value of i-th dimension of the pattern, and CDF_i – a marginal CDF of i-th dimension. Transformation of pattern is then defined as follows:

$$(\text{CDF}(x))_i := \text{CDF}_i(x_i)$$

Application of CDF transformation to the pattern space creates standardized space (denoted *CDF–Space*). Projection of training patterns into *CDF–Space* results in uniform distribution of patterns in each dimension (marginal distributions are $U[0, 1]$).

Estimation of CDF (denoted as *ECDF*) can be obtained either by parametric estimation (fitting parameters of arbitrarily chosen family of distributions) or by the use of simple non-parametric estimator defined as:

$$\text{ECDF}_i^{\text{Simple}}(x) = \frac{|\{z_i \in \text{TrSet} : z_i \leq x_i\}|}{|\text{TrSet}|},$$

where TrSet denotes the training set.

As the $\text{ECDF}^{\text{Simple}}$ function does not preserve the order of elements between the approximation knots (the function is constant between knots) , for the sake of practical applications – when training set size is limited – it is worth considering the continuous version of the function obtained with the use of linear interpolation between knots.

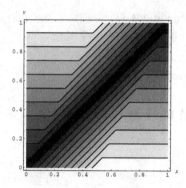

Fig. 1. Probabilistic distance from fixed point x to observation v

3.2   Model of Equivalence

The structure of discussed proximity measure can be decomposed into two components:

- *univariate proximity measure*
  (discussed in Sect 3.4) providing a fuzzy equivalence in a given dimension and
- *linking function*
  (discussed in Sect 3.5) which combines multiple univariate equivalences providing
  a univariate equivalence.

3.3   Probabilistic Distance between a Fixed Point and an Observation

The uniformity of marginal distributions in the *CDF–Space* provides the possibility of defining a distance between the fixed point in observation space and an observation.

Let v be an observed realization of a random variable $V \sim U[0, 1]$ (V is uniformly distributed over the interval $[0, 1]$) and x be a fixed point, $v, x \in [0, 1]$.

The p–value of the hypothesis $x = v$ vs. $x \neq v$ under the assumption of the model introduced in [1] can be expressed as:

$$p_{\text{Eq}}(x; v) = 1 - d(x; v),$$

where

$$d(x; v) = \min(1, x + |x - v|) - \max(0, x - |x - v|).$$

The function $d(x; v)$ can be regarded as the *probabilistic distance between the fixed point x and an observation v* [1].

The contour plot of function $d(x; v)$ is presented in Fig 1. It can be shown that random variable $d(X; V)$, where $U, V \sim U[0, 1]$, is uniformly distributed: $d(X; V) \sim U[0, 1]$.

Although function p_{Eq} is asymmetrical, it resembles a fuzzy equivalence.

3.4   Univariate Equivalences in CDF–Space

A distance measure on the CDF–Space is required to be symmetrical and to operate on observations rather than fixed values. This goal can be achieved by a combination of

$p_{Eq}(x; v)$ values that creates symmetrical function $E(u, v)$ by elimination of the fixed point x.

The following symmetrizations were proposed in [1]:

$$E_{Avg}(u, v) = \frac{p_{Eq}(u; v) + p_{Eq}(v; u)}{2},$$

$$E_{Ind}(u, v) = p_{Eq}(u; v)p_{Eq}(v; u),$$

$$E_{Min}(u, v) = \max_{x \in [0,1]} (p_{Eq}(x; u) + p_{Eq}(x; v)) = \max (p_{Eq}(u; v), p_{Eq}(v; u)),$$

expressed as respective distance measures.

It is easy to observe that all introduced symmetrizations fulfill the necessary conditions of the verification procedure presented in Sect. 2.4, rasing a question whether they are kernels and fuzzy equivallences. However, due to the complexity of the functions, the verification steps were performed numerically:

1. T_{cos}–equivalence of each symmetrization has been checked by evaluation of the expression
   $$sgn(T(E(x, z), E(z, y)) - E(x, y))$$
   over a grid of uniformly distributed knots (1 000 in each dimension) covering the expression domain $[0, 1]^3$,
2. positive semi-definition of each symmetrization has been checked using Monte–Carlo procedure verifying a sign of a determinant of a Gram matrix, constructed using uniformly distributed ($U[0, 1]$, i.i.d.) random vectors of length varying from 2 to 100 (for each vector length the procedure has been repeated 1 000 times).

During numerical verification none of the postulated symmetrizations provided a counter–example for properties being verified, giving a hope that each symmetrization is a fuzzy equivalence and a kernel.

3.5 Linking Function

In order to provide a unified equivalence in case of multidimensional CDF–space, the equivalences calculated independently in each dimension have to be combined. The proposed types of combinations are constructed with an assumption of data dimensions independency, made also in classical RBF kernels, as well as Naive Bayes classifier.

Equivalence Linking. A natural way of providing the combination of equivalences is the use of the triangular norm. Due to properties of t–norms such a combination is a T_{cos}–equivalence. In order to conclude that resulting function is a kernel it is necessary, however, to assure its semi-positive definition.

An example of such linking is the product t–norm T_P defined as

$$L_{Prod}(x, y) = T_P(x, y) = xy.$$

Since T_P is a one dimensional dot product it is semi-positively defined.

Kernel Linking. A combination of the kernel equivalences that is semi-positively defined can also be obtained – due to the *closeness property of kernels* [4] – using a linking function defined as a Taylor series with nonnegative coefficients. Resulting function can easily be verified for fuzzy equivalence properties using conditions listed in section 2.4. The application of described technique leads to the following linking functions:

- average linking

$$L_{\text{Avg}}(E_1, \ldots, E_n) = \frac{1}{n} \sum_{i=1}^{n} E_i,$$

- exponential average linking

$$L_{\text{ExpAvg}}(E_1, \ldots, E_n) = \exp(\frac{1}{n} \sum_{i=1}^{n} E_i - 1).$$

The exponential average linking is expected to outperform the product linking for high dimensionality data, due to bad asymptotical properties of L_{Prod} as the number of dimensions grows.

4   Data Sets

In order to provide experimental support for presented method's validity and generate results that can be compared to other sources, the data sets available in *UCI Machine Learning Repository* [7] were used. Benchmark sets were selected according to the following criteria and reasons:

- they represent binary classification problems,
- the number of observations is lower than 1 000 (due to the relatively high computational cost of creating a kernel matrix and SVM optimization procedure),
- they represent integer, real or binary categorical type of attributes.

A brief characteristics of selected data sets is presented in Table 1.

The data sets used in the following experiments were obtained by using the transformation described in Sect. 3.1 with the use of a continuous version of nonparametric estimation of *ECDF* which resulted in normalization of data and uniformity of marginal distributions. In order to provide the possibility to assess the significance of experimental results concerning postulated kernels, the linear standardization

$$x_i \mapsto \frac{x_i - \min_j(x_j)}{\max_j(x_j) - \min_j(x_j)}$$

was applied to the data sets used in case of SVMs with Gaussian and Laplace kernels. Standardization is necessary for the comparison with postulated kernels since they are defined on CDF–space, standardized by definition.

Table 1. A brief characteristics of selected data sets

data set name	number of instances	number of attributes	default classifier misclassification rate
BUPA Liver Disorders	345	7	42.03%
Pima Indians Diabetes	768	9	34.90%
Wisconsin Diagnostics Breast Cancer	569	31	37.26%
Sonar	208	61	46.63%
Ionosphere	351	34	35.90%
Wine	178	13	60.11%

5   Results

All data sets were evaluated with the use of an SVM classifier for each combination of the univariate equivalence and the linking function defined in sections 3.4 and 3.5, respectively. Results of misclassification rate estimation (in per cent) were obtained for each value of ν parameter using 10–fold crossvalidation repeated 10 times. The sample of ν values was randomly generated over the interval $[0.005, 0.9]$ and contained 300 elements.

Numerical results of the evaluation of the proposed kernels are presented in Table 2. Presented results are misclassification rates of 10–fold CV estimators for the best ν found in each case.

Table 2. SVM misclassification rate comparison for different equivalence kernels. The best results obtained for each data set are marked in bold.

kernel	BUPA	Pima	WDBC	Sonar	Ionosphere	Wine
$L_{\text{ExpAvg}}(E_{\text{Avg}})$	**23.94**	**22.53**	2.19	**9.62**	**6.01**	1.12
$L_{\text{Avg}}(E_{\text{Avg}})$	24.72	22.84	2.00	11.06	6.03	1.12
Gaussian RBF	26.64	22.89	**1.93**	11.02	*64.10*	**0.70**
$L_{\text{ExpAvg}}(E_{\text{Min}})$	25.59	23.29	2.34	13.61	6.21	1.12
$L_{\text{Avg}}(E_{\text{Min}})$	24.84	22.89	2.23	12.79	6.46	1.12
$L_{\text{ExpAvg}}(E_{\text{Ind}})$	24.63	23.39	2.65	12.93	6.15	1.29
$L_{\text{Avg}}(E_{\text{Ind}})$	25.65	23.49	2.44	*14.28*	6.81	1.29
Laplace RBF	*27.59*	23.08	2.17	11.06	*64.10*	0.77
$L_{\text{Prod}}(E_{\text{Avg}})$	24.58	*25.09*	*37.25*	44.64	34.76	*25.84*

The results presented in the table confirm the efficacy of the proposed approach to the problem of kernel construction: the models of proposed structure and components are comparable or better than standard RBF kernels, concerning a misclassification rate estimation. An importance of proper component selection is proven by an example of

T_{Prod} linking function. An advantage over classical RBF kernels is more distinctive in the case of the problems, in which the nature of events expresses certain amount of uncertainty, thus requiring more complex separation boundaries (diabetes, liver disorders).

In the case of E_{Ind} and E_{Avg} equivalences the use of L_{ExpAvg} linking leads to significantly better results than those of L_{Avg}. An opposite effect observed in the case of E_{Min} suggests different properties of this equivalence, and can be explained by significantly different distribution of equivalence values over its domain (which could be observed in Fig. ??).

Despite the noticeable difference between $L_{ExpAvg}(E_{Avg})$ and Gaussian kernel concerning the density of value set, both kernels produce comparable results. This interesting fact suggests, that combination of both types of kernels can lead to the results superior to each kernel. An exploration of this possibility is a part of our future plans.

Very promising results of L_{ExpAvg} linking function suggest the direction of future work should be in specialization of symmetrizations E and their linking with use of exponential kernel.

The results were obtained with use of LIBSVM library v. 2.90 ([8]) and R framework v. 2.12 ([9]).

6   Conclusions

In this paper a new class of kernels and equivalences defined using observations in the pattern space is proposed and experimentally evaluated with the use of SVM classifier in the context of binary classification problems. The main idea of the proposed kernels is the use of statistically–induced distance measures that extend the distance measurement with some statistical aspects of a given space.

It is shown that postulated models are significantly different from classical RBF kernels and capable of producing better results than training without their use. The results obtained during numerical experiments suggest interesting directions of further research. Other possible applications of presented kernels as well as combination of different types of equivalences selected individually for each dimension are also considered as future research plans.

Acknowledgement. This work was supported by the research grant from the Warsaw University of Technology.

References

1. Dendek, C., Mańdziuk, J.: Probability-Based Distance Function for Distance-Based Classifiers. In: Alippi, C., Polycarpou, M., Panayiotou, C., Ellinas, G. (eds.) ICANN 2009, Part I. LNCS, vol. 5768, pp. 141–150. Springer, Heidelberg (2009)
2. Dendek, C., Mańdziuk, J.: Improving Performance of a Binary Classifier by Training Set Selection. In: Kurková, V., Neruda, R., Koutník, J. (eds.) ICANN 2008, Part I. LNCS, vol. 5163, pp. 128–135. Springer, Heidelberg (2008)
3. Moser, B.: On the t–transivity of kernels. Fuzzy Sets and Systems 157(13), 1787–1796 (2006)

4. Moser, B.: On representing and generating kernels by fuzzy equivalence relations. Journal of Machine Learning Research 6, 2603–2620 (2006)
5. Mańdziuk, J., Shastri, L.: Incremental class learning approach and its application to handwritten digit recognition. Inf. Sci. Inf. Comput. Sci. 141(3-4), 193–217 (2002)
6. Klement, E., Mesiar, R., Pap, E.: Triangular norms (2000)
7. Asuncion, A., Newman, D.: UCI machine learning repository (2007)
8. Chang, C.C., Lin, C.J.: LIBSVM: a library for support vector machines (2001), http://www.csie.ntu.edu.tw/~cjlin/libsvm
9. R Development Core Team: R: A Language and Environment for Statistical Computing. R Foundation for Statistical Computing, Vienna, Austria (2009) ISBN 3-900051-07-0

Bandwidth Selection in Kernel Density Estimators for Multiple-Resolution Classification

Mateusz Kobos and Jacek Mańdziuk

Warsaw University of Technology,
Faculty of Mathematics and Information Science,
Plac Politechniki 1, 00-661 Warsaw, Poland
{M.Kobos,J.Mandziuk}@mini.pw.edu.pl

Abstract. We consider a problem of selection of parameters in a classifier based on the average of kernel density estimators where each estimator corresponds to a different data "resolution". The selection is based on adjusting parameters of the estimators to minimize a substitute of the misclassification ratio. We experimentally compare the misclassification ratio and parameters selected for benchmark data sets by the introduced algorithm with these values of the algorithm's baseline version. In order to place the classification results in a wider context, we compare them with results of other popular classifiers.

Keywords: kernel density estimation, classification based on density estimation, average of density estimators.

1 Introduction

The construction of the classifier examined in this paper is based on the idea of "multiple-resolution" or "multiscale" approach to data analysis. In this approach, we utilize information about the data when looked at with various precisions or "resolutions". In practice, we use the Bayes classifier where the density of each class is estimated by an average of Kernel Density Estimators (KDEs). Each KDE corresponds to a different "resolution", their parameters called "bandwidths" are adjusted on the training set to minimize the overall classification error. However, we do not directly minimize the misclassification ratio, which has a disadvantage of being a non-continuous function, but its substitute, the Mean Squared Error (MSE) estimated with a 10-fold cross-validation method on the training set. The minimization is done by a quasi-Newton constrained optimization algorithm called L-BFGS-B. A more detailed description of the presented method can be found in [8, Sect. 2].

The algorithms from the literature that seem to be the most similar to the one presented can be gathered in two groups. In the first one, there are methods which use a combination of density estimators to optimize the quality of density estimation ([3,15,13]), in the other one – methods where a combination of density estimation-based classifiers is used to optimize the classification quality ([5,4]). Our algorithm is situated between these two groups since it uses a combination

L. Rutkowski et al. (Eds.): ICAISC 2012, Part I, LNCS 7267, pp. 378–386, 2012.

of density estimators but it optimizes classification quality instead of density estimation. To our knowledge, the only other algorithm that is also situated between these two groups is the one introduced in [6]. Our approach, however, is different and simpler. The most fundamental difference is that we do not operate on pairs of bandwidths where each bandwidth corresponds to a single KDE assigned to one of the classes (as it is in the case of the algorithm from [6]); instead, for each class we use a couple of KDEs with their outputs averaged.

The results presented in this paper are a continuation of our previous works [9,8,10], and a direct extension of the results presented in [7]. The latter contains theoretical considerations and tests of the algorithm on artificial as well as benchmark data sets. In this paper we delve into the following additional issues. We analyze the number of KDEs selected by the algorithm for each of the artificial problems examined in [7] (Sect. 2). We also consider distribution of bandwidth values found for selected benchmark data sets, and present a visualization of a simplified error function optimized by the algorithm which gives an insight into obtained results (Sect. 3.1). Next, we provide more detailed results and analyses of direct experimental comparison of the introduced algorithm with other popular machine learning classifiers (Sect. 3.2), among them the Linear Discriminant Analysis which was not examined in [7].

2   Number of KDEs Selected for Artificial Data

In [7], the introduced algorithm was tested on various (but related) artificial classification problems and two sets of tests were executed. Here we consider and examine in more detail one of these sets consisting of "real-life" experiments, where a practical training algorithm is used to select the parameters. This version of the algorithm selects automatically the number of KDEs for the problem using "distance distribution-based" method (see [7, Sect. 3.1] for a detailed description).

All artificial classification problems considered in this paper have a property of "multiple-resolution" i.e. they consist of clusters of different densities. Such a property is in favor of producing low misclassification rate by our algorithm. The first of the considered classification problems, denoted as $W((0,0), 100, (10^5, 0), 1)$, defines large and small Gaussian Mixture Model clusters separated by a long distance in the feature space. For this problem, we produce training data sets with different number of samples. The second problem, denoted as $W((0,0), \sigma_1, (10^5, 0), 1)$, is a modification of the previous one with the training data sets generated for different ratio of clusters' densities defined by a scale parameter σ_1: the larger the parameter's value, the larger the difference. The last problem, denoted as $W((0,0), \sigma_1, (0,0), 1)$, is a modification of the previous one, where the clusters are not separated, but have their centers situated at the same point. It is worth noting that in all of these problems there are generally two clusters of different densities defined, though in some cases the difference between the densities is small or vanishes completely (as in the case of data sets generated from $W((0,0), \sigma_1, (10^5, 0), 1)$ problem with $\sigma_1 = 1$).

The main conclusion drawn from the experiments on the above data sets is that the introduced algorithm yields better classification results than the baseline version, but in order to obtain good results, the difference in densities of clusters has to be large enough. However, it would be informative to know how the method that automatically selects the number of KDEs works for these problems. Is it always selecting two KDEs to match the two clusters of different densities in the data?

We conducted appropriate experiments for each artificial problem to find out (see Fig. 1). The simplest problem $W((0,0), 100, (10^5, 0), 1)$ is easily dealt with by the algorithm – the number of KDEs is almost always two. In case of separated clusters (i.e. $W((0,0), \sigma_1, (10^5, 0), 1)$ problem), we can see that for small difference between scales of the clusters ($\sigma_1 < 7$) the method is not able to recognize that there are two clusters in the data, but for larger values it correctly selects two KDEs per class. This might seem unsettling, but there is a similar situation even in the case when there are two KDEs with their bandwidths selected optimally (see [7, Sect. 4.2.2]) – the difference between the baseline version and the examined version is quite small for small σ_1 and is becoming larger for larger σ_1 values. Thus, by using the practical implementation of the algorithm in this case, we are not loosing much of the model's optimal discriminative power. The situation is more complicated for the $W((0,0), \sigma_1, (0,0), 1)$ problem where the clusters are not separated. Here, the vicinity of points from different clusters makes selecting the right number of KDEs more difficult and the method is not working that well. Nevertheless, even if more KDEs are selected than necessary, the introduced algorithm is still able to significantly reduce the classification error when compared with the baseline $N = 1$ versions of the algorithm in case of larger differences between densities of clusters (see [7, Sect. 4.2.3]).

We can conclude the analysis of these experiments by saying that the desired outcome of selecting exactly two KDEs depends mainly on the structure of the classification problem. The more separated the clusters of different densities, and the larger the difference between the densities, the easier it is for the "distance distribution-based" method to select the right number of KDEs. Certainly, in the real-life situations the clusters would rarely be separated, but even in such cases, when the method selects more KDEs than necessary, the algorithm is still able to produce a good classification result.

3   Experiments on Benchmark Data Sets

The algorithm was tested not only on artificial classification problems characterized by certain properties, but also on benchmark data sets which were not selected specifically to be in favor of the algorithm. The motivation was to test the efficacy of the method on data sets reflecting the real-life problems.

The algorithm was tested on data sets used for comparison of various classifiers in [11] and [6]. Some other data sets from the UCI Machine Learning Repository (UCIMLR) (see [1]) were also used. In all, 19 data sets were used in the experiments, among them: *blood transfusion* (Blood Transfusion Service Center data,

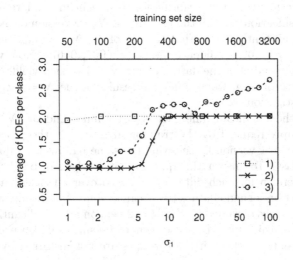

Fig. 1. Average number of KDEs per class selected by the algorithm in "real-life" experiments. The parameter of the experiments examined: 1) the training set size for the $W((0,0), 100, (10^5, 0), 1)$ problem, 2) the scale parameter σ_1 for the $W((0,0), \sigma_1, (10^5, 0), 1)$ problem, 3) the scale parameter σ_1 for the $W((0,0), \sigma_1, (0,0), 1)$ problem.

introduced in [17]), *breast cancer* (Wisconsin breast cancer data set, collected at the University of Wisconsin by W.H. Wolberg [12]), *glass* (forensic glass data), *heart* (SPECTF Heart Data Set), *image segmentation* (Statlog Image Segmentation), *Indian diabetes* (PIMA Indian diabetes), *liver disorders* (BUPA liver disorders), *satellite image* (StatLog satellite image), *vehicle silhouette* (StatLog vehicle silhouette), *vowel Deterding* (Vowel Recognition – Deterding Data), and *waveform* (waveform database generator – version 1). All data sets except *Ripley's synthetic* were downloaded from the UCIMLR. The *Ripley's synthetic* data set was obtained from [14]. The data sets were preprocessed the same way as in the original papers. If the data set was originally divided into the training set and the test set, we merged these two and executed cross-validation experiments on the merged version.

3.1 Comparison with Baseline Version

Two versions of the algorithm were tested and compared: the baseline with one KDE per class (denoted as $N = 1$) and one with two KDEs per class (denoted as $N = 2$). A version of the algorithm with fixed number of KDEs per class was used, because in preliminary experiments we observed that it yielded slightly better results than the version with automatic selection of number of KDEs (this is probably due to noise and complex structure of benchmark data sets). Samples in each class were standardized. A 10-fold cross-validation repeated 10 times was used to obtain the average results.

Taking into consideration the performance on all benchmark data sets, it turns out that the classification error of the introduced $N = 2$ version of the algorithm is statistically significantly better that the one of the $N = 1$ version (Wilcoxson signed-ranks test, $p \approx .02$, confidence interval: $[.0007, .0067]$). However, the difference is not large and on some data sets the $N = 2$ version yields results that are very similar to or even worse than the results of the $N = 1$ version. This needs some investigation.

First, maybe the significant difference is just a fluke, and the $N = 2$ version is in practice simply reduced by the training algorithm in the process of optimization to the $N = 1$ version by selecting the same bandwidth values for both KDEs in each class? To answer this question, an analysis of bandwidth values found by each version for each data set averaged over all classes and over all repeats of the test on a single data set was carried out. As a result, we observed that the average values obtained by the $N = 2$ version are significantly different, what suggests that this is not the case. But to be sure, we also need a deeper look at the raw data to check if these results are not distorted by averaging. It turns out that generally these values indeed differ significantly, but there are some data sets (like *ionosphere*) where the difference is not as large (see Fig. 2 for some examples).

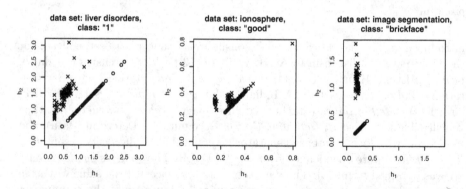

Fig. 2. Distribution of bandwidths for selected data sets in all experiments. The circle corresponds to the bandwidth of the basic $N = 1$ version of the algorithm (with coordinates of (h, h)), the cross corresponds to the bandwidths of the $N = 2$ version (with coordinates (h_1, h_2), where h_1 is the smaller bandwidth and h_2 is the larger one). The plot for *ionoshpere* data set shows an example of data where the bandwidth values of the $N = 2$ version are located near the values of the $N = 1$ version.

One of the reasons of small difference between misclassification ratios of the versions of the algorithm is probably lack of an appropriate "multi-resolution" structure of some data sets – the clusters of different density might not be present in the data or the difference in density might not be large enough for the $N = 2$ version to show its superiority over the baseline version. This results in a structure of the error function where minima found by the algorithm using two bandwidths are not much smaller then minima found when using one bandwidth.

This can be illustrated with a simpler version of the algorithm, namely one where bandwidth value is the same for each class (and not different as in the algorithm considered so far). The error function for such version is two-dimensional; thus, can be easily visualized. Note that the baseline algorithm ($N = 1$) can only achieve values of the error function at points belonging to the half-line (h, h), $h \in [0, \infty)$. This half-line might or might not include the global minimum of the $N = 2$ version, thus using more than one KDE might or might not improve the results. This situation may be seen in Fig. 3 where for the *liver disorders* data set the global minima are located far from the half-line; on the other hand, for the *yeast* data set, a minima of similar values are located on the half-line as well as far from it.

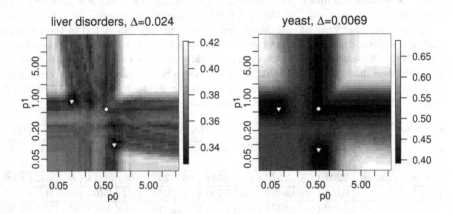

Fig. 3. Mean classification error on testing set for selected benchmark data sets for a version of the algorithm with the same bandwidth value for each class. The axes correspond to bandwidth values of each KDE. The darker the color of a point, the smaller the function value. The global minima of the function are marked with triangles, the minimum for points belonging to the diagonal is marked with a circle. The difference between minimal value of the function for points belonging to the diagonal and the global minimum is denoted as Δ.

3.2 Comparison with Popular Classifiers

The algorithm with two KDEs per class was also directly compared with a few popular classifiers: Naive Bayes, Nearest Neighbor (NN), Linear Discriminant Analysis (LDA), Support Vector Machine (SVM). All of these algorithms were tested using the same methodology as in Sect. 3.1. As before, to obtain more precise results, the same splits into the training and testing sets were used for all algorithms. The implementation of the algorithms used in the tests came from the R statistical environment (packages: class, e1071, MASS); the default parameter values were used. In case of Naive Bayes, the Gaussian distribution (given the target class) of continuous attributes is assumed; in case of SVM, a "radial" kernel is used; in case of NN two version are examined: with $k = 1$ and $k = 5$.

The method described in [2, Sect. 3.2.2] was used to compare the overall performance of the algorithms on all datasets (see Table 1). The Iman & Davenport test shows that there are statistically significant differences between the algorithms ($p \approx 1.42 \cdot 10^{-6}$). Next, the Holm test was used to compare the introduced algorithm with other classifiers. The algorithm's overall classification performance turned out to be statistically significantly better than those of Naive Bayes and 1-NN, while the results of SVM, LDA, and 5-NN were not statistically significantly different.

Table 1. Misclassification ratio of popular algorithms on benchmark data sets. The first column contains names of different data sets; the rest of the columns contain results of various classifiers. The columns with headers $N=2$ and NB contain results of the introduced method and the Naive Bayes algorithm respectively. The last row presents an average rank of each algorithm. The ranks are calculated in the following way: for a given data set, the best algorithm obtains rank 1, the second one obtains rank 2, etc. The average rank is computed over all data sets. One can see that the SVM algorithm has the best average rank, while the Naive Bayes has the worst average rank. Standard deviation value for all 100 results from a single 10 times repeated 10-fold cross-validation experiment is placed in parentheses.

data set	SVM	N=2	LDA	5-NN	1-NN	NB
blood transfusion	.2229 (.03)	.2202 (.03)	.2295 (.02)	.2301 (.04)	.2974 (.04)	.2479 (.03)
Boston housing	.2203 (.05)	.2323 (.06)	.2542 (.05)	.2575 (.05)	.2384 (.05)	.3134 (.06)
breast cancer	.0313 (.02)	.0315 (.02)	.0396 (.02)	.0308 (.02)	.0464 (.03)	.0378 (.02)
ecoli	.1289 (.05)	.1324 (.06)	.1275 (.05)	.1436 (.06)	.1902 (.06)	.2084 (.06)
glass	.3212 (.09)	.2906 (.09)	.4133 (.09)	.2807 (.08)	.2497 (.10)	.5046 (.09)
heart	.2059 (.02)	.2094 (.02)	.2427 (.06)	.2653 (.07)	.2811 (.09)	.3185 (.09)
image segmentation	.0579 (.01)	.0357 (.01)	.0840 (.02)	.0569 (.01)	.0352 (.01)	.2032 (.02)
Indian diabetes	.2423 (.05)	.2433 (.04)	.2277 (.04)	.2604 (.05)	.2966 (.05)	.2440 (.04)
ionosphere	.0573 (.04)	.0500 (.04)	.1361 (.05)	.1522 (.05)	.1332 (.04)	.0989 (.05)
iris	.0353 (.04)	.0473 (.05)	.0200 (.03)	.0527 (.05)	.0553 (.06)	.0473 (.05)
liver disorders	.3074 (.06)	.3684 (.07)	.3170 (.07)	.3939 (.06)	.3751 (.08)	.4470 (.08)
Ripley's synthetic	.0942 (.02)	.1001 (.03)	.1218 (.03)	.0975 (.03)	.1086 (.03)	.1152 (.03)
satellite image	.1008 (.01)	.0876 (.01)	.1606 (.01)	.0929 (.01)	.0934 (.01)	.2039 (.01)
sonar	.1574 (.08)	.1386 (.07)	.2243 (.11)	.1499 (.08)	.1595 (.08)	.3109 (.11)
vehicle silhouette	.2291 (.03)	.2906 (.04)	.2178 (.04)	.2807 (.04)	.2996 (.04)	.5411 (.05)
vowel Deterding	.0519 (.02)	.0146 (.01)	.3959 (.05)	.0648 (.03)	.0108 (.01)	.3319 (.05)
waveform	.1378 (.02)	.1586 (.02)	.1434 (.02)	.1914 (.02)	.2342 (.02)	.1896 (.02)
wine	.0185 (.03)	.0252 (.04)	.0113 (.02)	.0358 (.04)	.0451 (.05)	.0290 (.04)
yeast	.3996 (.04)	.3963 (.04)	.4142 (.04)	.4362 (.04)	.4688 (.04)	.8149 (.04)
average rank	2.16	2.34	3.37	3.74	4.26	5.13

Let us examine more closely the difference in results between the introduced algorithm $N = 2$ and the most successful and at the same time the most sophisticated of the algorithms tested, namely SVM. In the previous test we checked that when taking into consideration all of the algorithms and all of the data sets, these two are not significantly different, nevertheless we can test if there are any specific data sets for which one or the other is significantly superior. We used the corrected resampled t-test to compare results on each data set (see [16, Sect. 5.5]). Each obtained p-value was then multiplied by the number of the tests executed (there were 19 of them) in accordance to the conservative Bonferroni adjustment to account for multiple comparisons. The $N = 2$ algorithm yielded statistically significantly better results on *image segmentation* ($p \approx 5 \cdot 10^{-4}$), *satellite image* ($p \approx 1 \cdot 10^{-3}$), and *vowel Deterding* ($p \approx 1 \cdot 10^{-3}$) data sets, while the SVM yielded statistically better results on *vehicle silhouette* ($p \approx 6 \cdot 10^{-5}$) and *waveform* ($p \approx 1 \cdot 10^{-3}$) data sets.

These experiments show that the introduced algorithm fares quite well when compared with other popular methods. On some data sets it even obtains better results than the sophisticated SVM algorithm.

4   Conclusions and Future Work

We examined different aspects of bandwidth selection in the introduced algorithm. We observed that the less discernible the difference in densities of clusters in data sets, the harder it is to automatically select an appropriate number of KDEs. We also checked that on benchmark data sets the multiple-KDEs algorithm is not simply reduced by the training process to a baseline single-KDE algorithm. We argued as well about the inappropriate form of the error function as the cause of the small difference in results between the baseline and the introduced $N = 2$ version of the algorithm on some benchmark data sets. Finally, we experimentally compared the introduced algorithm with some other popular ones – the algorithm seems to be competitive; on some data sets it even yields better results than the popular and advanced SVM.

More work is needed to find a way of identifying the "multiple-resolution" property and other potential properties that are in favor of our algorithm in real data sets. With such method it would be easier to decide whether using the multiple-KDEs algorithm for a given data set would yield better classification result than using the baseline version or other popular classifier.

References

1. Asuncion, A., Newman, D.: UCI Machine Learning Repository (2007), http://www.ics.uci.edu/~mlearn/MLRepository.html
2. Demšar, J.: Statistical comparisons of classifiers over multiple data sets. Journal of Machine Learning Research 7, 1–30 (2006)
3. Di Marzio, M., Taylor, C.C.: Boosting kernel density estimates: A bias reduction technique? Biometrika 91(1), 226–233 (2004)

4. Di Marzio, M., Taylor, C.C.: Kernel density classification and boosting: an l2 analysis. Statistics and Computing 15, 113–123 (2005)
5. Di Marzio, M., Taylor, C.C.: On boosting kernel density methods for multivariate data: density estimation and classification. Statistical Methods and Applications 14, 163–178 (2005)
6. Ghosh, A.K., Chaudhuri, P., Sengupta, D.: Classification using kernel density estimates: Multiscale analysis and visualization. Technometrics 48(1), 120–132 (2006)
7. Kobos, M., Mańdziuk, J.: Multiple-resolution classification with combination of density estimators. Connection Science 23(4), 219–237 (2011)
8. Kobos, M.: Combination of independent kernel density estimators in classification. In: Ganzha, M., Paprzycki, M. (eds.) Proceedings of the International Multiconference on Computer Science and Information Technology, vol. 4, pp. 57–63 (2009)
9. Kobos, M., Mańdziuk, J.: Classification Based on Combination of Kernel Density Estimators. In: Alippi, C., Polycarpou, M., Panayiotou, C., Ellinas, G. (eds.) ICANN 2009. LNCS, vol. 5769, pp. 125–134. Springer, Heidelberg (2009)
10. Kobos, M., Mańdziuk, J.: Classification Based on Multiple-Resolution Data View. In: Diamantaras, K., Duch, W., Iliadis, L.S. (eds.) ICANN 2010. LNCS, vol. 6354, pp. 124–129. Springer, Heidelberg (2010)
11. Lim, T.S., Loh, W.Y., Shih, Y.S.: A comparison of prediction accuracy, complexity, and training time of thirty-three old and new classification algorithms. Machine Learning 40, 203–228 (2000)
12. Mangasarian, O., Wolberg, W.: Cancer diagnosis via linear programming. Siam News 23, 1–18 (1990)
13. Marchette, D.J., Priebe, C.E., Rogers, G.W., Solka, J.L.: Filtered kernel density estimation. Computational Statistics 11(2), 95–112 (1996)
14. Ripley, B.: Pattern recognition and neural networks datasets collection (1996), http://www.stats.ox.ac.uk/pub/PRNN/
15. Smyth, P., Wolpert, D.: Linearly combining density estimators via stacking. Machine Learning 36, 59–83 (1999)
16. Witten, I., Frank, E.: Data Mining: Practical Machine Learning Tools and Techniques, 2nd edn. Elsevier (2005)
17. Yeh, I.C., Yang, K.J., Ting, T.M.: Knowledge discovery on rfm model using bernoulli sequence. Expert Systems with Applications 36, 5866–5871 (2008)

Competing Risks and Survival Tree Ensemble

Małgorzata Krętowska

Faculty of Computer Science
Bialystok University of Technology
Wiejska 45a, 15-351 Białystok, Poland
m.kretowska@pb.edu.pl

Abstract. In the paper the ensemble of dipolar trees for analysis of competing risks is proposed. The tool is build on the base of the learning sets, which contain the data from clinical studies following patients response for a given treatment. In case of competing risks many types of response are investigated. The proposed method is able to cope with incomplete (censored) observations and as a result, for a given set of covariates and a type of event, returns the aggregated cumulative incidence function.

1 Introduction

Survival analysis, in its basic form, aims at prediction the time of failure occurrence. The failure, in medical domain, usually means death or disease relapse. Analyzing the survival data we are often interested not only in estimation of the exact time point when the failure would occur for a given patient, but we also want to observe the failure probability during a given period of time. It may be done by estimation of a distribution function (e.g. survival function, hazard function or cumulative incidence function).

In the presence of competing risks we are not only focused on prediction of one type of event. In such kind of data there are many types of event, which may be investigated. For one patient we register only the time of the first failure occurred. If the patient has not experienced any type of event we register only the follow-up time. This kind of observation is called censored one. Censored data contain incomplete information about the time of failure occurrence of any type of event. For such kind data we only know that the failure time is greater or equal to given follow-up time.

Since the survival data is to a large extent censored, the crucial point of methods for failure time prognosis, is using the information from censored cases. The use of ensemble of simple tree structure predictors is very common, recently. Hothorn et al. [4] proposes boosting survival trees to create aggregated survival function. Krętowska [7] developed the approach by using the dipolar regression trees instead of the structure proposed in [4]. The technique proposed by Ridgeway [11] allows minimizing the partial likelihood function (boosting Cox's proportional hazard model). The Hothorn et al. [5] developed two approaches for censored data: random forest and gradient boosting. Breiman [2] provided the software that allows induction of random forest for censored data.

L. Rutkowski et al. (Eds.): ICAISC 2012, Part I, LNCS 7267, pp. 387–393, 2012.

In case of competing risk the authors develop the tools on the base of single survival tree. Similar approaches are described in [3] and [6], where induction of the proposed between-node tree is based on the difference between cumulative incidence function. Presented in [3] a within-node tree uses event-specific martingale residuals.

The results received from the single tree are instable. It means that each tree inducted for the same data produces different outcomes. The application of ensemble based methods stabilizes the results. In the paper, the survival tree ensemble proposed in [8] is modified for competing risks data. The modifications are mainly connected with the way the dipoles are formed during a single survival tree induction and the way the results are presented. The idea of aggregated cumulative incidence function is introduced as a result of survival tree ensemble. The results are presented on the base of follicular type lymphoma data, which contain 541 observations.

The paper is organized as follows. Section 2 describes the survival data with competing risks and introduces the idea of cumulative incidence function as well as the Kaplan-Meier survival function. In Section 4 induction of single dipolar survival tree and ensemble of survival tree are presented. The algorithm of calculation of aggregated cumulative incidence function is described. Experimental results are presented in Section 4. They were carried out on the base of real dataset describing the patients with follicular type lymphoma [9]. Section 5 summarizes the results.

2   Survival Data with Competing Risks

In case of survival data with competing risks, the patient is at risk of p ($p > 1$) different types of failure. Assuming that the time of occurrence of the ith failure is T_i, we are interested only in the failure with the shortest time $T = \min(T_1, T_2, \ldots, T_n)$. The learning sample L for competing risk data is defined as $L = (\mathbf{x}_i, t_i, \delta_i)$, $i = 1, 2, \ldots, n$, where $\mathbf{x}_i$ is N-dimensional covariates vector, t_i is time to the first event observed and $\delta_i = \{0, 1, \ldots, p\}$ indicates the case of failure. δ_i equals to 0 represents censored observation, which means that for a given patient has not occurred any failure. Variable t_i represents the follow-up time.

The distribution of the random variable T (time), for an event of type i ($i = 1, 2, \ldots, p$) may be represented by several functions. One of the most popular is cumulative incidence function (CIF) defined as the probability that an event of type i occurs at or before time t [10]:

$$F_i(t) = P(T \leq t, \delta = i) \tag{1}$$

or survival function:

$$S_i(t) = P(T > t, \delta = i) \tag{2}$$

The estimator of the CIF function is calculated as

$$\hat{F}_i(t) = \sum_{j \mid t_j \leq t} \frac{d_{ij}}{n_j} \hat{S}(t_{j-1}) \tag{3}$$

where $t_{(1)} < t_{(2)} < \ldots < t_{(D)}$ are distinct, ordered uncensored time points from the learning sample L, d_{ij} is the number of events of type i at time $t_{(j)}$, n_j is the number of patients at risk at $t_{(j)}$ (i.e., the number of patients who are alive at $t_{(j)}$ or experience the event of interest at $t_{(j)}$) and $\hat{S}(t)$ is the Kaplan-Meier estimator of the probability of being free of any event by time t. It is calculated as:

$$\hat{S}(t) = \prod_{j|t_{(j)} \leq t} \left(\frac{n_j - d_j}{n_j} \right) \tag{4}$$

where d_j is the number of events at time $t_{(j)}$.

The "patients specific" cumulative incidence function for the event of type i is given by $F_i(t|x) = P(T \leq t, \delta = i|\mathbf{X} = (x))$. The conditional CIF for the new patient with covariate vector $\mathbf{x}_{new}$ is denoted by $\hat{F}_i(t|\mathbf{x}_{new})$.

3   Survival Tree Ensemble

Individual survival tree being a part of the complex predictor [7] is a kind of binary regression tree. Each internal node contains a split, which tests the value of an expression of the covariates. In the proposed approach the split is equivalent to the hyper-plane $H(\mathbf{w}, \theta) = \{(\mathbf{w}, \mathbf{x}) : <\mathbf{w}, \mathbf{x} >= \theta\}$.

Establishing the structure of the tree (the number of internal nodes) and the values of hyper-planes parameters $(\mathbf{w}, \theta)$ are based on the concept of dipoles [1]. The dipole is a pair of different covariate vectors $(\mathbf{x}_i, \mathbf{x}_j)$ from the learning set. Mixed and pure dipoles are distinguished. Assuming that the analysis aims at dividing the feature space into such areas, which would include the patients with the same case of failure and similar survival times, pure dipoles are created between pairs of feature vectors with the same failure type, for which the difference of failure times is small, mixed dipoles - between pairs with distant failure times. Taking into account censored cases the following rules of dipole construction can be formulated:

1. a pair of feature vectors $(\mathbf{x}_i, \mathbf{x}_j)$ forms the pure dipole, if
   - $\delta_i \neq 0$ and $\delta_i = \delta_j = z$ and $|t_i - t_j| < \eta_z$, $z = 1, 2, \ldots, p$.
2. a pair of feature vectors $(\mathbf{x}_i, \mathbf{x}_j)$ forms the mixed dipole, if
   - $\delta_i \neq 0$ and $\delta_i = \delta_j = z$ and $|t_i - t_j| > \zeta_z$, $z = 1, 2, \ldots, p$
   - $(\delta_i = 0, \delta_j = z$ and $t_i - t_j > \zeta_z)$ or $(\delta_i = z, \delta_j = 0$ and $t_j - t_i > \zeta_z)$, $z = 1, 2, \ldots, p$

Parameters η_z and ζ_z are equal to quartiles of absolute values of differences between uncensored survival times for zth type of failure, $z = 1, 2, \ldots, p$. Basing on the earlier experiments, the parameter η_z is fixed as 0.3 quantile and ζ_z - 0.6.

The increasing number of censored cases may decrease the number of pure dipoles as well as the mixed ones.

The hyper-planes $H(\mathbf{w}, \theta)$ in the internal nodes of a tree are calculated by minimization of dipolar criterion function (detailed description may be fond in [7]). This is equivalent with division of possibly high number of mixed dipoles and possibly low number of pure ones constructed for a given dataset. The tree induction algorithm starts from the root, so in the root node, the dipolar criterion function is calculated on the base of dipoles created for the whole learning set. The dipolar criterion function for consecutive nodes of a tree are designed on the base on those feature vectors that reached the node. The induction of survival tree is stopped if one of the following conditions is fulfilled: 1) all the mixed dipoles are divided; 2) the set that reaches the node consists of less than 5 uncensored cases.

The survival tree ensemble algorithm leading to receive the aggregated cumulative incidence function $\hat{F}_i(t|\mathbf{x}_n)$ is as follows:

1. Draw k bootstrap samples $(L_1, L_2, \ldots, L_k)$ of size n with replacement from L
2. Induction of dipolar survival tree $T(L_i)$ based on each bootstrap sample L_i
3. For each tree $T(L_i)$, distinguish the set of observations $L_i(\mathbf{x}_n)$ which belongs to the same terminal node as $\mathbf{x}_n$
4. Build aggregated sample $L_A(\mathbf{x}_n) = [L_1(\mathbf{x}_n), L_2(\mathbf{x}_n), \ldots, L_k(\mathbf{x}_n)]$
5. Compute the Kaplan-Meier aggregated survival function for a new observation $\mathbf{x}_n$ as $\hat{S}^A(t|\mathbf{x}_n)$.
6. Compute the aggregated CIF functions for the ith type of failure for a new observation $\mathbf{x}_n$ as $\hat{F}_i^A(t|\mathbf{x}_n)$.

The predicted value of exact time of ith type of failure for observation $\mathbf{x}_n$ may be calculated as the median value of $\hat{F}_i^A(t|\mathbf{x}_n)$.

4 Experimental Results

The experiments were done on the base of lymphoma patient data, which was created at Princess Margaret Hospital, Toronto [9]. In the experiments we use the subset of 541 patients having follicular type lymphoma, registered for treatment at the hospital between 1967 and 1996, with early stage disease (I or II) and treated with radiation alone or with radiation and chemotherapy. Each patient is described by four covariates, having the following characteristics:

age [years]: $Q_1 = 47$, $Me = 58$, $Q_3 = 67$
haemoglobin [g/l]: $Q_1 = 130$, $Me = 140$, $Q_3 = 150$
clinical stage : equal to 1 (66.9% observations) or 2
chemotherapy : 0-no (78.2% observations), 1-yes

where Q_1 is the lower quartile, Me - median, Q_3 - upper quartile.

The goal of this study was to report long-term outcome in this group of patient. The event of interest is failure from the disease: no response to treatment or relapse. Competing risk type of event is death without failure. There are 272 event of interest and 76 observations with death without relapse.

All the experiments were performed using the ensemble of 100 survival trees.

In figure 1 we can observe the cumulative incidence functions which were calculated for the patient described by the covariates equal to their median values:

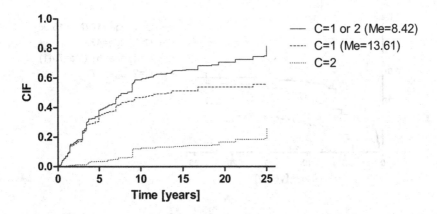

Fig. 1. CIF functions for disease failure (C=1), for competing risk (C=2) and without distinguishing two types of failure (C=1 or 2) (age=58, hgb=140, clinstg=1 and ch=0)

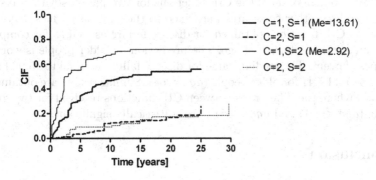

Fig. 2. CIF functions for disease failure (C=1) and for competing risk (C=2) for two values of clinical stage (S=1 and S=2) (age=58, hgb=140, ch=0)

age=58, hgb=140, clinstg=1 and ch=0. Three CIF functions are presented in figure 1: CIF function for disease failure (C=1), for competing risk (C=2) and the third one calculated for two types of failure (C=1 or 2). We can observe here that for each time point the probability of competing risk (death without failure) is lower than the probability of failure. The median value calculated for the event of interest is equal to 13.61, the median value for competing risk do not exist ($\hat{F}_2(t)$ is always less than 0.5).

Figure 2 presents the CIF functions for two values of clinical stage, other covariates were fixed to theirs median values. The functions calculated for competing risk do not differ significantly for two types of clinical stage. The difference is visible while comparing the functions calculated for disease failure. The prediction is worse for patient with clinical stage II (median value equal to 2.92 [years]), for stage I median value is 13.61 [years].

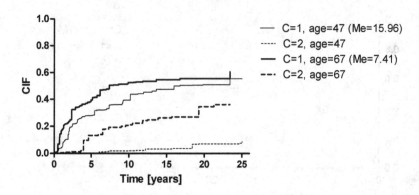

Fig. 3. CIF functions for disease failure (C=1) and for competing risk (C=2) for two values of age (hgb=140, clinstg=1, ch=0)

In figure 3 we can observe the CIF functions for two patients with two values of age: 47 and 68, other covariates were fixed to their median values. Analyzing the shape of CIF functions obtained for disease failure as well as for competing risk we can see the influence of age. The prediction for older people is worse for both types of event. The median value for disease failure is equal to 15.96 for age equals to 47 and 7.41 for older people ($age = 68$). Similar results are obtained by Pintilie [9], where the differences between CIF functions received for two groups of people ($age <= 65$ and $age > 65$) were statistically significant.

5   Conclusions

In the paper the ensemble of dipolar trees for analysis of competing risks is proposed. The method is an extension of the approach proposed in [8], where only one type of event was analyzed. In the described algorithm the information about the type of event is used during dipoles formation. Dipoles may be created only between these covariate vectors which represent the same type of event. The method produces aggregated cumulative incidence function (CIF) for a new patient described by **x**. The unknown time of occurrence of a given event type may be estimated by median value of the received function.

The results are conducted on the base of the set of patients with follicular type lymphoma, where two types of event were investigated: failure from the disease and death without failure. The influence of clinical stage and age were analyzed. The graphical representation of received CIF functions shows worse prediction of the first type of event for patients with clinical stage II. Age influences the CIF function for both types of event.

Acknowledgements. This work was supported by the grant S/WI/2/08 from Bialystok University of Technology.

References

1. Bobrowski, L., Krętowska, M., Krętowski, M.: Design of neural classifying networks by using dipolar criterions. In: Proc. of the Third Conference on Neural Networks and Their Applications, Kule, Poland, pp. 689–694 (1997)
2. Breiman, L.: How to use survival forest,
   http://stat-www.berkeley.edu/users/breiman
3. Callaghan, F.M.: Classification trees for survival data with competing risks, Univeristy of Pittsburgh, PhD. thesis (2008)
4. Hothorn, T., Lausen, B., Benner, A., Radespiel-Troger, M.: Bagging survival trees. Statistics in Medicine 23, 77–91 (2004)
5. Hothorn, T., Buhlmann, P., Dudoit, S., Molinaro, A.M., van der Laan, M.J.: Survival ensembles. U.C. Berkeley Division of Biostatistics Working Paper Series 174 (2005), http://www.bepress.com/ucbbiostat/paper174
6. Ibrahim, N.A., Kudus, A.: Decision tree for prognostic classification of multivariate survival data and competing risks. In: Strangio, M.A. (ed.) Recent Advances in Technologies (2009)
7. Krętowska, M.: Random Forest of Dipolar Trees for Survival Prediction. In: Rutkowski, L., Tadeusiewicz, R., Zadeh, L.A., Żurada, J.M. (eds.) ICAISC 2006. LNCS (LNAI), vol. 4029, pp. 909–918. Springer, Heidelberg (2006)
8. Krętowska, M.: Ensembles of dipolar trees for prediction of survival time. Biocybernetics and Biomedical Engineering 27(3), 67–75 (2007)
9. Pintilie, M.: Competing Risks: A Practical Perspective. John Willey & Sons (2006)
10. Putter, H., Fiocco, M., Geskus, R.B.: Tutorial in biostatistics: Competing risks and multi-stage models. Statistics in Medicine 26, 2389–2430 (2007)
11. Ridgeway, G.: The state of boosting. Computing Science and Statistics 31, 1722–1731 (1999)

Sign Language Recognition Using Kinect

Simon Lang, Marco Block, and Raúl Rojas

Freie Universität Berlin
Institut für Informatik und Mathematik
Takustr. 9, 14195 Berlin, Germany
{slang,block,rojas}@inf.fu-berlin.de

Abstract. An open source framework for general gesture recognition is presented and tested with isolated signs of sign language. Other than common systems for sign language recognition, this framework makes use of Kinect, a depth camera which makes real-time 3D-reconstruction easily applicable. Recognition is done using hidden Markov models with a continuous observation density. The framework also offers an easy way of initializing and training new gestures or signs by performing them several times in front of the camera. First results with a recognition rate of 97% show that depth cameras are well-suited for sign language recognition.

1 Motivation and Introduction

Using gestures as a natural communication interface between human beings and machines becomes more and more important. This involves controlling computers, as well as processing and translating sign language.

When Microsoft released Kinect in November 2010, it was mainly targeted at owners of a Microsoft Xbox 360 console, being advertised as a controller-free gaming experience. The device itself features an RGB camera, a depth sensor and a multiarray microphone, and is capable of tracking users' body movement [9,10]. The interest in the device has been high among developers, and thus, shortly after its release an unofficial open source driver was introduced, followed by many Kinect-based projects and technical demos. Even though Microsoft stated that "Kinect that is shipping [2010's] holiday will not support sign language", several demos show how it technically is capable of recognizing signs [11,12,13].

In sign languages, manual features are generally used along with facial expressions and different body postures to express words and grammatical features. The manual components can be split into four parameters: handshape, palm orientation, location, and movement. There are similar signs that differ in one of these components only, and thus without considering context, signs can only be recognized precisely when all of these components are known. Nevertheless, a great number of signs can be distinguished by only considering hand location and movement [6].

After the related work part in section 2, we present Dragonfly, an open source C++ framework for general gesture recognition that can be used to recognize signs of sign language, utilizing the two above-mentioned manual components. This is

L. Rutkowski et al. (Eds.): ICAISC 2012, Part I, LNCS 7267, pp. 394–402, 2012.

achieved by using hidden Markov models that allow training and recognition of isolated signs. In section 4, the framework is tested in several experiments, and an evaluation shows how well it performs when using optimal parameters. A conclusion in section 5 summarizes the achievements of this work and what future work may follow in order to improve it for better sign language recognition.

2   Related Work

This section summarizes the basics of hidden Markov models as well as their application on sign language recognition. Alternate methods of feature extraction are also presented.

2.1   Hidden Markov Models

Hidden Markov models (HMMs) are a type of stochastic model related to finite state machines. An HMM features a number N of states $S_1, S_2, \cdots, S_N$, being in exactly one of theses states at any time $t = 1, 2, 3, \cdots$, where the state at time t is referred to as q_t.

The initial probability distribution π describes the probability of starting in a specific state. Every state S_i features a probability of transitioning to a state S_j, stored in the transition probability matrix $A_{N \times N}$. A set of output probability distributions $B = \{b_j(k)\}$ describes the probability of observing the kth out of M observation symbols in state j. Observation sequences are denoted as $O = O_1 O_2 \ldots O_T$, where T is the number of observations in the sequence and each O_t represents one such observation.

If M is infinite (e. g. when observations are real numbers), the HMM features a continuous observation density. Each state then includes a mean vector μ and a covariance matrix Σ for use with a logarithmically concave function, e. g. a D-dimensional multivariate Gaussian distribution $\mathcal{N}$,

$$\mathcal{N}(O_t; \mu, \Sigma) = \frac{1}{(2\pi)^{\frac{D}{2}} |\Sigma|^{\frac{1}{2}}} \cdot \exp\left(-\frac{1}{2}(O_t - \mu)^{\mathrm{T}} \Sigma^{-1}(O_t - \mu)\right).$$

Given the triple $\lambda = (A, B, \pi)$ as a compact notation for HMMs, the three basic problems that come along can be summarized as follows [7,8,3]:

1. Given an observation sequence O, determine the probability of O being generated by λ, i. e. efficiently calculate $P(O|\lambda)$. This is done using a scaled version of the forward-backward procedure.
2. Determine the state sequence $Q = q_1 q_2 \ldots q_T$ that is most likely to be traversed, given an observation sequence O and a model λ. The scaled Viterbi algorithm takes care of this calculation.
3. Determine how to adjust the parameters of λ in order to maximize $P(O|\lambda)$. This is achieved by the Baum-Welch algorithm, modified to accept multiple observation sequences at once.

A method of initializating HMMs is proposed by Kelly et al. [1], where the initial parameters are calculated automatically with an optimal number of states.

2.2   Recognizing Sign Language

Recognizing sign language involves two major processes, namely extracting features and interpreting them. While the former is usually done using a 2D camera [2,5] and detecting the positions of hands and head, Vogler and Metaxas [4] use a set of three orthogonally placed 2D cameras to extract 3D data of the signers body parts. The results show that this method is more accurate than using 2D data.

In order to conveniently recognize signs and to handle the statistical variations when performing them, both intra- and interpersonal, HMMs are introduced and each sign is represented by a separate HMM. An observation sequence can be seen as a performance of one such sign, and each single observation represents a vector of body part information, e. g. a hand's position, movement speed, and the distance between both hands.

When a sign is performed, the probability of that performance given each HMM is calculated. The HMM with the highest probability is most likely to have produced that sign. This information is essential for actually building a sign language recognition framework.

3   Dragonfly Framework

The framework presented in this work is called Dragonfly (**Dr**aw gestures **on** the **fly**) and is capable of learning and recognizing gestures and signs. It is written in C++ and makes use of the free cross-platform Kinect driver OpenNI released by PrimeSense, including NITE skeletal tracking which automatically extracts users' body parts such as their hands and elbows.

The main classes to be included in other software are called `DepthCamera` and `Dragonfly`. The former acts as an interface to OpenNI and can easily be replaced to use a different Kinect driver with skeletal tracking. The latter is the actual interface to the framework which processes the skeleton data for gesture recognition.

Dragonfly features an own implementation of continuous density HMMs, offering automatic initialization, Baum-Welch re-estimation with multiple observation sequences, and serialization, among others. For vector and matrix calculations, the Vision Numerics Libraries are used. Boost provides several other helpful features such as an implementation of the observer pattern.

3.1   Gesture Recognition

Observations are recorded for every user separately, and consist of an N-dimensional feature vector. This can be data such as velocity or absolute position of each hand, or distance between hands.

By default, observations are recorded when the dominant (e. g. right) hand moves above a given threshold, such as the torso's y-position. Each of these observations is saved in a matrix which represents the entire observation sequence. Several of these matrices are stored in a list that can be seen as a set of observation sequences.

Observation recording can be turned on and off for each user separately. Every time the user's hand moves below the threshold, the probability of the newly recorded sequence given each existing HMM is calculated, and results are compared. This is done in order to determine the model that best matches the sequence.

To make use of this information, a system for callback functions has been implemented. Since HMMs must have distinct names, these can be uniquely associated with a signal using a hashmap. A signal can be linked to and unlinked from an HMM by calling appropriate methods in `Dragonfly`.

3.2 Learning New Gestures

Creating new gestures and training them is done successively in one method, by providing a maximum number of states, a set of observation sequences – used for initialization and re-estimating – and a set of negative test sequences that do not contain the actual gesture to be trained. An example of one out of several similar training sequences is shown in figure 1.

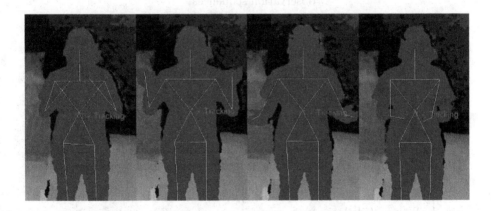

Fig. 1. Example training sequence of the sign PAKET (German for packet)

Cross validation splits observation sequences into sequences actually used for training (two third), and positive test sequences the model should recognize correctly without having them used for training (one third). Additionally, a set of existing HMMs that represent different gestures can be provided.

The algorithm then initializes and trains several HMMs using the training sequences, and determines the optimal HMM given the rest of the data, according to an optimality criterion that must be defined as well.

In detail, the algorithm works as follows:

1. Split provided observation sequences into training and positive test sequences. Two third are used for training and one third for positive testing.
2. Initialize with $N = 1$ states. Set the best HMM to NULL and the best value for each optimality criterion to the worst possible value.
3. Create $Q = 5$ HMMs, each with N states, from the given set of training sequences using automatic initialization, which works as follows:
   - Create a point cloud with every single observation of every sequence as a point.
   - Perform k-means clustering on the point cloud, initial prototypes are chosen randomly among its points. Empty clusters are avoided by determining a new prototype from the biggest cluster.
   - Sort the resulting clusters and assign each of them to a separate state.
   - Calculate the transition probability distribution A using data from all observation sequences, where

$$a_{ij} = \frac{\#\text{transitions from } S_i \text{ to } S_j}{\#\text{transitions from } S_i} \quad , 0 \leqslant i, j < N.$$

   - Compute the initial probability distribution π, where

$$\pi_i = \frac{\#\text{observation sequences starting in } S_i}{\#\text{observation sequences}} \quad , 0 \leqslant i < N.$$

   - Set each state's μ to the mean vector of the corresponding cluster.
   - Determine Σ for each state by calculating the covariance matrix for each corresponding cluster.

   Due to the randomness in k-means clustering, results may vary. Hence, several HMMs are created using the same algorithm.
4. Re-estimate these HMMs by the Baum-Welch algorithm, using the same training sequences as input.
5. Set $q = 1$.
6. Among the Q created HMMs, choose the one at position q.
7. If at least half of the observation sequences could not be processed due to underflow, discard this HMM and go to step 10.
8. Determine the values for all optimality criteria given the newly created model and all provided data, such as positive and negative test sequences, and HMMs of other gestures.
9. Update the best value for each optimality criterion. If this HMM is better than the stored best HMM according to the chosen criterion, define it as the new best HMM.
10. Increment q. If $q \leqslant Q$, go to step 6.
11. Increment N. If $N \leqslant S$ (where S is the maximum number of states), go to step 3.
12. If any of the three split combinations is left, split observation sequences accordingly and go to step 2.
13. Return the best HMM (which is NULL in case the procedure failed to create any HMM at all).

This procedure guarantees to deliver a re-estimated HMM that best matches the given data for the chosen criterion, depending on how well k-means clustering performs. Possible optimality criteria are σ_r (recognition rate), σ_v (variance), and σ_{np} (lowest negative above worst positive rate).

The first criterion σ_r uses positive test sequences only and tests them with the newly created HMM and all other HMMs. Negative test sequences are neglected. Each positive test sequence is tested with all HMMs and the number of correct results is saved and then summed up. A test result is correct when the sequence given the new HMM has a higher probability than the sequence given any other HMM. The summed number is divided by the total number of tests, and the resulting recognition rate is to be maximized.

The second criterion σ_v calculates the average logarithmic probability of all negative test sequences given the new model, and subtracts it from the average logarithmic probability of all positive test sequences given that model. Gestures of the new model can be distinguished from other gesture more clearly the higher this value is.

Determining σ_{np} is done by saving the lowest probability of any positive test sequence given the new model – i.e. saving the worst positive test sequence. Then, probabilities of all negative test sequences are calculated for the model. The number of negative test sequences with a probability higher than that of the worst positive test sequence, is divided by the total number of negative test sequences. The lower this value gets, the better the success rate of the new HMM is.

For equal values of the third criterion, the second criterion is used to determine which HMM is better. HMMs can be saved to and loaded from a file at any time during recognition.

4   Experiments and Results

First experiments were made with a vocabulary of 25 signs of German Sign Language that were trained with the help of fluent speakers. Best results could be achieved with a nine-dimensional feature vector, composed of ($RH_x, RH_x, RH_z,$ $LH_x, LH_y, LH_z, RH_v, LH_v, RE_x$), where RH and LH correspond to the right and left hand relative to the neck, respectively, v means velocity, and RE corresponds to the right elbow.

Every sign was tested 40 to 60 times, results show an overall recognition rate of 97,0%. Detailed results are shown in figure 2, where the recognition rate of each sign is shown next to a boxplot.

Each boxplot shows the distance between the actually performed sign and the best recognized sign that is unequal. This illustrates for positive values how well the recognized sign could be distinguished from others, and for negative values how much other signs were preferred. Since the logarithmic probabilities are negative, values have been normalized by $a \mapsto \frac{-700}{a}$ (higher values are better). The sign NEUKOELLN (a district in Berlin), for example, features a high

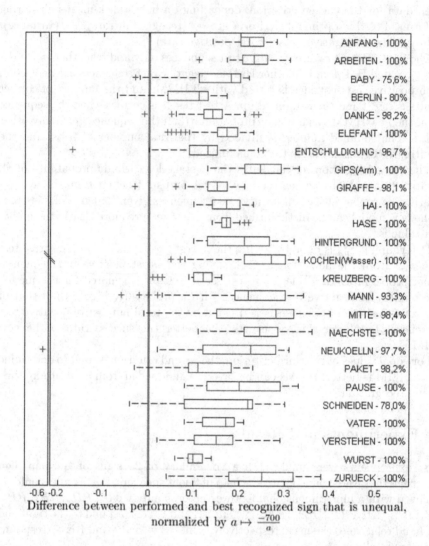

Fig. 2. Test results of the first experiment, the signs trained are ANFANG (beginning), ARBEITEN (to work), BABY, BERLIN, DANKE (thank you), ELEFANT (elephant), ENTSCHULDIGUNG (sorry), GIPS (gypsum), GIRAFFE, HAI (shark), HASE (rabbit), HINTERGRUND (background), KOCHEN (to boil), KREUZBERG (a district in Berlin), MANN (man), MITTE (a district in Berlin), NAECHSTE (next), NEUKOELLN (a district in Berlin), PAKET (packet), PAUSE, SCHNEIDEN (to cut), VATER (father), VERSTEHEN (to understand), WURST (sausage), and ZURUECK (back)

recognition rate and can usually be distinguished well from other signs, however one performance was not recognized correctly and is far off the sign that was recognized instead.

Signs that mainly contain movement towards the camera, such as DANKE (German for "thank you"), have a significantly worse recognition rate with a feature vector that does not contain the hands' z-positions. The right elbow's x-position (if the user is right-handed) helps distinguish other signs where the hand is near the face and the arm is either held away from or close to the body.

Since the depth of each body part is known, the recognition rate does not change when standing closer to the camera or further away from it, as long a minimum distance is kept in order for skeletal tracking to work. Especially the use of z-values shows an advantage of depth cameras over ordinary RGB cameras, where extracting depth information is generally harder and less reliable.

On a 2 GHz dual-core machine with 4 GB memory, the probabilities of a sequence given all 25 signs were calculated in less than 300 milliseconds.

5   Conclusion and Future Work

Kinect and other depth cameras offer 3D data without a complicated camera setup and efficiently extract the users' body parts, allowing for easier recognition of not just hands and head, but also other parts such as elbows that can further help distinguish similar signs. Another advantage is the independency of lighting conditions due to the use of infrared light, however thus, the cameras are limited to in-door use.

The presented framework offers recognition and learning of isolated signs, using NITE skeletal tracking and an own HMM implementation. This implementation includes a new way of initialization and several optimality criteria for HMM comparison. First experiments were made with a vocabulary of 25 signs of German Sign Language, and show a high recognition rate of 97,0% when using depth-camera-specific features. Future experiments will show how well the presented methods perform when using a larger vocabulary of more than 100 signs.

Accurately recognizing sign language, however, not only involves tracking hands. There are signs that only differ in mouthshape or handshape and are similar otherwise. Facial expression, body posture and head movement are often used to express grammatical features.

When detection of these essential components is supported by the backend, Dragonfly can be extended to support continuous sign language recognition. This also involves detecting a sign's start and end position, as well as movement epenthesis as described by Kelly et al. [1] in order to distinguish hand movement within a sign from movement between two signs.

In conclusion, this work shows that depth cameras are well-suited for sign language recognition. The approach is worth further consideration and features its own advantages, while leaving room for improvement of both the underlying technology as well as the framework itself.

The source code of Dragonfly is available under the terms of the GNU Lesser General Public License, version 3, at *https://bitbucket.org/Slang/dragonfly/*.

References

1. Kelly, D., McDonald, J., Markham, C.: Recognizing Spatiotemporal Gestures and Movement Epenthesis in Sign Language. In: 13th International Machine Vision and Image Processing Conference (IMVIP 2009). IEEE Computer Society, Washington, DC (2009)
2. Dreuw, P., Rybach, D., Deselaers, T., Zahedi, M., Ney, H.: Speech Recognition Techniques for a Sign Language Recognition System. In: INTERSPEECH 2007, 8th Annual Conference of the International Speech Communication Association (ISCA 2007), pp. 2513–2516 (2007)
3. Li, X., Parizeau, M., Plamondon, R.: Training Hidden Markov Models with Multiple Observations – A combinatorial Method. IEEE Transactions on PAMI PAMI-22(4), 371–377 (2000)
4. Vogler, C., Metaxas, D.: ASL Recognition Based on a Coupling Between HMMs and 3D Motion Analysis. In: Proceedings of the Sixth International Conference on Computer Vision, pp. 363–369. Narosa Publishing House (1998) ISBN: 978-8-17319-221-0
5. Starner, T., Pentland, A.: Real-Time American Sign Language Recognition from Video Using Hidden Markov Models. In: Proceedings of the International Symposium on Computer Vision, ISCV 1995, pp. 265–270. IEEE Publications, U.S (1995) ISBN: 978-0-81867-190-6
6. Boyes Braem, P.: Einführung in die Gebärdensprache und ihre Erforschung. In: Internationale Arbeiten zur Gebärdensprache und Kommunikation Gehörloser, 1st edn., vol. 11. SIGNUM-Verlag (1990) ISBN: 978-3-92773-110-3
7. Rabiner, L.R.: A Tutorial on Hidden Markov Models and Selected Applications in Speech Recognition. Proceedings of the IEEE 77(2), 257–286 (1989)
8. Rahimi, A.: An Erratum for "A Tutorial on Hidden Markov Models and Selected Applications in Speech Recognition", website of Ali Rahimi at MIT Media Laboratory, http://xenia.media.mit.edu/ rahimi/rabiner/rabiner-errata/ rabiner-errata.html
9. Official Microsoft Xbox website, introduction of Kinect, http://www.xbox.com/en-US/kinect
10. Countdown to Kinect: 17 Controller-Free Games Launch in November, Microsoft News Center, https://www.microsoft.com/presspass/press/2010/oct10/ 10-18mskinectuspr.mspx
11. Kinect Downgraded To Save Money, Can't Read Sign Language, News at Kotaku, http://kotaku.com/5609840/kinect-dumbed-down-to-save-money-cant-read-sign-language
12. CopyCat and Kinect, overview of the CopyCat Kinect demo on the website of the Center for Accessible Technology in Sign (CATS), http://cats.gatech.edu/content/copycat-and-kinect
13. Integrating Speech and Hearing Challenge Individuals, YouTube channel of Dr. Natheer Khasawneh, http://www.youtube.com/user/knatheer#p/a/u/1/vVL398dUU5Q

Investigation of Rotation Forest Method Applied to Property Price Prediction

Tadeusz Lasota[1], Tomasz Łuczak[2], and Bogdan Trawiński[2]

[1] Wrocław University of Environmental and Life Sciences,
Dept. of Spatial Management, Norwida 25/27, 50-375 Wrocław, Poland
tadeusz.lasota@up.wroc.pl
[2] Wrocław University of Technology, Institute of Informatics,
Wybrzeże Wyspiańskiego 27, 50-370 Wrocław, Poland
{tomasz.luczak,bogdan.trawinski}@pwr.wroc.pl

Abstract. A few years ago a new classifier ensemble method, called rotation forest, was devised. The technique applies Principal Component Analysis to rotate the original feature axes in order to obtain different training sets for learning base classifiers. In the paper we report the results of the investigation aimed to compare the predictive performance of rotation forest with random forest models, bagging ensembles and single models using two popular algorithms M5 tree and multilayer perceptron. All tests were carried out in the WEKA data mining system within the framework of 10-fold cross-validation and repeated holdout splits. A real-world dataset of sales/purchase transactions derived from a cadastral system served as basis for benchmarking the methods.

Keywords: rotation forest, random forest, bagging, property valuation.

1 Introduction

For some years we have been studying various machine learning techniques to create data driven models for property valuation. We have been investigating methods capable of solving regression problems. Our studies are spread in many directions including evolutionary fuzzy systems, neural networks, decision trees and statistical algorithms using MATLAB, KEEL, RapidMiner and WEKA data mining system [8], [13], [17]. Our long term goal is to build an automated system to aid in real estate appraisal devoted to information centres maintaining cadastral systems in Poland. A good performance revealed evolving fuzzy models applied to cadastral data [19], [20]. Last several studies we devoted to investigate ensemble models created applying various weak learners, resampling and subsampling techniques [11], [14], [18]. Ensemble learning is now an active area of our research. Many studies have proven that it is worth its attention.

Two of most popular and effective approaches in ensemble models are bagging and random forests. Bagging stands for bootstrap aggregating. It was first presented by Breiman [1] in 1995. Even though it is a very intuitive and straightforward algorithm it provides a very good performance. The idea standing behind

L. Rutkowski et al. (Eds.): ICAISC 2012, Part I, LNCS 7267, pp. 403–411, 2012.

this method is based on bootstrap selection. Each individual learner is supplied with training data drawn with replacements from original dataset. A given learning instance can occur several times in a for one component model and does not have to be taken into account when building other models. This way diversity is obtained. Finally, individual learners are combined through an algebraic expression, such as minimum, maximum, sum, mean, product, median, etc. [21]. Theoretical analyses and experimental results proved benefits of bagging, especially in terms of stability improvement and variance reduction of learners for both classification and regression problems [4], [5], [6].

Another approach to ensemble learning is called the random subspace method (RS), also known as attribute bagging [3]. It was first presented by Ho in 1995 [9]. This approach seeks learners diversity in feature space subsampling. All component models are built with the same training data, but each takes into account a randomly chosen subset of features bringing diversity to ensemble. For the most part, feature count is fixed at the same level for all committee components. Ho showed that RS can outperform bagging or in some cases even boosting [10]. While other methods are affected by the curse of dimensionality, RS can actually benefits out of it.

Both bagging and RS were devised to increase classifier or regressor accuracy, but each of them treats the problem from different point of view. Bagging provides diversity by operating on training set instances, whereas RS tries to find diversity in feature space subsampling. Breiman [2], developed a method called Random Forest (RF) which merges these two approaches. RF uses bootstrap selection for supplying individual learner with training data and limits feature space by random selection. Some recent studies have been focused on hybrid approaches combining random forests with other learning algorithms [7], [12], [22].

In this paper we focused on rotation forest (RTF). It is a relatively new approach, in ensembles methods, proposed by Rodríguez et al. in 2006 [22]. This method is based on Principal Component Analysis. Diversity is brought to ensemble by applying PCA to feature extraction. Using UCI repository benchmark classification datasets Rodriguez showed that RTF can outperform several popular ensemble methods [22]. It was also shown that for regression problems RTF performs at least equivalently to bagging [24], [15].

The main goal of the study presented in this paper was to compare empirically rotation forest models with bagging, random forest and single models (SM) in respect of its predictive accuracy. The algorithms were applied to real-world regression problem of predicting the prices of residential premises, based on historical data of sales/purchase transactions obtained from a cadastral system. The models were built using two weak learners including M5P pruned model tree and multilayer perceptron neural network implemented in WEKA.

2   Rotation Forest Algorithm

The main idea standing behind rotation forest is to use PCA to rotate the original feature axes in order to obtain different training sets for learning base classifiers or regressors. In general RTF learning process is similar to classical ensemble learning. Whole committee consists of component models. In regression problems ensemble output is given as a result of some arithmetical function (the most frequently it is an average). Each constituent is trained with the whole training dataset — it provides good accuracy. The difference is that for each component model RTF constructs a rotation matrix, which is then used to transform both training and test datasets. If we consider n dimensional learning problem, in traditional ensemble approach we supply our C_i regressor with $\mathscr{L}_i = [X^n Y]$, where X^n is an n-feature training dataset and $X^n \in \mathbb{R}$, Y are output labels and $Y \in \mathbb{R}$. RTF creates the rotation matrix R_i for each component model C_i, therefore in training phase each regressor C_i is supplied with $\mathscr{L}_i = [X^n R_i Y]$. The rotation matrix is also used in predicting phase. For a data point x regressor C_i output is computed as $C_i(xR_i)$. Figure 1 presents a pseudo code for creating the rotation matrix.

Given:

- C_i — ith regressor
- F — input feature space
- K — number of subsets of features
- P — percentage of instances to remove from training dataset

Create rotation matrix R_i for regressor C_i:

1. Randomly split F into K subsets $F_{i,j}$ $(j = 1, \ldots, K)$
2. For $(j = 1, \ldots, K)$
    (a) Compose a new matrix $X_{i,j}$ by selecting columns from X that correspond to attributes in $F_{i,j}$
    (b) Remove P randomly chosen instances from $X_{i,j}$
    (c) Apply PCA on $X_{i,j}$ creating a matrix $D_{i,j}$
3. Arrange matrices $D_{i,j}$ into a block diagonal matrix R_i
4. Rearrange the rows of R_i to match the order of the attributes in F

Fig. 1. Creating rotation matrix pseudo code

3   Methods Used and Experimental Setup

The main goal of our investigation was to compare the rotation forest (RTF) method with bagging ensemble (BE) and single (SM) models in respect of their predictive accuracy, using cadastral data on sales/purchase transaction of residential premises. All experiments were performed using WEKA (*Waikato Environment for Knowledge Analysis*) data mining framework. WEKA is an open source system [23] developed at University of Waikato which contains tools for data pre-processing, classification, regression, clustering, visualization and many more. For our purpose as base learners we chose two following WEKA algorithms, very often used for building and exploring ensemble methods:

M5P — Pruned Model Tree. Implements routines for generating M5 model trees. The algorithm is based on decision trees, however, instead of having values at tree's nodes, it contains a multivariate linear regression model at each node. The input space is divided into cells using training data and their outcomes, then a regression model is built in each cell as a leaf of the tree.

MLP — Multi Layer Perceptron. One of the most popular neural networks. It uses backpropagation for training. In our experiment we used one hidden layer containing three neurons. In output layer there was only one neuron presenting a prediction result.

The real-world dataset used in experiments was drawn from an unrefined dataset containing above 50,000 records referring to residential premises transactions accomplished in one Polish big city with the population of 640,000 within eleven years from 1998 to 2008. The problem is that most of these transactions do not reflect the real market value of premises. Due to that fact the dataset was cleansed by the experts. The final dataset counted 5213 records comprising nine following features pointed out by the experts as the main drivers of premises prices: usable area of premises, age of a building, number of rooms in a flat, floor on which a flat is located, number of storeys in a building, geodetic coordinates X_c and Y_c of a building, distance from the city centre and distance from the nearest shopping center. As target values total prices of premises were used, but not the prices per square meter, because the latter convey less information.

Due to the fact that the prices of premises change substantially in the course of time, the whole 11-year dataset cannot be used to create data-driven models, therefore it was split into 20 half-year subsets. Then, the prices of premises were updated according to the trends of the value changes over time. Starting from the second half-year of 1998 the prices were updated for the last day of consecutive half-years. The trends were modelled by polynomials of degree three. The sizes of half-year data subsets are given in Table 1. All data we used in experiments were normalized using the min-max approach. The next step in our study was to define algorithm validation schemata. We employed two commonly used approaches: 10-fold cross-validation (10cv) and holdout split in proportion 70% training set, 30% testing set, repeated ten times (H70). The ensembles consisted of 50 models each with averages as an aggregation function. The root mean square error (RMSE) was utilized as a performance function. For verifying the statistical significance of differences among all modeling methods, we applied the non-parametric Friedman and Wilcoxon tests using Statistica package.

Table 1. Number of instances in half-year datasets

1998-2	1999-1	1999-2	2000-1	2000-2	2001-1	2001-2	2002-1	2002-2	2003-1
202	213	264	162	167	228	235	267	263	267
2003-2	2004-1	2004-2	2005-1	2005-2	2006-1	2006-2	2007-1	2007-2	2008-1
386	278	268	244	336	300	377	289	286	181

4   Results of Experiments

Pursuing our goal we divided experiments into two series. The first preliminary series aimed to determine the best rotation forest configuration for both algorithms: MLP and M5P, within 10cv and H70 validation schemata. As a result of these tests we were able to select *the number of subsets K* and *percentage of removed instances P* for which RTF gave the best accuracy in corresponding experimental setup. The overall observation acknowledged what was pointed out by RTF authors. There is no general rule for fine tuning the algorithm. For each of experiment setup separate tuning was needed. The Friedman tests, performed for each combination of base algorithms and validation feamework and paramter P separately, showed that there are significant differences between models with different number of subsets. Average rank positions of tested models determined during Friedman test for different number of subsets are presented in Table 2.

Next, Wilcoxcon tests were conducted. Both tests together revealed that for M5P in 10cv for all values of P schema we got best accuracy for 5 subsets, but there was no significant difference among 4, 5 and 6 subsets. In H70 validation schema the best accuracy was gained mostly for 3 subsets, but again there was no significant difference among 2, 3, 4, 5, 6 and 7 subsets. As for MLP algorithms, in both 10cv and H70, two subsets outperformed other configurations and the difference was for the most cases statistically important. The results were not clearly decisive. However, taking into account the rank positions, for further tests we selected models which performed best in their groups. They were marked with bold font in Table 2.

The next step in tuning RTF was to find the best *percentage of removed instances P* for each algorithm within two validating schemata. Again, Friedman and Wilcoxon tests were made. Average rank positions of tested models are presented in Table 3. According to Friedman test the best results for M5P within 10cv were obtained for $P = 50$ and for MLP within both schemata for $P = 100$. M5P within H70 $P = 30$ was the best, however Wilcoxon tests revealed that differences were not significant statistically.

Due to lack of statistical differences for further testes models with the lowest average rank were selected (marked with bold font in Table 3. The second part of our study was intended to compare RTF performance with bagging, random forest and a single model. In our previous study the best results were obtained for bagging with a 100% bag size and random forest with seven features [16]. Results can not be averaged among all datasets, therefore as an examples table 4 presents root mean square error obtained by RTF ensembles and the models taken from the previous study for 2005-1 dataset. Table 5 presents average rank positions of mantioned modeles determined by Friedman test. B100 — stands for Bagging with bag size of 100%, RF — Random Forest with bag size of 100%, limited to 7 features. Both ensembles also consisted of 50 component models.

Table 2. Average rank positions of tested models determined during Friedman test for different feature subsets

Alg	Res	P	1	2	3	4	5	6	7	8	9
M5P	10cv	100	8.80	4.55	4.80	3.45	**3.20**	3.90	4.65	5.30	6.35
		90	8.40	4.70	4.50	3.85	**3.25**	3.40	4.85	5.60	6.45
		80	8.40	4.95	4.55	3.55	**3.20**	3.60	4.70	5.45	6.60
		70	8.70	4.60	4.75	3.35	**3.30**	3.80	4.70	5.40	6.40
		60	8.65	4.80	4.75	3.40	**3.15**	4.00	4.45	5.40	6.40
		50	8.55	5.00	4.55	3.60	**2.90**	3.75	4.70	5.55	6.40
	H70	100	6.80	4.90	**3.90**	3.90	5.40	4.35	5.60	4.10	6.05
		90	6.55	4.45	**4.10**	4.55	4.50	4.55	4.95	5.35	6.00
		80	6.70	4.85	5.40	**3.70**	5.40	3.95	4.55	5.10	5.35
		70	6.55	4.25	**4.05**	5.25	4.25	5.30	5.20	4.35	5.80
		60	6.05	4.55	**3.35**	5.25	4.20	4.70	5.20	5.40	6.30
		50	6.80	5.45	4.35	4.80	4.35	5.00	**3.45**	4.85	5.95
MLP	10cv	100	4.60	**2.60**	3.95	4.25	4.30	4.50	5.95	7.05	7.80
		90	4.60	**2.75**	4.10	4.20	4.45	4.70	6.10	6.50	7.60
		80	4.45	**2.70**	3.85	4.10	4.50	4.95	6.00	6.75	7.70
		70	4.40	**2.50**	4.80	3.80	4.45	4.40	6.35	6.90	7.40
		60	4.80	**2.85**	4.20	4.00	3.90	5.00	5.85	6.85	7.55
		50	4.50	**2.55**	4.05	4.05	4.55	4.70	5.85	7.25	7.50
	H70	100	5.40	**2.65**	3.85	5.65	5.45	5.45	5.30	5.10	6.15
		90	5.00	**3.35**	3.85	4.70	5.35	5.25	5.50	5.50	6.50
		80	4.75	**4.30**	4.70	5.00	4.55	4.95	4.60	5.40	6.75
		70	4.60	**3.35**	5.00	4.95	5.10	4.50	4.55	6.65	6.30
		60	4.65	**3.60**	5.25	4.80	5.90	3.90	5.70	5.15	6.05
		50	5.25	4.85	4.80	4.00	**3.70**	4.45	5.20	6.30	6.45

Table 3. Average rank positions of tested models determined during Friedman test for different percentage of instances removed from training dataset

Alg	Res	1st	2nd	3rd	4th	5th	6th
M5P	10cv	**50-5 (2.60)**	70-5 (3.45)	100-5 (3.50)	80-5 (3.60)	60-5 (3.65)	90-5 (4.20)
	H70	**80-4 (3.35)**	60-3 (3.40)	70-3 (3.50)	50-7 (3.50)	90-3 (3.55)	100-3 (3.70)
MLP	10cv	**100-2 (3.05)**	80-2 (3.35)	50-2 (3.35)	70-2 (3.55)	60-2 (3.70)	90-2 (4.00)
	H70	**100-2 (3.30)**	60-2 (3.45)	50-5 (3.50)	80-2 (3.55)	90-2 (3.60)	70-2 (3.60)

Table 4. RMSE of compared models obtained for 2005-1 dataset

Alg	Res	RTF-50-5	RF-7	B100	SM
M5P	10cv	0.0890	0.0893	0,0902	0,0872
	H70	0.0841	0.9553	0.1089	0.1241
MLP	10cv	0.0975	0.0942	0.0972	0.1108
	H70	0.0968	0.1120	0.1101	0.1273

Table 5. Average rank positions of compared models determined by Friedman test

Alg	Res	1st	2nd	3rd	4th
M5P	10cv	**RTF-50-5 (2.00)**	RF-7 (2.20)	B100 (2.35)	SM (3.45)
	H70	**RTF-80-4 (2.00)**	RF-7 (2.20)	B100 (2.60)	SM (3.20)
MLP	10cv	**RF-7 (1.20)**	B100 (2.05)	RTF-100-2 (2.75)	SM (4.00)
	H70	**RF-7 (1.65)**	B100 (2.15)	RTF-100-2 (2.20)	SM (4.00)

According to Friedman test RTF for M5P outperformed other models. However Wilcoxon test showed that it was equivalent to RF. For MLP within 10cv RTF performed worse than bagging and random forest. Although for MLP within H70 RTF got higher average rank position, but the differences were not statistically significant.

5 Conclusions and Future Work

The main goal of our study was to compare empirically the performance of rotation forest with bagging ensembles and single models in respect of their predictive accuracy. The experiments were conducted using WEKA implementation of M5 tree and multilayer perceptron algorithms. All tests were carried out within 10-fold cross validation and holdout split in a proportion of 70% training instances and 30% testing instances repeated ten times. A comprehensive real-world dataset including over 5200 samples and recorded during the time span of 11 years served as basis for benchmarking the methods.

Tuning of rotation forest parameters was necessary. Value of parameter K for which rotation forest obtained the best results depended on particular algorithm and testing framework. Tuning *percentage of removed instances* did not influence the overall results. The overall results of our investigation were as follows. For M5P rotation forest turned to be superior to other tested methods. However, it was not the case for MLP where random forest revealed the best performance for 10cv, and for H70 all ensemble methods were equivalent. Single models, in turn, provided worse prediction accuracy than any other ensemble technique for both learning algorithms.

It is planned to explore rotation forest methods with such weak learners as genetic fuzzy systems and genetic neural networks. Moreover, the techniques of determining the optimal sizes of multi-model solutions which lead to achieve both low prediction error and an appropriate balance between accuracy and complexity will be studied.

Acknowledgments. This work was funded partially by the Polish National Science Centre under grant no. N N516 483840.

References

1. Breiman, L.: Bagging Predictors. Machine Learning 24(2), 123–140 (1996)
2. Breiman, L.: Random Forests. Machine Learning 45(1), 5–32 (2001)
3. Bryll, R.: Attribute bagging: improving accuracy of classifier ensembles by using random feature subsets. Pattern Recognition 20(6), 1291–1302 (2003)
4. Bühlmann, P., Yu, B.: Analyzing bagging. Annals of Statistics 30, 927–961 (2002)
5. Friedman, J.H., Hall, P.: On bagging and nonlinear estimation. Journal of Statistical Planning and Inference 137(3), 669–683 (2007)
6. Fumera, G., Roli, F., Serrau, A.: A theoretical analysis of bagging as a linear combination of classifiers. IEEE Trans. Pattern Anal. Mach. Intell. 30(7), 1293–1299 (2008)
7. Gashler, M., Giraud-Carrier, C., Martinez, T.: Decision Tree Ensemble: Small Heterogeneous Is Better Than Large Homogeneous. In: 2008 Seventh International Conference on Machine Learning and Applications, ICMLA 2008, pp. 900–905 (2008)
8. Graczyk, M., Lasota, T., Trawiński, B.: Comparative Analysis of Premises Valuation Models Using KEEL, RapidMiner, and WEKA. In: Nguyen, N.T., Kowalczyk, R., Chen, S.-M. (eds.) ICCCI 2009. LNCS (LNAI), vol. 5796, pp. 800–812. Springer, Heidelberg (2009)
9. Ho, T.K.: Random Decision Forest. In: 3rd International Conference on Document Analysis and Recognition, pp. 278–282 (1995)
10. Ho, T.K.: The Random Subspace Method for Constructing Decision Forests. IEEE Transactions on Pattern Analysis and Machine Intelligence 20(8), 832–844 (1998)
11. Kempa, O., Lasota, T., Telec, Z., Trawiński, B.: Investigation of Bagging Ensembles of Genetic Neural Networks and Fuzzy Systems for Real Estate Appraisal. In: Nguyen, N.T., Kim, C.-G., Janiak, A. (eds.) ACIIDS 2011, Part II. LNCS (LNAI), vol. 6592, pp. 323–332. Springer, Heidelberg (2011)
12. Kotsiantis, S.: Combining bagging, boosting, rotation forest and random subspace methods. Artificial Intelligence Review 35(3), 223–240 (2010)
13. Król, D., Lasota, T., Trawiński, B., Trawiński, K.: Investigation of Evolutionary Optimization Methods of TSK Fuzzy Model for Real Estate Appraisal. International Journal of Hybrid Intelligent Systems 5(3), 111–128 (2008)
14. Krzystanek, M., Lasota, T., Telec, Z., Trawiński, B.: Analysis of Bagging Ensembles of Fuzzy Models for Premises Valuation. In: Nguyen, N.T., Le, M.T., Świątek, J. (eds.) ACIIDS 2010. LNCS (LNAI), vol. 5991, pp. 330–339. Springer, Heidelberg (2010)
15. Kotsiantis, S.B., Pintelas, P.E.: Local Rotation Forest of Decision Stumps for Regression Problems. In: 2nd IEEE International Conference on Computer Science and Information Technology, ICCSIT 2009, pp. 170–174 (2009)
16. Lasota, T., Łuczak, T., Trawiński, B.: Investigation of Random Subspace and Random Forest Methods Applied to Property Valuation Data. In: Jędrzejowicz, P., Nguyen, N.T., Hoang, K. (eds.) ICCCI 2011, Part I. LNCS (LNAI), vol. 6922, pp. 142–151. Springer, Heidelberg (2011)
17. Lasota, T., Mazurkiewicz, J., Trawiński, B., Trawiński, K.: Comparison of Data Driven Models for the Validation of Residential Premises using KEEL. International Journal of Hybrid Intelligent Systems 7(1), 3–16 (2010)
18. Lasota, T., Telec, Z., Trawiński, B., Trawiński, K.: Exploration of Bagging Ensembles Comprising Genetic Fuzzy Models to Assist with Real Estate Appraisals. In: Corchado, E., Yin, H. (eds.) IDEAL 2009. LNCS, vol. 5788, pp. 554–561. Springer, Heidelberg (2009)

19. Lasota, T., Telec, Z., Trawiński, B., Trawiński, K.: Investigation of the eTS Evolving Fuzzy Systems Applied to Real Estate Appraisal. Journal of Multiple-Valued Logic and Soft Computing 17(2-3), 229–253 (2011)
20. Lughofer, E., Trawiński, B., Trawiński, K., Kempa, O., Lasota, T.: On Employing Fuzzy Modeling Algorithms for the Valuation of Residential Premises. Information Sciences 181, 5123–5142 (2011)
21. Polikar, R.: Ensemble Learning. Scholarpedia 4(1), 2776 (2009)
22. Rodríguez, J.J., Kuncheva, L.I., Alonso, C.J.: Rotation Forest: A New Classifier Ensemble Method. IEEE Transactions on Pattern Analysis and Machine Intelligence 28(10), 1619–1630 (2006)
23. Witten, I.H., Frank, E.: Data Mining: Practical machine learning tools and techniques, 2nd edn. Morgan Kaufmann, San Francisco (2005)
24. Zhang, C.-X., Zhang, J.-S., Wang, G.-W.: An empirical study of using Rotation Forest to improve regressors. Appl. Math. Comput. 195(2), 618–629 (2008)

Locally Optimized Kernels

Tomasz Maszczyk and Włodzisław Duch

Department of Informatics, Nicolaus Copernicus University
Grudziądzka 5, 87-100 Toruń, Poland
{tmaszczyk,wduch}@is.umk.pl
http://www.is.umk.pl

Abstract. Support Vector Machines (SVM's) with various kernels have become very successful in pattern classification and regression. However, single kernels do not lead to optimal data models. Replacing the input space by a kernel-based feature space in which the linear discrimination problem with margin maximization is solved is a general method that allows for mixing various kernels and adding new types of features. We show here how to generate locally optimized kernels that facilitate multi-resolution and can handle complex data distributions using simpler models than the standard data formulation may provide.

1 Introduction

For more than a decade now kernel Support Vector Machines (SVM's) have become extremely successful approaches to pattern classification and regression problems. Excellent results have been reported in applying SVM's in multiple domains thanks to the ingenious use of various kernels, providing an equivalent of specific similarity measures in the kernel space [1]. However, the type of solution offered by a given data model obtained by SVM with a specific kernel may not be the most appropriate for particular data. Each data model defines a hypotheses space, that is a set of functions that this model may easily learn. Linear methods work best when decision borders are flat, but they are obviously not suitable for spherical distributions of data. For some problems (for example, high-dimensional parity and similar functions), neither linear nor radial decision borders are sufficient [2].

Kernel methods implicitly provide new, useful features $z_i(x) = k(x, x_i)$ constructed around support vectors x_i, a subset of input vectors relevant to the training objective. Prediction is supported by new features, most often distance functions from selected training vectors, weighted by a Gaussian function, making the decision borders flat in the kernel space. Multiple kernels may be used to construct new features, as shown in our Support Feature Machine algorithm [3]. In the second section standard approach to the SVM is described and linked to evaluation of similarity to support vectors in the space enhanced by $z_i(x) = k(x, x_i)$ kernel features. Linear models defined in the enhanced space are equivalent to kernel-based SVMs. In particular, one can use linear SVM to find discriminant in the enhanced space, preserving the wide margins. For special problems other linear discriminant techniques may be more appropriate [4].

Although most research in the SVM community has focused on the underlying learning algorithms the study of kernels has also gained importance recently. Standard kernels such as linear, Gaussian, or polynomial do not take full advantage of the nuances of

L. Rutkowski et al. (Eds.): ICAISC 2012, Part I, LNCS 7267, pp. 412–420, 2012.

specific data sets. This has motivated plenty of research into the use of alternative kernels. Various kernels may be used to create enhanced feature space. Here an approach that combines Gaussian kernels with selection of pure clusters, adopted from our Almost Random Projection Machines [5] algorithm, is investigated. In section 4 Locally Optimized Kernels are tested in a number of benchmark calculations. Brief discussion of further research directions concludes this paper.

2   Kernels and Support Vector Machines

2.1   Standard SVM Formulation

Since the seminal paper of Boser, Guyon and Vapnik in 1992 [6] Support Vector Machines quickly became the most popular method of classification and regression, finding numerous other applications [7,8,9]. In case of binary classification problems SVM algorithm minimizes average errors (or risk) over the set of data pairs $\langle x_i, y_i \rangle$. Depending on the choice of kernels and optimization of their parameters SVM can produce flexible nonlinear data models that, thanks to the optimization of classification margin, offer good generalization. This means that the minimum distance between the training vectors x_i and the hyperplane w should be maximized:

$$\max_{w,b} \min \|x - x_i\| \ : \ w \cdot x + b = 0, \ i = 1, \ldots, m \tag{1}$$

The w and b can be rescaled in such a way that the point closest to the hyperplane $w \cdot x + b = 0$, lies on one of the parallel hyperplanes defining the margin $w \cdot x + b = \pm 1$. This leads to the requirement that

$$\forall_{x_i} \ y_i[w \cdot x_i + b] \geq 1 \tag{2}$$

The width of the margin is equal to $2/\|w\|$. Therefore maximization of margins is equivalent to minimization:

$$\min_{w,b} \tau(w) = \frac{1}{2}\|w\|^2 \tag{3}$$

with constraints that guarantee correct classification:

$$y_i[w \cdot x_i + b] \geq 1 \quad i = 1, \ldots, m \tag{4}$$

Constraint optimization problems are solved by defining the Lagrangian:

$$L(w, b, \alpha) = \frac{1}{2}\|w\|^2 - \sum_{i=1}^{m} \alpha_i(y_i[x_i \cdot w + b] - 1) \tag{5}$$

where $\alpha_i > 0$ are Lagrange multipliers. Its minimization over b and w leads to two conditions:

$$\sum_{i=1}^{m} \alpha_i y_i = 0, \quad w = \sum_{i=1}^{m} \alpha_i y_i x_i \tag{6}$$

The vector $\boldsymbol{w}$ that defines the hyperplane is expressed as a combination of the training vectors, each component $\boldsymbol{w}[j]$ is a combination of j feature values for all vectors $\boldsymbol{x}_i[j]$. According to the Karush-Kuhn-Thucker conditions:

$$\alpha_i(y_i[\boldsymbol{x}_i \cdot \boldsymbol{w} + b] - 1) = 0, \quad i = 1, \ldots, m \tag{7}$$

For $\alpha_i \neq 0$ vectors must lie on one of the margin hyperplanes $y_i[\boldsymbol{x}_i \cdot \boldsymbol{w} + b] = 1$; these vectors "support" the hyperplane $\boldsymbol{w}$ that defines the solution of the optimization problem. Although the minimization may be performed in the primal form [10] the quadratic optimization problem is frequently redefined in a bit simpler dual form:

$$\max_{\alpha} \; \boldsymbol{w}(\alpha) = \sum_{i=1}^{m} \alpha_i - \frac{1}{2} \sum_{i,j=1}^{m} \alpha_i \alpha_j y_i y_j \boldsymbol{x}_i \boldsymbol{x}_j \tag{8}$$

with constraints:

$$\alpha_i \geq 0 \; i = 1, \ldots, m \quad \sum_{i=1}^{m} \alpha_i y_i = 0 \tag{9}$$

The discriminant function takes the form:

$$g(x) = \mathrm{sgn}\left(\sum_{i=1}^{m} \alpha_i y_i \boldsymbol{x} \cdot \boldsymbol{x}_i + b\right) \tag{10}$$

Now it is easy to replace dot product $\boldsymbol{x} \cdot \boldsymbol{x}_i$ by a kernel function $k(\boldsymbol{x}, \boldsymbol{x}') = \phi(\boldsymbol{x}) \cdot \phi(\boldsymbol{x}')$ where $\phi(\boldsymbol{x})$ represents an implicit transformation of the original vectors to a new kernel space. For any $\phi(\boldsymbol{x})$ vector the part orthogonal to the space spanned by $\phi(\boldsymbol{x}_i)$ does not contribute to the $\phi(\boldsymbol{x}) \cdot \phi(\boldsymbol{x}')$ products, therefore it is sufficient to express $\phi(\boldsymbol{x})$ and $\boldsymbol{w}$ as a combination of $\phi(\boldsymbol{x}_i)$ vectors. The dimensionality d of the input vectors is frequently lower than the number of training patterns $d < m$, and then $\phi(\boldsymbol{x})$ represents mapping into higher m-dimensional space. According to the Cover theorem [11] probability of linear separation of data points grows with the dimensional of the space in which data is embedded. However, in case of microarray data and some other problems the reverse situation is true: dimensionality is much higher than the number of patterns for training. Still weighted distances used as features for linear discrimination may be quite useful, providing some improvement in comparison to the nearest neighbor methods.

The discriminant function in the $\phi()$ space is:

$$g(\boldsymbol{x}) = \mathrm{sgn}\left(\sum_{i=1}^{m} \alpha_i y_i k(\boldsymbol{x}, \boldsymbol{x}_i) + b\right) \tag{11}$$

If the kernel function is linear the $\phi()$ space is simply the original space and the contributions to the discriminant function are based on the cosine distances to the reference vectors $\boldsymbol{x}_i$ from the y_i class. Thus the original features $\boldsymbol{x}[j], j = 1..d$ are replaced by new features $z_i(\boldsymbol{x}) = k(\boldsymbol{x}, \boldsymbol{x}_i)$ that evaluate how close (or how similar) the vector is from the training vectors. Incorporating signs in the coefficient vector $A_i = \alpha_i y_i$ discriminant functions is:

$$g(\boldsymbol{x}) = \mathrm{sgn}\left(\sum_{i=1}^{m} \alpha_i y_i z_i(\boldsymbol{x})) + b\right) = \mathrm{sgn}\left(\boldsymbol{A} \cdot \boldsymbol{z}(\boldsymbol{x})) + b\right) \tag{12}$$

With the proper choice of non-zero α coefficients this function provides a distance measure from the decision border, combining distances from the support vectors placed at the margins. In non-separable case instead of using cosine distance measures it is better to use localized similarity measures, for example by scaling the distance with Gaussian functions. This leads to one of the most useful kernels:

$$k_G(\boldsymbol{x}, \boldsymbol{x}') = \exp(-\beta\|\boldsymbol{x} - \boldsymbol{x}'\|^2) \tag{13}$$

Such kernels help to smooth decision borders because in the discriminant kernels anchored at the support vectors of one class are combined overcoming the influence of low-density data points from the opposite classes. Kernel-based methods use similarity in a special way in combination with linear discrimination, but similarity estimations may also be used in many other ways in pattern recognition problems [12,1].

2.2 Kernel Features Spaces

For each vector $\boldsymbol{x}$ we have m kernel features $z_i(\boldsymbol{x}) = k(\boldsymbol{x}, \boldsymbol{x}_i)$ defined for each training vector. For example taking the Gaussian kernel $k_G(\boldsymbol{x}, \boldsymbol{x}')$ and fixing the value of discriminant $g(\boldsymbol{x})$ =constant is equivalent to taking a weighted sum of gaussians centered at some support vectors that are near the border; for large dispersions all vectors may contribute, but a single one will have weak influence on the decision border. Because contours of discriminant function in the kernel space are approximately constant when $\boldsymbol{x}$ moves along the non-linear decision border in the input space, they lie on the hyperplane in the kernel space. Therefore in the space of kernel features linear discriminant methods may be applied directly, without the SVM machinery. This was demonstrated in computational experiments by comparing the results of SVM with Gaussian kernel solved by quadratic programming with direct linear solutions in the kernel-based feature space[3].

3 Locally Optimized Kernels

The Locally Optimized Kernels (LOK) approach presented in this paper is based on generation of new features using restricted gaussian kernels followed by the Winner Takes All (WTA) comparison of output activities (where a simple sum of the nodes assigned to class C is used to estimate the winning class), or by the linear discrimination. One may use many other machine learning algorithms in this new feature space [12,1], but here we have space to compare only the basic version of this approach with standard SVM approaches (see Algorithm 1).

To create LOK feature space for every training vector a candidate kernel feature is used: $g_i(\boldsymbol{x}) = \exp(-\|\boldsymbol{x}_i - \boldsymbol{x}\|^2/2\sigma^2)$. For every such feature g_i analyze $p(g_i|C)$ distributions to find relatively pure clusters in some $I_{iab} = [g_{ia}, g_{ib}]$ interval (here we have used only pure clusters, although in some problems it may be necessary to include some. This creates binary candidate features $B_{iab}(\boldsymbol{x})$. Good candidate feature should cover some minimum number η of training vectors. The optimal number may depend on the type of data, the domain expert may consider even a single vector to be a significant exception worth retaining. Below the η parameter has been optimized using results of crossvalidation. This condition avoids creation of overspecific features. In the implementation tested here LOK uses winner-takes-all mechanism or linear discrimination to find solutions in the new feature space.

The LOK algorithm is sketched below:

Algorithm 1 Locally Optimized Kernels

Require: Fix the values of internal parameters: η for minimum covering and σ for dispersion.

1: Standardize the dataset, m vectors, d features.
2: Create candidate kernel features $g_i(x) = \exp(-||x_i - x||^2/2\sigma^2)$.
3: Sort $g_i(x)$ values in descending order, with associated class labels.
4: Analyze $p(g_i|C)$ distribution to find all intervals with pure clusters defining binary features $B_{iab}(x; C)$.
5: **if** the number of vectors covered by the feature $B_{iab}(x; C) > \eta$ **then**
6:     accept this binary feature creating class-labeled hidden network node.
7: **end if**
8: Classify test data mapped into the enhanced space:
9: Sum the activity of hidden node subsets for each class to calculate network outputs (WTA).
10: Build linear model on the enhanced feature space (LDA).

In this version of LOK algorithm there are only two parameters to set: η determines the minimal size of a cluster (number of vectors per cluster), and σ controls dispersion of localized gaussian features. Clean clusters are found either in the local neighborhood of the support vector in the interval $[0, b]$, or if the support vector is surrounded by vectors from another class they may be quite far, with large values of both $a < b$. Thus even outliers may provide useful support features. Clean clusters and binary features may be quite useful to identify regions with vectors that may be correctly classified with high confidence. For very large datasets these vectors may be removed, leaving only areas close to the decision borders. In essence this solves the separable problem at a cost of high rejection rate. To deal with the remaining vectors one should introduce features based on clusters that are not pure.

For every candidate support vector point $b = g_i$ for which $p(g_i|C) = p(g_i|\neg C)$ is found and $\sigma_i = b/2$ is taken as dispersion, creating a new Gaussian kernel feature $g_i(x; b) = \exp(-||x_i - x||^2/b)$. A slightly smaller value of b could make the new feature more pure, but this would introduce at least one additional parameter, therefore we have not considered this possibility. With sufficient number of support features small impurities for small $g_i(x)$ feature values do not matter. In some cases more support features may be generated using large σ_i and analyzing $p(g_i|C)$ distribution for values larger than b, using intervals $I_{iab} = [g_{ia}, g_{ib}], a > 0$ where one of the classes dominates. These new features are obtained as differences of two gaussian functions $g_i(x; b) - g_i(x; a)$. Other types of functions could be used here to model the slopes of probability density distributions, for example differences of two sigmoidal functions [13]. In the comparison of results presented in Table 2 LOKLDA and LOKWTA are used with such additional features, if they were found useful improving the training results.

To find solution in the new feature space LOKLDA uses linear discrimination with margin maximization (optimal margin is selected using crossvalidation in a standard

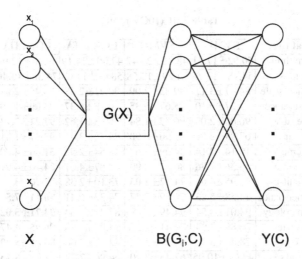

Fig. 1. Network structure of the LOK algorithm

way, as it is done also for SVM calculations). Features discovered by the LOK algorithm may be implemented as network nodes that represent kernel transformations. Additional layers of the network are then used to analyze the data in the feature space created in this way (see Fig. 1). LOK algorithm with Gaussian features may be called properly LOGK, as other functions may be used as kernels.

4 Illustrative Examples

In order to evaluate the effect of optimized kernels on SVM results 4 methods have been compared: standard SVM with linear kernel (SVML) and with Gaussian kernel

Table 1. Summary of datasets

Dataset	#Vectors	#Features	#Classes	Dataset	#Vectors	#Features	#Classes
arrhythmia	63	279	11	autos	159	25	6
balance-scale	625	4	3	breast-cancer	277	9	2
breast-w	683	9	2	car	1728	6	4
cmc	1473	9	3	credit-a	653	15	2
credit-g	1000	20	2	cylinder-bands	277	39	2
dermatology	358	34	6	diabetes	768	8	2
ecoli	336	7	8	glass	214	9	6
haberman	306	3	2	heart-c	296	13	2
heart-statlog	270	13	2	hepatitis	80	19	2
ionosphere	351	34	2	iris	150	4	3
kr-vs-kp	3196	36	2	liver-disorders	345	6	2
lymph	148	18	4	sonar	208	60	2
vote	232	16	2	vowel	990	13	11
				zoo	101	17	7

Table 2. 10x10CV results

Dataset	SVML	SVMG	LOKWTA	LOKLDA
arrhythmia	**50.92±17.31**	43.36±21.47	42.00±24.19	39.10±12.98
autos	54.48±13.75	74.29±12.58	58.69±11.03	**74.36±10.40**
balance-scale	84.47±3.17	89.83±2.09	90.71±2.38	**96.46±2.62**
breast-cancer	73.27±6.10	75.67±5.35	**76.58±6.37**	75.09±1.99
breast-w	96.60±2.07	96.77±1.84	96.93±1.62	**97.21±2.13**
car	67.99±2.61	**98.90±0.90**	84.72±3.44	93.57±1.81
cmc	19.14±2.14	34.09±3.67	48.54±2.52	**51.06±4.30**
credit-a	**86.36±2.86**	86.21±2.90	82.67±4.01	84.70±4.91
credit-g	73.95±4.69	**74.72±4.03**	73.10±2.38	72.70±3.86
cylinder-bands	74.58±5.23	76.89±7.57	74.32±6.41	**80.11±7.53**
dermatology	94.01±3.54	94.49±3.88	87.97±5.64	**94.71±3.02**
diabetes	76.88±4.94	76.41±4.22	74.88±3.88	**76.95±4.47**
ecoli	78.48±5.90	84.17±5.82	82.47±3.66	**85.66±5.40**
glass	42.61±10.05	62.43±8.70	64.96±7.72	**71.08±8.13**
haberman	72.54±1.96	72.91±5.93	**76.46±4.34**	73.53±0.72
heart-c	**82.62±6.36**	80.67±7.96	81.07±7.56	81.04±5.17
heart-statlog	**83.48±7.17**	83.40±6.56	81.48±8.73	83.33±7.46
hepatitis	83.25±11.54	84.87±11.98	**89.88±10.14**	84.05±4.40
ionosphere	87.72±4.63	94.61±3.68	85.18±6.28	**95.16±2.72**
iris	72.20±7.59	**94.86±5.75**	94.67±6.89	93.33±5.46
kr-vs-kp	96.03±0.86	**99.35±0.42**	83.73±2.58	98.25±0.45
liver-disorders	68.46±7.36	**70.30±7.90**	57.40±5.72	69.72±6.57
lymph	81.26±9.79	**83.61±9.82**	76.96±13.07	80.52±7.91
sonar	73.71±9.62	86.42±7.65	**86.57±7.01**	86.52±8.39
vote	96.12±3.85	**96.89±3.11**	92.57±7.52	93.95±4.18
vowel	23.73±3.13	**98.05±1.90**	92.49±3.37	97.58±1.52
zoo	91.61±6.67	93.27±7.53	88.47±5.35	**94.07±6.97**

(SVMG), LOK with the Winner Takes All (WTA) estimation (LOKWTA) and LOK with linear discrimination (LOKLDA), equivalent to the linear SVM in the extended space. These 4 approaches have been applied to the 27 standard benchmark datasets, summarized in Table 1, downloaded from the UCI Machine Learning Repository [14]. Vectors with missing feature values (if any) have been removed. Each calculation has been performed using the 10-fold stratified crossvalidation, and repeated 10 times to obtain reliable estimates of accuracies and standard deviations. The SVM parameters C (best value from the $[2^{-5} \dots 2^5]$ range) and σ (best value from the $[2^{-10} \dots 2^3]$ range) have been fully optimized for each dataset in an automatic way, using crossvalidation estimations on the training partition to be sure that no information about the test data has been used at any stage. Results for each dataset are collected in Table 2, with the best results marked in bold.

Results using Locally Optimized Kernels are in all cases not significantly worse than SVM, and in most cases better. As should be expected LOKWTA achieved best results only in a few (exactly 4) cases, in case of *cmc* data outperforming SVM by a large margin. SVML also achieved best results in 4 cases, in case of *arrhythmia* (only 63 vectors with 11 classes and 279 features) strongly outperforming other methods, but in this case variance is quite big and the difference is not statistically significant.

For 11 datasets LOKLDA outperformed all other methods, while SVMG was the best for 8 datasets, and only in the case of *car* data the difference becomes significant. These results show that in most cases local optimization of kernels leads to an improvement over the single kernel SVM algorithms, and may achieve the best results comparing to all state-of-the-art classifiers (Maszczyk, PhD thesis, in prep.). The computational complexity of the LOKLDA approach is dominated by solution of linear discrimination problem and thus is comparable to the original linear SVM. For d-dimensional problems and m vectors estimation of optimal kernel size requires $O(dm \log m)$ operations. This is the computational complexity of the LOKWTA approach that in many cases has not been significantly worse than SVM, while the method may be used with very large datasets, where solving linear discrimination becomes costly.

5 Conclusions

Locally Optimized Kernels (LOK) algorithm introduced in this paper is focused on generation of new useful kernel features. It is not restricted to gaussian kernels, and may be treated as one variant of our general Support Feature Machine approach [3] for generation of features that extract more information from the data than may be derived using simple kernels. The purpose of this paper is to show that the LOK approach despite its simplicity generates enhanced feature space that improves construction of the original SVM kernel space. While a lot of effort has been devoted to improvements of the SVM learning algorithm much less attention has been paid to methods that extract information from data, making the linear discrimination simpler and more accurate. In the case of gaussian kernel features there is no reason why the same dispersion should be used for all support vectors. Those support vectors that are far from decision border on the correct side should have large dispersions, and vectors closer to decision borders should have smaller dispersions. Support vectors on the wrong side should provide kernel features that exclude local neighborhood. LOK algorithm creates such locally optimized gaussian kernels. It may also be easily combined with many methods of feature selection for additional improvement.

A fruitful question is: what is the limit of accuracy for a given dataset that can be achieved in a given feature space? Progress in the recent years in classification and approximation methods shows that for simple data results are probably close to this limit. However, there is still an ample room for improvement in generation of enhanced features spaces that contain more information. Of course not only kernel-based features are useful. Several ways of creating new features have recently been introduced [15,3,16], overcoming the limitation of algorithms that work in original features spaces, where discrimination or similarity-based methods operate. The final goal is to create meta-learning approaches [17] that construct in automatical way optimal, and in most cases the simplest, models of data.

Acknowledgment. This work was supported by the Nicolaus Copernicus University under research grant for young scientists no. 407-F, and by the Polish Ministry of Education and Science through Grant No N516 500539.

References

1. Duch, W.: Similarity based methods: a general framework for classification, approximation and association. Control and Cybernetics 29, 937–968 (2000)
2. Duch, W.: K-Separability. In: Kollias, S.D., Stafylopatis, A., Duch, W., Oja, E. (eds.) ICANN 2006. LNCS, vol. 4131, pp. 188–197. Springer, Heidelberg (2006)
3. Maszczyk, T., Duch, W.: Support feature machines: Support vectors are not enough. In: World Congress on Computational Intelligence, pp. 3852–3859. IEEE Press (2010)
4. Tebbens, J., Schlesinger, P.: Improving implementation of linear discriminant analysis for the small sample size problem. Computational Statistics & Data Analysis 52, 423–437 (2007)
5. Duch, W., Maszczyk, T.: Almost Random Projection Machine. In: Alippi, C., Polycarpou, M., Panayiotou, C., Ellinas, G. (eds.) ICANN 2009. LNCS, vol. 5768, pp. 789–798. Springer, Heidelberg (2009)
6. Boser, B.E., Guyon, I.M., Vapnik, V.N.: A training algorithm for optimal margin classifiers. In: Haussler, D. (ed.) 5th Annual ACM Workshop on COLT, pp. 144–152. ACM Press, Pittsburgh (1992)
7. Schölkopf, B., Smola, A.J.: Learning with Kernels. Support Vector Machines, Regularization, Optimization, and Beyond. MIT Press, Cambridge (2001)
8. Schölkopf, B., Burges, C., Smola, A.: Advances in Kernel Methods: Support Vector Machines. MIT Press, Cambridge (1998)
9. Diederich, J. (ed.): Rule Extraction from Support Vector Machines. SCI, vol. 80. Springer (2008)
10. Chapelle, O.: Training a support vector machine in the primal. Neural Computation 19, 1155–1178 (2007)
11. Cover, T.M.: Geometrical and statistical properties of systems of linear inequalities with applications in pattern recognition. IEEE Transactions on Electronic Computers 14, 326–334 (1965)
12. Duch, W., Adamczak, R., Diercksen, G.H.F.: Classification, association and pattern completion using neural similarity based methods. Applied Mathematics and Computer Science 10, 101–120 (2000)
13. Duch, W., Jankowski, N.: Survey of neural transfer functions. Neural Computing Surveys 2, 163–213 (1999)
14. Asuncion, A., Newman, D.: UCI machine learning repository (2007), http://www.ics.uci.edu/~mlearn/MLRepository.html
15. Duch, W., Maszczyk, T.: Universal Learning Machines. In: Leung, C.S., Lee, M., Chan, J.H. (eds.) ICONIP 2009. LNCS, vol. 5864, pp. 206–215. Springer, Heidelberg (2009)
16. Maszczyk, T., Grochowski, M., Duch, W.: Discovering Data Structures using Meta-learning, Visualization and Constructive Neural Networks. In: Advances in Machine Learning II. SCI, vol. 262, pp. 467–484. Springer, Heidelberg (2010)
17. Jankowski, N., Duch, W., Grąbczewski, K. (eds.): Meta-Learning in Computational Intelligence. SCI, vol. 358. Springer, Heidelberg (2011)

Application of Hierarchical Classifier to Minimal Synchronizing Word Problem

Igor T. Podolak, Adam Roman, and Dariusz Jędrzejczyk

Institute of Computer Science, Jagiellonian University
{podolak,roman}@ii.uj.edu.pl, dariusz.jedrzejczyk@gmail.com

Abstract. We present a practical application of Hierarchical Classifier with overlapping clusters to the problem of finding the minimal synchronizing word length of a given finite automaton. We compare our approach with a single neural network model. Using a certain representation of automaton as the classifier's input we improve HC efficiency and we are able to analyze the relation between particular automata features and minimal synchronizing lengths.

1 Introduction

Synchronizing sequences play an important role in the model-based testing of reactive systems [1], part orienters [8], finding one's location on a map/graph [6], resetting biocomputers [20], networking (determining a leader in a network [6]), and recently – in communication protocols [16,5,22]. Synchronizing words allow us to bring the machine into one state, no matter which state it is in. This helps much in designing effective test cases, e.g. for sequential circuits. In [15] authors show a class of faults for which a synchronizing sequence for the faulty circuit can be easily determined from the synchronizing word of the fault free circuit. They also consider circuits that have a reset mechanism and show how reset can ensure that no single fault would cause the circuit to become unsynchronizable.

The central problem in the approach based on the synchronizing words is to find the shortest one (called the minimal synchronizing word, MSW) for a given automaton. As the problem is $\mathcal{DP}$-complete [9], the polynomial algorithms cannot be optimal, that is they cannot find the *shortest* possible synchronizing sequences (unless $\mathcal{P} = \mathcal{NP}$, which is strongly believed to be false).

In recent years some efforts were made in the field of algorithmic approach for finding possibly short synchronizing sequences [3]. Pixley et al. [10] presented an efficient method based upon the universal alignment theorem and binary decision diagrams to compute a synchronization sequence. There are also Natarajan [8] and Eppstein [4] algorithms. The problem of synchronizing finite state automata has a long history. While its statement is simple (find a word that sends all states to one state), there are some important questions still to be answered. One of the most intriguing issues is the so-called Černý Conjecture [2], which states that for any n-state synchronizing automaton there exists a synchronizing word of length at most $(n-1)^2$. Should the conjecture be true, this would be a strict upper

L. Rutkowski et al. (Eds.): ICAISC 2012, Part I, LNCS 7267, pp. 421–429, 2012.

bound, as there exist automata that reach this value. The Černý Conjecture has profound theoretical significance (remaining one of the last "basic" unanswered questions in the field of finite state automata, especially after the Road Coloring Conjecture has been proved by Trahtman [18]).

The problem of finding MSW length for a given automaton $\mathcal{A}$ can be re-stated as a classification problem, where the output class for $\mathcal{A}$ is labeled by this length. In this work we use the concept of Hierarchical Classifier (in short: HC) [11] to solve this problem. The crucial idea is to represent the input automaton not directly (by its transition function), but as a vector of some real-valued parameters that describe different automaton features. This approach allows us to obtain two results: first, the application of HC to solve the problem of finding MSW lengths. The second result shows the correlation between particular automata features and the MSW length. This result allows theoretical computer scientists, who work on the Černý conjecture, to focus on features that give the best results.

If we have the estimation of the MSW length (not the word itself), we may take advantage on this fact in several algorithms which find possibly short synchronizing words. For example, this is the case of the genetic algorithm [17], where we have to know in advance the estimate chromosome length. The other application is in numerical experiments, where, for example, we search for some extremal automata (the ones with long synchronizing words; such automata are very rare and have very interesting properties, see [21]). Exponential algorithm – which returns the real MSW – has a long execution time, so we may first check quickly the estimated length of the MSW and if it is below some predefined threshold, we may assume that this automaton is not an extremal one and that we do not have to run the exponential algorithm. This will help to save our time.

HC is a machine learning algorithm designed to cope with problems with a very large number of output classes. In every step of it's training process, the problem is divided into several sub-problems. Each is composed of groups of classes (clusters in HC's nomenclature) which are found to be similar at that step. Let K be the number of classes of the original problem, classes which are recognized in HC's root. In the next level the maximum number of classes in each sub-problem is $K/2$ (this ratio can be set as a parameter).

If we encode the synchronizing problem of predicting the MSW length, where each word length represents a class, then HC is perfectly fit for this problem. Because HC can divide the output space effectively, and the number of possible classes (all lengths from 0 to $(n-1)^2$) is high, the application of HC is natural.

Additionally, each individual classifier in the HC tree is designed to be *weak*, *i.e.* with accuracy only a small value higher than a random classifier (the minimal accuracy for a K-class classifier is given with $\alpha(K)$ [12]). Because of that, it is *not* necessary to train each node to be almost perfect, and the whole tree can be constructed in a manageable time. Also, the actual HC's architecture for a given problem is being designed during training, it is not predefined.

2   Preliminaries

An *automaton* is a triple $\mathcal{A} = (Q, A, \delta)$, where Q is a nonempty, finite set of states, A is a finite alphabet and $\delta : Q \times A \to Q$ is a *transition function* called also the automaton action. By A^* we denote a free monoid over A consisting of all finite words over A. By ε we denote the empty word of length 0. We define $A^+ = A^* \setminus \{\varepsilon\}$ and $A^n = \{w \in A^* : |w| = n\}$. For the sake of simplicity, we will write $p.a = q$ instead of $\delta(p, a) = q$. It is convenient to extend δ to the subsets of Q in the usual way: for $P \subset Q$ we define $P.\varepsilon = P$, $P.a = \bigcup_{p \in P}\{p.a\}$ and $P.a\omega = (P.a).\omega$ for all $\omega \in A^+$. We say that $W \in A^*$ *synchronizes* $\mathcal{A} = (Q, A, \delta)$ if $|Q.W| = 1$. If such a word exists, $\mathcal{A}$ is called a *synchronizing automaton*. Sometimes we will be interested in the "local" synchronization only: if $P \subset Q$, then we say that $W \in A^*$ is P-synchronizing (or that W synchronizes P) if $|P.W| = 1$. By $q.a^{-1}$ we understand the set $\{p : p.a = q\}$. We extend this notion to the subsets: for $P \subset Q$ we define $P.a^{-1} = \bigcup_{p \in P} p.a^{-1}$.

The decision problem of finding the MSW for a given automaton has been recently shown to be $\mathcal{DP}$-complete [9]. It is well-known that the length of MSW for an n-state synchronizing automaton is at most $(n^3 - n)/6$ [7]. The Černý conjecture states that this length can be bounded by $(n - 1)^2$. Černý showed [2] that for each $n \geq 1$ there exists an automaton with SSW of length $(n - 1)^2$, so the conjectured bound is tight. These automata are called the Černý automata. An n-state Černý automaton will be denoted by $\mathcal{C}_n$. Černý automaton is defined over the two-element alphabet $A = \{a, b\}$ and its transition function is as follows (states are denoted by $1, 2, ..., n$):

$$\delta(q, x) = \begin{cases} (q \bmod n) + 1 & \text{if } x = a \\ q & \text{if } x = b \wedge q \neq n \\ 1 & \text{if } x = b \wedge q = n \end{cases} \qquad (1)$$

Černý automata are very important, as automata with $|MSW| = (n - 1)^2$ are very rare. Only eight such automata are known that are not isomorphic with the Černý automata [19].

Now we will introduce the important notion of the pair automaton. This construction is used in greedy synchronizing algorithms and, as it will be shown later, some property of this construction is highly correlated with the length of MSW. Let $\mathcal{A} = (Q, A, \delta)$ be a synchronizing automaton. A *pair automaton* for $\mathcal{A}$ is the automaton $\mathcal{A}^2 = (Q', A, \delta')$, where:

$$Q' = \bigcup_{p,q \in Q \wedge p \neq q} \{\{p, q\}\} \cup \{0\}, \; \delta' : Q' \times A \to Q',$$

$$\delta'(\{p, q\}, l) = \begin{cases} \{\delta(p, l), \delta(q, l)\} & \text{if } \delta(p, l) \neq \delta(q, l) \\ 0 & \text{otherwise,} \end{cases} \; \delta'(0, l) = 0 \; \forall l \in A.$$

Pair automaton shows how the pairs of states behave when words are applied to the original automaton. If $p, q \in S \subseteq Q$ and w is a path leading from $\{p, q\}$ to 0, it means that $|\delta(S, w)| < |S|$, where $p, q \in S$. In such a situation we say that pair

$\{p, q\}$ of states is *synchronized* by w. By $h(\{p, q\})$ we will denote the shortest path from $\{p, q\} \in Q'$ to "sink state" 0. The next proposition is a straightforward, but very important fact, also utilized in all heuristic algorithms.

Proposition 1. *A word $w \in A^*$ synchronizes $\mathcal{A}^2$ iff w synchronizes $\mathcal{A}$.*   □

This is a very important fact, as checking if pair-automaton is synchronizing is very easy because of the existence of 0 "sink state" ($\mathcal{A}^2$ is synchronizing if for each state q there is a path from q to 0). Proposition 1 implies the following necessary and sufficient condition for $\mathcal{A}$ to be synchronized:

Proposition 2. *$\mathcal{A}$ is synchronizing iff each pair of its states is synchronizing.* □

2.1   The Hierarchical Classifier

HC is a type of boosting machine learning algorithm [14]. Suppose we have a K-class classification problem. Denote by $\mathcal{C} = \{C_1, \ldots, C_K\}$ the set of all classes. HC is a triple (V, V^0, par), where $V = \{V^i = (Cl^i, F^i)\}_{i \in I}$ is a set of nodes which form a tree structure. $V^0 \in V$ is a root of this tree and $par : V \mapsto V \cup \{\emptyset\}$ returns a parent classifier for a given node. We put $par(V^0) = \emptyset$. Each V^i is composed of a classifier $Cl^i : X \mapsto \mathcal{C}^i$, $\mathcal{C}^i \subseteq \mathcal{C}$ and a clustering matrix F^i.

$$F^i = \begin{cases} \emptyset & \text{if } V^i \text{ is a leaf node} \\ K^i \times L^i \text{ matrix} & \text{otherwise,} \end{cases}$$

where L^i is the number of child nodes of V^i. It is a binary matrix which describes which of V^i's children node recognizes which classes in a way that $f^i_{kl} = 1 \Leftrightarrow$ l-th child of V^i recognizes class C_k. If Cl^i has no children, we put $F^i = \emptyset$. Each classifier Cl^i in the HC structure is able to solve some subproblem $\mathcal{C}^i$ of the original problem $\mathcal{C}$. If V^i is a child of V^j, then $\mathcal{C}^i \subsetneq \mathcal{C}^j$. An example HC is shown in Fig.1.

In each training step the classifier in the current node V^i is trained and then the problem is divided into several sub-problems, each described with a subset of classes $\mathcal{C}^j \subsetneq \mathcal{C}^i, j = 1, \ldots, L^i$. This generation of smaller (in the sense of the number of recognized classes) sub-problems is done basing on how well the parent classifier Cl^i recognized individual classes. If some two classes C_k and C_m are frequently mistaken by Cl^i, then both are put in the same sub-problem. In that case, even if some example $x \in C_k$ is mistakenly classified as being from C_m, then the classification can be corrected one level down the HC tree. As the sub-problems are smaller, so are the errors of the corresponding classifiers. Clusters may *overlap*, *i.e.* some class may belong to more than one cluster. This improves the whole classification process.

For each non-leaf node V^i and for a given input attribute vector x a weight function $w^i(x)$ is defined, $w^i(x) = [w^i_1(x), \ldots, w^i_{L^i}(x)]$. Weights $w^i_j(x)$ describe the belief of Cl^i that an attribute vector x belongs to a sub-cluster $Q^i_j \subsetneq \mathcal{C}^i$ of V^i node. Clusters Q^i_j are defined by F^i: j-th column of F^i is the characteristic vector of Q^i_j.

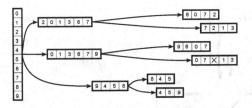

Fig. 1. An example HC. Original problem of 10 classes is first divided into 3 sub-problems, which are then divided into smaller ones. The × symbol denotes that class 2 is not included in that cluster.

Weights are used to compute the final classification in the evaluation process. Let Cl^0 recognize K classes. For an attribute vector x the vector $Cl^0(x)$ is computed, together with weights $w_l^0 = \sum_{k=1}^{K} f_{kl}^0 Cl_k^0(x) / \sum_{l'=1}^{L'} \sum_{k=1}^{K} f_{kl}^0 Cl_k^0(x)$ for $l = 1, \dots, L^0$. The final classification is found as a weighted sum $HC_k(x) = \sum_{l=1}^{L} w_l^0(x) Cl_k^l(x)$, where $Cl_k^l(x)$ are the activations of child classifiers for class C_k. If Cl^l is not a leaf node classifier but a sub-HC, a recursive procedure is used. The rule described above (named ALL-SUBTREES) uses classifications of all child nodes in a HC tree which may be both computationally expensive and also error prone – a node which does not recognize the true class of x would also generate some answers, *i.e.* noise. There are also some other rules, like: SINGLE-PATH (follow only one path from root to final leaf), RESTRICTED (follow only paths to these sub-classifiers that at least one class C_k has activation higher than the class prior, *i.e.* $Cl_k^i(x) > P(C_k)$), α-RESTRICTED (follow only paths where at least one class has activation higher than a pre-defined weakness value), see [14] for details.

The main problem in successful HC training is the way to obtain the correct clustering matrix F^i. The basic algorithm analyzes the misclassifications of Cl^i. It is based on the Bayes rule: it starts with K (equal to the number of Cl^i recognized classes) single element clusters adding successfully classes which are frequently mistaken with other classes that are already in a cluster. The clusters are then glued together if one includes the other. The process is stopped when either some threshold on the minimal number of clusters is reached or some fitness function is maximized [14]. Other clustering algorithms include those based on SAHN, GNG machine learning, or on genetic [13].

3   Problem

The problem is to predict the MSW length for a given automaton treating it as a classification problem. Each class represents an MSW length. Since the class labels form a quotient scale, it is possible to compute the classifiers error as the difference between the labels of the true and predicted class. The very important thing is the way automata are presented to HC. They are not represented directly by their transition functions, but as vectors of so-called features.

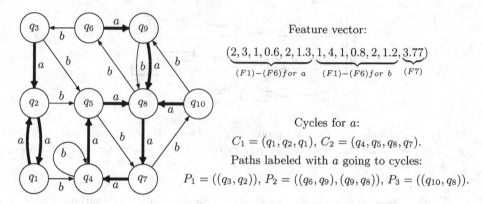

Feature vector:

$$(\underbrace{2,3,1,0.6,2,1.3}_{(F1)-(F6)for\ a},\underbrace{1,4,1,0.8,2,1.2}_{(F1)-(F6)for\ b},\underbrace{3.77}_{(F7)})$$

Cycles for a:

$C_1 = (q_1, q_2, q_1)$, $C_2 = (q_4, q_5, q_8, q_7)$.

Paths labeled with a going to cycles:

$P_1 = ((q_3, q_2))$, $P_2 = ((q_6, q_9), (q_9, q_8))$, $P_3 = ((q_{10}, q_8))$.

Fig. 2. Example automaton with $Q = \{q_1, \ldots, q_{10}\}$. Edges labeled by a are bolded. Feature values for letter a: (F1) $=\gcd(|C_1|, |C_2|) =\gcd(2, 4) = 2$; (F2) $= (|C_1|+|C_2|)/2 = 3$; (F3) $= \max\{|P_1|, |P_2|, |P_3|\} = 2$; (F4) $= (|C_1| + |C_2|)/|Q| = 0.6$; (F5) $= |\{q_2, q_8\}| = 2$, because $|q_2.a^{-1}| = |\{1, 3\}| = 2$, $|q_8.a^{-1}| = |\{5, 9, 10\}| = 3$ and $|q_i.a^{-1}| = 1$ for $i \notin \{2, 8\}$; (F6) $= (8 \cdot 1 + 1 \cdot 2 + 1 \cdot 3)/10 = 1.3$; (F7) ≈ 3.77. To compute (F7) for each pair of states we compute the length of the shortest word that synchronize this pair. For example, there are words of length 1 for pairs $\{1, 3\}$, $\{1, 4\}$, $\{5, 9\}$, $\{5, 10\}$, $\{9, 10\}$ and $\{2, 3\}$. For 6 pairs there are words of length 2, for 6 pairs – of length 3, for 9 – of length 4, for 11 – of length 5, for 6 – of length 6 and for 1 ($\{7, 8\}$) – of length 7, so (F7) $= \frac{1}{45}(6 + 12 + 18 + 36 + 55 + 36 + 7) \approx 3.77$.

We introduce the following automata features: (F1) g.c.d. of all cycles for a given letter $a \in A$; (F2) mean length of cycle for a given $a \in A$; (F3) maximal length of path going to some cycle (for a given $a \in A$); (F4) ratio of states lying on a cycle to all states (for a given $a \in A$); (F5) size of "synchronizable" part of automaton, that is $|\{q \in Q : |q.a^{-1}| > 1\}|$; (F6) mean "synchronizability level" for a given $a \in A$, that is $(1/|Q|) \cdot \sum_{q \in Q} |q.a^{-1}|$; (F7) mean "height" of states (except 0 state) in pair automaton, that is $(1/(|Q'|-1)) \sum_{\{p,q\} \in Q' \setminus \{0\}} h(\{p, q\})$. The example automaton with all of its feature values is given in Fig. 2.

4   Experiments and Results

Experiments were performed for automata with $|Q| = 4, 5, 6, 8$ states and $|A| = 2, 3, 4$ letters. For each $|Q|$ and $|A|$ we generated a 1000-element set of random automata. The set was split into train and test sets. The HC results were then compared with a single neural network model. Table 1 shows the results of this experiment. Column ℓ_{01} shows classification error (ratio of examples for which predicted class was different than the true one); column "diff err" gives the most important error: the mean difference between the true and predicted length of MSW; column MSE gives the standard mean squared error. Errors are given for test sets. Each experiment was executed in 100 runs for different number of hidden neurons (3, 5, 8). We give the mean error value together with its standard deviation, computed from 100 runs of each experiment. Also, for each experiment we give the errors for the best found HC and the best single neural network. Column hid gives the number of hidden neurons used in HC classifiers that gave the best results in terms of "diff err". In experiments with single neural networks the best networks had 3 hidden neurons, except $|Q| = 4, |A| = 2$, where the best network had 5 hidden neurons.

Table 1. Results for HC prediction of the minimal synchronizing word lengths compared to a single neural network model. Each error is a mean error computed from 100 experiment runs. ℓ_{01} is the ratio of examples incorrectly classified; "diff err" is the absolute difference between MSW and predicted length; MSE is a standard mean square error. For each experiment the errors for the best run are also shown. Hid is the number of neurons in HC nodes that gave the best results for each experiment.

$|Q|$	$|A|$	hid	Hierarchical Classifier			Neural Network		
			ℓ_{01}	diff err	MSE	ℓ_{01}	diff err	MSE
4	2	8	0.31 ± 0.03	0.42 ± 0.04	0.77 ± 0.14	0.71 ± 0.10	1.62 ± 0.60	5.19 ± 2.80
			0.25	0.32	0.50	0.37	0.43	0.57
4	3	3	0.43 ± 0.06	0.60 ± 0.13	1.07 ± 0.40	0.66 ± 0.14	1.20 ± 0.38	2.82 ± 1.24
			0.34	0.44	0.71	0.43	0.59	0.97
4	4	8	0.47 ± 0.04	0.61 ± 0.08	0.97 ± 0.22	0.71 ± 0.09	1.22 ± 0.27	2.4 ± 0.80
			0.40	0.47	0.62	0.60	0.77	1.17
5	2	8	0.55 ± 0.03	0.89 ± 0.07	1.86 ± 0.25	0.82 ± 0.11	2.57 ± 0.90	11.4 ± 6.53
			0.50	0.73	1.37	0.51	0.70	1.24
5	3	5	0.49 ± 0.05	0.71 ± 0.29	1.37 ± 1.63	0.70 ± 0.18	1.48 ± 0.72	4.27 ± 2.92
			0.44	0.58	0.94	0.47	0.64	1.05
5	4	8	0.44 ± 0.02	0.60 ± 0.05	1.14 ± 0.16	0.74 ± 0.17	1.86 ± 0.72	6.84 ± 3.21
			0.40	0.52	0.94	0.40	0.53	0.94
6	2	3	0.63 ± 0.05	1.11 ± 0.21	2.75 ± 1.00	0.85 ± 0.12	3.24 ± 1.31	18.8 ± 12.0
			0.58	0.93	1.97	0.59	0.88	1.67
6	3	8	0.64 ± 0.01	1.11 ± 0.06	2.75 ± 0.35	0.82 ± 0.13	2.93 ± 1.54	17.2 ± 12.9
			0.61	1.01	2.36	0.64	0.97	1.98
6	4	8	0.55 ± 0.05	0.80 ± 0.48	1.83 ± 4.26	0.82 ± 0.11	2.61 ± 1.06	13.6 ± 7.88
			0.51	0.67	1.07	0.51	0.69	1.23
8	2	5	0.76 ± 0.02	1.90 ± 0.15	7.04 ± 1.08	0.86 ± 0.10	4.25 ± 2.66	38.2 ± 36.3
			0.73	1.70	5.67	0.71	1.61	5.09
8	3	8	0.70 ± 0.02	1.44 ± 0.13	4.67 ± 0.91	0.88 ± 0.08	4.00 ± 1.58	29.7 ± 16.8
			0.67	1.31	3.79	0.70	1.28	3.60
8	4	5	0.77 ± 0.01	2.20 ± 0.21	10.29 ± 2.05	0.91 ± 0.05	5.00 ± 1.72	42.4 ± 27.1
			0.74	1.75	6.41	0.77	1.71	5.52

Table 2. Correlations between feature values and MSW lengths

$|Q|$	$|A|$	F1	F2	F3	F4	F5	F6	F7	$|Q|$	$|A|$	F1	F2	F3	F4	F5	F6	F7
4	2	.23	.33	-.07	.28	-.15	-.27	.93	6	2	.19	.35	-.26	.50	-.28	-.34	.93
4	3	.24	.29	-.10	.30	-.22	-.33	.90	6	3	.10	.16	-.32	.50	-.36	-.40	.94
4	4	.18	.26	-.20	.38	-.26	-.37	.90	6	4	.12	.20	-.42	.56	-.48	-.48	.95
5	2	.27	.35	-.15	.38	-.21	-.33	.90	8	2	.10	.31	-.40	.63	-.30	-.32	.94
5	3	.18	.34	-.27	.50	-.32	-.41	.92	8	3	.04	.11	-.32	.50	-.30	-.38	.92
5	4	.10	.19	-.27	.44	-.31	-.39	.93	8	4	-.07	-.03	-.35	.48	-.36	-.40	.90

Table 2 shows the Pearson's correlations between feature values and MSW lengths. Fig. 3 (right part) shows the histogram of differences between true and predicted length of MSW for experiment $|Q| = 8, |A| = 2$. Notice that HC usually returns the true value or value that is very close to the true one. Left part of Fig. 3 shows the x-y plot of true MSW length vs. the value of F7 feature for the same experiment.

HC architecture is designed to handle many classes. Assuming the Černý conjecture is true, for class of n-state automata we have $(n-1)^2 + 1$ classes, so it is quadratic in state set size. Standard deviation for all HC errors in Table 1 are

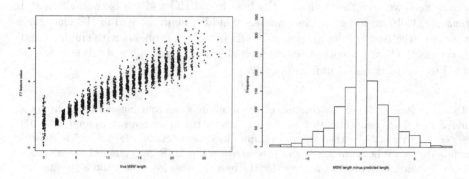

Fig. 3. Correlation between MSW length and F7 feature value for experiment $|Q| = 8$, $|A| = 2$

usually small, which means that HC prediction is stable, contrary to the single NN model, which has much bigger both mean error values and their standard deviations. HC, in terms of "diff" error, works very well – it finds almost exact values of the MSW lengths. These above facts allow us to claim that HC is a very good tool to predict MSW length.

Correlations between MSW length and values of some features F3 and F4 grow with the number of states. These features should be the good predictors of MSW lengths for automata with larger number of states. Feature F7 (mean height of a node in the pair automaton tree) is strongly correlated with MSW length. The relation between pair automaton structure and the input automaton should be the subject of future theoretical research. This may lead to some new results on the upper bound of the MSW length.

The future work in this area should concentrate on the proper choice of predictive automata features. Well chosen set of features cannot only decrease classification error, but also may allow us to understand deeply what are the main factors that make MSW lengths so long in some automata. Such result can be then utilized in new, effective algorithms for finding possibly short synchronizing words.

References

1. Broy, M., Jonsson, B., Katoen, J.-P., Leucker, M., Pretschner, A. (eds.): Model-Based Testing of Reactive Systems. LNCS, vol. 3472, pp. 5–33. Springer, Heidelberg (2005)
2. Černý, J., Pirická, A., Rosenauerová, B.: On directable automata. Kybernetika 7(4), 289–298 (1971)
3. Deshmukh, R.G., Hawat, G.N.: An algorithm to determine shortest length distinguishing, homing, and synchronizing sequences for sequential machines. In: Proc. Southcon 1994 Conference, pp. 496–501 (1994)
4. Eppstein, D.: Reset sequences for monotonic automata. SIAM Journal on Computing 19(3), 500–510 (1990)

5. Fukada, A., Nakata, A., Kitamichi, J., Higashino, T., Cavalli, A.: A conformance testing method for communication protocols modeled as concurrent DFSMs. Treatment of non-observable non-determinism. In: Proc. IEEE 15th Int. Conf. on Information Networking, pp. 155–162 (2001)
6. Kari, J.: Synchronizing and Stability of Finite Automata. Journal of Universal Computer Science 8, 270–277 (2002)
7. Klyachko, A.A., Rystsov, I., Spivak, M.A.: An extremal combinatorial problem associated with the bound on the length of a synchronizing word in an automaton. Kybernetika 2, 16–20 (1987)
8. Natarajan, B.K.: An Algorithmic Approach to the Automated Design of Part Orienters. In: Proc. IEEE Symp. Foundations of Computer Science (FOCS 1986), pp. 132–142 (1986)
9. Olschewski, J., Ummels, M.: The Complexity of Finding Reset Words in Finite Automata. In: Hliněný, P., Kučera, A. (eds.) MFCS 2010. LNCS, vol. 6281, pp. 568–579. Springer, Heidelberg (2010)
10. Pixley, C., Jeong, S.W., Hachtel, G.D.: Exact calculation of synchronizing sequences based on binary decision diagrams. In: Proc. ACM/IEEE 29th Design Automation Conference, pp. 620–623 (1992)
11. Podolak, I.T.: Hierarchical Classifier with Overlapping Class Groups. Expert Systems with Applications 34(1), 673–682 (2008)
12. Podolak, I.T., Roman, A.: A new notion of weakness in classification theory. Advances in Intelligent and Soft Computing 57, 239–245 (2009)
13. Podolak, I.T., Bartocha, K.: A Hierarchical Classifier with Growing Neural Gas Clustering. In: Kolehmainen, M., Toivanen, P., Beliczynski, B. (eds.) ICANNGA 2009. LNCS, vol. 5495, pp. 283–292. Springer, Heidelberg (2009)
14. Podolak, I.T., Roman, A.: Fusion of supervised and unsupervised training methods for a multi-class classification problem. Pattern Analysis and Applications 14(4), 395–413 (2011)
15. Pomeranz, I., Reddy, S.M.: On synchronizing sequences and test sequence partitioning. In: Proc. IEEE 16th VLSI Test Symp., pp. 158–167 (1998)
16. Ponce, A.M., Csopaki, G., Tarnay, K.: Formal specification of conformance testing documents for communication protocols. In: 5th IEEE Int. Symp. on Personal, Indoor and Mobile Radio Communications (PIMRC 1994), vol. 4, pp. 1167–1172 (1994)
17. Roman, A.: Genetic Algorithm for Synchronization. In: Dediu, A.H., Ionescu, A.M., Martín-Vide, C. (eds.) LATA 2009. LNCS, vol. 5457, pp. 684–695. Springer, Heidelberg (2009)
18. Trahtman, A.N.: The road coloring problem. Israel Journal of Mathematics 1(172), 51–60 (2009)
19. Trahtman, A.N.: An Efficient Algorithm Finds Noticeable Trends and Examples Concerning the Černy Conjecture. In: Královič, R., Urzyczyn, P. (eds.) MFCS 2006. LNCS, vol. 4162, pp. 789–800. Springer, Heidelberg (2006)
20. Ananichev, D.S., Volkov, M.V.: Synchronizing Monotonic Automata. In: Ésik, Z., Fülöp, Z. (eds.) DLT 2003. LNCS, vol. 2710, pp. 270–382. Springer, Heidelberg (2003)
21. Volkov, M.V.: Exponents of labeled digraphs and synchronizing automata. In: First Russian-Finish Symposium on Discrete Mathematics (2011) (not published)
22. Zhao, Y., Liu, Y., Guo, X., Zhang, C.: Conformance testing for IS-IS protocol based on E-LOTOS. In: IEEE Int. Conf. on Information Theory and Information Security (ICITIS 2010), pp. 54–57 (2010)

Dimensionality Reduction Using External Context in Pattern Recognition Problems with Ordered Labels

Ewa Skubalska-Rafajłowicz[1], Adam Krzyżak[2], and Ewaryst Rafajłowicz[1]

[1] Institute of Computer Engineering, Control & Robotics,
Wrocław University of Technology, Wrocław, Poland
`ewaryst.rafajlowicz@pwr.wroc.pl`
[2] Department of Computer Science and Software Engineering,
Concordia University, Montreal, Canada

Abstract. Our aim is to propose a new look at the dimensionality reduction in pattern recognition problems by extracting part of variables that are further called external context variables. We show how to incorporate them into the Bayes classification scheme with loss functions that depend on class labels that are ordered. Then, the general form of the optimal context sensitive classifier is derived and the learning method that is based on kernel approximation is proposed.

1 Introduction

Our aim in this paper is to propose a new approach that incorporates external context variables, as introduced in [11], into the Bayesian model with loss function that takes into account label ordering (see [8] and the bibliography cited therein). By external context we mean variables that influence our classification process but they are not features of an object to be recognized. For example, let us suppose that our classifier equipped with a watch-dog camera has to distinguish whether a vehicle 500 meters in front of it is a car, a van or a truck. Weather conditions, such as rain, snow or a direct sunlight may essentially influence our decision, but are not features of a vehicle to be recognized. Clearly, the weather conditions can be artificially incorporated into a feature vector for vehicle recognition, but – as we shall see later – it is not advisable. The same example explains why it is reasonable to order labels of a car (label 1), a van (label 2) and a truck (label 3). We intuitively feel that misclassifying a small car as a truck should yield higher loss than when it is misclassified as a van.

One can consider the proposed approach as information fusion, coming from features of an object to be recognized and the context in which this object was observed as well as incorporating additional knowledge on relative importance of recognition errors when class labels are far away from our decisions.

A deeper insight into the role of context variables reveals that they lead to the dimensionality reduction unlike the traditional approach that incorporates them directly into the vector of features. This statement is illustrated in Fig. 1 and Fig. 2. The former illustrates the traditional approach, i.e., we have two

L. Rutkowski et al. (Eds.): ICAISC 2012, Part I, LNCS 7267, pp. 430–438, 2012.

features X and Y and additional variable Z that can assume two levels $Z1$ and $Z2$, say. We have two classes, the first one (marked by the oblique lines) can be separated by a plane from the second one (marked by the crossed lines). In the left panel of Fig. 1 one can notice that the recognition task is much more difficult when we ignore information provided by Z variable that is considered here as a context variable. In the middle and in the right panel of this figure we illustrate how easy is the recognition task when the context variable is taken into account. Note that this time we have to select two two-dimensional separating surfaces instead of one in three dimensional space as it was in the case when Z was treated in the same way as features X and Y. The dimensionality reducing effect attained by introducing context is even more apparent when Z assumes more than two levels and the dimensionality of the features space is larger. On the other hand, the proposed approach can be considered as a fusion of classifiers such that each of them is designed to operate in a different external context.

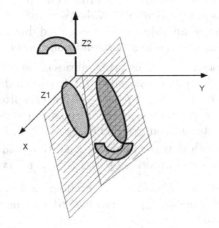

Fig. 1. Example of three dimensional pattern recognition problem when context variable Z is considered in the same way as original features

It should be mentioned that internal context has been known in the pattern recognition theory for a long time, at least from 60's. By internal context we mean the one that appears as the result of previous decisions or outputs or in multistage decision processes (see [4], [15]), [10], [9], [19]), [5]). Another way of using internal context can be found in image processing tasks in which it is provided by pixels from a neighborhood providing contextual information (see, e.g.,[2]).

2   Augmentation of the Bayesian Scheme

Let $X \in R^{d_X}$ denote d_X-dimensional vector of features of a pattern to be recognized that was drawn at random from one of $L \geq 2$ classes, where $\mathcal{L} \stackrel{def}{=} \{1, 2, \ldots, L\}$ denotes the set of labels.

432   E. Skubalska-Rafajłowicz, A. Krzyżak, and E. Rafajłowicz

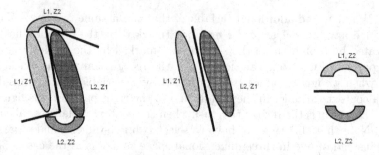

Fig. 2. The same pattern recognition task as in Fig. 1 when context variable Z is ignored (left panel) and when it is properly taken into account (the middle and the right panel) leading to two two-dimensional and easier problems

Incorporating Context. We also observe $Z \in \mathcal{Z} \overset{def}{=} \{\kappa_1, \kappa_2, \ldots, \kappa_J\}$, which is interpreted as a discrete level of an external context. Z is also a random a random variable that is independent of X. Z helps us in a proper classification of X, but it does not describe an object to be recognized, but rather circumstances of our decision problem such as weather conditions, level of air pollution etc. Denote by $\Pi \overset{def}{=} \{\pi_1, \pi_2, \ldots, \pi_J\}$ the probabilities of observing κ_j's.

Thus, the triple (X, Z, i) describes pattern X from i-th class, which appeared in context Z. Denote by $f_i(x; \kappa_j)$ a density of patterns from i-th class, which depends on context κ_j. A priori class probabilities, denoted as q_i, $i = 1, 2, \ldots, L$, may also depend on external context Z, i.e., $q_i(\kappa_j) \geq 0$, $i = 1, 2, \ldots, L$, $i = 1, 2, \ldots, J$, which are such that the following condition holds: $\sum_{i=1}^{L} q_i(\kappa_j) = 1$ for all $\kappa_j \in \mathcal{Z}$. The scheme of observing patterns is as follows:

1) An observed context $Z_0 \in \mathcal{Z}$ is drawn at random, according to Π.
2) A priori class probabilities $q_i(Z_0)$ are established and the class label, $i^{(0)}$, say, is drawn according to them.
3) The vector of features X_0, say, is drawn at random, according to the probability density (p.d.f.) $f_{i^{(0)}}(x; Z_0)$.

It is clear that the above scheme reduces the classical pattern recognition problem when only one level of the context is assumed.

For a while, we shall assume that f_i's and q_i's are known. Later, we shall discuss the learning problem.

Corollary 1. *Denote by $P(i|x, z)$ the a posteriori probability that pattern x, observed in context $z \in \mathcal{Z}$ is a member of i-th class. Then,*

$$P(i|x, z) = q_i(z) \, f_i(x; z) / f(x; z), \quad i = 1, 2, \ldots, L. \tag{1}$$

where

$$f(x; z) \overset{def}{=} \sum_{i=1}^{L} q_i(z) \, f_i(x; z). \tag{2}$$

Taking into account that $\mathcal{Z}$ is finite, we can interpret $P(i|x, z)$ as a family, indexed by $z \in \mathcal{Z}$, of a posteriori probabilities that x is from i-th class.

Loss Function with Ordered Labels. We attach loss $S(i, k) \geq 0$, if a pattern from i-th class is classified to k-th class, $k, i \in \mathcal{L}$. We consider a special class of loss functions of the form: $S(i, k) = (i - k)^2$ that reflects the fact that class labels are ordered in the sense that our loss is higher when X is erroneously classified to class $(k + 1)$ and smaller, if it is (also erroneously) classified to class k, while a proper class label is $i < k$. Clearly, one can formalize this idea in other ways, e.g., as $S(i, k) = |i - k|$, but the quadratic loss is more manageable and leads to simpler classifiers. One can also consider weights attached to $(i - k)^2$ or other generalizations, but here we stay within a simpler scheme.

Optimal, Context Sensitive Classifier for Classes with Ordered Labels. Denote by $\Psi : R^{d_X} \times \mathcal{Z} \to \mathcal{L}$ a classifier, which is a measurable function $\Psi(X, Z)$ of X for each $Z \in \mathcal{Z}$. The overall risk of classifier Ψ is defined as

$$R(\Psi) = \mathbf{E}_{X, Z} \left[\sum_{i=1}^{L} (i - \Psi(X, Z))^2 \, P(i|X, Z) \right] \tag{3}$$

or

$$R(\Psi) = \sum_{j=1}^{J} \pi_j \int_{R^{d_X}} \left[\sum_{i=1}^{L} (i - \Psi(x, z))^2 \, P(i|x, z) \right] f(x; \kappa_j) \, dx. \tag{4}$$

Corollary 2. *Classifier Ψ^* that minimizes $R(\Psi)$ in the class of all measurable functions $\Psi(x, z)$ of x for each $z \in \mathcal{Z}$ is of the form:*

$$\Psi^*(x, z) = ROUND \left[\sum_{i=1}^{L} i \, P(i|x, z) \right], \tag{5}$$

where $ROUND[a]$ denotes the nearest integer for a.

Indeed, the conditional risk $r(j, x, z)$, given x and z, can be expressed as

$$r(j, x, z) = \sum_{i=1}^{L} (i - j)^2 \, P(i|x, z). \tag{6}$$

Then, the overall risk can be rewritten as

$$R(\Psi) = \sum_{j=1}^{J} \int_{R^{d_X}} r(j, x, z) \, \pi_j \, f(x; \kappa_j) \, dx \tag{7}$$

and it is clear that it suffices to minimize $r(j, x, z)$, due to the fact that $\pi_j f(x; z)$'s are nonnegative. Formal differentiation of (6) w.r.t. j yields (5), while strict convexity of the quadratic function allows to convince oneself that the $ROUND[.]$ operation provides the minimizer of $r(j, x, z)$.

Let us note that Ψ^* does not depend on Π, i.e., on the distribution of context variables. This is in sharp contrast with the influence of X variables (features), indicating that the role of the context in our model is different than those of features. Clearly, the overall risk depends on Π (see (7)). In order to justify the fact that Ψ^* does not depend on Π it suffices to analyze (1).

All the above finite case formulas approach smoothly the case when the number of classes is countable, but infinite, i.e. $L = \infty$, provided that all the corresponding sums are convergent.

Optimal Classifier for the Exponential Family. In our example it will be more convenient to label classes from "0" (instead of "1") and to admit $L = \infty$. Consider the following class densities, dependent on context $z \in \mathcal{Z}$:

$$f_i(x; z) = \frac{\lambda^i(x; z) \exp(-\lambda(x; z))}{\alpha_i(z) \, i!}, \quad i = 0, 1, 2, \ldots \tag{8}$$

where $\lambda(x; z)$ is a positive function that depends on pattern x and context $z \in \mathcal{Z}$, while $\alpha_i(z)$ are normalizing factors, which are selected in such a way that $\int f_i(x; z) \, dx = 1$ for each $i = 0, 1, 2, \ldots$ and $z \in \mathcal{Z}$. In our example we select $\lambda(x; z)$ as a linear function of features, i.e., $\lambda(x; z) = c^T(z) \, x$ with d_X dimensional column vector of nonnegative coefficients $c(z)$ that depends on $z \in \mathcal{Z}$. As the feature space we take the positive ortant, i.e., all elements of x are nonnegative. In this case (note that we write d instead of d_X for brevity)

$$\alpha_i(z) = \frac{(i + d - 1)!}{(d - 1)! \, i! \, \prod_{l=1}^d c_l(z)} \tag{9}$$

Suppose the a priori distribution has the form:

$$q_i(z) = (1 - \gamma(z)) \, \gamma(z)^i, \quad i = 0, 1, 2, \ldots, \tag{10}$$

where $0 < \gamma(z) < 1$ may depend on context variables. Later, we shall write γ instead of $\gamma(z)$ for brevity. Under these assumptions we obtain from (2):

$$f(x; z) = -c^T(z) \, x \, (\gamma - 1) \, \gamma \left[\prod_{l=1}^d c_l(z) \right] e^{c^T(z) \, x \, (\gamma - 1)} (c^T(z) \, x \, \gamma)^{-d} \times \tag{11}$$

$$\times \left(\Gamma(d) - (d - 1) \, \Gamma(d - 1, c^T(z) \, x \, \gamma) \right)$$

Similarly, defining $\mathcal{N}(x; z)$ as $\sum_{i=0}^{\infty} i \, q_i(z) \, f_i(x; z)$, we obtain

$$\mathcal{N}(x; z) = c^T(z) \, x \, e^{-c^T(z) \, x} \, (\gamma - 1) \, \gamma \left[\prod_{l=1}^d c_l(z) \right] \Gamma(d)(c^T(z) \, x \, \gamma)^{-d} \times \tag{12}$$

$$\left(e^{c^T(z) \, x \, \gamma} (-c^T(z) \, x \, \gamma + d - 1) \, (\Gamma(d + 1) - d \, \Gamma(d, c^T(z) \, x \, \gamma)) - d \, (c^T(z) \, x \, \gamma)^d \right) / d!,$$

where $\Gamma(a, b)$ is the incomplete gamma function.

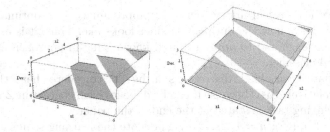

Fig. 3. Example of the decision rule (15) in two different contexts (see the text)

Noticing that $\sum_{i=0}^{\infty} i\, P(i|x, z) = \mathcal{N}(x; z)/f(x; z)$, we obtain:

Corollary 3. *For class densities (8) with $\lambda(x; z) = c^T(z)\,x$ and a priori probabilities (10) we obtain the following decision rule:*

$$\Psi^*(x; z, c(z)) = ROUND[\psi^*(x; z, c(z))], \tag{13}$$

where $\psi^*(x; z, c(z))$ is defined as follows:

$$\frac{e^{-c^T(z)\,x\gamma}\,\Gamma(d)\left(d\,(c^T(z)\,x\gamma)^d + e^{c^T(z)\,x\gamma}(c^T(z)\,x\gamma - d + 1)\Omega(d)\right)}{d!\,\Omega(d-1)} \tag{14}$$

where $\Omega(d) \overset{def}{=} (\Gamma(d+1) - d\,\Gamma(d, c^T(z)\,x\gamma))$ (note that the rest of variables in the definition of Ω is omitted for brevity).
For $d_X = d = 2$ (14) simplifies to

$$\psi^*(x; z) = c^T(z)\,x\gamma\left(\frac{1}{e^{c^T(z)\,x\gamma} - 1} + 1\right) - 1, \tag{15}$$

while for $d_X = d = 1$ we obtain: $\psi^*(x; z) = c(z)\,x\gamma$.

If $c(z)$ and γ are known (or estimated), then (14) can be calculated (almost) exactly, because the incomplete gamma function can be evaluated to arbitrary numerical precision.

Fig. 3 illustrates how Ψ^* may looks like for $d_X = d = 2$ in two different contexts, $z_1 = 1$ (left panel) and $z_2 = 2$ (right panel). In the both cases $\gamma = 0.5$ was used and for $z_1 = 1$ vector $c^T(z_1) = (0.8, 0.6)$, while for $z_2 = 2$ vector $c^T(z_2) = (0.36, 0.86)$.

3   Learning Context Sensitive Classifiers with Ordered Labels

In the previous section it was assumed that we know class densities $f_i(x; z)$'s and priors $q_i(z)$'s for each context variables. These assumptions were necessary in order to develop the theory. In practice, however, we do not have such knowledge, but then we need a learning sequence for approximating an optimal classifier. Corollary 2 shows how the optimal classifier looks like. Thus, it is expedient to use this knowledge and to apply the well known plug-in approach for building an empirical classifier.

When context variable is discrete, as in the case considered here, the learning process is relatively easy, because it can be done for each context in $\mathcal{Z}$ separately. More challenging task is stated at the end of the paper.

Let $(x_n(z), i_n(z))$, $n = 1, 2, \ldots, N(z)$ denote the learning sequence observed in context $z \in \mathcal{Z}$, where $N(z)$ is the length of this sequence, $x_n(z)$ is n-th vector of features, while $i_n(z)$ is a true label attached to $x_n(z)$ in context z. Note that we need $Card(\mathcal{Z})$ learning sequences of the form described above and having such sequences, the estimation of a priori distributions in each context is easy.

Parametric Case. By the parametric case of learning we mean the following task: build an empirical decision rule when underlying distributions are known to within a vector of unknown parameters and we have a learning sequence for their estimation. We sketch the idea of a learning algorithm in the parametric case using Corollary 3 as a vehicle for presenting it.

Let us note that when context variable $z \in \mathcal{Z}$ is fixed, then the decision rule (13) and $\psi^*(x; z, c(z))$ depend on a fixed vector $c = c(z)$ of unknown parameters. Thus, it suffices to minimize the following empirical loss function:

$$\hat{Q}_z(c) = \sum_{n=1}^{N(z)} \left[i_n(z) - ROUND[\psi^*(x_n(z), z, c)] \right]^2 \tag{16}$$

with respect to $c \in R^{d_X}$, taking into account, as constraints of the optimization problem, that all elements of c should be nonnegative. An unpleasant feature of $\hat{Q}_z(c)$ as the goal function is the presence of the $ROUND[.]$ operation, which

- may lead to non-unique solutions,
- precludes the possibility of using fast optimization solvers such as the Levenberg-Marquardt algorithm.

For these reasons, we propose to minimize

$$\tilde{Q}_z(c) = \sum_{n=1}^{N(z)} \left[i_n(z) - \psi^*(x_n(z), z, c) \right]^2 \tag{17}$$

with respect to $c \in R^{d_X}$. Note that for $d_X = 1$ this task has the well known closed form solution.

Now, it remains to repeat the minimization of $\tilde{Q}_z(c)$ for each context $z \in \mathcal{Z}$ and to plug-in the resulting $\tilde{c}(z)$ into (13).

Nonparametric Case. By the nonparametric case of learning we mean that class densities in each context $f_i(x; z)$ are completely unknown. In fact, it is even not necessary to postulate their existence, because the result presented below holds for every distribution of X variables.

Let $K(t) \geq 0$ be a kernel, for which the following conditions hold:

$$\int K(t)\,dt = 1, \quad \int t\,K(t)\,dt = 0, \quad \int t^2\,K(t)\,dt < \infty, \tag{18}$$

$$\alpha H(\|x\|) \leq K(x) \leq \beta H(\|x\|), \quad x \in \mathcal{R}^{dx} \tag{19}$$

for some $0 < \alpha < \beta < \infty$ and nonincreasing $H : \mathcal{R}_+ \to \mathcal{R}_+$ with $H(+0) > 0$, $\|.\|$ is a norm in R^{dx}.

Following general ideas from [6], [3] of constructing an empirical nonparametric classification rules and [7] when the least squared loss is involved and interpreting Ψ^* in Corollary 2 as the conditional expectation, we suggest the following estimator of the classification rule for fixed context $z \in \mathcal{Z}$:

$$\hat{\Psi}_{N(z)}(x;\, z) = ROUND \left[\frac{U_{N(z)}(x;\, z)}{V_{N(z)}(x;\, z)} \right], \tag{20}$$

where

$$U_{N(z)}(x;\, z) = \sum_{n=1}^{N(z)} i_n(z)\, K\left(\frac{\|x - X_n(z)\|}{h(n)} \right), \tag{21}$$

$$V_{N(z)}(x;\, z) = \sum_{n=1}^{N(z)} K\left(\frac{\|x - X_n(z)\|}{h(n)} \right), \tag{22}$$

where $X_n(z)$ are independent, identically distributed random vectors drawn according to $f_i(x;\, z)$. When (20) is used we insert observations $x_n(z)$ instead of $X_n(z)$ in (21) and (22). Let us note that (21) and (22) can be written in the recursive form. Let us note that (20) can be interpreted as a bank of classifiers, indexed by $z \in \mathcal{Z}$. A proper classifier is activated by the context variable.

Theorem 31. *Let kernel K satisfy conditions (18) and (19) and assume that*

$$h(n) \to 0 \quad and \quad \sum_{k=1}^{n} h^{dx}(k) \to \infty \quad as \quad n \to \infty. \tag{23}$$

Then the rule (20) is universally consistent for each context $z \in \mathcal{Z}$ separately:

$$R(\hat{\Psi}_{N(z)} | \mathcal{Z} = z) - R(\Psi^* | \mathcal{Z} = z) \to 0 \quad as \quad N(z) \to \infty \tag{24}$$

for all distributions of X variables in every context. In (24) the risk is conditioned on the context variable, i.e.,

$$R(\Psi | \mathcal{Z} = \kappa_j) = \int_{R^{dx}} \left[\sum_{i=1}^{L} (i - \Psi(x, z))^2\, P(i|x, z) \right] f(x;\kappa_j)\,dx, \ j = 1, 2, \ldots, J.$$

The proof of this results is an extension of the proof for the context free case that can be found in [8].

The real challenge is the case when z is not discrete but takes values from an interval or a hypercube $\mathcal{Z}$. In this case one can cover $\mathcal{Z}$ by sets with centers $\kappa_j \in \mathcal{Z}$ and repeat al the above considerations. However, the proof of consistency is much more difficult, because the covering sets should have decreasing size as the length of the learning sequence increases.

References

1. Ciskowski, P., Rafajłowicz, E.: Context-Dependent Neural Nets–Structures and Learning. IEEE Trans. Neural Networks 15, 1367–1377 (2004)
2. Davies, E.R.: Machine Vision. Morgan Kaufmann, San Francisco (2005)
3. Devroye, L., Györfi, L., Lugosi, G.: Probabilistic Theory of Pattern Recognition. Springer, New York (1996)
4. Eden, M.: Handwriting and Pattern Recognition. IRE Transactions on Information Theory, 100–166 (February 1962)
5. Elman, J.L.: Finding structure in time. Cognitive Sci. 15(2), 179–211 (1990)
6. Greblicki, W.: Asymptotically Optimal Pattern Recognition Procedures with Density Estimates. IEEE Trans. Information Theory IT 24, 250–251 (1978)
7. Gyorfi, L., Kohler, M., Krzyżak, A., Walk, H.: A Distribution-Free Theory of Nonparametric Regression. Springer, New York (2002)
8. Krzyżak, A., Rafajłowicz, E.: Pattern Recognition with Linearly Structured Labels Using Recursive Kernel Estimator. In: Rutkowski, L., Scherer, R., Tadeusiewicz, R., Zadeh, L.A., Zurada, J.M. (eds.) ICAISC 2010. LNCS (LNAI), vol. 6113, pp. 422–429. Springer, Heidelberg (2010)
9. Kurzyński, M.: On the identity of optimal strategies for multistage classifiers. Pattern Recognition Letters 10, 39–46 (1989)
10. Lee, K.T.: Context-dependent phonetic hidden Markov models for speaker-independent continuous speech recognition. IEEE Transactions on Acoustics, Speech and Signal Processing 38(4), 599–609 (1990)
11. Rafajłowicz, E.: Classifiers sensitive to external context – theory and applications to video sequences. Expert Systems (2011), doi:10.1111/j.1468-0394.2010.00564
12. Rafajłowicz, E.: Context-dependent neural nets – Problem statement and examples. In: Proceedings 3rd Conference on Neural Networks Applications, Zakopane, Poland, pp. 557–562 (May 1999)
13. Rafajłowicz, E.: Learning context dependent neural nets. In: Proceedings 3rd Conference on Neural Networks Applications, Zakopane, Poland, pp. 551–556 (May 1999)
14. Rafajłowicz, E., Skubalska-Rafajłowicz, E.: MAD Loss in Pattern Recognition and RBF Learning. In: Rutkowski, L., Tadeusiewicz, R., Zadeh, L.A., Zurada, J.M. (eds.) ICAISC 2008. LNCS (LNAI), vol. 5097, pp. 671–680. Springer, Heidelberg (2008)
15. Raviv, J.: Decision Making in Markov Chains Applied to the Problem of Pattern Recognition. IEEE Transactions on Information Theory IT-3(4), 536–551 (1967)
16. Skubalska-Rafajłowicz, E.: Clustering of Data and Nearest Neighbors Search for Pattern Recognition with Dimensionality Reduction Using Random Projections. In: Rutkowski, L., Scherer, R., Tadeusiewicz, R., Zadeh, L.A., Zurada, J.M. (eds.) ICAISC 2010. LNCS (LNAI), vol. 6113, pp. 462–470. Springer, Heidelberg (2010)
17. Skubalska-Rafajłowicz, E.: Neural networks with sigmoidal activation functions-dimension reduction using normal random projection. Nonlinear Analysis, Theory, Methods & Applications. Series A, Theory and Methods 71(12), 1255–1263 (2009)
18. Skubalska-Rafajłowicz, E.: Pattern recognition algorithms based on space-filling curves and orthogonal expansions. IEEE Transactions on Information Theory 47(5), 1915–1927 (2001)
19. Turney, P.: The identification of context-sensitive features: A formal definition of context for concept learning. In: Proceedings 13th Int. Conf. Machine Learning (ICML 1996), Bari, Italy, pp. 53–59 (1996)

SVM with CUDA Accelerated Kernels for Big Sparse Problems

Krzysztof Sopyła, Paweł Drozda, and Przemysław Górecki

Department of Mathematics and Computer Sciences,
University of Warmia and Mazury, Olsztyn, Poland
ksopyla@uwm.edu.pl, {pdrozda,pgorecki}@matman.uwm.edu.pl

Abstract. The SVM algorithm is one of the most frequently used methods for the classification process. For many domains, where the classification problems have many features as well as numerous instances, classification is a difficult and time-consuming task. For this reason, the following paper presents the CSR-GPU-SVM algorithm which accelerates SVM training for large and sparse problems with the use of the CUDA technology. Implementation is based on the SMO (Sequential Minimal Optimization) algorithm and utilizes the CSR(Compressed Sparse Row) sparse matrix format. The proposed solution allows us to perform efficient classification of big datasets, for example rcv1 and newsgroup20, for which classification with dense representation is not possible. The performed experiments have proven the accelerations in the order of 6 - 35 training times compared to original LibSVM implementation.

Keywords: SVM, GPGPU, CUDA, Classification, Sparse Matrix.

1 Introduction

Many of the problems associated with dynamically developing fields of computer science such as Music Retrieval, Information Retrieval or Content Base Image Retrieval have a representation with a great number of attributes as well as instances. As a result, the calculation of an effective model for Machine Learning tasks (for example: classification) becomes difficult and time-consuming [12]. This creates a need for methods and algorithms for forming a model within a reasonable time, which deal well with multidimensional data. It is worth mentioning that the "multidimensionality" is often accompanied by the "sparsity" of data.

Recent studies show that the SVM algorithm copes well with the multidimensional classification problems [10],[7]. The essence of teaching the SVM involves solving a quadratic optimization task, where in order to assess the similarity of objects, the kernel function is used. To obtain the model, computation of m^2 kernel executions (scalar products) is required in the worst case, where m is the number of objects. Therefore, this operation can be considered the most time-consuming part of the SVM training process and creating a model for a collection that contains a huge number of instances becomes impossible within a reasonable time.

L. Rutkowski et al. (Eds.): ICAISC 2012, Part I, LNCS 7267, pp. 439–447, 2012.

This introduces the necessity for methods which will accelerate the computation of kernel function. One of the possible solution is the utilization of the NVidia CUDA (Compute Unified Device Architecture) technology, which allows us to perform part of calculations simultaneously on the graphics processing unit (GPU). Recently, this technology arouses the interest of many researchers, who try to implement existing algorithms on CUDA. In many cases, it accelerates computing processes by 10 to 100 times.

The algorithm presented in this paper also exploits CUDA. In particular, the computations of SVM kernel function are transferred to the GPU, which allows us to fully leverage the potential of the GPU and obtain the result in a reasonable time. Moreover, the described algorithm takes advantage of data sparsity, which allows for a possibility to perform the SVM method for big datasets.

The paper is organized as follows. In the next section we review the existing SVM implementations on the CPU and the GPU. The main contribution of this paper, the CSR-GPU-SVM algorithm, is introduced in Section 3. Next, Section 4 evaluates the proposed approach based on experimental results. We conclude and point future directions in Section 5.

2   Support Vector Machines

The SVM algorithm described in [2],[5] is a binary classifier which divides the training set into two classes using the optimal hyperplane. It can be done by solving the quadratic optimization task. Given a set of instance-label pairs (x_i, y_i); $i = 1, \ldots, l$; $x_i \in R^n$; $y_i \in \{-1, +1\}$, SVM solves the following dual problem (1) derived from the primal problem described in [5]:

$$\min_{\alpha} \frac{1}{2}\alpha^T Q\alpha - e^T\alpha, \tag{1}$$

subject to

$$y^T\alpha = 0; \quad 0 \le \alpha_i \le C; i = 1, \ldots, l; \tag{2}$$

having $C > 0$ as a penalty parameter that sets the tradeoff between the margin size and the amount of error in training. α is a vector of Lagrange multipliers introduced during conversion from primal to dual problem, e is the unit vector, Q is an l by l positive semidefinite matrix such that $Q_{ij} = y_i y_j K(x_i, x_j)$ and $K(x_i, x_j) = \phi(x_i)^T \phi(x_j)$ is the kernel function, which maps training vectors into a higher dimensional space via function ϕ.

Frequently, the problems can not be solved by means of a linear separation. In such cases, the "Kernel Trick" is applied, where a linear kernel is replaced by a non-linear one. The most frequently used non-linear kernels of SVM are RBF and polynomial from which we examine the RBF kernel (3).

$$K(x_i, x_j) = \exp(-\gamma\|x_i - x_j\|^2), \tag{3}$$

having x_i, x_j as observations and $\gamma > 0$.

The label $F(x)$ of the feature vector x is calculated by the following equation:

$$F(x_{new}) = sign\left(\sum_{i=1}^{l} y_i \alpha_i K(x_i, x_{new}) + b\right).$$

$$(4)$$

2.1 SVM Solvers on CPU

Currently, LibSVM [5] and SVMLight [10] are the most commonly used SVM implementations. They are based on decomposition methods of the quadratic optimization problem, which only use the selected variables in each step of the algorithm. The main difference between mentioned solutions lies in the type of decomposition. LibSVM applies SMO-type decomposition [15],[11] with second order information [8] to choose appropriate working set when SVMLight uses the decomposition idea of Osuna [14].

For accelerating calculation of the kernel function both methods apply caching of recently obtained scalar products as well as shrinking. However, SVMlight and LibSVM use only computational power of CPU.

Our implementation utilizes SMO-type decomposition with second order information similar to LibSVM, where all evaluations of kernel function are transfered to the GPU, which allows distributed and parallel batch computations.

2.2 SVM Implementation on CUDA with Dense Format

Many SVM methods require processing of N scalar products, which is equivalent to multiplying the matrix by the chosen vector in a given iteration step. The main task of SVM implementation on the GPU is the calculation of the scalar products mentioned above in a parallel manner. It will significantly accelerate the whole process.

Recent solutions such as GPU-SVM [4], CuSVM [3] or MultiSVM [9] apply dense matrix format during Kernel Matrix evaluation which considerably limits the usage of these methods for big datasets. Memory size of modern graphics cards varies from 1GB (GeForce GTX 460) to 6GB (TESLA C2070) which is not sufficient for processing such well-known datasets as rcv1 or newsgroup20.

2.3 SVM Implementation on CUDA with Sparse Format

The data processed in a machine learning domain is often characterized by the sparse format as well as a great amount of instances and features. Storage of such datasets in naive dense format would involve memory in the range from tens to hundreds GB. In particular, dataset newsgroup20 occupies 99.46 GB, having 19 996 instances and 1335191 features of each element. Due to such large memory involvement, it is not possible to process such datasets in RAM of modern computers as well as using the GPU. One of the methods employed to overcome this restriction is the application of the sparse matrix format.

Choosing the appropriate format depends on the occurrence regularity of nonzero elements, among which we can distinguish Diagonal (DIA), ELLPACK

(ELL), Compressed Sparse Row (CSR) or Coordinate Format (COO). The choice of sparse data representation for SVM should cover all possible nonzero distributions, so that the chosen format should be sufficiently universal. Among the above mentioned, the most suitable for use in our case are ELLPACK, COO and CSR. The ELLPACK format is best suited for processing on the GPU because of its regularity, but it requires much more memory than others for a dataset of a highly diverse number of nonzero elements in each row.

For example, the modification of the ELLPACK format is applied in [13], in which the authors reached the acceleration of approximately 130x in relation to LibSVM. However, research was only focused on the fact of calculation acceleration without taking into account the problem of memory usage. This makes the algorithm not applicable for big irregular datasets.

To overcome the size limit of dataset, we use the CSR format, which in addition to its versatility also ensures maximum utilization of available memory. Moreover, the CSR vector implementation is proposed in [1], which effectively deals with CSR matrix multiplication on the GPU.

3   CSR-GPU-SVM Algorithm

Code profiling results for standard implementation of SVM presented in [3], [9], [10] proves that kernel evaluation is the most time-consuming part of the whole algorithm and takes up to 80% of overall time. It is obvious that the acceleration of these operations will speed up SVM training process. The CSR-GPU-SVM algorithm focuses on the acceleration of generating Kernel Matrix columns for extremely sparse big collections, which is achieved by transferring all kernel computations to the GPU.

3.1   Algorithm Architecture

The algorithm presented in this paper is largely based on the skeleton of LibSVM method, since this method turned out to be very effective [8], when dealing with classification. Similar to LibSVM, we utilize SMO, and as it was mentioned in previous section, we store the dataset in the CSR format. The part of the algorithm including the working set selection, updating gradients and checking optimality condition is processed on the CPU in the same manner as in LibSVM, while the whole kernel invocation is transferred to the GPU.

The main task of kernel evaluation in the SVM training process is reduced to matrix-vector multiplication. First, the i-th vector x_i named 'main vector', where i is index found during working set selection step, is transformed to the dense format from CSR and moved to the GPU in each iteration. Then, the matrix in the CSR format is multiplied by the main vector with the use of the CUDA technology. Next, for the $j-th$ vector the same computation is performed. The results of these multiplications are copied back to the CPU for next step of iteration.

3.2   Kernel Evaluation on CUDA

The algorithm presented in this paper applies the CUDA technology for kernel evaluation. The most difficult part in CUDA programming is to write the device function in such a way that it will fully utilize the computational power of the GPU. In particular, all treads in warp (group of 32 CUDA threads) should process the same instruction, which will improve the instruction throughput, and as a result any flow control should be avoided. Moreover, all access to global memory should be coalesced, which means that treads in warp read data from the continuous global memory block.

In this paper CUDA functions for computing 'SVM kernels' are based on CSR Vector [1] method, which uses 32-thread warp for multiplying one sparse matrix row by a dense vector. Listing below presents the main part of CUDA RBF implementation.

```
for(int k = warp_id; k < num_rows; k+= num_warps){
    const int row_start = vecPointers[k];;
    const int row_end   = vecPointers[k+1];
    float sum = 0;
    for(int j = row_start+thread_lane; j<row_end; j+= WARP_SIZE)
        sum += vals[j] * tex1Dfetch(mainVectorTexRef,idx[j]);

    volatile float* smem = sdata;
    smem[threadIdx.x] = sum; __syncthreads();
    smem[threadIdx.x] = sum = sum + smem[threadIdx.x + 16];
    smem[threadIdx.x] = sum = sum + smem[threadIdx.x +  8];
    smem[threadIdx.x] = sum = sum + smem[threadIdx.x +  4];
    smem[threadIdx.x] = sum = sum + smem[threadIdx.x +  2];
    smem[threadIdx.x] = sum = sum + smem[threadIdx.x +  1];
    if (thread_lane == 0)
        results[k]=labels[k]*labels[mainVecIndex]*
            expf(-Gamma*(selfDot[k]+mainSelfDot-2*smem[threadIdx.x]));
}
```

Each thread from a particular warp accumulates in the local variable sum results for $x_{kj}, x_{k(j+WARP\_SIZE)}, \cdots, x_{k(j+n*WARP\_SIZE)}$ where k is the matrix row index, $j \in \{1 \cdots 32\}$ is thread id in this warp and n is the lowest number such as $n*WARP\_SIZE$ is greater or equal to nonzero values in $k-th$ row. These partial results are stored in shared memory $smem$, from which a warp-wide parallel reduction is performed in order to obtain final dot product written to $results$ array. This improves memory pattern access for CSR format matrix and decreases thread divergence in warp.

Besides simultaneous calculations, the acceleration is achieved by storing part of data in cache memory. In particular, each SVM kernel matrix column evaluation has a different 'main vector' which has to be transformed to dense format and copied to device memory. All threads can access this memory simultaneously, thus to speed up this process the 'main vector' is kept in the graphic card

Table 1. Datasets used in experiments

Data set name	#instances (train/test)	#features
Web (w8a)	49749 / 14951	300
Adult (a9a)	32561 / 16281	123
20 Newsgroup (newsgroup20.binary)	19996/ 19996	1335191
Real vs. Simulated (real-sim)	72309/ 72309	20958
RCV1 (rcv1.binary)	20242 / 677399	47236
RCV1 (rcv1.binary reverse)	677399 / 20242	47236
Mnist (even vs odd)	60000 / 10000	784

texture cache *mainVectorTexRef*. Moreover, the *results* array must be transferred back to host many times during the algorithm process. The allocation of this array as page-locked memory in CSR-GRU-SVM algorithm increases memory bandwidth.

Apart from the training phase described above the CSR-GPU-SVM algorithm performs a testing phase on CUDA. Obtaining the instance label is provided by the dot product between support vectors and this instance (4), which is equal to sparse matrix - matrix multiplication. CSR-GPU-SVM prediction was organized as k sparse matrix dense vector multiplications, where k is the number of objects to classify. This operation is performed using CSR Vector CUDA kernel. Each multiplication requires copying the vector into the GPU memory to obtain higher memory bandwidth kernel computation and next vector memory transfers are performed asynchronously with the use of CUDA stream API.

For implementation details please download open source KMLib library [16] and browse KMLib.GPU project.

4   Experimental Results

The goal of the experimental session was to test the acceleration of SVM with the use of the CSR-GPU-SVM method compared to LibSVM library and multiSVM. For this purpose, the GPU code was tested on two Nvidia cards: GeForce 240 (96 cores) and GeForce GTX 460 (336 cores) both with 1GB device memory. The stopping criterion in SVM formulation was set to 0.001, I/O time was excluded and as a kernel RBF ($C = 4, \gamma = 0.5$) was chosen.

All tested files were downloaded from LibSVM web page [6] which contains most of popular binary classification datasets, specially preprocessed for SVM. Tests were run on the datasets presented in Table 1.

The RCV1 dataset was examined twice. For training and testing we first used rcv1_train and rcv1_test files, while for the second run the files were reversed. Mnist dataset was preprocessed in order to adjust it to the binary classifier. In particular, all even labels were changed to '-1', and odd labels were changed to '+1'.

Table 2. SVM training times (in seconds) with RBF kernel, parameters C=4, gamma=0.5 for CSR-GPU-SVM and LibSvm algorithms

Data set name	LibSVM	CSR-GPU-SVM GeForce 240	CSR-GPU-SVM GeForce 460	Speedup
Web(w8a)	586.2	108.1	85.7	6.8x
Adult(a9a)	353.1	89.3	71.3	5.5x
20 Newsgroup (newsgroup20.binary)	3456	576.3	325.5	10.6x
Real vs. Simulated(real-sim)	3422.2	230.2	160	21.3x
RCV1(rcv1.binary)	353.4	48.9	27.5	12.8x
RCV1(rcv1.binary reverse)	114421.6	21032.7	10470.9	10.9x
Mnist (even vs odd)	24141.3	888.1	681.1	35.4x

Table 2 presents training times of the CSR-GPU-SVM algorithm in comparison with LibSVM. The accuracies in all cases were the same (with 0.001 precision).

The obtained acceleration ratio varies from 5 to 35 times over standard Lib-SVM for GeForce 460 graphic card implementation. It is worth mentioning that the training times on GeForce 240 do not deviate significantly in comparison with GeForce 460, which suggests that the computation can be limited by memory bandwidth. As concerning the level of acceleration, the biggest speed up was achieved for Mnist collection, where average number of nonzero elements is high, equal to 149. On the other hand, the lowest acceleration was obtained for A9A dataset, which contains only 13.8 nonzero values per row and 123 features. This shows that CSR-GPU-SVM is most suitable for big sparse collections, where the average number of nonzero elements per row is greater than 32 (warp size). The next important achievement that should be noted is the possibility of classifying such collections as newsgroup20 or rcv1, which can not be performed by standard GPU classifiers.

The testing part of SVM proceeded in the same manner as training and the detailed results are shown in Table 3.

Subsequent experiments which were carried out involved comparing training times of the CSR-GPU-SVM and multiSVM algorithms [9]. The results are obtained for the following datasets: Adult, Web and Mnist. The RBF kernel parameters were taken from multiSVM paper [9] in order to make the comparison of the results possible. This comparison, presented in Table 4, shows that for the sets with a small number of features (Adult, Web) our implementation achieves worse results, but for the Mnist dataset we managed to get comparable results with significantly reduced memory consumption.

Table 3. SVM classification times (in seconds) with RBF kernel, parameters C=4, gamma=0.5for CSR-GPU-SVM and LibSvm algorithms

Data set name	LibSVM	CSR-GPU-SVM GeForce 240	CSR-GPU-SVM GeForce 460	Speedup
Web (w8a)	53	16.3	12.3	4.2x
Adult (a9a)	39	14.1	10.1	3.8x
20 Newsgroup (newsgroup20.binary)	575	1254	64.4	9.2x
Real vs. Simulated (real-sim)	399	35.5	34	11.6x
RCV1 (rcv1.binary)	2961	254	161.2	18.3x
RCV1 (rcv1.binary reverse)	90	99.2	66.6	1.3
Mnist (even vs odd)	609	108	150.8	4x

Table 4. SVM training time comparison, multiSVM versus CSR-GPU-SVM, results taken from multiSVM paper

	multiSVM paper			this work		
	LibSVM	multiSVM	Speedup	LibSVM	CSR-GPU-SVM	Speedup
Adult	341.5	32.6	10.4x	412.2	75.9	5.4x
Web	2350	156.9	14.9x	1777.4	202.3	8.7x
Mnist	13963.4	425.9	32.7x	14307.8	391	36.5x

5   Conclusion and Future Work

This work presents GPU accelerated SVM kernel computation for an SMO type algorithm, which utilizes a CSR sparse matrix format for classifying big sparse problems emerging in a machine learning task. Compared to LibSVM, the acceleration of training times is satisfactory. In relation to multiSVM, the CSR-GPU-SVM algorithm works better for datasets such as Mnist. Moreover, the use of the CSR sparse matrix format allowed us to minimize the memory usage, which made it possible to classify big sparse collections.

The CSR-GPU-SVM implementation is a part of the free, open source KMLib library [16].

In the future we plan to improve the algorithm by shifting the search of working set on the GPU, which can significantly reduce the time of SVM training. In addition, we are going to perform more experiments with the use of different SVM kernels.

Acknowledgments. The research has been supported by grant N N516 480940 from The National Science Center of the Republic of Poland.

References

1. Bell, N., Garl, M.: Efficient sparse matrix-vector multiplication on cuda. Tech. rep., NVidia (2008)
2. Boser, B.E., Guyon, I.M., Vapnik, V.N.: A training algorithm for optimal margin classifiers. In: Proceedings of the Fifth Annual Workshop on Computational Learning Theory, COLT 1992, pp. 144–152. ACM, New York (1992)
3. Carpenter, A.: Cusvm: A cuda implementation of support vector classification and regression. Tech. rep. (2005)
4. Catanzaro, B., Sundaram, N., Keutzer, K.: Fast support vector machine training and classification on graphics processors. In: Proceedings of the 25th International Conference on Machine Learning, ICML 2008, pp. 104–111. ACM, New York (2008)
5. Chang, C.C., Lin, C.J.: LIBSVM: A library for support vector machines. ACM Transactions on Intelligent Systems and Technology 2, 27:1–27:27 (2011)
6. Chang, C.C., Lin, C.J.: Libsvm datasets (2011), http://www.csie.ntu.edu.tw/~cjlin/libsvmtools/datasets/binary.html
7. Chapelle, O., Haffner, P., Vapnik, V.N.: Support vector machines for histogram-based image classification. IEEE Transactions on Neural Networks 10(5), 1055–1064 (1999)
8. Fan, R.-E., Chen, P.-H., Lin, C.-J.: Working set selection using the second order information for training svm. Journal of Machine Learning Research 6, 1889–1918 (2005)
9. Herrero-Lopez, S., Williams, J.R., Sanchez, A.: Parallel multiclass classification using svms on gpus. In: Proceedings of the 3rd Workshop on General-Purpose Computation on Graphics Processing Units, GPGPU 2010, pp. 2–11. ACM, New York (2010)
10. Joachims, T.: Text Categorization with Support Vector Machines: Learning with Many Relevant Features. In: Nédellec, C., Rouveirol, C. (eds.) ECML 1998. LNCS, vol. 1398, pp. 137–142. Springer, Heidelberg (1998)
11. Keerthi, S., Shevade, S., Bhattacharyya, C., Murthy, K.: Improvements to platt's smo algorithm for svm classifier design. Neural Computation 13(3), 637–649 (2001)
12. Korytkowski, M., Rutkowski, L., Scherer, R.: From Ensemble of Fuzzy Classifiers to Single Fuzzy Rule Base Classifier. In: Rutkowski, L., Tadeusiewicz, R., Zadeh, L.A., Zurada, J.M. (eds.) ICAISC 2008. LNCS (LNAI), vol. 5097, pp. 265–272. Springer, Heidelberg (2008)
13. Lin, T.K., Chien, S.Y.: Support vector machines on gpu with sparse matrix format. In: Fourth International Conference on Machine Learning and Applications, pp. 313–318 (2010)
14. Osuna, E., Freund, R., Girosi, F.: Training support vector machines: an application to face detection. In: Proceedings of IEEE Computer Society Conference on Computer Vision and Pattern Recognition, vol. 6, pp. 130–136 (1997)
15. Platt, J.: Fast training of support vector machines using sequential minimal optimization. In: Schoelkopf, B., Burges, C., Smola, A. (eds.) Advances in Kernel Methods - Support Vector Learning. MIT Press (1998)
16. Sopyła, K.: Kmlib - kernel machine library for .net (2011), https://github.com/ksirg/KMLib

Initialization of Nonnegative Matrix Factorization with Vertices of Convex Polytope

Rafal Zdunek

Institute of Telecommunications, Teleinformatics and Acoustics,
Wroclaw University of Technology, Wybrzeze Wyspianskiego 27,
50-370 Wroclaw, Poland
rafal.zdunek@pwr.wroc.pl

Abstract. Nonnegative Matrix Factorization (NMF) is an emerging un-supervised learning technique that has already found many applications in machine learning and multivariate nonnegative data processing. NMF problems are usually solved with an alternating minimization of a given cost function, which leads to non-convex optimization. For this approach, an initialization for the factors to be estimated plays an essential role, not only for a fast convergence rate but also for selection of the desired local minima. If the observations are modeled by the exact factorization model (consistent data), NMF can be easily obtained by finding vertices of the convex polytope determined by the observed data projected on the probability simplex. For an inconsistent case, this model can be relaxed by approximating mean localizations of the vertices. In this paper, we discuss these issues and propose the initialization algorithm based on the analysis of a geometrical structure of the observed data. This approach is demonstrated to be robust, even for moderately noisy data.

1 Introduction

Since an alternating minimization procedure in NMF is non-convex, an initialization for the factors to be estimated plays a predominate role. There are several strategies for initializing the factors in the standard NMF model [1]. A typical approach assumes both factors are initialized with uniformly distributed random numbers [1,2]. However, this strategy involves many iterations to convergence, especially as the estimated factors are very sparse.

To avoid convergence to unfavorable local minima, the multi-start random initialization [3] can be applied. In this technique, the estimated factors are initialized several times with random initializers, and the initializer that ensures the steepest descent in the objective function after a fixed number of alternating steps is selected. This strategy combined with the multilayer technique [4] significantly improves the performance if the observed data is sparse and weakly redundant.

Another approach involves the centroid decomposition or spherical k-means [5,6]. Unfortunately, this is computationally expensive preprocessing that is also non-convex, and may not guarantee the right initializer.

L. Rutkowski et al. (Eds.): ICAISC 2012, Part I, LNCS 7267, pp. 448–455, 2012.

Langville *et al.* proposed in [2] four strategies for initialization of NMF. One of them assumes the SVD-centroid initialization, that is, the centroid decomposition that is applied to the right singular vectors of the observation matrix. This way is computationally attractive since the space of right singular vectors is considerably smaller than the observation space. Nevertheless, it involves computations of the SVD of a large matrix of observations. Another approach assumes averaging of randomly selected data columns. However, this strategy usually gives only slightly better performance than the random initialization. An improved version assumes random selection of the data columns that have the longest length, which usually means the selection of the densest columns. The last approach involves construction of the co-occurrence matrix, which is computationally very expensive.

The SVD-based initialization has been also considered by Boutsidis and Gallopoulos in [7]. This strategy initializes both factors in NMF by certain positive parts of rank-1 matrices obtained by the leading left and right singular vectors of the observation matrix.

To better model sparse part-based image representations from NMF, Kim and Choi [8] discussed the initialization based on the hierarchical clustering of the observed data with a similarity measure reflecting "closeness to rank-one". Unfortunately, when an observation matrix is large, a computational complexity of this approach is quite large due to its iterative cluster merging character.

The clustering-based initialization has been also proposed in [9]. This is an iterative strategy that is based on the k-means clustering, however, a similarity measure between samples and their centroids is determined by the generalized Kullback-Leibler (KL) divergence. Geometrically, this approach is equivalent to finding centroid vectors that are collinear with extreme rays of the convex cone spanned by the observation vectors [10]. For noise-free case, the extreme rays may determine vertices of the convex polytope created from data points. Similarly as for the centroid decomposition, a computational complexity of this approach is rather high.

Our approach is somehow related to the latter but instead of using computationally expensive k-means clustering, we attempt to find the vertices of the convex polytope by searching the observation vectors that maximize its volume. For a noise-free case, this approach ensures an exact model of NMF. For an inconsistent case, the locations of the vertices are approximated by averaging a few observation vectors in their neighborhood.

The paper is organized as follows: Section 2 discusses a geometrical aspect of NMF. The initialization algorithm is presented in Section 3. The experiments are described in Section 4. Finally, the conclusions are drawn in Section 5.

2   Geometrical Interpretation

The aim of NMF is to find such lower-rank nonnegative matrices $\boldsymbol{A} = [a_{ij}] \in \mathbb{R}_+^{I \times J}$ and $\boldsymbol{X} = [x_{jt}] \in \mathbb{R}_+^{J \times T}$ that $\boldsymbol{Y} = [y_{it}] \cong \boldsymbol{AX} \in \mathbb{R}_+^{I \times T}$, given the data matrix $\boldsymbol{Y}$, the lower rank J, and possibly some prior knowledge on the matrices

$\boldsymbol{A}$ or $\boldsymbol{X}$. The orthant of nonnegative real numbers is denoted by $\mathbb{R}_+$. Typically we have high redundancy, i.e. $J << \frac{IT}{I+T}$ but in our considerations we assume $J \leq \min\{I, T\}$ and $T >> I$.

The exact nonnegative factorization $\boldsymbol{Y} = \boldsymbol{AX}$ means that each column vector in $\boldsymbol{Y}$ is a convex combination of the column vectors in $\boldsymbol{A}$. The vectors $\{\boldsymbol{a}_a, \ldots, \boldsymbol{a}_J\}$ form the simplicial cone [10] in $\mathbb{R}^I$ that lies inside the nonnegative orthant $\mathbb{R}_+^I$.

Definition 1. *The $(I-1)$-dimensional probability simplex $\mathcal{S}_I = \{\boldsymbol{y} = [y_i] \in \mathbb{R}_+^I : y_i \geq 0, \boldsymbol{1}_I^T \boldsymbol{y} = 1\}$ contains all the points of $\mathbb{R}_+^I$ located onto the hyperplane $\Pi : \|\boldsymbol{y}\|_1 = 1$. Its vertices are determined by the versors (unit vectors) of the Cartesian coordinate system.*

Definition 2. *The matrix $\boldsymbol{X} = [\boldsymbol{x}_1, \ldots, \boldsymbol{x}_T] \in \mathbb{R}_+^{J \times T}$ is sufficiently sparse if there exists a square diagonal full-rank submatrix $\tilde{\boldsymbol{X}} \in \mathbb{R}_+^{J \times J}$ created from a subset of its column vectors.*

The projection of the nonzero columns in $\boldsymbol{Y}$ onto $\mathcal{S}_I$ can be expressed as

$$\mathcal{P}_{\mathcal{S}_I}(\boldsymbol{Y}) = \bar{\boldsymbol{Y}} = \left\{ \frac{\boldsymbol{y}_1}{\|\boldsymbol{y}_1\|_1}, \ldots, \frac{\boldsymbol{y}_T}{\|\boldsymbol{y}_T\|_1} \right\}. \tag{1}$$

The projected columns onto $\mathcal{S}_I$ form the convex polytope $\mathcal{C}(\boldsymbol{Y})$ [11]. If the matrix $\boldsymbol{X}$ is sufficiently sparse (see Def. 2), the vertices of $\mathcal{C}(\boldsymbol{Y})$ correspond to the column vectors of $\boldsymbol{A}$ projected onto $\mathcal{S}_I$. Any column vector $\bar{\boldsymbol{y}}_t$ whose the corresponding vector $\boldsymbol{x}_t$ contains at most 2 positive entries lies on the boundary of the convex polytope $\mathcal{C}(\boldsymbol{Y})$.

Example 1. Assuming $I = J = 3$ and $T = 1000$, we generated $\boldsymbol{A} \in \mathbb{R}_+^{3 \times 3}$ from an uniform distribution (cond($\boldsymbol{A}$) $\cong 5.2$) and $\boldsymbol{X} \in \mathbb{R}^{3 \times 1000}$ from a normal distribution $\mathcal{N}(0, 1)$, replacing the negative entries with a zero-value. Thus sparsity($\boldsymbol{X}$) $\cong 50\%$. The column vectors of $\boldsymbol{Y} = \boldsymbol{AX}$ plotted in $\mathbb{R}^I$ are shown in Fig. 1(a) as the blue points. The red squares indicate directions of the column vectors in $\boldsymbol{A}$. Note that all the blue points are contained inside the simplicial cone determined by the column vectors of $\boldsymbol{A}$.

Fig. 1(b) shows the observation points (blue points) projected onto the 2D probability simplex (the equilateral triangle marked with the black lines). The red squares denotes the projected columns of $\boldsymbol{A}$. Note that all the observation points are contained inside the convex polytope (triangle) $\mathcal{C}(\boldsymbol{Y})$.

Figs. 1(c) and (d) refer to the noisy cases when the observation data is corrupted with a zero-mean Gaussian noise with the variance adopted to (c) $SNR = 30$ dB and (d) $SNR = 20$ dB. Note that even for a very weak noise ($SNR = 30$ dB), the smallest convex polytope (the smallest triangle) that contains all the observation points is considerably different than marked by the red squares. For a moderate noisy case ($SNR = 20$ dB), the locations of the columns of $\boldsymbol{A}$ can be estimated with a statistical approach, e.g. by searching the highest density of observation points (provided that the observed data is very sparse). The negative entries of noisy observations where replaced with a zero-value, hence many entries of $\bar{Y}$ lie on the boundary of the probability simplex $\mathcal{S}_I$.

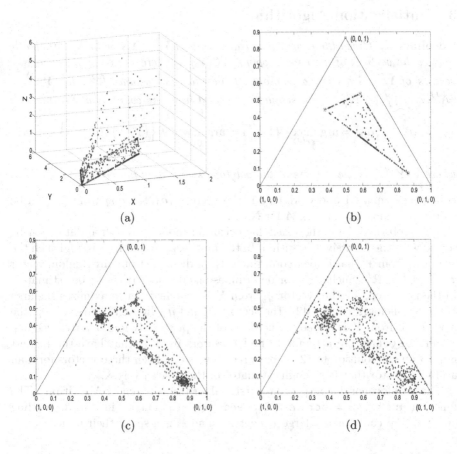

(a)

(b)

(c)

(d)

Fig. 1. Geometric visualization of column vectors (blue points) of Y and the columns vectors of A (red squares) for $I = J = 3$, $T = 1000$: (a) noise-free observation points in $\mathbb{R}^3$, (b) noise-free observation points projected onto the $(I - 1)$-dimensional probability simplex, (c) noisy observation points with $SNR = 30$dB projected onto the $(I - 1)$-dimensional probability simplex, (d) noisy observation points with $SNR = 20$dB projected onto the $(I - 1)$-dimensional probability simplex.

Remark 1. From Example 1 we may conclude that if the underlying matrix X is sufficiently sparse and the factorization model $Y = AX$ is exact, the columns of the matrix A can be readily estimated by finding the vertices of the convex polytope $\mathcal{C}(Y)$, that is, the columns in $\bar{Y}$ that correspond to the vertices. For moderately noisy data, exact locations of the columns in A cannot be found but they can be roughly estimated considering the mean locations for cluster centroid points of observations. These estimations may also serve as the initial vectors of A.

3   Initialization Algorithm

Corollary 1. *Given the exact factorization model $Y = AX$ with X sufficiently sparse, the vertices of the convex polytope $\mathcal{C}(Y)$ are determined by these column vectors of $\bar{Y}$ which span a polytope of the maximal volume [12]. Let $\bar{Y}^{(J)} = [\bar{y}_1^{(J)}, \ldots, y_J^{(J)}] \in \mathbb{R}_+^{I \times J}$ be a submatrix created from the columns of $\bar{Y}$, then*

$$[a_1, \ldots, a_J] = \arg \max_{\bar{Y}^{(J)}} V(\bar{Y}^{(J)}) = \arg \max_{\bar{Y}^{(J)}} \det \left\{ (\bar{Y}^{(J)})^T (\bar{Y}^{(J)}) \right\}, \qquad (2)$$

where $V(\bar{Y}^{(J)})$ is the volume of the polytope spanned by the vectors in $\bar{Y}^{(J)}$.

Following Remark 1 and Corollary 1, the vectors $\{a_1, \ldots, a_J\}$ from (2) can be used to initialize the matrix A for NMF.

The problem (2) for the exact factorization model (noise-free data) can be solved with the recursive algorithm. In the first step, we attempt to find such the vector $\bar{y}_t$ from $\bar{Y}$ that is located in the furthest distance from any random vector $z \sim \mathcal{U}[0, 1] \in \mathbb{R}_+^I$. Such a vector determines one of the vertices to be estimated. In the next step, another vector $\bar{y}_s$ from $\bar{Y}$ is searched that maximizes the area of the parallelogram formed by the vectors $\bar{y}_t$ and $\bar{y}_s$. In each recursive step, the new vector from $\bar{Y}$ is added to the basis of the previously found vertex vectors.

For noisy-data, we attempt to find p vectors from $\bar{Y}$ that have the highest impact on the solution to (2) in each recursive step. Then these vectors form an averaged vector that is a rough estimator of the desired vertex.

The final form of the proposed recursive algorithm is given by Algorithm 1. The function $[c^{(sort)}, \mathcal{K}] = \texttt{sort}(c, p, \texttt{descend})$ sorts the entries in c in descending order, $c^{(sort)}$ contains the largest p entries, and $\mathcal{K}$ is a set of their indices.

4   Experiments

The experiments are carried out for some Blind Source Separation (BSS) problem, using the benchmark of 7 synthetic sparse nonnegative signals (the file AC-7_2noi.mat) taken from the Matlab toolbox *NMFLAB for Signal Processing*[1] [13]. Thus $X \in \mathbb{R}_+^{7 \times 1000}$, and this is a sufficiently sparse matrix according to Definition 2. The entries of the mixing matrix $A \in \mathbb{R}_+^{21 \times 7}$ were generated from a normal distribution $\mathcal{N}(0, 1)$, with $\text{cond}(A) \cong 4.3$, where the negative entries are replaced with a zero-value.

To estimate the matrices A and X from Y, we use the standard Lee-Seung algorithm [1] (denoted here by the MUE acronym) for minimizing the Euclidean distance, using 500 iterations.

---

[1] http://www.bsp.brain.riken.jp

Algorithm 1. SimplexMax

Input : $Y \in \mathbb{R}_+^{I \times T}$, J - number of lateral components, p - number of nearest neighbors

Output: $A \in \mathbb{R}_+^{I \times J}$ - estimated initial basis matrix

1 **Initialize**: $A = 0$, Replace negative entries (if any) in Y with zero-value,
2 and remove zero-value columns in Y ;
3 $\bar{Y} = \left\{ \frac{y_1}{\|y_1\|_1}, \ldots, \frac{y_T}{\|y_T\|_1} \right\}$;   // Projection onto the probability simplex
4 $z \sim \mathcal{U}[0,1] \in \mathbb{R}_+^I$;
5 $r_t = \|\bar{y}_t - z\|_2$;
6 $\left[r^{(sort)}, \mathcal{K}_p^{(0)} \right] = \text{sort}(r, p, \text{descend})$,   where $r = [r_t] \in \mathbb{R}^T$;

$$a_1 = \frac{1}{p} \sum_{k \in \mathcal{K}_p^{(0)}} \bar{y}_k \ ;$$

7

8 **for** $j = 1, 2, \ldots, J - 1$ **do**
9     $d = [d_t] = 0$;
10   **for** $t = 1, 2, \ldots, T$ **do**
11        $D = [a_1, \ldots, a_j, \bar{y}_t] \in \mathbb{R}_+^{I \times (j+1)}$;
12        $d_t = \det(D^T D)$;
13     $\left[d^{(sort)}, \mathcal{K}_p \right] = \text{sort}(d, p, \text{descend})$,   where $d = [d_t] \in \mathbb{R}^T$;
14     $a_{j+1} = \frac{1}{p} \sum_{k \in \mathcal{K}_p} \bar{y}_k$;

To test the efficiency of the discussed initialization methods, 100 Monte Carlo (MC) runs of NMF were performed, each time the initial matrix A was estimated with the tested initialization method but X is randomly generated from an uniform distribution.

We tested the following initialization methods: random, multilayer with multistart [3] (3 layers and 30 restarts), ALS-based initialization [3], SVD-based initialization [7], and the proposed SimplexMax.

The efficiency of the initializers was evaluated with the Signal-to-Interference Ratio (SIR) [3] between the true matrix A and estimated one. Fig. 2 shows the SIR statistics for estimating the mixing matrix A using the MUE algorithm initialized with various initialization methods.

We analyzed 3 cases: noise-free, weakly noisy data with $SNR = 30$ dB, and moderately noisy data with $SNR = 20$ dB. The SIR statistics plotted in Fig. 2 concerns only the noisy cases. We set $p = 1$ and $p = 3$ for $SNR = 30$ dB and $SNR = 20$ dB, respectively. For the noise-free data, the SimplexMax method estimates the columns in the matrix A with $SIR > 200 \ dB$ for $p = 1$, and hence, no further alternating steps of NMF is needed (see Table 1).

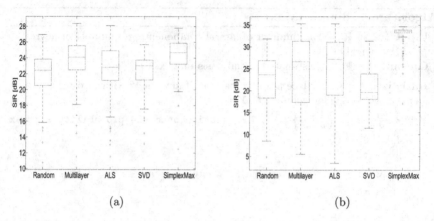

(a)   (b)

Fig. 2. SIR statistics for estimating the mixing matrix A from noisy observations, using the MUE algorithm with various initialization methods (random, multilayer, ALS, SVD, and Simplex Volume Maximization): (a) SNR = 20 dB, (b) SNR = 30 dB. For noise-free data, the Simplex Max method estimates the matrix A with $SIR > 200$ dB.

Table 1. Mean-SIR values [dB] and standard deviations (in parenthesis) averaged over 100 MC runs of the the SimplexMax method (without the MUE algorithm)

Data	$p = 1$	$p = 3$	$p = 5$	$p = 10$
noise-free	276 (1.43)	151.8 (2.62)	63.23 (10.42)	10.93 (3.05)
$SNR = 30$ dB	21.23 (0.81)	17.91 (1.83)	15.13 (2.82)	9.91 (2.17)
$SNR = 20$ dB	7.27 (1.36)	10.18 (2.06)	8.69 (1.85)	8.37 (1.67)

5   Conclusions

Fig. 2 demonstrates that for the observations with $SNR \geq 20$ dB the proposed SimplexMax method provides the best initializer for A among the tested methods. For noise-free data that satisfies the sufficiency sparsity condition (Definition 2), the SimplexMax method gives the exact estimator. However, such data is difficult to obtain in practice, hence the SimplexMax should be nearly always combined with some alternating optimization algorithm for NMF. The performance of Algorithm 1 for $p = 1$ considerably depends on the SNR of observations. We noticed that for $SNR \cong 30$ dB and $p = 1$, the mean-SIR of the estimated initial matrix A with the SimplexMax is about 21 dB (Table 1) but after using the MUE algorithm, the SIR grows up to about 33 dB. When the observed data is stronger corrupted with noise, the SimplexMax needs adaptation of the parameter p. A further study is needed to determine the relation of p with a level of noise.

Summing up, the proposed SimplexMax method seems to be efficient for initialization of the basis vectors in NMF when the observations are sufficiently sparse and corrupted with moderate noise. For a noise-free case, the proposed method gives exact estimators.

Acknowledgment. This work was supported by the habilitation grant N N515 603139 (2010-2012) from the Ministry of Science and Higher Education, Poland.

References

[1] Lee, D.D., Seung, H.S.: Learning the parts of objects by non-negative matrix factorization. Nature 401, 788–791 (1999)

[2] Langville, A.N., Meyer, C.D., Albright, R.: Initializations for the nonnegative matrix factorization. In: Proc. of the Twelfth ACM SIGKDD International Conference on Knowledge Discovery and Data Mining, Philadelphia, USA (2006)

[3] Cichocki, A., Zdunek, R., Phan, A.H., Amari, S.I.: Nonnegative Matrix and Tensor Factorizations: Applications to Exploratory Multi-way Data Analysis and Blind Source Separation. Wiley and Sons (2009)

[4] Cichocki, A., Zdunek, R.: Multilayer nonnegative matrix factorization. Electronics Letters 42(16), 947–948 (2006)

[5] Wild, S.: Seeding non-negative matrix factorization with the spherical k-means clustering. M.Sc. Thesis, University of Colorado (2000)

[6] Wild, S., Curry, J., Dougherty, A.: Improving non-negative matrix factorizations through structured initialization. Pattern Recognition 37(11), 2217–2232 (2004)

[7] Boutsidis, C., Gallopoulos, E.: SVD based initialization: A head start for nonnegative matrix factorization. Pattern Recognition 41, 1350–1362 (2008)

[8] Kim, Y.D., Choi, S.: A method of initialization for nonnegative matrix factorization. In: Proc. IEEE International Conference on Acoustics, Speech, and Signal Processing (ICASSP 2007), Honolulu, Hawaii, USA, vol. II, pp. 537–540 (2007)

[9] Xue, Y., Tong, C.S., Chen, Y., Chen, W.S.: Clustering-based initialization for non-negative matrix factorization. Applied Mathematics and Computation 205(2), 525–536 (2008); Special Issue on Advanced Intelligent Computing Theory and Methodology in Applied Mathematics and Computation

[10] Donoho, D., Stodden, V.: When does non-negative matrix factorization give a correct decomposition into parts? In: Thrun, S., Saul, L., Schölkopf, B. (eds.) Advances in Neural Information Processing Systems (NIPS), vol. 16. MIT Press, Cambridge (2004)

[11] Chu, M.T., Lin, M.M.: Low dimensional polytype approximation and its applications to nonnegative matrix factorization. SIAM Journal of Scientific Computing 30, 1131–1151 (2008)

[12] Wang, F.Y., Chi, C.Y., Chan, T.H., Wang, Y.: Nonnegative least-correlated component analysis for separation of dependent sources by volume maximization. IEEE Transactions Pattern Analysis and Machine Intelligence 32(5), 875–888 (2010)

[13] Cichocki, A., Zdunek, R.: NMFLAB for Signal and Image Processing. Technical report, Laboratory for Advanced Brain Signal Processing, BSI, RIKEN, Saitama, Japan (2006)

Part IV

Computer Vision, Image and Speech Analysis

Comparison of Corner Detectors
for Revolving Objects Matching Task

Grzegorz Bagrowski and Marcin Luckner

Warsaw University of Technology, Faculty of Mathematics and Information Science,
pl. Politechniki 1, 00-661 Warsaw, Poland
{gbagrowski,mluckner}@mini.pw.edu.pl
http://www.mini.pw.edu.pl/~lucknerm/en/

Abstract. The paper contains test of corner detectors applied in finding characteristic points on 3D revolving objects. Five different algorithm are presented starting from historical Moravec detector and ending at newest ones, such as SUSAN and Trajkovic.

Since the algorithms are compared from the perspective of use for 3D modeling, the count of detected points and their localization is compared. The modeling process uses a series of photos and requires finding a projection of 3D point to two or three subsequent photos. The quality of algorithms is discussed on the base of the ability to detect modeled objects' corners and immunity to noise. The last researched aspect is the computation cost.

The presented tests show that the best results are given by Shi–Tomasi operator. The detector does find false corners on noisy images, thus SU-SAN operator may be used instead.

Keywords: Computer vision, Corner detectors, 3D modeling.

1 Introduction

The paper presents the analysis of corner detectors, designed for plain images, in a 3D revolving objects matching task. The aim of the analysis was to select corner detectors, which would be used in 3D modeling task [10].

In this task a series of revolved object's photos is created. Such series consist of 24–36 images, which present different views of an object that is placed on a revolving pedestal. For a 3D modeling it is necessary to detect 7 points present on each pair of adjacent photos in a series or 6 points present on each of the tree adjacent photos. In the first case the fundamental matrix is used in the modeling, while the in the second a trifocal tensor is created [3].

A problem of matching points between images of revolving objects is much more complex than an equivalent in a satellite photogrammetry, where modeled objects can be discussed as a plain. Projections of 3D points have various representations on different photos and some of them can be ignored by a detector.

For given reasons corner detectors should be analyzed from a number of perspectives. First, a the count of corners detected on each objects should be sufficient to create a model. Second, the same point has to be detected on two

L. Rutkowski et al. (Eds.): ICAISC 2012, Part I, LNCS 7267, pp. 459–467, 2012.

or three subsequent photos. Next, the quality of the result will be discussed, detected points should represent corners of an object. The last aspect is a computation time, which cannot be ignored in application for multi–image series.

The rest of article briefly presents discussed corner detectors (Section 2) and tests performed (Section 3). Finally, the conclusions are presented (Section 4).

2   Corner Detectors

Each of the described corner detection algorithms follows a similar outline. The first step is to calculate a detector–dependent cornerness measure of a pixel. Next, corners with a response below certain threshold are removed. Finally, local maxima are extracted from remaining points using the non-maximal suppression.

The first step is detector–specific and thus has a decisive impact on the result of the algorithm, as well as its running time. Subsequent steps are common to all algorithms, however some detectors apply certain steps multiple times.

Additionally, each algorithm uses a concept of a window (also referred to as a kernel) which, placed over the pixel in question, defines the background pixels used for evaluation of point's cornerness measure.

2.1   Corner Detection Algorithms

One of the earliest algorithms for the class of problems is Moravec corner detector [5]. The corner response of a pixel is evaluated as the minimum of the sum of square differences between pixels included in a window placed over given pixel and its shifts in all of the 8 principle directions.

Harris [2] developed the idea further by expanding the analytic expression of Moravec operator and directly using the derivatives of the image by the x and y coordinates. Since square mask does not cover the same area when rotated, the image is additionally filtered by convolving with a Gaussian window. Thus less value is attributed to the points further from the center imitates the use of a more resistant to rotation, round mask.

An improved version of the idea of Haris' corner detector took the form of the Shi–Tomasi–Kanade operator [6], [8] in which the detector uses a modified statistic for distinguishing between feature classes (corner, line, flat area).

Different approach was used in the SUSAN (Smallest Univariate Segment Assimilating Nucleus) detector [7]. This detector places a circular mask (called USAN) over the point in question and evaluates the similarity of it's intensity to that of surrounding pixels. Further steps can be employed to reject false corners, namely: verifying the center of gravity and contiguity of USAN.

Trajkovic [9] corner detector was built based on the strategy utilized by SUSAN detector. As per the idea of SUSAN, a circular mask is used, but the amount of straight lines having the same intensity and passing through the middle is considered instead and it is measured taking into account only the points on the circle and the center point. This significantly reduces the number of pixels compared.

2.2   Algorithm Parameters

As mentioned earlier in this section, algorithms share two steps that extract the final results from the cornerness map created by the first step.

Threshold filter must be calibrated carefully to remove false responses, but retain valid corners. Too high threshold value would remove groups of local minima containing corners that have lower response value, this applies especially to methods assigning the response based on pixel intensities. On the other hand, a sufficient compromise must be found to remove enough false responses. Each detector was manually assigned two values of threshold: high and low, to compare the actual impact of threshold on finding of desired features. Higher value would elliminate more corners and thus requires less restriction from other parameters, contrary to lower thresholds, for which the number of corners found must be reduced using other methods.

After thresholding, the corner map contains a number of groups of pixels, from which the actual corners are extracted using the the non-maximal suppression. The only parameter here is the radius (which defines the size of $2n + 1 \times 2n + 1$ box used), which has to be small enough not to remove correct corners and high enough to produce sparse enough map of corners. It is convenient to use this filter to remove even an amount of correctly recognized corners in order to limit the number of results both speeding up computation and preparing a simpler problem for the matching algorithm.

Algorithms share one more parameter, the radius of window used. In case of Moravec, Harris and Shi–Tomasi it is a 3 by 3 square, as increasing the size did not bring significant improvement, while increasing the computation time. SUSAN algorithm approximates the circular mask by a square bit mask, in our case the 7 by 7 version was used. Trajkovic algorithm does not compare a mask per se and the algorithm uses notation of 4 or 8 neighbor variants, of which the 8 neighbor version produces far better results.

Additionally to the above–mentioned parameters, there is a number of detector-specific values. Harris algorithm requires specifying of k constant parameter which influences the decision boundaries use for point classification, values 0.13 was chosen empirically. Please not that although the Shi–Tomasi corner detector follows Harris detector it does not require this constant, because of different corner statistic being used.

Another parameter used by both Harris and Shi–Tomasi algorithms is the standard deviation of the Gaussian filter. Value 1 is used typically, as increased blurring would influence corner localization. SUSAN algorithm rejects a number of false matches by checking the distance of each points' centroid and its center of gravity [7]. The value used was set to 1.4, removing a great amount of edge points. Trajkovic algorithm requires scaling the image to a smaller size and performing simplified corner detection on the produced image. Therefore, the algorithm is supplied with a scale parameter being a power of 2. In our case, $\frac{1}{4}$ proved to be sufficient. Additionally, two thresholds must be specified for this algorithm: for the scaled and for the input image.

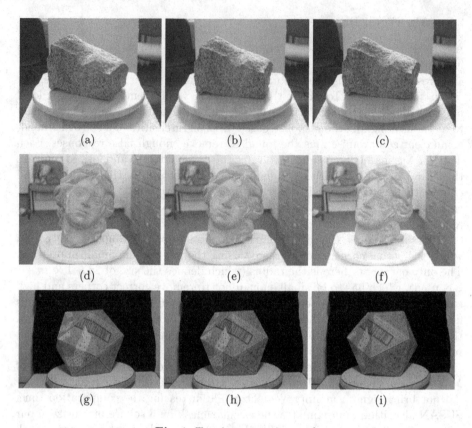

Fig. 1. Test images series used

3 Tests

There exist a number of well known benchmark images for corner detection algorithms, unfortunately, none of them contains two or more images.

Corner matching problem is usually considered for 2 images and there are no widely used benchmark image sets - authors usually provide their own test sets.

Moreover, this article is focused on researching the problem for 3D model acquisition, more specifically - from a revolving 3D object. Thus sets of 3 images depicting the same object, but from different angles are required. Such data sets for real objects are unique among popular benchmarks, which are focused on images taken in the same plane [4].

Data sets could be generated from objects commonly used in computer graphics, for example the so called 'Stanford Bunny'[1] and so forth. On the other hand, artificially generated images contain unnatural smooth background that could significantly bias the result. Therefore we propose three benchmark sets, displaying three solids varying in texture and structure. Additionally, the lighting does vary among the photographs in 1(a)–1(c) (direct sunlight) and 1(d)–1(f)image series.

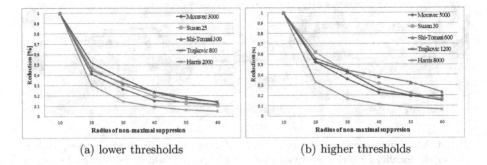

(a) lower thresholds   (b) higher thresholds

Fig. 2. Influence of non-maximal suppression for number of detected points

Grayscale versions of the images were used for the tests. A common practice to improve the results of the detection process is to reduce the size of the images, thus, the size of the images used are 539×404 for two first series and 539×359 for the last one. All three photo series are presented in Figure 1.

3.1   Parameters Selection

The problem of parameters optimization is very complex task. Both characteristic detector parameters and parameters of general detection procedure have to be found. An influence of different parameters is presented in Figure 2. For an increased radius of non-maximal suppression a percentage of point from an initial image, which are not eliminated is presented. The results are given both for lower 2(a) and higher 2(b) values of individual detector parameters.

An ideal parameter set allows recognition of 6 points, which are present on all three images or 7–8 for images pairs. However, this task is not trivial even for a small number of parameters.

For that reason all parameters of detectors are fixed on typical values, suggested by authors or obtained experimentally as described in Section 2.2. Next a non–maximal suppression radius is decreased by 5 starting from 50. Given the size of images, radius of 50 is enough to eliminate all but a few points, while relaxing this parameter would increase the detected points set. When the numbers of points with a projection on all three images reaches 6 algorithm stops.

3.2   Corners Detection and Matching

For each image series detectors were run with fixed parameters calculated as above–mentioned. For each photo set the number of detected points was counted as well as the number of matches between photo pairs and triples.

Corresponding points on each two adjacent images were found using a moified version of area-based matching. First, for each point, only candidates having coordinates in a certain radius were considered. Next, for each potential match, the distance was calculated as the correlation between points' backgrounds of $n \times n$

Fig. 3. Matching procedure. For projections of 3D point on the first photo equivalent points are localized on the next two photos. The points, which are on all photos are connected with black lines. The rest of matched points is connected with gray lines.

pixels. Pairs having correlation below 80% were rejected at this step. The matching was performed in both directions, eliminating non-bijective pairs of corners. Finally a 3-dimensional projection was estimated by RANSAC algorithm based on the remaining matches. Hence the random nature of RANSAC algorithm, a number of trials was performed, choosing the best result. All pairs fitting to the estimated models were considered correct matches.

Table 1. Statistics for detected points. For each series results for 5 detectors are presented. The number of detected points and the number of pairs are given. A percentage of points, which are double or triple projection of 3D point is in last columns.

Model	Detector	Points	Pairs	Double projections [%]	Triple projections [%]
Stone	Harris	361	46	22.99	7.48
1(a)–1(c)	Moravec	63	16	38.31	28.57
	Shi-Thomasi	43	21	83.72	41.86
	SUSAN	48	18	62.50	37.50
	Trajkovic	74	21	48.65	24.32
Head	Harris	52	18	57.69	34.62
1(d)–1(f)	Moravec	39	17	71.79	46.15
	Shi-Thomasi	57	21	63.16	31.58
	SUSAN	77	26	59.74	23.38
	Trajkovic	498	49	18.07	4.82
Solid	Harris	192	28	26.04	9.38
1(g)–1(i)	Moravec	368	39	18.75	7.34
	Shi-Thomasi	38	14	55.26	55.26
	SUSAN	57	22	66.67	31.58
	Trajkovic	223	24	18.83	8.07

First, corners corresponding to 3D points were detected on each photo. Then, matching was found between adjacent images, producing left (between image 1 and 2) and right (between images 2 and 3) match sets. Finally, pairs were combined into triples using by matching points on the middle image, common to

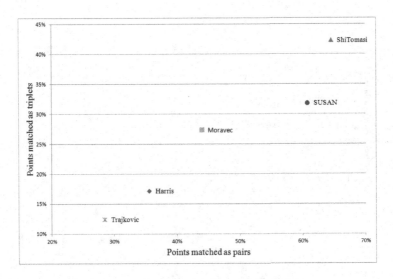

Fig. 4. Detected pairs and triples among points

both matchings. Matches not included in a triple were counted as a pairs. The matching procedure is presented in Figure 3.

Statistics for all detectors and series are presented in Table 1. The best algorithm should assure both high percent of detected pairs and triples. Average values of these two parameters are compared, as it is shown in Figure 4.

This diagram gives a well ordered hierarchy of detectors and it is clear that the best results are obtained by Shi–Thomasi detector. Moreover, it can be said that the estimated number of detected triplets should be in ratio $\frac{3}{5}$ to the number of detected pairs for all discussed detectors.

3.3   Detection of Correct Corners

In 3D modeling a correct detection of objects' corners is essential for a quality of the model. In theory all discussed operators detect corners. In practice a lot of detected points lie on edges or on a surface of the modeled object. A detector that detects correct corners of the object is preferred. However, a detector that is prone to noise detection can detect a high number of correct corners as well as other points. For that reason a good detector should maximize a localization of correct corners in respect to minimalization of different points detection.

In many cases it is hard to define correct corners of an analyzed object. For example objects presented in 1(a)– 1(f) do not have well defined corners. On the other hand, the object from 1(g)– 1(i) is a well defined solid.

This object was selected for the test of correct corners detection. As a measure a correct corners detection quality the number of detected corners of the solid among all detected points is used. As it was said, a detector, which is prone to noise can have a relatively high correct corners detection level. For that reason

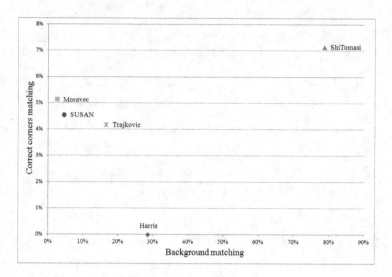

Fig. 5. The percent of matched correct corners (corners of the solid) against the percent of matched points detected on a background

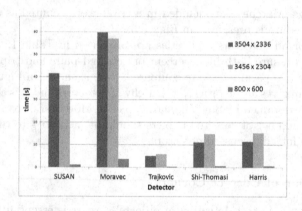

Fig. 6. Comparison of computation time for two images

a susceptibility to noise will be also estimated as a percent of points detected outside of the solid among all detected points.

In the modeling process only points included in doubles or triplets are used and only such points were taken into consideration in the quality of correct corners detection and noise estimation. The results for all compared algorithms are presented in the Figure 5.

The highest number of correct corners was detected by Shi–Thomasi operator. However, this detector is also prone to noise detection. The reason lies in a low level of the rejection threshold.

A reasonable quality level with a much better noise immunity was presented by Moravec and SUSAN detectors. The results show that Harris operator did not detect any correct corners. Despite of that, a detected points may be characteristic points, which are useful in the matching process, but the quality of created 3D model will be probably lower.

3.4 Time Consumption

The comparison of algorithm running times is presented in Figure 6. The computation time was compared for images of different size. In all cases the slowest algorithm was Moravec. The SUSAN algorithm also was relatively slow. Both Shi-Thomasi and Harris have similar results, which is not surprising because of their nearly identical construction. The fastest algorithm is Trajkovic.

4   Conclusions

When the number of detected pairs and triples is compared as in Figure 4, then Shi–Thomasi operator seems to be the best choice. This operator has also a good quality of correct corner detection (detection of points, which are projections of a modeling object corners), but with sensitivity to noise on a significant level (Figure 5). For that reason, if the noise cannot be reduced with other methods a good solution may be using the SUSAN detector instead. In such case, a the computational cost will grow significantly (Figure 6).

References

1. The stanford 3d scanning repository,
   http://www.graphics.stanford.edu/data/3Dscanrep/
2. Harris, C., Stephens, M.: A combined corner and edge detector. In: Proceedings of the 4th Alvey Vision Conference, pp. 147–151 (1988)
3. Hartley, R.I., Zisserman, A.: Multiple View Geometry in Computer Vision. Cambridge University Press (2000) ISBN: 0521623049
4. Mikolajczyk, K., Schmid, C.: Scale & affine invariant interest point detectors. Int. J. Comput. Vision 60, 63–86 (2004)
5. Moravec, H.: Visual mapping by a robot rover. In: Proceedings of the 6th International Joint Conference on Artificial Intelligence, pp. 599–601 (August 1979)
6. Shi, J., Tomasi, C.: Good features to track. In: Proceedings of 9th IEEE Conference on Computer Vision and Pattern Recognition (1994)
7. Smith, S., Brady, J.: Susan - a new approach to low level image processing. International Journal of Computer Vision 23(1), 45–78 (1997)
8. Tomasi, C., Kanade, T.: Detection and tracking of point features. Tech. rep., International Journal of Computer Vision (1991)
9. Trajkovic, M., Hedley, M.: Fast corner detection. Image and Vision Computing 16(2), 75–87 (1998)
10. Zawieska, D.: Analysis of operators for detection of corners set in automatic image matching. In: Proceedings of 7th International Symposium on Mobile Mapping Technology (2011)

A Hierarchical Action Recognition System Applying Fisher Discrimination Dictionary Learning via Sparse Representation

Ruihan Bao and Tadashi Shibata

Department of Electrical Engineering and Information System,
The University of Tokyo,
7-3-1 Hongo Bunkyo-ku, Tokyo, Japan, 113-8656
ray@if.t.u-tokyo.ac.jp, shibata@ee.t.u-tokyo.ac.jp

Abstract. In this paper, we propose a hierarchical action recognition system applying Fisher discrimination dictionary learning via sparse representation classifier. Feature vectors used to represent certain actions are first generated by employing local features extracted from motion field maps. Sparse representation classification (SRC) are then employed on those feature vectors, in which a structured dictionary for classification is learned applying Fisher discrimination dictionary learning (FDDL). We tested our algorithms on Weizmann human database and KTH human database, and compared the recognition rates with other modeling methods such as k-nearest neighbor. Results showed that the action recognition system applying FDDL can achieve better performance despite that the learning stage for the Fisher discrimination dictionary can converge within only several iterations.

Keywords: Action Recognition, Motion Field, Sparse Representation Classification, Spatio-temporal Patches.

1 Introduction

Action recognition is receiving growing attentions due to its applications in smart surveillance[9], sign language interpretation[22], advanced user interface[21,13] and intelligent robotics. Compared with the object recognition from static images, action recognition usually takes videos as inputs. In addition, if actions are subjected to cluttered background in videos, recognition rates from current algorithms may decline to lower levels, unless some additional methods are adopted, e.g. imposing tracking windows or estimating background by other information.

Designing the systems for action recognition usually involves two issues, i.e. how to represent actions in given videos and how to label unknown actions. To solve the first issue, algorithms usually fall into two categories, depending on whether global features or local features are employed. In the first category [18,7], human bodies as a whole are modeled and actions are represented by the trajectories of body parts. In the other category such as [10,4,14], local features

L. Rutkowski et al. (Eds.): ICAISC 2012, Part I, LNCS 7267, pp. 468–476, 2012.

(called patches or bag-of-words) are often utilized to represent actions because they can preserve details rather than absolute positions.

In order to address another issue, several groups applied algorithms from machine learning, and their efforts can be classified as either generative approaches [6] or discriminative approaches [20], depending on how they model the actions in videos [16]. Recently a novel model called sparse representation classification(SRC) has been widely studied in face recognition, due to its success in image restoration [12] and image compression [3]. There are generally two steps [23] involved in the SRC, namely, building dictionaries from training data and classifying unlabeled data by solving coding coefficients. While most of SRC methods directly use training data as dictionaries, latest researches in [24] proposed a more efficient algorithm for dictionary learning, in which Fisher discrimination criterion was applied. Although SRC and its variations are widely used in face recognition, there are few researches in action recognition utilizing the methods, mainly because of current models cannot be easily combined with the SRC.

In this paper, we try to solve the two issues by introducing a hierarchical action recognition system, which is an extension to our previous works [1] on gesture perception. In our system, motion field maps capturing lower features such as speed and directions are estimated at first, followed by feature vector calculations from matchings between query videos and template patches which can be thought of as *visual words* for actions. Once feature vectors are computed, classification based on Fisher discrimination dictionary learning(FDDL) is carried out and unknown actions are labeled by solving coding coefficients from fisher discrimination dictionary. Compared with our previous works in [1] which addressed the problem of how to efficiently generate feature vectors for gestures, this paper focuses on comprehensive solutions for action recognition problems, and for the first time incorporates state-of-the-art models from face recognition to the action recognition system. We tested our system on popular action database, and promising results were reported.

2   Hierarchical System via Spatio-temporal Patches

The proposed architecture employs a hierarchical structure similar to the one described in [1]. At the lower level, global features such as speed and directions are extracted. While at the higher level, invariance to positions is achieved by applying matchings between template patches and query videos.

2.1   Lower Level Processing

The lower level processing includes calculating motion field maps and blurring them by max operations[1]. In this stage, vertical and horizontal edge flags in Directional Edge Displacement(DED) maps are projected onto x-axis or y-axis in local windows and histograms are generated for consecutive DED maps, separately. Shift-and-matching between two histograms in the consecutive frames is carried out so that the important information such as directions and speed is estimated. Once motion field maps are calculated, the invariance of the system is increased by blurring motion fields in a $w \times w$ window at each frame, using either max filters or average filters. In reality we follow the previous method[1] by sampling maximum values from $w \times w$ windows and the window is shifted by a step of $w/2$, thus resulting in a $(w/2)^2$ factor reduction in scale for each frame. Blurred motion field maps at both directions are further half-wave rectified into four non-negative channels like [5].

2.2   Higher Level Processing

The system at higher levels provides functionalities that are similar to those of visual cortex [17], and local features are detected while absolute positions of features become irrelevant. There are two different processes existing at the higher level: template learning and feature vector calculation. Both processes involve so called spatio-temporal patches [1] which can be seen as a small portion of videos.

Template Learning. Once motion field maps are available, a number of spatio-temporal patches are extracted randomly in space and time from learning samples and served as template patches. Along with the extraction, a simple detecting algorithm is adopted, that is, patches only containing enough non-zero values are kept. Because most of the noises are eliminated at the lower stage and only essential motions from video sequences are preserved, our selection of patches based on this algorithm is well-tuned to the strong motions.

Once numbers of patches are extracted randomly from different action categories, they are converted to descriptor representations [1]. The K-means is then applied to those descriptors so that the number of patches extracted from the learning stage is reduced.

Feature Vector Calculation. As described in [2], when video sequences to be recognized enter the system, features at the lower layers are first calculated by motion field estimation and further blurred by taking maximum values from local windows, which are identical to the steps used in template learning stage. During feature vector generation, spatio-temporal patches with the same size of the template patches are extracted from the input video sequences. The differences compared with the learning stage are that the extraction is carried out in sequential order rather than random selection. Similar threshold algorithm is adopted, which selects patches that contain enough non-zero values. Since then only small numbers of meaningful patches are calculated, computation can be reduced significantly.

3   Fisher Discrimination Dictionary Learning (FDDL) via Sparse Feature Classification(SRC)

Sparse representation classification (SRC) is first proposed by [23] for face recognition. The underlying principles are simple and elegant, which based on the observation that the query sample can be represented by a linear combination of training samples. Though related researches shows that the SRC may lead to minimal reconstruction error for recognition tasks with even significant occlusions, it may be not effective to represent the query samples directly by training samples, due to the uncertainty in the training samples. In order to improve the classification accuracy for sparse representation classification, Fisher discrimination dictionary learning (FDDL) is proposed by [24] for face recognition and the dictionary used for sparse classifier is learned by optimizing a FDDL function.

3.1 Sparse Representation Classification(SRC)

Suppose we have c classes of samples, and let $A = [A_1, A_2, ..., A_c]$ be the set of original training samples, where A_k represents the subset of training set k. Assume that f is the feature vector for query sample, the class for the given query sample is found by,

$$identity(f) = arg \min_i \{\|f - A_i \hat{a}_i\|_2\} \tag{1}$$

where $\hat{a}_i$ is the subset for sparse codes $\hat{a} = [\hat{a}_1; \hat{a}_2; ...; \hat{a}_c]$, which is calculated by solving the following l_1-norm minimization problem:

$$\hat{a} = arg \min_a \{\|f - A\hat{a}\|_2^2 + \gamma\|\hat{a} - m_i\|_1\} \tag{2}$$

in which γ is a scalar constant.

3.2 FDDL Models

Instead of using raw training samples for classification, a structured dictionary $D = [D_1, D_2, ..., D_c]$ has been learned [24], where D_k is the sub-dictionary for the class k. With this dictionary, we can classify a given query sample using reconstruction errors defined by Equation.1.

Firstly, in order to learn the structure dictionary, an FDDL model is constructed in the following way,

$$J_{(D,X)} = arg \min_{(D,X)} \{r(A, D, X) + \lambda_1\|X\|_1 + \lambda_2 g(x)\} \tag{3}$$

where $r(A, D, X)$ is called discriminative fidelity term, $\|X\|_1$ is called sparsity constraint, and $g(x)$ is the discrimination constraint imposed on the coefficient matrix X [24]. In order to train the FDDL model, a special strategy has been adopted in which dictionary and coefficient matrix are updated alternatively. It also shows that FDDL can converge efficiently within limited number of iterations(see Figure.1).

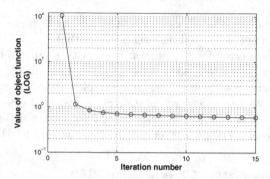

Fig. 1. Values of object function for each iteration(Weizmann database). It shows that after several iteration, the objective function can actually converge very well.

(a) Weizmann human database(including nine actions in all)

(b) KTH human database(including six actions with variations)

Fig. 2. Database used in the experiment

3.3 SRC Based on FDDL Model

Once the dictionary is available, we can apply the similar idea from SRC for classification,

$$identity(\boldsymbol{f}) = arg \min_i \left\{ \|\boldsymbol{f} - D_i \hat{a}_i\|_2 + w\|\hat{a} - m_i\|_2^2 \right\} \tag{4}$$

where D_i is the sub-dictionary for class i, $\hat{a}_i$ the sparse codes learned in the similar way from Equation.1 except using dictionary D instead of training samples A. m_i is the mean vector of the class i and w is a preset weight to balance the two terms.

4 Experiment Results

We have tested the algorithm on both Weizmann database and KTH human database. In addition, we compare our algorithm with the one applying k-Nearest

Table 1. Experiment results for Weizmann human database

Approaches	Recognition Rate	Testing Methods
1-NN	91.53%	Split
1-NN	93.02%	Leave-one-out(LOO)
FDDL	100.00%	Split

Neighbor(1-NN) classifier. In order to test the robustness of the system, we divided the samples so that 50% of the them are served as training samples and the rests are served as testing samples.

4.1   Weizmann Database

The Weizmann human action database (see Figure.2a) [8] contains 81 low resolution video sequences(180×144 pixels) with nine subjects. It contains nine actions, including bending, jumping at the same places, jumping from one side to the other side, galloping-sideways, waving two hands, waving one hands, running, walking and jumping-jack. For the simplicity, we adjusted the size of each frame to 256×256 for our system. The database also contains an extra video sequences for background, which can be used for foreground emergence [8]. In our experiment, nevertheless, we did not utilize this extra information.

The results showed that the algorithm that applied FDDL models generally performed better than 1-NN as well as other similar algorithms, and we also listed the results of leave-one-out test for comparison. Moreover, Figures.1 shows that the learning for dictionary D can be done within 15 iterations without losing much accuracy, which can be used to further reduce the computational cost of the model.

4.2   KTH Human Database

The KTH human action database (see Figure.2b) [19] contains 25x6x4=600 video files for each combination of 25 subjects, 6 actions and 4 scenarios. For the simplicity, we adjusted the size of each frame to 256×256 for our system. We have generated $k = 2400$ prototypes from only one learning sample under 1st scenarios (d1) which contains six actions.

The experiment results show FDDL outperform 1-NN significantly, and the confusion matrix shows that the mismatch usually happened between actions that are similar to each other. In addition, we also compared our recognition rates with latest researches, though some of them used additional background estimation methods as pre-processing steps [10]. Despite the recognition results in the table, the performance can be further improved, since during the experiment we used only one sample (about 1% of total videos) to learn the template patches.

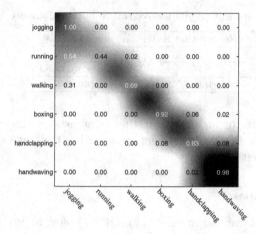

Fig. 3. Confusion Matrix for the KTH human database

Table 2. Experiment results for KTH human database

Approaches	Recognition Rate	Testing Methods
Liu&Shah [11]	94.16%	LOO
Jhuang et al.[10]	91.70%	Split
Ours (**FDDL**)	87.15%	Split
Nowozin et al.[15]	87.04%	Split
Niebles et al.[14]	81.50%	LOO
Dollar et al.[4]	81.17%	LOO
Ours (1NN)	75.00%	LOO

5   Conclusion

In this paper, we proposed a hierarchical system for action recognition. Inspired by the latest researches in face recognition, we extended the FDDL models to video recognition and experiment results showed that the sparse representation based on FDDL may be a promising model for action recognition. As the future researches, we would like to explore more about the sparse representation and incorporate the SRC into the template learning, given that the two processes are quite similar to each other in the way they process.

References

1. Bao, R., Shibata, T.: A gesture perception algorithm using compact one-dimensional representation of spatio-temporal motion-field patches. In: 3rd International Conference on Signal Processing and Communication Systems, ICSPCS 2009, pp. 1–5. IEEE (2009)

2. Bao, R., Shibata, T.: Spatio-Temporal Motion Field Descriptors for The Hierarchical Action Recognition System. In: 5th International Conference on Signal Processing and Communication Systems, ICSPCS 2011. IEEE (2011)
3. Candès, E.: Compressive sampling. In: Proceedings oh the International Congress of Mathematicians, Madrid, August 22-30, pp. 1433–1452 (2006) (invited lectures)
4. Dollar, P., Rabaud, V., Cottrell, G., Belongie, S.: Behavior recognition via sparse spatio-temporal features. In: VS-PETS, pp. 65–72 (2005)
5. Efros, A.A., Berg, A.C., Berg, E.C., Mori, G., Malik, J.: Recognizing action at a distance. In: ICCV, pp. 726–733 (2003)
6. Feng, X., Perona, P.: Human action recognition by sequence of movelet codewords. In: Proceedings of the First International Symposium on 3D Data Processing Visualization and Transmission, pp. 717–721. IEEE (2002)
7. Ferrari, V., Marin-Jimenez, M., Zisserman, A.: Progressive search space reduction for human pose estimation. In: IEEE Conference on Computer Vision and Pattern Recognition, CVPR 2008, pp. 1–8. IEEE (2008)
8. Gorelick, L., Blank, M., Shechtman, E., Irani, M., Basri, R.: Actions as space-time shapes. In: ICCV, pp. 1395–1402 (2005)
9. Hampapur, A., Brown, L., Connell, J., Ekin, A., Haas, N., Lu, M., Merkl, H., Pankanti, S.: Smart video surveillance: exploring the concept of multiscale spatiotemporal tracking. IEEE Signal Processing Magazine 22(2), 38–51 (2005)
10. Jhuang, H., Serre, T., Wolf, L., Poggio, T.: A biologically inspired system for action recognition. In: ICCV, pp. 1–8 (2007)
11. Liu, J., Shah, M.: Learning human actions via information maximization. In: IEEE Conference on Computer Vision and Pattern Recognition, CVPR 2008, pp. 1–8. IEEE (2008)
12. Mairal, J., Elad, M., Sapiro, G.: Sparse representation for color image restoration. IEEE Transactions on Image Processing 17(1), 53–69 (2008)
13. Meng, H., Pears, N., Bailey, C.: A human action recognition system for embedded computer vision application. In: 2007 IEEE Conference on Computer Vision and Pattern Recognition, pp. 1–6. IEEE (2007)
14. Niebles, J., Wang, H., Fei-Fei, L.: Unsupervised learning of human action categories using spatial-temporal words. International Journal of Computer Vision 79(3), 299–318 (2008)
15. Nowozin, S., Bakir, G., Tsuda, K.: Discriminative subsequence mining for action classification. In: IEEE 11th International Conference on Computer Vision, ICCV 2007, pp. 1–8. IEEE (2007)
16. Poppe, R.: A survey on vision-based human action recognition. Image and Vision Computing 28(6), 976–990 (2010)
17. Quiroga, R., Reddy, L., Kreiman, G., Koch, C., Fried, I.: Invariant visual representation by single neurons in the human brain. Nature 435(7045), 1102–1107 (2005)
18. Ramanan, D.: Learning to parse images of articulated bodies. In: NIPS 2007. NIPS (2006)
19. Schuldt, C., Laptev, I., Caputo, B.: Recognizing human actions: A local svm approach. In: ICPR (2004)
20. Sminchisescu, C., Kanaujia, A., Li, Z., Metaxas, D.: Conditional models for contextual human motion recognition. In: Tenth IEEE International Conference on Computer Vision, ICCV 2005, vol. 2, pp. 1808–1815. IEEE (2005)

21. Touyama, H., Aotsuka, M., Hirose, M.: A pilot study on virtual camera control via Steady-State VEP in immersing virtual environments. In: Proceedings of the Third IASTED International Conference on Human Computer Interaction, pp. 43–48. ACTA Press (2008)

22. Vogler, C., Metaxas, D.: Handshapes and Movements: Multiple-Channel American Sign Language Recognition. In: Camurri, A., Volpe, G. (eds.) GW 2003. LNCS (LNAI), vol. 2915, pp. 247–258. Springer, Heidelberg (2004)

23. Wright, J., Yang, A., Ganesh, A., Sastry, S., Ma, Y.: Robust face recognition via sparse representation. IEEE Transactions on Pattern Analysis and Machine Intelligence, 210–227 (2008)

24. Yang, M., Zhang, L., Feng, X., Zhang, D.: Fisher discrimination dictionary learning for sparse representation. In: ICCV. IEEE (2011)

Do We Need Complex Models for Gestures? A Comparison of Data Representation and Preprocessing Methods for Hand Gesture Recognition

Marcin Blachnik[1] and Przemysław Głomb[2]

[1] Silesian University of Technology, Department of Management and Informatics,
Katowice, Krasinskiego 8, Poland
marcin.blachnik@polsl.pl
[2] The Institute of Theoretical and Applied Informatics, Polish Academy of Sciences,
Gliwice, Baltycka 5, Poland
przemg@iitis.pl

Abstract. Human-Computer Interaction (HCI) is one of the most rapidly developing fields of computer applications. One of approaches to HCI is based on gestures which are in many cases more natural and effective than conventional inputs. In the paper the problem of gesture recognition is investigated. The gestures are gathered from the dedicated motion capture system, and further evaluated by 3 different preprocessing procedures and 4 different classifier. Our results suggest that most of the combinations produce adequate recognition rate, with appropriate signal normalization being the key element.

Keywords: Human-Computer Interaction, gesture recognition, signal processing, machine learning.

1 Introduction

Human-Computer Interaction (HCI) using gestures is for many tasks more natural and effective than conventional input. In most cases, the key to an effective application of gesture HCI system is the performance of gesture recognition, which, in turn, depends on the characteristics of data source. A common approach, combining low cost with being non-intrusive, is to use video cameras. Unfortunately, this source of data is sensitive to acquisition conditions, and requires complex preprocessing algorithms (as seen for example on a large set of competitions organized by the Pascal-Network [1]). To facilitate the recognition, special acquisition systems have been designed, from special painted gloves (e.g. [15]), through devices targeted for games (e.g. Nintendo Wii Remote[TM] and Microsoft Kinect[TM]), to dedicated motion capture systems (e.g. Cyberglove[TM]or DGTech DG5VHand[TM]).

We can view gesture recording with motion capture devices as corresponding to simultaneous recording and preprocessing / information extraction from cameras. That is, our data contains information relating to movement characteristics (e.g. time change of finger bend, hand orientation) extracted from that of registration process (e.g. position configuration, lighting). This data is often complete enough to allow visualization

L. Rutkowski et al. (Eds.): ICAISC 2012, Part I, LNCS 7267, pp. 477–485, 2012.

of a gesture and human recognition. Given enough examples of natural gestures (those that have a widespread use in human communication) we could attempt to analyze the *space of gestures*[1] and answer the questions: what is the expected complexity of the task of gesture classification? Are additional preprocessing steps (of the captured data) required to achieve high recognition rate?

Our work presents an approach to analyze this need of preprocessing and complexity by a series of experiments with natural gestures data. We used a database of $d = 22$ natural gestures captured with motion capture gloves [6]. We have prepared an experimental testbed of 3 preprocessing methods and 4 classifiers to evaluate the effect of different preprocessing and class modelling. Our results suggest that most of the combinations produce adequate recognition rate, with appropriate signal normalization being the key element.

1.1 Related Work

The idea of glove-based human gesture recognition is still under the development. There has be proposed many sophisticated methods to deal with universal time series (UTM) [17]. Some of the ideas are based on dynamic time wrapping (DTW)[5] which allows to measure the similarity between two signals of different length. Other approaches are based on singular value decomposition of the signals what was proposed in [9], and further extended in [11] by the use of more robust Segmented Singular Value Decomposition, which focused on local properties of the signals. Chuanjun Li et al. proposed a similarity measure based on SVD decomposition, where one of the applications was hand gesture recognition [10]. Another system for gesture recognition and multivariate time series processing was proposed in the dissertation of M. Kadous [8] where author described a novel system called TClass. In the literature many other methods can be found, however, we have noticed that most of these methods are computationally very expensive, and there is a lack of a comparison to the simple standard approaches used in signal processing. In the following section (2) we describe the gestures dataset and present our solution; in section 3 three different preprocessing and feature extraction algorithms are described. Section 4 discuss algorithms used for classification, with an empirical comparison. The last section concludes the paper with discussion and directions of further research.

2 Our Approach

The gesture recognition process can be divided into two subsystems as presented on fig.(1). The first stage is responsible for recognition if the recoded signals belong to any of the known set of gestures denoted as class $c = [c_1, c_2, \ldots, c_d]$, so it can be seen as a kind of filter, filtering only known gestures and rejecting the unknown ones. This can be realized as a novelty detection system where any novel gestures will be automatically rejected (e.g. by the One Class SVM [14] or a Hidden Markov Model) or, as it is usually done in image processing, by generating negative samples (here negative gestures) and

---

[1] As opposed to *space of gesture images*, when the data analyzed would be camera based.

establishing two class classification problem. In the second stage, launched only for known gestures, the system will make the final recognition and assign appropriate class label. In presented paper only this second stage will be discussed.

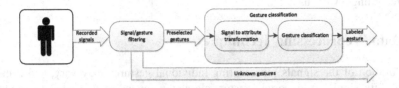

Fig. 1. Gesture processing scheme

The main problem of the second stage is to design a system which consists of two building blocks fig.(2):

- **Feature Extraction** - this first building block should prepare data for the final classification problem, with the goal to represent recorded signals of a gesture as a vector in some n dimensional feature space
- **Discrimination** - this processing step is responsible for final decision by assigning appropriate class label c_i form the set of gestures **c**.

In this paper we would like to address the problem of selecting appropriate feature extraction and discrimination methods by comparing several simple and intuitive methods with low computational complexity. In our experiments we have compared:

- Resampling of the signals
- Classification based on Fast Fourier Transformation coefficients
- Classification based on coefficients extracted form polynomial approximation of that signal.

Also three different classifiers were used to classify the signals which are: decision trees (with a random forest of decision trees), support vector machine (SVM) and nearest neighbor classifier.

2.1 Natural Gesture Database

For the experiments a subset of 'IITiS Gesture Database' (see [6] for details) was used. This database contains $d = 22$ natural hand gesture classes (e.g. „A-OK", „thumbs up", „come here"). In the experiments only the subset of this database recorded with DGTech DG5VHand^{TM2} motion capture glove was used. The glove was equipped with $a = 10$ sensors: 5 finger bend sensors (resistance type) and three-axis accelerometer producing three acceleration and two orientation readings. The sampling frequency was approximately 33 Hz.

Each recording was performed with participant sitting at the table with motion capture glove on his right hand, with the hand in fixed initial position. At the command

---

[2] http://www.dg-tech.it/vhand

given by the operator sitting in front of the participant, the participant performed the gestures. Each gesture was performed six times at natural pace, two times at a rapid pace and two times at a slow pace. The operator decided the start and stop of the recording.

In the experiments the data for 5 participants, $m = 1100$ samples (from the 4195 total recordings) were used.

3   Data Preprocessing Techniques

The duration of the signals representing individual gestures may vary, and even the length of the singles from certain gesture class may depend on the speed related to the gesture execution. This requires normalization of the signals or transformation into a time independent domain. In our experiments all signals were normalized to a fixed length interval such that each signal starts at $t_0 = 0$ and ends in $t_N = 1$.

In the next step all the signals for each gesture were also normalized to obtain a comparable signals amplitude. However in opposite to the time normalization, the maximum and the minimum value was set based on the analysis of all the signals recorded from a single glove sensor and stored in the databased. The simple normalization of each signal independent is inappropriate introducing noise to the system by maximizing the fluctuation for sensors which recorded constant value like for example for „hello" gesture where fingers are not bending. Assuming the notation where $s_k^{j,i}$ denotes i-th value of k-th signal, of j-th recorded gestures, and denoting m as the total number of recorded gestures, and N_j as the number of values of the signal of j-th recorded gestures, the normalization process can be written as:

$$\underset{k\in[1,a]}{\forall}\ s_k^{min} = \min_{j\in[1,m];i\in[0,N_j]}\left(s_k^{j,i}\right)$$

$$\underset{k\in[1,a]}{\forall}\ s_k^{max} = \max_{j\in[1,m];i\in[0,N_j]}\left(s_k^{j,i}\right) \tag{1}$$

$$\underset{k\in[1,a];j\in[1,m];i\in[0,N_j]}{\forall}\ s_k^{j,i} = \frac{s_k^{j,i} - s_k^{min}}{s_k^{max} - s_k^{min}}$$

where s_k^{min} and s_k^{max} represents the maximum and minimum value for all recorded signals of k'th sensor, and N_j is the length or the last index of gesture j.

In the next step three different preprocessing methods were used to create a feature set:

Simple Resampling - in this approach all of the signals were first resampled to the fixed number of samples r. The resampling process allows for fixing the time interval between samples in all signals. This further allows for concatenation, such that the single instance x represented in the input space of the classifier was defined as $x = [s_1^j \oplus s_2^j \oplus s_a^j]$, where $\oplus$ denotes the concatenation operator. Finally the feature set consists of $n = (a \cdot r)$ attributes, and each instance was annotated with an appropriate class label.

Fast Fourier Transformation - This approach includes all the previous steps, also the resampling process however with higher number of samples, typically $r = 55$ followed by the fast Fourier transform (FFT) [12].

$$g_k = \sum_{t=0}^{N-1} x_t e^{-i2\pi k \frac{t}{N}} \tag{2}$$

Where g_k is a complex number describing the parameters of k'th harmonic frequency, x_t is an t'th sample of some signal s_j, and N - is a total number of samples in that signal.

According to the properties of the FFT transform, bypassing the resampling process may lead to inconsistent feature space, because the values of estimated harmonic frequences depends on the number of samples of the processed signal. In this scenario the feature space is obtained by concatenation of the module of the most relevant p harmonic frequences, so the final dataset consists of m samples and $n = (a \cdot p)$ features.

Polynomial Signal Approximation - In this method the input space of the classifier is created by concatenation of the coefficients of the polynomials of order l used for approximation of singles describing single gesture, so $n = (l + 1 \cdot a)$. This method also requires additional preprocessing. However in opposite to two previous methods the resampling process is not required and only the time and signal normalization steps were used. In the formula below z_l denotes the polynomial parameters stored as a values of the attribute set.

$$y_k = z_0 x^0 + z_1 x^1 + z2 x^2 + \ldots + z_l x^l \tag{3}$$

4   Numerical Experiments

4.1   Discrimination Methods

In our experiments we have compared several well known classification algorithms. The selected ones were the Support Vector Machines (SVM) with Gaussian kernel (G-SVM) which is well known as the most universal shape of a kernel function [7], also the RandomForests (RF) [3] which is also known as powerful classifier, and proved it in the feature selection challenge organized in 2003 by Isabel Guyon [14, 15] during the NIPS conference. Because this algorithm is based on a set of trees a classic single tree was also used for the comparison - C4.5 [13]. The last algorithm used in all experiments is the nearest neighbor classifier (kNN).

4.2   Testing Procedure Definition

In all experiments the performance of the classifier was estimated using 10 fold cross validation. However the preprocessing steps were done separately before the cross validation. This shouldn't affect the overall performance and estimated accuracy because

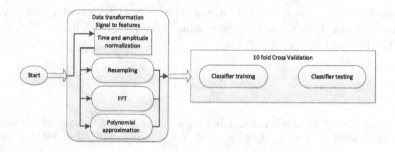

Fig. 2. Data processing steps during gesture recognition process

the preprocessing steps didn't take into account class labels. The processing procedure is presented on figure fig (2).

In the beginning all the classification algorithms were applied to the resampled dataset with $r = 55$. This value is the highest reasonable value of that parameter, because the minimum number of samples is equal to 55. In this scenario all the parameters were optimized to maximize the accuracy. For the G-SVM the model was optimized checking all combinations of $C = [0.0001 \cdot 10^{0,\dots,7}]$ (the trade-off between training error and margin) and $\gamma = [0.1 + 2 \cdot (0.1 \cdot [0,\dots,9])]$ (the spread of the Gaussian kernel). In all calculations LibSVM [4] implementation was used. Then for RF and C4.5 the Weka [16] implementation was used with the default set of parameters for C4.5 and similarly for the RF except that 100 trees were build without any feature preselection. All of the experiments were performed using RapidMiner software [2], except the preprocessing techniques, which were implemented in Matlab.

4.3 Classifiers Comparison

Obtained best results for each classifier, and the hyperparameters are presented in the table tab.(1).

Table 1. Empirical comparison of different classifiers of resampled dataset

dataset	G-SVM	kNN	RF	C4.5
Accuracy [%]	96.37±1.28	94.75±1.38	96.03±1.93	77.95±2.79
Parameters	$C = 1000, \gamma = 1.9$	$k = 1$	$TN = 100, FN = inf$ Where: TN - number of trees, FN - number of features	Default weka values

Very interesting results were obtained for G-SVM. The set of optimal parameters C and γ suggest that the decision border is very jagged so the SVM behaves like an kNN classifier. On the other hand results obtained by a single decision tree and a random forest algorithm differ a lot. This shows that the support of other tree in the forest is crucial for the decision making.

4.4 Comparison of Preprocessing Methods

For the process of preprocessing methods comparison only single classifier was selected. As a reference algorithm for the validation of preprocessing methods the kNN classifier was selected with $k = 1$. This model was selected because of several reasons. Its performance is sensitive to the normalization process by the distance evaluation, and thus may be more sensitive on the properties of the preprocessing parameters. Also its performance was comparable to the other methods, however evaluation was much faster, both in training and testing. Based on that classifier we have first evaluated the quality based on the number of resampled instances. The results are presented on fig.(3.a). As it can be seen as the number of resampled values reach around $r = 15$ samples per signal the accuracy starts fluctuating around $acc = 94\%$ without any significant improvement. Then the influence of the number of harmonic frequences selected on the error rate of the classification process was estimated. As the number of harmonic the range between $[1 \ldots 30]$ was tested. The results are presented on figure fig.(3.b). For this preprocessing technique the maximum accuracy is reached for $p = 5$ and then

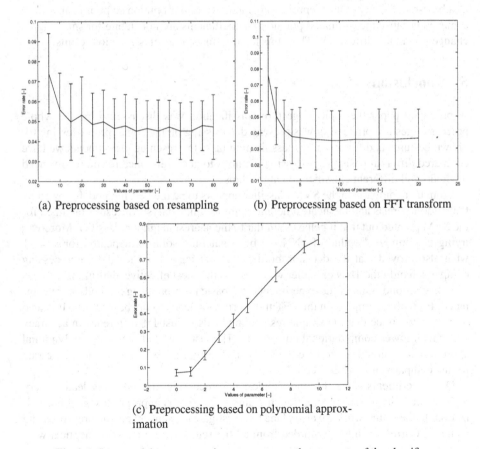

(a) Preprocessing based on resampling   (b) Preprocessing based on FFT transform

(c) Preprocessing based on polynomial approximation

Fig. 3. Influence of the preprocessing parameter on the error rate of the classifier

remain almost constant without any statistically significant difference. The best accuracy obtained by the 1NN classifier is $acc = 96.64 \pm 1.46$ As the SVM obtained the best results for the preprocessing based on resampled data, we have also tried to optimize it for the FFT preprocessing but for fixed number of harmonic. Because as we have already mentioned the accuracy of the 1NN model remains constant for $p > 5$ we have optimized the SVM classifier for $p = 10$. The value of p was selected based on the principle to move away from the border values, close to minimum error presented on fig.3.b. Obtained maximum accuracy $acc = 97.38 \pm 1.21$ was reached for $\gamma = 6$ and $C = 1000$. It is worth to note that the accuracy differs form that obtained for resampling based preprocessing just in 1% in both cases for SVM and kNN classifiers, while the computational complexity of FFT is much higher.

Finally the preprocessing based on polynomial approximation was tested with the order of the polynomial varying in range $l = [0, \ldots, 10]$. Obtained results are presented on figure fig.(3.c). Surprisingly in this method increasing the order of the polynomial decreases the accuracy, and the best results are obtained for order $l = 0$. This suggests that simple averaging of the signals (after initial amplitude normalization) may be enough to classify signals with the accuracy of $acc = 92\%$, and should be treated as a base-rate for any other preprocessing methods. In our opinion so poor results were achieved because the estimated polynomial coefficients are not stabile for small signal changes, and may differ a lot. Thus, this leads to inaccurate classification results.

5   Conclusions

In presented paper the topic of gesture classification was discussed. First the whole process of gesture processing was presented, focussing on the signal preprocessing for known gestures and followed by classification task. In presented experiments we have compared different basic preprocessing methods to get a reference for more advanced methods, and different classification algorithms.

From that comparison the SVM classifier appears to be the best method, followed by the random forests and the nearest neighbor algorithm. Analysis of results obtained for the SVM pointed out that it behaves similar to the nearest neighbor classifier. Moreover trying to optimize k value of kNN the best matching solution appeared for $k = 1$ what also proved that the decision border is rather jagged. So for the preprocessing comparison only the 1NN classifier was used, as the most effective algorithm.

In that second stage of the experiment three basic preprocessing methods were compared. From that comparison the FFT transformation leads to the best results. It is also important to notice that the simple resampling leads to just 1% difference in accuracy with much lower computational complexity. The last of tested methods - polynomial approximation turned out to be completely useless, but allows as to define a base-rate for the comparison to other methods.

Our experiments show that the simplest preprocessing methods may lead to very high accuracy in gesture recognition, the only restriction is appropriate signal normalization. In the future work we also plane to investigate the sensor specific preprocessing methods. Currently signals recorded from all the sensors are process in identical way, however it may be important to adjust preprocessing methods for individual sensors. We also plan to compare these simple methods with more advanced ones, to analyze the real gains and losses of all these methods.

Acknowledgment. The work was sponsored by the Polish Ministry of Science and Higher Education, project No. 4421/B/T02/2010/38 (N516 442138) and NN516405137 'User interface based on natural gestures for exploration of virtual 3D spaces'.

References

1. Pascal network, http://www.pascal-network.org/
2. Rapidminer, http://www.rapid-i.com
3. Breiman, L.: Random forests. Machine Learning 45(1), 5–32 (2001)
4. Chang, C.C., Lin, C.J.: LIBSVM: A library for support vector machines. ACM Transactions on Intelligent Systems and Technology 2, 27:1–27:27 (2011), Software http://www.csie.ntu.edu.tw/~cjlin/libsvm
5. Corradini, A.: Dynamic time warping for off-line recognition of a small gesture vocabulary. In: Proceedings of IEEE ICCV Workshop on Recognition, Analysis, and Tracking of Faces and Gestures in Real-Time Systems (2001)
6. Głomb, P., Romaszewski, M., Opozda, S., Sochan, A.: Choosing and modeling hand gesture database for natural user interface. In: Proc. of GW 2011: The 9th International Gesture Workshop Gesture in Embodied Communication and Human-Computer Interaction (2011)
7. Hsu, C.W., Chang, C.C., Lin, C.J.: A practical guide to support vector classification. Tech. rep., Department of Computer Science, National Taiwan University (2003), http://www.csie.ntu.edu.tw/~cjlin/papers.html
8. Kadous, M.: Temporal Classification: Extending the Classification Paradigm to Multivariate Time Series. Ph.D. thesis, University of New South Wales (2002)
9. Li, C., Zhai, P., Zheng, S., Prabhakaran, B.: Segmentation and recognition of multi-attribute motion sequences. In: Proceedings of the 12th Annual ACM International Conference on Multimedia, pp. 836–843 (2004)
10. Li, C., Prabhakaran, B.: A similarity measure for motion stream segmentation and recognition. In: Proceedings of the MDM (2005)
11. Liu, J., Kavakli, M.: Hand Gesture Recognition Based on Segmented Singular Value Decomposition. In: Setchi, R., Jordanov, I., Howlett, R.J., Jain, L.C. (eds.) KES 2010, Part II. LNCS, vol. 6277, pp. 214–223. Springer, Heidelberg (2010)
12. Oppenheim, A.V., Schafer, R.W.: Discrete-time signal processing. Prentice Hall (2010)
13. Quinlan, J.: C 4.5: Programs for machine learning. Morgan Kaufmann, San Mateo (1993)
14. Schölkopf, B., Smola, A.: Learning with Kernels. In: Support Vector Machines, Regularization, Optimization, and Beyond. MIT Press, Cambridge (2001)
15. Wang, R., Popovic, J.: Real time hand tracking with a color glove 28(3) (2009)
16. Witten, I., Frank, E.: Data Mining: Practical machine learning tools and techniques, 2nd edn. Morgan Kaufmann (2005)
17. Yang, K., Shahabi, C.: A pca-based kernel for kernel pca on multivariate time series. In: Proceedings of ICDM 2005 Workshop on Temporal Data Mining: Algorithms, Theory and Applications, pp. 149–156 (2005)

Learning 3D AAM Fitting with Kernel Methods

Marina A. Cidota[1], Dragos Datcu[2], and Leon J.M. Rothkrantz[2]

[1] Faculty of Mathematics and Computer Science, University of Bucharest,
Academiei Street No. 14, Bucharest, Romania
cidota@fmi.unibuc.ro
[2] Netherlands Defense Academy, Den Helder, The Netherlands
{D.Datcu,l.j.m.rothkrantz}@tudelft.nl

Abstract. The active appearance model (AAM) has proven to be a powerful tool for modeling deformable visual objects. AAMs are nonlinear parametric models in terms of the relation between the pixel intensities and the parameters of the model. In this paper, we propose a fitting procedure for a 3D AAM based on kernel methods for regression. The use of kernel functions provides a powerful way of detecting nonlinear relations using linear algorithms in an appropriate feature space. For analysis, we have chosen the relevance vector machines (RVM) and the kernel ridge method. The statistics computed on data generated with our 3D AAM implementation show that the kernel methods give better results compared to the linear regression models. Although they are less computational efficient, due to their higher accuracy the kernel methods have the advantage of reducing the searching space for the 3D AAM fitting algorithm.

Keywords: 3D-Active Appearance Models, nonlinear optimization, kernel methods.

1 Introduction

First proposed by Cootes et al. [3], the active appearance model (AAM) has attracted much interest in the computer vision community for modeling deformable visual objects. Using principal component analysis (PCA), the method allows a linear representation of both shape and texture.

In a typical application, the first step is to fit the AAM to an input image, i.e. model parameters are found to minimize the difference between the model instance and the input image. The model parameters may be used then in different applications, such as classification to yield a face recognition algorithm.

Despite its simplicity, the linear update model has been shown not to capture accurately the relationship between the AAM's texture residual and the optimal parameter updates. Fitting an AAM to an image is a non-linear optimization problem [13,14].

In this work, a fitting procedure based on kernel regression methods for a 3D implementation of AAM is proposed. Fitting an AAM to an image consists of minimizing the error between the input image and the closest model instance; i.e. solving a nonlinear optimization problem. In such a context, the RVM has proven to be an attractive technique because of the advantages it provides. The RVMs are based on a Bayesian

L. Rutkowski et al. (Eds.): ICAISC 2012, Part I, LNCS 7267, pp. 486–494, 2012.
© Springer-Verlag Berlin Heidelberg 2012

formulation of a linear model with the outputs being formulated as posterior probabilities in a sparse representation [1,18]. As a consequence, they can generalize well and provide inferences at low computational cost [1]. The advantages of a 3D implementation over a 2D AAM would be a more efficient detection for faces that are rotated in the 3D space and a more accurate modeling of faces for emotion recognition [5].

2 Related Work

In several papers, the detection of faces in images has been approached by deformable models which represent the variations in either shape or texture of the face object. The active shape models - ASM [4] and active appearance models - AAM [9] are two deformable models that have been extensively researched and used with good results in the literature. Point distribution models - PDMs relate to a class of methods used to represent flexible objects through sets of feature points that indicate deformable shapes. 3D face models have been proposed as an alternative to 2D face analysis for better handling the face pose and face gestures. Edwards et al. [9] introduced the AAM as a method to analyze faces using both shape and grey-level appearances. The spatial relationships are determined using principal components analysis - PCA that build statistical models of shape variation. In a similar way, statistical models of grey-level appearance are derived by applying PCA on shape-free samples obtained by wrapping the face images using triangulation. The models of shape appearance and grey-level appearance are finally combined using PCA, to derive appearance vectors that control both grey-level and shape data. Dornaika and Ahlberg [7] propose two appearance-based methods that use locally exhaustive and directed search for both simultaneous and decoupled computation of 3D head pose and facial expressions. Marcel et al. [11] use ASMs and local binary patterns - LBPs to localize the faces within image samples. Tong et al. [19] propose a two-level hierarchical face shape model to simultaneously characterize the global shape of a human face and the local structural details of each facial component. The shape variations of facial components are handled using multi-state local shape models. Datcu and Rothkrantz [6] proposed a bimodal semantic data fusion model that determines the most probable emotion. The approach uses 2D active appearance models and support vector machine classifiers. Lefvre and Odobez [10] present an approach that makes use of view-based templates learned online and an extension of a deformable 3D face model to collect appearance information from head sides and from the face. The method has a high robustness in tracking natural and fake facial actions as well as specific head movements.

3 Kernel Methods for Regression

3.1 Linear and Ridge Regression

Given a training set $S = \{(x_1, y_1), ..., (x_l, y_l)\}$ of points $x_i \in X \subseteq \Re^n$ with corresponding label $y_i \in Y \subseteq \Re$, we consider the problem of finding a linear function $g(x) = \langle w, x \rangle = w'x$ that best interpolates S [16]. The problem is reduced to determining the vector w that minimizes the loss function defined as:

$$L(w, S) = (y - Xw)'(y - Xw) \tag{1}$$

where X is the matrix whose rows are $x_1', ..., x_l'$ and $y = (y_1, ..., y_l)'$. If the inverse of $X'X$ exists, the solution is

$$w = (X'X)^{-1} X'y. \qquad (2)$$

If $X'X$ is singular, we can solve this linear problem using ridge regression that corresponds to the optimization problem

$$\min_w L_\lambda(w, S) = \min_w \left(\lambda \|w\|^2 + \sum_{i=1}^{l} (y_i - g(x_i))^2 \right), \qquad (3)$$

where λ is the trade-off between norm and loss and controls the degree of regularization. The dual solution is

$$g(x) = \langle w, x \rangle = y'(G + \lambda I_l)^{-1} \kappa, \qquad (4)$$

where $\kappa_i = \langle x_i, x \rangle$ and $G_{ij} = \langle x_i, x_j \rangle$.

3.2 Kernel Ridge Regression

If we consider the function Φ that transforms the initial data into a feature space F where the nonlinear pattern become linear

$$\Phi : x \in \Re^n \to \Phi(x) \in F \subseteq \Re^n \qquad (5)$$

then the kernel is defined as a function κ that satisfies

$$\kappa(x, z) = \langle \Phi(x), \Phi(z) \rangle \quad \text{for all } x, z \in X. \qquad (6)$$

The solution for the kernel ridge regression is

$$g(x) = \sum_{j=1}^{l} \alpha_j^* \kappa(x_j, x), \qquad (7)$$

where $\alpha^* = (K + \lambda I_l)^{-1} y$, $\lambda > 0$ and $K = (\kappa(x_i, x_j))_{i,j=1}^{l}$.

3.3 Relevance Vector Machine

The relevance vector machine (RVM) is a Bayesian sparse kernel technique for regression that shares many of the characteristics of the support vector machines (SVM) [1,18]. By a sparse solution we understand the fact that the outputs corresponding to new inputs depend only on the kernel function evaluated at a subset of the training data points. The smaller the subset is, the sparser the model we get. The RVM has two main advantages over the SVM. First, it leads to much sparser models while maintaining comparable generalization error and second, the hyperparameters governing complexity and noise variance are found automatically, whereas in the support vector machines the parameters C and ε are determined using cross-validation.

The non-linear relation between x and y can be expressed as

$$y(x) = \sum_{i=1}^{l} w_i \kappa(x, x_i) + b, \qquad (8)$$

where b is a bias parameter and κ is a kernel function. In contrast to the SVM, there is no restriction to positive definite kernels.

We assume that each target t_i is representative of the true model y_i, but with the addition of noise ε_i:

$$t_i = y_i + \varepsilon_i, \tag{9}$$

where ε_i are assumed to be independent samples from a Gaussian noise process with zero mean and variance σ^2, i.e. $\varepsilon_i \sim N(0; \sigma^2)$. This means that the RVM model can be defined as a conditional distribution for a real valued target variable t, given an input vector x

$$p(t|x, w, \beta) = N(t|y(x), \beta^{-1}), \tag{10}$$

where $N(x|\mu, \sigma^2)$ is the Gaussian distribution of mean μ and variance σ^2. Here $\beta = \sigma^{-2}$ is the noise precision.

The relevance vector machine is a specific instance of this model, whose parameters are determined using the maximum likelihood method.

4   The 3D Face Model

The 3D active appearance model was generated by combining a model of shape variation with a model of the appearance variations [3,8]. The 3D shapes were aligned in a 256×256 pixel frame such that the positions of the center of the eyes is the same for each of the faces we took from the Bosphorus database [15]. We used a training set of 102 3D labeled faces, each annotated with 111 landmark points. We apply a principal component analysis or PCA for the shapes, so any example can be approximated using

$$x = \bar{x} + P_s b_s, \tag{11}$$

where $\bar{x}$ is the mean shape, P_s is a set of orthogonal modes of variation and b_s is a set of shape parameters. For the statistical model of the appearance, first we warp each face so that its landmark points match those of the mean shape and second, we normalize the textures to minimize the effect of global lighting variations using the recursive method described in [8]. By applying PCA to the warped normalized textures, we obtain the linear model:

$$g = \bar{g} + P_g b_g, \tag{12}$$

where $\bar{g}$ is the mean normalized gray-level texture vector, shape, P_g is a set of orthogonal modes of variation and b_g is a set of shape parameters. Since there may be correlations between the shape and the texture, we apply a third PCA on the combined shape and texture vectors and thus we obtained a 68 element vector to represent a face in our 3D AAM.

5   Generating Data for the Regression Model

Each artificial face generated by the AAM is characterized by 2 vectors: a 6 element pose vector that gives the position and the orientation of the face in the 3D space and a

68 element vector from which we can reconstruct the shape and the gray-level normalized texture of the face. To be able to model a real face with an artificial one, we used a kernel regression model to learn these parameters based on error vectors computed as differences between a real image and one synthesized by the AAM. The components of the pose vector are: $(t_x, t_y, s\cos(\theta_x) - 1, s\sin(\theta_x), \theta_y, \theta_z)$ where t_x and t_y represent translations on the axes Ox, respectively Oy, s is the scale parameter and θ_x, θ_y and θ_z are the rotation angles around the three principle axes (Oz, Ox, Oy). The combination of the two parameters s and θ_x is useful in retaining linearity for the similarity transformations (translations, scaling and rotations) denoted by T, i.e. $T_{\delta t_1}(T_{\delta t_2}(x)) \approx T_{(\delta t_1 + \delta t_2)}(x)$ for small changes δt_1 and δt_2 [3].

For the pose experiments, we generated new faces with the 3D AAM, and for each face we applied a similarity transformation (one at a time). For example, in Figure 1 we translated a face with 10 pixels to the left. The difference between the mean face and the translated face is associated with the update value $\delta t_x = 10$ for the t_x parameter. We used 10 different faces for each value of a parameter.

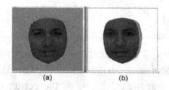

(a)   (b)

Fig. 1. (a) The mean face; (b) A new generated face, translated with 10 pixels to the left

For the appearance experiments we used all of the 102 faces that we took from the Bosphorus database. We tried to model the relation between the values for updating each of the 68 parameters and the error obtained as a difference between the mean face and a face from the database (see Figure 2).

(a)   (b)   (c)

Fig. 2. (a) The mean face; (b) A face from the database, reconstructed with the 3D AAM;(c) The image cut from (b) with the shape from (a)

6   Results

6.1   Simulations

To test the kernel regression models for the 3D AAM, we generated 240 pose and 102 appearance experiments and used the cross-validation method in comparing the results.

For each regression model, we considered randomly 66% of data for training and the rest of 33% for testing, and we repeated the simulation for one hundred times. Each time we compute the mean square error (MSE) for each regression model and based on these values we obtained the statistics displayed in Table 1 and Table 2. Each row in the tables refers to a single parameter (appearance or pose). We made a comparison between the kernel methods and the linear regression models. As kernel methods, we considered the kernel ridge regression and the RVM and for linear methods, we took the simple linear regression and the ridge regression.

For the kernel ridge regression and the RVM, we considered the Gaussian kernels for two reasons: they proved to work good for a many variety of applications and second, their properties have been extensively studied in neighboring fields [16]. The Gaussian kernels are defined as:

$$\kappa(x,z) = \exp\left(-\frac{\|x-z\|^2}{2\sigma^2}\right). \tag{13}$$

The parameter σ controls the capacity of learning and generalization for the models that use the Gaussian kernels. Small values of σ allow a good learning, but risk overfitting. On the other hand, large values of σ gradually reduce the kernel to a constant function. Usually, a good choice for σ depends on the magnitude of data and it is found using a cross validation method.

As a comparison basis between the four regression methods presented above, we used the mean square error (MSE) defined for the data set $S = \{(x_1,y_1),...,(x_l,y_l)\}$ as

$$MSE = \frac{1}{l}\sum_{i=1}^{l}(y_i - \hat{y}_i)^2, \tag{14}$$

where $\hat{y}_i$ is the output value of a regression model associated with the input x_i.

We can see from Tables 1 and 2 that the kernel methods give better results compared to the linear techniques. But the higher accuracy has the price of requiring a higher time complexity than the linear regression. Although, this disadvantage is compensated with a reduced searching space for the fitting algorithm.

The large values of MSE in Table 1 for the linear regression case are due to the near singularity of the matrix $X'X$ and from the loss of precision that occurs when the inverse matrix is computed. From the same table we can see that this problem is solved by a proper choice of the trade-off parameter λ that controls the degree of regularization in the linear ridge regression.

6.2   Testing the 3D Model on Real Faces

We implemented the 3D Active Appearance Model in C++/Matlab using the openGL and openCV libraries [2,17]. In the fitting module, we first apply the Viola-Jones algorithm to detect the face we want to model [20] and thus to reduce the searching space. For the initialization phase, we considered the idea suggested by the pseudo grand tour method in exploratory data analysis [12]. From this, we retain only the part with the projection of the data to a plane that is rotated through all possible angles, obtaining thus a continuous space-filling path through the manifold of planes. Through different

Table 1. Statistics for the MSE values for the first 6 appearance parameters

	RVM			kernel ridge regression		
	min	mean	max	min	mean	max
app1	0.0315	0.0566	0.1081	0.0240	0.0459	0.0864
app2	0.0250	0.0436	0.0813	0.0173	0.0329	0.0659
app3	0.0103	0.0231	0.0419	0.0063	0.0164	0.0337
app4	0.0061	0.0160	0.0356	0.0042	0.0121	0.0286
app5	0.0073	0.0181	0.0319	0.0054	0.0138	0.0250
app6	0.0078	0.0138	0.0244	0.0047	0.0108	0.0207

	ridge regression			linear regression		
	min	mean	max	min	mean	max
app1	0.1375	0.8373	3.1133	0.5952	162.0633	5961
app2	0.1386	0.5217	1.7150	0.2685	212.5090	1526.5
app3	0.0544	0.2256	1.1084	0.1734	140.0996	6942
app4	0.0345	0.1629	0.6975	0.0762	35.9547	1594
app5	0.0281	0.1713	0.7464	0.0638	71.5733	4313
app6	0.0243	0.1342	0.7212	0.0987	97.8225	3995

simulations, we reached the conclusion that in our problem 8 initialization points are enough to achieve reasonable results. We initialize the searching algorithm by positioning the mean shape in each one of these 8 points situated on a circle centered in the center of the frame returned by Viola-Jones algorithm. As for the regression method, we used the RVM because of its sparsity advantage over the kernel ridge regression. In Figure 3 we show the results obtained by running the fitting procedure for 4 faces taken from the training sample. In Figure 4 the results for fitting 4 new faces, also taken from the same database, are displayed. The white rectangles in both figures represent the searching space for the fitting algorithm and are obtained, as we already mentioned, by Viola-Jones face detection algorithm. From the tests we made with many other different faces we noticed that, in the cases of bad fitting, the problem is usually in the region around the mouth. A possible explanation could be the number of annotated faces (102 faces) we used for training our model, that don't cover a wide range of positions and shapes of lips.

Fig. 3. A good fitting results for faces used in our 3D AAM training

Fig. 4. Fitting results for new faces

Table 2. Statistics for the MSE values for the pose parameters

	RVM			kernel ridge regression		
	min	mean	max	min	mean	max
pose1	0.0326	0.1072	0.2255	0.0296	0.0685	0.1454
pose2	0.0336	0.2440	0.7031	0.0270	0.1130	0.3854
pose3	0.0593	0.1359	0.4126	0.0593	0.0939	0.2244
pose4	0.0319	0.0965	0.2192	0.0246	0.0632	0.1472
pose5	0.0749	0.1169	0.1846	0.0609	0.1004	0.1617
pose6	0.1725	0.3464	0.6822	0.1570	0.2622	0.4994

	ridge regression			linear regression		
	min	mean	max	min	mean	max
pose1	0.1052	0.3581	2.0127	0.1050	0.3561	2.0215
pose2	0.0674	0.2496	1.1061	0.0687	0.2564	1.2093
pose3	0.1519	0.6314	2.4635	0.1680	0.6993	3.0627
pose4	0.0652	0.1718	0.5874	0.0658	0.1716	0.6014
pose5	0.2044	0.7473	11.3829	0.2306	0.8623	13.7641
pose6	0.4437	1.4512	9.0153	0.4436	1.4167	9.0053

7 Conclusion

In this paper we proposed the kernel regression methods for solving the non-linear optimization problem of minimizing the error between the input image and the closest 3D AAM instance. As we could see from the tests we made, this approach brings a substantial improvement in comparison with the linear solutions. Despite its computational complexity, the advantage of providing a sparse non-linear solution makes the RVM an attractive alternative for implementing a fitting 3D AAM algorithm. To build and train the 3D AAM, we used 102 faces taken from the Bosphorus database. To improve the generalization for new faces, we intend to annotate more faces from the database in our future work.

Acknowledgments. This work was supported by the strategic grant POSDRU/89/1.5/S/ 58852, Project "Postdoctoral programme for training scientific researchers" cofinanced by the European Social Found within the Sectorial Operational Program Human Resources Development 2007-2013.

References

1. Bishop, C.: Pattern Recognition and Machine Learning, 1st edn. Springer Science+Business Media, New York (2006)
2. Bradski, G., Kaehler, A.: Learning OpenCV, 1st edn. Reilly Media, Inc., Sebastopol (2008)
3. Cootes, T., Edwards, G., Taylor, C.: Active Appearance Models. In: Burkhardt, H., Neumann, B. (eds.) ECCV 1998, Part II. LNCS, vol. 1407, pp. 484–498. Springer, Heidelberg (1998)
4. Cootes, T., Taylor, C.J., Cooper, D.H., Graham, J.: Active shape models: their training and application. Computer Vision and Image Understanding 61(1), 38–59 (1995)
5. Datcu, D., Rothkrantz, L.: The use of active appearance model for facial expression recognition in crisis environments. In: Proceedings of ISCRAM, pp. 515–524 (2007)
6. Datcu, D., Rothkrantz, L.: Semantic audio-visual data fusion for automatic emotion recognition. In: Euromedia 2008, Porto, Eurosis, Ghent, pp. 58–65 (April 2008) ISBN: 978-9077381-38-0
7. Dornaika, F., Ahlberg, J.: Fitting 3D face models for tracking and active appearance model training. Image and Vision Computing 24(9), 1010–1024 (2006)
8. Edwards, G., Taylor, C., Cootes, T.: Face Recognition Using Active Appearance Models. In: Burkhardt, H., Neumann, B. (eds.) ECCV 1998, Part II. LNCS, vol. 1407, pp. 581–595. Springer, Heidelberg (1998)
9. Edwards, G., Taylor, C., Cootes, T.: Interpreting face images using active appearance models. In: FG 1998: Proceedings of the 3rd International Conference on Face & Gesture Recognition. IEEE Computer Society, Washington, DC (1998)
10. Lefèvre, S., Odobez, J.M.: View-Based Appearance Model Online Learning for 3D Deformable Face Tracking. In: Proc. Int. Conf. on Computer Vision Theory and Applications (VISAPP), Angers (May 2010)
11. Marcel, S., Keomany, J., Rodriguez, Y.: Robust to illumination face localization using shape models and local binary patterns. Technical report, IDIAP (2006)
12. Martinez, W., Martinez, A.: Computational Statistics HandBook with MATLAB. Chapman&Hall/CRC, New York (2002)
13. Matthews, I., Baker, S.: Active appearance models revisited. International Journal of Computer Vision, 135–164 (2004)
14. Saragih, J., Gocke, R.: Learning aam fitting through simulation. Pattern Recognition (42), 2628–2636 (2009)
15. Savran, A., Alyüz, N., Dibeklioğlu, H., Çeliktutan, O., Gökberk, B., Sankur, B., Akarun, L.: Bosphorus Database for 3D Face Analysis. In: Schouten, B., Juul, N.C., Drygajlo, A., Tistarelli, M. (eds.) BIOID 2008. LNCS, vol. 5372, pp. 47–56. Springer, Heidelberg (2008)
16. Shawe-Taylor, J., Cristianini, N.: Kernel Methods for Pattern Analysis. Cambridge University Press, New York (2004)
17. Stegmann, M.: The AAM-API: An Open Source Active Appearance Model Implementation. In: Ellis, R.E., Peters, T.M. (eds.) MICCAI 2003. LNCS, vol. 2879, pp. 951–952. Springer, Heidelberg (2003)
18. Tipping, M.: Sparse bayesian learning and the relevance vector machine. The Journal of Machine Learning Research 1 (2001)
19. Tong, Y., Liao, W., Ji, Q.: Facial action unit recognition by exploiting their dynamic and semantic relationships. IEEE Transactions on Pattern Analysis and Machine Intelligence 29(10), 1683–1699 (2007)
20. Viola, P., Jones, M.: Robust real-time face detection. International Journal of Computer Vision 57(2), 137–154 (2004)

An Analytical Approach to the Image Reconstruction Problem Using EM Algorithm

Piotr Dobosz

Technical University of Czestochowa,
Departament of Computer Engineering,
Armii Krajowej 36, 42-200
Czestochowa, Poland

Abstract. In this paper an analytical iterative approach to the problem of image reconstruction from parallel projections is presented. The reconstruction process is performed using Expectation Minimization algorithm. Experimental results show that the appropriately designed reconstruction procedure is able to reconstruct an image with better quality than obtained using the traditional convolution/ back-projection algorithm.

1 Introduction

The image reconstruction from projections problem remains the primary concern for scientists in area of computed tomography. The images in computed tomography are obtained by applying a method of projections acquisition and an appropriate image reconstruction algorithm. There are several well-known reconstruction methods to solve this problem. The most popular reconstruction algorithms are these using filtered back-projection methodology (FBP) and the algebraic reconstruction technique (ART) [1]. Beside those methods, there exist iterative reconstruction techniques which can be exploited to reduce influence of the measurement noise on quality of the reconstructed image [2]. Recently, statistical reconstruction methods, such as the maximum *a posteriori* probability (MAP) algebraic approach, are dynamically developed (see e.g. [3]). It seems to be more feasible to implement reconstruction algoritms based on algebraic methodology of image processing, such as was presented in the following papers [4], [5], [6], [7]. Thanks to its analytical origins, the reconstruction method formulated in this way avoids most of the difficulties connected with the use of ART methodology. Although it is necessary to establish certain coefficients in analytical approach, this can be performed much more easily than in ART methods. Additionally, this concept can be extended in easy way on spiral cone-beam geometry of scanner. In our paper, we show a new approach to this concept, where the Expected Maximization (EM) algorithm instead of the gradient methods is used. We show that the analytical approach to the image reconstruction from projections problem with implemented EM algorithm can give some benefits. In particular, it is a convergence acceleration of the iterative algorithm, and quality improving of reconstructed image (in this case in absence of measurement noise).

L. Rutkowski et al. (Eds.): ICAISC 2012, Part I, LNCS 7267, pp. 495–500, 2012.

2 Image Reconstruction Algorithm

Described in this paper a reconstruction algorithm for scanner with parallel x-ray beams is based on designed earlier reconstruction method presented in papers [4], [5], [6], [7]. The scheme of the proposed reconstruction method using the Expected Maximization algorithm is shown in Fig.1, where the parallel-beam geometry of collected projections is taken into consideration.

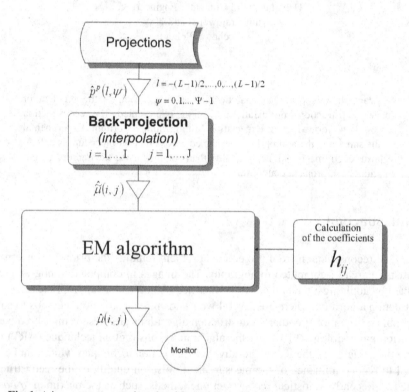

Fig. 1. A image reconstruction algorithm with parallel-beam geometry of the scanner

2.1 The Back-Projection Operation

Suppose that function $\mu(x,y)$ discribes a distribution of the attenuation coefficient of x-rays in an investigated cross-section. The first step in the proceeding sequence is the standart back-projection operation (see e.g. in [7]). It is highly probable that for any given projection no ray passes through a certain point (x,y) of the image. To establish a projection value for a ray passing through this point we can apply interpolation expressed by the following relation

$$\dot{p}(\dot{s},\alpha) = \int\limits_{-\infty}^{+\infty} p(s,\alpha) \cdot Int(\dot{s}-s)\,ds, \qquad (1)$$

where $Int(\Delta s)$ is an interpolation function. After the back-projection operation we obtain a blurred image $\tilde{\mu}(x,y)$ which can be expressed by the following expression

$$\tilde{\mu}(x,y) = \int_0^\pi \dot{p}(s,\alpha)\,d\alpha. \tag{2}$$

Taking into account relations (1) and (2) it is possible to define the obtained, after back-projection operation, image in the following way

$$\tilde{\mu}(x,y) = \int_{-\infty}^{+\infty}\int_{-\infty}^{+\infty} \mu(\ddot{x},\ddot{y})\left(\int_0^\pi I(\ddot{x}\cos\alpha + \ddot{y}\sin\alpha - x\cos\alpha - y\sin\alpha)\,d\alpha\right)d\ddot{x}d\ddot{y}. \tag{3}$$

In further considerations we will take into account the discrete form of images $\mu(x,y)$ and $\tilde{\mu}(x,y)$. In this case, we present approximation of the relation (3) as follows

$$\hat{\mu}(i,j) \approx \sum_k \sum_l \hat{\mu}(l,k)\cdot h(i-k,j-l), \tag{4}$$

where

$$h(\Delta i, \Delta j) = \Delta_\alpha(\Delta_s)^2\cdot\sum_{\psi=0}^{\Psi-1} I(i\Delta_s\cos\psi\Delta_\alpha + j\Delta_s\sin\psi\Delta_\alpha), \tag{5}$$

and $i,k = 0,1,\ldots,I$; $j,l = 0,1,\ldots,J$; I and J are numbers of pixels in horizontal and vertical directions, respectively.

As one can see from equation (4), the image obtained after back-projection operation is equal to the amalgamation of this image and the geometrical distortion element given by (5).

The number of coefficients $h_{\Delta i,\Delta j}$ is equal to $I\cdot J$ and owing to expression (5) values of these coefficients can be easily calculated in numerical way.

2.2 The Reconstruction Process Using EM-Type Algorithm

According to the considerations of Snyder et al. [8], the deconvolution problem (deblurring problem) can be presented in the following scheme

$$\int_{x\in X} h(\mathbf{y}|\mathbf{x})c(\mathbf{x})\,d\mathbf{x} = a(\mathbf{y}), \tag{6}$$

where $a(\mathbf{y})$; $\mathbf{y}\in \mathbf{Y}$ is an observed function, $h(\mathbf{y}|\mathbf{x})$ is a blurring kernel, $c(\mathbf{x})$ is a function which has to be reconstructed.

An iterative reconstruction algorithm was proposed in [8] which minimizes monotonically Csiszár I-divergence (it is worth to note that this divergence is a generalization of the Kullback-Leibler divergence). That divergence is observed between a reconstructed function $c(\mathbf{x})$ and a based on measurement function $a(\mathbf{y})$. The original iterative deblurring algorithm was written in the following way

$$c_{t+1}(\mathbf{x}) = c_t(\mathbf{x}) \frac{1}{H(\mathbf{x})} \cdot \int\limits_{\mathbf{y} \in Y} \frac{h(\mathbf{y}|\mathbf{x})}{\int\limits_{\mathbf{x} \in X} h(\mathbf{y}|\mathbf{x})c_t(\mathbf{x})} a(\mathbf{y}) d\mathbf{y}, \tag{7}$$

where

$$H(\mathbf{x}) = \int\limits_{\mathbf{y} \in Y} h(\mathbf{y}|\mathbf{x}) d\mathbf{y}, \tag{8}$$

and $c_{t+1}(\mathbf{x})$; $c_t(\mathbf{x})$ are current and updated versions of the functions $c(\mathbf{x})$, respectively.

Taking into account the form of the invariant system (4) and basing on the scheme (8), we can formulate an iterative EM-type reconstruction algorithm as follows

$$\hat{\mu}_{t+1}(i,j) = \hat{\mu}_t(i,j) \frac{\hat{\mu}(i,j)}{\sum_k \sum_l \hat{\mu}_t(l,k) \cdot h(i-k,j-l)}. \tag{9}$$

Above iterative expression is fundamental for our new concept of image reconstruction procesure.

3   Experimental Results

A mathematical model of the projected object, a so-called phantom, is used to obtain projections during simulations. The most common matematical phantom of head was proposed by Kak (see eg. [9]). In our experiment the size of the image was fixed at $I \times J = 128 \times 128$ pixels.

The discret approximation of the interpolation operation expressed by equation (5) takes the form

$$\hat{p}(s,\psi) = \sum_{l=-L/2}^{L/2-1} \hat{p}(l,\psi) \cdot I(s - l\Delta_\psi). \tag{10}$$

The interpolation function $Int(\Delta s)$ can be defined for example as linear interpolation function

$$Int_L(\Delta s) = \begin{cases} \frac{1}{\Delta_s}\left(1 - \frac{|\Delta s|}{\Delta_s}\right) & if\,|\Delta s| \geq \Delta_s \\ 0, & if\,|\Delta s| > \Delta_s \end{cases}, \tag{11}$$

where $\Delta s = (i\cos\psi\Delta_\alpha + j\sin\psi\Delta_\alpha)$.

The obtained after back-projection operation image was next subject to a process of reconstruction using iterative reconstruction process described by (9).

The differences between reconstructed images obtained using: the standart convolution/back-projection method using Shep-Logan kernel, the gradient descent algorithm described in in papers [4], [5], [6], [7], and presented originally in this paper algorithm are depicted in Fig. 3. For comparison, the original image in Fig. 2 is shown.

Fig. 2. Original image: the Shepp-Logan mathematical model of the head

The quality of the reconstructed image has been evaluated in this case by error measure defined as follows

$$MSE = \frac{1}{I \cdot J} \sum_{i=1}^{I} \sum_{j=1}^{J} [\mu(i,j) - \hat{\mu}(i,j)]^2, \tag{12}$$

where discrete function $\mu(i,j)$ describes an original image of reconstructed cross-section.

These images are obtained using window described in [10]. In this case we used the following parameters of the window $C = 1.02$, $W = 0.2$.

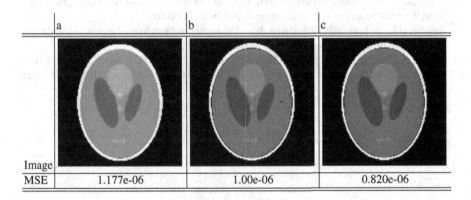

Image	a	b	c
MSE	1.177e-06	1.00e-06	0.820e-06

Fig. 3. View of the reconstructed image using: standard reconstruction method (convoluation/back-projection with rebinning method) (a); reconstruction algorithm with gradient descent optimization (b); EM-type reconstruction algorithm described in this paper (c)

4   Conclusions

The carried out computer simulations demonstrated a stability of the image reconstruction process using EM-type methodology. Presented in this paper algorithm converges to the solution much faster than reconstruction using the gradient descent optimization strategy. The reconstructed image obtained after 2000 iterations, shown in Fig.2, has achieved better level of quality in comparison to the result of the standard convolution/back-projection method. Our iterative reconstruction algorithm can be in the easy way reformulated to the form of neural network structure, what allows to parallize the performed calculations.

References

1. Cierniak, R.: Tomografia komputerowa. Akademicka Oficyna Wydawnicza EXIT, Warsaw (2005)
2. Cierniak, R.: X-ray computed tomography in biomedical engineering. Springer, London (2011)
3. Thibault, J.-B., Sauer, K.D., Bouman, C.A., Hsieh, J.: A three-dimensional statistical approach to improved image quality for multislice helical CT. Medical Physics 34, 4526–4544 (2007)
4. Cierniak, R.: A new approach to image reconstruction from projections problem using a recurrent neural network. Applied Mathematics and Computer Science 18, 147–157 (2008)
5. Cierniak, R.: A new approach to tomographic image reconstruction using a Hopfield-type neural network. International Journal Artificial Intelligence in Medicine 43, 113–125 (2008)
6. Cierniak, R.: A Novel Approach to Image Reconstruction Problem from Fan-Beam Projections Using Recurrent Neural Network. In: Rutkowski, L., Tadeusiewicz, R., Zadeh, L.A., Zurada, J.M. (eds.) ICAISC 2008. LNCS (LNAI), vol. 5097, pp. 752–761. Springer, Heidelberg (2008)
7. Cierniak, R.: New neural network algorithm for image reconstruction from fan-beam projections. Elsevier Science: Neurocomputing 72, 3238–3244 (2009)
8. Snyder, D.L., Schulz, T.J., O'Sullivan, J.A.: Deblurring subject to nonnegativity constraints. IEEE Trans. on Signal Processing 40, 1143–1150 (1992)
9. Jain, A.K.: Fundamentals of Digital Image Processing. Prentice Hall, New Jersey (1989)
10. Kak, A.C., Slanley, M.: Principles of Computerized Tomographic Imaging. IEEE Press, New York (1988)

Recognition of Two-Dimensional Shapes Based on Dependence Vectors

Krzysztof Gdawiec and Diana Domańska

Institute of Computer Science, University of Silesia, Poland
kgdawiec@ux2.math.us.edu.pl, ddomanska@poczta.onet.pl

Abstract. The aim of this paper is to present a new method of two-dimensional shape recognition. The method is based on dependence vectors which are fractal features extracted from the partitioned iterated function system. The dependence vectors show the dependency between range blocks used in the fractal compression. The effectiveness of our method is shown on four test databases. The first database was created by the authors and the other ones are: MPEG7 CE-Shape-1PartB, Kimia-99, Kimia-216. Obtained results have shown that the proposed method is better than the other fractal recognition methods of two-dimensional shapes.

1 Introduction

Nowadays recognition of objects is very important task. Because of that the research on methods of recognition is very intensive and most diverse area of machine vision. Often object is represented by its shape so good shape descriptors and matching measures are the central issue in the research. The shape descriptors can be divided into two groups: based on the silhouette and based on the contour of the object. In both of the groups there are many known methods [1].

From the beginning fractals gain much attention. First in the computer graphics, because the images of fractals were perceived as very interesting and beautiful. Later fractals found applications in other areas of our life, e.g. in economics, medicine, image compression [2]. With the help of fractals we were able to represent real world objects much better than with the help of the classical Euclidean geometry, so this was the motivation to use fractal as a shape descriptor for the recognition. The methods based on fractal description of the shape found applications in: face recognition [3], character recognition [9], general recognition method [10], etc.

In the paper we present a new method which is based on fractal features. The features are called dependence vectors and are extracted from the partitioned iterated function system, which is obtained from the fractal compression of the image containing the object.

In Section 2 we briefly introduce the definition of a fractal and the fractal compression scheme, which will be later used in our method. Next, in Section 3

L. Rutkowski et al. (Eds.): ICAISC 2012, Part I, LNCS 7267, pp. 501–508, 2012.

we present the notion of dependence vectors and a method of recognizing two-dimensional shapes. Later, in Section 4 we give the description of conducted experiments and used test bases. Finally, in Section 5 we give some conclusions.

2   Fractals and Fractal Image Compression

In this section we will present the fractal image compression scheme used later in the proposed recognition method. But first we need to introduce the notion of a fractal, because there are several non-equivalent definitions. The definition we use in this work is fractal as attractor [2].

First we must define the notion of an iterated function system (IFS) [2].

Definition 1. *Let (X, d) be a metric space. We say that a set of mappings $W = \{w_1, \ldots, w_N\}$, where $w_n : X \to X$ is a contraction mapping for $i = 1, \ldots, N$ is an iterated function system.*

Any IFS $W = \{w_1, \ldots, w_N\}$ determines the so-called Hutchinson operator which is contrative mapping on the space $(\mathcal{H}(X), h)$, where $\mathcal{H}(X)$ is the space of non-empty, compact subsets of X and h is the Haussdorf distance [2]. The Hutchinson operator is given by following formula:

$$\forall_{A \in \mathcal{H}(X)} \quad W(A) = \bigcup_{n=1}^{N} w_n(A) = \bigcup_{n=1}^{N} \{w_n(a) : a \in A\}. \tag{1}$$

Definition 2. *We say that the limit $\lim_{n \to \infty} W^k(A)$, where $A \in \mathcal{H}(X)$ is called an attractor of the IFS $W = \{w_1, \ldots, w_N\}$.*

The fractals poses the property of self-similarity, i.e. any part of the fractal is similar to the whole fractal. The real world objects do not have this property. Instead they have partial self-similarity, i.e. smaller parts of object are similar to bigger parts of the object [7]. The fractal image compression is based on the partial self-similarity and the notion of a partitioned iterated function system (PIFS).

Definition 3. *We say that a set $P = \{(F_1, A_1), \ldots, (F_N, A_N)\}$ is a partitioned iterated function system, where F_n is a contraction mapping and A_n is an area of the image which is transformed with the help of F_n for $n = 1, \ldots, N$.*

In practice as the mappings from the Definition 3 we use affine mappings of the space $\mathbb{R}^3$ of the following form:

$$F\left(\begin{bmatrix} x \\ y \\ z \end{bmatrix}\right) = \begin{bmatrix} a_1 & a_2 & 0 \\ a_3 & a_4 & 0 \\ 0 & 0 & a_7 \end{bmatrix} \begin{bmatrix} x \\ y \\ z \end{bmatrix} + \begin{bmatrix} a_5 \\ a_6 \\ a_8 \end{bmatrix}, \tag{2}$$

where coefficients $a_1, \ldots, a_6 \in \mathbb{R}$ describe a geometric transformation, coefficients $a_7, a_8 \in \mathbb{R}$ are responsible for the contrast and brightness and x, y are the co-ordinates in image, z is pixel intensity.

In the coding scheme given later we have two types of blocks: range and domain. The set of range blocks consists of non-overlapping blocks of the same size that cover the image. The number of range blocks is fixed before we start the coding. The set of domain blocks consists of overlapping blocks bigger than the range blocks (usually two times bigger) and transformed using four mappings: identity, rotation through 180°, two symmetries of a rectangle.

The fractal coding scheme is following:

1. Create a set of range blocks $\mathcal{R}$ and domain blocks $\mathcal{D}$.
2. For each range block $R \in \mathcal{R}$ find domain block $D \in \mathcal{D}$ such that

$$D = \arg \min_{D' \in \mathcal{D}} \rho(R, F(D')), \tag{3}$$

where ρ is a metric (usually Euclidean), F is a mapping of the form (2) determined by the position of R and D', the size of the blocks in relation to itself, one of the four mappings used to transform D' and the coefficients a_7, a_8 are calculated by following formulas:

$$a_7 = \frac{k \sum_{i=1}^{k} g_i h_i - \sum_{i=1}^{k} g_i \sum_{i=1}^{k} h_i}{k \sum_{i=1}^{k} g_i^2 - \left(\sum_{i=1}^{k} g_i\right)^2}, \tag{4}$$

$$a_8 = \frac{1}{k} \left[\sum_{i=1}^{k} h_i - a_7 \sum_{i=1}^{k} g_i \right], \tag{5}$$

where k is the number of pixels in the range block, $g_1, \ldots, g_k$ are the pixel intensities of the transformed and resized domain block, $h_1, \ldots, h_k$ are the pixel intensities of the range block. If $k \sum_{i=1}^{k} g_i^2 - \left(\sum_{i=1}^{k} g_i\right)^2 = 0$, then $a_7 = 0$ and $a_8 = \frac{1}{k} \sum_{i=1}^{k} h_i$.
3. Remember the coefficients of F and block D.

The search process in step 2 is the most time-consuming step of the coding algorithm [7].

This algorithm is very simple and therefore used only in fractal image recognition. Moreover, in recognition of two-dimensional shapes in binary images the coefficients a_7 and a_8 are omitted. In practice, when we compress an image we use adaptive methods of partitioning such as quad-tree, HV partition and others [7].

3   Dependence Vectors Method

In our previous works [4] [5] [6] we have shown some weaknesses of the fractal recognition methods and how to improve them. In [5] [6] we proposed division of the image into sub-images and compression of each sub-image independently. Better improvement was obtained in [4] using the pseudofractal approach in which we use fixed image as the source for domain blocks in the fractal compression algorithm. The pseudofractal approach will be used in the proposed method which we call dependence vectors method (DVM).

Before we give the dependence vectors method we need to introduce the definition of the dependence vectors.

Definition 4. *Let W be the PIFS with a set o range blocks $\mathcal{R}$. For each $R \in \mathcal{R}$ we define* dependence vectors *of R as a set of vectors between the range block R and the range blocks that overlap the domain block corresponding to R. Set $V = \{V^1, \ldots, V^N\}$, where V^i are dependence vectors of R_i for $i = 1, \ldots, |\mathcal{R}|$ is* called *set of dependence vectors.*

Figure 1 presents one range blocks, corresponding domain block (bold line), range blocks that overlap the domain block (dashed grey line) and the dependence vectors.

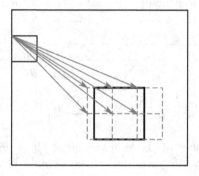

Fig. 1. Range block and its dependence vectors

The DVM method is following:

1. extract object from the image,
2. find a set o correct orientations Γ,
3. choose a correct orientation $\gamma \in \Gamma$ and rotate the object through γ,
4. resize the image to 128×128 pixels,
5. find normalized PIFS W using the pseudofractal approach,
6. determine the set of dependence vectors V_W of W,
7. in the base $\mathcal{B}$ find a set of dependence vectors V such that

$$V = \arg \min_{V_B \in \mathcal{B}} \sum_{i=1}^{N} h(V_B^i, V_W^i), \tag{6}$$

   where N is the number of range blocks, h is the Haussdorf distance based on the Euclidean distance,
8. choose an image from the base which corresponds to V.

Some of the points in the method need further explanations. First one is the notion of correct orientation. A correct orientation is an angle by which we need to rotate an object so that it fulfils following conditions: area of the bounding box is the smallest, height of the bounding box is smaller than the width and the left half of the object has at least as many pixels as the right. The correct orientation is needed because we want the method to be rotation invariant.

Resizing the image to 128 × 128 pixels is used to speed up the fractal coding process and the normalization is needed to make the method translation and scale invariant.

4   Experiments

To show effectiveness of the proposed method we compare it with other existing fractal methods. These methods are: Neil-Curtis method (NC) [10], Multiple Mapping Vector Accumulator (MMVA) [9], method which uses the PIFS coefficients (CM) [3], Mapping Vectors Similarity Method (MVSM) [5], Fractal Dependence Graph Method (FDGM) [6]. All the methods will be tested in the original form. Moreover all the methods, except the Neil-Curtis method, will be tested using the pseudofractal approach presented by the authors in [4] and in this case the abbreviations of the methods will begin with the letter P, e.g. PMMVA for the pseudofractal MMVA.

In the test we used division into 16 × 16 range blocks, so PIFS consists of 256 transformations. As the source for domain blocks in the pseudofractal approach we used one image showed in Fig. 2.

The description of the databases used in the tests and the obtained results are shown in the next subsections.

Fig. 2. Source for the domain blocks used in the tests

4.1   Authors Base

Our base consists of three datasets. In each of the datasets we have 5 classes of objects, 20 images per class. In the first dataset we have base objects changed by elementary transformations, i.e. rotation, scaling, translation. In the second dataset we have objects changed by elementary transformations and we add small changes to the shape locally, e.g. shapes are cut and/or they have something added. Finally, in the third set, similar to the other two sets, the objects

were modified by elementary transformations and we add to the shape large
changes locally. The large changes are made in such a way that the shape is still
recognizable.

In the tests on our three datasets to estimate the error rate we used leave-
one-out method. The results of the tests are shown in Tables 1(a)-1(c). From
the Table 1(a) we see that the lowest values of error (2%) obtained almost all
methods so we can say that they are robust to elementary transformations. For
the base with locally small changes (Table 1(b)) we see that the best result
(2%) was obtained by the PPMVA method. The proposed method with other
two methods (PMVSM, PFDGM) obtained error rate equal to 3%. Finally, from
the Table 1(c) we see that the proposed method with the PFDGM method
obtained the best result (3%). Two other methods: PMMVA and PCM obtained
error rate equal to 4% and the rest of the methods obtained error rate greater
than 10%.

Table 1. Results of the test for the authors base

(a) elementary		(b) locally small		(c) locally large	
Method	Error [%]	Method	Error [%]	Method	Error [%]
DVM	2.0	DVM	3.0	DVM	3.0
NC	2.0	NC	4.0	NC	11.0
MMVA	10.0	MMVA	18.0	MMVA	32.0
PMMVA	2.0	PMMVA	2.0	PMMVA	4.0
CM	4.0	CM	11.0	CM	37.0
PCM	2.0	PCM	4.0	PCM	4.0
MVSM	3.0	MVSM	6.0	MVSM	14.0
PMVSM	2.0	PMVSM	3.0	PMVSM	10.0
FDGM	2.0	FDGM	6.0	FDGM	14.0
PFDGM	2.0	PFDGM	3.0	PFDGM	3.0

4.2   MPEG7 CE-Shape-1 Part B Database

The MPEG7 CE-Shape-1 Part B database [8] consists of 1400 silhouette images
from 70 classes. Each class has 20 different shapes.

For the estimation of the error rate we used the stratified 10-fold cross validation. The obtained results are shown in Table 2. From the results we see that
the proposed method obtained the lowest value of the error (13.15%). Moreover
we see that the pseudofractal versions of the methods have values of the error
very close to the error of the DVM method.

4.3   Kimia Databases

The Kimia-99 database [11] consists of object images from 9 different classes. In
each class we have 11 shapes. The last database used in the test is Kimia-216
[11]. The base consist of 216 images selected from the MPEG7 CE-Shape-1 Part
B. The images are divided into 18 classes, 12 images per class.

Table 2. Results of the test for the MPEG7 CE-Shape-1 Part B base

Method	Error [%]
DVM	13.15
NC	29.45
MMVA	49.03
PMMVA	19.22
CM	52.74
PCM	18.15
MVSM	30.45
PMVSM	17.58
FDGM	35.88
PFDGM	14.72

Like in the case of authors base for the Kimia databases we used the leave-one-out method for the estimation of the error rate. The obtained results for the Kimia-99 are shown in Table 3(a) and for Kimia-216 in Table 3(b). From the obtained results we clearly see that the DVM method obtained the best results (12.12% for the Kimia-99, 13.42% for the Kimia-216). Similarly like for the MPEG7 base only the pseudofractal versions of the methods obtained results close to the best result.

Table 3. Results of the test for the Kimia bases

(a) Kimia-99			(b) Kimia-216	
Method	Error [%]		Method	Error [%]
DVM	12.12		DVM	13.42
NC	15.15		NC	14.81
MMVA	45.45		MMVA	33.79
PMMVA	17.17		PMMVA	14.81
CM	43.43		CM	31.48
PCM	14.14		PCM	14.81
MVSM	32.32		MVSM	27.31
PMVSM	22.22		PMVSM	17.12
FDGM	29.29		FDGM	26.38
PFDGM	13.13		PFDGM	14.35

5   Conclusions

In the paper we have presented a new method of two-dimensional shape recognition, which we called Dependence Vectors Method. In the method as the features we used dependence vectors and also we used the psuedofractal approach proposed by the authors in [4]. The experiments have shown that the proposed method obtained smaller error rates comparing to the other known fractal recognition methods.

In our further work we will concentrate on improving the effectiveness of our method with the help of using different types of classifiers, other similarity measures. Moreover we will conduct further research to check if the pseudofractal approach depends on the image chosen for the creation of the domain set. All the tested methods used descriptors from the whole shape, so we will try to find contour descriptor which is based on fractal description.

References

1. Amit, Y.: 2D Object Detection and Recognition: Models, Algorithms, and Networks. MIT Press, Cambridge (2002)
2. Barnsley, M.: Fractals Everywhere. Academic Press, Boston (1988)
3. Chandran, S., Kar, S.: Retrieving Faces by the PIFS Fractal Code. In: Proceedings 6th IEEE Workshop on Applications of Computer Vision, pp. 8–12 (December 2002)
4. Gdawiec, K.: Pseudofractal 2D Shape Recognition. In: Yu, J., Greco, S., Lingras, P., Wang, G., Skowron, A. (eds.) RSKT 2010. LNCS (LNAI), vol. 6401, pp. 403–410. Springer, Heidelberg (2010)
5. Gdawiec, K.: Shape Recognition Using Partitioned Iterated Function Systems. In: Cyran, K.A., Kozielski, S., Peters, J.F., Stańczyk, U., Wakulicz-Deja, A. (eds.) Man-Machine Interactions. AISC, vol. 59, pp. 451–458. Springer, Heidelberg (2009)
6. Gdawiec, K., Domańska, D.: Partitioned Iterated Function Systems with Division and Fractal Dependence Graph in Recognition of 2D Shapes. International Journal of Applied Mathematics and Computer Science 21(4), 757–767 (2011)
7. Fisher, Y.: Fractal Image Compression: Theory and Application. Springer, New York (1995)
8. Latecki, L.J., Lakamper, R., Eckhardt, T.: Shape Descriptors for Non-rigid Shapes with a Single Closed Contour. In: Proceedings IEEE Conference on Computer Vision and Pattern Recognition, vol. 1, pp. 424–429 (June 2000)
9. Mozaffari, S., Faez, K., Faradji, F.: One Dimensional Fractal Coder for Online Signature Recognition. In: Proceedings of the 18th International Conference on Pattern Recognition, vol. 2, pp. 857–860 (August 2006)
10. Neil, G., Curtis, K.M.: Shape Recognition Using Fractal Geometry. Pattern Recognition 30(12), 1957–1969 (1997)
11. Sebastian, T.B., Klein, P.N., Kimia, B.B.: Recognition of Shapes by Editing Their Shock Graphs. IEEE Transactions on Pattern Analysis and Machine Intelligence 26(5), 550–571 (2004)

Ranking by K-Means Voting Algorithm for Similar Image Retrieval

Przemysław Górecki, Krzysztof Sopyła, and Paweł Drozda

Department of Mathematics and Computer Sciences,
University of Warmia and Mazury, Olsztyn, Poland
{pgorecki,pdrozda}@matman.uwm.edu.pl, ksopyla@uwm.edu.pl

Abstract. Recently, the field of CBIR has attracted a lot of attention in the literature. In this paper, the problem of visually similar image retrieval has been investigated. For this task we use the methods derived from the Bag of Visual Words approach, such as Scale Invariant Feature Transform (SIFT) for identifying image keypoints and K-means to build a visual dictionary. To create a ranking of similar images, a novel Ranking by K-means Voting algorithm is proposed. The experimental section shows that our method works well for similar image retrieval. It turned out that our results are more accurate in comparison with a classical similarity measure based on the Euclidean metric in the order of 6% - 15%.

Keywords: Image ranking, CBIR, SIFT, K-means.

1 Introduction

The amount of information available on the Internet is increasing at a tremendous rate in recent times. This necessitates the need to develop methods and algorithms to effectively search in large data collections [14]. The first systems which dealt with this problem have focused on textual information retrieval. The development of image processing and computer vision methods allowed us to search for information encoded in images, giving birth to Content Based Image Retrieval (CBIR).

CBIR systems allow users to query for relevant images either using words describing the content of the image, or using an example image provided by the user. This paper studies the latter approach. In particular, we focus on the problem of retrieving images which contain similar object within a specific category. This issue is of major importance and is examined in many scientific fields. For instance, eCommerce offers the possibility to search for a similar products (like bags, shoes, watches, etc.), which greatly facilitates finding the right product [17]. Medicine is another area that should be mentioned, where CBIR is widely used and is of great importance [1]. In radiology, CBIR techniques assist radiologists in the assessment of medical images and accurate diagnosing by allowing to search for similar images.

L. Rutkowski et al. (Eds.): ICAISC 2012, Part I, LNCS 7267, pp. 509–517, 2012.

Existing CBIR methods are widely based on the well-known descriptors, described in Section 2. These descriptors encode the image features concerning color, texture, shapes and the length of edges, which are then subsequently employed to measure the similarity between images. Recent scientific reports [4] introduced the dictionary methods (Bag of Words), previously applied successfully in Information Retrieval, in the field of image analysis. Bag of Visual Words technique (BoVW) introduces the image representation as a vector containing frequency of similar image patches.

In order to obtain such representation, one should perform the detection of image keypoints. The most frequently used keypoint detectors are Speeded Up Robust Features (SURF) [3] and Scale-Invariant Feature Transform (SIFT) [18]. After the image representation is obtained, it is possible to create the ranking of similar images on the basis of a similarity measure, such as the Euclidean distance.

This paper takes advantage of Bag of Visual Words and SIFT detector to obtain image representations, while for similarity ranking we introduce a novel method, called Ranking by K-means Voting algorithm, where the clustering is repeated multiple times to get the images ranked by similarity.

The paper is organized as follows. In the next section we review the existing image feature extraction algorithms as well as various image representations. Section 3 describes the chosen methods and the main contribution of this work: Ranking by K-means Voting algorithm. Next, section 4 evaluates the proposed approach based on experimental results. We conclude the article and discuss future directions in section 5.

2   State of the Art

In every CBIR system, two main components can be identified. The first one, called feature extractor, is intended to quantitatively express the information encoded in the basic elements of the image, such as color and texture, edges, shapes or spatial layout of objects. The second one, called ranking component, uses the previously extracted features to calculate the similarity between the query image and all other images in the dataset. It can be accomplished using the simple similarity measure, or more complex approach such as machine-learned ranking [11]. In this paper we propose the ranking component based on unsupervised clustering.

Regarding the feature extraction process, we can distinguish methods which capture the global characteristics of an image (global feature extraction) as well as those which indicate locally relevant areas, known as keypoints. Global feature-based algorithms strive to imitate the human way of perception, that is to discern an object in the picture as a whole. The most popular methods are based on color histograms. In particular, in [6] the classic color histogram is proposed, authors of [8] introduce Fuzzy Color Histogram, while in [10] Color Correlogram method is used. Another way of dealing with global feature extraction is related to the study of information encoded in the image texture. Examples of the algorithms that follow this approach are Steerable Pyramid [21], Gabor Wavelet Transform [9], Contourlet Transform [5] or Complex Directional Filter Bank [23].

Global features algorithms are generally considered to be simple and fast, which often results in the lack of invariance to change of perspective or illumination. To overcome these problems local features methods were introduced [16]. For instance, Schmid and Mohr [20] utilize Harris corner detector to identify interest points which is insensitive to change of image orientation.

Lowe [18] introduced Scale Invariant Feature Transform (SIFT), which proved to be robust against variations in rotation, scale and light intensity. The improvement of the SIFT method can be found in Ke & Sukthankar paper [12]. The authors apply Principal Components Analysis (PCA) for relevant keypoints selection, which results in an increased resistance against image deformations. Finally, Bay et al. proposed Speeded Up Robust Feature (SURF) detector [3], which is several times faster then SIFT while retaining similar stability extracted keypoints.

On the basis of the extracted features the image representation can be formed, which is used for the purpose of determining the similarity between any given images. In case of Bag of Visual Words technique [4] image representation consists of histogram of local image features. Such representation does not encode any spatial relationships. In contrast, representations based on graph theory can be applied [1] if interrelation of features is essential eg. their relative spatial distribution. The choice of image representation has a significant impact on the manner in which the similarity is calculated. In case of feature vectors, it is common to use distance functions, i.e. Euclidean or cosine distance. On the other hand, when an image is represented by a graph, the similarity is defined as graph matching [13] or by the effort required to transform one graph into another [2].

Many of the techniques described above were implemented in the existing CBIR systems, from which the following are worth mentioning: ALIPR `alipr.com` automatic photo tagging and visual image search, BRISC a pulmonary nodule image retrieval framework [15], Tineye `tineye.com` commercial online visual search or `like.com` system for visual shopping.

3 Methodology

This section presents the details of our CBIR method. The feature extraction phase involves creation of the visual words dictionary for which SIFT [18] and k-means algorithms are applied. Then, for the given query image, the ranking of similar images is formed using the Ranking by K-means Voting algorithm detailed in section 3.3. Finally, the accuracy of the proposed method is assessed in the experimental session.

3.1 Dictionary of Visual Words

It has been confirmed by numerous research projects [19], [22] that SIFT is one of the most effective and robust keypoint detectors. Therefore, we follow this approach in our work. Keypoint detection by SIFT proceeds as follows: initially, the potential interest points are localized by means of difference-of-Gaussians. Then, unstable keypoints are rejected. In the next phase, for each keypoint, the additional information concerning its relative orientation, scale and location is added. Finally, on the basis of the histograms of local gradients, keypoint descriptors are computed and have the form of numerical vectors. The number of keypoints extracted from an image depends largely on the complexity of the image elements and may oscillate between a hundred and several thousand.

The goal of the next phase is to group the keypoints into k "visual words". This is achieved using k-means clustering, where each cluster contains the keypoints with the smallest distance to the center of a centroid. As a result, a k-visual size dictionary is formed. This allows to unify the number of features for each image and leads to simpler image representation. An important task is the appropriate selection of parameter k, which significantly affects the quality of results as well as the speed of calculation. If the number of clusters is too small, strongly differing key points can be represented by the same visual word and conversely, if the clusters are too many, similar descriptors can be described by different visual words. This may result in a reduced precision of the obtained results. The experiments with different values of the k parameter in Section 4 are presented.

3.2   Image Representation

Given the image keypoints and the visual dictionary, it is possible to assign visual word to each keypoint. From this point, the image can be represented as a histogram of its visual words. In Information Retrieval, such representation is referred to as term frequency (TF). Taking into account only TF histograms can lead to unsatisfactory results, as TF does not include information about its importance among all images. Thus, for the representation of image we also consider TFIDF (TF - term frequency, IDF - inverse document frequency) from the field of Information Retrieval. The idea of TFIDF is to weight each word according to number of its occurrences among entire dataset of images. Visual word which occurs in few images is more informative that the one appearing in many images. Therefore, the weight value for a particular word is calculated by the following formula:

$$(\text{tf-idf})_{i,j} = \frac{n_{i,j}}{\sum_k n_{k,j}} \times \log \frac{|D|}{|\{d : t_i \in d\}|}, \tag{1}$$

where $n_{i,j}$ is the number of occurrences of $i-th$ visual word at $j-th$ image, the denominator of the former fraction is equal to the number of all visual words at $j-th$ image, $|D|$ is number of images and $|\{d : t_i \in d\}|$ is a number of images containing $i-th$ visual word.

Moreover, our previous studies [7] proved that normalizing histograms significantly improves classification based on Bag of Visual Words method. Therefore, we apply the Euclidean norm (2), so that each histogram can be interpreted as a unit-length vector.

$$\|\mathbf{x}\|_2 := \left(\sum_{i=1}^{n} |x_i|^2 \right)^{1/2}. \tag{2}$$

3.3 Ranking by K-Means Voting Algorithm

The next step of proposed methodology is the creation of a similarity ranking for the query image on the basis of the image representations. For this task a novel Ranking by K-means Voting procedure is proposed. A series of k-means clustering is executed to divide all images in the dataset (including the query image) into varying number of groups. After each clustering, the pictures from the same centroid receive a vote which is accumulated in the similarity matrix SM. In particular, for each images pair (s,t) in the same cluster, the value of similarity matrix at position (s,t) is incremented. The general outline of the proposed method is presented in Algorithm 1.

Algorithm 1. Ranking by K-means Voting Algorithm

Require: $N > 0$ {number of images}, $M > 0$ {number of iterations}
1: var SM[N,N] {similarity matrix of size NxN}
2: **for** $i = 1 \rightarrow M$ **do**
3:    **for** $k = 2, 3, \ldots, \lfloor \lg_2 N \rfloor$ **do**
4:       Do k-means clustering procedure
5:       **for all** $s, t \in 1..N$ in the same cluster **do**
6:          SM[s,t] = SM[s,t] + 1
7:       **end for**
8:    **end for**
9: **end for**

After the execution of algorithm the similarity matrix SM is obtained, which holds the similarity value between any two given images. This similarity is expressed by the number of votes that particular pair of images has received. Having the similarity matrix SM, the ranking for image s can be easily obtained by sorting $s - th$ row of SM in descending order. It should be noted that the clustering is repeated $M \text{x} \lfloor \lg_2 N \rfloor$ times to minimize the effect of stucking in local minimum solutions.

4 Experimental Results

The goal of the experimental session was to test the effectiveness of our CBIR approach. The dataset, which can be downloaded from wmii.uwm.edu.pl/~kmmi consisted of 166 shoe images from four distinctive shoe categories containing 59, 20, 29, and 58 images in each collection (figure 2 presents the exemplary

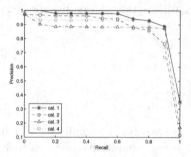

Fig. 1. Precision/Recall graph for Ranking by K-means Voting Algorithm, $k=2000$ and TF+normalization representation

Fig. 2. Representative images from each category

images from each category). Such structure of the dataset allowed us to preserve the straightforward notion of relevant and irrelevant images for the purpose of retrieval evaluation. In particular, all images from the same category as the query image were considered to be relevant, while images from other category were considered to be irrelevant.

Given the dataset, the visual dictionary was constructed as follows. Initially, SIFT keypoints we extracted from all of the images. Successively, keypoints were clustered into k visual words, using the k-means algorithm, as described in section 3.1. In order to determine the most suitable number of words for the dataset, the image retrieval evaluation was repeated for the following values of k: 50, 100, 250, 500, 1000, 1500, 2000. In addition to different vocabulary sizes, we tested the following term weighting schemes: TF, TF' (normalized TF), TFIDF and TFIDF' (normalized TFIDF), as described in section 3.2. The proposed Ranking by K-means Voting algorithm was compared with the ranking based on the Euclidean distance between the histograms of the query image and all other images in the dataset.

To quantitatively express the quality of the results, we employed standard measures for evaluating retrieval results in unranked datasets, such as precision and recall. Each image in the dataset was used as a query, and its precision and recall values were calculated. This allowed us to obtain the average precision for each query, and the mean average precision (MAP) for each category. Finally, the overall precision among all categories was calculated as the mean of the mean average precisions (MMAP).

The MMAP results obtained for Ranking by K-means Voting are presented in Table 1. In the similar way, the MMAP results for the ranking based on the Euclidean distance are shown in Table 2. It can be noted, that the best results were obtained for theRanking by K-means Voting with the dictionary containing 2000 words and the TF' image representation. In such case MMAP reached over 91 percent. Additionally, it can be observed that Ranking by K-means Voting generally performs better that the ranking based on the Euclidean distance, regardless of the number of words and the weighting scheme used. In particular, when taking into account k values greater than 500, the results were significantly better and the increase of MMAP value oscillated between 6 and 15 percent. Moreover, we examined the effect of the weighting forms applied to visual vocabulary. Considering the TF and TFIDF representations, it can be concluded that the application of the former or the latter slightly affects the results. Figure 1 presents precision/recall graphs for all image categories, that were obtained for Ranking by K-means Voting, $k = 2000$ and TF' weighting.

Table 1. Mean of the mean average precisions (MMAP) for Ranking by K-means Voting Algorithm

	Number of Visual Words						
	50	100	250	500	1000	1500	2000
TF	84.13	83.23	83.18	78.77	67.24	67.72	66.46
TF'	76.37	84.4	87.49	87.52	88.02	88.17	91.85
TFIDF	72.21	74.73	69.63	80.17	75.32	74.27	77.57
TFIDF'	75.01	74.45	81.54	82.85	89.55	90.96	91.38

Table 2. Mean of the mean average precisions (MMAP) for Euclidean distance as similarity measure

	Number of Visual Words						
	50	100	250	500	1000	1500	2000
TF	81,69	80.19	75.8	70.78	64.5	61.98	61.16
TF'	70.34	72.48	74.98	76.03	74.22	74.19	76.01
TFIDF	75.87	77.49	76.69	70.36	64.09	61.89	60.61
TFIDF'	65.66	69.48	74.92	74.89	74.24	74.76	77.27

5   Conclusion and Future Work

The main contribution of this work is the Ranking by K-means Voting algorithm, whose purpose is to create a ranking of similar images. The results obtained in the experimental session show the advantage of the method proposed in this paper over the standard similarity measures, in our case over the Euclidean distance. In particular, we obtained accuracy better by from 6 to 15 percent. In addition, it should be noted that the normalization of image representation has a great impact on the result quality. In most cases, the application of the Euclidean normalization caused a significant increase in accuracy. Finally, studies on the optimal number of "visual words" were undertaken. The results of the experiments show that with the Euclidean normalization the best quality is obtained for $k = 2000$. On the basis of the encouraging results, we plan to test our algorithm on commonly available datasets and compare it with other ranking methods. Other future goals include the verification of the algorithm performance and improving its accuracy.

Acknowledgments. The research described here has been supported by the National Science Center of the Republic of Poland grant N N516 480940. We would like to thank Geox and Salomon companies for providing a set of shoes images for scientific purposes.

References

1. Akgül, C.B., Rubin, D.L., Napel, S., Beaulieu, C.F., Greenspan, H., Acar, B.: Content-based image retrieval in radiology: Current status and future directions. J. Digital Imaging 24(2), 208–222 (2011)
2. Aschkenasy, S.V., Jansen, C., Osterwalder, R., Linka, A., Unser, M., Marsch, S., Hunziker, P.: Unsupervised image classification of medical ultrasound data by multiresolution elastic registration. Ultrasound Med. Biol. 32(7), 1047–1054 (2006)
3. Bay, H., Tuytelaars, T., Van Gool, L.: SURF: Speeded up robust features. In: Leonardis, A., Bischof, H., Pinz, A. (eds.) ECCV 2006, Part I. LNCS, vol. 3951, pp. 404–417. Springer, Heidelberg (2006)
4. Csurka, G., Dance, C.R., Fan, L., Willamowski, J., Bray, C.: Visual categorization with bags of keypoints. In: Workshop on Statistical Learning in Computer Vision, ECCV, pp. 1–22 (2004)
5. Do, M.N., Vetterli, M.: The contourlet transform: an efficient directional multiresolution image representation. IEEE Transactions on Image Processing 14(12), 2091–2106 (2005)
6. Ee, P., Report, P.: Histogram-based color image retrieval. Image Rochester NY, pp. 1–21 (2008)
7. Górecki, P., Artiemjew, P., Drozda, P., Sopyła, K.: Categorization of Similar Objects using Bag of Visual Words and Support Vector Machines. Accepted for Fourth International Conference on Agents and Artificial Intelligence. IEEE (2012)
8. Han, J., Ma, K.K.: Fuzzy color histogram and its use in color image retrieval. IEEE Transactions on Image Processing 11(8), 944–952 (2002)
9. He, C., Zheng, Y.F., Ahalt, S.C.: Object tracking using the gabor wavelet transform and the golden section algorithm. IEEE Trans. Multimedia 4, 528–538 (2002)
10. Huang, J., Kumar, S.R., Mitra, M., Zhu, W.J., Zabih, R.: Image indexing using color correlograms. In: Proceedings of the 1997 Conference on Computer Vision and Pattern Recognition (CVPR 1997), pp. 762–768. IEEE Computer Society, Washington, DC (1997)
11. Joachims, T.: Optimizing search engines using clickthrough data. In: ACM SIGKDD Conference on Knowledge Discovery and Data Mining (KDD), pp. 133–142 (2002)
12. Ke, Y., Sukthankar, R.: Pca-sift: a more distinctive representation for local image descriptors. In: Proceedings of IEEE Conference on Computer Vision and Pattern Recognition, vol. 2, pp. 506–513 (2004)
13. Keysers, D., Dahmen, J., Ney, H., Wein, B.B., Lehmann, T.M.: Statistical framework for model-based image retrieval in medical applications. Journal of Electronic Imaging 12(1), 59–68 (2003)

14. Korytkowski, M., Scherer, R., Rutkowski, L.: On combining backpropagation with boosting. In: 2006 International Joint Conference on Neural Networks, IEEE World Congress on Computational Intelligence, Vancouver, BC, Canada, pp. 1274–1277 (2006)
15. Lam, M.O., Disney, T., Raicu, D.S., Furst, J., Channin, D.S.: Briscan open source pulmonary nodule image retrieval framework. Journal of Digital Imaging 20(suppl. 1), 63–71 (2007)
16. Lee, Y., Lee, K., Pan, S.: Local and Global Feature Extraction for Face Recognition. In: Kanade, T., Jain, A., Ratha, N.K. (eds.) AVBPA 2005. LNCS, vol. 3546, pp. 219–228. Springer, Heidelberg (2005)
17. Li, J.: The application of cbir-based system for the product in electronic retailing. In: 2010 IEEE 11th International Conference on Computer-Aided Industrial Design and Conceptual Design (CAIDCD), pp. 1327–1330 (November 2010)
18. Lowe, D.G.: Distinctive image features from scale-invariant keypoints. Int. J. Comput. Vision 60, 91–110 (2004)
19. Mikolajczyk, K., Leibe, B., Schiele, B.: Local Features for Object Class Recognition. In: Tenth IEEE International Conference on Computer Vision (ICCV 2005), vol. 1, pp. 1792–1799. IEEE (2005)
20. Schmid, C., Mohr, R.: Local grayvalue invariants for image retrieval. IEEE Transactions on Pattern Analysis and Machine Intelligence 19, 530–535 (1997)
21. Simoncelli, E.P., Freeman, W.T.: The steerable pyramid: A flexible architecture for multi-scale derivative computation, pp. 444–447 (1995)
22. Tuytelaars, T., Mikolajczyk, K.: Local invariant feature detectors: a survey. Found. Trends. Comput. Graph. Vis. 3, 177–280 (2008)
23. Vo, A.P.N., Nguyen, T.T., Oraintara, S.: Texture image retrieval using complex directional filter bank. In: ISCAS (2006)

Shape Parametrization and Contour Curvature Using Method of Hurwitz-Radon Matrices

Dariusz Jakóbczak[1] and Witold Kosiński[2,3]

[1] Technical University of Koszalin, Śniadeckich 2, 75-453 Koszalin, Poland
[2] Polish-Japanese Institute of Information Technology, Warsaw, Poland
[3] Kazimierz-Wielki University, 85-064 Bydgoszcz, Poland
djakob@ie.tu.koszalin.pl, wkos@pjwstk.edu.pl

Abstract. A method of Hurwitz-Radon Matrices (MHR) is proposed to be used in parametrization and interpolation of contours in the plane. Suitable parametrization leads to curvature calculations. Points with local maximum curvature are treated as feature points in object recognition and image analysis. The matrices are skew-symmetric and possess columns composed of orthogonal vectors. The operator of Hurwitz-Radon (OHR), built from these matrices, is described. It is shown how to create the orthogonal OHR and how to use it in a process of contour parametrization and curvature calculation.

1 Introduction

A significant problem in computer vision [1] and object recognition [2] is that of suitable contour parametrization and calculations for points with local maximum curvature [3]. The explicit form of the function $y = h(x)$ or implicit representation of the curve $f(x, y) = 0$ are not always good enough for image analysis. Parametrization of the contour [4] is a better way to compute feature points of the object. This paper is dealing with the novel Hurwitz-Radon Matrices method (MHR) of contour interpolation and parametrization by using a family of Hurwitz-Radon matrices. Contour is parameterized for each pair of successive interpolation nodes. Contour points $(x(\alpha), y(\alpha))$ are computed for $\alpha \in [0; 1]$ between nodes $(x_i, y_i) = (x(1), y(1))$ and $(x_{i+1}, y_{i+1}) = (x(0), y(0))$. Appropriate parametrization leads to possibility of curvature calculation $C(\alpha)$:

$$C(\alpha) = \frac{|x'(\alpha)y''(\alpha) - x''(\alpha)y'(\alpha)|}{\sqrt{[(x'(\alpha))^2 + (y'(\alpha))^2]^3}} \qquad (1)$$

Points with local maximum curvature are fixed with condition $C'(\alpha) = 0$ and checking the monotonicity of $C(\alpha)$. The proposed method is used in object contour parametrization and then calculations for local maximum curvature are described. So suitable contour parametrization and precise reconstruction of the curve [5] is a key factor in many applications [6] of manufacturing [7], image analysis, object recognition and computer vision [8].

L. Rutkowski et al. (Eds.): ICAISC 2012, Part I, LNCS 7267, pp. 518–526, 2012.
© Springer-Verlag Berlin Heidelberg 2012

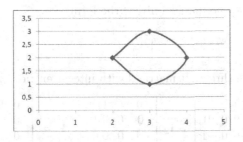

Fig. 1. Four nodes and the contour (MS EXCEL graph)

2   Contour Interpolation

In the proposed method a contour is described by the set of nodes $(x_i, y_i) \in \mathbf{R}^2$ as follows:

1. nodes (interpolation points) are settled at key points: local extremum (maximum or minimum) of one of coordinates and at least one point between two successive local extremum;
2. one contour is represented by at least four nodes;
3. nodes are indexed in accordance with course of the contour.

Conditions 1 and 3 are done for the most appropriate description of the contour. In condition 2 first node is the last, so proposed method uses in calculations minimum five nodes. The following question is important in mathematics and computer sciences: is it possible to find an interpolation method for a curve [9] and a parametrization without building interpolation polynomials or Bézier curves, NURBS [10] neither spline functions [11]? Our paper aims at giving the positive answer to this question. The contour or function in MHR method is parameterized for value $\alpha \in [0; 1]$ in the range of two successive interpolation nodes.

2.1   The Operator of Hurwitz-Radon

Adolf Hurwitz (1859-1919) and Johann Radon (1887-1956) published the papers about a specific class of matrices in 1923, working on the problem of quadratic forms. Matrices $A_i, i = 1, 2, ...m$ satisfying

$$A_j A_k + A_k A_j = 0 \,, A_k^2 = -I \,, j \neq k, \tag{2}$$

for $j, k = 1, 2, ..., m$, where I is the unit matrix, are called a family of Hurwitz-Radon matrices(HR).

The family has significant features [12]:

1. HR matrices are skew-symmetric, i.e. $A_i^T = -A_i$,
2. inverse matrices are easy to find, i.e. $A_i^{-1} = -A_i$, and
3. only for dimensions $N = 2, 4$ or 8 the family of HR matrices consists of $N - 1$ matrices;

4. for $N = 2$ there is one matrix only, of the form

$$\begin{bmatrix} 0 & -1 \\ -1 & 0 \end{bmatrix}. \tag{3}$$

For $N = 4$ there are three HR matrices with integer entries, they are

$$A_1 = \begin{bmatrix} 0 & 1 & 0 & 0 \\ -1 & 0 & 0 & 0 \\ 0 & 0 & 0 & -1 \\ 0 & 0 & 1 & 0 \end{bmatrix}, A_2 = \begin{bmatrix} 0 & 0 & 1 & 0 \\ 0 & 0 & 0 & 1 \\ -1 & 0 & 0 & 0 \\ 0 & -1 & 0 & 0 \end{bmatrix}, A_3 = \begin{bmatrix} 0 & 0 & 0 & 1 \\ 0 & 0 & -1 & 0 \\ 0 & 1 & 0 & 0 \\ -1 & 0 & 0 & 0 \end{bmatrix}. \tag{4}$$

For $N = 8$ we have seven HR matrices with elements $0, 1$. So far HR matrices are applied in electronics [13]: in Space-Time Block Coding (STBC) and orthogonal design [14], also in signal processing [15] and Hamiltonian Neural Nets [16]. HR matrices, together with the identity matrix I_N, are used to build the orthogonal and discrete Hurwitz - Radon Operator (OHR). For nodes $(x_1, y_1), (x_2, y_2)$ the matrix M of dimension $N = 2$ is constructed:

$$M = \frac{1}{x_1^2 + x_2^2} \begin{bmatrix} x_1 y_1 + x_2 y_2 & x_2 y_1 - x_1 y_2 \\ x_1 y_2 - x_2 y_1 & x_1 y_1 + x_2 y_2 \end{bmatrix} \tag{5}$$

For nodes $(x_1, y_1), (x_2, y_2), (x_3, y_3)$ and (x_4, y_4) the discrete OHR of dimension $N = 4$ is constructed:

$$M = \frac{1}{x_1^2 + x_2^2 + x_3^2 + x_4^2} \begin{bmatrix} u_0 & u_1 & u_2 & u_3 \\ -u_1 & u_0 & -u_3 & u_2 \\ -u_2 & u_3 & u_0 & -u_1 \\ -u_3 & -u_2 & u_1 & u_0 \end{bmatrix}, \tag{6}$$

where

$$u_0 = x_1 y_1 + x_2 y_2 + x_3 y_3 + x_4 y_4 , u_1 = -x_1 y_2 + x_2 y_1 + x_3 y_4 - x_4 y_3 ,$$

$$u_2 = -x_1 y_3 - x_2 y_4 + x_3 y_1 + x_4 y_2 , u_3 = -x_1 y_4 + x_2 y_3 - x_3 y_2 + x_4 y_1 .$$

For nodes $(x_1, y_1), (x_2, y_2), ..., (x_8, y_8)$ the discrete OHR of dimension $N = 8$ is built [17] similarly as (5) or (6):

$$M = \frac{1}{\sum_{i=1}^{8} x_i^2} \begin{bmatrix} u_0 & u_1 & u_2 & u_3 & u_4 & u_5 & u_6 & u_7 \\ -u_1 & u_0 & u_3 & -u_2 & u_5 & -u_4 & -u_7 & u_6 \\ -u_2 & -u_3 & u_0 & u_1 & u_6 & u_7 & -u_4 & -u_5 \\ -u_3 & u_2 & -u_1 & u_0 & u_7 & -u_6 & u_5 & -u_4 \\ -u_4 & -u_5 & -u_6 & -u_7 & u_0 & u_1 & u_2 & u_3 \\ -u_5 & u_4 & -u_7 & u_6 & -u_1 & u_0 & -u_3 & u_2 \\ -u_6 & u_7 & u_4 & -u_5 & -u_2 & u_3 & u_0 & -u_1 \\ -u_7 & -u_6 & u_5 & u_4 & -u_3 & -u_2 & u_1 & u_0 \end{bmatrix}, \tag{7}$$

where the components $u_0, u_1, ..., u_7$ formed as the vector $\boldsymbol{u}$ are calculated in the similar way to those of 4 dimensional vector appearing (5) but now in terms of the coordinates of the above 8 nodes,

$$
u = \begin{bmatrix}
y_1 & y_2 & y_3 & y_4 & y_5 & y_6 & y_7 & y_8 \\
-y_2 & y_1 & -y_4 & y_3 & -y_6 & y_5 & y_8 & -y_7 \\
-y_3 & y_4 & y_1 & -y_2 & -y_7 & -y_8 & y_5 & y_6 \\
-y_4 & -y_3 & y_2 & y_1 & -y_8 & y_7 & -y_6 & y_5 \\
-y_5 & y_6 & y_7 & y_8 & y_1 & -y_2 & -y_3 & -y_4 \\
-y_6 & -y_5 & y_8 & -y_7 & y_2 & y_1 & y_4 & -y_3 \\
-y_7 & -y_8 & -y_5 & y_6 & y_3 & -y_4 & y_1 & y_2 \\
-y_8 & y_7 & -y_6 & -y_5 & y_4 & y_3 & -y_2 & y_1
\end{bmatrix}
\begin{bmatrix}
x_1 \\ x_2 \\ x_3 \\ x_4 \\ x_5 \\ x_6 \\ x_7 \\ x_8
\end{bmatrix}.
\tag{8}
$$

Note that the all OHR operators M appearing in (5)-(7) satisfy the condition of interpolations

$$
Mx = y \tag{9}
$$

for $x = (x_1, x_2, ..., x_N)^T \in \mathbf{R}^N$, $x \neq 0$, $y = (y_1, y_2, ..., y_N)^T \in \mathbf{R}^N$, with $N = 2, 4$ or $N = 8$. If for each matrix M appearing so far we use the general denotation

$$
M = \{\sum_{i=1}^{N} x_i^2\}^{-1}(u_0 I_N + D) \tag{10}
$$

with the matrix D possessing 0 on the main diagonal and elements $u_1, u_2, ..., u_{N-1}$ on the remaining positions, then the reverse discrete operator OHR, denoted by M^{-1}, will have the form

$$
M^{-1} = \{\sum_{i=1}^{N} y_i^2\}^{-1}(u_0 I_N - D). \tag{11}
$$

The reverse OHR operator in (11) satisfies, of course, the interpolation condition

$$
M^{-1}y = x \tag{12}
$$

for $x = (x_1, x_2, ..., x_N)^T \in \mathbf{R}^N$, $y = (y_1, y_2, ..., y_N)^T \in \mathbf{R}^N$, $y \neq 0$ with $N = 2, 4$ or $N = 8$.

2.2   MHR Method and Contour Parametrization

Key questions look as follows: how can we compute coordinates of points settled between the interpolation nodes [18] and how the object contour is parameterized? The answers are connected with the novel MHR method [19]. On a segment of a line every number "c" situated between "a" and "b" is described by a linear (convex) combination $c = \alpha a + (1 - \alpha)b$ for

$$
\alpha = \frac{b - c}{b - a} \in [0, 1]. \tag{13}
$$

New average OHR operator M_2 of dimension $N = 2, 4$ or $N = 8$ is constructed

$$
M_2 = \alpha M_0 + (1 - \alpha) M_1 \tag{14}
$$

with two operators: M_0 constructed according to the previous methods (5)-(7), however with new nodes $(x_1 = a, y_1), (x_3, y_3), .., (x_{2N-1}, y_{2N-1})$, and M_1 constructed according to the same methods, however, with new nodes $(x_2 = b, y_2), (x_4, y_4), ..., (x_{2N}, y_{2N})$. Having the operator M_2 it is possible to reconstruct the second coordinate (i.e. y) of each point (x, y) in terms of the vector $C = (c_1, c_2, ..., c_N)^T$ defined by

$$c_i = \alpha x_{2i-1} + (1 - \alpha)x_{2i}, \text{with } i = 1, 2, ..., N. \tag{15}$$

The required formula for those coordinates is similar to (9)

$$Y(C) = M_2 C \tag{16}$$

if we use components of the vector $Y(C)$ for the second coordinate of each point (x, y), corresponding to the first coordinate.

On the other hand, having the operator M_2^{-1} it is possible to reconstruct the first coordinate of each point (x, y) as follows

$$M_2^{-1} = \alpha M_0^{-1} + (1 - \alpha)M_1^{-1}, \text{with }, c_i = \alpha y_{2i-1} + (1 - \alpha)y_{2i},$$

$$X(C) = M_2^{-1}C \tag{17}$$

with the obvious meaning of the symbols used.

Calculation of unknown coordinates for curve points using (13)-(17) is called here the method of Hurwitz - Radon Matrices (MHR) [20]. Here some applications of MHR method for functions $h(x) = 1/x$ (nodes with $y_i = 0.2, 0.6, 1, 1.4, 1.8$) and $f(x) = 1/(1 + 25x^2)$ with nodes of $x_i = -1, -0.5, 0, 0.5, 1$ are presented.

Using MHR parametrization and (13)-(16) for $N = 2$ and $\beta = 1 - \alpha$ give

$$M_0 = \frac{1}{x_1^2 + x_3^2} \begin{bmatrix} x_1 y_1 + x_3 y_3 & x_3 y_1 - x_1 y_3 \\ x_1 y_3 - x_3 y_1 & x_1 y_1 + x_3 y_3 \end{bmatrix},$$

$$M_1 = \frac{1}{x_2^2 + x_4^2} \begin{bmatrix} x_2 y_2 + x_4 y_4 & x_4 y_2 - x_2 y_4 \\ x_2 y_4 - x_4 y_2 & x_2 y_2 + x_4 y_4 \end{bmatrix},$$

$$\begin{bmatrix} Y(c_1) \\ Y(c_2) \end{bmatrix} = (\alpha M_0 + \beta M_1) \begin{bmatrix} \alpha x_1 + \beta x_2 \\ \alpha x_3 + \beta x_4 \end{bmatrix},$$

where, for example, in the explicit form $Y(c_1)$ is given by

$$Y(c_1) = \alpha^2 y_1 + \beta^2 y_2 + \frac{\alpha\beta}{x_1^2 + x_3^2}(x_1 x_2 y_1 + x_2 x_3 y_3 + x_3 x_4 y_1 - x_1 x_4 y_3)+$$

$$+\frac{\alpha\beta}{x_2^2 + x_4^2}(x_1 x_2 y_2 + x_1 x_4 y_4 + x_3 x_4 y_2 - x_2 x_3 y_4).$$

Parametrization of contour points $(x(\alpha), y(\alpha))$ situated between nodes (x_1, y_1) and (x_2, y_2), calculated with OHR operators of dimension $N = 2$, is:

$$x(\alpha) = \alpha x_1 + (1 - \alpha)x_2, \alpha \in [0; 1] \tag{18}$$
$$y(\alpha) = \alpha^2 y_1 + (1 - \alpha)^2 y_2 + \alpha(1 - \alpha)r,$$

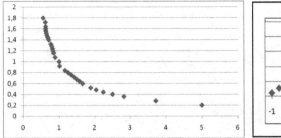 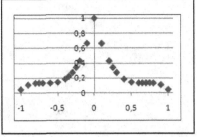

Fig. 2. Twenty six interpolation points of the functions: $h(x) = 1/x$, on the left, and $f(x) = 1/(1 + 25x^2)$, on the right, using the MHR method with 5 nodes

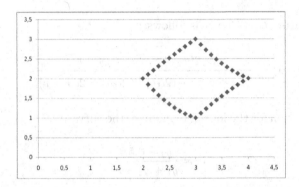

Fig. 3. Thirty six interpolation points calculated by MHR method with 4 nodes

where $r = \frac{1}{x_1^2 + x_3^2}(x_1x_2y_1 + x_2x_3y_3 + x_3x_4y_1 - x_1x_4y_3) + \frac{1}{x_2^2 + x_4^2}(x_1x_2y_2 + x_1x_4y_4 + x_3x_4y_2 - x_2x_3y_4)$. Parametrization of contour points situated between each pair of successive nodes (x_i, y_i) and (x_{i+1}, y_{i+1}) looks similarly to (18). For the contour presented in Fig.1 our MHR method with nodes at corners (2;2), (3;1), (4;2) and (3;3) gives the result on Fig. 3.

3   Curvature

The formula for curvature (1) consists of elements given by the parametrization (18), and hence are solutions of the system of equations

$$x'(\alpha) = x_1 - x_2 \ , x''(\alpha) = 0 \ , \tag{19}$$
$$y'(\alpha) = 2\alpha y_1 - 2(1 - \alpha)y_2 + (1 - 2\alpha)r \ ,$$
$$y''(\alpha) = 2y_1 + 2y_2 - 2r \ .$$

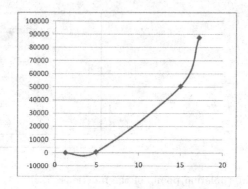

Fig. 4. A curve with 4 nodes (MS EXCEL graph)

Then the curvature $C(\alpha)$ looks as follows:

$$C(\alpha) = \frac{2(x_2 - x_1)|y_1 + y_2 - r|}{[(x_2 - x_1)^2 + (2\alpha y_1 + 2\alpha y_2 - 2\alpha r + r)^2]^{\frac{3}{2}}}. \tag{20}$$

Hence the condition for the local maximum of the curvature $C'(\alpha) = 0$ is fulfilled when

$$\alpha = \frac{y_2 - 0.5r}{y_1 + y_2 - r}. \tag{21}$$

Now let us consider three examples.

- Linear (affine) function: $y_1 + y_2 - r = 0$, and then $C(\alpha) = 0$.
- A curve with interpolation nodes:

$$(0.5; 2), (3; 0.333), (6.5; 0.154), (20; 0.05),$$

then the local maximum of the curvature is at $\alpha_0 = 0.709$ (cf. (21)) and is equal to $C(\alpha_0) = 1.278$ (cf.(20)), and appears at the curve point $(1.229; 2.339)$ situated between the first and the second node.
- For the function presented in Fig. 4 with interpolation nodes

$$(1.2; 2.074), (4.9; 576.48), (15; 50630), (17.2; 87520)$$

the local maximum of the curvature is $C(\alpha_1) = 401.296$ with $\alpha_1 = 0.605$ and at the curve point with coordinate $x = 2.663$ situated between the first and the second node (Fig.5).

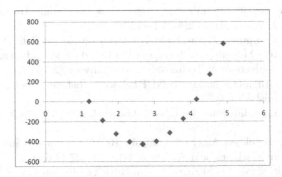

Fig. 5. Ten points of the curve from Fig.4, calculated by MHR method; between the first and the second node we have the local minimum of the curvature for $x = 2.663$

4 Conclusions

The method of Hurwitz-Radon Matrices leads to object contour interpolation and parametrization in the range of two successive nodes, depending on the number and location of nodes [21]. The only condition is to have a set of contour points according to assumptions of MHR method. Main features of MHR method are accuracy of data reconstruction depending on number of nodes. Interpolation of the contour consisting of L points leads the computational cost of rank $O(L)$. MHR method deals with local operators: average OHR operators are built by successive 4, 8 or 16 curve points, what is connected with smaller computational costs then using all nodes. Moreover, MHR method is not an affine interpolation [22]. Future works are related to: parametrization and curvature reconstruction using 8 or 16 nodes, possibility to apply MHR method to three-dimensional curves (3D data), object recognition [23], data extrapolation and decision making [24].

References

1. Ballard, D.H.: Computer Vision. Prentice Hall, New York (1982)
2. Tadeusiewicz, R., Flasiński, M.: Image Recognition. PWN, Warszawa (1991) (in Polish)
3. Saber, E., Xu, Y., Murat Tekalp, A.: Partial Shape Recognition by Sub-matrix Matching for Partial Matching Guided Image Labeling. Pattern Recognition 38, 1560–1573 (2005)
4. Kiciak, P.: Modelling of curves and surfaces: applications in computer graphics. WNT, Warsaw (2005) (in Polish)
5. Soussen, C., Mohammad-Djafari, A.: Polygonal and Polyhedral Contour Reconstruction in Computed Tomography. IEEE Transactions on Image Processing 11(13), 1507–1523 (2004)
6. Jakóbczak, D., Kosiński, W.: Application of Hurwitz - Radon Matrices in Monochromatic Medical Images Decompression. In: Kowalczuk, Z., Wiszniewski, B. (eds.) Intelligent Data Mining in Diagnostic Purposes: Automatics and Informatics, pp. 389–398. PWNT, Gdansk (2007) (in Polish)

7. Tang, K.: Geometric Optimization Algorithms in Manufacturing. Computer - Aided Design & Applications 2(6), 747–757 (2005)
8. Choraś, R.S.: Computer Vision. Exit, Warszawa (2005) (in Polish)
9. Kozera, R.: Curve Modeling via Interpolation Based on Multidimensional Reduced Data. Silesian University of Technology Press, Gliwice (2004)
10. Rogers, D.F.: An introduction to NURBS with Historical Perspective. Morgan Kaufmann Publishers (2001)
11. Schumaker, L.L.: Spline Functions: Basic Theory. Cambridge Mathematical Library (2007)
12. Eckmann, B.: Topology, Algebra, Analysis- Relations and Missing Links. Notices of the American Mathematical Society 5(46), 520–527 (1999)
13. Citko, W., Jakóbczak, D., Sieńko, W.: On Hurwitz - Radon Matrices Based Signal Processing. In: Workshop Signal Processing at Poznań University of Technology (2005)
14. Tarokh, V., Jafarkhani, H., Calderbank, R.: Space-Time Block Codes from Orthogonal Designs. IEEE Transactions on Information Theory 5(45), 1456–1467 (1999)
15. Sieńko, W., Citko, W., Wilamowski, B.: Hamiltonian Neural Nets as a Universal Signal Processor. In: 28th Annual Conference of the IEEE Industrial Electronics Society IECON (2002)
16. Sieńko, W., Citko, W.: Hamiltonian Neural Net Based Signal Processing. In: The International Conference on Signal and Electronic System ICSES (2002)
17. Jakóbczak, D.: 2D and 3D Image Modeling Using Hurwitz-Radon Matrices. Polish Journal of Environmental Studies 4A(16), 104–107 (2007)
18. Jakóbczak, D.: Shape Representation and Shape Coefficients via Method of Hurwitz-Radon Matrices. In: Bolc, L., Tadeusiewicz, R., Chmielewski, L.J., Wojciechowski, K. (eds.) ICCVG 2010, Part I. LNCS, vol. 6374, pp. 411–419. Springer, Heidelberg (2010)
19. Jakóbczak, D.: Curve Interpolation Using Hurwitz-Radon Matrices. Polish Journal of Environmental Studies 3B(18), 126–130 (2009)
20. Jakóbczak, D.: Application of Hurwitz-Radon Matrices in Shape Representation. In: Banaszak, Z., Świć, A. (eds.) Applied Computer Science: Modelling of Production Processes, vol. 1(6), pp. 63–74. Lublin University of Technology Press, Lublin (2010)
21. Jakóbczak, D.: Object Modeling Using Method of Hurwitz-Radon Matrices of Rank k. In: Wolski, W., Borawski, M. (eds.) Computer Graphics: Selected Issues, pp. 79–90. University of Szczecin Press, Szczecin (2010)
22. Jakóbczak, D.: Implementation of Hurwitz-Radon Matrices in Shape Representation. In: Choraś, R.S. (ed.) Image Processing and Communications Challenges 2. AISC, vol. 84, pp. 39–50. Springer, Heidelberg (2010)
23. Jakóbczak, D.: Object Recognition via Contour Points Reconstruction Using Hurwitz-Radon Matrices. In: Józefczyk, J., Orski, D. (eds.) Knowledge-Based Intelligent System Advancements: Systemic and Cybernetic Approaches, pp. 87–107. IGI Global, Hershey (2011)
24. Jakóbczak, D.: Data Extrapolation and Decision Making via Method of Hurwitz-Radon Matrices. In: Jędrzejowicz, P., Nguyen, N.T., Hoang, K. (eds.) ICCCI 2011, Part I. LNCS (LNAI), vol. 6922, pp. 173–182. Springer, Heidelberg (2011)

Vision-Based Recognition of Fingerspelled Acronyms Using Hierarchical Temporal Memory

Tomasz Kapuscinski

Rzeszow University of Technology,
Department of Computer and Control Engineering,
W. Pola 2, 35-959 Rzeszow, Poland
tomekkap@prz-rzeszow.pl

Abstract. In this paper, a new, glove-free method for recognition of fingerspelled acronyms using hierarchical temporal memory has been proposed. The task is challenging because many signs look similar from the camera viewpoint. Moreover handshapes are distorted strongly as a result of coarticulation and motion blur, especially in the fluent fingerspelling. In the described work, the problem has been tackled by applying the new, bio-inspired recognition engine, based on structural and functional properties of mammalian neocortex, robust to local changes shape descriptors, and a training scheme allowing for capture possible handshape deformations in a manner that is lexicon independent.

Keywords: gesture recognition, hierarchical temporal memory, image processing and recognition, human-computer interaction.

1 Introduction

Fingerspelling consists on spelling words using hand gestures that correspond to the letters in the alphabet. It is used by hard-of-hearing when no sign exists for a desired word, for spelling proper nouns, technical terms, acronyms, loan signs, words from foreign languages, or to clarify a sign unfamiliar to the interlocutor.

In many sign languages, unlike word-level signs, fingerspelling gestures use a single hand and are mostly static. The meaning is conveyed by the hand shape, therefore the discrimination between letters should be based on hand and finger configurations, rather than on global hand and arm motions. The hand configurations are complex and contains finger occlusions. Some signs are ambiguous from the observer's viewpoint (Fig. 1).

For this reason the majority of proposed methods rely on active sensors, such as data-gloves or magnetic trackers, which provide information about finger configurations, e.g. [1,2]. These devices are both expensive and intrusive therefore the passive sensing with vision-based approaches is preferable. Many researchers have proposed different vision-based methods to recognize finger alphabets. In [3] the algorithm that recognize fingerspelling images using neural networks with pattern recognition model has been proposed. The 46 hand postures from Japanese kana fingerspelling, performed by 5 persons, have been recognized with

L. Rutkowski et al. (Eds.): ICAISC 2012, Part I, LNCS 7267, pp. 527–534, 2012.

(a) *A - P*   (b) *D - Z*   (c) *F - T*   (d) *O - S*

Fig. 1. Selected pairs of similar letters in Polish finger alphabet

accuracy up to 85.2%. Good recognition rates, up to 99%, have been reported by Altun et all. [4]. They have developed a handshape alignment method and tested it with different classifiers, trying to recognize 29 static letters of Turkish finger alphabet, performed by 3 signers. In [5] the authors have used an appearance-based model with a sort of pre-processing operations. They have achieved the recognition rate up to 86.7% for 24 letters performed by 20 users. Liwicki et al. [6] have demonstrated that using the modified histogram of oriented gradients as the appearance descriptor with a simple hidden Markov models can give highly accurate fingerspelling recognition on a large vocabulary. They have recognized 100 words performed by a single novice signer with the accuracy up to 84.1%.

Recognition is more difficult when the letters are shown in a sequence, what is the case investigated in this paper. The majority of existing systems tries to tackle this problem by an initial time segmentation. The various techniques have been used to identify frames with a slow motion. In [3] the recognition worked only when the same spelling was observed for more than 0.8 seconds. In [4] authors select for recognition frames whose distance to its successor, given by the sum of the city block distances between corresponding pixels, is minimum. However, at conversational speed, proficient signers are able to produce 40-45 words per minute and they do not pause at each letter. Moreover, in the fluent, high-speed fingerspelling, individual letters are not formed exactly, but combined with neighboring letters. This phenomenon is called coarticulation. Even if a signer pass through the exact hand configuration corresponding to the given letter, the aliasing resulting from a low frame rate can cause this sign to be missed (Fig. 2). Recognition of distorted handshapes is particularly difficult.

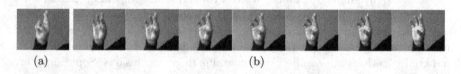

(a)   (b)

Fig. 2. Exact performance of the letter *R* (a), and the frames captured between letters *F* and *O* in the acronym *PFRON* (b)

An interesting approach has been proposed in [7], where the transitions between letters are recognized instead of isolated signs. The drawback of this solution is the increase in the number of recognized classes which also means the need for more training data. In [7] authors have also suggested a division of the hand into smaller parts (a palm and fingers), distinguished using morphological operations.

Indeed fingerspelled words can be treated as entities having a hierarchical structure in space and time. The spatial hierarchy manifests itself by building handshapes from smaller pieces, whereas the temporal one, by concatenation of subsequent letters into a given word. Taking this observation into account, an idea to use hierarchical temporal memory (HTM), a new computing paradigm replicating the structural and functional properties of mammalian neocortex [8], has been proposed in this paper. The method relies on building a hierarchical model of an observed part of world. In this model various appearances of the same object manifest themselves by different configurations of pieces from lower levels within hierarchy. However these configurations, called coincidences, can be grouped together, because they occur closely in time.

There is a chance that highly deformed handshapes will be still recognized as the same class provided the similar distortions will be shown sequentially during the training phase. This has been achieved by a special training scheme, proposed in this paper.

HTM is able to learn the new deformation of the object, using the small number of examples [9,10]. This is because fragments remembered in lower levels within hierarchy constitute building blocks, which are repeatedly used by other objects. HTM deals well with ambiguities thanks to belief propagation technique, multiple feedback and feed-forward connections within hierarchy and interaction of the bottom-up input signals with the top-down predicted expectations.

The remaining part of this article is organized as follows. The section 2 contains a brief overview of HTM. In the section 3 details concerning the proposed approach are given. Obtained results are presented in the section 4. Section 5 concludes the paper.

2   Hierarchical Temporal Memory

Recently the Hierarchical Temporal Memory (HTM), the new computing paradigm, has been developed [8]. HTM is based on neuroanatomical research of mammalian neocortex and observations how living creatures solve the vision problem. We can pretty well recognize objects even from a single static snapshot but to learn we use a sequence of views showing objects in motion. As children, when we are confronted with a new and confusing object, we pick it up and move it about in front of our eyes. As the object moves, patterns on our retina are changing, and our cortical system is able to build an invariant model. This model is not stored in our brain in one place. It is hierarchically spread throughout nodes of the neocortex. Fine, instantaneous and concrete details are stored in lower nodes, whereas larger, temporarily stable and abstract structures are represented higher within hierarchy. Models created in our brain are composed from reusable units. This leads to good scalability and helps to solve ambiguities. As the information propagates up the hierarchy, it becomes more stable and unambiguous.

Hierarchical temporal memory is a technology that replicates the structural and algorithmic properties of the neocortex. HTM receives spatio-temporal patterns coming from the senses. Through a learning process, HTM discovers and memorizes the causes of these patterns. Then, taking into account the new sensory stimuli, HTM can infer which of the known causes occurred at that time.

HTM is organized as a tree-shaped hierarchy of nodes which may work in the learning or inference mode. In the learning mode, the basic operation of each node is divided into two steps. The first step is to assign the input pattern to one of the so-called quantization points (spatial clustering). Then, each node forms common groups of quantization points using their temporal proximity (time clustering). Two points belong to the same group if they follow each other frequently in the training set. Stored groups represent causes discovered by HTM. They contain all observed variations in the appearance of objects. In the inference mode, the belief distribution over all known causes is determined. This is done by searching for the occurrence of the input pattern in one of the memorized groups. The output of the node is distribution of beliefs across all the learned causes, whereas its input is the concatenation of outputs of all connected nodes from the previous level. The variation of belief propagation technique used in hierarchy assures that the system very quickly resolves possible ambiguities. The detailed description can be found in [8].

3 Proposed Solution

The proposed method does not require any special gloves. At the beginning, skin areas are determined in each frame based on skin chrominance model built in the normalized RGB space (Fig. 3). Only areas larger than a predefined threshold are taken into account. They correspond to the face and hands of a signer under the assumption that there are no other skin-colored objects in the background (Fig. 3b). Unlike word-level gestures, letters of Polish finger alphabet should be

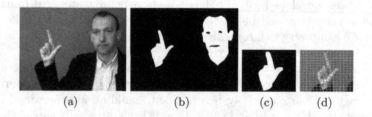

(a)   (b)   (c)   (d)

Fig. 3. Image processing: (a) input color image (shown here in gray levels), (b) skin-colored regions, (c) hand's binary mask, (d) extracted luminance window with the centered hand and the grid of receptive fields of HTM's sensors

performed at a distance of 20 cm from the face on the right side of the head therefore the region lying closest to the left edge of the image corresponds to the dominant hand of a signer. This binary object is used as a mask roughly indicating the position of the hand in the image.

Even under controlled laboratory conditions, a binary object obtained in this way, may not correspond exactly to the actual shape of the hand. Therefore, to make sure that most of the hand edges will be covered by the mask, the morphological dilation is applied to the binary object and holes in its interior are filled (Fig. 3c). Based on the mask position, the rectangular window of size 320 x 240, containing the dominant hand, is extracted from the luminance component of the input image and selected for further processing.

This window is divided into 16 x 16 = 256 rectangular patches, each measuring 20 x 15 pixels (Fig. 3d) and constituting the receptive fields of HTM sensors. Then for each patch, a histogram of quantized orientation is calculated. Currently only four different orientations are distinguished: horizontal, vertical and two slanting. Only orientations calculated at points covered by the binary mask are accumulated, with each orientation weighted by the corresponding gradient magnitude. For empty patches a vector filled with zeros is returned.

Each histogram constitutes the output of the HTM's sensor, put over the corresponding fragment of the image, and describes the local appearance of the hand. It has been selected as a result of experiments with recordings registered in different conditions and it was quite resistant to changes in illumination. The whole handshape is described as a joint histogram over quantized gradient orientation and position. Gradient based descriptors are biologically justified because neurons in primary visual cortex respond to a gradient at a particular orientation and spatial frequency.

After many experiments with the various network structures and parameters the following two-layer HTM has been proposed (Fig. 4). Sensor layer consists of

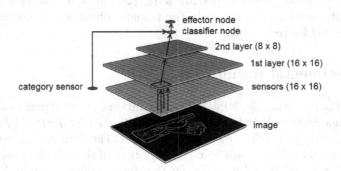

Fig. 4. The HTM topology

16 x 16 elements placed over the corresponding parts of the image. The category sensor is connected only in the learning phase and provides the information about the label of the currently processed gesture. The hierarchy is mapped by putting two layers containing 16x16 and 8x8 nodes respectively. Each of the nodes located in these two layers make the spatial and temporal clustering [8]. Above these layers the classifier and the effector nodes are put. The effector node

writes the results to the file. The hierarchy manifests itself in linking the nodes between the particular layers.

To achieve the invariance from the hand position, the nodes in the first layer share their internal states. In other words, each node is aware of what parts of the hand can appear anywhere in the image. The second layer of the network perceives the given shape as the particular coincidence of lower-level features (local descriptors), memorized in the nodes of the first layer. These features are invariant to local deformations only within some range. However, due to the factors mentioned in the introduction, hand deformations can be so large that the second layer will see a completely different coincidence of lower level features. During the learning stage, HTM is able to group together completely different configurations, provided they occur closely in time. Therefore, the following learning scheme was proposed.

It was assumed that there is no additional class for transitions between letters. Deformed shapes, which appear between accurate performances were classified as preceding or following letter. To create the training set, the video sequences containing all possible pairs of letters have been recorded. For each pair, the separate HTM has been trained using accurate performances of two letters, segmented by hand from the training sequence. Then, the HTM has been switched into the inference mode and used to separate the sequence into two parts, corresponding to the first and second letter of the processed pair. Obtained in this way, appearances of distorted letters have been added to the global training set. After processing all recorded pairs, the new HTM has been trained on exact and deformed realizations of all letters and used to recognize the fingerspelled acronyms. The idea was to capture the natural deformations when letters are performed in a sequence. Using all possible letter pairs instead of specific acronyms assures that coarticulation shown in the training phase, is not specific to the lexicon selected for recognition.

4   Experimental Results

The following acronyms, denoting Polish institutions, political parties and international organizations have been considered: *MPK*, *NATO*, *PFRON*, *PIS*, *PKO*, *PKP*, *PKS*, *PO*, *PSL*, *PZG*, *PZU*, *RP*, and *SLD*. The data set consisted of 30 frame-per-second video of each acronym performed 6 times by two persons, denoted further A and B. Additionally, for the training purposes, each letter pair has been performed once by person A and B. The signers have been asked to wear long-sleeved clothes. The color of clothing and objects in the background was different from the skin color. Each frame was originally 640 x 480 pixels, with the hand occupying a region no larger than 320 x 240 pixels. The person A is the professional sign language interpreter. She has performed the gestures accurately with the average speed about 45 acronyms per minute. Person B is hard-of-hearing and sign language is his primary means of communication.

His gestures have been performed more spontaneously and a bit carelessly with the average speed about 50 acronyms per minute.

HTM returns the label of the recognized class for each image in a sequence. Therefore a simple post-processing has been applied. Identical labels, occurring immediately after each other, have been merged into larger segments. Then, fragments shorter than the predefined threshold have been glued to the previous or next segment (to the shorter one).

The table 1 reports results in terms of acronyms recognition. Recognition was considered correct, if labels of the consecutive segments matched letters occurring in a given acronym.

The experiments have shown that the proposed method does not depend heavily on the feature extraction task. Errors in determining the mask, which occur due to fast fingerspelling (person B) do not degrade overall performance significantly.

Solution seems to be user dependent. However, the transition between the letters in each pair has been shown by a given person only once. When the list of acronyms is fixed a priori, one may consider enriching the training set by adding transitions characteristic for the considered vocabulary. It has been done for the person A by moving one utterance of each acronym from the testing to training set. The obtained recognition rate was 94.9%.

Table 1. Acronyms recognition accuracy

training (pairs of letters)	testing (acronyms)	recognition rate [%]
person A	person A	92.3
person B	person B	88.5
person A	person B	82.1
person B	person A	87.2
person A, B	person A	92.3
person A, B	person B	87.2

5   Conclusions and Future Work

A new method for recognition of fingerspelled acronyms using hierarchical temporal memory has been proposed. The method is glove free. It uses a new, bio-inspired computing paradigm, replicating the structural and functional properties of mammalian neocortex. Applied training scheme assures that the captured coarticulation is not specific to lexicons selected for recognition. The normal speed and careless gesturing are possible. The errors in the feature extraction, inevitable in the fluent fingerspelling, do not degrade the overall performance.

However, there are some issues requiring further research. The imaging conditions were only moderately challenging. Further works will involve investigation of the image processing methods robust enough to deal with arbitrary conditions. Selecting the proper parameters controlling the HTM training process is a bit troublesome. For the highest levels in the hierarchy, it relies on user intuition and experience. Elaborating systematic training procedures which can be run automatically is a great challenge. The long term goal of research is to develop a method allowing continuous sign language recognition. This will require, among other things, elaborating a method to distinguish between conscious gestures and involuntary hand movements. An integration of the acronyms recognition procedure with the word-level recognizer will be also needed.

Acknowledgments. This research was supported by the Polish Ministry of Higher Education under grant N N516 369736.

References

1. Oz, C., Leu, M.C.: Recognition of Finger Spelling of American Sign Language with Artificial Neural Network Using Position/Orientation Sensors and Data Glove. In: Wang, J., Liao, X.-F., Yi, Z. (eds.) ISNN 2005. LNCS, vol. 3497, pp. 157–164. Springer, Heidelberg (2005)
2. Tabata, Y., Kuroda, T.: Finger Spelling Recognition using Distinctive Features of Hand Shape. In: Proceedings of International Conference on Disability, Virtual Reality and Associated Technologies, pp. 287–292 (2008)
3. Shimada, M., Iwasaki, S., Asakura, T.: Finger Spelling Recognition using Neural Network with Pattern Recognition Model. In: SICE Annual Conference, pp. 2458–2463 (2003)
4. Altun, O., Albayrak, S., Ekinci, A., Bükün, B.: Turkish Fingerspelling Recognition System Using Axis of Least Inertia Based Fast Alignment. In: Sattar, A., Kang, B.-h. (eds.) AI 2006. LNCS (LNAI), vol. 4304, pp. 473–481. Springer, Heidelberg (2006)
5. Suraj, M.G., Guru, D.S.: Appearance Based Recognition Methodology for Recognising Fingerspelling Alphabets. In: International Joint Conference on Artificial Intelligence, pp. 605–610 (2007)
6. Liwicki, S., Everingham, M.: Automatic recognition of fingerspelled words in British sign language. In: Proceedings of the 2nd IEEE Workshop on CVPR for Human Communicative Behavior Analysis (CVPR4HB 2009), in conjunction with CVPR 2009, pp. 50–57 (2009)
7. Ricco, S., Tomasi, C.: Fingerspelling Recognition through Classification of Letter-to-Letter Transitions. In: Zha, H., Taniguchi, R.-i., Maybank, S. (eds.) ACCV 2009, Part III. LNCS, vol. 5996, pp. 214–225. Springer, Heidelberg (2010)
8. George, D., Hawkins, J.: Towards a Mathematical Theory of Cortical Microcircuits. PLoS Computational Biology, e1000532 (2009)
9. Kapuscinski, T.: Using Hierarchical Temporal Memory for Vision-Based Hand Shape Recognition under Large Variations in Hand"s Rotation. In: Rutkowski, L., Scherer, R., Tadeusiewicz, R., Zadeh, L.A., Zurada, J.M. (eds.) ICAISC 2010. LNCS (LNAI), vol. 6114, pp. 272–279. Springer, Heidelberg (2010)
10. Kapuściński, T.: Hand Shape Recognition in Real Images Using Hierarchical Temporal Memory Trained on Synthetic Data. In: Choraś, R.S. (ed.) Image Processing and Communications Challenges 2. AISC, vol. 84, pp. 193–200. Springer, Heidelberg (2010)

Lip Tracking Method for the System of Audio-Visual Polish Speech Recognition

Mariusz Kubanek, Janusz Bobulski, and Lukasz Adrjanowicz

Czestochowa University of Technology
Institute of Computer and Information Science
Dabrowskiego Street 73, 42-200 Czestochowa, Poland
{mariusz.kubanek,januszb,lukasz.adrjanowicz}@icis.pcz.pl

Abstract. This paper proposes a method of tracking the lips in the system of audio-visual speech recognition. Presented methods consists of a face detector, face tracker, lip detector, lip tracker, and word classifier. In speech recognition systems, the audio signal is exposed to a large amount of acoustic noise, therefor scientists are looking for ways to reduce audio interference on recognition results. Visual speech is one of the sources that is not perturbed by the acoustic environment and noise. To analyze the video speech one has to develop a method of lip tracking. This work presents a method for automatic detection of the outer edges of the lips, which was used to identify individual words in audio-visual speech recognition. Additionally the paper also shows how to use video speech to divide the audio signal into phonemes.

Keywords: lip reading, visual speech, audio visual speech recognition.

1 Introduction

Automatic speech recognition (ASR) is widely used as an effective interface in many devices: personal computers, robots, mobile phones and car navigation. For ASR systems, in low noise-level environments, the word correct rate (WCR) for audio channel only is over 95%. However in noisy environments, the WCR is significantly reduced [1]. To overcome this problem, we consider a lip reading method. Automatic recognition of audio-visual speech provokes a new and challenging tasks of comparison and competition with automatic recognition of the audio speech. It's well known that the visual modality contains some complementary information to the audio modality. The use of visual features in audio-visual speech recognition (AVSR) is motivated by the bimodal nature of the speech formation and the ability of humans to better distinguish spoken sounds when both audio and video are available [2,3,4]. Audio-visual speech recognition examines two separate streams of information, in comparison to only audio speech. The combination of these streams should provide better performance in contrast with modern approaches that utilise each source separately. The issue of video characteristics extraction and fusion of audio and video characteristics are difficult

L. Rutkowski et al. (Eds.): ICAISC 2012, Part I, LNCS 7267, pp. 535–542, 2012.

problems, that generate a lot of research in the scientific community. Since E. Petajan demonstrated in his work [5] that audio-visual systems are more effective than either speech or vision systems alone, many researchers started to investigate audio-visual recognition systems [6].

The paper presents a method for automatic detection of the outer edges of the lips. In addition, it shows how to improve the distinguish ability of video sounds, by analyzing the position of tongue and how to use video speech to divide the audio signal into phonemes. Because it is difficult to evaluate the effectiveness of lip-tracking, as the tracking accuracy may be verified only by observation. Therefore performance tests where based on isolated words recognition of audio-visual Polish speech. Moreover this work focuses on hidden Markov models (HMM) and presents a method of automatic lip tracking.

2   Face, Eye and Area of the Lip Detection

The first step in the process of creating a video observation vectors of speech, is the location of the user's face in a video. Because the system was designed to operate with only one user at any given time, it is assumed that the frame contains only a single face of one individual. The process of face localization involves the reduction of entire frame to the area containing only the face. This work uses haar-like features [7,8] as the detection method to locate the face area.

After determining the coordinates of vertices rectangular mask, a new video sequence of statements containing the limited area of the image to the user's face is creates from the original sequence of frames. For a lip-reading system, it is essential to track the lip region of the speaker. This can be achieved by tracking the lip-corners. It is difficult to locate or track lip-corners alone. In order to find the lip-corners within a face, it is possible to search other facial features using certain constraints and heuristics. Some facial features are easier to locate than lip-corners. For example, within a face, the pupils are two dark regions that satisfy certain geometric constraints, such as: position inside the face, symmetry according to the facial symmetric axis and minimum and maximum width between each other.

When designating mouth image area it is well known that individual frames contains the entire face of the user. Therefore eye coordinates can be used to determine the exact position of the mouth. For this reason Gradient Method and Integral Projection (GMIP) [9] is applied to find horizontal and vertical lines of eyes.

3   Lip Edge Detection and Video Encoding Speech

During natural speech, lips move vertically, the lip corners are in place or, alternatively, move horizontally, and the distance between the inner and outer edge of the lower and upper lip remains unchanged. Therefore, the system uses only the corners and outer edges of the lips as the main features in the process of lip tracking [10].

An important element of the extraction characteristics of the lips is to locate the lip corners. The exact position of the mouth corners is crucial, so that later on the basis of their location the outer edges of the mouth could be detection, as well as the landmark distribution. This paper proposes a method based on the specifics of lips color and shape. In this method, the localization process of lip corners is realized on a color image. Lips have a very distinct color and by properly manipulating the various components of the RGB color space, isolated borders between the lips and the rest of the face might be obtained by thresholding. Operations performed on the RGB channels could be described by the following relationship:

$$
lipregion = \begin{cases} \frac{B}{G} - 1 < T1 \\ \qquad and \\ \frac{R}{G} - \frac{B}{G} < T2 \\ \qquad and \\ \frac{R}{G} - 1 < T3 \end{cases} \tag{1}
$$

where: $T1$, $T2$ and $T3$ are empirically chosen thresholding values.

In this way, the values of the pixels corresponding to the specific color of the lips are set. Knowing the structure shape of lips, corners of the mouth may be designated as the extreme levels of specific color of mouth pixels. Searching for the pixels has to be done within a limited area of the mouth, near the horizontal axis of the lips.

Correct determination of the lip corners is so important that a round grid is built on its basis to determine the points on the outer edges of the lips. Based on the corners of the mouth the center of the circle can be determined at half of the distance between the corners of the lips. When moving around the circle the radius is determined as the angle α. Starting from one of designated corner we can differentiate between $2\pi/\alpha$ of rays. Then, moving along each of the rays toward the center of the circle we can designated a characteristic point of the outer edge of the lips, as the first encountered mouth pixel. The offset of rays is chosen accordingly to the accuracy with which the outer edges of the lips should be reproduce. The study assumed that each of the rays is at about 22.5 degree, which gives 16 points, including two characteristic corners of the mouth.

The system is based on HMM. For the HMM model, the input signal has to be introduced as a vector of observations, so for each frame based on the coordinates of characteristic points a symbol could be assigned that best describes the characteristics of that frame. The proposed method for encoding frames incorporates a simplified method that uses the location of each of the characteristic points of the straight line defined by the corners of the mouth. For each frame, we calculate the sum of relative distances m from all points of a straight line, defined by the corners of the mouth. We adopted 16 characteristic points, so each of the calculated relationships could be divided by 16. The sum of obtained value, when multiplied by 100 is in the range from 11 to 60, obviously if properly located in characteristic points on the outer edges of the lips:

$$y = \frac{\sum_{i=1}^{N} \frac{m_i}{d}}{N} \cdot 100 \tag{2}$$

where: N - is the number of points, m and d - see Fig. 1.

Fig. 1 shows scheme of assumed location of corners of mouth, definition of external edges of mouth and video speech encoding method.

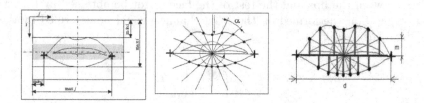

Fig. 1. Scheme of assumed location of corners of mouth, definition of external edges of mouth and video speech encoding method

It was assumed that the resulting symbols should be in the range from 1 to 50, so the minimum value of the code for each user must be specified accordingly and on this basis the code values need to be reduced to the objective range.

4   The Method of Supporting the Division of Phonemes

The division of the speech signal into phonemes is very important for systems that perform continuous speech recognition. The most often used method currently uses constant-time segmentation. This methods benefit from simplicity of implementation and the ease of comparing blocks of the same length. Clearly, however, the boundaries of speech elements such as phonemes do not lie on fixed position boundaries; phonemes naturally vary in length both because of their structure and due to speaker variations. Constant segmentation therefore risks losing information about the phonemes. Different sounds may be merged into single blocks and individual phonemes lost completely.

Spectral analysis of the speech signal is the most appropriate method for extracting information from speech signals. The analysis of the power in different frequency bands offers potential for distinguishing the start and end of phonemes. Many phonemes exhibit rapid changes in particular sub bands which can be used to detect their start and endpoints. However, for many boundaries, there is no discernible drop in overall power, and at some frequencies, the power is broadly constant over the lifetime of the phoneme.

We propose a method that combines analysis of the frequency signal, and an analysis of the key changes from the video frames of speech. In our approach, we analyze the significant changes in the video frames and synchronize those changes with an acoustic signal. The idea of the described method is shown in Fig. 2

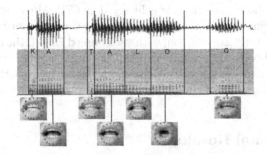

Fig. 2. The method of divide the audio signal into phonemes with use video frame

5   System of Audio Visual Speech Recognition

The accuracy of automatic lip tracking method was tested in audio-visual speech recognition system, that incorporates the hidden Markov models as a probabilistic data classifier. Audio-visual speech recognition is based on the extraction of recording features of audio and features of video. In such system video and audio channels are analyzed separately, then a proper fusion of designated features is made.

The input to HMM has to be presented in the form of vectors of observation. Such an observation vectors can be obtained by making a vector quantization. In audio speech analysis Mel Frequency Cepstral Coefficients (MFCC) were used for the extraction of audio features. To create a codebook Lloyd algorithm was used. In speech recognition systems based on HMM, each frame represented by a vector of observation is coded as a symbol of observation. In our system, all the individual words can be encoded using 37 code symbols, corresponding to the number of phonemes of the Polish language.

The result of audio signal analysis is the extraction of required characteristics of the signal, whereas the result of video analysis being the process of encoding each frame containing the shape of the lips with the use of appropriate symbol observation.

Vectors of observations of audio and video signals have a similar length. The audio signal is sampled at a frequency of 8000 samples per second. After the encoding process one second of audio contains about 50 symbols. Consequently the video signal is sampled at a frequency of 50 frames per second, to synchronize audio and video streams.

In the method of fusion, the audio and visual observation sequences are integrated using a coupled hidden Markov model (CHMM) [11,12]. The feature fusion system using a multi-stream HMM assumes that the audio and video sequences are state synchronous, but allows the audio and video components to have different contributions to the overall observation likelihood. The audio visual product HMM can be seen as an extension of the multi-stream HMM that allows for audio-visual state asynchrony. The CHMM can model the audio-visual state asynchrony and preserve at the same time the natural audio visual dependencies over time. In addition, with the coupled HMM, the audio and video observation likelihoods are computed independently, significantly reducing the parameter space and complexity of the model compared to the models that require the concatenation of the audio and visual observations [12].

6   Experimental Results

To perform research, we applied a set of seventy-command, recorded for 40 different users. In order to show the correctness of functioning method of automatic tracking of the lips, and the level of error recognition system of audio-video speech, experiments were performed for different levels of audio noise (at SNR of 20, 15, 10, 5, and 0 dB).

Many scientists in the world deal with the analysis of audio-visual speech. In their studies, they examine the various factors of processing audio-visual speech. Therefore, to compare the obtained results with those of other researchers, we chose only those leading the work that analyzed in a similar way audio-visual recognition of speech. In order to compare the developed method with the popular methods of audio-visual recognition of speech, developed by leading researchers in this field, we adopted similar conditions for noisy audio signal. Effectiveness compared with those of [2,13,14,15,16], in which the authors have adopted similar solutions by encoding both signals, and using CHMM for learning and testing. Assumptions may differ in terms of quantity of the analyzed words, different amounts of CHMM states and various means of fusion of audio and video signals. But the sense of studies was similar, so it was concluded that the comparison will be reliable. The results of comparing the level of recognition errors of audio-visual speech was showed in Tab. 1.

Table 1. The results of comparing the level of recognition errors of audio-visual speech

Method	Recognition Accuracy [%]				
	SNR 20dB	SNR 15dB	SNR 10dB	SNR 5dB	SNR 0dB
AV-Concat [2]	88,37	80,66	73,95	66,36	53,73
AV-HiLDA [2]	88,44	81,92	75,91	66,77	56,49
AV-Enhanced [2]	87,28	79,84	70,28	56,88	41,04
AV-MS-Joint [2]	88,63	82,52	77,08	69,97	59,11
AV-LSNR [17]	93,13	88,26	83,05	78,64	71,27
AV-CHMM [18]	98,56	90,08	85,09	75,23	70,51
Audiovisual [19]	94,72	88,16	84,72	74,12	68,96
AV Combined [20]	97,20	93,40	79,50	58,40	50,80
A Mowa PL	**96,02**	**77,35**	**52,30**	**37,84**	**29,73**
AV Mowa PL	**96,12**	**89,76**	**83,33**	**77,11**	**71,32**

7   Conclusion and Future Work

Conducted tests indicate that the method of automatic lip tracking is working properly and performs well in real life. Test results show that the accuracy of speech recognition is largely affected by the fact of whether the environment is disturbed or not.

In comparison of recognition accuracy our method obtains similar or better results to other existing audio-visual speech recognition methods, published in scientific literature. Fig. 3. shows results of comparing the level of recognition errors of audio-visual speech for different methods.

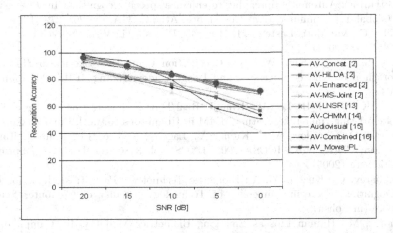

Fig. 3. Results of comparing the level of recognition errors of audio-visual speech for different methods

The results show also that this method should be developed. There are plans to expand the method of automatic detection of the position of the tongue, for each of the spoken video phonemes. In future work we plan to build a system for Polish speech recognition, based on analysis of individual phonemes. Such an approach would allow for continuous speech recognition. The method of audio-visual recognition of Polish speech was used in the system to control the camera movement using voice commands. To increase the efficiency of the method to make the system work properly in real time, can be used to support at the hardware level.

An advantage of the proposed method is the satisfactory effectiveness created by the lip-tracking procedures, and the simplicity and functionality by the proposed methods, which fuse together the audio and visual signals. A decisively lower level of mistakes was obtained in audio-visual speech recognition, and speaker identification, in comparison to only audio speech, particularly in facilities, where the audio signal is strongly disrupted.

References

1. Shin, J., Lee, J., Kim, D.: Real-time lip reading system for isolated Korean word recognition. Pattern Recognition 44, 559–571 (2011)
2. Neti, C., Potamianos, G., Luttin, J., Mattews, I., Glotin, H., Vergyri, D., Sison, J., Mashari, A., Zhou, J.: Audio Visual Speech-Recognition. 2000 Final Report (2000)
3. Zhi, Q., Kaynak, M.N.N., Sengupta, K., Cheok, A.D., Ko, C.C.: A study of the modeling aspects in bimodal speech recognition. In: Proc. 2001 IEEE International Conference on Multimedia and Expo, ICME 2001 (2001)
4. Jian, Z., Kaynak, M.N.N., Cheok, A.D., Chung, K.C.: Real-time Lip-tracking For Virtual Lip Implementation in Virtual Environments and Computer Games. In: Proc. 2001 International Fuzzy Systems Conference (2001)
5. Petajan, E.: Automatic lipreading to enhance speech recognition. In: Proceedings of Global Telecommunications Conference, Atlanta, GA, pp. 265–272 (1984)
6. Bailly, G., Vatikiotis-Basteson, E., Pierrier, P.: Issues in Visual Speech Processing. MIT Press (2004)
7. Park, S., Lee, J., Kim, W.: Face Recognition Using Haar-like feature/LDA. In: Workshop on Image Processing and Image Understanding, IPIU 2004 (January 2004)
8. Hong, K., Min, J.-H., Lee, W., Kim, J.: Real Time Face Detection and Recognition System Using Haar-Like Feature/HMM in Ubiquitous Network Environments. In: Gervasi, O., Gavrilova, M.L., Kumar, V., Laganá, A., Lee, H.P., Mun, Y., Taniar, D., Tan, C.J.K. (eds.) ICCSA 2005. LNCS, vol. 3480, pp. 1154–1161. Springer, Heidelberg (2005)
9. Kukharev, G., Kuzminski, A.: Biometric Technology, Part. 1: Methods for Face Recognition. Szczecin University of Technology, Faculty of Computer Science (2003) (in Polish)
10. Choraś, M.: Human Lips as Emerging Biometrics Modality. In: Campilho, A., Kamel, M.S. (eds.) ICIAR 2008. LNCS, vol. 5112, pp. 993–1002. Springer, Heidelberg (2008)
11. Kaynak, M.N.N., Zhi, Q., Cheok, A.D., Sengupta, K., Chung, K.C.: Audio - Visual Modeling for Bimodal Speech Recognition. In: Proc. 2001 International Fuzzy Systems Conference (2001)
12. Liu, X., Zhao, Y., Pi, X., Liang, L., Nefian, A.V.: Audio-visual continuous speechr ecognition using a coupled hidden Markov model. In: ICSLP 2002, pp. 213–216 (2002)
13. Hasegawa-Johnson, M., Livescu, K., Lal, P., Saenko, K.: Audiovisual speech recognition with articulator positions as hidden variables. In: Proc. International Congress of Phonetic Sciences (ICPhS) (2007)
14. Shao, X., Barker, J.: Stream weight estimation for multistream audio-visual speech recognition in a multispeaker environment. Speech Communication 50, 337–353 (2008)
15. Nefian, A.V., Liang, L., Pi, X., Xiaoxiang, L., Mao, C., Murphy, K.: A coupled HMM for audio-visual speech recognition. In: IEEE International Conference on Acoustics, Speech, and Signal Processing, ICASSP (2002)
16. Nefian, A.V., Liang, L., Pi, X., Liu, X., Mao, C.: An coupled hidden Markov model for audio-visual speech recognition. In: International Conference on Acoustics, Speech and Signal Processing (2002)

Object Recognition
Using Summed Features Classifier

Marcus Lindner, Marco Block, and Raúl Rojas

Free University of Berlin
Institut für Informatik und Mathematik
Takustr. 9, 14195 Berlin, Germany
{lindner,block,rojas}@inf.fu-berlin.de

Abstract. A common task in the field of document digitization for information retrieval is separating text and non-text elements. In this paper an innovative approach of recognizing patterns is presented. Statistical and structural features in arbitrary number are combined into a rating tree, which is an adapted decision tree. Such a tree is trained for character patterns to distinguish text elements from non-text elements. First experiments in a binarization application have shown promising results in significant reduction of false-positives without producing false-negatives.

1 Introduction

Application of pattern recognition methods often takes place after many stages of image preprocessing. Especially at the binarization step, when foreground objects are separated from the background, a lot of information reduction is done (a common survey to binarization methods is [14]).

Another method of binarization is the local contrast segmentation (LCS), which uses continuous edge intensities to identify connected components, that have a high probability of being text elements due to their local properties [2]. Figure 1 shows the results of the LCS algorithm on a shadowed document. The algorithm yields no false-negatives but some false-positives due to its defensive operation. For subsequent processing steps, such as the document layout determination, the number of false-positives must be reduced without introducing false-negatives.

We present a novel classifier, which interprets objects as the characteristic sum of their properties. The paper is organized as follows: Section 2 reviews some related work from the state of current research. Section 3 explains the new classifier in detail with the training and recognition stages. In section 4, we evaluate our classifier with a practical binarization application, where false-positives from a preceding character classifier are reduced significantly, without increasing the number of false-negatives. Finally, section 5 concludes the paper with a prospect to aspects of future work.

L. Rutkowski et al. (Eds.): ICAISC 2012, Part I, LNCS 7267, pp. 543–550, 2012.
© Springer-Verlag Berlin Heidelberg 2012

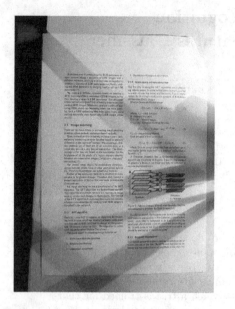

Fig. 1. left: grey-scale document image with a lot of shadows; right: the binarized result image of the LCS algorithm

2   Related Work

There are statistical and structural approaches for pattern recognition systems [18]. The main difference is the necessity of having domain knowledge for the structural approaches. The proposed system uses generalized structural feature extraction without relying on domain knowledge spezialized for time-series. Behnke et al. present an off-line graph based method for handwritten digits [19]. They vectorize the pixel image for structural analysis and generate a structural graph. This method uses only one very specialized feature for classification - the structural graph. Al-Taani et al. propose an approach for handwritten arabic digits. They calculate a slope change chain using the drawn pixels, which is used to identify and extract primitives. Each digit is a unique sequence of primitives. A finite transition network is used to find a matching grammar for the primitives sequence in the classification step [11,6]. Elgammal et al. use a graph- and primitives-based approach. Structural features are extracted and represented in a line adjacency graph. This graph is used to map the structural features in topological relation to the baseline and segment the characters into primitives. Regular grammars, which describe the composition of primitives for the specific characters, are used for pattern recognition [17].

A standard technique for unsupervised learning is agglomerative clustering and is used in many applications like data mining and other [7]. During the training stage of our rating tree, we use agglomerative clustering to determine the childnodes.

Algorithms for object recognition, like k-NN [10,3,21,20], k-means [9,12] and others [4], use pattern matching techniques that rely on the difference between positive and negative samples, in fact they depend on it. The several approaches use either features of one particular type in any count [15,13,9] or single features of various types [1,8], but not both at the same time.

We present a completely new approach to the field of pattern recognition problems. We think an object is the sum of its properties and thus we propose a method to combine any type of feature, statistical as well as structural features. Our approach is not restricted to one specialized feature or type of features. We define an extendable set of different features and train a special decision tree. The feature set is highly application specific and therefore it is necessary to have domain knowledge. The decision tree can be interpreted as a grammar verifier at the classification stage. Each symbol has one or more paths, depending on its variation presented during the training phase.

3   Summed Features Classifier

A special classifier for object recognition combines features of different types with varying count and thus constitutes a summed features classifier (SFC).

The classifier is trained during an offline phase. Therfor sets of different features are extracted from each training object and then combined to a specialized decision tree. The tree stores the individual composition of the features for each object. There is no need of negative samples for the training of the classifier.

At the online stage the classifier is used to determine the class label for an unknown connected component. It can be used for binary classification as well, if no distinction between the objects is needed or all objects are unlabeled and have to be distinguished from clutter only.

For the application of character recognition we identified many patterns in latin letters and arabic digits, for which we built fast and simple feature extractors. For example, we used a modified RANSAC [23,24] algorithm to find straight lines and line segments as well as circles and semicircles in a connected component. The set of found line segments is searched for triangle and rectangle structures, as they are contained in characters. This is done by application of the following criteria: one phantom line segment or at least one horizontally or vertically oriented line segment is included in a subset. There are many more statistical and structural features like closed surfaces, junctions and their degree or line ends on the character skeleton, holes with horizontal or vertical direction in the character topology, the best axis of symmetry and the associated degree of symmetry, the ratio between foreground and whole image area or the centroid of the character.

The used feature set is customized for latin letters and arabic digits. With an application specific feature set, our classifier can also be used for another class of problems. Visualizations of some features can be seen in figure 2.

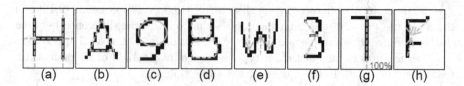

Fig. 2. selection of some used features for SFC: (a) straight lines; (b) triangle; (c) circle; (d) closed surface; (e) 2 northern openings and 1 southern opening; (f) junction points and edges between them on the character skeleton; (g) axis of symmetry with perfect degree of symmetry and (h) centroid point

3.1   Train Classifier

The tree is built by a recursive algorithm: Sets T and V contain all training and validation samples at the beginning. At each recursion step a certain feature type $m_i \in M$ is manually chosen, for which the features were extracted from T and V. All feature vectors of type m_i of T are clustered with an unsupervised cluster analysis algorithm (i.e. agglomerative cluster analysis) to r clusters C_d with $d = 0 \ldots r - 1$. The current node gets $r + 1$ child nodes, one for each found cluster and one for the rest of the feature space. This special child node represents non-classified objects. Connected components with a path to such a leaf in the tree will be rejected. Figure 3 shows the clusters (as Gaussian distributions) found in the 1-dimensional feature space of vertical straight lines (x coordinate).

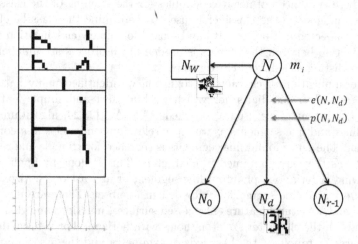

Fig. 3. left: multivariate normal distribution as specification for 1-dimensional clusters found in the feature space of vertical lines; right: generic creation scheme of a node N during the recursive training algorithm, with chosen feature type m_i, children $N_{0 \ldots r-1}$ for determined clusters and child node N_W for the remaining feature space, as well as annotated edges

A cluster is represented as a Gaussian distribution by its mean vector $\mu(C_d)$ and covariance matrix $\Sigma(C_d)$. Additionally all labels of training samples, that have at least one feature vector, which is inside C_d (three standard deviations), are in the set of labels stored at the child node edge d:

$$e(N, N_d) = [\{l_1, l_2, \ldots\}, \mu(C_d), \Sigma(C_d)]$$

Next the training error is computed with the validation samples and stored as a probability distribution function $p(N, N_d)$ for each child node. Assuming there is validation sample v of class A from which two feature vectors f_1^i and f_2^i of type m_i are extracted as shown in figure 4. Each feature vector belongs to one cluster and adjusts the probability function respectively to its own class label and the class labels stored at the edge. For example feature vector f_1^i falls into cluster C_1 at node N_1, that means the path to node N_1 in distribution function $p(N, N_1)$ must be incremented. This has to be done for every validation sample and is normalized afterwards.

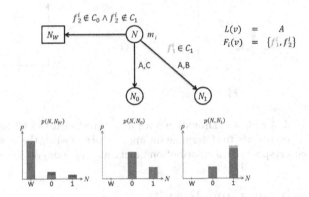

Fig. 4. example for computation of distribution functions: validation image v with label A has 2 feature vectors of type m_i, f_1^i falls into cluster C_1 and f_2^i neither in cluster C_1 nor C_2; that is $p(N, N_1)$ and $p(N, N_W)$ have to be adjusted

Before continuing with child node N_d, the sets of training and validation samples have to be reduced by all samples, which have no feature vector in the appropriate cluster C_d. The set M is reduced by m_i only if none of the samples in the reduced sets T' and V' has an unused feature vector of type m_i on the path from the root down to the node N_d.

3.2 Object Recognition

Recognition of unknown objects is done by a random Monte Carlo [22,5,16] depth-first search traversal with respect to the distribution functions stored at each edge on the path down to a leaf. While going down the tree, the specific feature type m_i is extracted of the unknown object at each node. One of the vectors and its appropriate edge are chosen randomly (if more than one is available).

Depending on the probability distribution function for this edge the next node is determined randomly, as shown in figure 5. At the end all probability values on the chosen path down to the leaf are normalized using the path length. This is done for a given number of n iterations. The path with the highest value is the best fit for the unknown object and the returned class.

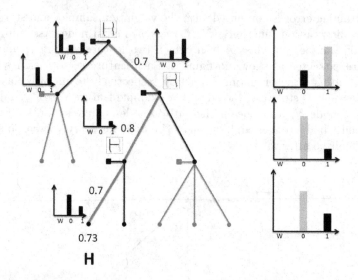

Fig. 5. example for class examination with a Summed Features Classifier: one feature is selected at each node to determine an appropriate cluster, the next node is chosen randomly with respect to the distribution function (right side) of that particular cluster

4   Experiments and Results

We test our approach on an Intel Core2Duo based computer with 2.0GHz/4GB RAM and a set of 2209 connected components, that result on an application of LCS. LCS yields a number of connected components it identifies as characters. Not all of them are truly characters. Each connected component is classified by a human afterwards. This means we have a number of objects which are positives and false-positives. The aim is to discard as many as possible of false-positive objects without rejecting real characters.

We train a summed features classifier for the ten arabic digits. Figure 6(a) shows the distribution of our used object set before application of SFC. The set of 259 positive samples contains every connected component which was classified as an arabic digit and the set of 1950 false-positives all other. We apply the SFC as a binary classifier to this set of objects. Figure 6(b) shows the results after application of the SFC, where are 59 false-positives only, 1891 negatives and no false-negative. The time to traverse the rating tree for one object is less than 10ms.

With SFC we are able to decrease dramatically the false-positives and discard them as non-characters. Furthermore no digits are rejected (false-negatives). It is possible to increase the rejection rate of false-positives by adjusting the probability distribution functions to be less tolerant towards errors. But this results also in discarding positives.

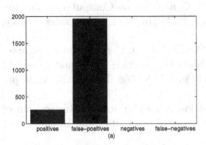 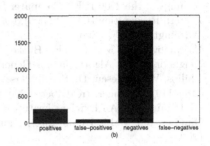

Fig. 6. distribution of connected components (a) after LCS with many background objects and (b) after SFC, where most false-positives and no positives are rejected

5 Conclusion and Future Work

We presented the classifier SFC, which interprets objects as the characteristic sum of their properties. In the first experiment we could significantly reduce the set of false-positives by more than 96% without producing false-negatives. With that the results of LCS binarization can be improved considerably.

However, the algorithm is currently not suitable for applications, that need to compute the binarization in realtime. Therefore we are working on a more performant solution. Additionally, the configuration of the feature selection during the training phase will be adjusted automatically in future.

References

1. He, D., Liang, S., Fang, Y.: A Multi-Descriptor, Multi-Nearest Neighbor Approach for Image Classification. In: Huang, D.-S., Zhao, Z., Bevilacqua, V., Figueroa, J.C. (eds.) ICIC 2010. LNCS, vol. 6215, pp. 515–523. Springer, Heidelberg (2010)
2. Block, M., Rojas, R.: Local Contrast Segmentation to Binarize Images. In: Third International Conference on Digital Society (ICDS 2009), Cancun/Mexiko, vol. 1(1), pp. 294–299. IEEE Computer Society (2009)
3. Boiman, O., Shechtman, E., Irani, M.: In defense of nearest-neighbor based image classication. In: IEEE Conference on Computer Vision and Pattern Recognition (CVPR), pp. 1–8 (2008)
4. Wu, X., Kumar, V., Quinlan, J.R., Ghosh, J., et al.: Top 10 Algorithms in Data Mining. Knowledge and Information Systems 14(1), 1–37 (2008)
5. Kalos, M.H., Whitlock, P.A.: Monte Carlo Methods. Wiley-VCH (2008)
6. Al-Taani, A.T., Maen, H.: Recognition of On-line Handwritten Arabic Digits Using Structural Features and Transition Network. Informatica 32, 275–281 (2008)

7. Walter, B., Bala, K., Kulkarni, M., Pingali, K.: Fast Agglomerative Clustering for Rendering. In: IEEE Symposium on Interactive Ray Tracing (RT), pp. 81–86 (2008)
8. Zhang, Q., Izquierdo, E.: A Multi-feature Optimization Approach to Object-Based Image Classification. In: Sundaram, H., Naphade, M., Smith, J.R., Rui, Y. (eds.) CIVR 2006. LNCS, vol. 4071, pp. 310–319. Springer, Heidelberg (2006)
9. Nister, D., Stewenius, H.: Scalable recognition with a vocabulary tree. In: Proceedings of the 2006 IEEE Computer Society Conference on Computer Vision and Pattern Recognition (CVPR 2006), vol. 2, pp. 2161–2168. IEEE Computer Society, Washington, DC (2006)
10. Bajramovic, F., Mattern, F., Butko, N., Denzler, J.: A Comparison of Nearest Neighbor Search Algorithms for Generic Object Recognition. In: Blanc-Talon, J., Philips, W., Popescu, D., Scheunders, P. (eds.) ACIVS 2006. LNCS, vol. 4179, pp. 1186–1197. Springer, Heidelberg (2006)
11. Al-Taani, A.T.: An Efficient Feature Extraction Algorithm for the Recognition of Handwritten Arabic Digits. International Journal of Computational Intelligence 2 (2005)
12. Fei-Fei, L., Perona, P.: A Bayesian Hierarchical Model for Learning Natural Scene Categories. In: Proc. of IEEE Computer Vision and Pattern Recognition, pp. 524–531 (2005)
13. Lowe, D.G.: Distinctive image features from scale-invariant keypoints. Int. J. Comput. Vision 60, 91–110 (2004)
14. Sezgin, M., Sankur, B.: Survey over image thresholding techniques and quatitative performance evaluation. Journal of Electronic Imaging 13(1), 146–165 (2004)
15. Viola, P., Jones, M.J.: Robust real-time face detection. Int. J. Comput. Vision 57, 137–154 (2004)
16. Andrieu, C., de Freitas, N., Doucet, A., Jordan, M.I.: An Introduction to MCMC for Machine Learning. Machine Learning 50(1), 5–43 (2003)
17. Elgammal, A.M., Ismail, M.A.: A Graph-Based Segmentation and Feature-Extraction Framework for Arabic Text Recognition. In: Sixth International Conference on Document Analysis and Recognition (ICDAR 2001), pp. 622–626 (2001)
18. Olszewski, R.T.: Generalized Feature Extraction for Structural Pattern Recognition in Time-Series Data. PhD thesis, University Pittsburgh (2001)
19. Behnke, S., Pfister, M., Rojas, R.: Recognition of Handwritten Digits using Structural Information. In: Proceedings ICNN 1997, pp. 1391–1396 (1997)
20. Lebourgeois, F., Henry, J.: An evolutive ocr system based on continuous learning. In: IEEE Workshop on Applications of Computer Vision, pp. 272–277 (1996)
21. Hong, T., Lam, S.W., Hull, J.J., Srihari, S.N.: The design of a nearest-neighbor classier and its use for japanese character recognition. In: Proceedings of the Third International Conference on Document Analysis and Recognition (ICDAR 1995), vol. 1, pp. 270–273. IEEE Computer Society, Washington, DC (1995)
22. Neal, R.M.: Probabilistic inference using markov chain monte carlo methods. In: Technical Report CRG-TR-93-1, Dept. of Computer Science, University of Toronto, 144 pages (1993)
23. Rousseeuw, P.J.: Least median of squares regression. Journal of the American Statistical Association 79(388), 871–880 (1984)
24. Fischler, M.A., Bolles, R.C.: Random sample consensus: a paradigm for model fitting with applications to image analysis and automated cartography. Commun. ACM 24, 381–395 (1981)

Novel Method for Parasite Detection in Microscopic Samples

Patryk Najgebauer, Tomasz Nowak, Jakub Romanowski,
Janusz Rygał, Marcin Korytkowski, and Rafał Scherer

Department of Computer Engineering, Częstochowa University of Technology
al. Armii Krajowej 36, 42-200 Częstochowa, Poland
{patryk.najgebauer,tomasz.nowak,jakub.romanowski,janusz.rygal,
marcin.korytkowski,rafal.scherer}@kik.pcz.pl
http://kik.pcz.pl

Abstract. This paper describes a novel image retrieval method for parasite detection based on the analysis of digital images captured by the
camera from a microscope. In our approach we use several image processing methods to find known parasite shapes. At first, we use an edge
detection method with edge representation by vectors. The next step consists in clustering edges fragments by their normal vectors and positions.
Then grouped edges fragments are used to perform elliptical or circular
shapes fitting as they resemble most parasite forms. This approach is
invariant from rotation of parasites eggs or the analyzed sample. It is
also invariant to scale of digital images and it is robust to overlapping
shapes of parasites eggs thanks to the ability to reconstructing elliptical
or other symmetric shapes that represent the eggs of parasites. With this
solution we can also reconstruct incomplete shape of parasite egg which
can be visible only in some part of the retrieved image.

Keywords: edge detection, shape recognition, objects detection, image
processing.

1 Introduction

Content-Based Image Retrieval (CBIR) is a branch of science based on advanced
mathematical and computer science methods for analyzing digital images. In
truth, the process of computer image analysis is still far from the way in which
images are analyzed by the human brain. Nevertheless, existing methods and
algorithms allow the use of CBIR-related technologies in many areas of daily life
or work. One of the areas in which CBIR gains the immense popularity is analysis
of medical imaging (e.g. computed tomography, USG or RTG). The current
literature studies do not show, however, real-world solutions in the field of image
analysis in parasitological domain. Parasitology is the study of parasites and
parasitism, which deals with morphology, anatomy and development of parasites.
One of the primary examinations used in parasitology is taking samples and
test them under a microscope to identify a parasite on the basis of its physical

L. Rutkowski et al. (Eds.): ICAISC 2012, Part I, LNCS 7267, pp. 551–558, 2012.

characteristics. Each parasite has individual characteristics, which identify its species. The examination itself is time consuming, even for an experienced doctor or lab technician; there are also frequent errors in determining parasite species, resulting in inadequate treatment that can lead to rapid health deterioration and even death of patient.

For many years content-based image retrieval systems (CBIR)[6] have been used in many different areas, such as medicine, biometrics or automotive. Major research areas combining image processing and medical analysis are computed tomography, magnetic resonance and ultrasound scan [8][1][7][2]. Currently, these systems support the work of medical doctors in many different fields of medicine. However, there is no specific application dedicated to parasitology, i.e. to detect and identify parasites in raw laboratory samples. Certain works focused on building knowledge bases, which contained images of selected parasites [10] and were used primarily for academic purposes. In most samples there exists different pollution that can obscure parasites. In many samples there are also structures that can resemble parasites. There are many algorithms for processing images [11][14][4] used in medicine, which specialize in finding specific objects (e.g. bacteria, tumors, fractures, different unwanted changes). An example may be algorithms, which allow searching for strains of malaria in blood [12], or specific algorithms analyzing organs in tomography [13]. General methods used in image processing are not suitable for search of parasites. They can only locate the object (provided that the sample was previously cleaned), but are not able to identify the parasite species. In the case where the sample is contaminated with other structures (such as hair or grass), these structures will be also treated as important objects.

The proposed method can detect edges of objects, which could be parasites, and can supplement the missing parts of the detected edges. In samples obtained directly from the parasite tests there can exist many different objects such as air bubbles, blood, grass, fur, and other non-parasitic objects. Objects can overlap, which may hinder their detection by existing algorithms. A helpful feature here is the shape of the parasite eggs as they are characterized by elliptical construction and have distinctive shell. These features can be a starting point to detect the edges of the object. Often in the samples only a part of the essential object is visible and the next important stage of this method is to develop an algorithm that will be able to predict (reconstruct) the missing elements of the parasites. This is possible because the eggs of parasites are characterized by symmetrical oval shapes, and have similar size [9]. Methods that were presented in the literature are very general and do not provide a solution to this problem. The next problem will be converting the detected edges of objects and their classification.

The remainder of this paper is organized as follows. Section 2 describes the problem of the edge extraction in digital images and the current CBIR methods used in parasitology. Section 3 describes the proposed method of the edge recognition. Section 4 reports the experimental results on a set of real images.

2   Problem Description and Existing Methods

Problems with computer-aided parasites detection start at the edge detection step. Most edges of parasite eggs are blurred. Edges blur is mainly caused by focus loss of the microscope and reflections of the backlight. The second problem is transparent egg bodies, because some pollution are visible in the background. The standard Canny edge algorithm cannot detect blurred edges; this problem can be resolved by using various size of edge detection masks.

After edge detection, we have to deal with a problem with vague egg edges and edges noise from objects texture and pollution. Noise edges from textures and small pollution can be eliminated by curvature test. Vague or invisible edges are caused by close extensive pollutions and other parasite eggs. The extensive pollution can be e.g. crystals, air bubbles or undigested debris. Problems with these pollutions are hard to solve because they exist in different sizes and shapes. Moreover, some of their shapes are similar to parasite eggs. Second problem occurring with the lack of pronounced edges is that edges are sometimes connected with other nearly located objects what increases problem for recognition of objects. To overcome this problem we present a method that transforms edges pixels to vectors to speed up filtering and grouping process.

In the last step of parasites egg detection the main problem is the comparison of their shape to ellipse. The problem outcomes from the fact that the shapes of parasite eggs are not accurately symmetrical. Symmetries and ellipses matched to the shape can be determined only approximately.

There are many algorithms for processing images [11] [14] [4] used in medicine, which specialize in finding specific objects (bacteria, tumors, fractures, different unwanted changes). These specific as well as general methods used in image processing are not suitable for search of parasites. They can only locate objects (provided that the sample was previously cleaned), but are not able to identify the parasite species. In the case when the sample is contaminated with other structures (e.g. hair, grass, crystals, air bubbles), existing algorithms will also classify them as important objects.

The literature shows that previous work focused on building knowledge bases containing images of selected parasites (see e.g. [10]), which are used primarily for academic purposes. None of the previous work was dedicated to an attempt to detect and identify parasites in raw laboratory samples. In most samples there exist various pollutions and in result parasites can be obscured. In many samples there are also structures that can resemble parasites. Existing databases [9] [5] mainly contain parasites isolated from the samples. Moreover they are prepared on various hardware, in different scales and using various methods. These databases are not suitable to for the development of CBIR algorithms for parasite identification.

3   Novel Method for Parasite Egg Detection

Proposed method is designed to detect and to enhance edges of parasite eggs or cyst and finally to estimate the best fit ellipse to their shape. The proposed method detects parasites in following steps.

3.1   Multi-scale Edge Detection

The presented solution is based on the Canny edge detection algorithm [3]. First, the median filter is used to remove noise and small reflections (backlight from microscope), that appear on the test material. The proposed method uses the Sobel filter mask in X and Y axis direction. Frequent blurring on the edge of the examined objects caused by inaccurate focus calibration of microscope forced detection of edges at several scales (Fig. 1). We used 8x8 (Fig. 1b) and larger, 16x16 mask sizes (Fig. 1c). Such action also allowed skipping the part of small impurities and isolating the edges of larger objects from each other. The last

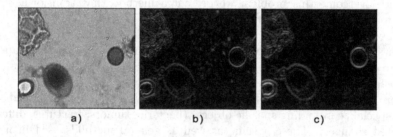

Fig. 1. Multi scale edge detection. (a) Input image. (b) Sobel filter with mask size 8x8 pixels. (c) Sobel filter with mask size 16x16 pixels.

step of the process of edge detection in the presented solution is to search for local extremes among the determined edges. In the result we obtain enhanced edges and steeper gradients of edges. The outcome of this stage is an array of local gradient maximum values in the X and Y direction for each pixel.

3.2   Vector-Based Edge Representation

To speed up the method and to allow for additional filtration of image, edges are converted to a vector form as presented in Fig 2. With this action the amount of data to be analyzed is dramatically reduced. Each part of the edge has information about its location and position of his arms. For this purpose, the image with detected edges is analyzed by means of a grid at a minimum of 10 pixels in x and y axes. This solution speeds up the search for egg edges and ignores the edges of small, unimportant parts of the background. The edges of larger objects will be sliced by the grid at multiple points to provide an outline of the object. For each detected by the grid of edge pixel neighboring pixels are examined.

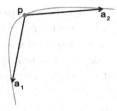

Fig. 2. Edge vector based representation. p - position of edges. a_1, a_2 - vectors of edge arm

The algorithm follows the edge of the pixel tracking in two opposite directions relative to the axis in which the component value of the gradient was the highest. After the passing of the distance in pixels equal to the number of pixels between grid lines are designated as vectors for the edges of each arm from the starting point. An example of vector representation of image edges is shown in Fig 3a.

3.3   Edge Filtration

Filtering of the detected edges is possible thanks to the determined arm vectors from the previous stage. At the beginning we remove the edges where the angle

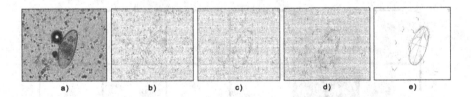

Fig. 3. Vector-based edge representation with filtering and grouping. (a) Input image. (b) Image of vector-based representation of detected edges . (c) Edges filtered by angle between arm vectors. (d) Edge filtered by relation between neighbor edges.

between their arms is less than $140°$. For that purpose, we determine cosine of the angle (dot product) between their normal vectors

$$A = \overrightarrow{an} \cdot \overrightarrow{bn} \tag{1}$$

where $\overrightarrow{an}$, $\overrightarrow{bn}$ are normal vectors of edge arms. In this way, we remove part of the detected edges which represent object texture or small pollution (see Fig. 3b). The second step of filtering is removing isolated edges, i.e. without near placed edges of the same direction, forming continuous line (Fig. 3c). The degree of linkage between the lines is determined by the following formula

$$B = |\overrightarrow{n} \cdot \overrightarrow{abn_1}| \cdot |\overrightarrow{n} \cdot \overrightarrow{abn_2}| \tag{2}$$

where: $\overrightarrow{n}$ specifies the normal vector between positions of the edge fragments, and $\overrightarrow{abn_1}$ normal vector between the positions of the first edge arms and $\overrightarrow{abn_2}$ normal vector between the positions of second edge arms. Edges of the value of the coefficient B above values of 0.7 are treated as related edges. All the edges that are not related with at least one edge are removed from the list of edges.

3.4   Edge Grouping and Ellipse Approximation

In this step of the proposed method we group related edges in similar way to filtering by the coefficient B from Section 3.3. However, one edge can be joined only with two related edges, one per arm. Additionally, the method rejects groups composed of less than three edges. Now, only a few groups of edges remain from the entire image. At the final step, the algorithm finds ellipses which are best fit to edges groups by last square estimation.

4   Experiments

In the experiments we use images directly from the clinical parasitological laboratory at a resolution of 720x576 pixels. Images were captured directly from the camera which is built into the microscope. Presented method was implemented in C# language. The first step of analysis was to use median filter with mask

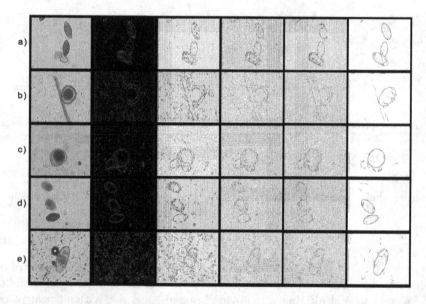

Fig. 4. Experimental results for parasite edge detection on 5 real images. First column, original images; second column, Canny edge detection with Sobel 8x8 filter; third column, created vectors from edges pixels; fourth column, the rejection of sharp edges; fifth column, rejection of the edges that do not form a continuity with the neighbor; sixth column, edge grouping by the proposed method.

of 4x4 pixels to denoise image. The next stage is the process of edge detection which uses Canny edge algorithm with Sobel mask of size 4x4 and 8x8 pixels. Figure 3 shows the step-by-step algorithm. The next step was to replace the detected edges by vector based representation - this operation is described in detail in section 3.2. The resulting vectors are filtered and grouped by their normal vectors (Section 3.3). The last step in the proposed solution is the detection of ellipses based on the created groups of the edges, using the least squares method (chapter 3.4). Fig. 4 shows 5 real images taken in different focus which were used during the experiments. As shown in the presented experimental examples the goal of the method is to find the edges of parasites and to remove all edges that belong to the impurities.

5   Conclusions

Existing algorithms used in image analysis of are not suitable for the analysis of images from parasitological examinations in a way that would enable the detection and identification of the parasite. After consultation with the parasitological clinical laboratory and preliminary research, it can be assumed that the creation of new algorithms targeted for parasitological examination will enable more profound research of such images. The result of the algorithms should be to locate and identify parasites. Characteristics that allow for proper classification of objects similar to parasite eggs and cysts are elliptical shapes with smooth edges.

Acknowledgements. The authors would like to thank Dr Andrzej Połozowski from Wrocław University of Environmental and Life Sciences for the opportunity to capture microscopic parasite video and inspiring talks.

The project was funded by the National Center for Science under decision number DEC-2011/01/D/ST6/06957.

References

1. Akgül, C.B., Rubin, D.L., Napel, S., Beaulieu, C.F., Greenspan, H., Acar, B.: Content-based image retrieval in radiology: current status and future directions. J. Digit. Imaging 2, 208–222 (2011)
2. Antonie, M.L., Zaiane, O.R., Coman, A.: Application of Data Mining Techniques for Medical Image Classification. In: Proceedings of the Second International Workshop on Multimedia Data Mining (2001)
3. Canny, J.: A computational approach to edge detection. IEEE Trans. Pattern Anal. Mach. Intell. 8(6), 679–698 (1986)
4. Chuctaya, H., Portugal, C., Beltran, C., Gutierrez, J., Lopez, C., Tupac, Y.: M-CBIR: A medical content-based image retrieval system using metric datastructures. JCC (2011)
5. Gardner, S.L.: The parasite collection search page in the Manter Laboratory of Prasitology, http://manter.unl.edu/hwml

6. Gudivada, V.N., Raghavan, V.V.: Content based image retrieval systems, vol. 28(9), pp. 18–22. IEEE Computer Society (1995)
7. Gueld, M.O., Keysers, D., Deselaers, T., Leisten, M., Schubert, H., Ney, H., Lehmann, T.M.: Comparison of global features for categorization of medical images. Medical Imaging (2004)
8. Hsua, W., Antani, S., Long, L.R., Neve, L., Thoma, G.R.: SPIRS: a Web-based image retrieval system for large biomedical databases. Int. J. Med. Inform. 78, 13–24 (2009)
9. Mallik, J., Samal, A.K., Gardner, S.L.: A Content Based Pattern Analysis System for a Biological Specimen Collection. In: 7th IEEE International Conference on Data Mining (2007)
10. Meduri, R., Samal, A., Gardner, S.L.: Worm-Web Search: A Content-Based Image Retrieval (CBIR) System for the Parasite Image Collection in the Harold W. Manter Laboratory of Parasitology, University of Nebraska State Mueum (2008)
11. Muller, H., Michoux, N., Bandon, D., Geissbuhler, A.: A Review of Content - Based Image Retrieval Systems in Medical Applications - Clinical Benefits and Future Directions. Int. J. Med. Inform. (2009)
12. Tek, F.B., Dempster, A.G., Kale, I.: Malaria Parasite Detection in Peripheral Blood Images. In: British Machine Vision Conference (2006)
13. Urschler, M., Mayer, H., Bolter, R., Leberl, F.: The LiveWire Approach for the Segmentation of Let Ventricle Electron-Beam CT Images. OCG 160, 319–326 (2002)
14. Wanjale, K., Borawake, T., Chaudhari, S.: Content Based Image Retrieval for Medical Images Techniques and Storage Methods-Review Paper. IJCA Journal 1(19) (2010)

Lipreading Procedure
Based on Dynamic Programming

Agnieszka Owczarek and Krzysztof Ślot

Institute of Electronics, Technical University of Lodz
Wolczanska Street 211/215, 90-924 Lodz, Poland
{agnieszka.owczarek,k.slot}@p.lodz.pl

Abstract. The following paper describes a novel lipreading procedure based on dynamic programming. We proposed a new method of outer lip contour extraction and representation. Lip shapes, corresponding to selected group of visems, are firstly extracted using dynamic programming and then approximated by B-splines. Coordinates of B-spline control points form final feature vector used for visem recognition task. The discontinuity of lip gradient image is addressed by dynamic programming technique. This has the advantage of global minimum detection and consequently optimal lip contour extraction. Experiments for Polish language utterances show that seven classes of visems can be recognized with 75% accuracy.

Keywords: lip contour extraction, dynamic programming, lipreading.

1 Introduction

Using visual information for automatic speech recognition (ASR) has been an active research area for over two decades. It is mainly used for improving recognition performance in audio speech recognition systems [1,2,3]. Lipreading contains information that is not always present in the acoustic signal and mimics human visual perception of speech recognition [4] that lets to better determine the phonetic content of the message.

Various sets of visual features for automatic speech-reading have been proposed by researchers so far. They can be categorized into three groups [5]: high-level features (lip contour based), low-level features (pixel based) and combinations of the aforementioned approaches. In the first group inner or outer lip contour is extracted and parameters of parametric or statistical model are used as visual features [6,7,8]. For example in [9,10] active shape models (ASM) are used, whereas in [11] snakes are exploited for contour extraction. In the second approach the entire mouth region is considered as region of interest and appropriate image transformations are applied [12,13]. For example in [14] discrete cosine transform (DCT) coefficients of gray-scale lip images have been adopted for visem representation and in [15] principal component analysis has been performed on raw lip intensity images. Researches show that combination of both

L. Rutkowski et al. (Eds.): ICAISC 2012, Part I, LNCS 7267, pp. 559–566, 2012.

techniques lets to build efficient solution to deal with drawbacks of individual techniques. High-level, lip-contour based approaches suffer from high computational effort whereas low-level features, although more computationally efficient, are very sensitive on varying illumination. For example, this problem is investigated in [16], where snakes are used to extract geometric features and KLT is applied to extract principal components in the color eigenspace, which provide auxiliary basis for classification.

In this paper a novel lipreading procedure is proposed. A set of seven visems of Polish language, characterized by the highest discriminative properties, was selected and a new approach for lip feature extraction was presented. Visems are modeled by coordinates of control points of B-splines that approximate outer lip contours. These contours, in turn, are extracted using dynamic programming technique. Since dynamic programming is capable of handling the problem of discontinuity of image gradients, extraction of optimal lip contours can be guaranteed. Experiments show good performance of the proposed solution for visem recognition purposes.

2   Proposed Solution

The proposed lipreading procedure consists of three processing stages as presented in Fig. 1. Firstly, the initial preprocessing is performed in order to roughly estimate lip area in video frames subject to further analysis (I). In the next step the exact lips contour is extracted using dynamic programming technique and initial feature vector is built (II). In order to reduce descriptor dimensionality, in the final step, supervised principal components analysis (S-PCA) is performed and appropriate final feature vector is found (III).

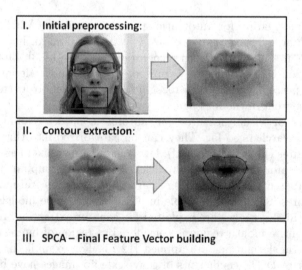

Fig. 1. The proposed lipreading procedure components

2.1   Initial Preprocessing

In order to roughly estimate lip region and to find lip key points the initial preprocessing is done as presented in Fig. 2. Firstly, the Haar classifier [17] is applied to determine face position in the image. Lip area is estimated on the basis of typical human face proportions as a region between 30-70% of face width and 60-90% of face height (a). The identified mouth region is a subject to further analysis.

Lip key points (left and right lip corners and uppermost and lowermost points of lips) are searched for in a modified LAB color space. Contrast enhancement between lip and skin colors is achieved by subtracting the channel 'A' from the channel 'B' (b) as proposed in [18]. Then, the resultant image is thresholded using Otsu method [19] (c). Because different skin artifacts such as hyperpigmentation or spots can cause errors, blob detection is applied and the biggest region is left as belonging to mouth (d). Finally, the resultant binary image is scanned for terminal lip points (e).

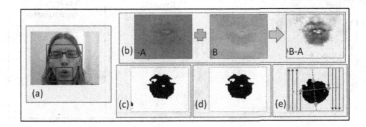

Fig. 2. The initial preprocessing stages

2.2   Lip Contour Extraction

Lip contour extraction procedure is presented in Fig. 3. Firstly, the outer lip contour is extracted using dynamic programming (I). Dynamic programming enables to solve complex optimization problems by breaking them down into smaller subproblems and searching for optimal subsolutions. Because, lip contour extraction can be viewed as a search for an optimal path (in the sense of a cost) between two vertices in a 2D graph, dynamic programming approach can be applied to this task. This requires defining a cost function, transition rules (b) and the corresponding 2D graph.

The cost function to be minimized through dynamic programming is defined as:

$$c_k^{opt} = min_{w(k-1)} \left\{ c_{k-1}^{opt} + d\left[(i_{k-1}, j_{k-1}) \rightarrow (i_k, j_k) \right] \right\} . \tag{1}$$

where: c_k^{opt} - is the optimal cost of reaching a node k, c_{k-1}^{opt} - the optimal cost of reaching a node $k-1$, $d\left[(i_{k-1}, j_{k-1}) \rightarrow (i_k, j_k) \right]$ - is a cost of transition from node $k-1$ to node k.

The transition cost consists of two components - a cost associated with branches of 2D graph structure and a cost of visiting a node. In the proposed solution the first component is not considered. Hence, the total cost of transition reduces to a node-visiting cost, which is defined as a value of a pixel of a modified gradient map (a). This map is created by inverting gradients and by masking-out strong teeth-contours.

Although, the outer lip contour, extracted separately for every quarter of lips using dynamic programming, is optimal in the sense of Bellman theory [20], it is not smooth. Therefore the final lip contour is obtained by B-spline approximation [21] of the dynamic programming results. Upper and lower lip contours are approximated separately. Experiments have shown that the best results can be achieved by modeling upper lip contour with 7 control points and the lower one with 4 control points. The 3rd order B-splines were used.

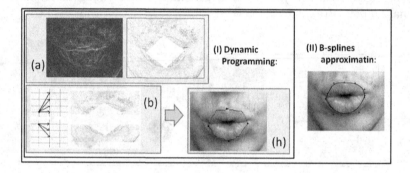

Fig. 3. Lip contour extraction stages

2.3   Building Feature Descriptor

Coordinates of B-spline control points that model lip shape represent initial feature descriptor. In the proposed procedure it consist of 22 elements. To remove information redundancy and to reduce descriptor dimensionality, the Supervised Principle Component Analysis (S-PCA) is performed [22]. Contrary to the standard Principle Component Analysis (PCA) it lets to eliminate impact of within class scatter by involving a-priori knowledge on class affinity.

A matrix containing initial feature vectors for N observation is an input for S-PCA procedure. Firstly, standard PCA analysis is done for all samples. As a result eigenvectors $E = [e_0, e_1, ..., e_{N-1}]$ and corresponding eigenvalues $L = [l_0, l_1, ..., l_{N-1}]$ are calculated. Next, the standard PCA analysis is repeated for all considered visems separately. Contrary to the first step, where directions of the largest scatter for all visems are found, this step lets to identify directions of the highest within-class variability. Denoting $E_k = [e_0^k, e_1^k, ..., e_{N-1}^k]$ and $L_k = [l_0^k, l_1^k, ..., l_{N-1}^k]$ as eigenvectors and eigenvalues for a class k, correction weight of within-class scatter can be calculated as follows:

$$w_i = \sum_{j=1}^{N} \sum_{k=1}^{K} \left| l_j^k \left(e_i \right)^T e_j^k \right|. \tag{2}$$

where: K - number of all classes, N - number of eigenvectors, l_j^k - i-th eigenvalue for class k, e_j^k - i-th eigenvector for class k.

These coefficients represent cumulative within-class variation in a direction of principal components found for all samples. By modifying original eigenvalues L according to:

$$l_i' = \frac{l_i}{w_i}. \tag{3}$$

the new feature space, built from directions featuring the highest between-class scatter only, is found, where: l_i' - i-th corrected eigenvalue, l_i - i-th eigenvalue calculated for all observations, w_i - i-th correction coefficient.

The presented procedure lets to reduce the feature vector to 9-10 elements (depends on a speaker) while preserving 90% of information associated with input data.

3   Experimental Evaluation

For experimental purposes an audio-visual database was recorded. Resolution of images was 960x720. Speakers were prompted to repeat 100 randomly generated sequences of syllables (10 syllables per sentence). Each syllable contains at least one out of seven visems selected as a basis for verification (these were: 'A', 'M', 'U', 'O', 'W', 'S', 'SZ'). All recordings were manually labeled.

To validate the proposed approach the prepared database was used for identifying visems in single images. For classification purposes Ada Boost method [23] was used (training set contains ca. 600 samples, test sets contain ca. 200 samples for every visem). Results for four sample speakers are presented in Table 1 and in Fig. 4. Average classification rate for all speakers was 75%.

In general, the best recognition rates were achieved for the vowel 'U' (89.8%) and the consonant 'W' (77.3%), the worse for phonemes 'O' and 'S' (ca. 60.0%). Recognition accuracy strongly depends on speaker and for example for the speaker A visem 'A' is recognized correctly only in 36.4% cases whereas for other speakers, in about 82.3% of all cases. Similarly for the speaker C recognition of the consonant 'W' is only 38.3% that is much lower than for the others. This is caused by the learnt uttering style, which do not use significant participation of mouth movements in speech production.

Achieved results (75% for 7 classes) seem to be comparable with the ones that can be found in literature (as presented in Table 2). Unfortunately strict comparison is not possible because of using different databases (not available publicly). Additionally, most of lipreading publications focus on isolated word (mainly digits) recognition task, making isolated visem recognition results difficult for objective comparison.

Table 1. Isolated visem recognition results for four speakers

Visem	Speaker A Efficiency [%]	Speaker B Efficiency [%]	Speaker C Efficiency [%]	Speaker D Efficiency [%]
A	36.4	74.0	79.5	93.3
M	88.1	83.0	85.5	42.8
O	38.2	77.6	64.8	59.0
S	64.8	67.1	48.9	64.2
U	98.7	82.4	92.7	85.4
W	68.6	82.5	38.3	74.6
SZ	74.0	92.4	61.5	68.5
Avg.	72.9%	80.8%	74.1%	72.7%

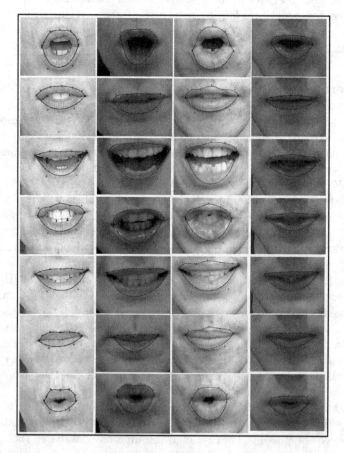

Fig. 4. Results for outer lip contour extraction for recognized visems (from first row: O','W','A','SZ','S','M','U')

Table 2. Comparison of different lipreading approaches 1st column - dynamic programming with BSplines approximation - the proposed approach; 2nd column - discriminative deformable models; 3rd - sieve decomposition)

	DP + BSplines	DDM [18]	SD [24]
Recognition task	Isolated visems	Isolated phones	Isolated letters
No. of classes	7	8	26
Average effectiveness	76%	83%	50%

4   Conclusion

A novel approach of outer lip contour extraction, based on dynamic programming, was presented and evaluated. Experiments performed for the prepared database confirm reliability of the presented approach for visem recognition.

The main directions of further research will include efforts to improve robustness of image preprocessing stage (as poor illumination or skin artifacts can cause erroneous lip key point detection and, consequently, erroneous visem classification). Simultaneously, attempts will be taken to evaluate proposed lipreading procedure for liveness verification in visual authentication systems. Decision, if biometric data presented to a system is captured from a physically present person and as a result access to the system can be granted, can be based on the following procedure: a system prompts random sequences of predefined syllables to be uttered by the user. For each syllable, it is checked if in a set of frames corresponding to this syllable, some expected visem was identified. If some minimum correct visem identification rate in syllable sequence is achieved, liveness verification test is successfully passed.

References

1. Dupont, S., Luettin, J.: Audio-visual speech modeling for continuous speech recognition. IEEE Trans. Multimedia 2, 141–151 (2000)
2. Faraj, M.I., Bigun, J.: Synergy of Lip-Motion and Acoustic Features in Biometric Speech and Speaker Recognition. IEEE Transactions on Computers 56(9), 1169–1175 (2007)
3. Chibelushi, C.C., Deravi, F., Mason, J.S.D.: A Review of Speech-Based Bimodal Recognition. IEEE Transaction on Multimedia 4(1), 23–36 (2002)
4. Gurbuz, S., Tufekci, Z., Patterson, E., Gowdy, J.N.: Application of affine-invariant Fourier descriptors to lipreading for audio-visual speech recognition. In: 2001 IEEE International Conference on Acoustics, Speech and Signal Processing, vol. 1, pp. 177–180 (2001)
5. Potamianos, G., Neti, C.: Improved ROI and within frame discriminant features for lipreading. In: International Conference on Image Processing, vol. 3, pp. 250–253 (2002)

6. Hennecke, M.E., Stork, D.G., Prasad, K.V.: Visionary speech: Looking ahead to practical speechreading systems. In: Speechreading by Humans and Machines, pp. 331–349 (1996)
7. Adjoudani, A. Benoit, C.: On the integration of auditory and visual, parameters in an HMM-based ASR. In: Speechreading by Humans and Machines, pp. 461–471 (1996)
8. Rogozan, A., Deltglise, P., Alissali, M.: Adaptive determination of audio and visual weights for automatic speech recognition. In: Proc. Europ. Tut. Res. Work. Audio-Visual Speech Process, pp. 61–64 (1997)
9. Wang, S.L., Lau, W.H., Leung, S.H., Yan, H.: A real-time automatic lipreading system. In: Proc. 2004 Int. Symp. Circuits and Systems, vol. 2, pp. 101–104 (2004)
10. Perez, J.F.G., Frangi, A.F., Solano, E.L., Lukas, K.: Lip reading for robust speech recognition on embedded devices. In: Proc. Int. Conf. Acoustics, Speech and Signal Processing, vol. I, pp. 473–476 (2005)
11. Kass, M., Witkin, A., Terzopoulos, D.: Snakes: Active contour models. Internaltional Journal of Computer Vision, 321–331 (1987)
12. Matthews, I., Potamianos, G., Neti, C., Luettin, J.: A comparison of model and transform-based visual features for audio-visual LVCSR. In: Proc. Int. Conf. Multimedia Expo. (2001)
13. Duchnowski, P., Hunke, M., Biisching, D., Meier, U., Waibel, A.: Toward movement-invariant automatic lip-reading and speech recognition. In: Proc. Int. Conf. Acoust. Speech Signal Process., vol. 1, pp. 109–112 (1995)
14. Potamianos, G., Neti, C., Gravier, G., Garg, A., Senior, A.W.: Recent advances in the automatic recognition of audio-visual speech. Proc. IEEE 91(9), 1306–1326 (2003)
15. Bregler, C., Konig, Y.: Eigenlips for robust speech recognition. In: Proc. IEEE Conf. Acoustics, Speech and Signal Processing, pp. 669–672 (1994)
16. Chiou, G.I., Hwang, J.-N.: Lipreading from color video. Trans. Image Processing 6, 1192–1195 (1997)
17. Viola, P., Jones, M.J.: Robust Real-Time Face Detection. Information Journal of Computer Vision 57(2), 137–154 (2004)
18. Nowak, H.: Lip-reading with discriminative deformable models. Machine Graphic and Vision International Journal 15, 567–575 (2006)
19. Otsu, N.: A threshold selection method from gray-level histograms. IEEE Trans. Sys., Man., Cyber. 9(1), 62–66 (1979)
20. Bellman, R.E., Dreyfus, S.E.: Applied dynamic programming. Princeton University Press (1971)
21. Lee, E.T.Y.: Comments on some B-spline algorithms. Computing 36(3), 229–238
22. Slot, K.: Biometric Recognition, pp. 101–103. WKL Press, Warszawa (2010)
23. Schapire, R.E.: The boosting approach to machine learning: An overview: Nonlinear Estimation and Classification. Springer, Heidelberg (2003)
24. Matthews, I., Bangham, J.A., Cox, S.: Audio-visual speech recognition using multiscale nonlinear image decomposition. In: Proc. Znt. Gonf. Speech Lang. Process., Philadelphia, pp. 38–41 (1996)

Meshes vs. Depth Maps
in Face Recognition Systems

Sebastian Pabiasz and Janusz T. Starczewski

Department of Computer Engineering,
Czestochowa University of Technology, Czestochowa, Poland
{sebastian.pabiasz,janusz.starczewski}@kik.pcz.pl

Abstract. The goal of this paper is to present data structures in 3D face recognition systems emphasizing the role of meshes and depth maps. 3D face recognition systems are still in development since they use different data structures. There is no standarized form of 3D face data. Dedicated hardware (3D scanners) usually provide depth maps of objects, which is not sufficiently flexible data sturcture. Meshes are huge structures and operating on them is difficult and requieres a lot of resources. In this paper, we present advantages and disadvantages of both types of data structures in 3d face recognition systems.

Keywords: biometric, 3D face, mesh, depth map.

1 Introduction

Over the past 20 years many different face recognition techniques were proposed. Originally they were based on flat images. Turk and Pentland [1] used eigenfaces for face detection and identification. Zhao et al. [2] presented the use of the LDA algorithm in face recognition. A classification method using the SVM technique was presented by Heisele et al.[3]; they developed a whole set of tools for processing and comparing facial photographs. However, these solutions do not work well in applications where reliability is a priority. The solution may be systems based on 3D data. In 2D facial biometrics research, the material is provided by a photography, which is a basic data structure. In 3D facial biometrics, we have few data structures, such as normals maps, depth maps, meshes and corresponding to them photographs. Such a number of different types of data makes the system difficult to operates on them. Already, there exist a number of public methods for 3D reconstruction (e.g. [4], [5], [6]). Depending on the method we have a limited number of data structures. A typical 3D scanner gives us a depth map so thus we can generate a mesh based on it. Other methods, that use a flat as a data source give us differential data structures.

2 Data in 3D Biometric

In 3D face biometrics, we distinguish multiple types of data. The kind of them depends on the method of acquisition. Typical dedicated hardware, like 3D

L. Rutkowski et al. (Eds.): ICAISC 2012, Part I, LNCS 7267, pp. 567–573, 2012.

scanner, give us depth map of surface, which is our basic structure that we can generate a mesh based on it. An alternative method is to use photometry stereo to reconstruct a face from flat images. In this case, our basic structure is a map of normals, from which we can generate a depth map and then a mesh.

2.1 From Normals to Depth Map

Methods based on bidirectional transmittance distribution function (BRTF, e.g. [7], [8]), as a first result, give a map of normals of an object. To build a depth map, we apply the least-squares technique. We use the fact that if the normal is perpendicular to the surface, then it will be perpendicular to any vector on it. We can construct vectors on the surface using neighbor pixels, more precisely, we employ a pixel from the right and below. The normal at a surface must be orthogonal to the vector Vec1, i.e.,

$$Vec1 = (x + 1, y, Z_{x+1,y} - (x, y, Z_{x,y}))$$
$$Vec1 = (1, 0, z_{x+1,y} - Z_{x,y})$$
$$Normal.Vec1 = 0$$
$$(N_x, N_y, N_z).(1, 0, Z_{x+1,y} - Z_{x,y}) = 0$$

$$N_x + N_z(Z_{x+1,y} - Z_{x,y}) = 0$$

and to the vector Vec2 leads to

$$Vec2 = (x, y + 1, Z_{x,y+1} - (x, y, Z_{x,y}))$$
$$Vec2 = (0, 1, Z_{x,y+1} - Z_{x,y})$$
$$Normal.Vec2 = 0$$
$$(N_x, N_y, N_z).(0, 1, Z_{x,y+1} - Z_{x,y}) = 0$$

$$N_y + N_z(Z_{x,y+1} - Z_{x,y}) = 0$$

If the pixel does not belong to an object, we describe this as

$$- N_x + N_z(Z_{x-1,y} - Z_{x,y}) = 0 \tag{1}$$
$$-N_y + N_z(Z_{x,y-1} - Z_{x,y}) = 0 \tag{2}$$

For each pixel of an object, we construct two entries so our main matrix will be of the form $M(2 * number\_of\_pixels, number\_of\_pixels)$. We can express our matrix equation as $MZ = Vec$, but the least squares method solves the equation $M^T M Z = M^T Vec$, so thus the main matrix $M^T M$ will be extremely big.

2.2 Depth Map

A depth map is a matrix, which elements represent the height of a particular pixel. Fig.1 presents an objects which depth map is in Table 1. In this case, resolution is 8x8. 3D scanners usually deliver data in the form of a depth map, additionally they can deliver information which pixel is valid (belongs to the object).

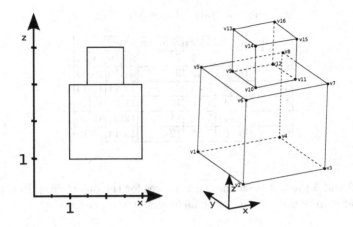

Fig. 1. Exaple of a 3D picture

Table 1. Depth map of figure from Fig.1

0	0	0	0	0	0	0	0
0	0	0	0	0	0	0	0
0	0	3	3	3	3	0	0
0	0	3	4	4	3	0	0
0	0	3	4	4	3	0	0
0	0	3	3	3	3	0	0
0	0	0	0	0	0	0	0
0	0	0	0	0	0	0	0

2.3   Meshes

Meshes are more complex data structures than depth maps. The mesh is usually a collection of vertices, edges and faces. The face usually consist of triangles or quadrilaterals.

Table 2. Coordinates of verticles from Fig.1

Number	x	y	z	Number	x	y	z
1	1	-1	1	9	0.5	-0.5	3
2	1	1	1	10	0.5	0.5	3
3	3	1	1	11	2.5	-0.5	3
4	3	-1	1	12	2.5	0.5	3
5	1	-1	3	13	0.5	-0.5	4
6	1	1	3	14	0.5	0.5	4
7	3	1	3	15	2.5	-0.5	4
8	3	-1	3	16	2.5	0.5	4

Table 3. Table of faces from Fig.1

Number	v1	v2	v3	v4	Number	v1	v2	v3	v4
1	1	2	3	4	7	9	10	11	12
2	1	2	6	7	8	9	10	14	13
3	2	3	7	6	9	10	11	15	14
4	3	4	8	7	10	11	12	15	16
5	4	1	5	8	11	12	9	13	16
6	5	6	7	8	12	13	14	15	16

Table 2 and 3 present basic mesh structures for the object from Fig. 1. In this case, squares were used as the basic faces shape.

2.4   Building a Mesh from a Depth Map

The depth map is the main data source for building the mesh. First step in this process is to select such points that are basic to build faces. We also have to make a decision about a shape of the faces (usually triangles are used). Use all points from a depth map, the resultant mesh can be extremely big and can require large resources and time. To reduce the number of the basic points, we can apply a simply algorithm (Alg. 1).

Algorithm 1. Depth map reduction algorithm

```
for x = 1 → MAXX do
   for y = 1 → MAXY do
      if i = factor then
         reduced[x, y] ⇐ source[x, y]
         i ⇐ 0
      else
         i ⇐ i + 1
      end if
   end for
end for
```

The results of Algorithm 1 are presented in Fig. 2. As we can observe, this solution reduce the mesh uniformly. Some important points may be lost. A significant improvement of quality can be obtained by key selection points and reduction. Key points can be obtained by filtration. Mesh construction is, in this case, difficult because a depth map is not uniformly reduced. Algorithm 2 presents our solution to build mesh from a uniform depth map, and Fig. 3 presents results of reduction with factor 20 and key point selection.

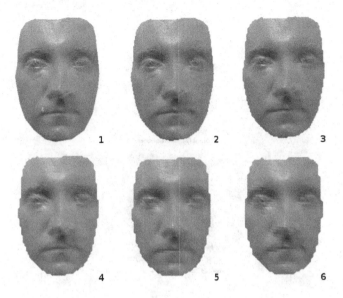

Fig. 2. Reduction factor (1-6)

Algorithm 2. Building mesh from uniforlmy depth map

---

for $x = 1 \rightarrow MAXX$ **do**
  for $y = 1 \rightarrow MAXY$ **do**
    findSection {2 points y1 and y2}
    $findPoints(x - 1)$
    $findPoints(x + 1)$ {In lines x-1 and x+1 from y1 to y2}
    for $point = 1 to foundedPoints$ **do**
      $buildTriangle(y1, y2, point)$
    end for
  end for
end for

---

3 Comparison

Comparison is the most important process in verification and identification of faces. In the past years, many solutions have been proposed (e.g. [9], [10], [11]). They operate on different principles and are effective to varying degrees.

3.1 Depth Map vs. Depth Map

The comparison of two depth maps directly is difficult because values in one cell on the first depth maps must correspond exactly to the same cell on the second depth map. The process of acquisition must be very accurate, what is often feasible. The second solution is to calibrate depth maps based on landmarks.

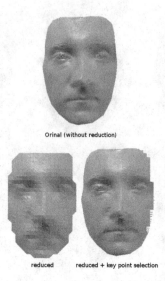

Fig. 3. Reduction with the key points selection

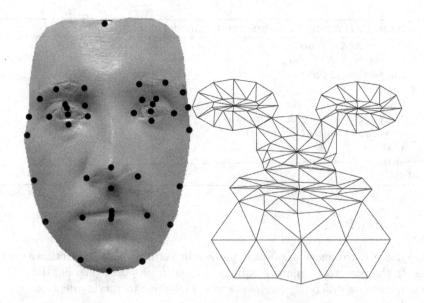

Fig. 4. Mesh based on landmarks

It is much more better solution; however, we must take into attention errors of acquisition apparatus. Summarizing, obtaining two identical maps of the same object is very difficult and laborious.

3.2   Mesh vs. Mesh

A medium-sized facial mesh consists of about 50000 points. The comparison of two meshes in this form is very resource-intensive and time consuming. As in the case of depth maps, calibration is required; however, to perform the comparison is much easier since we compare two faces which need not coincide perfectly. Fig. 3 presents a mesh build on landmarks, which results in that the number of points is always constant.

4   Final Remarks

Depth maps and meshes are inextricably connected data structures, they complement each other. In 3D biometric systems, we can use intelligently reduced meshes, which are more flexible and they are not restrictive as depth maps in comparison. In this area, is still much work to do.

References

1. Turk, M.A., Pentland, A.P.: Face recognition using eigenface. In: Internat. Conf. on Pattern Recognition, pp. 586–592 (1991)
2. Zhao, W., Chellappa, R., Krishnaswamy, A.: Discriminant analysis of principal component for face recognition. In: 3rd IEEE Internat. Conf. on Automatic Face and Gesture Recognition, pp. 336–341 (1998)
3. Heisele, B., Ho, P., Poggio, T.: Face recognition with support vector machines: Global versus component-based approach. In: 8th IEEE Internat. Conf. on Computer Vision, pp. 668–694 (2001)
4. Levine, M.D., Yu, Y.: State-of-the-art of 3D facial reconstruction methods for face recognition based on a single 3D training image per person. Pattern Recognition Letters 30, 908–913 (2009)
5. Mahoor, M.H., Abdel-Mottaled, M.: Face recognition based on 3D ridge images obtained from range data. Pattern Recognition 42, 445–451 (2009)
6. Jiang, D., Hu, Y., Yan, S., Zhang, L., Zhang, H., Gao, W.: Efficient 3D reconstruction for face recognition. Pattern Recognition 38, 787–798 (2005)
7. Song, P., Wu, X., Wang, M.Y.: Volumetric stereo and silhouette fusion for image-based modeling. Vis. Comput. 26, 1435–1450 (2010)
8. Pabiasz, S., Starczewski, J.T.: Face reconstruction for 3d systems. Selected Topics in Computer Science Applications, 54–64 (2011)
9. Huang, J., Blanz, V., Heisele, B.: Face recognition with support vector machines and 3D head models. In: Internat. Workshop on Pattern Recognition with SVM, pp. 334–341 (2002)
10. Blanz, V., Vetter, T.: Face recognition based on fitting a 3D morphable model. IEEE Transaction on Pattern Analysis and Machine Intelligence, 1063–1074 (2003)
11. Lu, X., Zhang, H.: Adapting geometric attributes for expression-invariant 3D face recognition. IEEE Transactions on Pattern Analysis and Machine Intelligence 30, 1346–1357 (2008)

Facial Expression Recognition
for Detecting Human Aggression

Ewa Piątkowska[1] and Jerzy Martyna[2]

[1] Institute of Applied Computer Science, Jagiellonian University,
ul. Reymonta 4, 30-059 Cracow, Poland
[2] Institute of Computer Science, Faculty of Mathematics and Computer Science,
Jagiellonian University, ul. Prof. S. Łojasiewicza 6, 30-348 Cracow, Poland

Abstract. This paper presents a system for facial expression recognition which is designed to detect spontaneous emotions. The goal was to detect human aggression. Using a face detection algorithm, a representation of the human face was created. Then, the face texture was encoded with Gabor filter and Local Binary Pattern (LBP) operator. These techniques were used to find the feature set in emotion recognition. As a classifier, a Support Vector Machine (SVM) was applied. The system constructed was tested with spontaneous emotions for aggression detection. The numerical results indicate that the presented classifier achieved an 85% correctness recognition coefficient.

Keywords: facial expression recognition, aggression detection, classification.

1   Introduction

Computational spontaneous facial expression recognition is a challenging research topic in computer vision. It is required by many application such as human-computer interaction and computer graphic animation. Automatic recognition of facial expressions did not really start until 1990s. To classify expressions in still images, many techniques have been developed such as those based on neural networks and Gabor wavelets [1]. Recently, more attention has been given to capture the temporal pattern in the sequence of feature vectors related to each frame such as the Hidden Markov Models based methods [3]. However, the methods presented in these surveys did not address the aggression detection nor the facial expression recognition.

Facial Expression Recognition and Analysis (FERA), in particular the Facial Action Coding System (FACS) recognition and discrete emotion detection, have been an a popular topic in computer science for some time now, and many promising methods have been published [6]. The first survey of the field was reported in 1992 [7] and has been continued by several others [4, 11]. However, none of these methods can track the facial actions and recognize the expressions over time in a monocular video sequence.

The main purpose of the paper is to analyze spontaneous facial expressions, paying special attention to the detection of aggression. Using the method introduced here, face representation was defined by means of the set of points, which are tracked in the video sequence. Thanks to using the special filter and the developed coding of a texture, an extraction of face features was made. Then, the use of the SVM classifier allowed us to

L. Rutkowski et al. (Eds.): ICAISC 2012, Part I, LNCS 7267, pp. 574–582, 2012.
© Springer-Verlag Berlin Heidelberg 2012

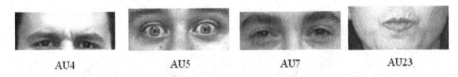

AU4   AU5   AU7   AU23

Fig. 1. Facial expressions corresponding to human aggression

detect aggression features in the examined face. Conducted numerical tests confirmed correctness of the approach in detecting aggression.

In chapter 2, the adopted concept of face representation and tracking their selected points is presented. Chapter 3 is devoted to the extraction of features to the trajectory of particular points and changes in the texture which correspond to aggression facial changes and the Support Vector Machine (SVM) classifier. Chapter 4 presents results of the numerical research. In chapter 5, final conclusions are presented.

2   Representation of Face and Tracking Its Selected Points

In this section we investigate the representation of face and tracking its selected points.

We recall that in the FACS method facial expressions are described by means of units, the so called Action Units (AUs). The AU unit constitutes the observable and indivisible facial movement, caused by a tone or relaxation of a muscle or a group of muscles. The authors of the FACS method have distinguished 46 independent AUs units. However, over 7000 combinations were isolated, where these units can occur. In addition, the FACS system also determines intensity of a particular facial expression in a scale from A to E, where A means the trace intensity, and E is the maximum intensity.

According to the FACS, aggression is described by 4 AU units (see Fig. 1), namely:

1) AU4 lowering eyebrows,
2) AU5 lifting upper eyelids,
3) AU7 tightening of eyelids,
4) AU23 tightening of mouth.

Systems of the facial expression analysis generally consist of 4 parts: face detection, face representation, feature extraction and classification. The proposed solution also retains the 4-phase scheme used.

For the sake of representation of the face the anthropometric method, mentioned in the paper [8], which consists in the determination of 18 points (Fig. 2a) and the relating regions (Fig. 2b). Selected points describe individual elements of a face, such as eyes, forehead, chin, and mouth. Additionally, together with these points the areas of a face are isolated, which will still be analyzed, according to the changes in the texture. For the object tracking in the video sequence (25 frames per second), an estimation of dynamics of the objects in time should be made, which will allow for the reproducing the trajectory of such object. In the proposed solution, a particle filter [2] was used, also called the sequential Monte Carlo method.

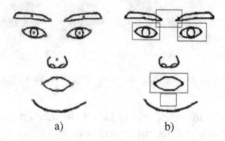

a)   b)

Fig. 2. Facial points (a) and the relating regions (b)

The operation of a particle filter consists in the estimation of a non-linear dynamic system, in which the measuring error does not have the Gaussian character. Filtering by means of this filter consists in the determination of the density function of marginal distribution $p(x_t \mid y_{1:t})$, or the distribution calculated a posteriori on the basis of the observation history from moment 1 up to t.

The recursive Bayes filter is used as particle filter, in which the evaluation of the probability $p(x_t \mid y_{1:t})$ distribution is carried out within a set of the weighted samples:

$$s = \{(s^n, \pi^n) \mid n = 1, \ldots, N\} \tag{1}$$

Each sample represents a hypothesis of the object state in time, together with the corresponding discrete π probability, where $\sum_{n=1}^{N} \pi^n = 1$. In each step (frame) N samples are taken at random with the probability

$$\pi^n = p(y_t \mid X_t = s_t^n) \tag{2}$$

The averag state of the object is given according to the formula:

$$E[S] = \sum_{n=1}^{N} \pi^n s^n \tag{3}$$

In order to locate the objects in each frame of the video sequence, it is necessary to define the representation of the object by means of some characteristic features. Here it was assumed that colour is such a characteristic feature.

Using colour in the partial filter requires that each x_i pixel belonging to the object is assigned to the appropriate range in the histogram by means of $h(x_i)$ function. Then, colour variable of the object being tracked is analyzed.

Due to high sensitivity of the color variable distribution to the changes in illumination, the Hue Saturation Value (HSV) model was used here, in which it was assumed, that histogram consists of $8 \times 8 \times 4$ ranges, assigning the smaller stress to the component V. In addition, it was assumed that higher weights were assigned to the colours from the area of the central object, while colours of pixels in marginal areas were considered less significant. This helped to avoid false readings connected with the probability of the object's contours. The weights are assigned according to the distance from the center of the ellipse circumscribing the object, namely:

$$k(r) = \begin{cases} 1 - r^2, & r < 1 \\ 0, & r \geq 1 \end{cases} \tag{4}$$

Then, distribution $\{p_j^n\}_{u=1,...,m}$ of the $\{p_j^n\}_{u=1,...,m}$ colour variable for pixels belonging to the object is calculated according to the formula:

$$p_j^u = f \sum_{i=1}^{I} k \left(\frac{\| f - x_i \|}{a} \right) \delta(h(x_i) - u) \qquad (5)$$

where m is a number of ranges in the histogram, I is a number of pixels in the object, δ is the Kronecker delta. Parameter a is responsible for adaptation of the size of the ellipse circumscribing the object and is defined as follows:

$$a = \sqrt{H_x^2 + H_y^2} \qquad (6)$$

In addition, in order to fulfill the condition $\sum_{u=1}^{m} p_j^u = 1$, a normalizing parameter f equal to $1/\sum_{i=1}^{I} k(\frac{\|j-x_i\|}{a})$ was applied.

In the object tracking problem, the object's state is evaluated for each frame of the sequence on the basis of new observations. This is why the so called measure of similarity between the objects with the given representation must necessarily be defined. Here, the Bhattacharyya coefficient ρ was applied in order to compare two discrete distributions $\{p_j^u\}_{u=1,...,m}$ and $\{q_j^u\}_{u=1,...,m}$, in the following way:

$$\rho[p, q] = \int \sqrt{p^u q^u} \qquad (7)$$

Each sample (particle) is defined by vector $s = \{x, y, \dot{x}, \dot{y}, H_x, H_y, \dot{a}\}$, where (x, y) are the position of the ellipse describing the object, $(\dot{x}, \dot{y})$ describes the movement, (H_x, H_y) are the lengths of the big and small semi-axes, while $\dot{a}$ is the parameter of change of the object's size over time.

The algorithm for tracking the object in the form of the distribution of the colour variable q for a given set of samples s has the form:

1) Sampling of N samples from the set S_{t-1} with the probability π_{t-1}^n.
2) Propagation of each sample through $s_t^n = As_{t-1}^n + w_{t-1}^n$, where A is the matrix of transition which defines the deterministic model of the dynamics, w_{t-1} is a multi-dimensional random variable G of the distributions,
3) Observation of the colour variables: (a) calculation of colour distribution p_s^n for each sample from the set S_t, (b) calculation of the Bhattacharya coefficient (distance) between object model q and hypothesis p_s^n, (c) assigning weights to each sample with the changing values of the Bhattacharya coefficient, which means that the most significant are the samples with the highest similarity to the model of the object q,
4) Assessment of the averaging state of the set S_t, namely $E(S_t) = \sum_{n=1}^{N} \pi_t^n s_t^n$.

3   Extraction of Features and SVM Classifier

In the two-dimensional area the Gabor filter is defined as the Gaussian function modulated by the sine and cosine waves:

$$\Psi_G(x, y; f_{0G}, \theta_G) = \frac{f_{0G}^2}{\pi \cdot \gamma_G \cdot \eta_G} \cdot e^A \cdot e^B \qquad (8)$$

where $A = -(\frac{f_{0G}^2}{\gamma_G^2} \cdot x'^2 + \frac{f_{0G}^2}{\gamma_G^2} \cdot y'^2)$, $B = 2\pi j \cdot f_{0G} \cdot x'$, $x' = x \cdot \cos\theta_G + y \cdot \sin\theta_G$, $y' = -x \cdot \sin\theta_G + y \cdot \cos\theta_G$.

Parameters of the Gabor filter are the sharpness along the longer axis of γ_G and shorter axis of η_G, the filter central, the frequency of filter f_{0G} and the angle of rotation θ_G of the main filter axis. In order to analyze the texture, the convolution of the input image is conducted with the Gabor filter kit. From the representation obtained this way, a histogram is calculated which is the vector of features.

An LBP operator [5] with R radius and a number of pixels P can code the image by means of $2P$ different values (codes). The image after processing into the LBP representation $lbp(x, y)$ is analyzed by means of a histogram, which can be defined as follows:

$$H_i = \sum_{x,y}^{I} (lbp(x, y) = i), \quad i = 0, \ldots, n - 1 \tag{9}$$

where n is a number of possible values of LBP codes. Function $I(.)$ returns 1, when expression $(.)$ is true, otherwise it returns 0. The obtained histogram describes statistical distribution of individual standards.

Support Vector Machine (SVM) [9] is a popular technique for classification. SVM performs an implicit mapping of data into a higher dimensional feature space, where linear algebra and geometry can be used to separate data that is only separable with nonlinear rules in the input space.

Given a training set of labeled examples $\{(x_i, y_i), i = 1, \ldots, l\}$ where $x_i \in R^n$ and $y_i \in \{1, -1\}$, the new test data x is classified by the following function:

$$f(x) = sgn(\sum_{i=1}^{l} \alpha_i y_i K(x_i, x) + b) \tag{10}$$

where α_i are Lagrange multipliers of a dual optimization problem, $K(x_i, x)$ is a kernel function. Given a nonlinear mapping Φ that embeds input data into feature space, kernels have the form of $K(x_i, x_j) = \langle \Phi(x_i \cdot \Phi(x_j) \rangle$. SVM finds a linear separating hyperplane with the maximal margin to separate the training data in feature space. b is the parameter of the optimal hyperplane.

4   The Experimental Results

In our analysis, we have used data contained in the FEED [10] base. This base was prepared in the framework of the FG-NET project at the University of Munich.

The base consists of video sequences acquired during the recording of 18 persons of whom were 9 women and 9 men. The data are stored in the form of MPGE4 files with a frame-rate equal to 25 frames/second, dimensions 320×240 and 8-bit depth of colour. For each person, 3 samples were gathered, where the first two make the teaching set, while the third serves for testing. The presented emotions have been labelled in accordance with the theory of six universal emotions. The base also contains sequences in which persons keep neutral face, i.e., they do not express emotions.

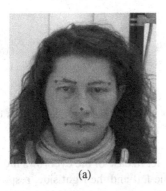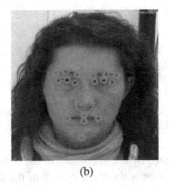

(a)   (b)

Fig. 3. Face described as a set of 18 points (a) and the relating regions (b)

The proposed method was implemented in the environment of MATLAB using the Image Processing and Bioinformatics Toolboxes. The obtained algorithm consists of the following stages:

1) matching of the model in the first model frame,
2) tracking the model points in each frame,
3) definition of the feature vector, extraction of texture and analysis of the point movement trajectory,
4) classification, or detection of aggression.

The face was described using a set of 18 points (Fig. 3a). The location of the face model in the sequence is determined manually in the first frame of the sequence. Coordinates of points are stored in the file. Next, the areas defined defined around the face model (Fig. 3b) are tracked by means of the particle filtering algorithm described in section 2. Points of the model have been circumscribed by an ellipse, the area of which is then

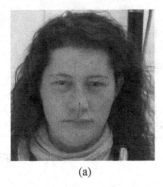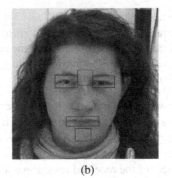

(a)   (b)

Fig. 4. Change of location of mouth corners (a) and measured position of the eyes, forehead, chin and mouth regions (b)

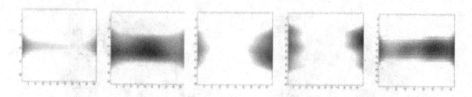

Fig. 5. Face regions after the Gabor method filtering. From left side are face regions of chin, forehead, right eye, left eye, mouth.

represented by the histogram of the colour variable. In case of the eyebrows movement such a point is the inner corner of the eye, on the left and the right side, respectively. On the other hand, change of location of mouth corners is measured with reference to the tip of the nose (Fig. 4a). In order to maintain constant value of the features vector, the video sequences have been normalized according to the number of frames. As a result of this, the algorithm operates on the sequences consisting of 100 frames. On the basis of the face model location in particular frames we have assessed position of the eyes, forehead, chin and mouth regions (Fig. 4b), which are then analysed according to the changes in the texture. Particular regions have been subjected to the process of normalization, the effect of which is that the areas the areas of the eyes have been rescaled to the size of 40 x 35, forehead - 30×30, mouth - 60×25 and chin - 40×20.

In the proposed approach, the texture was analyzed by means of two methods: Gabor filter and LBP operator. Firstly, the areas were transformed into the appropriate representation, and then they were described in the form of a histogram. The histograms for each area were connected into one vector of features.

Filtering by means of the Gabor method meant that filter banks with 8 orientations and 9 rates were used (Fig. 5). As a result of this method, the vector of features obtained consists of 432000 elements. In case of the LBP operator, the basic operation (3 x 3) version was used. Number of the histogram ranges was 256, and the size of each vector of features was 1280. As the input set, various combinations of the vector of features were fed:

– geometrical features in time,
– a histogram of texture obtained by means of the Gabor filters,
– a histogram of texture obtained by means of the LBP operator,
– a concatenation of geometrical features and histograms of the texture (for both methods).

The system was tested by means of 10 video sequences, demonstrating aggression and 10 sequences expressing other emotions. The set of texts contained 4 examples, 2 positive cases (aggression) and 2 negative cases (no aggression).

Effectiveness in detecting the expression was measured by the correctness recognition coefficient of the received results, namely

$$R = \frac{\text{number of correctly recognized examples}}{\text{number of all examples in the test}} \times 100\% \qquad (11)$$

The presented results are in conformity with the tested configurations of the vector of features. For the analysis of the face points movements trajectory a vector was defined with dimensions of 1000 features, containing the information concerning the change in the face geometry in the determined time slice (frames). The correctness recognition coefficient obtained here is equal to 78%.

Texture of the face was acquired from the most representative frame of the sequence, where the presented emotion is in the phase of culmination. When coding the texture with the Gabor filters the system achieved the correctness recognition coefficient of 81%, while when using the LBP method - 72%. Combining the two categories, or the methods describing both the geometry, and the face texture, the tested examples were classified with a correctness recognition coefficient of 82.5%. The overall results of the classification in different configurations of the vector of features presented in Table 1.

Table 1. The overall results of the classification in different configurations of features

Vector of features in time	Number of features	R
Geometrical features	1000	78%
Coding the texture with Gabor filter	432 000	81%
Coding the texture with LBP method	1280	72%
Geometrical features in time plus Gabor filter	433 000	80%
Geometrical features in time plus LBP method	2 280	85%

5   Conclusions

The conducted experiment demonstrated that a detection of aggression in people, from a given video sequence containing spontaneous facial reactions, was possible. The best results for the analysis of a human face texture have been obtained by means of the Gabor filter. Results of the classification for the texture analysis prove that a relatively large amount of information is coded in the face's texture, and in particular in the analyzed regions of the eyes, forehead, mouth and chin. It is for this reason that the texture of the face was combined during the experiment with the dynamics and geometry. For this way of adopting configuration the system analyzing the vector of features, built of the dynamic features and histograms of the texture obtained by the LBP operator, has the highest accuracy reaching 85%, which can also correctly classify new objects.

References

[1]   Bartlett, M., Littlewort, G., Lainscsek, C., Fasel, I., Movellan, J.: Machine Learning Methods for Fully Automatic Recognition of Facial Expressions and Facial Actions. In: IEEE Int. Conf. on Systems, Man and Cybernetics, pp. 592–597 (2004)

[2]   Brzozowska, K., Dawidowicz, A.L.: Partial Filter Method. Applied Mathematics 10 (2009)

[3]   Cohen, I., Sebe, N., Garg, A., Chen, L., Huang, T.: Facial Expression Recognition from Video Sequences: Temporal and Static Modeling. Computer Vision and Image Understanding 91(1-2), 160–187 (2003)

[4]   Fasel, B., Luettin, J.: Automatic Facial Expression Analysis: A Survey. Pattern Recognition 36(1), 259–275 (2003)

[5]   Ojala, T., Pietikainen, M., Maenpaa, T.: Multiresolution Gray-scale and Rotation Invariant Texture with Local Binary Patterns. IEEE Trans. on Pattern Analysis and Machine Intelligence 7(7), 971–987 (2002)

[6]   Pantic, M., Rothkrantz, L.: Automatic Analysis of Facial Expressions: The State of the Art. IEEE Trans. on Pattern Analysis and Machine Intelligence 22(12), 1424–1445 (2000)

[7]   Samal, A., Iyengar, P.A.: Automatic Recognition and Analysis of Human Faces and Facial Expressions: A Survey. Pattern Recognition 25(1), 65–77 (1992)

[8]   Sohail, A.S.M., Bhattacharya, P.: Detection of Facial Feature Points Using Anthropometric Face Model. In: Signal Processing for Image Enhancement and Multimedia Processing, pp. 189–200. Springer (2008)

[9]   Vapnik, V.N.: The Nature of Statistical Learning Theory. Springer, New York (1995)

[10] Wallhoff, F.: Facial Expressions and Emotion Database, Technische Univesität München (2006), http://www.mmk.ei.tum.de/~waf/fgnet/feedtum.html

[11] Zeng, Z., Pantic, M., Roisman, G.I., Huang, T.S.: A Survey of Affect Recognition Methods: Audio, Visual, and Spontaneous Expressions. IEEE Trans. on Pattern Analysis and Machine Intelligence 31(1), 39–58 (2009)

Combining Color and Haar Wavelet Responses for Aerial Image Classification

Ricardo C.B. Rodrigues[1], Sergio Pellegrino[1], and Hemerson Pistori[2]

[1] Instituto Tecnológico de Aeronáutica
P. Marechal Eduardo Gomes, 50 Sao Jose dos Campos, SP, Brazil
{rcezar,pell}@ita.br
http://www.ita.br
[2] INOVISAO, Universidade Católica Dom Bosco
Av. Tamandaré 6000, Campo Grande, MS 79117-900, Brazil
pistori@ucdb.br

Abstract. A new set of attributes combining color and SURF-based histograms coupled with a SVM classifier to enhance visual based autonomous aerial navigation is proposed. These new features are used for region classification with aerial images in order to speed up the UAV (Unmanned Aerial Vehicles) localization performed by image matching using only reference images according to the region classification. Experimental results comparing the proposal with color or SURF only attributes are presented. In the experiments the UAV localization task can be performed four times faster using the proposed approach, however the performance gain can be still bigger for large datasets of reference images.

Keywords: unmaned aerial vehicles, vision based navigation, feature extraction, SURF.

1 Introduction

During the last two decades the interest in UAVs had an exponential growth. They became an essential weapon in military fields especially after 2001 with the successful record of North American model MQ-1 Predator in missions in Pakistan, Uzbekistan and Afghanistan [1]. With the development of small and mature applicable technologies such as digital cameras and GPS (Global Positioning System) UAVs have also emerged as solution for many civil applications such surveillance, firefighting, remote sensing, etc [2].

Currently there is a large variety of UAV models with different sizes, shapes and characteristics, such diversity boosted the development of UAV flight hardware [2]. But what remains as a challenge is the study on how to provide autonomy to UAV's and what degree of autonomy can be reached. In this sense, image-based robots navigation has been a subject investigated by many research groups and some works have exploited the supervised approaches to perform unmanned aerial vehicle (UAV) autonomous navigation [3,4,5,6].

L. Rutkowski et al. (Eds.): ICAISC 2012, Part I, LNCS 7267, pp. 583–591, 2012.
© Springer-Verlag Berlin Heidelberg 2012

One important computer vision supervised approach for robots navigation is the image registration, a supervised method which register target images in a database and match them with current images during navigation. For each match performed, the robot can use georeferences associated to images in database (knowledge base) and then estimate robot position. In [6] Conte uses the image registration approach to update the accumulated error of a visual odometer. So whenever a match is reliable it restores absolute UAV position and the filter is updated. The result of this work shows that this technique can reproduce a similar path to the GPS navigation system. But the image matching used is based on border filters that may be not so effective for some variances in scales, perspective or other changes in the environment.

Today there are many available databases of georeferenced aerial images, also called waypoint images or simply waypoints, which could be used to aid in UAV's autonomous navigation. The problem is how to match current images with database considering image variances in scale, rotation, perspective illumination and so on. The work [7] presents an evaluation of a supervised method based on image registration approach using robust scale-invariant algorithms like SIFT and SURF for waypoint recognition. The results demonstrate that these algorithms are able to accurately match the images, however this approach could be unfeasible to real time aircrafts navigation due to high processing time required for image matching using large databases.

In this context this work proposes a coarse geografical region classification step using color and SURF based descriptors. In this way, the search for waypoints using image match will be bounded to the images in the dataset that are related only to one region previously found and not to the entire waypoints dataset. The next section presents the proposed approach and is followed by the experiments section which reports the evaluation of three different classifiers and three sets of image descriptors. Conclusions and future works are presented in the last section.

2   Background

The scale-invariant SURF algorithm is used to detect interest points, named here keypoints, and describe local features of the images. This algorithm was chosen due to its performance and accuracy in detecting and matching keypoints in images. SURF is based on SIFT algorithm, a robust method proposed by Lowe in 1999 [8] to find keypoints and describe local features invariant to image scaling and rotation, and partially invariant to change in illumination and 3D camera viewpoint.

Roughly speaking, SURF detects keypoints by using scale-space as an image pyramid, where the image is iteratively convolved with Gaussian kernel and repeatedly sub-sampled at different scales [9].

Those pyramid layers are subtracted in order to get the DoG (Difference of Gaussians) images where edges and blobs can be found [10]. Keypoints are local maxima/minima in a 3x3x3 neighborhood in the image over scales.

One dominant orientation is assigned to each interest point found in the image by calculating the sum of all responses from a sliding orientation window Haar filter [10]. Thus a 64 dimension vector of wavelet (Haar) responses relative to dominant orientation is extracted.

Finally, each image is composed of n keypoints and each keypoint contains local descriptor represented by a 64 dimension features vector extracted by SURF. More details can be found in [10].

3   Proposed Approach

This work proposes a feature vector containing orientation gradients information combined with color histograms to identify visual patterns of interest regions in aerial images. Such information will be available for regions classification, which allows test images to be matched only with waypoints inside the chosen region. Therefore the aim of this approach is to use regions classification as a filter which reduces the number of comparisons during image matching phase and then speed up the UAV location during navigation.

Given a set of images of an environment, colors may be an important feature to describe a regions. Considering regions are a limited area with some objects inside, the colors distribution of images from the same region tends to be similar. In this sense the Hue histogram from HSV (Hue, Saturation and Value) color model is proposed to compose the region descriptor. Hue could be described as the color value by itself, it is invariant and independent from other channels in HSV model, for more details see [11].

The Hue value is measured in degrees and it goes from 0 to 180. The histogram is composed by 30 bins, in sets of 6 degrees intervals, reducing the number of attributes in the feature vector to speed up classification time and making the histograms less variant to noise.

Many works have used color histograms to describe images [12,13], but when color distribution in different regions are too similar the classifier could not distinguish them, since traditional histogram does not take into account spatial information.

Having this problem in mind this approach proposes in addition to the hue histogram an orientation gradient histogram, called here SURF histogram, it will compose the region descriptor in order to represent structural features of images.

SURF algorithm has successfully been used to describe local features, however the goal of region descriptor in this work is to represent a global context of the image (scene) instead of a single pixel region. In this sense a single vector of orientation features is constructed in order to represent the whole content of a scene.

The first step for constructing SURF histogram is to use SURF to find keypoints and describe local features; each keypoint has a 64 features vector of Haar wavelet responses (gradients orientation). Then the next step is to calculate the mean average of each vector value using all keypoints in the image. It will result in a single vector of 64 features per image. Since keypoints are supposed to describe common and singular objects in the images, if images are representing the same region, the average of keypoints descriptors should be similar.

Combining color and orientation features the final vector for describing regions has 94 attributes, 30 from color histogram and 64 from SURF histogram. Supervised learning algorithms can be trained with these features extracted from samples of interest regions and finally used for region classification.

4 Experimental Evaluation

Having in mind the goal of evaluating region classification step and comparing the results obtained by the selected classifiers, this section describes the details of this experiment including an analysis of results.

4.1 Training Dataset

In order to create the training dataset for experimentation, 161 aerial images were selected from the SURF recognized waypoints set in the experiment presented in [7]. In this previous work, a set of test and sample images where matched using SURF algorithm in the conventional approach where every test image is compared to all samples in the dataset. Now the goal is to validate if the images are classified in the proper region which the waypoint belongs and also estimate the improvements of time processing using this additional classification step.

In the sequence, a set of 94 attributes for each sample were extracted using SURF histogram and the Hue histogram.

For each of the 161 region examples, a feature vector was calculated and stored into the dataset. The training examples were manually labeled with one of the following classes: Region 1, Region 2, Region 3, Region 4 and Region 5, see Figure 1. The distribution of classes is: 21 images in Region 1, 31 in Region 2, 40 in Region 3, 23 in Region 4 and 47 in Region 5. The number of samples for each class was extracted from the available images of each region in the environment, see examples of sample images in Figure 2.

4.2 Experimental Settings

The experiments were conducted using OpenCV 1.1 for dataset building and the latest developer version of Weka software[1] [14] for classifiers evaluation.

The supervised algorithm Support Vector Machines (SVM) was tested in conjunction with the well known algorithms Multi Layer Perceptron (MLP) and K-nearest neighbors (KNN). All classifiers implementations were performed using Weka default configuration. SVM uses a polynomial function, complexity parameter separation $C=1.0$ and $\epsilon = 1.0E\text{-}12$.

---

[1] Weka is open source software which has a collection of machine learning algorithms for data mining tasks, more details in http://www.cs.waikato.ac.nz/ml/weka/

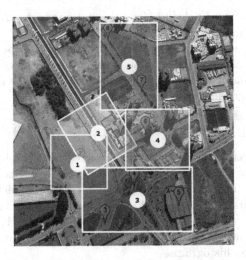

Fig. 1. Visual representation of the five regions covering all waypoints in the environment

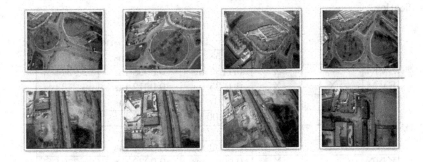

Fig. 2. Samples: Top images contain samples of Region 3 and Bottom images samples of Region 2

SVM classifier was chosen due to its generalization capability and fast classification time [15]. The experiments uses Sequential Minimal Optimization (SMO), a implementation SVM developed by John C. Platt [16], who claims that SMO is a simple and fast technique to solve the SVMs quadratic problem.

The MLP was chosen because of its ability of Neural Networks to implicitly detect complex nonlinear relationships between attributes of training data, this classifier uses backpropagation method and parameters hidden Layers = (number of attributes + number of classes), learning Rate=0.3, momentum =0.2 and trainingTime = 500, more details of these parameters can be obtained in [17].

KNN classifier was selected as a weak classifier to be compared with SVM and MLP and then evaluate the complexity of the classification problem, it uses a linear search applying Eucledian distance and parameter $K=1$, more details of parameters can be found in [18].

For each of the algorithms 5-fold cross validation was performed over the dataset in order to certify a more reliable estimation of the generalization error [19]. A paired-samples t-test was also conducted to compare the set of features combining color and orientation histograms.

4.3   Results and Analysis

The experiments were exploratory and conducted with the intention of evaluating the specificity (Precision), sensitivity (Recall) and efficiency (processing time x accuracy) of algorithms for region classification problem using Color and SURF based histograms. The Table 1 shows the CPU training time, CPU classification time and overall accuracy of the three classifiers. Each classifier was trained and tested with three different combinations of features vector using color and orientation histograms.

Table 1. Results of SVM, MLP and KNN classifiers for region classification problem using aerial images. The mark X means the feature in the column was used for classification.

	Color Hist.	Ori. Hist	Train. time	Classif. Time	Accuracy
SVM	X	-	0.1158 ms	0.0006 ms	92.5956%
SVM	-	X	0.1186 ms	0.0008 ms	92.9044 %
SVM	X	X	0.1535 ms	0.0012 ms	96.2733 %
MLP	X	-	12.9218 ms	0.0016 ms	92.6336%
MLP	-	X	11.6400 ms	0.0016 ms	91.6544 %
MLP	X	X	34.6597 ms	0.0106 ms	**96.8944 %**
KNN	X	-	0.0002 ms	0.0051 ms	91.4130 %
KNN	-	X	0.0000 ms	0.0039 ms	89.7794 %
KNN	X	X	0.0000 ms	0.0218 ms	92.5466 %

In the conventional approach of image matching presented in [7], all test images are matched with all sample images in the dataset. Then the global processing time Gt is given by:

$$Gt = Tim \times Mt \times Sim \qquad (1)$$

where Tim is the number of test images, Mt is the average time of image matching process and Sim the number of sample images in the database.

Considering the region classification step proposed in this work, test images would be matched only with the samples images of the region it was classified, therefore the new global time NGt would be reduced to:

$$NGt = (\sum_{i=1}^{n} Ri \times Mt) + Tim \times Ct \qquad (2)$$

Where Ri is the number of images in the region i, n is the number of regions and Ct is the classification time for one instance.

Considering $Mt = 0.163$ ms (according on experiments in [7]), $Si=8$ and $Ti = 161$ (number of test images in this work) the $Gt = \mathbf{209.944}$ **ms**. Based on the distribution of the regions and the classification time presented in Table 1, the Table 2 presents, for each classifier, the new global time NGt and the timing performance gain.

Table 2. Timing performance gain using regions classification before matching step

	NGt (ms)	Perf. Gain (× faster)
SVM	52.353	**4.01**
MLP	53.866	3.89
KNN	55.669	3.77

The Table 3 shows the standard deviations of results for percentage correct classifications. Results marked with • are significantly different at confidence $p < 0.05$, based on a pared t-test.

Table 3. Standard deviation results based on pared t-test. SVM and KNN classifiers are compared to MLP in the first column. The symbols ○, • mean that the results have statistically significant improvement or degradation with confidence $p < 0.05$.

Dataset	MLP	SVM	KNN
Color H.	± 4.95	± 4.59	± 4.32
Orient. H.	± 2.56	± 3.70	± 4.52
Color+Orient.	± 2.65	± 2.71	± 3.88 •

Although MLP has performed the best classification (Table 1), its possible to see in Table 3 that the results achieved by MLP are not statistically significant better than SVM classifier. Nevertheless, the efficiency of the algorithms during the testing phase is of interest as well. Note that the processing time of testing phase of SVM is by far the best in terms of efficiency. It is justified by the fact that the time for evaluating test cases is proportional only to the final number of support vectors. Nevertheless KNN presents the best time during training and the SVM with the second best time.

The classification results using the combination of color plus orientation histograms obtained the best accuracy, from the set of 161 instances, SVM classified only 6 instances incorrectly, MLP 5 and KNN 12. SVM algorithm has the best overall performance and the low numbers of instances incorrect classified only shows that all selected classifiers are very suitable for the region classification problem using aerial images.

The results confirm that the set features can discriminate the regions very accurately. Note that SURF-based histogram features could discriminate the region classes very precisely. The final features vector also including the color histogram increased significantly the classification rate that reached more than 96% of accuracy.

In the Table 4 is possible to observe the behavior of the classifiers using color and orientation histograms with respect to precision, recall, and the F-measure.

Table 4. True Positives, False Positives, Precision, Recall, F-Measure and ROC curve averages for SVM, MLP and KNN algorithms

	TP Rate	FP Rate	Precision	Recall	F-Measure	ROC curve
SVM	0.963	0.01	0.964	0.963	0.963	0.986
MLP	0.969	0.008	0.97	0.969	0.969	0.997
KNN	0.925	0.017	0.932	0.925	0.926	0.958

5   Conclusions

The image descriptor presented in this work was able to represent global context in the set of aerial images experimented and provided excellent results with more than 95 % of accuracy. With that, waypoints can be grouped by regions reducing the processing time of recognition step during navigation. The results of experiments in this work showed a gain of performance that speeds up the global processing up to 4 times faster. But note that some of regions evaluated here had only one or two waypoints. Therefore, this approach can be still better if considering large environments with dense grids of mapped waypoints.

In order to better evaluate the model, a natural step is the application of similar solutions at different environments and larger datasets in both urban and rural areas. It is also of interest to perform experiments using satellite images, such the ones obtained from Google Earth, for matching with UAV images.

A future research direction is the exploitation of presented image descriptors to the improvement of classification and also reduction of the number of parameters using feature selection algorithms in order to decrease processing time and then to satisfy real industry needs.

References

1. Shah, P.Z.: Pakistan says u.s. drone kills 13. New York Times (2009)
2. Valavanis, K.P.: Advances in Unmanned Aerial Vehicles: State of the Art and the Road to Autonomy, 1st edn. Springer Publishing Company, Incorporated (2007)
3. Shiguemori, E.H., Martins, M.P., Monteiro, M.V.T.: Landmarks recognition for autonomous aerial navigation by neural networks and gabor transform. In: IPAS, 64970 (2007)
4. Rodrigues, R.C.B., Shiguemori, E.H., Forster, C.H.Q., Pellegrino, S.R.M.: Color and texture features for landmarks recognition on uav navigation, Sao Jose dos Campos, Simpósio Brasileiro de Sensoriamento Remoto, 14 (SBSR), Instituto Nacional de Pesquisas Espaciais (INPE), pp. 7111–7118 (2009)

5. Royer, E., Lhuillier, M., Dhome, M., Lavest, J.M.: Monocular vision for mobile robot localization and autonomous navigation. Int. J. Comput. Vision 74(3), 237–260 (2007)
6. Conte, G., Doherty, P.: An integrated uav navigation system based on aerial image matching. In: Proceedings of the 2008 IEEE Aerospace Conference, Big Sky Montana, USA (2008)
7. Rodrigues, R.C.B., Pellegrino, S.R.M.: An experimental evaluation of algorithms for aerial image matching. In: 17th International Conference on Systems, Signals and Image Processing, Rio de Janeiro, Brazil, EdUFF, pp. 416–419 (2010)
8. Brown, M., Lowe, D.: Invariant features from interest point groups. In: Proceedings of the British Machine Vision Conference, BMVC 2002, Cardiff, UK, pp. 656–665. British Machine Vision Association (2002)
9. Evans, C.: Notes on the opensurf library. Technical report, University of Bristol, Bristol, UK (2009)
10. Bay, H., Ess, A., Tuytelaars, T., Gool, L.V.: Speeded-up robust features (surf). Computer Vision and Image Understanding 110(3), 346–359 (2008), Similarity Matching in Computer Vision and Multimedia
11. Schwarz, M.W., Cowan, W.B., Beatty, J.C.: An experimental comparison of rgb, yiq, lab, hsv, and opponent color models. ACM Trans. Graph. 6(2), 123–158 (1987)
12. Arjunan, R.V., Kumar, V.V.: Image classification in cbir systems with color histogram features. In: International Conference on Advances in Recent Technologies in Communication and Computing, pp. 593–595 (2009)
13. Cheng, Y.C., Chen, S.Y.: Image classification using color, texture and regions. Image and Vision Computing 21(9), 759–776 (2003)
14. Weka Machine Learning Project: Weka (2008), http://www.cs.waikato.ac.nz/~ml/weka
15. Vapnik, V.N.: The nature of statistical learning theory. Springer-Verlag New York, Inc., New York (1995)
16. Platt, J.: Sequential minimal optimization: A fast algorithm for training support vector machines (1998)
17. Haykin, S.: Neural Networks: A Comprehensive Foundation. Prentice Hall PTR, Upper Saddle River (1998)
18. Bremner, D., Demaine, E., Erickson, J., Iacono, J., Langerman, S., Morin, P., Toussaint, G.: Output-sensitive algorithms for computing nearest-neighbour decision boundaries. Discrete and Computational Geometry 33, 593–604 (2005), doi:10.1007/s00454-004-1152-0
19. Imbault, F., Lebart, K.: A stochastic optimization approach for parameter tuning of support vector machines. In: Proceedings of the 17th International Conference on Pattern Recognition (ICPR 2004), vol. 4, pp. 597–600. IEEE Computer Society, Washington, DC (2004)

Properties and Structure of Fast Text Search Engine in Context of Semantic Image Analysis

Janusz Rygał, Patryk Najgebauer, Tomasz Nowak,
Jakub Romanowski, Marcin Gabryel, and Rafał Scherer

Department of Computer Engineering, Częstochowa University of Technology
al. Armii Krajowej 36, 42-200 Częstochowa, Poland
{janusz.rygal,patryk.najgebauer,tomasz.nowak,
jakub.romanowski,marcin.gabryel,rafal.scherer}@kik.pcz.pl
http://kik.pcz.pl

Abstract. In the world of computer imaging, we still do not have a good and fast enough method for image searching. This is because science is still not able to imitate fully functions of the human brain. When humans think about images, they do not think about mathematical formulas, matrices, histograms etc. Those mathematical and algorithmic methods are very good for e.g. computer face detection or number plate recognition, but we cannot directly use them for analyzing a whole image and for searching in a set of thousands or even millions of images. On the other hand, computers are able to scan millions of documents, searching for some phrase or even a single word. Fast text search is fully supported by a majority of significant database systems such as Oracle, PostgreSQL or MS SQL Server. The paper presents fast text search engine from another point of view, that is, its application in content based image retrieval.

Keywords: semantic image analysis, fast text search, CBIR.

1 Introduction

In the existing state of the art there are various ways to process images and to perform object recognition. Generally, there are two main approaches to object recognition and several stand-alone algorithms which are used as components in various, more complex CBIR methods. The first approach is object recognition by appearance which uses algorithms of edge detection such as Canny edge detector [1], Sobel [10] or Harris corner detection [6]. The second approach is object recognition based on features where object finding methods are often based on geometry or tree algorithms [7]. In feature-based methods, the most frequently used feature detection algorithms are SURF[2][15] , SIFT [15] and their modification such as GLOH [11], PCA-SIFT [16] and others. We can also try to utilize some soft computing techniques in image recognition [5][8][9][12][14]. All of these methods work in certain cases and constraints. They are associated with the precise shapes of objects whose mappings are visible in the image or consisting in homographic [3][4] mapping of key-points allowing some changes in scale

L. Rutkowski et al. (Eds.): ICAISC 2012, Part I, LNCS 7267, pp. 592–599, 2012.

and view point. The experiments performed by the authors have shown that these methods are not resistant to view point change or scale changes when the changes of scale or view position are too large for the test pattern. These factors are, among others, reasons staying behind the idea proposed in this article.

The solution presented in the paper is a combination of two streams of data transformation methods: heuristic and mathematical analysis of the structure of dependencies. Image transformation methods will be used in the preprocessing and data preparation phase. These two steps will prepare data for next steps, which will convert digital image data into finite text strings and store them in the database.

In this paper we wish to introduce results of test experiments on text data stored in data base with German selected as dictionary language. On this data set we were make a set of variously complicated queries for custom strings which are not in the German dictionary but they are the encoded segments of the digital image. Additionally, we aim to improve the way how the lexically encoded images could be retrieved by SQL queries and full text search algorithms. Now we present more advanced concepts of the proposed solution. Firstly, the idea presented in the paper is a part of a large, complicated system for content based image retrieval. The system will be applied to compare digital images and searching for them in a data base using methods that rely on text search algorithms rather than the direct geometric analysis or key points analysis. In first step of our image analysis approach we cut image into segments which will represent single objects extracted from the image like cars, trees or any other thing or person which could be depicted by digital imaging. Then, extracted segments of the image are translated to the lexical form using novel algorithms and language. Each segment of the image could be treated like single word which can be stored to data base or it can be grouped with other single words to create a sentence of translated image segments. Presented concept would help to increase the speed of searching data for images translated into the text and it could reduce the time of image content analysis comparing to the solutions presented in the literature.

In the paper we mainly focus on the last stage of the whole, above mentioned, solution, i.e. the text search engine and its application to search custom "words" (text chunks) that are beyond the dictionary of selected language (German in our experiments). We examined if the Fast Text Search algorithms can be used to find strings that have no substantive meaning by using them to search for hashed word. We performed the tests that correspond to searching words derived from the encoded image segments using SQL queries with various degree of complexity. Queries and test results are presented in the Section 4. We used data collected by the system created for the purpose of research which we have called "Mosquito Explorer". The system is described in the next section. Proposed idea proved to be accurate and it was more efficient than the standard implementation of Fast Text Search Algorithms in most tests.

2   Fast Text Search Engine Properties

There are many relational database systems, but only three of them were chosen for further consideration i.e. Oracle, PostrgeSQL and MS SQL Server. Each of them is a professional database systems, which have been used in countless applications and systems. Oracle and MS SQL Server are commercial systems and PostgreSQL is an open source project. During tests and research we have decided to use PostgreSQL database system. It offers professional full text search engine, which can be used with success in the experiments. What is also the great advantage of that choice is that the PostgreDB can be easily extended with any extensions and solutions, for example, in our case with parsers or converters. PostgreSQL offers also special types of data and indexes designed for full text search.

We can single out following database structures usually used in the fast text search: special data types, indexes, converting and ranking functions, dictionary, parsers. In the next subsections we will describe each type of these objects.

2.1   Special Data Types

- Tsvector is a specific PostgreSQL data type, created for full text search. This is a sorted list, containing distinct lexemes with a position in document. Lexeme is a normalized word.
Example: ... 'version':60 'view':208 'vorbeleg':5,14 'warum':176 ...
- Tsquery is another specific PostgreSQL data type, which stores lexemes, which are to be searched for. Applying our search phrase, we have to make a conversion from text to the tsquery.

2.2   Indexes

- GIST (Generalized Search Tree) index, this is the first type of indexes in PostgreSQL Database system for full text search. This type of index can produce false results, because of its design. Thus, searching using this type of index is slower, because of other necessary checks, which have to eliminate false matches. But it has also a big advantage, it is fast for updating. Thus, it is better to use this type of index in dynamic systems, where the performance of update statement is very important.
- GIN (Generalized Inverted Index) this type of index is not lossy as the GIST index, but an index of this type needs three times more disk space, needs three times more time to build and needs ten times more time to be updated but it is three times faster for lookups then the GIST index.

2.3   Converting and Ranking Functions

- To_tsvector, when we want to fill a column of type tsvector, we have to use this converting function, it can be done for example as a trigger function. This function parses a document and produces a list of lexemes together with their positions in the document at the input.

- To_tsquery converts a value in parameter into tsquery, given value must be in special format, row of single tokens separated by Boolean operators. For simple conversion from text to tsquery was designed a function called plainto_tsquery.
- Ts_rank is ranking values in tsvectors by the frequency of matching lexemes.
- Ts_rank_cd creates cover density ranking.

2.4 Dictionaries

In a nutshell, a dictionary is used to eliminate the information which is not valuable for searching. Thus, an indexing system removes stop words and converts words into lexemes (normalization) with a help of the dictionary.

2.5 Parsers

Parser has to split a document into tokens and identify a type of each of them. Default implementation of the parser is usually optimal for a majority of possible usages, but in specific applications it has to be refactored.

3 Design of the Test Application

We have developed software for indexing Internet resources, which offers fast text search ability in the most convenient and easy way. To achieve that goal we had to create an multi module application. Only several parts of this software are presented in the paper. Separated modules of Mosquito Explorer are shown in the Figure 1. For the purpose of this paper we use only the database structure, data and the Search Module of the Mosquito Explorer. The Search Service is

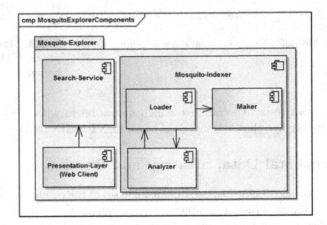

Fig. 1. Mosquito Explorer – diagram of components

only one part of the whole system, but this is needed for the purpose of presented experiments. Mosquito Explorer Release data:

- System Version: Beta 1
- Release Date: 19-12-2011
- Web Client Compatibility: Firefox 8.0, Internet Explorer 8.0, Opera 11.60
- Authors: Janusz Rygal.

To develop the test software we used the following technologies: Core modules (java 1.6, postgreSQL 9.0), Presentation Layer, Web Client (php, extjs 3.0, javascript, xhtml, css). We also the following libraries: POI Library ver. 3.7, Xmlbeans ver. 2.5.0, Dom4j ver. 1.6.1, Jericho-html ver. 3.2.

As already mentioned, for our experiment only the Search Service is relevant, and it will be tested in the context of semantic image analysis. In a nutshell, we want to check the behavior of the search engine, working with various types of words and sentences.

Table schema of Mosquito Explorer ver. Beta 1 contains 17 tables (see Figure 2) and dozens of other database objects. Only the table A_ITEM (Figure 3.)

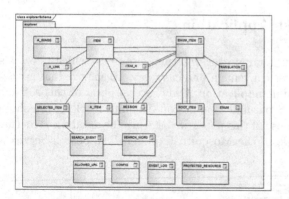

Fig. 2. Mosquito Explorer – database schema

Fig. 3. Mosquito Explorer – AItem table properties

is relevant for our tests. All columns, which names begin with 'TSV_ %' were defined as tsvector. On the column TSV_ITEM_TEXT a GIN index was created.

4   Experimental Data, Strategy and Results

Strategy of tests was designed as two dimensional set of the combination of a type of query and a search phrase. This approach ensures satisfying test covering level. Moreover it tests the system in two different directions;first one is a structure of test data and the second one are different types of queries.

4.1   Test Data Properties (Table A_ITEM)

Testing data contains various types of textual information; all of them are documentation of some project. Majority of those documents were written in German. Language information is very important for our application, because we must know, which dictionary should be used. Text persisted in the table A_ITEM, was extracted from diverse types of files for example: web pages (html), doc, xls, ppt or common txt files. A resource of our experimental data is:

- Size in disk : 4.6 GB
- Number of rows: 78855
- Average length of text : 10264.81 characters.

4.2   Test Strategy

The most important part of test is a test strategy. The strategy was designed as a matrix of query types and search phrases. We used the following query types:

1. Simple query SELECT "ID" FROM "explorer"."A_ITEM", to_tsquery ('pg_catalog.german', 'phrase') query
   WHERE "TSV_ITEM_TEXT" @@ query;

2. Limited simple query SELECT "ID" FROM "explorer"."A_ITEM", to_tsquery ('pg_catalog.german', 'phrase') query
   WHERE "TSV_ITEM_TEXT" @@ query LIMIT 10;

3. Ranked query SELECT "ID", ts_rank("TSV_ITEM_TEXT", query) as "RANK" FROM "explorer"."A_ITEM", to_tsquery('pg_catalog.german', 'phrase') query
   WHERE "TSV_ITEM_TEXT" @@ query ORDER BY "RANK" DESC

4. Limited ranked query SELECT "ID", ts_rank("TSV_ITEM_TEXT", query) as "RANK" FROM "explorer"."A_ITEM", to_tsquery('pg_catalog.german', 'phrase') query
   WHERE "TSV_ITEM_TEXT" @@ query ORDER BY "RANK" DESC LIMIT 10 ;

And we searched for the following phrases: "Fehler", "xyz", "123", "test ticket", "Der Fehler wurde behoben." Test results are presented in Table 1, every cell contains the result of a single test, i.e. the following information: execution time of first query [ms], average execution time of next 10 executions [ms], the number of items which were found [u].

Table 1. Test results. Every cell contains the result of single test, i.e. the following information: execution time of first query [ms], average execution time of next 10 executions [ms], the number of items which were found [u].

SearchPhrase /Query	"Fehler"	"xyz"	"123"	"test ticket"	"Der Fehler wurde behoben."
Simple query	562[ms] 469.8[ms] 54374[u]	25 [ms] 16.6 [ms] 62 [u]	71[ms] 13.5[ms] 236[u]	179[ms] 121.5[ms] 11157[u]	231[ms] 87.1[ms] 5801[u]
Limited simple query	11 [ms] 13.9 [ms] 10[u]	1362 [ms] 4343.2[ms] 10[u]	1352[ms] 2371.4[ms] 10[u]	12[ms] 14.2[ms] 10[u]	22[ms] 17.3[ms] 10[u]
Ranked query	10123[ms] 2762.4[ms] 54374[u]	43 [ms] 18.4 [ms] 62[u]	322[ms] 45.4[ms] 236[u]	2984[ms] 751.5[ms] 11157[u]	2285[ms] 463[ms] 5801[u]
Limited ranked query	1914 [ms] 1894.5[ms] 10[u]	12 [ms] 17.3 [ms] 10 [u]	52[ms] 43.8[ms] 10[u]	555[ms] 551[ms] 10[u]	392[ms] 394.2[ms] 10[u]

5   Conclusions

In results of tests we can see the satisfactory behavior of the database engine. In the search results of phrases which theoretically are not from the database dictionary (German) such as "xyz" and "123", query execution time is smaller than other phrases which are included in dictionary. It follows that this method could be used to lexical image search with new special language not specified in standards. In addition phrases from the outside of the dictionary could be correctly ranked in queries, similarly to phrases from the dictionary. In image retrieval it is very important because some parts of the image could be searched individually or in combination with others, so mapping it into the text there could be searched one phrase or its combination with others phrases. Depending on occurrences of a phrase or several (optional) phrases and their density in the text, an image containing the most searched phrases will be chosen most likely.

Acknowledgements. The project was funded by the National Center for Science under decision number DEC-2011/01/D/ST6/06957.

References

1. Ali, M., Clausi, D.: Using the Canny edge detector for feature extraction and enhancement of remote sensing images. IGARSS 2001 Scanning the Present and Resolving the Future Proceedings IEEE 2001 International Geoscience and Remote Sensing Symposium Cat No01CH37217, pp. 2298–2300 (2001)
2. Bay, H., Tuytelaars, T., Van Gool, L.: SURF: Speeded Up Robust Features. In: Leonardis, A., Bischof, H., Pinz, A. (eds.) ECCV 2006, Part I. LNCS, vol. 3951, pp. 404–417. Springer, Heidelberg (2006)

3. Brown, M., Lowe, D.: Recognising Panoramas. In: Proceedings of the 9th International Conference on Computer Vision (ICCV 2003), Nice, France, pp. 1218–1225 (2003)
4. Brown, M., Lowe, D.: Automatic Panoramic Image Stitching using Invariant Features. International Journal of Computer Vision 74(1), 59–73 (2007)
5. Cpałka, K.: On evolutionary designing and learning of flexible neuro-fuzzy structures for nonlinear classification. Nonlinear Analysis: Theory, Methods & Applications 71(12), 1659–1672 (2009)
6. Derpanis, K.G.: The Harris Corner Detector (2004), www.cse.yorku.ca/~kosta/CompVis_Notes/harris_detector.pdf
7. Ghahroudi, M.R., Sarshar, M.R., Sabzevari, R.: A Novel Content-Base Image Retrieval Techniques Using Tree matching. In: Proceedings of the World Congress on Engineering 2008, London, U.K., vol. III (2008)
8. Grąbczewski, K., Jankowski, N.: Saving time and memory in computational intelligence system with machine unification and task spooling. Knowledge-Based Systems 24(5), 570–588 (2011)
9. Jankowski, N., Grąbczewski, K.: Universal Meta-Learning Architecture and Algorithms. In: Jankowski, N., Duch, W., Grąbczewski, K. (eds.) Meta-Learning in Computational Intelligence. SCI, vol. 358, pp. 1–76. Springer, Heidelberg (2011)
10. Kazakova, N., Margala, M., Durdle, N.G.: Sobel edge detection processor for a real-time volume rendering system. In: Proceedings of the 2004 International Symposium on Circuits and Systems, ISCAS 2004, vol. 2, II-913–II-916 (2004)
11. Mikołajczyk, K., Schmid, C.: A Performance of Local Descriptors. IEEE Transactions on Pattern Analysis and Machine Inteligence 27(10), 1615–1630 (2005)
12. Nowicki, R., Rutkowski, L.: Soft Techniques for Bayesian Classification. In: Rutkowski, L., Kacprzyk, J. (eds.) Neural Networks and Soft Computing. AISC, pp. 537–544. Springer Physica-Verlag (2003)
13. PostgreSQL 9.1.2 Documentation, http://www.postgresql.org/docs/9.1/static/textsearch.html
14. Rutkowski, L., Cierniak, R.: On image compression by competitive neural networks and optimal linear predictors. Signal Processing: Image Communication - a Eurosip Journal 15(6), 559–565 (2000)
15. Valgren, C., Lilienthal, A.: SIFT, SURF and Seasons: Long-term Outdoor Localization Using Local Features. In: Proc. European Conference on Mobile Robots, pp. 253–258 (2007)
16. Yan, K., Sukthankar, R.: PCA-SIFT: a more distinctive representation for local image descriptors. In: Proceedings of the 2004 IEEE Computer Society Conference on Computer Vision and Pattern Recognition, CVPR 2004, vol. 2, pp. II-506–II-513 (2004)

Full Body Motion Tracking in Monocular Images Using Particle Swarm Optimization

Bogusław Rymut, Tomasz Krzeszowski, and Bogdan Kwolek

Polish-Japanese Institute of Information Technology
Koszykowa 86, 02-008 Warszawa, Poland
bytom@pjwstk.edu.pl

Abstract. The estimation of full body pose in monocular images is a very difficult problem. In 3D-model based motion tracking the challenges arise as at least one-third of degrees of freedom of the human pose that needs to be recovered is nearly unobservable in any given monocular image. In this paper, we deal with high dimensionality of the search space through estimating the pose in a hierarchical manner using Particle Swarm Optimization. Our method fits the projected body parts of an articulated model to detected body parts at color images with support of edge distance transform. The algorithm was evaluated quantitatively through the use of the motion capture data as ground truth.

1 Introduction

At present human behavior understanding is becoming one of the most active and extensive research topics of artificial intelligence and cognitive sciences. The strong interest is driven by broad spectrum of applications in several areas such as visual surveillance, human-machine-interaction and augmented reality. Tracking of human behavior inherently involves localization of body parts and estimation of the body pose [11]. Pose estimation can be approached with different ways depending on the image sensor configuration and the scenarios. The approaches can be categorized as either model-based and model-free ones [9]. In [13], an example-based approach for view-invariant estimation of 3D pose of upper body using single image has been proposed. In model-based approach, which uses a priori model of the subject to guide the pose estimation, the markerless motion tracking is typically more robust and accurate. In such an approach, the pose estimation is usually formulated as an optimization problem aiming at seeking the pose parameters, which minimize the errors between the projected 3D body segments and the image observations. One of the major difficulties in recovering human pose from 2D images is the high number of degrees-of-freedom (DOF) in the body's movement that has to be estimated. Generally, a human body consists of no less than 10 large body parts, equating to more than 20 DOF that are needed for describing realistic human movements.

Reconstructing 3D human poses from monocular images is considerably more difficult than 3D pose estimate from multiple views. The challenges to be addressed in single camera-based pose estimation are depth and observation ambiguities, self-occlusions, and last but not least the matching imperfect and very

---

L. Rutkowski et al. (Eds.): ICAISC 2012, Part I, LNCS 7267, pp. 600–607, 2012.

flexible model to cluttered images. Observation ambiguities take place since any image observation can be mapped to several 3D human poses. Besides the difficulties mentioned above, for any realistic human model at least one-third of DOFs are almost unobservable in any given monocular image. In consequence, without depth information it is challenging to reconstruct skeleton in 3D. A successful approach to recovering 3D human body pose from monocular images is presented in [1], which consists in the use of direct nonlinear regression of join angles against histogram-of-shape-context silhouette shape descriptors. The most successful algorithm to date is based on propagating a mixture of Gaussians, which approximate the probability density functions representing the probable 3D poses [14]. The key contribution is efficient and exhaustive searching of the cost surface relating the candidate body configurations to image features. However, it is unclear if without explicit mechanism for re-initialization the propagation of multimodal distribution over longer period of time remains reliable.

The typical framework to human pose estimation is to fit the geometrical models to the image features by the use a deterministic or stochastic strategy. In 3D model based estimation of the human pose in monocular image sequences the particle filters are widely used. Particle filters [3] are recursive Bayesian filters that are based on Monte Carlo simulations. They approximate a posterior distribution for the configuration of a human body given a series of observations. The high dimensionality of articulated body motion requires huge number of particles to represent well the posterior probability of the states. In such spaces, sample impoverishment may prevent particle filters from maintaining multimodal distribution for long periods of time. Therefore, many efforts have been spent in developing methods for confining the search space to promising regions with true body pose. In [12], Schmidt et al. proposed a kernel particle filter to effectively explore the probability distributions and achieved reliable real-time tracking of the upper-body in monocular image sequences. Another possibility to constrain the configuration space is to use hierarchical search. In such an approach, a part of the articulated model is localized independently in advance, and then its location is used to constrain the search for the remaining limbs. In [4], an approach called search space decomposition is proposed, where on the basis of color cues the torso is localized first and then it is used to confine the search for the limbs. Recently, Particle Swarm Optimization (PSO) algorithm was proposed to achieve full body motion tracking using single [8] and multiple cameras [15][5]. PSO is a population based stochastic optimization technique [6], which shares many similarities with evolutionary computation techniques. It has been shown to perform well on many nonlinear and multimodal optimization problems.

In this paper, we present an approach for 3D model based reconstructing the 3-dimensional motions of human figure in monocularly-viewed image sequences. Full body pose estimation is performed in a hierarchical manner using PSO. At the beginning of each frame we determine the pose of the torso and afterwards the pose of the remaining limbs. To obtain reliable motion tracking we segment of the person's silhouette into torso and limbs. In order to obtain better orientation of the torso we take into account the direction of person's walking.

2   PSO for Dynamic Optimization

PSO maintains a swarm of particles, where each one represents a candidate solution. Every particle determines its own position, moves with its own velocity in
the multidimensional search space and determines its fitness using an objective
function $f(x)$. At the beginning each individual is initialized with a random position and velocity. During searching for the best fitness each particle is attracted
towards the position that is affected by the best position p_i found so far by itself
and the global best position g found by the whole swarm. The i-th particle's
velocity and position are updated according to the following two equations:

$$v_i^{k+1} = \omega v_i^k + c_1 r_1 (p_i - x_i^k) + c_2 r_2 (g - x_i^k) \tag{1}$$

$$x_i^{k+1} = x_i^k + v_i^{k+1} \tag{2}$$

where the constants c_1 and c_2 are used to balance the influence of the individual's
knowledge and that of the group, respectively, r_1 and r_2 are uniformly distributed
random numbers, x_i is position of the i-th particle, p_i is the local best position
of particle i, whereas g stands for the global best position, and ω is an inertia
constant. The swarm stops the updating when a termination criterion is met.
Because the pose tracking is a dynamic optimization problem, in order to cover
possible pose changes the particles are propagated according to weak transition
model when a new image becomes available.

3   3D Body Model and Cost Function

3.1   Human Body Model

The articulated human body model is represented as a kinematic tree consisting
of 11 segments. It is made of truncated cones that model the pelvis, torso/head,
upper and lower arm and legs. Its 3D pose is defined by 26 DOF and it is
determined by position and orientation of the pelvis in the global coordinate
system and the relative angles between the connected limbs. The perspective
projection is used in mapping the model onto 2D image plane. In this way we
attain the image of the 3D model in a given configuration, which can then be
matched to the person extracted through image analysis. The aim of the tracking
is to estimate the pose of the pelvis and the joint angles and this is achieved by
maximizing the fitting cost.

3.2   Body Part Detection

Our approach to full body motion tracking in monocular images is motivated
by findings from other previous work, which stresses the importance of good 2D
features to achieve reliable human pose estimation, cf. [10]. However, detection
of body parts, such as torso and the limbs in color images is difficult due to
variations caused by varying shape, appearance, clothing, etc.

In first stage of our algorithm the background subtraction is performed using algorithm [2]. The binary foreground image is then employed in determining the silhouette-overlap degree. The silhouette features extracted via background subtraction are complemented by image edges, which contribute towards more precise aligning the body parts. At this stage a cost of fitting the projected model edges to the image edges is determined. The most common approach to edge detection is based on image gradient, which shares many properties with optical flow. In particular, the gradient features are independent from background subtraction. Gradient angle is invariant to global changes of image intensities. In contrast to optical flow, gradients features are discriminative for both moving and non-moving body parts. In our approach, the gradient magnitude is masked by the closed image of the foreground. In this fashion we obtain edges belonging only to the person undergoing tracking. They are then employed to generate the edge distance map, see also Fig. 1. The distance map assigns each pixel a value that is the distance between that pixel and the nearest nonzero edge pixel. In our implementation we employ chessboard distance and limit the number of iterations on the chain propagation to three. A color histogram in HSI color space, quantized into $8 \times 8 \times 8$ bins was used to approximate the distribution of the skin color. The skin color areas were detected via histogram backprojection and then refined using a skin-locus [7]. Owing to skin-locus it is possible to successfully delineate the skin areas even in front of wooden planking, see also images in first row at Fig. 1. The torso has been detected using histogram-based model of color distribution in HSI color space. The remaining part of the foreground blob was segmented as legs.

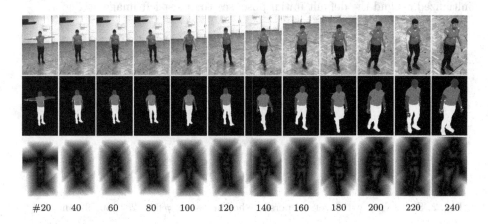

#20   40   60   80   100   120   140   160   180   200   220   240

Fig. 1. Input images (upper row), segmented body parts (middle row), edge distance map (bottom row)

3.3   Hierarchical Optimization and Objective Function

In hierarchical fitting the pose of the body parts, which are the most predictable should be estimated first. Therefore, at the beginning of each time step we estimate the position of the torso. The location is determined with regard to the torso area delineated in the image. During determining the orientation of the torso we take into account the direction of motion of the walking person. With the help of camera calibration we determine the contact point with the floor for both legs or single leg. Given such contact point(s), we determine the pose of the legs. Finally, using the segmented forearms and/or arms we estimate the pose of both hands. In hierarchical PSO we used the following fitness function: $f(x) = o_z(x)^{\alpha_1} \times e_z(x)^{1-\alpha_1} \mid z \in \{\text{torso,legs,skin}\}$, where o_z denotes the silhouette overlap term, whereas e_z stands for the edge distance-based fitness. In ordinary PSO we utilized the following fitness function: $f(x) = o(x)^{\alpha_1} \times e(x)^{1-\alpha_1}$, where $o(x) = \alpha T(x) + \beta L(x) + \gamma S(x)$, where $\alpha + \beta + \gamma = 1$ and $T(x), L(x), S(x)$ stand for silhouette overlap term for torso, legs and skin, respectively.

4   Experimental Results

The PSO-based algorithms for full body motion tracking were compared by analyses carried out both through qualitative visual evaluations as well as quantitatively through the use of the motion capture data as ground truth. A GigE vision camera was used to acquire the color images of size 1920×1080 at 25 fps. Human motion tracking was performed on the cropped images with spatial resolution 740×800 pixels, see Fig. 2. An average silhouette height was approximately 300 pixels and varied from 250 pixels to 425 pixels. The swarm was initialized around the default initial pose, see the most left image at Fig. 1.

Fig. 2. Scene view with overlaid person, shot in frames #64, 128, 160,192 and 240

At Fig. 3 are shown some tracking results that were obtained by ordinary and hierarchical PSO. The overlap of the projected 3D model on the subject undergoing tracking is shown to illustrate the quality of tracking. In the experiments presented below we focused on analyses of motion of walking people with bared and freely swinging arms. The analysis of the human way of walking, termed gait analysis, has attracted considerable attention in recent years and can be utilized in several applications ranging from medical applications to surveillance.

#20 40 60 80 100 120 140 160 180 200 220 240

Fig. 3. Full body motion tracking in monocular images

We evaluated the accuracy of the PSO-based algorithm for motion tracking on a number of image sequences of a walking person taken from a fixed viewpoint. In Table 1 are depicted some quantitative results, which are averages over ten runs of the motion tracker with unlike initializations. The results were obtained on image sequence consisting of 240 frames, see Fig. 3, in 40 iterations using PSO consisting of 512 particles, and a configuration for hierarchical PSO with 40 iterations, 102 particles for torso, 205 for legs, and 205 particles for hands.

Table 1. Average errors for $M = 39$ markers

		full body	torso	left hand	right hand	left ankle	right ankle
PSO	avg. err [mm]	222.3	112.6	258.5	660.8	225.8	227.1
	std. dev. [mm]	83.9	40.1	122.8	150.7	95.4	153.0
HPSO	avg. err [mm]	167.8	110.1	242.4	223.8	228.8	239.4
	std. dev. [mm]	66.7	22.9	128.1	123.0	86.5	105.8

The results for the full body, see also first column in Table 1, were obtained for $M = 39$ markers. From the above set of markers, 4 markers were placed on the head, 7 markers on each arm, 12 on the legs, 5 on the torso and 4 markers were attached to the pelvis. Given such a placement of the markers on the human body and the estimated human pose, which has been calculated by our algorithm, the corresponding positions of virtual markers were determined and then utilized in calculating the average Euclidean distance between corresponding markers. The average Euclidean distance $\bar{d}_i$ for each marker i was calculated using real world locations $m_i \in R^3$ on the basis of the following equation:

$$\bar{d}_i = \frac{1}{T} \sum_{t=1}^{T} ||m_i(\hat{x}_t) - m_i(x_t)|| \tag{3}$$

where $m_i(\hat{x})$ stands for marker's position that was calculated using the estimated pose, $m_i(x)$ denotes the position, which has been determined using ground-truth, whereas T stands for the number of frames. The errors reported in columns 2-6 of Table 1 indicate the distance errors for single markers on the considered limbs. For each marker i the standard deviation σ_i was calculated as follows:

$$\sigma_i = \sqrt{\frac{1}{T-1} \sum_{t=1}^{T} \left(\|m_i(\hat{x}_t) - m_i(x_t)\| - \overline{d}_i \right)^2} \qquad (4)$$

The standard deviation $\overline{\sigma}$ shown in Table 1 is the average over all markers. The errors were obtained in scenarios with walking person, see Fig. 3. As we can observe, the hierarchical PSO algorithm outperforms the PSO based tracker. The results shown in Table 1 demonstrate that in our scenario with walking person that was shot by a monocular HD camera, the Particle Swarm Optimization algorithm is capable of estimating the full body motion with promising accuracy. The 3D reconstruction of human motion in monocular walking sequences is reliable in almost the whole sequence. The errors of the left hand are slightly larger for the reason that it has undergone complete occlusion in considerable number of frames. The mean distance error for *Lee walk* sequence recorded at 30 fps and 20 fps, that was obtained in [5] is equal to 283.6 ± 113.0 and 299.0 ± 121.9, respectively. The error obtained by our method on our walking sequence is far smaller owing to person segmentation into individual body parts as well as taking into account the direction of walking and the points of floor contact. Since the full body pose is estimated hierarchically, a large distance error of the torso can lead to considerable distance error of the whole body. A demo illustrating full body pose tracking using single monocular camera is available at: `http://prz.edu.pl/~bkwolek/res/icaisc12/sv_hmt.avi`.

The complete human motion capture system was written in C/C++. The system runs on Windows in both 32 bit and 64 bit modes. The entire tracking process takes approximately 7 sec. per frame on a PC with dual CPU Intel Xeon X5690 3.46 GHz using a configuration with 512 particles and 40 iterations for PSO and a configuration for hierarchical PSO with 40 iterations, 102 particles for torso, 205 for legs, 205 for hands. The image processing and analysis takes about 0.45 sec. Although the customization of the model can be completed automatically, the model is adjusted manually for each person to be tracked.

5   Conclusions

In this paper, we have shown that a successful full body motion tracking in monocular image sequences can be achieved using Particle Swarm Optimization and reliable segmentation of person into body parts. To show the advantages of the hierarchical PSO algorithm, we have conducted several experiments on sequences with a walking individual. The ordinary and hierarchical PSO algorithms were compared by analyses carried out both through qualitative visual evaluations as well as quantitatively through the use of the motion capture data as ground truth.

Acknowledgment. This paper has been supported by the research project OR00002111: "Application of video surveillance systems to person and behavior identification and threat detection, using biometrics and inference of 3D human model from video."

References

1. Agarwal, A., Triggs, B.: Recovering 3D human pose from monocular images. IEEE Trans. Pattern Anal. Mach. Intell. 28, 44–58 (2006)
2. Arsic, D., Lyutskanov, A., Rigoll, G., Kwolek, B.: Multi camera person tracking applying a graph-cuts based foreground segmentation in a homography framework. In: IEEE Int. Workshop on Performance Evaluation of Tracking and Surveillance, pp. 30–37. IEEE Press, Piscataway (2009)
3. Doucet, A., Godsill, S., Andrieu, C.: On sequential Monte Carlo sampling methods for bayesian filtering. Statistics and Computing 10(1), 197–208 (2000)
4. Gavrila, D.M., Davis, L.S.: 3-D model-based tracking of humans in action: a multi-view approach. In: Proc. of the Conf. on Computer Vision and Pattern Recognition (CVPR 1996), pp. 73–80. IEEE Computer Society, Washington, DC (1996)
5. John, V., Trucco, E., Ivekovic, S.: Markerless human articulated tracking using hierarchical Particle Swarm Optimisation. Image Vis. Comput. 28, 1530–1547 (2010)
6. Kennedy, J., Eberhart, R.: Particle swarm optimization. In: Proc. of IEEE Int. Conf. on Neural Networks, pp. 1942–1948. IEEE Press, Piscataway (1995)
7. Kovac, J., Peer, P., Solina, F.: Human skin color clustering for face detection. In: Int. Conf. on Computer as a Tool, EUROCON 2003, vol. 2, pp. 144–148 (2003)
8. Krzeszowski, T., Kwolek, B., Wojciechowski, K.: GPU-Accelerated Tracking of the Motion of 3D Articulated Figure. In: Bolc, L., Tadeusiewicz, R., Chmielewski, L.J., Wojciechowski, K. (eds.) ICCVG 2010. LNCS, vol. 6374, pp. 155–162. Springer, Heidelberg (2010)
9. Moeslund, T.B., Hilton, A., Krüger, V.: A survey of advances in vision-based human motion capture and analysis. Computer Vision and Image Understanding 104(2-3), 90–126 (2006)
10. Mori, G., Ren, X., Efros, A.A., Malik, J.: Recovering human body configurations: Combining segmentation and recognition. In: Proc. of the Conf. on Computer Vision and Pattern Recognition, vol. 2, pp. 326–333. IEEE Comp. Society (2004)
11. Salah, A.A., Gevers, T., Sebe, N., Vinciarelli, A.: Challenges of Human Behavior Understanding. In: Salah, A.A., Gevers, T., Sebe, N., Vinciarelli, A. (eds.) HBU 2010. LNCS, vol. 6219, pp. 1–12. Springer, Heidelberg (2010)
12. Schmidt, J., Fritsch, J., Kwolek, B.: Kernel particle filter for real-time 3D body tracking in monocular color images. In: IEEE Int. Conf. on Face and Gesture Rec., Southampton, UK, pp. 567–572. IEEE Computer Society Press (2006)
13. Shakhnarovich, G., Viola, P., Darrell, T.: Fast pose estimation with parameter-sensitive hashing. In: Proc. of IEEE Int. Conf. on Computer Vision, ICCV 2003, vol. 2, pp. 750–757. IEEE Computer Society, Washington, DC (2003)
14. Sminchisescu, C., Triggs, B.: Kinematic jump processes for monocular 3D human tracking. In: Proc. of the IEEE Computer Society Conf. on Computer Vision and Pattern Recognition, CVPR 2003, pp. 69–76. IEEE Computer Society (2003)
15. Zhang, X., Hu, W., Wang, X., Kong, Y., Xie, N., Wang, H., Ling, H., Maybank, S.: A swarm intelligence based searching strategy for articulated 3D human body tracking. In: IEEE Workshop on 3D Information Extraction for Video Analysis and Mining in conjuction with CVPR, pp. 45–50. IEEE Press, Piscataway (2010)

DriastSystem: A Computer Vision Based Device for Real Time Traffic Sign Detection and Recognition

Marcin Tekieli and Marek Słoński

Institute for Computational Civil Engineering
Faculty of Civil Engineering
Cracow University of Technology
{mtekieli,mslonski}@l5.pk.edu.pl
http://www.l5.pk.edu.pl

Abstract. This paper presents the design and application of novel device for real time traffic sign detection and recognition on a hardware platform powered by Intel® Atom™ processor. Image frames from standard and relatively cheap web cameras are processed using OpenCV library [7][2]. An innovative method is proposed for traffic sign detection phase. Two color models are used for image segmentation and detection of traffic sign. Many well-known and described tactics have been tested and rated. Implemented in OpenCV Library functions for pattern recognition method are also used in main algorithm. Experimental results of traffic sign detection and recognition are described. The prototype was implemented as part of the Master Thesis at Cracow University of Technology [1].

Keywords: computer vision, traffic sign detection and recognition, OpenCV library, color model, pattern recognition, fuzzy logic.

1 Introduction and Motivation

The problem of traffic sign recognition is quite popular in the field of computer vision technology, but it is very often processed with previously collected data. In many cases these data are represented by several short videos recorded in similar weather conditions. Nowadays, this type of approach is useless because system is adapted to the specific type of circumstances and it will be ineffective for new data.

There were many attempts to solve this problem undertaken by teams of scientists and corporations dealing with modern technologies, as well as car companies. On the other hand, commercial proposals are not documented in terms of their construction and actual quality of the recognition effectiveness. What's more, they are inaccessible to regular user because of their price and intellectual property protection.

Due to the miniaturization of high speed computing systems and the systematic decrease in their prices, it is possible to build mobile device that would tackle

L. Rutkowski et al. (Eds.): ICAISC 2012, Part I, LNCS 7267, pp. 608–616, 2012.

the problem in real time on the vehicle's board. Designed prototype meets this requirement. For proper operate performance it requires only a standard 12V power supply available in each vehicle. The device is relatively inexpensive, as well as fully mobile. It can also be regularly updated without affecting software installed in on-board computer.

Fig. 1. Different templates of traffic signs in some countries

Individual templates of traffic signs depend on the country where they are approved. It was additional motivation to build a device adapted to Polish conditions. In each country traffic signs differ not only in shape and color but also the pictograms placed on them are different. The found solutions are designed in U.S.A. and Japan, so probably they would not be effective in Poland. As may be seen in figure 1 traffic signs differ in shape and color.

Related Works. At present - the end of 2011, in addition to the above mentioned Ford Focus, traffic signs recognition systems are available in several car models, which are among the most expensive. Such improvements can be found among others in the Audi A8, Saab 9-5 and the productions of the Mercedes-Benz S Class. However, these are high-end vehicles, also equipped with other intelligent systems, and traffic sign recognition module is only one of many subsystems. None of these solutions has officially available documentation clearly defining their structure and effectiveness.

Siemens's project was implemented in 2008. Its primary purpose was to reduce the number of breaking the speed limits on highways, therefore it was limited to the recognition of speed limit signs. It is integrated with on-board computer and in some car models, it can automatically influence the speed of the vehicle [3]. Wider approach to the problem has been suggested at the IEEE Computer Society International Conference on Computer Vision and Pattern Recognition by Michael Shneier. His project included a methodology that allows to recognize the signs of all subgroups [4]. The prototype version of the camera device that downloads images from the road environment was placed on the roof of the car. The quality of detection and recognition was determined on the basis of several pre-prepared videos and amounted to about 88% and 78%. Also an interesting solution for the circular traffic signs recognition has been proposed by a team of researchers from Nagaoka University of Technology in Japan and the Institut

Teknologi Nasional Malang in Indonesia [5]. At the beginning, fragments from the collected samples were isolated. To isolate them, researchers used the geometric fragmentation, which is similar in its assumptions to Genetic Algorithms.

2   System Design

The components of the system can be divided into two main groups. The first is the hardware part, which brings all the components together. All of them can perform required operations in a relatively simple way for implementation. The second group combines the application modules, and running processes which performs various tasks. Graphical application interface was developed in an environment with Qt signals and slots mechanism[6]. Additionally, to notify driver about passing traffic sign, voice messages are played and information is presented on the monitor. Instead of using embedded operating system, Ubuntu Server edition is used.

2.1   Hardware

During the selection of hardware platform many solutions including the AVR and ARM microprocessors have been tested but their performance is low for this type of system. Finally, the platform with built in Intel Atom Processor has been chosen. Atom series processors are a relatively new solution proposed by Intel Corporation to build small, energy-efficient computing system fully compatible with 32 and 64 bit architecture. Small size motherboard, low power consumption of the entire set (50W) and low emission of heat in conjunction with the performance of the standard unit makes this solution ideal for this project implementation.

Asus motherboard AT3GC-I has been chosen as a stable foundation for the Intel Atom CPU and 2GB DDR2 800Mhz RAM. Instead of the standard 2.5" or 3.5" hard drive, system uses a Ultra CompactFlash card with a capacity of 8GB and write speed of 30MB/s. All components have been installed in a compact computer case in MiniITX format and powered with a universal power supply used in portable computers.

2.2   Main Algorithm

The central element of the system and the entire device is the algorithm responsible for traffic signs identification. Each video frame taken from camera mounted in the vehicle is subjected to preliminary processing in order to prepare it for the next steps of the main algorithm. The effect called 'digital image noise' causes the appearance of erroneous final results. To overcome it, a series of transformations has been applied to the image. Also an appropriate sequence of actions and transformations has been developed in order to increase the effectiveness of the algorithm. Image smoothing was performed and the technique of image pyramids has been used. Source image has been converted to HSV color space, and each channel of RGB and HSV models has been isolated into separate arrays.

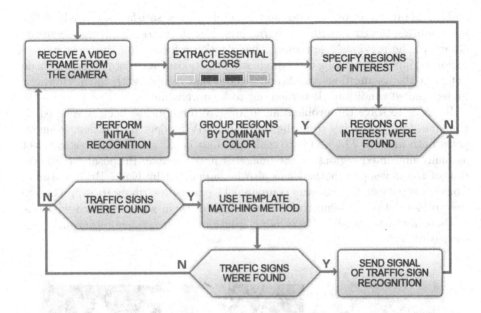

Fig. 2. System workflow diagram

Detection Phase. Following the initial stage of processing and standardization of the camera image is a phase of traffic signs detection. It involves the segmentation of a single image to isolate smaller areas, which may contain essential objects. The rejection of as many fragments of the original image as it is possible significantly affects the efficiency of subsequent steps. It directly involves a number of calculations that must be made in the recognition phase.

The main idea used at this stage of processing is to identify parts of the image, which have specific characteristics - for example, hue and saturation in the HSV model. So-called 'color maps' are created and used in logical sentences as arguments. They determine the logical group of pixels of given properties. With the characteristic structure of the HSV color space it is possible to determine the approximate location of three existing traffic sign colors - yellow, red and blue in this color space. Hue frequency distributions for each group of signs were determined by additional program, which was designed for this task. This was done by analyzing the components of hue (H) and saturation (S) of the HSV model in individual pixels located on the prepared samples of signs. 200 samples were prepared for warning signs, 100 for regulatory and 100 for prohibition signs. Distributions were then normalized to the interval $< 0; 1 >$.

In the standard approach to the problem, detected areas are compared with the distribution of the averaged just by using the membership function. Subjects of fuzzy logic, such as fuzzy set are used here. Then the probability when a given area may be an interesting object is determined.

This approach is often used and generally gives satisfactory results. The schema using the HSV model is characterized by the extracting image segments closest to the previously set color. This algorithm focuses on the most narrow region of interest through the systematic rejection of all fragments, which do not meet the assumptions and keeping those that comply with them. However, under studied conditions, it turned out to be unreliable.

In order to solve the problem an innovative method has been developed. It combines the approaches from the RGB and HSV models. In addition, it aggregates both models. The aim is to make the best detection of traffic signs reject as many unwanted regions of the image as it is possible. Proposal for innovation of the developed method can also be supported by Karla Brkic's studies from University of Zagreb, who compared 11 papers describing the approach to the problem of recognizing traffic signs. Each of them was connected with one of the color space model. There is no solution which uses simultaneously two models [9].

Fig. 3. Improving the extraction process by using the proposed method

Intervals containing acceptable hue and saturation values for each color have been extended to prevent rejection of too many important areas. The new values are presented in table 1. What's more, the analysis of each pixel is derived by its properties in two color space models - RGB and HSV. In most cases it is much easier to discover dependencies involving image segmentation based on two or more models. For each pixel hue and saturation value from HSV model and red, green and blue value from RGB model are checked simultaneously. Only if all of these assumptions are satisfied the pixel is considered to be significant and it is placed in the set of pixels of a given color e.g. for yellow pixel the following conditions must be met in HSV color space model:

$$H_{val} \in (10; 85) \wedge S_{val} \in (45; 255); . \tag{1}$$

and RGB color space model:

$$R_{val} \in (125; 220) \wedge G_{val} \in (90; 145) \wedge B_{val} \in (0; 45) . \tag{2}$$

Green and red pixels are classified in the same way but with different ranges. It has been observed that for blue pixels this procedure is not necessary and standard approach also gives satisfactory results.

In the project it has also been proposed to use CMYK for the extraction of the regions with white and black color. The CMYK color space model is rather used in polygraphy - not in issues related to the computer vision, but preliminary tests showed that using this model could be beneficial in this case. It should be noted that this model has also a separate channel 'Y' for yellow color, as it is important in the case of Polish traffic signs.

Table 1. The modified components of hue and saturation for the four colors

COMPONENT	RED	YELLOW	BLUE	GREEN
(H) Hue	(0; 35)	(10; 85)	(90; 155)	(10; 110)
(S) Saturation	(50; 255)	(45; 255)	(40; 205)	(0; 180)

Expanding ranges of hue and saturation parameters showed in table 1 imply a further innovation in this approach. The color already extracted are used for the following extraction of the areas in specified color. In addition, exploration field is not drastically but gradually narrowed in each step. For example, in order to detect the warning signs, first determined regions are colored yellow, orange and red. Then, extraction of yellow color is carried out, which is easier when the search area was initially narrowed. This is done with adaptive thresholding, which in this case highlights its advantages over standard thresholding. The described approach can be traced in the figure 4.

Fig. 4. Gradual extraction of yellow areas

Extraction of colors that do not appear on traffic signs brings positive results. An example would be a green color which is not seen on the relevant traffic signs and its extraction helps to indicate the yellow colored areas by the application of a logical difference operator. Green mask is subtracted from the mask containing yellow color. This makes sense due to the fact that these two colors are near each other in both color space models - RGB and HSV.

Recognition Phase. At the moment the device has a lower efficiency in this phase as compared to competitive solutions. More sophisticated methods like neural networks or SVM have not been applied yet. Features defining tests have been carried out so that they would be sent to SVM, but none of them has given satisfactory results. All areas that have been classified at the previous stage, as segments, which may include a traffic sign are sent to the recognition phase. They are initially grouped according to the dominant color - yellow warning signs, red - prohibition signs and blue - mandatory and information signs.

On most road signs there are pictograms that define their meaning. To prevent a situation where the sign's template would be incomplete, new method has been developed called 'Expanding the Region of Interest Method'. Area sent from the detection phase is enlarged for so long that within it there are important pixels described by a given color mask. Note, that there have been many transformations with image segment which is processed, including blurring and smoothing, so it is suggested to do the kind of one step back. Portion of the image is taken from the untransformed sample source for analysis. This is advantageous because the operations useful at detection stage are not necessarily useful at the moment of recognition.

Pattern Matching Method has been used to recognize the traffic signs. To maximize the chance of correct identification of all not rejected segments, all areas are scaled to the same size 100x100 pixels. The next step involves using the cvMatchTemplate function, which is available in OpenCV library. It returns the maximum and minimum fit of the pattern to the part of the image. These values are normalized to the range $< -1; 1 >$. The decision to recognize a traffic sign is based on the best fit value. In algorithm the correlation coefficient method has been used, where correlation coefficient is between -1.0 and 1.0. Extreme values represent the worst and the best fit. Value 0.0 represents no correlation. This method matches a template T relative to its mean against the image I relative to its mean and the result R is given by the following formula[2]:

$$R_{ccoeff}(x,y) = \sum_{x',y'} [T'(x',y') * I'(x+x', y+y')]^2 .$$ (3)

where:

$$T'(x',y') = T(x',y') - \frac{1}{(w * h) \sum_{x'',y''} T(x'',y'')} .$$ (4)

$$I'(x+x', y+y') = I(x+x', y+y') - \frac{1}{(w * h) \sum_{x'',y''} I(x+x'', y+y'')} .$$ (5)

To save resources, pattern matching is done in stages. For each color group of signs, first attempt to identify the characteristic signs is taken. In case of prohibition signs, STOP sign is recognized at the beginning. If the established conditions are met, the search is terminated at this stage. Otherwise, an attempt is made to recognize B-35 or B-36 sign. Finally, all other prohibition signs are searched.

Table 2. DriastSystem and other solutions comparison

SYSTEM	(1)	(2) [%]	(3) [%]	(4) [%]	(5)
Siemens VDO	n/a	n/a	n/a	n/a	YES
Road Sign Det. and Rec.	92	88.0	78.0	6.5 - 58.0	NO
Intell. Machine Vision	n/a	n/a	95.5	n/a	NO
Driast System	714	88.2 (94.8)	71.2 (91.0)	22.1 (4.2)	YES

(1) - Number of signs on samples, (2) - Detection quality, (3) - Recognition quality

(4) - Percent of faulty recognitions, (5) - Real time tests

3 Experiments

Tests for each traffic sign appearing in a set of recognized signs has been carried out using collected samples. In each case 20 representative images with a sign, and 80 random samples with other sign or only background have been selected. Most important signs, indicating the priority on the road were also separated. In this case the number of test samples has increased twice. This group included D-1, D-2, A-7 and B-20 signs. In case of these signs tests have been made in real time during regular travel by car. Due to the very limited time, official tests for other signs were limited to samples in the form of images. Comparison of the average efficiency of the prototype built with the described solutions is presented in the table 2.

During tests there were also numerous false indications, number of which should be reduced. The applied patterns are fragments of the original signs templates. Using averaged image pattern, modeled on the slices of test samples, better results could be obtained. But this would require some time to prepare templates. It is noteworthy that beside the simplicity of the pattern preparation process, this method has already given satisfactory results at this stage and could be further developed or supported by other mechanisms. Currently, mechanisms enabling recognition of more than 30 traffic signs of various types have been implemented in the main algorithm.

4 Summary

So far, a solid foundation for the development of our device has been built. Already at this stage fairly good results has been achieved, especially for the detection phase. However, they require further improvements for the recognition phase. Developed tool clearly shows the capabilities of vision systems, and digital image processing algorithms. A few dependencies that can be used in a similar type projects have been noticed.

The greatest innovation which is characterized by the algorithm is a completely different approach to the given problem than the one which have already been described by the developers of such tools. Simultaneous use of two color space models has given much better results than relying on only one of them. Another advantage was achieved by the introduction of methods for expanding the region of interest and by dividing almost all steps into smaller threads. The progressive narrowing of the problem field is a more effective approach than trying to achieve high results at the very beginning.

While working at main algorithm several methods for this purpose have been tested e.g. Cyganek's method of essential points[8]. However, they have not given satisfactory results for recognition in real time.

Development Possibilities. Like any prototype device it requires a further contribution of the work. It could be improved and developed at the hardware and software level. To make it more attractive to potential users, it should be miniaturized. A software layer also requires permanent improvements in performance and quality.

Using the experience gained so far in the field of computer vision and structure of OpenCV library, it would be possible to introduce additional functionality, such as the detection of horizontal signs and traffic lights. Set of recognized signs also should be expanded, but it involves additional tests and re-execution phase of data collection.

References

1. Tekieli, M., Worek, K.: Design of Computer Vision Based Device for Real Time Traffic Sign Detection and Recognition. Master Thesis, Cracow University of Technology, Cracow (2011) (in Polish)
2. Bradski, G., Kaehler, A.: Learning OpenCV. O'Reilly (2008)
3. Siemens, VDO - Traffic Sign Recognition (2007),
   http://www.siemens.com/press/en/pp_cc/2007/02_feb/sosep200702_27_mt_special_mobility_1434304.html
4. Shneier, M.: Road Sign Detection and Recognition. In: ICCVPR 2005 (2005)
5. Yamada, K., Limpraptono, Y.: Intelligent Machine Vision System For Road Traffic Sign Recognition. In: Proc. of Seminar Nasional Teknoin (2008)
6. Nokia Corporation: Signals and Slots (2011),
   http://doc.qt.nokia.com/4.7/signalsandslots.html
7. Willow Garage: OpenCV Wiki (2010), http://opencv.willowgarage.com/wiki/
8. Cyganek, B.: Methods and Algorithms of Object Recognition in Digital Images. AGH University of Science and Technology Press (2009)
9. Brkic, K.: An overview of traffic sign detection methods (2010),
   http://www.fer.hr/_download/repository/BrkicQualifyingExam.pdf

Real-Time Object Tracking Algorithm Employing On-Line Support Vector Machine and Multiple Candidate Regeneration

Pushe Zhao, Renyuan Zhang, and Tadashi Shibata

Department of Electrical Engineering and Information Systems
The University of Tokyo
7-3-1 Hongo, Bunkyo-ku, Tokyo 113-8656, Japan
{zhao,tyoninen}@if.t.u-tokyo.ac.jp, shibata@ee.t.u-tokyo.ac.jp

Abstract. A real-time object tracking algorithm is presented based on the on-line support vector machine (SVM) scheme. A new training framework is proposed, which enables us to select reliable training samples from the image sequence for tracking. Multiple candidate regeneration, a statistical method, is employed to decrease the computational cost, and a directional-edge-based feature representation algorithm is used to represent images robustly as well as compactly. The structure of the algorithm is designed especially for real-time performance, which can extend the advantages of SVM to most of the general tracking applications. The algorithm has been evaluated on challenging video sequences and showed robust tracking ability with accurate tracking results. The hardware implementation is also discussed, while verification has been done to prove the real-time ability of this algorithm.

Keywords: object tracking, real-time, on-line learning SVM, multiple candidate regeneration.

1 Introduction

Object tracking is a critical and well-studied problem with many practical applications. A number of algorithms have been developed based on various mechanisms. One promising direction is to consider the object tracking as a binary classification problem, and employ discriminative methods in the tracking framework. Support vector machine (SVM), as a powerful classification scheme, has been used in many tracking algorithms, benefiting the algorithms with accurate localization and flexible modeling of the target [1,2,3]. The SVM works as an appearance model of the target in these algorithms. One feature of SVM is that the decision boundary is represented as a linear combination of support vectors, and the number of support vectors is usually small compared with the entire training dataset. Since the hardware resources always have limitation, this feature is very important when considering the implementation of the tracking algorithm on hardware.

L. Rutkowski et al. (Eds.): ICAISC 2012, Part I, LNCS 7267, pp. 617–625, 2012.

Despite the good performance of the existing algorithms, they suffer from several practical problems. The work in [1] builds a superior SVM classifier and gives good results in tracking vehicles. However, the off-line training mechanism employed in the work requires a large number of training samples selected manually and does not support updating the training samples. In [2], all samples learned from each frame of an image sequence are stored for training the SVM. This causes a large memory cost if it is used in a long-duration task. In [3], a simple strategy is employed to determine new training samples, which may cause "drift problem" as described in [4]. Moreover, these algorithms do not consider their real-time performances, which is in fact of great importance in object tracking applications. This is mainly because of the complex computation of SVM. Especially for the on-line learning SVMs, frequently repeated training and predictions make this problem even worse. Therefore, in order to extend the power of SVM in most of the general tracking applications, it is necessary to develop a proper tracking framework and a VLSI-hardware-implementation-friendly structure for the SVM-based algorithm.

The tracking framework includes how to update training samples and how to select test samples and make prediction of the target location. In this work, a new improved tracking framework is proposed. Different from other algorithms, this framework gives a rule guiding the selection of target training samples. When the target changes its appearance significantly, the system may fail to localize the target because the classifier misclassifies the target image to the background image category. In order to solve this problem, background samples are utilized to predict the location of the target image. Unlike the moving target image, most of the background sample images are stable. As a result, high-accuracy tracking has been established. In addition, regarding the selection of target samples for on-line training of SVM, a new selection rule has been introduced.

As mentioned, the on-line SVM learning requires repeated training and predicting. The predicting process always contains computation of thousands of test samples in conventional algorithms, preventing these algorithms from working in real-time. In this process, not only the SVM, but also the feature extraction of each sample will cost lots of time. Based on a SVM chip developed in [10], the most complex part in this algorithm can be computed efficiently. At the same time, multiple candidate regeneration [8] is employed to reduce the computational cost without sacrificing the tracking accuracy. In addition, the directional-edge-feature vector representation [11], whose VLSI implementation has been proposed in [12], is employed to represent the sample images. By using this hardware-friendly structure, real-time tracking ability can be achieved.

In this paper, a real-time object tracking algorithm employing on-line learning SVM is proposed. Tracking framework with new specific training strategy is designed, while simple hardware implementation is considered as an essential goal. The tracking performance is evaluated by several challenging publicly available video clips, and the core function is verified on hardware to prove its hardware-friendly structure.

2   Object Tracking Algorithm

2.1   On-Line Learning SVM

The basic mechanism of on-line learning SVM is to train the SVM classifier repeatedly with new training samples. How to update the training samples affects the training result greatly. In [5] a training strategy is proposed, in which in each iteration of training the support vector machine is trained by a new data set and the support vectors determined by the previous learning iteration. The reasoning behind this is that the resulting decision function of an SVM depends only on its support vectors so that training an SVM on the support vectors alone results in the same decision function as training on the whole data set. This strategy is suitable to implement on hardware because of its simplicity. The following researches claimed that this strategy only give a proximate learning result [6,7], and proposed accurate approaches dealing with huge amount of data. Although the computational complexity has been decreased in these strategies, massive memory is necessary to store all the data. In this work, we took advantage of the strategy in [5] and designed an on-line learning strategy for object tracking, which is explained in the following section.

2.2   Training Framework

Fig. 1 shows the basic configuration of the on-line learning SVM in tracking algorithms. In this work, sample images are represented by directional feature vector proposed in [11]. At the beginning, the SVM is trained by labeled samples from previous iteration or the initialization stage. Then, in the present image, test samples extracted from a certain region (shown as square in Fig.1(b)) are classified by the trained SVM into two classes: the target and the background. Then a confidence map is generated (shown on the top left corner of the image) using the locations of the test samples and their decision function values. The target location is predicted based on the confidence map. After this step, new samples for training in the next frame are selected and the next iteration starts.

The following parts focus on how to select reliable training samples in each iteration. The training samples which are not support vectors are discarded in the strategy in [5] to remove redundant training samples. In this work, the same rule is applied only to the background training samples. The target training samples are all stored and never discarded, because the target samples are more important than the background samples in the tracking application, and the quantity of the target samples does not explode as the background samples do in complex situations.

Besides the support vectors retained as mentioned above, new training samples from each frame of image are also added to the background training samples. Suppose that the algorithm has finished predicting the target location in the present frame. Then, several image patches around the predicted target location are stored as new background samples, as shown in Fig. 2. This is based on the assumption that in the next frame, the background images at these locations

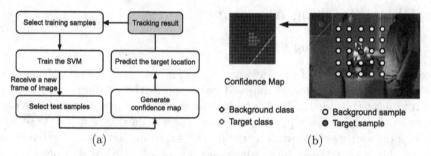

(a)   (b)

Fig. 1. Basic mechanism of the online learning SVM-based tracking algorithm: (a) Training samples and the confidence map and (b) Basic process of the algorithm

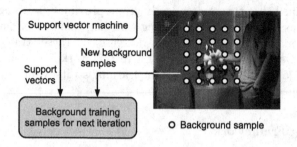

Fig. 2. Selection of the background training samples

tend to be critical distracters. Together with the background support vectors, the newly generated samples are stored as new background training samples for the next frame.

For the target samples, we developed an approach to select reliable new training samples. Different from the conventional algorithms, the image patch at the predicted target location in each frame is not added as new training sample. Since the prediction of the target location always has small location error, adding the image patches brings inaccurate training samples into the SVM. The error may accumulate after a long time of tracking, and cause the tracker drift away from the real target. In this work, whether to add a new target training sample is determined by the decision function values of the test samples, as shown in Fig. 3. If there are candidates with large function values in target class, it indicates the knowledge in the SVM is sufficient at present and no new target sample is added. However, when the target changes its appearance, it may happen that the decision function values of the samples in the target class become very small, or even there is no test samples falling in the target class. In this situation, it is difficult to predict the target location in the present frame, which also means new target sample should be learnt. From the confidence map in Fig. 3, it can be observed that although the target images are not found (no samples are classified into the target class), most of the background images are classified with large confidence values (shown in brighter color). Among the background samples, some samples

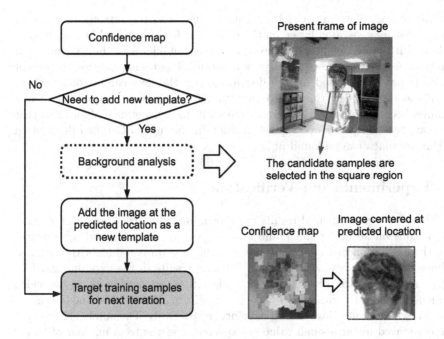

Fig. 3. Selection of the target training samples

own small confidence values (shown in darker color) because a certain region of the background is occluded by the target. Based on this assumption, the center of gravity of the background samples with small confidence values is calculated, and the image at this location is stored as a new target training sample.

In summary, the training samples are composed of the initial target sample, the target samples generated by background analysis, background support vectors and new back ground samples generated in the present frame.

2.3 Multiple Candidate Regeneration

The multiple candidate regeneration (MCR) is first proposed in [8] as a solution of real-time object tracking. It is a statistical approach which is similar with the particle filter, but simplified for hardware implementation. It has shown good performance in solving the object tracking problem. This work employs the MCR to determine the test samples in order to reduce the computational cost in the predicting process.

The candidates in the MCR are used to represent the test samples. The candidates are all distributed around the previous target location. In the present frame of image, feature vectors are generated from the candidate images centered at these candidate locations and sent to SVM as test samples. The function values returned by the SVM are used to calculate weight values for the candidates. The candidate with larger decision function value is assigned a weight with larger absolute value. The positive weight and negative weight stand for the target candidate and the background candidate, respectively. Then, new candidates are generated based on the criteria as follows: in each iteration, candidates with large weight value have more new candidates in their vicinity and the total number of the candidates is constant. The target location in present frame is predicted based on the distribution of the new candidate locations. In this work, by using this approach with 256 candidates the quantity of test samples becomes much smaller compared with the conventional algorithms that generate test sample at every pixel location in the image. Detailed description of this approach can be found in [8].

3   Experiments and Verification

In this section experimental results are shown, including the simulation results, evaluations on accuracy and number of support vectors. The video sequences and the evaluation method are proposed in [9]. The proposed algorithm showed robust tracking ability with accurate tracking results in the experiments. Fig. 4(b) and (f) compare this work with the algorithm proposed in [9] on two video sequences. Under the threshold of 20, this algorithm achieved 0.90 and 0.95 accuracy in Sylvester and David video sequence, respectively. The number of support vectors stayed under a small value as expected, and the total number of target samples is 68 and 82, respectively. Some examples of the target samples are also shown. More experimental results on publicly available videos are shown in Table 1. The algorithm shows a high-accuracy tracking ability in the experiments. Since this algorithm does not include a specific solution to heavy occlusion between objects, it shows less accurate results in the last two face occlusion videos, in which the target (human face) is partially or almost fully occluded by other object.

Table 1. Evaluation of tracking accuracy at a fixed threshold of 20

	Sylvester	David Indoor	Cola Can	Occluded Face	Occluded Face 2
MILTrack [9]	0.90	0.52	0.55	0.43	0.60
This work	0.90	0.95	0.93	0.27	0.44

In order to give a hardware-friendly solution to the object tracking task, we considered the implementation of each part of the algorithm. For the training of SVM, a dedicated VLSI chip proposed in [10] can be employed. It is a fully-parallel self-training SVM system with high training speed. Based on this chip, computational time caused by SVM computation can be decreased dramatically. A functional verification of this algorithm on the chip is shown in Fig. 5. Vectors were extracted from the image in advance and sent to the chip in real-time. After $100ns$ of training process (not shown), the chip received and gave out the

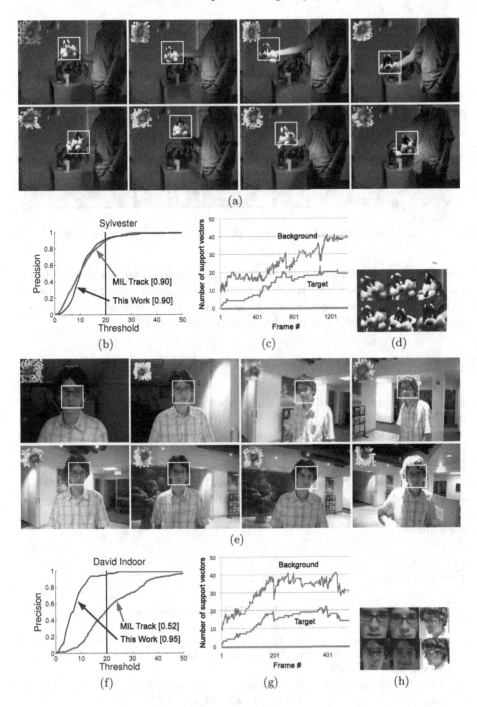

Fig. 4. Evaluation of this algorithm with Sylvester and David video sequences: (a)(e) tracking result; (b)(f) precision evaluation; (c)(g) number of support vectors and (d)(h) examples of target training samples

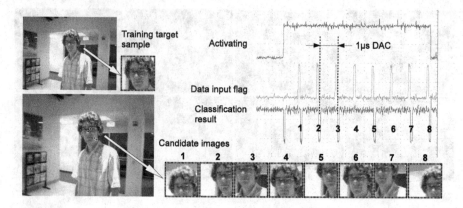

Fig. 5. Verification of the training and predicting process on SVM chip

classification result for each vector every $1\mu s$, in which the 4th and 6th candidate images were classified into the target class. In addition, we also employed a directional-edge-based representation algorithm [11] to represent sample images, for which a dedicated VLSI chip has been proposed in [12].

4   Conclusion

In this work, we proposed a real-time object tracking algorithm based on the on-line learning support vector machine with hardware-friendly structure and a newly proposed training framework. The tracking framework give a solution to the problem of updating reliable training samples in object tracking. The hardware structure employs several real-time algorithms which have been implemented into VLSI chips. Software simulation results were evaluated, which showed robust and accurate tracking ability. Hardware verification was carried out on a VLSI SVM chip, which proved the real-time performance of this algorithm.

References

1. Avidan, S.: Support Vector Tracking. IEEE Transactions on Pattern Analysis and Machine Intelligence 26, 1064–1072 (2004)
2. Tang, F., Brennan, S., Zhao, Q., Tao, H.: Co-Tracking Using Semi-Supervised Support Vector Machines. In: IEEE 11th International Conference on Computer Vision, pp. 1–8 (2007)
3. Tian, M., Zhang, W., Liu, F.: On-Line Ensemble SVM for Robust Object Tracking. In: Yagi, Y., Kang, S., Kweon, I., Zha, H. (eds.) ACCV 2007, Part I. LNCS, vol. 4843, pp. 355–364. Springer, Heidelberg (2007)
4. Matthews, L., Ishikawa, T., Baker, S.: The Template Update Problem. IEEE Transactions on Pattern Analysis and Machine Intelligence 26, 810–815 (2004)

5. Syed, N., Liu, H., Sung, K.: Incremental Learning with Support Vector Machines. In: Proceedings of the Workshop on Support Vector Machines at the International Joint Conference on Articial Intelligence, Stockholm, Sweden (1999)
6. Cauwenberghs, G., Poggio, T.: Incremental and Decremental Support Vector Machine Learning. In: Advances in Neural Information Processing Systems, vol. 13 (2001)
7. Ruping, S.: Incremental Learning with Support Vector Machines. In: Proceedings IEEE International Conference on Data Mining, San Jose, CA, USA, pp. 641–642 (2001)
8. Zhu, H., Zhao, P., Shibata, T.: Directional-edge-based Object Tracking Employing On-line Learning and Regeneration of Multiple Candidate Locations. In: Proceedings of 2010 IEEE International Symposium on Circuits and Systems (ISCAS), pp. 2630–2633 (2010)
9. Babenko, B., Yang, M., Belongie, S.: Robust Object Tracking with Online Multiple Instance Learning. IEEE Transactions on Pattern Analysis and Machine Intelligence 33, 1619–1632 (2011)
10. Zhang, R., Shibata, T.: A Fully-Parallel Self-Learning Analog Support Vector Machine Employing Compact Gaussian-Generation Circuits. In: International Conference on Solid State Devices and Materials (SSDM), Nagoya, pp. 174–175 (2011)
11. Suzuki, Y., Shibata, T.: Multiple-clue Face Detection Algorithm Using Edge-Based Feature Vectors. In: IEEE International Conference on Acoustics, Speech, and Signal Processing, vol. 5, pp. V-737–V-740 (2004)
12. Zhu, H., Shibata, T.: A Real-Time Image Recognition System Using a Global Directional-Edge-Feature Extraction VLSI Processor. In: Proceedings of ESSCIRC, pp. 248–251 (2009)

Part V

The 4th International Workshop on Engineering Knowledge and Semantic Systems

On the Complexity
of Shared Conceptualizations*

Gonzalo A. Aranda-Corral[1], Joaquín Borrego-Díaz[2], and Jesús Giráldez-Cru[3]

[1] Universidad de Huelva, Department of Information Technology,
Crta. Palos de La Frontera s/n, 21819 Palos de La Frontera, Spain
[2] Universidad de Sevilla, Department of Computer Science and Artificial Intelligence,
Avda. Reina Mercedes s/n. 41012 Sevilla, Spain
[3] Artificial Intelligence Research Institute (IIIA-CSIC)
Campus Universidad Autónoma de Barcelona, Barcelona, Spain

Abstract. In the Social Web, folksonomies and other similar knowledge organization techniques may suffer limitations due to both different users' tagging behaviours and semantic heterogeneity. In order to estimate how a social tagging network organizes its resources, focusing on sharing (implicit) conceptual schemes, we apply an agent-based reconciliation knowledge system based on Formal Concept Analysis. This article describes various experiments that focus on conceptual structures of the reconciliation process as applied to Delicious bookmarking service. Results will show the prevalence of sharing tagged resources in order to be used by other users as recommendations.

1 Introduction

The availability of powerful technologies for sharing information among users (social network members) empowers the organization of social resources. Among them, collaborative tagging represents a very useful process for users that aim to add metadata to documents, objects or, even, urls.

As with other social behaviours, tagging shows advantages but also deficiencies, e.g. semantic heterogeneity. Projects like *Faviki* (http://www.faviki.com) or CommonTag (http://commontag.org) attempt to resolve these deficiencies. Within the network, and also based on user preferences, different tagging behaviours exist that actually obstruct automated interoperability. Although solutions exist that assist the user's folksonomy (tag clouds, tools based on related tag ideas, collective intelligence methods, data mining, etc.), personal organization of information leads to implicit logical conditions that often differ from the global interpretation of these conditions. Tagging provides a manner of weak organization for information that, although useful, is mediated by the individual user's behaviour. In order to make the concept of semantic heterogeneity explicit,

---

* Supported by TIN2009-09492 project of Spanish Ministry of Science and Innovation and *Excellence project* TIC-6064 of *Junta de Andalucía* cofinanced with FEDER founds.

L. Rutkowski et al. (Eds.): ICAISC 2012, Part I, LNCS 7267, pp. 629–638, 2012.

we use Formal Concept Analysis (FCA) [5]. FCA is a mathematical theory that, applied to tagging systems, results in explicit sets of concepts that users manage by tagging, thereby organizing information into structured relationships.

As is argued in [6], tagging is essentially about sensemaking, a process where information is categorized, labeled and, most importantly, through which meaning emerges [8]. Even in a personal tagging structure, concept boundaries and categories are vague, so some items can be doubtfully labeled. Finally, users also use tagging task for their own benefit, but nevertheless they contribute usefully to the public good [6]. Therefore, it seems interesting to apply concept mining technologies to facilitate semantic interoperability. Since the users' tagging reflects their own set of concepts about documents, tag-driven navigation among different resources could be insufficient due to semantic heterogeneity. Thus, to ensure an efficient use of another user's tag sets, some thought must be given to tags in order to achieve some consensus (also using FCA based tools), which allows us to navigate between different conceptual structures. In this scenario, it could be very important to attempt to delegate these tasks to intelligent agents. In [2], an agent-based knowledge conciliation method is presented.

The aim of this paper is to show how a Multiagent System (MAS) can be applied to shape the complexity of users' conceptual structures into a social bookmarking service, by comparing the *resource sharing* relationship among users against the *tagging sharing* relationship between users. The first relationship comprises a complex network where semantic similarities could be weak, while one expects that the second allows us some understanding about semantic interoperability based on tags and achieved by conciliation. The paper aims to show the prevalence of semantic similarity (knowledge conciliation) in *tagging sharing* relation.

The following paper is organized as follows. Section 2 is devoted to the introduction of FCA. Section 3 reviews original agent-based reconciliation, which is applied in this paper. Section 4 describes the relational structure of tagging in Delicious. Sect. 5 provides a specific implementation of knowledge reconciliation. Section 6 presents the experiments and some results. Finally, Sect. 7 discusses some conclusions.

2   Formal Concept Analisys

Convergence between Mobile Web 2.0 and Semantic Web will depend on the specific management of ontologies. Ontologies and tags/folksonomies must be reconciled in these kinds of projects. A useful bridge between these two kinds of knowledge representation could be *Formal Concept Analysis* [5]. According to Wille, FCA mathematizes the philosophical understanding of a concept as a unit of thought, composed by the *extent* and the *intent*. The extent covers all objects belonging to the concept, while the intent comprises all of the common attributes valid for all the objects under consideration. FCA also allows us to compute concept hierarchies from data tables.

The process of transforming data into structured information by means of FCA starts from an entity called *Formal Context*. This formal context is a tupla

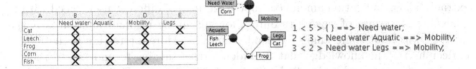

Fig. 1. Formal context and associated concept lattice and Stem Basis

$M = (O, A, I)$ composed of two sets, O (objects) and A (attributes), and a relation $I \subseteq O \times A$. Given $X \subseteq O$ and $Y \subseteq A$, a derivative operator can be defined such as

$$X' := \{a \in A \mid oIa \text{ for all } o \in X\}, \quad Y' := \{o \in O \mid oIa \text{ for all } a \in Y\}$$

From this, a definition of (formal) concept can be obtained as a pair (X, Y) which holds $X' = Y$ and $Y' = X$. If we define the subconcept relation, $C_1 \subseteq C_2$ if $O_1 \subseteq O_2$, a hierarchy among concepts can be obtained and represented as a lattice.

Finally, logical expressions in FCA are *implications between attributes*, a pair of sets of attributes, written as $Y_1 \to Y_2$. This expression holds in M if for all $o \in O$, its derivative set, $\{o\}'$, models $Y_1 \to Y_2$, and it is said that $Y_1 \to Y_2$ is an implication of M. A set $\mathcal{L}$ of implications is a (implication) basis, for M, if $\mathcal{L}$ is complete and non-redundant. Also, FCA defines a method to calculate an implication basis [5], which is called Stem Basis. It is important to note that the Stem Basis is only a particular case of implication basis, any other implication basis could be used as well. SB will be used as set of rules in production systems for reasoning (as in [2]). This rules (implication) support can be defined as the number of objects that contain all attributes Y_1 and hold the implication. Based on this property, a variant of implicational basis is defined, called Stem Kernel basis (SKB), the SB's subset where support of each rule is greater than zero.

To illustrate these three entities -formal context, concept lattice, and Stem Basis- an example based on a living being is depicted in fig. 1, left, center, and right, respectively.

2.1   Tagging, Contexts and Concepts

There are several limitations to collaborative tagging in sites such as Delicious. The first is that a tag can be used to refer to different concepts, i.e. there is a context dependent feature of the tag associated with the user. This dependence -called "Context Dependent Knowledge Heterogeneity" (CDKH)- limits both the effectiveness and adequacy of collaborative tagging. The second is the Classical Ambiguity (CA) of terms, inherited from natural language and/or the consideration of different "basic levels" among users [6]. CA would not be critical when users work with urls (content of url induces, in fact, a disambiguation of terms because of its specific topic). In this case, the contextualization of tags in a graph structure (by means of clustering analysis) distinguishes the different terms associated with the same tag [4]. However, CDKH is associated with concept structures that users do not represent in the system, but that FCA can extract. Thus, navigation among concept structures of different users faced with CDKH. So, the use of tagged resources for automatic recommendation is not advisable without some kind of semantic analysis. More interesting is the idea of deciphering the knowledge that is hidden in user tagging to understand their tagging behaviour and its implied meaning. In sites such as Delicious, CDKH is the main problem, because tags perform several functions as bookmarks [6].

3   Agent-Based Reconciliation

Users's Knowledge Conciliation aims to exploit an important benefit of the Web 2.0, namely information and knowledge sharing. A potential threat is that semantic techniques are adapted to each user. Over time, the user's knowledge can vary a great deal, and this difference could create knowledge incompatibility issues. In order to navigate through the set of tags and documents from different users, SinNet[1] has delegated this process to agents in order to make these different conceptualizations compatible. A agent-based conciliation algorithm was presented in [2]. It is based on the idea that conceptual structure associated with tags gives more information about the user's tagging. The algorithm runs in six steps:

1. Agent Creation: It starts creating two Jade[2] agents, passing through agent names and SinNet data as parameters.

2. Each Agent Then Builds Its Own Formal Contexts and Stem Basis

3. Initializing Dialogue Step: The agent executes tasks related to communications: It sends its own language (attribute set) to the other agent, and also prepares itself to receive the same kind of messages from the other agent.

4. Restrictions of Formal Contexts: After this brief communication, each agent creates a new (reduced) set of common attributes, and with them a new context to which are added all of the objects from the original context, along with the values and attributes of the common language.

5. Extraction of the Production System. (Stem Basis) for the new contexts.

6. Knowledge Negotiation between Agents: Agents establish a conversation based on objects, accepting them (or not) according to their tag set and their own Stem Kernel Basis: if the object matches the rules, it is accepted, if not the production system is applied, considering the object's tags as facts, getting the answer (new facts which should be added in order to be accepted as a valid object) that is added to the object and re-sent to the other agent to be accepted.

---

[1] http://www.semanticville.org/sinnet/
[2] http://jade.tilab.com

Once this process is completed, the agents will achieve a common context. So, they can extract new concepts and suggestions from a common context, and therefore, a shared conceptualization.

4   Delicious Bookmarking Service

We have chosen the bookmarking service Delicious (http://www.delicious.com/) due to its large volume of data. In Delicious, objects are web links (urls), and attributes are tags. Users save their personal web links tagged with their personal tags. But several users may share common objects (with different attributes for each one), or common attributes (tagged in different links). The structure and dynamics of tagging with Delicious have been extensively analyzed [6]. Because of limited computing capacity, certain reduction operations must be performed in order to ensure the normal functioning of the solution presented in this paper. Therefore, a subset of public Delicious data has been extracted, in which all the links are tagged with the tag *haskell*, and saved in a private database (DB) used to drive experiments.

The process of obtaining this data is achieved through a query by tag (*haskell*), and the extraction of the associated results content: link, user, and others tags, which have been saved in the DB. Thereafter, we optimize this data. For example, one of the optimization operations achieved consisted of simplifying equal and equivalent links that have different registers in DB. Our DB is composed of 4259 users, 3028 links, 2427 tags, and 45079 tuples of {user, link, tag}. Data extraction was performed on March 1st, 2011. This data set has a volume large enough to expect significant results. However, this set of data does not encompass all the links related to the *haskell* tag, instead only the first query results.

4.1   The Relational Structure of Tags

In order to estimate the complexity of the relationships among tags of data source, a graph was generated, in which nodes appear as tags, which were interconnected by weighted edges, whose weight represents the amount of links commonly shared according to a Delicious user. To understand the structure of the graph and the number of relevant tags, some simplifications have to be made.

Fig. 2 shows data resulting from *semantic communities* computing (using the method [3]), which is a simplified graph. This graph shows 5 different communities, demonstrating that tags of a same community are very interconnected, unlike tags of different communities, which display little connectivity. In the graph, each node is characterized by its color (determining the community it belongs to), its size (scaled according to its degree), and by the width of its edges (scaled according to the weight of the edge). Finally, only the most relevant nodes (27) and edges (138) are shown - accordingly measured by their importance in terms of degree and weight, respectively.

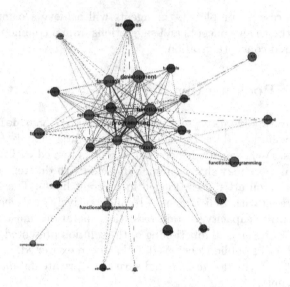

Fig. 2. Analysis of tag communities induced by *haskell* tag in Delicious (simplified)

5   Multiagent System

Our aim is to find a good strategy in order to apply the reconciliation algorithm presented above in Delicious. This algorithm allows us to calculate the reconciled knowledge. However, this algorithm requires high computational resources. Hence, choosing the right pairs of users to execute the algorithm, among the whole community, remains a problematic issue. In order to execute a solution that calculates reconciled knowledge for the whole tagging system, a negotiation based on MAS is proposed, in which agents represent tagging system users. They interact with each other to generate new common knowledge using the above mentioned algorithm. In the following section, the results we obtained are presented for different parameters used in the negotiation process. The MAS has also been implemented in Jade, where the implementation of the previous algorithm can be easily integrated. The execution of MAS can be described as the following steps:

1. Initialization: In this step, as many user agents as needed are created. Only users sharing a minimum number of tags (threshold) participate in the MAS. Execution starts by creating an agent, called *control*, which passes this threshold as a parameter. This agent searches the DB for all pairs of users satisfying the threshold condition, and creates them within the MAS. Therefore, the presented agents in the system are known by the *control* agent. The control agent may be useful to manage the MAS when integrated in more complex systems. Every *User_i* must know its personal information (username, links and tags), and initialize itself by creating its own request queue. This queue contains references of all users having an equal or greater number of common attributes. It is sorted by the common attributes number, in descending order. Additional methods are equally needed to verify that a pair of users is only referenced in one of their request queues. Further experiments use the number of common objects of a pair of users as the threshold in order to compare results from both executions.

2. Negotiation: User agents must execute a dual behaviour in order to perform the negotiation process: sending and receiving requests. This negotiation establishes a very simple method to decide when a pair of users starts the reconciliation process. Each user is only allowed to perform one reconciliation process at a time. Furthermore, received requests have priority over the sent ones. Two possible states for each user are defined: *free*, if it is not performing any reconciliation at the moment, and otherwise, *busy*. As such, only free users may send or receive requests. On one hand, every user sends proposals to the user having the highest priority in its request queue. If it receives a response, the reconciliation process with the addressee starts. Should this not be the case, it reiterates with the user having the next highest priority. On the other hand, every free user accepts any incoming proposals, even if it has already sent another proposal, which will be cancelled by timeout. The following conditions ensure that all of the conciliations will be processed: their number is finite, and there is always free users ready to accept new conciliations, reducing the number of unsolved processes. When starting a reconciliation, user's state switches from free to busy.

3. Reconciliation: The algorithm presented in section 3 is used to calculate the common knowledge between two users. The steps 1 and 2 (user's concept lattice and SB) are executed only once, when the user runs it for the first time. The rest of the steps (3-6), are executed each time the user runs the algorithm. The obtained common knowledge, a formal context with objects and common attributes, is stored in the DB. Both users switch from busy to a free state.

4. Finalization: When a user's request queue becomes empty, its behaviour is limited to receiving incoming proposals. However, if all the users' request queues are empty, no proposal is received by any of them. Therefore, this situation requires that the execution stops. The *control* agent is used to manage it. It is informed by every user when its request queue becomes empty. When all the users have completed this action, the control agent stops the MAS execution.

6   Experiments

Different experiments have been conducted with data described in section 4 using several criteria. The first criterion is setting a threshold of common attributes (tags) between users. The second criterion is setting a different threshold of common objects (urls). In both cases, the threshold is a necessary condition of a minimum number of attributes or objects that two users must have in common in order to execute the reconciliation algorithm. For each executed reconciliation process, a common knowledge is obtained. This knowledge is a formal context where the attributes are common to both users, and objects belong either to one of them, or both. In this way, the global result is a set of reconciled contexts.

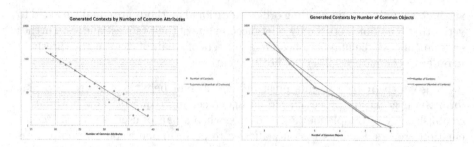

Fig. 3. Contexts generated by number of common attributes or objects

The results obtained for both experiments using numerical and graphic representations are presented bellow. In order to do so, the results have been measured with five parameters for a fixed value of the threshold. They are the number of contexts obtained (there are as many contexts as number of executed reconciliation processes), and the average values of objects, attributes, concepts and implications per context. Finally, both experiments are compared.

Reconciliation from Common Attributes: In this experiment, the threshold value is set to 18. It implicates that two users having a language[3] size greater or equal to 18, reconcile their knowledge. It is assumed that users having a number of common attributes less than 18 do not share a relevant amount of information. In fig. 3 (left), the graphics are plotted in logarithmic scale.

A total of 908 contexts were obtained, with an average value of 44.18 objects, 18 attributes, 6.91 concepts, and 17.20 implications per context. As the threshold value increases, the number of generated contexts decreases exponentially. However, the four average values tend to increase. Although the number of contexts is smaller, they are semantically better, since the two users generating these contexts share more information. In this DB, the maximum number of common attributes is 64. Such a threshold value results in one matching context. It is concluded that one pair of users share a minimum of 64 common attributes. In this context, 138 objects, 38 concepts, and 114 implications are obtained.

Reconciliation from Common Objects: In the second experiment, the threshold value is set to 3. The implication is that two users having a set of common objects with size greater or equal than 3 reconcile their knowledge. As previously mentioned, it is assumed that sharing less than 3 objects is not relevant for the purpose of this study. In fig. 3 (right), the results are represented. This case shows a total of 663 contexts, with an average value of 33.55 objects, 9.41 attributes, 6.09 concepts, and 79.75 implications per context. As the threshold value increases, the number of obtained contexts also decreases, but in this case, more than exponentially. The maximum number of common objects is 11, which is very small: We obtain 98 objects, 37 attributes, 29 concepts, and 56 implications.

---

[3] The language between two users is the set of common tags that both of them use, independent of wether or not these tags have been used in different urls or not.

6.1   Results

The results draw the conclusion that common attributes criterion is better than common objects criterion. On one hand, the decrease in generated contexts is higher when using common objects rather than common attributes. In the first case, this decrease is higher than exponential (more curved than an exponential line). On the contrary, the second case shows a exponential progression. On the other hand, the *semantic* validity of the generated contexts, measured along with their average values, is higher using attributes rather than objects. In the first case, average values increase linearly. It is then thought that the higher number of common attributes, the more reconciled context. Unlike the first case, the second shows a constant function from a certain value of the number of common objects. It seems that the validity of the generated contexts does not depend on the number of common objects.

In conclusion, previous results lead us to think that the common attributes criterion separates more effectively the sample of generated contexts. Indeed, despite the fact that it returns a smaller amount of contexts, increasing the threshold value leads to results *semantically* better. Therefore, it is a good measurement of the semantic similarity of two users.

7   Conclusions and Future Work

The experiments described in this paper show the prevalence of semantic techniques (tags) in resource sharing when users aim to exploit knowledge organization from other users in Delicious as a recommendation source. Although this result seems evident, Web 2.0 shows several examples where url sharing by social networks represent a powerful method for information diffusion (e.g. Twitter).

Therefore, we have empirical evidence that semantic similarity between users is better supported by using the method of reconciling the knowledge among users that have a large set of common attributes, rather than any other method. One of our lines of research is the intensive application of definability methods based on completion [1] in order to enrich the bookmarking system and to facilitate the reconciliation.

References

1. Alonso-Jiménez, J.A., Aranda-Corral, G.A., Borrego-Díaz, J., Fernández-Lebrón, M.M. and Hidalgo-Doblado, M.J. Extending Attribute Exploration by Means of Boolean Derivatives. In: Proc. 6th Int. Conf. on Concept Lattices and Their Applications. CEUR Workshops Proc., vol. 433 (2008)
2. Aranda-Corral, G.A., Borrego-Díaz, J.: Reconciling Knowledge in Social Tagging Web Services. In: Corchado, E., Graña Romay, M., Manhaes Savio, A. (eds.) HAIS 2010. LNCS (LNAI), vol. 6077, pp. 383–390. Springer, Heidelberg (2010)
3. Blondel, V.D., Guillaume, J.L., Lambiotte, R., Lefebvre, E.: Fast unfolding of communities in large networks. Journal of Statistical Mechanics: Theory and Experiment (10) (2008)

4. Au Yeung, C.M., Gibbins, N., Shadbolt, N.: Contextualising Tags in Collaborative Tagging Systems. In: Proceedings of the 20th ACM Conference on Hypertext and Hypermedia (2009)
5. Ganter, B., Wille, R.: Formal Concept Analysis - Mathematical Foundations. Springer, Heidelberg (1999)
6. Golder, S., Huberman, B.A.: The structure of collaborative tagging systems. Journal of Information Science 32(2), 98–208 (2006)
7. Jäschke, R., Hotho, A., Schmitz, C., Ganter, B., Stumme, G.: Discovering shared conceptualizations in folksonomies. Journal of Web Semantics 6(1), 38–53 (2008)
8. Weick, K.E., Sutcliffe, K.M., Obstfeld, D.: Organizing and the Process of Sensemaking. Organization Science 16(4), 409–421 (2005)

Local Controlled Vocabulary
for Modern Web Service Description

Konstanty Haniewicz

Poznan University of Economics, Poland
konstanty.haniewicz@ue.poznan.pl

Abstract. This works contains a proposition for a modern Web service description, where functionality of Web service operations is defined with a set of federated Local Controlled Vocabularies (LCV). The LCVs serve as a referral platform for functionality definition with a phrase schema. This schema allows for describing every Web service operation in terms of main action associated with some object extended with an arbitrary number of supplements and marked with desired non functional properties. The proposed description argues for federated LCV instead of centralised fully fledged ontology based effort due to the cost, scalability and performance issues simultaneously maintaining the high level of expressivity unreachable for standard Information Retrieval systems used in Web service retrieval. This work concludes in presentation of mechanism that allows for query matching on envisioned structure along with experiment results and discussion on possible enhancements.

Keywords: federated local controlled vocabularies, Web service description, functionality description, knowledge engineering, knowledge representation, Information Retrieval.

1 Introduction

The model and mechanism presented here are a result of the ongoing research on a modern functionality description for Web services. It was inspired by close analysis of available solutions that propose a retrieval scenario for Web service repositories. The importance of such repository is enormous especially in case of Service Oriented Architecture ([12]) and electronic markets ([3]) of Web services, as a repository is a key tool to find an entity that satisfies some particular needs.

Available solutions for Web service retrieval range from those using fully fledged ontologies to augmented repositories indexing Web services as regular text documents. A good review of available in [9]. There is trend of preparing a solution that introduces a balance between the two extreme cases by incorporation of various additional features and relaxation of some requirements as in [8], [7] and [5]. This work follows the mentioned trend with additional focus on following aspects of the following qualities:

- effectiveness - ability to supply results meeting requirements, encoded in user queries in time comparable with modern search engines,

L. Rutkowski et al. (Eds.): ICAISC 2012, Part I, LNCS 7267, pp. 639–646, 2012.
© Springer-Verlag Berlin Heidelberg 2012

- cost - an effort that shall be spent for a proper description, time spent on learning necessary description techniques and a prognosis on a timewise performance of analyzed solution,
- scalability - how soon and to what degree a performance shall drop along with an increase in a number of handled Web services,
- scope - any important additions to a baseline of Web service description by WSDL documents in terms of an identification of vital, not previously addressed areas of a importance to user,
- purpose statement - stating the purpose of a Web service along with its operations.

The structure of work is now given. First, a model overview is presented along with discussion on its various aspects available to interested parties. Following that a functional Web service description is introduced with details on its structure and capabilities. The introduced model is further investigated as a base for mechanism of query matching which is detailed in subsequent section with experiment description and discussion on its results. Summary section concludes this work.

2 Model Overview

The most important quality that any model shall take into account is its effectiveness as is perceived by users. This can be summarised as a high precision of results from issued queries.

Semantic languages allow for that, yet they incur a considerable additional cost to achieve this high precision. This cost is a combination of time invested into a training and a description of every Web service. Many a time, this description is yet another addition to already long list of product documentation.

Therefore, one could think of a perfect situation, where Web services expressed as WSDL documents were annotated at the same time they are being documented. What is more, a further optimization shall directly force anyone documenting and annotating WSDL documents include a number of words from a controlled vocabulary. This vocabulary might be either a thesaurus or semantic net. As inferring is out of the scope of this work, both of mentioned structures offer a good combination of efficiency (in terms of speed) and transparency for the end user. Annotation shall be performed so that each atomic element of a Web service must be annotated with words from the Local Controlled Vocabulary. It is important to make an assumption that, an atomic element should be an Web service operation.

It is easy to notice that a sum of all words use to describe each operation of a Web service might not yield a coherent picture of its functionality. Alas, this is a very common situation in Web services gathered from the open Internet.

As organizations might be of an arbitrary size, a one centrally managed vocabulary might be counterproductive due to a number of various obstacles, therefore a federated structure of vocabularies is postulated. This postulate introduces some caveats as there is a risk of repetition of some words. To overcome this problem a well known solution of namespaces is to be used. Every controlled vocabulary must be described in terms of a unit or a group that is responsible for it. While searching for an operation by a set of words, results will be grouped by their namespaces. This is an interesting feature, as after retrieval a user can quickly inspect results and notice whether a hit is stored in a namespace that posses some interest for him. Therefore, from now on one shall refer to Local Controlled Vocabulary.

To increase expressiveness of controlled vocabularies a simple language that allows for writing queries similar to natural language is envisioned. This language emphasizes simplicity and restricts queries to a set of formalized phrases.

The obvious advantages of this scheme over formal descriptions (implemented with one of the semantic description languages) is its straightforwardness for a user. There is no learning curve that descends deeper than absorption of vocabulary that is used on daily basis in user's closest environment. When a user is to break boundaries of his everyday interests he is aided with a list of namespaces mapping other organization units on software artifacts. This is important, as when one is to step beyond known procedures one is more likely to consult search service in order to answer a question of whether similar service exists in a organisation. One may think of this as a utility that helps to avoid suboptimal decisions by providing necessary data.

The cost side of the envisioned solution, at this point, is covered by intra organizational agreement on documenting Web services in a specific manner and honouring organizational policies. More, a controlled vocabulary must be assembled to make it work. Cost of this operation shall be manageable as even when started as an organization-wide effort the actual expenditure is at a unit level. One is to assume that the unit size is limited.

Additional effort shall be recuperated when additional elements of systems are requested and when new team members are taking over maintenance tasks of some specific project. As previously highlighted all investment in extra description shall enable quicker and more confident decisions when a request for new functionality arrives.

Local Controlled Vocabularies shall be most effective if and only if, organization implementing them agrees to give a complete control over an atomic namespace to a single management. Preferably a single person shall wield the control over vocabulary as there is no risk of decision conflicts. The management role is of utmost importance because it has the ability to define the structure of queries and decide what verb noun pairs are acceptable in a given namespace. This allows for further features such as clustering of Web services based on their functionality described with the controlled vocabulary. This resembles semantic networks as structures for representing a language. Instead of describing entities in terms of subtypes and instances, one is interested in relations such as more general, more specific or vogue equivalent.

Additional measure, that shall help user experience is ranking functionality. This ranking functionality centres on a number of requests of given Web service, level of match of users query and number of times when other users chose a Web service in question and user's affiliation in terms of organizational structure. This is another method of simplifying access to potentially valuable data with minimum effort on specifying additional criteria.

Link between the demand stream (projects, organizational units, business goals) and Web services has to be underlined as it must be a first class citizen. Many a time this channel of information is neglected and it should not be. Information on inclusion of specific tools enables a business user to navigate in terms that he understands. This might be viewed as a bridge between technology centric Information Technology personnel and task oriented business users. Traditionally, this resources are people and their skills and necessary additional tangible and intangible assets. This model postulates that a mandatory extension is explicit markup of Web services used for any project. This is a benefit for all parties involved as a business user does not have to identify technical details. He only needs to point which project or projects he is interested in (in terms of similarity or further maintenance) and all involved Web services are presented to development team. This short circuit the overall process of gathering information resources necessary for any given project to launch. An overview is given in figure 1.

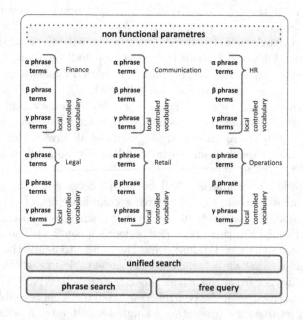

Fig. 1. Local controlled vocabulary for modern Web service description along with the phrase queries described in detail in this work and free queries which were omitted from the discussion

3   Functional Web Service Description

As balance between flexibility and precision is to be achieved, some prerequisites for description must be met. First of all, any operation serves some purpose, thus it is being expressed by a verb term that denotes this action. Later a context for this action is given. By a context, one is to understand a set of targets and additional clarifications. General pattern of description must be based on the form: do something - to what/whom - in what manner. Every Web service operation can be accompanied by a non-empty vector storing the non functional parameters and its values for operation in question.

Web service: $\langle (\alpha, \beta, \gamma), \mathbf{nfp} \rangle$

- α – action
- β – object
- γ – action-object supplement
- $\mathbf{nfp}$ – vector of NFP and its values.

As the first two parts are fairly obvious stating the target and the action, the third clause is the most interesting one as it can vary a lot across different domains. To differentiate the third claus from the first two one is to make an assertion that both action and its target must be single terms. When one is to describe them in compound fashion, this terms must be separated with underscores. On the other hand, third clause can contain a number of terms from the semantic network in given organisation. Each term is automatically branded with information on what project/namespace it originates. For Web services that span across different systems and substructure groups it might contain terms annotated with foreign projects/namespaces.

When one is to examine already existing Web services that are invocable on the open Internet he is quick to observe that the underlying pattern proposed earlier is readily available to some degree. This was an exact source of inspiration, a description method that does not completely break the efforts of earlier efforts but tries to organize them with the criteria that are agreed upon in some organization. Providing a common structure of every description allows for semi-automated relation building between various suborganization units and their namespaces.

When one is dealing with an organisation which software products are designed by software architects one can expect a layered or otherwise structured model that apart from clarity in terms of structure introduces order into naming scheme of the software in question. Such order is a great cornerstone for description. One has to remember that not all functionality is eligible for being made available as Web service operation. The eligibility depends upon the effects of its invocation to its user or system itself. This is to be depicted in a variety of reporting, checking, transforming and combining functionality given by Web services. Lower level functionality is seldom available and by many it can seem that such exposure is simply unnecessary or dangerous from system security point of view.

Thanks to introduction of a structure into a description of Web services, queries on available operations can be performed in a manner allowing for presentation of viable transitions between actions, objects and their complementary phrases.

4 Query Matching

The search for Web service operations is made fast in comparison with fully fledged ontology description thanks to a solution acting as an automaton which allows for rapid narrowing of the set of the feasible Web services. It has 4 ways of narrowing the search space, as there are three key phrases that can be of interest to a user and a forth one which is devoted to non functional parameters.

The simplest manner in which one can narrow the search space is with starting with the non functional parameter vector. The operation of narrowing is just a simple filter on available Web service operations that can be augmented to the search of Web services where every operation has some desired trait and a value of this frame matches the filtering query. This is especially important when a high level overview has to be delivered so that decisions can be made which are in scope of key business objectives - boosting delivery of some type of services, revoking this type of services, changing scope and terms of agreements concerning quality and warranties. To developers this information can be of small importance, yet for the business users and executives this is a real benefit as its direct mapping of business concepts to Web service operations.

Addressing the three key phrases of Web service operation description (α, β and γ) is achieved thanks to inputting one or many possibly desired terms into the automaton. As all the possible terms are handled by the envisioned system for some given namespace, and additional terms from other namespace are also reachable, query operates on the cache in form of hashes that contain terms as keys and Web service operations as values. A situation traditionally viewed as a key collision is perfectly acceptable one, as a list of Web service operations is a valid value and algorithm can continue so that a query yields at some time a possible solution. The results yielded by this stage are to be stored in a data structure with traits of a set. With this assumption, a set arithmetic operations shall lead directly to production of outputs satisfying requirements in a efficient manner.

Stage results are to be combined by an aggregation procedure which reduces outputs from the previously obtained phase in order to single out Web service operations satisfying all of the requirements obtained from the user defined query. If assumption on a set of traits of the outputs holds, this part is satisfied with an operation of a set intersection, therefore efficiently computed even for large data sets (with the same assumptions as presented in [2]).

5 Experiment

Table 1 presents the results of the experiment. The obtained complexity is quadratic due to the fact that Web service descriptions had to be generated

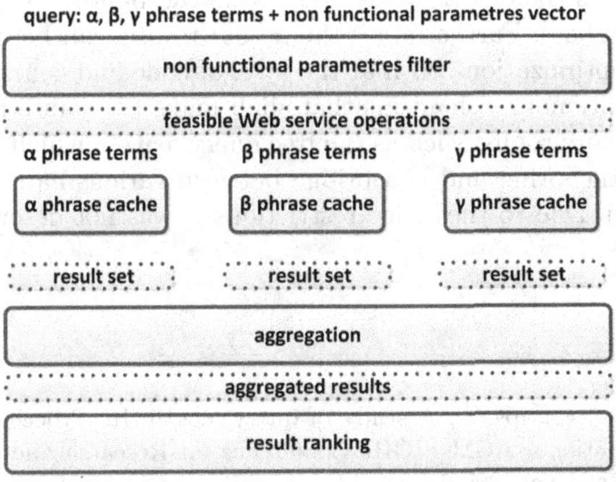

Fig. 2. Query resolution - operation flow is to be viewed from top to bottom

randomly, therefore a distribution of terms varied greatly in comparison to one that is coherent with Zipf's law what was discussed in greater detailed in [2]. The worst case scenario is that the intersection of two sets shall have complexity of $O(n * m)$ and the best case scenario with a specially crafted intersection algorithm can yield complexity of $O(n * logm)$ where m and n are the sizes of sets to be intersected. The experiment was performed on the corpus of randomly generated Web service descriptions. It was repeated ten times and the number of Web service descriptions was changed from 100 to 1000000. Every Web service description was prepared according to previously discussed model. α and β phrases were to contain a single term, γ phase and nfp vector could contain a number of terms from the controlled vocabulary (ranging from 1 to 8). Overall length of the query was modelled to be rather short due to the nature of Web queries (please refer to [4] and [1]).

Table 1. Result of experiment on query matching times with modern Web service description. Time is expressed in seconds.

Number of descriptions:	100	1000	10000	100000	10000000
Best time on 10 runs:	0.0001	0.0006	0.0064	0.0644	1.0950
Worst time on 10 runs:	0.0023	0.0008	0.0068	0.0821	1.3167
Averaged time on 10 runs:	0.0003	0.0007	0.0065	0.0736	1.2000

6   Summary

The model presented here along with query matching mechanism is an example of a solution that breaks with traditional bipolar schema of Web service retrieval. It values greatly a number of aspects often omitted in those solutions.

Presented results demonstrate feasibility of the mechanism implementing functionality in the model. Furthermore, the actual results can be even better due to a number of optimizations both at the level of code and general use strategy.

There are additional mechanisms that shall make the solution implementing the model even more robust such as the free query feature which is supported by Local Context Anchoring and is a bridge between various namespaces existing in a organization. Due to the space restrictions it was not described in greater detail.

References

1. Arampatzis, A., Kamps, J.: A study of query length. In: Proceedings of the 31st Annual International ACM SIGIR Conference on Research and Development in Information Retrieval (2008)
2. Baeza-Yates, R.: A Fast Set Intersection Algorithm for Sorted Sequences. In: Sahinalp, S.C., Muthukrishnan, S.M., Dogrusoz, U. (eds.) CPM 2004. LNCS, vol. 3109, pp. 400–408. Springer, Heidelberg (2004)
3. Bakos, Y.: The Emerging Role of Electronic Marketplaces on the Internet. Communications of the ACM 41(8), 35–42 (2008)
4. Belkin, N.J., Kelly, D., Kim, G., Kim, J.Y., Lee, H.J., Muresan, G., Tang, M.C., Yuan, X.J., Cool, C.: Query length in interactive information retrieval. In: Proceedings of the 26th Annual International ACM SIGIR Conference on Research and Development in Informaion Retrieval (2003)
5. Cardoso, J., Barros, A., May, N., Kylau, U.: Towards a Unified Service Description Language for the Internet of Services: Requirements and First Developments. In: 2010 IEEE International Conference on Services Computing (SCC) (2010)
6. Haniewicz, K.: A Motivation for a Modern Web Service Description. In: ICE-B 2011 - Proceedings of the International Conference on e-Business, Seville, Spain (2011)
7. Hu, L., Ying, S., Zhao, K., Chen, R.: A Semantic Web Service Description Language. In: WASE International Conference on Information Engineering (2009)
8. Kona, S., Bansal, A., Simon, L., Mallya, A., Gupta, G., Hite, T.D.: USDL: A Service-Semantics Description Language for Automatic Service Discovery and Composition. In: E-Commerce Technology and the Eighh IEEE Conference on Enterprise Computing, E-Commerce and E-Services (2006)
9. D'Mello, D.A., Ananthanarayana, V.S.: A Review of Dynamic Web Service Description and Discovery Techniques. In: First International Conference on Integrated Intelligent Computing, pp. 246–251 (2010)
10. Mili, R., Mili, A., Mittermeir R.T.: Storing and Retrieving Software Components. In: A Refinement Based System, pp. 445–460 (1997)
11. Papazoglou, M.P., Traverso, P., Dustdar, S., Leymann, F.: Service-Oriented Computing: State of the Art and Research Challenges. Computer 40(11), 38–45 (2007)
12. Vitvar, T., et al.: Semantically-Enabled Service-Oriented Architecture: Concepts, Technology and Application. Service Oriented Computing and Applications 2(2) (2007)

Semantics and Reasoning
for Control Application Engineering Models

David Hästbacka and Seppo Kuikka

Tampere University of Technology,
Department of Automation Science and Engineering,
P.O. Box 692, FI-33101 Tampere, Finland
{david.hastbacka,seppo.kuikka}@tut.fi
http://www.tut.fi/ase

Abstract. Development of advanced systems requires new methods to improve quality and efficiency of engineering processes, and to assist management of complex models encompassing different engineering disciplines. Methods such as model-driven development and domain-specific modeling facilitate development from this perspective but reduce interoperability and other prospects of rationalizing processes, on the other hand. An approach applying OWL semantics and reasoning to models is presented with examples to support industrial control application engineering. Using the methods, generalized classifications are inferred from instance models and combined with generic engineering knowledge maintained in ontologies. Reasoning allows identifying assemblies and structures outside the scope of traditional modeling to detect flaws and error-prone designs. The results indicate that OWL semantics and reasoning can be used as a supplement furthering typical development practices.

Keywords: control application engineering, software models, semantic web, owl, rules, reasoning.

1 Introduction

Advanced control systems and applications are essential in monitoring and controlling industrial processes and manufacturing operations. The increase in the level of automation and intelligent features as well as the requirements on performance, reliability and safety of these systems has resulted in engineering challenges. There is a demand for new methods to improve development and engineering in order to address these requirements, and also to improve efficiency of engineering processes and reduce the total costs of system development.

In system development, models are used to develop, document and communicate engineering artefacts. For advanced systems the models easily become large including tens of thousands of engineering objects. Especially when people from different engineering disciplines use these models to communicate and collaborate, and as input for automatic imports and transformations there is a risk for error when potential problems and dependencies in models are not detected.

In our previous work, model-driven development (MDD) of industrial process control applications has been studied with emphasis on development processes

L. Rutkowski et al. (Eds.): ICAISC 2012, Part I, LNCS 7267, pp. 647–655, 2012.

and domain-specific modeling constructs [1]. The developed engineering process along with UML Automation Profile (UML AP) concepts enables the designer to focus on significant engineering challenges while much of the work between design phases is automated. Nevertheless, situations can be identified where the development process and the modeling foundation is not sufficient in providing the interoperability and support for further improving the engineering processes.

Interest in ontologies and related formalisms for industrial applications has increased during the last years [2]. The use of Semantic Web technologies can improve software engineering throughout the life-cycle by providing logic-based formalisms and semantics to concepts [3]. Despite many benefits it is problematic to shift to an entirely ontology-based modeling due to the differing nature of the approach. The varying granularity, freedom in expressivity, and the required complexity in modeling detailed semantics are examples of some of the impediments. Semantic Web technologies can regardless of the above mentioned be used as a supplement to MDD practices. For example, to provide added semantics and interoperability during engineering phases to improve understandability, knowledge management and reuse, automatic reasoning and classification, and even assisting in automatic transformations. Semantic descriptions generated from models could also be used for run-time operations [4][5].

From modeling perspective OWL does not allow syntactical enforcement of specific restrictions as opposed to typical modeling languages. However, this point of view can be neglected as the metamodel of the MDD approach typically caters for those aspects. The purpose of using semantic methods is to capture elements and features outside the scope of the metamodel. It is acknowledged that Object Constraint Language (OCL) can be used in many cases for defining constraints and rules to identify structures, related to the metamodel. OCL, however, is restricted to known types of the modeling language making it challenging for maintaining more advanced knowledge of a more generic nature.

This paper presents application of semantics and reasoning on MDD models in engineering of control applications using OWL 2 DL and SWRL. Knowledge management and reuse of engineering information and existing know-how is also discussed. Section 2 presents related work and background. The organization of information in engineering ontologies is presented in section 3 and OWL reasoning challenges for control application models are presented in section 4. The developed prototypes, examples and the results are discussed in section 5. Finally, section 6 contains the discussion and section 7 concludes the paper.

2 Related Work and Background

The complexity of consistency checking of UML class diagrams has been studied by using first-order predicate logic [6]. Description Logics based reasoning has been considered and applied to UML class diagrams to check for inconsistencies and redundancy [7] and the authors opinion is that state-of-the-art DL-based systems are ready to serve as a core reasoning engine in advanced case tools. Also a framework for integrated use of UML class-based models and OWL has been proposed [8]. Semantics in ontologies have been used to enhance modeling capabilities and transformations in MDD of service-based software [9].

The use of ontology-based query retrieval for reusing UML class diagram designs during development has also been studied [10]. The results highlight the importance of the domain ontology and the added semantics the ontologies bring. The adoption of OMG MDA principles to ontology development have been studied by [11] to facilitate transformations between different ontology languages.

Ways to combine ontologies with metamodeling have been studied by [12] and [13]. This paper enhances and deepens the discussion in [13] on the relationship between ontologies and meta-modeling, and the model-driven development paradigm by applying classification and reasoning to models in process control application development to support engineering tasks.

3   Control Application Engineering Knowledge

Knowledge management in engineering of control applications can be organized into three categories; domain knowledge, model instances, and use case specific knowledge, as presented in figure 1. Domain knowledge represents information related to the area of interest, e.g. a specific engineering discipline or a type of systems or devices, and knowledge and practices such as modeling languages and standards. From a modeling perspective a domain ontology (DO) provides the central building blocks and constructs used in the application domain but with additional semantic interoperability. The domain knowledge is of a static nature, i.e. the ontologies do not change very often. This type of information can be generated automatically from existing sources such as metamodels or standards, for instance. Domain knowledge can also be mined and the extraction of domain ontologies from engineering domain handbooks has been proposed [14].

UML AP modeling concepts [1] extend both UML and Systems Modeling Language (SysML), and hence there are three metamodels with corresponding domain ontologies defining the semantics and the relationships. In this case the ontologies are taxonomies that primarily reflect relationships in the sense of classification and generalization of concepts. In OWL a too detailed DO easily causes unwanted inferences if all property domains and ranges are considered.

Model instance knowledge represents models under development or being studied, i.e. model instances serialized as an individual or instance ontology (IO). A plain representation of the individuals that relies on the corresponding DO allows for the transformation between the modeling paradigms to remain sufficiently simple [13]. The IO contains the individual class types, the associated data properties, and structural ownership relations of the source instance model.

Use case specific knowledge refers to knowledge that can be described as information used in analysis and reasoning, e.g. rules on typical design issues and pattern-like structures, company specific conventions, and concerns where special attention is desired. This knowledge is typically of a generic nature and not restricted to a particular modeling or development method. In this sense, also mapping and alignment of different ontologies fall into this category when information from various sources needs to be combined. The ability to combine and reuse existing knowledge in different ontologies is also a justification for using ontologies to support development, e.g. applying generic engineering knowledge to the IO of a UML AP model while performing automatic structural analysis.

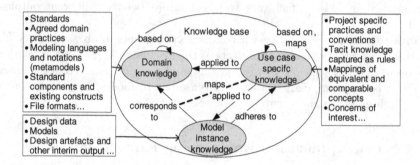

Fig. 1. The knowledge in engineering scenarios can be divided into three main categories: domain knowledge, model instance knowledge, and use case specific knowledge

4   Reasoning with OWL

OWL and SWRL are based on an open world assumption (OWA) meaning that anything that is not stated is unknown and cannot be used to deduce negation as a failure, for instance. As OWL DL (and SWRL) is based on description logics it supports only monotonic inference. Altering a fact based on some condition is not possible and requires an additional layer, e.g. program code, to be implemented. Also domain and range conditions are not constraints in the sense that they are checked for consistency. In reasoning they are used as axioms to infer further knowledge which can easily lead to unexpected effects e.g. in classification.

The impacts of open world semantics can be limited with techniques to close the world or restrict different possibilities. Traditional programming languages have often been used in combination with OWL to overcome these restrictions. Recently there has also been a RDF/SPARQL based proposal [15] for circumventing some of the limitations that is also applicable to OWL.

The management of truth in the knowledge base is of importance in scenarios where the knowledge is frequently updated, such as engineering environments. The challenge in forward chaining is that facts can be both explicit and implicit, and the same fact entailment can be based on a number of facts making the management difficult. On the other hand, inferring all the entailments each time can be too intensive from a performance point of view. This is worth noting as OWL DL, for instance, is computationally hard and in the NExpTime complexity class. Backward chaining is more attractive in the case of rapidly changing knowledge bases where inference is conducted only when needed and the additional entailments do not have to be stored and maintained.

Typically a lot of work is required backtracking different possibilities and reasoning is non-deterministic. Considering this, it can be argued that reasoning easily becomes computationally challenging even for simple-appearing problems. Although information can be stated more explicitly requiring less reasoning it is an important issue especially when integrating other information sources.

5 Applications in Control Application Engineering

The prototypes developed implement the concepts of knowledge management presented in section 3 with information distributed in separate OWL DL ontologies. The reasoning examples are performed mainly in Protege 4 but implementation as a Web Service in Java using OWLAPI has also been evaluated and proved working as well. The Pellet reasoner has been used in all of the examples both in Protege and the Java based OWLAPI implementation.

The SWRL based inferences are implemented DL Safe to retain decidability and are embedded in the engineering knowledge ontology (EKO) and the Mapping ontology (MO). UML AP model transformations to instance ontologies are performed using a refined version of the XSLT developed in [13]. Present are also the domain ontologies for UML AP, UML, and SysML metamodels.

5.1 Examples

Figure 2 illustrates some of the inferences using the developed ontologies for a subset of a control application model. UML AP model elements are connected with nested AutomationFunctionPort and InterlockPort elements that are linked using a UML Connector with ConnectorEnd sub elements identifying the Port elements. The structure is complicated and rules can be used to infer direct connections between model elements instead. The following MO rule considers UML AP elements (DO concepts and IO individuals) in the antecedent part and makes an inference of a simplified connection (EKO concepts) in the consequent.

```
AutomationFunctionPort(?prtA), AutomationFunctionPort(?prtB),
Connector(?cnn), ConnectorEnd(?cnnendA), ConnectorEnd(?cnnendB),
hasPart(?cnn, ?cnnendA), hasPart(?cnn, ?cnnendB),
hasLinkId(?cnnendA, ?idA), hasLinkId(?cnnendB, ?idB),
direction(?prtA, "out"^^string), id(?prtA, ?idA), id(?prtB, ?idB),
DifferentFrom (?prtA, ?prtB) -> hasPortConnectionOut(?prtA, ?prtB)
```

OWL allows declaring conditions for which new inferences can be made but the use of rules allows more powerful expressing of deductive reasoning than OWL alone. A similar example infers a tracedBy relation between Requirements and AutomationFunctions from a TraceRelation contained in the Requirement.

```
AutomationFunction(?af), Requirement(?r), TraceRelation(?tr),
hasPart(?r, ?tr), modelId(?tr, ?id), sourceDomainId(?af, ?id)
-> tracedBy(?af, ?r)
```

In addition to the inferred connections presented, also specific interlock connections are identified as well as relations between measurements that via a controller are connected to an actuator. For example the Primary and Secondary Controller inferences are reasoned based on an OWL class expression identifying a set point coming from another controller. The existence of cascade controllers in the organizing control loop also classifies it as a Cascade ControlLoop. In addition there is a Complete Connected ControlLoop inference that has identified all parts of the control loop to have the minimum amount of required connections.

If developing systems with safety requirements it could be required that all interlocks implemented must have a separate measurement for the interlock that is not used in the normal regulatory control of the actuator, for example. For this an inference can be made that identifies those actuators that have an interlock based on the same measurement that also the controller is utilizing.

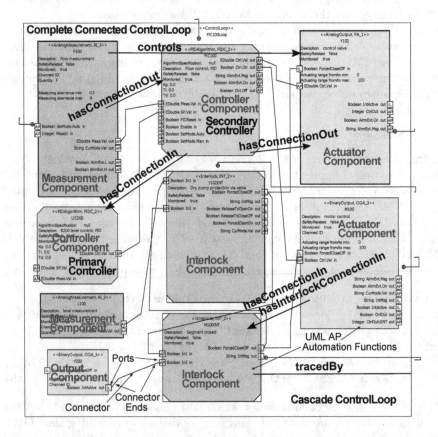

Fig. 2. Example of some of the generalized classifications and inferred connections for elements in a subset of a control application model. The red markings (lighter shade) represent the result of mapping assertions from UML AP ontology concepts to generic engineering concepts and the black markings further inferred facts about the model.

5.2   Results and Experiences

Classifications and inferences enable many use cases for the method to support engineering tasks and assist the developer by highlighting potential error-prone designs and structures, for example. It also enables the use of automatic checking of consistency and structures that the metamodel might not address.

Trace relations, for example, are used to relate requirements to functions in the model as a means to improve quality. Inferring the trace is of little use if broken or missing traces cannot be identified. Inferring this, the different interlock measurement or incompletely connected control loops, for example, is impossible using OWL mechanisms due to the OWA. In practice one can get around this if not developing applications that rely only on OWL. As the interesting concepts or structures could be defined as complements of those identifiable with OWL it was straightforward to make a complement using programming language constructs as a middle layer in the Java based prototype.

Rules were used to infer direct relationships between elements to simplify connections to the engineering knowledge. Rules were chosen because OWL does not allow mixing of object and data properties in chains. The rule based approach inferring simplified relationships based on linking sub elements proved to be challenging for models containing hundreds of Ports. In comparison, deducing the same connection assertions in the instance transformation phase, using XPath and XSLT, the typical ontology classification time was reduced to a tenth of the time required when the connection and interlock connection rules were included.

Using the reasoner also for the different individuals declaration of OWL was found decreasing performance significantly with more than one thousand individuals. An alternative approach using a functional data property to differentiate the individuals proved out more efficient.

A generic way to tackle large numbers of individuals is to perform reasoning only on a subset of the model and iterate the complete model one package at a time, for example. The feasibility of this, in general, depends on the source domain model structure of how sub models are connected. For rules performance a division of the reasoning tasks can be implemented by grouping rules to be executed according to the needs of each task. When there are a lot of rules involved it is, according to our experiences, usually quicker to run several smaller and even partially redundant reasoning tasks than a large one including all of the axioms.

Because UML AP is based on UML and SysML, and via its implementation on the Eclipse platform also on the Ecore metamodel, it is worth considering which of those equivalent ontologies are needed in reasoning. Unless utilization of knowledge in UML or SysML is not required in inferences, the DOs may be omitted from reasoning. For many purposes it is a feasible solution for UML AP because the model semantics are present in UML AP with its own class hierarchies, and the structures and semantics of UML and SysML are mainly utilized for the modeling tool support. Nevertheless, classification and operating with UML and SysML concepts is also possible for UML AP models if desired.

5.3   Additional Requirements for Design-Time Reasoning

Off-line analysis of models, e.g. in project repositories, can be implemented with less consideration on space and time complexity as it can be performed separately from design. In order to implement on-line reasoning properly, e.g. for integrated development environments (IDE), some additional issues have to be considered.

Reasoning performance is an important concern for support to be useful and assisting in development tasks. Therefore it is not practical to do all reasoning tasks as on-line background processing. A plausible approach could be to limit on-line reasoning only to a subset of selected objects and performing more extensive analysis less frequently, e.g. when saving or changing views.

Another issue to consider is the way the model instances in the IDE are transformed to the knowledge base. A practical transformation approach instead of the XSLT could be to use an incremental transformation that simultaneously maintains a semantic knowledge base of the model being developed.

6   Discussion

Interpreting models as ontologies enables various classifications and inferences to be performed. When knowledge about instances is combined with other information new inferences can be made to support development and give an indication about structures that designers should pay attention to, for example.

OWL provides capabilities for describing concepts beyond typical modeling languages. Additionally, OWL provides semantic interoperability which is an increasingly important feature both for networked engineering environments and the systems being designed. Using OWL, pattern-like structures can be identified and generic platform agnostic engineering knowledge can be applied and reused to classification and analysis of model instances.

In addition to practical issues which currently prevent adoption of pure OWL based engineering, it is also limited by some of its inherent design patterns originating from Description Logics. The OWA is a considerable restriction when reasoning on application models that reflect more a closed space. To close the assertional box an additional layer of program code or other techniques are required that e.g. operate on the less restricted OWL FULL or RDF level.

7   Conclusion

Development of advanced systems, such as industrial control applications, requires new methods to improve quality and efficiency of engineering, and to assist in handling of complex design models. Typical modeling methods, however, often fall short in interoperability, expressing additional knowledge, and reasoning on structures and features beyond single elements.

This paper presented application of OWL semantics and reasoning to models when developing control applications. Using the developed method, elements in models can be classified and generic engineering knowledge can be applied to detect inconsistencies and anomalies in model instances. According to our experiences OWL can be used as a supplement to MDD to provide interoperability and support in various engineering operations developing complex systems. The presented implementation and experiments are of an off-line nature but the general approach and some of the implementations, i.e. classifying a subset of a model, can also be adapted to on-line reasoning in an IDE as well.

References

1. Hästbacka, D., Vepsäläinen, T., Kuikka, S.: Model-driven development of industrial process control applications. Journal of Systems and Software 84(7), 1100–1113 (2011)
2. Breslin, J.G., O'Sullivan, D., Passant, A., Vasiliu, L.: Semantic web computing in industry. Computers in Industry 61(8), 729–741 (2010)
3. Happel, H.J., Seedorf, S.: Applications of ontologies in software engineering. In: International Workshop on Semantic Web Enabled Software Engineering (SWESE 2006), Athens, USA (November 2006)
4. Albert, M., Cabot, J., Gómez, C., Pelechano, V.: Generating operation specifications from uml class diagrams: A model transformation approach. Data & Knowledge Engineering 70(4), 365–389 (2011)
5. Serral, E., Valderas, P., Pelechano, V.: Towards the model driven development of context-aware pervasive systems. Pervasive and Mobile Computing 6(2), 254–280 (2010)
6. Kaneiwa, K., Satoh, K.: On the complexities of consistency checking for restricted uml class diagrams. Theoretical Computer Science 411(2), 301–323 (2010)
7. Berardi, D., Calvanese, D., Giacomo, G.D.: Reasoning on uml class diagrams. Artificial Intelligence 168(1-2), 70–118 (2005)
8. Parreiras, F.S., Staab, S.: Using ontologies with uml class-based modeling: The twouse approach. Data & Knowledge Engineering 69(11), 1194 –1207 (2010), special issue on contribution of ontologies in designing advanced information systems
9. Claus, P.: Semantic model-driven architecting of service-based software systems. Information and Software Technology 49(8), 838–850 (2007)
10. Robles, K., Fraga, A., Morato, J., Llorens, J.: Towards an ontology-based retrieval of uml class diagrams. Information and Software Technology 54(1), 72–86 (2012)
11. Cranefield, S., Pan, J.: Bridging the gap between the model-driven architecture and ontology engineering. International Journal of Human-Computer Studies 65(7), 595–609 (2007)
12. Henderson-Sellers, B.: Bridging metamodels and ontologies in software engineering. Journal of Systems and Software 84(2), 301–313 (2011)
13. Hästbacka, D., Kuikka, S.: Bridging uml profile based models and owl ontologies in model-driven development — industrial control application. In: International Joint Workshop on Information Value Management, Future Trends of Model-Driven Development, Recent Trends in SOA Based Information Systems and Modelling and Simulation, Verification and Validation, pp. 13–23
14. Hsieh, S.H., Lin, H.T., Chi, N.W., Chou, K.W., Lin, K.Y.: Enabling the development of base domain ontology through extraction of knowledge from engineering domain handbooks. Advanced Engineering Informatics 25(2), 288–296 (2011)
15. Knublauch, H., Hendler, J.A., Idehen, K.: Spin - overview and motivation. Technical report (2011)

MapReduce Approach to Collective Classification for Networks

Wojciech Indyk, Tomasz Kajdanowicz,
Przemysław Kazienko, and Sławomir Plamowski

Wroclaw University of Technology, Wroclaw, Poland
Faculty of Computer Science and Management
{wojciech.indyk,tomasz.kajdanowicz,kazienko,
slawomir.plamowski}@pwr.wroc.pl

Abstract. The collective classification problem for big data sets using MapReduce programming model was considered in the paper. We introduced a proposal for implementation of label propagation algorithm in the network. The method was examined on real dataset in telecommunication domain. The results indicated that it can be used to classify nodes in order to propose new offerings or tariffs to customers.

Keywords: MapReduce, collective classification, classification in networks, label propagation.

1 Introduction

Relations between objects in many various systems are commonly modelled by networks. For instance, those are hyperlinks connecting web pages, papers citations, conversations via email or social interaction in social portals. Network models are further a base for different types of processing and analyses. One of them is node classification (labelling of the nodes in the network). Node classification has a deep theoretical background, however, due to new phenomenon appearing in artificial environments like social networks on the Internet, the problem of node classification is being recently re-invented and re-implemented.

Nodes may be classified in networks either by inference based on known profiles of these nodes (regular concept of classification) or based on relational information derived from the network. This second approach utilizes information about connections between nodes (structure of the network) and can be very useful in assigning labels to the nodes being classified. For example, it is very likely that a given web page x is related to sport (label *sport*), if x is linked by many other web pages about sport.

Hence, a form of collective classification should be provided, with simultaneous decision making on every node's label rather than classifying each node separately. Such approach allows taking into account correlations between connected nodes, which deliver usually undervalued knowledge.

Moreover, arising trend of data explosion in transactional systems requires more sophisticated methods in order to analyse enormous amount of data. There

L. Rutkowski et al. (Eds.): ICAISC 2012, Part I, LNCS 7267, pp. 656–663, 2012.

is a huge need to process big data in parallel, especially in complex analysis like collective classification.

MapReduce approach to collective classification which is able to perform processing on huge data is proposed and examined in the paper. Section 2 covers related work while in Section 3 appears a proposal of MapReduce approach to label propagation in the network. Section 4, contain description of the experimental setup and obtained results. The paper is concluded in Section 5.

2 Related Work

2.1 Collective Classification

Collective classification problems, may be solved using two main approaches: within-network and across-network inference. Within-network classification, for which training entities are connected directly to entities, whose labels are to be classified, stays in contrast to across-network classification, where models learnt from one network are applied to another similar network [8]. Overall, the networked data have several unique characteristics that simultaneously complicate and provide leverage to learning and classification.

Among others, statistical relational learning (SRL) techniques were introduced, including probabilistic relational models, relational Markov networks, and probabilistic entity-relationship models [9,10]. Two distinct types of classification in networks may be distinguished: based on collection of local conditional classifiers and based on the classification stated as one global objective function. The most known implementations of the first approach are iterative classification (ICA) and Gibbs sampling algorithm (GS), whereas example of the latter are loopy belief propagation (LBP) and mean-field relaxation labeling (MF) [11].

2.2 MapReduce Programming Model

MapReduce is a programming model for data processing derived from functional language[3]. MapReduce breaks the processing into two consecutive phases: the map and the reduce phase. Usually, big data processing requires parallel execution and MapReduce provides and manages such functions. It starts with data splitting into separate chunks. Each data chunk must meet the requirement of $< key, value >$ format, according to input file configuration. Then each data chunk is processed by a Map function. Map, takes an input pair and results with a set of $< key, value >$ pairs. All values associated with the same key are grouped together and propagated to Reduce phase. The Reduce function, accepts a key and a set of values for that key. The function performs some processing of entered values and returns a new pair $< key, value >$ to be saved as an output of processing. Usually reducers results in one $< key, value >$ pair. Both, Map and Reduce phases need to be specified and implemented by user[1,2]. The aforementioned process is presented in figure 2.2.

The MapReduce is able to process very large datasets thanks to initial split of data into small chunks. The most common open-source implementation of

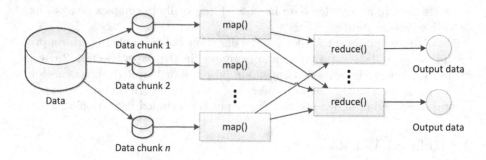

Fig. 1. The MapReduce programming model

MapReduce model is Apache Hadoop library[4]. Apache Hadoop is a framework that allows distributed processing of large data sets. It can be done across clusters of computers and offers local computation and storage. The architectural properties of Hadoop deliver high-availability not due to hardware but application layer failures handling. The single MapReduce phase in Hadoop is named *Job*. The Job consist of map method, reduce method, data inputFiles and configuration.

3   Collective Classification by Means of Label Propagation Using MapReduce

The most common way to utilize the information of labelled and unlabelled data is to construct a graph from data and perform a Markov random walk on it. The idea of Markov random walk has been used multiple times [5,6,7] and involves defining a probability distribution over the labels for each node in the graph. In case of labelled nodes the distribution reflects the true labels. The aim then is to recover this distribution for the unlabelled nodes. Using such a Label Propagation approach allows performing classification based on relational data.

Let $G(V, E, W)$ denote a graph with vertices V, edges E and an $n \times n$ edge weight matrix W. According to [6] in a weighted graph G(V,E,W) with $n = |V|$ vertices, label propagation may be solved by linear equations 1 and 2.

$$\forall i, j \in V \sum_{(i,j) \in E} w_{ij} F_i = \sum_{(i,j) \in E} w_{ij} F_j \tag{1}$$

$$\forall i \in V \sum_{c \in classes(i)} F_i = 1 \tag{2}$$

where F_i denotes the probability density of classes for node i. Let assume the set of nodes V is partitioned into labelled V_L and unlabelled V_U vertices, $V = V_L \cup V_U$. Let F_u denote the probability distribution over the labels associated with vertex $u \in V$. For each node $v \in V_L$, for which F_v is known, a dummy node v' is inserted such that $w_{vv'} = 1$ and $F_{v'} = F_v$. This operation is equivalent to 'clamping' discussed in [6]. Let V_D be the set of dummy nodes. Then solution of equations 1 and 2 can be performed according to Iterative Label Propagation algorithm 3.

Algorithm 1. The pseudo code of Iterative Label Propagation algorithm

1: **repeat**
2:     **for all** $v \in (V \cup V_D)$ **do**
3:         $F_v = \frac{\sum_{(u,v) \in E} w_{uv} F_u}{\sum_{(u,v)} w_{uv}}$
4:     **end for**
5: **until** convergence

As it can be observed, at each iteration of Iterative Label Propagation certain operations on each of nodes are performed. These operations are calculated basing on local information only, namely node's neighbourhoods. This fact can be utilized in parallel version of algorithm, see algorithm 2.

Algorithm 2. The pseudo code of MapReduce approach to Iterative Label Propagation algorithm

1: $map < node; adjacencyList >$
2: **for all** $n \in adjacencyList$ **do**
3:     $propagate< n; node.label, n.weight >$
4: **end for**
1: $reduce < n, list(node.label, weight) >$
2: $propagate< n, \frac{\sum node.label \cdot weigth}{\sum weight} >$

MapReduce version of Iterative Label Propagation algorithm consist of two phase. The Map phase gets all labelled and dummy nodes and propagate their labels to all nodes in adjacency list taking into account edge weights between nodes. The Reduce phase calculates new label for each node with at least one labelled neighbour. Reducers calculates new label for nodes based on a list of labelled neighbours and relation strength between nodes (weight). The final result, namely – a new label for a particular node, is computed as weighted sum of labels' probabilities from neighbourhood.

4   Experiments and Results

For the purpose of experimental setup the telecommunication network was built over 3 months history of phone calls from leading European telecommunication company. The original dataset consisted of about 500 000 000 phone calls and more than 16 million unique users.

All communication facts (phone calls) were performed using one of 38 tariffs, of 4 types each. In order to limit the amount of data and simplify the task to meet hardware environment limitations only two types of phone calls were extracted and utilized in experiments.

Users were labelled with class conditional probability of tariffs, namely sum of outcoming phone calls durations in particular tariff was divided by summarized duration of all outcoming calls. Eventually, final dataset consisted of 38585 users.

Afterwards, the users' network was calculated, where connection strength between particular users was calculated according to equation 3.

$$e_{ij} = \frac{2 \cdot d_{ij}}{d_i + d_j} \tag{3}$$

where d_{ij} denotes summarized duration of calls between user i and j, d_i - summarized duration of ith outcoming calls and d_j - summarized duration of jth incoming calls. Obtained network was composed of 55297 weighted edges between aforementioned users.

The goal of the experiment was to predict class conditional probability of tariff for unlabelled users.

Initial amount of labelled nodes (training set) for collective prediction was established to 37% randomly chosen users, according to uniform distribution. The rest of nodes should potentially belong to test set, however due to the property of examined algorithm some of nodes were unable to be reached and this same to have a label assigned. This mean that some of nodes did not posses incoming edges and the algorithm was not able to propagate the probability of labels to them. Eventually, the final test set was composed of only 2% of users distributed over the whole network. Nevertheless, the rest of nodes were utilized to keep the structure of network and propagation of labels, please see figure 4.

The collective classification algorithm was implemented in MapReduce programming model. It consists of six Jobs, each accomplishing map-reduce phases. Detailed description of Jobs is presented in table 1. The convergence criterion in the algorithm has been controlled by ϵ change of conditional probability for each node. The algorithm was iterating until the this change was greater than ϵ. The experiment was organised in order to examine the computational time devoted for each of map-reduce steps as well as the number of iterations of the algorithm. The time was measured for three distinct values of $\epsilon = \{0.01, 0.001, 0.0001\}$.

The final assessment of implemented algorithm was measured using mean square error between predicted label probability and known (true) label probability. The Mean Square Error (MSE) equals 0.1522 for all three ϵ values. Therefore we did not observe significant changes in the performance of algorithm while examining different values of convergence criterion ϵ.

However, as presented in table 2 and figure 3 the value of convergence criterion ϵ has an impact on number of executions of implemented jobs. The less restrictive it is, the less executions of jobs to be performed.

The results obtained during experiments (MSE, execution time) indicate that proposed MapReduce approach for implementation of Iterative Label

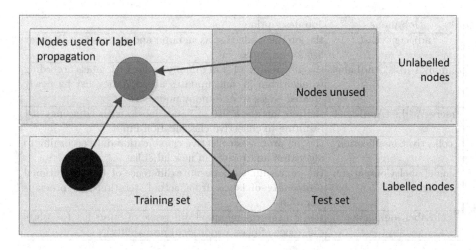

Fig. 2. Types of nodes that have been utilized in the experiments: labelled and unlabelled, training and testing ones, used only for label propagation and omitted

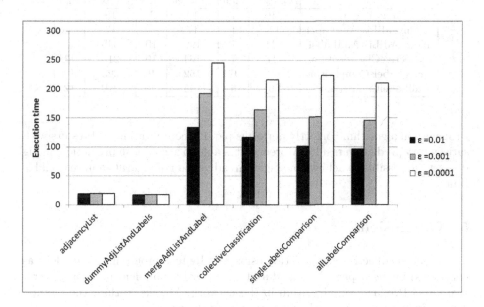

Fig. 3. Execution time in [s] of map-reduce jobs for distinct convergence criterion ϵ

Table 1. MapReduce jobs implemented in the algorithm

Job name	Job description
adjacencyList	the job takes edge list as an input and returns an adjacency list for all nodes
dummyAdjListAndLabels	the job creates a list of dummy nodes with labels according to algorithm [9] and updates an adjacency list by newly created edges from dummy nodes
mergeAdjListAndLabel	the job merges a list of nodes labels with adjacency list resulting in collective classification input
collectiveClassification	the job processes collective classification data according to algorithm and results in new label list
singleLabelsComparison	the job results with absolute difference of class conditional probability of labels from actual iteration and previous iteration
allLabelComparison	the job returns maximal difference of input list (absolute difference of class conditional probability)

Table 2. Execution time in [s] and number of executions of map-reduce jobs for distinct convergence criterion ϵ

Job name	$\epsilon = 0.01$		$\epsilon = 0.001$		$\epsilon = 0.0001$	
	No. exec.	Time	No. exec.	Time	No. exec.	Time
adjacencyList	19	1	19	1	19	1
dummyAdjListAndLabels	17	1	17	1	17	1
mergeAdjListAndLabel	134	7	192	10	245	13
collectiveClassification	117	7	164	10	216	13
singleLabelsComparison	101	6	152	9	223	12
allLabelComparison	96	6	145	9	210	12

Propagation algorithm correctly performs parallel computation and results with satisfactory prediction results. Moreover it is able to accomplish prediction on big dataset, impossible to achieve in single thread version of algorithm in reasonable time.

5 Conclusions

The problem collective classification using MapReduce programming model was considered in the paper. We introduced a proposal for implementation of Iterative Label Propagation algorithm in the network. Thanks to that, the method can perform complicated calculation using big data sets.

The proposed method was examined on real dataset in telecommunication domain. The results indicated that it can be used to classify nodes in order to propose new offerings or tariffs to customers.

Further experimentation will consider a comparison of the presented method with other approaches. Moreover, further studies with much bigger data will be conducted.

Acknowledgement. This work was supported by The Polish National Center of Science the research project 2011-2012, 2011-2014 and Fellowship co-financed by The European Union within The European Social Fund.

References

1. Ekanayake, J., Pallickara, S., Fox, G.: MapReduce for Data Intensive Scientific Analyses. In: Proceedings of the 2008 Fourth IEEE International Conference on eScience (2008)
2. Dean, J., Ghemawat, S.: Mapreduce: simplified data processing on large clusters. In: Proceedings of the 6th Conference on Symposium on Opearting Systems Design & Implementation, pp. 10–24. USENIX Association, Berkeley (2004)
3. White, T.: Hadoop: The Definitive Guide. O'Reilly (2009)
4. Hadoop official web site (November 05, 2011), `hadoop.apache.org`
5. Szummer, M., Jaakkola, T.: Clustering and efficient use of unlabeled examples. In: Proceedings of Neural Information Processing Systems, NIPS (2001)
6. Zhu, X., Ghahramani, Z., Lafferty, J.: Semi-supervised learning using Gaussian fields and harmonic functions. In: Proceedings of the International Conference on Machine Learning, ICML (2003)
7. Azran, A.: The rendezvous algorithm: Multiclass semi-supervised learning with markov random walks. In: Proceedings of the International Conference on Machine Learning, ICML (2007)
8. Jensen, D., Neville, J., Gallagher, B.: Why collective inference improves relational classification. In: The Proceedings of the 10th ACM SIGKDD International Conference on Knowledge Discovery and Data Mining, pp. 593–598 (2004)
9. Desrosiers, C., Karypis, G.: Within-Network Classification Using Local Structure Similarity. In: Buntine, W., Grobelnik, M., Mladenić, D., Shawe-Taylor, J. (eds.) ECML PKDD 2009. LNCS, vol. 5781, pp. 260–275. Springer, Heidelberg (2009)
10. Knobbe, A., de Haas, M., Siebes, A.: Propositionalisation and Aggregates. In: Siebes, A., De Raedt, L. (eds.) PKDD 2001. LNCS (LNAI), vol. 2168, pp. 277–288. Springer, Heidelberg (2001)
11. Kramer, S., Lavrac, N., Flach, P.: Propositionalization approaches to relational data mining. In: Dezeroski, S. (ed.) Relational Data Mining, pp. 262–286. Springer (2001)

Semantic Wiki-Based Knowledge Management System by Interleaving Ontology Mapping Tool

Jason J. Jung and Dariusz Król

[1] Department of Computer Engineering
Yeungnam University
Dae-Dong, Gyeongsan, Korea 712-749
j2jung@gmail.com
[2] Wroclaw University of Technology
Wroclaw, Poland
dariusz.krol@pwr.wroc.pl

Abstract. In this paper, we propose a novel KMS by using semantic wiki framework based on a centralized Global Wiki Ontology (GWO). The main aim of this system is i) to collect as many organizational resources as possible, and ii) to maintain semantic consistency of the system. During enriching the KMS in a particular domain, not only linguistic resources but also conceptual structures can be efficiently captured from multiple users, and more importantly, the resources can be automatically integrated with the GWO of the KMS in the real time. Once users add new organization resources, the proposed KMS can formalize and contextualize them into a set of triplets by referring to a predefined pattern-triplet mapping table and the GWO. Especially, since the ontology matcher is interleaved, the KMS can determine whether the new resources are semantically conflicted with the GWO.

Keywords: Knowledge management system, Semantic wiki, Ontology matching, Semantic annotation, Collaborative editing, Semantic consistency.

1 Introduction

Wiki systems have been regarded as the most successful application for realizing collective intelligence. Users in these wiki systems are able to collaboratively publish resources (e.g., information and knowledge) through web pages as well as to take various activities (e.g., discussion and correction) [1,2]. However, since the amount of resources in the wiki has been extremely increasing, it is difficult to support efficient collaborations among the wiki users. The wiki users can not recognize the whole structure inside the wiki, as well as the latest information published by the other users. It means that the information published by different users tends to be inconsistent and semantically heterogeneous. Even though consensus (e.g., reconciliation) among wiki users may deal with such inconsistencies, it takes a long time to foster a number of interactions among the wiki users for building the consensus.

To solve the problem more efficiently, many *semantic* wiki platforms have been proposed as an extension of general wiki systems by using semantic technologies [3]. The

L. Rutkowski et al. (Eds.): ICAISC 2012, Part I, LNCS 7267, pp. 664–672, 2012.

main feature of the semantic wiki systems is to support useful annotation facilities for attaching semantic metadata to the resources that the users want to insert into the wiki. Essentially, a centralized ontology[1] has been employed to the wiki system for allowing users from various organizations (e.g., universities and companies) to efficiently work together on knowledge-enhanced tasks [4].

While conventional hyperlinks on the web are indicating physical links between web pages or resources, the relationships between the resources on semantic wikis are described by a specific vocabulary. This process is referred to as *semantic annotation* for describing the resources of the wiki. For example, in Fig. 1, given two wiki pages of a city Seoul and a country Korea, a wiki user can define a semantic relationship isCapitalOf between them.

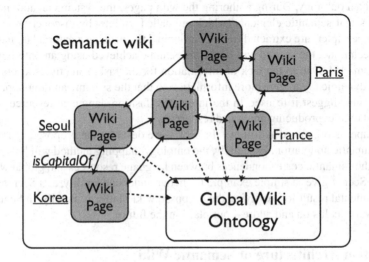

Fig. 1. An ontology-based semantic annotation of wiki resources

So far, most of the current semantic wiki systems have directly asked users to explicitly assert the definitions of the wiki resources as well as the relationships between them by referring to the semantics derived from the centralized GWO. This "manual" process requires much effort of the wiki users in minimizing the inconsistency problems, even though the precision of the manual process might be high. It means that another wiki user needs to find out whether any matched semantics exist for defining two wiki resources. For instance, when the user is trying to add Paris and France, he has to learn that there already exists the same semantics (i.e., isCapitalOf) in the GWO.

Of course, more seriously, as wiki resources are inserted, updated, and removed by the users, the GWO can dynamically change over time.

The aim of this work is to support wiki users by interleaving ontology mapping tools. While the user is inserting the resources, the proposed semantic wiki system can *i*) be aware of his/her contexts, *ii*) match the context with the GWO, and *iii*) recommend the

---

[1] In this paper, we call this ontology as a Global Wiki Ontology (GWO).

matched semantics to the user. Through these processes, the wiki resources from the users are semi-automatically annotated, and consequently, knowledge of the semantic wiki is effectively managed with increasing semantic enrichments.

While most of the existing studies have focused on annotating the collected resources by converting them to machine-readable resources (i.e., two steps of authoring and annotation), the proposed semantic wiki in this paper wants to emphasize that wiki resources (semantic wiki pages) can be annotated during an authoring process (i.e., one step of annotation-based authoring). Thus, the users do not need to consider how to conduct semantic annotation, except for describing the wiki resources in natural language sentences.

Thereby, in this work, semantic annotation based on GWO can be viewed as identifying semantics expressed in each principal terms and then creating instances populated from a given ontology. During authoring the wiki pages, the system can automatically extract a set of semantic elements (which are called triplets) by discovering principal terms. Once triplets are extracted from the principal terms using a natural language processing technique, the second part of the task can be achieved using an ontology mapping schema [5]. Due to the lack of information for the task, sometimes, users would be asked dynamically to give more information so that the system can infer appropriate relations and suggest it to user. In the interactive fashion, language resources can be annotated online, producing annotated resources.

The paper is organized as follows. In Sect 3, we describe the proposed approach to online semantic annotation. Especially, the ontology mapping method will be shown to find out the semantic correspondences between language resources and global wiki ontologies. Sect. 4 gives a simple example for better understandability, and Sect. 5 shows an experimental result for justifying the proposed wiki platform. Finally, in Sect. 6, we will draw a conclusion and address our plans in the future.

2   System Architecture of Semantic Wiki

The proposed semantic wiki system is based on a centralized ontology (called GWO) which can be referred by all of the wiki users. The system is composed of three main components, which are user interface, a database, and a core module for semantic annotation.

As the first component, user interface module is to interact with multiple wiki users. Through this user interface, the users can generate new wiki pages and update them. Also, the users can find the semantic annotations provided from the system, during editing the wiki pages. Second main component is a database. Basically, the goal of this database is to record all activities taken by wiki users within the wiki system. Such activities include any access histories (e.g., login time).

The third component for semantic annotation is the most important one in this system. As previously described, this component can find out how the user inputs are semantically related with the GWO, and also how to enrich the GWO.

Definition 1 (Global wiki ontology [13]). *A global wiki ontology $\mathbb{O}$ is represented as*

$$\mathbb{O} := (\mathcal{C}, \mathcal{R}, \mathcal{E}_{\mathcal{R}}, \mathcal{I}_{\mathcal{C}}) \tag{1}$$

where C and R are a set of classes (or concepts), a set of relations (e.g., equivalence, subsumption, disjunction, etc), respectively. $\mathcal{E}_R \subseteq C \times C$ is a set of relationships between classes, represented as a set of triples $\{\langle c_i, r, c_j \rangle | c_i, c_j \in C, r \in R\}$, and $\mathcal{I}_C$ is a power set of instance sets of a class $c_i \in C$.

While user edit a wiki page, triplet extractor should be interleaving in real time. Technically, this triplet extractor is based on AJAX method which can refer to the triplet pattern repository (TPR). A set of triplets matched with the TRP can be compared with GWO by the ontology mapper (OM). Finally, the mapping results, which are regarded as the semantic annotation in this work, are sent to the user interface module and shown to the wiki users. The extracted triplet is semantically matched to the GWO.

3   Online Semantic Annotation

In this work, online semantic annotation is regarded as a semi-automatic process that takes as input a stream of words entered by a user and simultaneously generates annotated resources in which each words are described using vocabulary from given ontology. In opposition, offline semantic annotation takes as input a document that had already been written and then annotates it. It should be noted that output of both approaches are much the same, e.g. annotated resources. The difference is in that while the former approach parses incomplete sentences entered in real-time, the later approach parses relatively well-formed sentences in already existing documents. Moreover, the online semantic annotation has some advantages in that it can obtain necessary information in real-time by asking the writer to provide more information. For example, the meaning of a multi-sense word can be clarified by asking the writer to specify domain to which it belongs. Thereby, we divide the problem into two phases;

1. The first phase is to extract triplets from a stream of words which a user is entering.
2. The second phase is to automatically map the resulting triplets into a global wiki ontology (GWO) for annotating the resources.

On its way of processing, in the case that input words are unidentifiable, it suggests alternative words to allow to select another one that is identifiable for itself. More importantly, ontology mapping module is interleaved with extracting triples. It means once we have extracted any triple, the ontology mapping module has to find out the best mapping to the given global wiki ontologies.

3.1   Online Triplets Extraction from a Word Stream

In this section, we present how to extract triplets from a stream of words user enters. By the stream of words, we indicate a sequence of words. If it is the point at which the user does not finish to write a sentence, the word stream at that moment would be the first part of the sentence. Because the system takes as input words at each time user enters, it has an opportunity to bother users to stop and enter the next word in an way in which its annotation task proceeds as desired.

Suppose, for example, that the word stream, "The capital city of", is the current snapshot. By referring to a global wiki ontology or language resources, it can be inferred that the next word must be of a country name, such as "Korea". If users entered the word "Seoul" instead of "Korea", the system lets users know that a typographical error or semantic mismatch occurs, since "Seoul" is not a name of country. In this fashion, it is ensured that in a systemic way every words user entered are correctly analyzed and converted into meaningful triplets, although the user is not allowed to enter whose semantics is not recognized using language resources it bases. Fortunately, WordNet already indexes a number of terms with its synset terms, which might be effectively used for word sense disambiguation.

While regular expressions are not enough to parse complex natural language sentences, it could effectively be used in parsing very simple word streams acquired from the interactive approach mentioned above. A hand-made pattern-triplet mapping table, which is used for mapping a string pattern into a triplet, is shown in Table 1. It is composed of 2-tuples that consist of a regular expression-like pattern and corresponding triplet.

Table 1. An example of pattern-triplet mapping table. * indicate a blank node whose value is assigned later when sufficient information is found in the next input by user.

Pattern	Triplet
The capital of ARG1	<ARG1> <hasCaptialCity> <*>
ARG1 is ARG2	<ARG1> <isA> <ARG2>
ARG1 express ARG2	<ARG1> <definedAs> <ARG2>
ARG1 aim at ARG2	<ARG1> <motivationOf> <ARG2>

Given a word stream, before extracting triplets from it, it is firstly figured out which patterns are matched to it. To find out its corresponding pattern, all of patterns are individually taken and tested by using a classical string matching technique. For instance, "The capital" as the first term in the word stream has no corresponding pattern. Note that the first pattern, "the capital of ARG1" was rejected, since it was not matched as a whole. Once an appropriate pattern is found, a triplet is automatically extracted whose argument slots are replaced with some principal terms. For the word stream, "The capital of ARG1" resulting triplet would be "<Korea> <hasCaptial> <*>". The character "*" is marked to indicate a blank node, since principal words that can be assigned in that place has not been entered yet. Using a heuristic, the slot is filled by observing the next a few words, "[T1] is Seoul", where T1 corresponds to the already-extracted triplet. The second pattern, "ARG1 is ARG2", would be selected whose first argument, ARG1, comes with the triplet, "<Korea> <hasCapital> <*>". Combining two triplets, we are able to obtain linked triplets, "<Korea> <hasCapital> <R1>", "<R1> <isA> <Seoul>".

3.2 Mapping to Global Wiki Ontology

In this section, we describe how the resulting triplets be mapped into the global wiki ontology. The main purpose of this task is to assign semantics to the resulting triplets so that a complete form of annotated resources referring to the global wiki ontology is produced. The main idea of this mapping process is based on finding out the optimized alignment state which is maximizing the summation of similarities between all pairs of ontologies elements [14,15].

By allowing different users to edit the same page, collaborative editing involves some risk, e.g., inconsistent semantic wiki pages. In other words, relationships among sentences are hard to be captured if these were annotated using heterogeneous ontologies. In most cases, however, readers expect to see a semantic wiki page based on the same context. Most of applications that utilize such a machine-readable document often assume that single domain-specific knowledge is sufficient to analyze one document.

Furthermore, we can take into account multiple ontologies. In this case, an ontology alignment task [16] can also help to integrate sentences which were annotated using different ontologies. Thus, one of drawbacks of collaborative editing on semantic wikis can be resolved by using this ontology mapping method.

4   Example

Wiki platform has been regarded as an important media to support online communications between multiple users. This work has extended the generic wiki platform to be aware of semantic relationships between the resources in the wiki.

Now, we want to present a simple example. Suppose that a user is entering the sentence "The capital of Korea is Seoul". In a specific moment, the word stream could be "The capital of". If he enters the word, "Seoul", then the system will tell him that the word is wrong, since it is not a country name. After realizing his fault, he can correct it to "Korea", which is an appropriate word. Based on the pattern list in Table 1, the triplet labeled with T1 is extracted, as shown in Table 2. Continuing this procedure, two triplets are extracted.

Table 2. As user enters words, corresponding triplets are extracted simultaneously

Word stream	Triplets
The capital of apple	None
The capital of Korea	T1 : <Korea> <hasCapital> <*>
T1 is	T1 : <Korea> <hasCapital> <*>
T1 is Seoul	T1 : <Korea> <hasCapital> <R1>
	T2 : <R1> <isA> <Seoul>

Once patterns have been found, we need not taken into account whether the sentence is grammatically correct or not. Given a global wiki ontology, we are able to create a semantically annotated document as desired. Information about the author and original sentence, which is a wiki-specific one, is also added to it.

We now review the approach described in this paper. In order to successfully extract triplets from sentences which a user is entering, Due to the limitation of NLP processes, so far we have been assuming that users enter very simple sentences with no complex dependency among words, . It is because we use a pattern-based approach which can hardly be robust against complex sentences if not sufficient patterns is available. If we are allowed to assume that the purpose of authoring semantic wiki pages is to produce a machine-readable document in a collaborative way, such limitation is reasonably acceptable. It is very difficult to create machine-readable documents from the scratch, because even state-of-art technology such as OWL (Web Ontology Language) offers very complex for human. So, we argue that it might be an efficient approach to allow human to author a document in a controlled language, and then converts it into a machine-readable format. In addition, by mapping to a global wiki ontology, semantic wiki pages which were created based on it can share its semantics, making them consistent according to the ontology.

5   Experimental Results and Discussion

In order to evaluate the proposed semantic wiki system, we have implemented the basic platform, and employed it to build an efficient KMS for e-learning in the purpose of training college students. As a use case, 40 faculty members in Inha university, Korea were invited to use the proposed semantic wiki platform for developing the curriculum in three departments. The users are divided into two groups which are denoted by G_A and G_B, respectively. While the users in G_A could use only simple online communications (e.g., email and bulletin board), users in G_B can use only the proposed semantic wiki platform for communication. They had to describe what each course is about, and assert the relationships between courses.

We have compared two different situations with the same users. Both situations are indicating two different semesters, i.e., i) Fall 2009 and ii) Spring 2010. We have measured the number of terms added by multiple users every two hours, and the time to determine the final decision in each case (i.e., how long it took to reach the final consensus).

We found out that most of users in both groups have added new terms for wiki pages over time. Particularly, in the final stage, the total numbers of wiki terms by both groups were almost same. It means that once enrichment of ontology has been done, the size of ontologies seems quite identical.

However, the most important finding in this experimentation is the convergence rate, which means how quickly and efficiently the ontologies have been enriched. In case of G_A, the converging rate has been monotonically increasing. On contrast, the converging rate of G_B has been dramatically increasing, until it has reached to a certain moment. Based on these patterns, we can understand that semantic wiki-based annotation helps the users (i.e., G_B) to collaborate with each other.

6   Conclusion and Future Work

We proposed the design of an semantic wiki authoring system that automatically annotate terms user enters online by referring to a global wiki ontology. We argue that more informative data can be obtained in the case of online annotation, by asking users to give more information. By using that information, the system suggests appropriate words user needs to enter, thereby reducing a change that rubbish triplets are extracted.

By utilizing an ontology aligner, semantic-inconsistency that might be occurred when collaborative editing is allowed can be gone way.

We plan to implement the system and experiment on it to evaluate whether it operates according to expectation. At the same time, more functionalities are expected to be available on the system as follows. Being equipped with more sophisticated natural language techniques, user is allowed to enter more complex natural language sentence in convenience. Multilingual language resource can be produced if the ontology aligner is capable of mapping resulting triplets into another ontology written in another language. Finally, semantic crawler [17] will be employed to find relevant semantics from external sources

Acknowledgments. This work was supported by the National Research Foundation of Korea(NRF) grant funded by the Korea government(MEST) (No. 2011-0017156).

References

1. Jung, J.J., Król, D.: Engineering Knowledge and Semantic Systems. The Computer Journal, doi: 10.1093/comjnl/bxr088
2. Hepp, M., Siorpaes, K., Bachlechner, D.: Harvesting wiki consensus - using wikipedia entries as vocabulary for knowledge management. IEEE Internet Computing 11(5), 54–65 (2007)
3. Souzis, A.: Building a semantic wiki. IEEE Intelligent Systems 20(5), 87–91 (2005)
4. Schaffert, S., Bry, F., Baumeister, J., Kiesel, M.: Semantic wikis. IEEE Software 25(4), 8–11 (2008)
5. Jung, J.J.: Ontology mapping composition for query transformation on distributed environments. Expert Systems with Applications 37(12), 8401–8405 (2010)
6. Heflin, J., Hendler, J., Luke, S.: SHOE: A blueprint for the semantic web. In: Spinning the Semantic Web: Bringing the World Wide Web to Its Full Potential, pp. 29–63. MIT Press (2003)
7. Handschuh, S., Staab, S.: Authoring and annotation of web pages in cream. In: Proceedings of the 11th International World Wide Web Conference (WWW), pp. 462–473. ACM, New York (2002)
8. Jung, B., Yoon, I., Lim, H., Ramirez-Weber, F.A., Petkovic, D.: Annotizer: User-friendly www annotation system for collaboration in research and education environments. In: Proceedings of the IASTED International Conference on Web Technolgies, Applciations and Services, WTAS 2006 (2006)
9. Glover, I., Hardaker, G., Xu, Z.: Collaborative annotation system environment (case) for online learning. Campus-Wide Information Systems 21, 72–80 (2004)
10. Oren, E., Gerke, S., Decker, S.: Simple Algorithms for Predicate Suggestions Using Similarity and Co-occurrence. In: Franconi, E., Kifer, M., May, W. (eds.) ESWC 2007. LNCS, vol. 4519, pp. 160–174. Springer, Heidelberg (2007)
11. Backhaus, M., Kelso, J., Bacher, J., Herre, H., Hoehndorf, R., Loebe, F., Visagie, J.: Bowiki a collaborative annotation and ontology curation framework. In: Proceedings of the Workshop on Social and Collaborative Construction of Structured Knowledge (CKC 2007) at the 16th International World Wide Web Conference (WWW 2007), Banff, Canada, May 8. CEUR Workshop Proceedings, vol. 273, CEUR-WS.org (2007)
12. Kiesel, M., Schwarz, S., van Elst, L., Buscher, G.: Mymory: Enhancing a Semantic Wiki with Context Annotations. In: Bechhofer, S., Hauswirth, M., Hoffmann, J., Koubarakis, M. (eds.) ESWC 2008. LNCS, vol. 5021, pp. 817–821. Springer, Heidelberg (2008)

13. Jung, J.J.: Ontology-based context synchronization for ad-hoc social collaborations. Knowledge-Based Systems 21(7), 573–580 (2008)
14. Euzenat, J., Valtchev, P.: Similarity-based ontology alignment in OWL-Lite. In: Proceedings of the 16th European Conference on Artificial Intelligence (ECAI 2004), Valencia, Spain, August 22-27, pp. 333–337. IOS Press (2004)
15. Jung, J.J.: Ontological framework based on contextual mediation for collaborative information retrieval. Information Retrieval 10(1), 85–109 (2007)
16. Euzenat, J., Shvaiko, P.: Ontology matching. Springer, Heidelberg (2007)
17. Jung, J.J.: Towards open decision support systems based on semantic focused crawling. Expert Systems with Applications 36(2), 3914–3922 (2009)

A Method for Tuning User Profiles Based on Analysis of User Preference Dynamics in Document Retrieval Systems

Bernadetta Mianowska and Ngoc Thanh Nguyen

Institute of Informatics, Wroclaw University of Technology,
Wybrzeze Wyspianskiego 27, 50-370, Wroclaw, Poland
Bernadetta.Mianowska@pwr.wroc.pl, Ngoc-Thanh.Nguyen@pwr.edu.pl

Abstract. Modeling users' information interests and needs is one of
the most important tasks in the area of personalization in information
retrieval domain. In this paper the statistical model of information retrieval system is considered. A method for tuning the user profile based
on analysis of user preferences dynamics is experimentally evaluated to
check whether with growing history of user activity the created user profile can come closer to his preferences. As statistical analysis of series of
simulations have shown, proposed method of user profile actualization is
effective in the sense of distance between user preferences and his profile.

Keywords: user profile tuning method, user behaviour simulation.

1 Introduction

User modeling is a very popular problem in information retrieval domain. The
main objective of user personalization in information retrieval systems is to recommend to the user the documents that are useful for him and relevant to his
information needs.

In our previous papers [4], [5] and [6] the model of user behaviour in information retrieval system was proposed. On one hand we had a user preferences as
the user interests and on the other – user profile generated by the system based
on observations of user activities in the system and dynamics of his preferences.
In the middle we had a system with a database of documents to retrieve. User
asked queries to the system and judged the obtained documents if they were
relevant to his needs and queries. Based on this information, the system tried to
guess the user preferences and built a user profile. The most important issue of
this idea was a method of user profile tuning when his preferences were changing
with time. Researches performed in above mentioned papers have shown that the
user profile updated with proposed method is getting closer to user preferences
with subsequent steps of profile adaptation series.

In this paper we extend the works [4] and [6], where the method of user
profile updating was explored. In those previous works we have used existing
documents' set in the Library of Wroclaw University of Technology. This paper

L. Rutkowski et al. (Eds.): ICAISC 2012, Part I, LNCS 7267, pp. 673–681, 2012.
© Springer-Verlag Berlin Heidelberg 2012

is based on randomly generated set of documents. We were checking the effectiveness of proposed method for building and updating user profile understood as the distance between user preferences and user profile. The aim of updating procedure is building the user profile as close to user preferences as possible. In this paper we check if the distance between user preferences and user profile built and updated with proposed methods is decreasing in the statistical sense.

The rest of the paper is organized as follows. In the Section 2 we present the overview of approaches to modeling information retrieval systems. Section 3 describes the details of user modeling. In the Section 4 the experimental evaluations are presented and obtained results are discussed. In the last Section 5 we gather the main conclusions and future works.

2   Related Works

The most popular model of information retrieval system was designed and described by Rijsbergen [11]: suppose there is a store of documents and a person (user of the store) formulates a question (request or query) to which the answer is a set of documents satisfying the information need expressed by his question. He can obtain the set by reading all the documents in the store, retaining the relevant documents and discarding all the others. In a sense, this constitutes „perfect" retrieval. In this model, the basic operation is considered as the comparison of a document with a query. Nie [9] has developed Rijsbergen's approach using modal logics which can be applied to define all existing models. According to this model, the more knowledge the system has acquired, the more inference capabilities it has, the more precise answer it will be able to give.

In many information retrieval system the effectiveness is understood in terms of precision and recall [3]. Unfortunately, these two popular measures are useless when there is no information about relevance of documents and they seem to ignore the user preferences. Even if two users have a common interest, a document relevant to the first user can be irrelevant to the second user. Ren and Racewell [10] noted that current information retrieval systems are designed to achieve high recall and precision, which is of course desired, but ignores user satisfaction. They claim that future systems must make user satisfaction one of their top priorities. Similar notes can be found in works of Wang and Forgionne [12]. They also affirm that popular effective measure of information retrieval process like precision and recall evaluates only the IR outcome, and ignores the IR process. The second major limitation is that the user dimension is absent from the evaluation. As a result, information needs and relevance are set by the system rather than the user.

Hider [2] pointed out that „search goals" are defined as goals that the user has in mind when he enters a query into an IR system, representing a particular information need. He hoped that this goal will be satisfied by one or more documents retrieved, either directly or indirectly, as a result of the query.

A desirable model of user in information retrieval system should represent user interests and preferences. In literature one can find a lot of different approaches to user modeling. The most popular of them assumes some parameters that describe the user. Mostafa et al. [7] proposed a model of information retrieval where documents are represented in vector space model and classified into some clusters. A user is represented as a profile with appropriate relevance values for the various classes because conducting many experiments with actual users is expensive and, in terms of time requirements, can be impractical.

3   Model of Information Retrieval System

In this paper we present the model of the user in information retrieval system and a personalization method based on user activities in this system. In Fig. 1 we present a schema of interactions between the user and the personalization system. At the beginning the user sends a query to the browser. The system searches the documents' set and chooses all documents that have any of the terms obtained from the user query. The list of results is ranked by the system and presented to the user.

System observes user activities connected with the results rating, e.g. user can select the document (open, print, in library system – order the book). In this way the system obtains the information about the relevancy of the presented documents (relevant/irrelevant) the user has used – user chooses the most important documents for him and ranks them according to his preferences. In the next step, system can compare lists of results: presented at the beginning and given by the user. Based on those information, the user profile is built (the first user profile) or updated (when the user profile already exists) using proposed tuning method. User profile should contain the terms that the user has used in his queries (if he asks about a specific term, he is probably interested in this terms) and for each term a value of its weight is calculated.

To check if this method is effective, we calculate the distance between user preferences and user profile. The desirable trend is decreasing values of distances calculated in subsequent series of user activity.

In this section we present a way of modeling all components of proposed system. We would like to simulate library and the user behaviour instead of using a real library system or a real user. The aim of the simulation is to show that user profile built and updated using the proposed method is getting closer to user preferences with the subsequent steps of user activities in the system.

3.1   Document Description

In the simulation a set of documents is generated. In other works [1], [8] the authors proposed the ontological structure of terms set containing information about the relationships between terms that can be used to describe the documents in libraries or documents' bases.

In real library systems each document has its index terms (keywords) given by the author or obtained by indexing procedure. We assume that every document is described by a set of weighted terms. In real systems weights can be

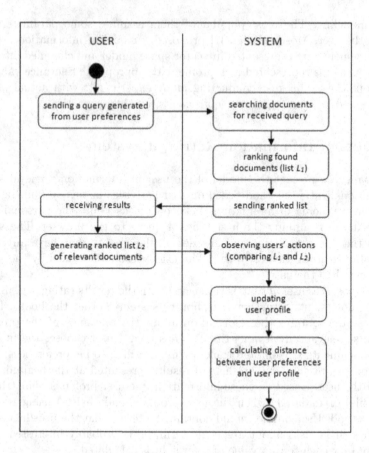

Fig. 1. Model of interactions between the user and the system

e.g. calculated as a frequency of keywords occurring. The library consists of the documents set: $D = \{(t_i, w_i) : t_i \in T \wedge w_i \in [0.5, 1), i = 1, 2, \ldots, n_d\}$ where t_i is index term, w_i is appropriate weight and n_d is a number of index terms that describe the document. Each document can have from 2 to 5 index terms with a weight in the $[0.5, 1)$ interval. Terms are randomly selected from the set T of index terms and weights are generated with fixed distribution.

Searching process can be described as follows. When the user enters his query, the system finds every document that is described by at least one of query terms (logical alternative). In the next step, obtained documents are rated by the system - an extended cosine measures: between document description (keywords) and user query and between document description and the user profile are calculated. The system presents to the user a ranked list of documents that distance function calculated as a convex combination of these two values for them are greater than assumed threshold.

3.2   User Preferences

In many document retrieval systems the effectiveness of proposed method is checked experimentally by inviting many users (volunteers) to interact with the system and to judge if the effects are correct or not. In our approach we do not involve any real user. We have proposed a method of simulating user behaviour in an information retrieval system. We assume that user is described by a set of weighted terms T_U, where $T_U \cap T \neq \varnothing$. Weight can be interpreted as a level of user interests in particular term: $T_U = \{(t_j, v_j) : t_j \in T \wedge v_j \in [0.5, 1), j = 1, 2, \ldots, n_u\}$ where t_j is index term, v_j is appropriate weight of user interests in particular term and n_u is a number of user preferences at the moment. The most important aspects of user behaviour is the generation of queries and modification of user preferences over time. User query contains a few terms randomly selected from his preferences. The second problem connected with modeling user behaviour is dynamic of user preferences. In real life, users' preferences are changing with time, so we also assume that in the subsequent series of user activity in the system, some of user preferences should be replaced by a new one or the level of user interests in each term can be changed to a small extend.

In a real system the user sends the query to the browser and selects the documents relevant to him from the obtained results. In our simulation there is a need to judge the list of results based on user preferences as the real user would do. The assumption in this place is that every document from the list is compared with user query and his preferences using extended cosine measure and the convex combination of these two numbers is calculated. Based on the obtained values the ranking of documents is generated for the documents with the value greater than assumed threshold th_u.

3.3   User Profile

When user is interacting with the system, history of his activities is saved in the system. User asks queries and marks appropriate documents as relevant. Based on this information, the system creates a user profile. The aim of building a user profile is to gather information about the users' interests. Such knowledge can be used in the future to recommend better documents to the user.

User profile should become more similar to the user preferences when the system has more information about user activities. The system knows neither the terms nor the weights in the user preferences. Only information about the user can be obtained from his activity. In other words, the system treats the user as a black box, where an input is a set of terms (user query) and in the output there are a few documents that are relevant to this query and user preferences.

In our previous works [4], [5] and [6] we have proposed a method of building and updating the user profile. The main idea of it is here in short presented. User activities with the system are divided into sessions. A session is set of user activities from login to logout of the system. In every session user submits a few queries (here we assume 5 queries) and to each query he obtains a list of documents: $D(s) = \{(q_i^{(s)}, d_{i_j}^{(s)}) : i_j = 1, 2, \ldots, i_J\}$, where s is session's number,

i is query's number and i_J is a number of documents relevant to query $q_i^{(s)}$. Every document has its description in the form of weighted terms so the system can calculate the mean value of weights connected with appropriate terms coming from the set $D(s)$ of relevant documents in every session s. The objective of the system is to guess user preferences based on his activities, so the system calculate the relative change of user interest in particular term between two sessions. Calculated relative change of user interests is a basis to build and update the user profile. The user profile consists of terms that have appeared in user queries and appropriate weights calculated with the following formula 1:

$$w_{t_l}(s+1) = \alpha \cdot w_{t_l}(s) + (1 - \alpha) \cdot \frac{A}{1 + \exp(-B \cdot \Delta w_{t_l}(s) + C)} \tag{1}$$

where $w_{t_l}(s+1)$ is weight of term t_l in user profile in session $s+1$; A, B, C and α are parameters that should be attuned in experimental evaluation.

4   Experimental Evaluation

For the purposes of our research we have implemented a prototype information retrieval system to test our approach. The simulations were performed using Java Standard Edition Environment.

In the experiments the following parameters were assumed: size of library $\overline{D} = 10000$; size of terms' set $\overline{T} = 100$. Each document is described by 2 to 5 index terms with weights generated from $[0.5; 1)$ interval. User preferences are gathered in a set of 6 to 10 terms randomly selected from the set T with weights also generated from $[0.5; 1)$ interval. User query contains 2 to 4 terms from his preferences. Every session has 5 queries and every 30 sessions forms a block of sessions. In accordance to real life a session can be treated as a day – in this context statistical user asks 5 question a day on average; after 7 sessions (a week) the weights of up to 2 preferences may change by at most 20%.

The second user activity that needs to be modeled is user relevance in accordance to obtained documents. As described in Section 3.2, a cosine measure is calculated between the document and user preferences and between the document and user query. Next, the convex combination of these two values is calculated and based on the obtained values, the ranking of documents is generated. Only a part of $th_u = 30\%$ documents from the final list is treated as relevant for the user. User profile is built based on data from a month of user interaction with the system. After each next block of sessions, user profile is updated according to the method described in Section 3.3. The goal of experiments was to show that user profile built and updated using proposed methods is getting closer to user preferences in subsequent series. The obtained results were gathered in Fig. 2. The first figure presents the distance between user preferences and user profile in 100 timestamps. The trend of the obtained distances is decreasing with subsequent blocks of sessions which means that user profile becomes closer to user preferences. In this sense proposed method of user profile updating is effective. The value of distance in particular timestamps may grow

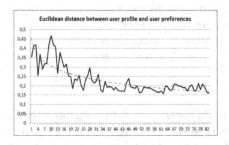 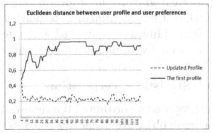

Fig. 2. Euclidean distance between user profile and user preferences

up in comparison to previous timestamp because user preferences are changing randomly and the effect of those changes is registered by the user profile in a few timestamps. The obtained results show that for assumed parameters, the 6 to 8 updates are sufficient for the system to identify the user preferences. Further fluctuations in value of distance are connected only with the fact that user preferences are modified with time.

The second diagram in Fig. 2 presents the differences between the profile built at the beginning of user interaction with the system and the profile updated based on current user activities. It shows that adaptation method is needed to keep user profile up-to-date. The system can work properly (rates the documents similarly as the user) only based on the current information of user interests.

A great part of simulations were connected with tuning the parameters of proposed model. One of the considered aspects of our investigation was the way of generating a set of documents. Descriptions of documents (index terms) were generated with uniform distribution (each term from a set of terms T can appear with the same probability) and with exponential distribution where a part of terms occurred very frequently (about 50%), some of them less frequent and a few terms (10%) can not appear at all. In Fig. 3 these two approaches are presented. In the both cases, the trends are decreasing, what is desirable but we can note that the amplitude of distance values is greater in the approaches with exponential distribution. The reason for this situation is that user can have some interests that can not be found in documents descriptions and as the result the weights of these

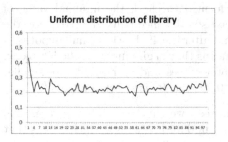 

Fig. 3. Euclidean distance between user profile and user preferences

terms are 0 while the appropriate weights in user preferences are nonzero. An approach with exponential distribution is justified in real life because there are many specialized libraries connected with one or a few domain. Users' preferences can be connected with many domains which are not all in one library.

4.1   Statistical Verification

The proposed algorithm of tuning user profile generates a list of weighted terms. The main objective of the statistical tests is to show that the distances between weights of terms coming from user preferences and obtained in result of user profile tuning are getting smaller in the statistical meaning. Formally we have defined a random variable as the distance between two weights of the same terms in user preferences and in user profile: $X = w_{pref}(t_i) - w_{prof}(t_i)$. The statistically tested feature is the null hypothesis $H_0 : m = m_0$ and the alternative hypothesis $H_1 : m < m_0$, where m is the mean value of distances obtained from empirical data and m_0 is assumed mean value of weights distances. It is not possible to show that the limit of weights distances in infinite number of series equals zero because the user preferences are changing. In the performed tests we have tried to find the minimal mean value m_0 that the null hypothesis can be rejected.

We have calculated and analyzed the null hypothesis after every block of sessions. An exemplary calculations for $m_0 = 0,11$ and data about weights after exemplary block of sessions are presented below. There are no information considering standard deviation and the tested sample is small, that is why for testing the null hypothesis the Student's t-distribution is assumed: $t = \frac{X - m_0}{\sigma}\sqrt{p - 1}$ with $p - 1$ degrees of freedom, where p is sample size, m_0 – assumed average value, σ – standard deviation. The significance level of 0.05 is assumed.

$$t = \frac{-0,032 - 0,11}{0,234}\sqrt{16 - 1} = -2,344; \qquad t_{cr} = t_{(0,05;15)} = 2,131$$

The following inequality $|t| > t_{cr} = t_{(0,05;15)}$ is satisfied, that is why the null hypothesis is rejected and alternate hypothesis is assumed.

Conclusion: The average distance between weights in user preferences and user profile is smaller than assumed $m_0 = 0,11$ with the certainty level of 95%, which means that almost all weights of terms in user profile are closer than $0,11$ to weights of appropriate terms in user preferences.

A series of statistical tests were performed to check the minimal value of m_0 that the obtained result of t can satisfy the inequality $|t| > t_{cr}$ for the subsequent blocks. We have calculated that after the 4th block the null hypothesis $H_0 : m = m_0 = 0,14$ is rejected, which means that beginning from the 5th block, the distances between weights in user preferences and user profile are smaller than $0,14$ and for the assumption $m_0 = 0,11$, the H_0 is rejected after 5th block.

Conclusion: The average distances between weights in user preferences and user profile are smaller than $0,11$ after 5th update procedure, which means that the method for user profile tuning requires about 6 series (updates) to tune the weights for terms in user profile.

5 Summary and Future Works

In this paper we have presented a way of modeling user behaviour in information retrieval system. A lot of intuitive assumptions were made about the user activities in such system. A method of user profile building was experimentally evaluated to check whether with growing history of user activity the built user profile can come closer to his preferences. Statistical verification have shown that only about 6 series of updates is sufficient condition to tune the user profile.

Acknowledgments. This research was partially supported by Polish Ministry of Science and Higher Education – research project no. B10065.

References

1. Duong, T.H., Jo, G.S., Jung, J.J., Nguyen, N.T.: Complexity Analysis of Ontology Integration Methodologies: A Comparative Study. Journal of Universal Computer Science 15(4), 877–897 (2009)
2. Hider, P.: Search goal revision in models of information retrieval. Journal of Information Science 32(4), 352–361 (2006)
3. Manning, C.D., Raghavan, P., Schütze, H.: Introduction to Information Retrieval. Cambridge University Press (2009)
4. Mianowska, B., Nguyen, N.T.: A Method of User Modeling and Relevance Simulation in Document Retrieval Systems. In: O'Shea, J., Nguyen, N.T., Crockett, K., Howlett, R.J., Jain, L.C. (eds.) KES-AMSTA 2011. LNCS (LNAI), vol. 6682, pp. 138–147. Springer, Heidelberg (2011)
5. Mianowska, B., Nguyen, N.T.: A Method for User Profile Adaptation in Document Retrieval. In: Nguyen, N.T., Kim, C.-G., Janiak, A. (eds.) ACIIDS 2011, Part II. LNCS (LNAI), vol. 6592, pp. 181–192. Springer, Heidelberg (2011)
6. Mianowska, B., Nguyen, N.T.: Using Knowledge Integration Techniques for User Profile Adaptation Method in Document Retrieval Systems. In: Nguyen, N.T. (ed.) Transactions on Computational Collective Intelligence V. LNCS, vol. 6910, pp. 140–156. Springer, Heidelberg (2011)
7. Mostafa, J., Mukhopadhyay, S., Lam, W., Palakal, M.: A Multilevel Approach to Intelligent Information Filtering: Model, System, and Evaluation. ACM Transactions on Information Systems 15(4), 368–399 (1997)
8. Nguyen, N.T.: Conflicts of Ontologies – Classification and Consensus-based Methods for Resolving. In: Gabrys, B., Howlett, R.J., Jain, L.C. (eds.) KES 2006, Part II. LNCS (LNAI), vol. 4252, pp. 267–274. Springer, Heidelberg (2006)
9. Nie, J.: An Outline of a General Model for Information Retrieval Systems. In: Proceedings of the 11th Annual International ACM SIGIR Conference on Research and Development in Information Retrieval. ACM, New York (1988)
10. Ren, F., Bracewell, D.B.: Advanced Information Retrieval. Electronic Notes in Theoretical Computer Science 225, 303–317 (2009)
11. Rijsbergen, C.J.: Information Retrieval. Information Retrieval Group, University of Glasgow (1979)
12. Wang, Y.D., Forgionne, G.: Testing a Decision-Theoretic Approach to the Evaluation of Information Retrieval Systems. Journal of Information Science 34(6), 861–876 (2008)

A Term Normalization Method for Better Performance of Terminology Construction

Myunggwon Hwang[1], Do-Heon Jeong[1,*], Hanmin Jung[1], Won-Kyoung Sung[1],
Juhyun Shin[2], and Pankoo Kim[2]

[1] Korea Institute of Science and Technology Information (KISTI)
245 Daehak-ro, Yuseong-gu, Daejeon, South Korea
mg.hwang@gmail.com, {heon,jhm,wksung}@kisti.re.kr
[2] Chosun University
375 Seoseok-dong, Dong-gu, Gwangju, South Korea
{jhshinkr,pkkim}@chosun.ac.kr

Abstract. The importance of research on knowledge management is growing due to recent issues with big data. The most fundamental steps in knowledge management are the extraction and construction of terminologies. Terms are often expressed in various forms and the term variations play a negative role, becoming an obstacle which causes knowledge systems to extract unnecessary knowledge. To solve the problem, we propose a method of term normalization which finds a normalized form (original and standard form defined in dictionaries) of variant terms. The method employs a couple of characteristics of terms: one is appearance similarity, which measures how similar terms are, and the other is context similarity which measures how many clue words they share. Through experiment, we show its positive influence of both similarities in the term normalization.

Keywords: Term Normalization, Terminology, Appearance Similarity.

1 Introduction

Text resources are increasing explosively, due the large amount of data. Methods for efficient text resource management are of great importance and an area of recent concentration. The management begins with terminology construction, and term extraction is the most fundamental work in the construction. However, terms can be expressed in various forms in documents and this is big obstacle to quality terminology. Technical terms especially, which consist of two words at least, have more variations than general words. In the case of general words, the forms are differently expressed according to singular/plural types (ex. 'word' and 'words') and sometimes mistyping; the case of technical terms has additional expressions such as semantic replacement (ex. '**head** mounted display' and '**helmet** mounted display') and re-arrangement (ex. '**visna maedi** virus' and '**maedi visna** virus') of component word(s). These expressions cause a large

---

* Corresponding author.

L. Rutkowski et al. (Eds.): ICAISC 2012, Part I, LNCS 7267, pp. 682–690, 2012.

quantity of unnecessary information, resulting in data sparseness of knowledge extraction [5], feature selection for machine learning [7], and knowledge integration/merging [8, 9], and so on. Even though such term variations need to be solved, research on normalization has been dealt with in only a few works [1, 2].

In order to cover the issue, we suggest a normalization method. First, we prepare a set of technical terms which are extracted from a huge corpus and divide the set into a normalized term set (NTS) and a variant term set (VTS). The method finds the variant terms original forms from NTS. We utilize Wikipedia[1] to collect the NTS and employ a couple of similarities, such as appearance similarity and context similarity. Through experimental evaluation, it is confirmed that both of the similarities can be positive factors for term normalization.

This paper is organized as follows: Section 2 describes our term normalization method. In Section 3, we evaluate the method through experiment. Finally, we summarize our research in the Fourth Section.

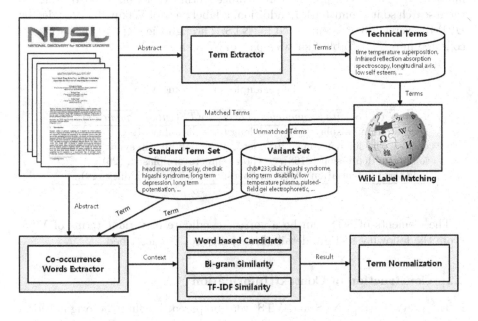

Fig. 1. System architecture for term normalization

2   Term Normalization Method

To construct terminology, many efforts are needed to extract and filter out terms. This current work is that kind of effort, and mainly consists of three parts for the term normalization as shown in Fig. 1. The first constructs a normalized term set (NTS) and a variant term set (VTS). The second step is to collect context

---

[1] Wikipedia, The Free Encyclopedia: http://en.wikipedia.org/wiki/Main_Page

information based on co-occurrence nouns of NT and VT. The last is to measure similarities by using the appearance feature and context information together. In this section, each step is described in detail with examples.

2.1 Construction of NTS and VTS

Terms can be expressed in various forms and a part of them is already generalized to the public and defined in dictionaries. The remaining part is considered to be variants or new words (in the research, the new word is not dealt with). The defined terms may be used more frequently than the other terms, but the undefined terms become an obstacle resulting in low performance in the works related to terminology. In order to resolve the obstacle, we divide terms into two groups: NTS, which is defined in a dictionary, and VTS, which is not defined. Through processing a huge paper abstract set of NDSL[2], 89,231 basic terms, which consist of only multi-words, have been prepared in advance (term extraction is out of range of the research so it is omitted). In addition, a label page of Wikipedia provided by DBPedia version 3.6[3] is employed for NTS. Through the step, 10,684 terms are collected into NTS. Table 1 shows a part of NTS and VTS.

Table 1. The examples of NTS and VTS

$Terms in NTS (with frequencies)$	$Terms in VTS (with frequencies)$
head mounted display (64),	long term disability (19),
chediak higashi syndrome (308),	chédiak higashi syndrome (80),
long term depression (2168),	low temperature plasma (26),
long term potentiation (8417),...	madine darby canine kidney (29),...

The elements of NTS can be a correct candidate of variant terms of VTS. From the following section, detail of the processes are described.

2.2 Construction of Context Information

In the previous step, NTS and VTS were prepared. To find the original form of VT, the work uses appearance similarity and context similarity together. For context similarity, co-occurrence nouns (clue words) are gathered as the context. After this step, each term of the NT and the VT has its co-occurrence nouns with their frequencies. In extracting nouns, the Stanford POStagger[4] is applied to tag part-of-speech to each word [4] and the Porter stemmer[5] is used for noun

---

[2] NDSL (National Discovery for Science Leaders): http://www.ndsl.kr/index.do

[3] DBPedia: http://dbpedia.org/About

[4] The Stanford Natural Language Processing Group:
http://nlp.stanford.edu/software/tagger.shtml

[5] Porter Stemmer (The Porter Stemming Algorithm):
http://tartarus.org/martin/PorterStemmer/

normalization [3][6]. Table 2 shows clue words and their frequencies as a part of terms in Table 1.

Table 2. The example of context information

Set	Terms	ClueWords(ContextInformation)withFrequencies
NTS	chediak higashi syndrome (308)	active (30), blood (12), cell (103), patient (45), rel (3), heterozyg (2), control (16), individu (2), enzym (7), protein (16), membran (19), gene (20), ...
VTS	chédiak higashi syndrome (80)	capac (8), neutrophil (18), monocyt (8), electron (5), microscopi (4), phagocytosi (2), leucocyt (1), aureu (1), vitro (1), abnorm (6), chemotaxi (2), ...

The context information of each term is utilized for context similarity between NTs and VTs.

2.3   Selecting Correct Candidates of VT

If the system tries to measure the similarity between all elements of NTS and VTS in order to find a NT as original forms of VTs, it wastes time and cost and causes low precision as well. Therefore the research selects correct candidates for all VTs. The terms the research deals with consist of multi-words, so if they share one word at least between a VT and a NT, the NT is added to the correct candidate set for the VT. Here, propositions, conjunctions and stop-words such as 'of,' 'for,' 'by,' 'an,' 'the,' 'and,' and 'or' are not involved in the selection process. Table 3 shows examples of candidate terms selected for VTs.

Table 3. Examples of lists of candidate terms

Variantterms	Listsofcandidateterms
vaso occlusive crises	hepatic veno **occlusive** disease, vaso **occlusive** crisis, **veno occlusive** disease, aorto iliac **occlusive** disease, **vaso** vagal syncope, **veno occlusive**
voltage operated ca2+ channels	**voltage** gated, l type calcium **channels**, **voltage** controlled filter, **voltage** sensitive calcium channel, plasma membrane **ca2+** atpase, voltage gated **ca2+** channel, store **operated** calcium channel, **voltage** dependent anion **channels**, ...

In order to find the correct NT (normalized term or original form), the work measures similarities between VT and each element of its candidate list. The next section explains the similarities.

---

[6] Term normalization and word normalization are different in a point of authors view. The motivation of both normalizations is to find original form but term normalization is more complex than that of the word. Please refer to the introduction of the paper for details.

2.4   Similarities for Term Normalization

The VTS may have two types of terms such as VTs and new words. For finding VTs which have a high possibility of variation we have two basic clues like the following.

- Decisive Clue 1. Similar appearance: The variations of multi-word terms could happen due to semantic replacement, re-arrangement, word inflection, and mistyping. If one term is originated from a NT, their term appearances are strongly similar.

- Decisive Clue 2. Similar context information: Even though two terms are similar on appearances, one is not always originated from the other, such as the case between 'vitamin c' and 'vitamin d'. Therefore the context similarity is additionally utilized.

Appearance Similarity. Terms contain a few words and each word consists of letter(s). The term variations occur due to additions, substitutions and removals of letter(s) or word(s) and thus a measure which inspects those specific changes is needed. The appearance similarity can grasp the changes and it measures bigram based word similarity. For the explanation, a set of words consisting of terms and a set of bigrams of each word are expressed by (1) and (2) respectively.

$$term_t = \{w_i, 1 \le i \le n\} \tag{1}$$

$$bigram_w = \{b_j, 1 \le j \le |w| - 1\} \tag{2}$$

where, $term_t$ is a term, w_i is i-th word of termt, n and b mean count of words and bigram of each word (w_i) individually. The count of bigrams of a word is different with word length by 1. For example, 'vaso occlusive crises' in Table 3 is expressed as: $term_{vasoocclusivecrises} = \{vaso, occlusive, crises\}$, $bigram_{vaso} = \{va, as, so\}$, $bigram_{occlusive} = \{oc, cc, cl, lu, us, si, iv, ve\}$, $bigram_{crises} = \{cr, ri, is, se, es\}$.

To measure bigram based word similarity, Dice's coefficient is used and (3) shows the equation.

$$s(w_k, w_l) = \frac{2 \times P(bigram_{w_k} \cap bigram_{w_l})}{|w_k| + |w_l| - 2}, w_k \in VT, w_l \in NT \tag{3}$$

To inspect word re-arrangement, the order of words can be ignored in (3). Its reason is indicated with Table 4 later. The results by (3) are used for appearance similarity of (4).

$$s(term_{VT}, term_{NT}) = \frac{2 \times \Sigma arg\ max\ (s(w_k, w_l))}{|term_{VT}| + |term_{NT}|} \tag{4}$$

Where $term_{VT}$ and $term_{NT}$ are a variant term and candidate term respectively. Tables 4 and 5 show the examples of the appearance similarities, and bold typed result means the maximum.

Table 4 is an example of the word re-arrangement, and Table 5 is about the substitution or the mistyping. For the word re-arrangement case, we should

Table 4. An appearance similarity of re-arrangement case

terms	{visna, maedi, virus}	{maedi, visna, virus}
Bigram	$bigram_{visna}$ = {vi,is,sn,na} $bigram_{maedi}$ = {ma,ae,ed,di} $bigram_{virus}$ = {vi,ir,ru,us}	$bigram_{maedi}$ = {ma,ae,ed,di} $bigram_{visna}$ = {vi,is,sn,na} $bigram_{virus}$ = {vi,ir,ru,us}
$s(w_k, w_l)$	$s(w_{visna},w_{maedi})$=0, $s(w_{visna}, w_{visna})$=1 {vi,is,sn,na}, $s(w_{visna},w_{virus})$=0.25 {vi}, $s(w_{maedi}, w_{maedi})$ = 1 {ma,ae,ed,di}, $s(w_{maedi},w_{visna})$=0, $s(w_{maedi}, w_{virus})$ = 0, $s(w_{virus},w_{maedi})$=0, $s(w_{virus},w_{visna})$=0.25 {vi}, $s(w_{virus}, w_{virus})$ = 1 {vi,ir,ru,us}.	
$s(term_p, term_q)$	$(2*(1+1+1))/(3+3) = 1$.	

Table 5. An appearance similarity of mistyping or substitution case

terms	{chediak, higashi, syndrome}	{chédiak, higashi, syndrome}
Bigram	$bigram_{chediak}$ = {ch,he,...,ak} $bigram_{higashi}$ = {hi,ig,...,hi} $bigram_{syndrome}$ = {sy,yn,...,me}	$bigram_{ch\&\#233;diak}$ = {ch,h&,...,ak} $bigram_{higashi}$ = {hi,ig,...,hi} $bigram_{syndrome}$ = {sy,yn,...,me}
$s(w_k, w_l)$	$s(w_{chediak},w_{ch\&\#233;diak})$=0.471 {ch,di,ia,ak}, $s(w_{higashi},w_{higashi})$=1 {hi,ig,ga,as,sh,hi}, $s(w_{syndrome},w_{syndrome})$=1 {sy,yn,nd,dr,ro,om,me}.	
$s(term_p, term_q)$	$(2*(0.471+1+1))/(3+3) = 0.824$.	

follow that the word order is not important. The appearance similarity is utilized as one factor for the normalization.

Context Similarity. As described previously, the appearance similarity is not sufficient to find an original form. As a supplement, the context similarity is additionally considered. From the section 2.2, the context information of each term has been collected. This section measures context similarity between NT and VT. For the similarity, clue (co-occurrence noun) weights of NT are calculated by TF-IDF (Term Frequency-Inverse Document Frequency). Table 6 is an example (chediak higashi syndrome) of NT.

The weights about all clues of every NT are applied to context similarity which measures how many clues they share.

$$Context\_Similarity\,(term_{VT}, term_{NT}) = \Sigma weight\,(matched\_clue) \quad (5)$$

where *matched_clue* is a clue which appears with $term_{VT}$ and $term_{NT}$ together. Table 7 shows an example of context similarity measure of a VT and each element of its candidate set.

3 Experimental Evaluation

For evaluation of the normalization method, we chose 171 variant terms *(vt)* randomly and selected their normalized terms *(nt)* which have the term similarity

Table 6. An example of target term

Term(Occ.)	Clues	Occ.	TF	IDF	TF − IDF
Chediak higashi syndrome (308)	mk	9	0.029	2.478	0.072
	cell	103	0.334	0.686	0.229
	enzym	7	0.023	1.151	0.026
	protein	16	0.052	0.836	0.043
	studi	29	0.094	0.439	0.041
	blood	12	0.039	0.981	0.038
	clone	4	0.013	1.469	0.019
	phosphatas	4	0.013	1.722	0.022
	fetus	3	0.010	2.023	0.020
	cytotox	5	0.016	1.741	0.028
	...		...	...	...

Table 7. An example of target term

Variantterm	Candidateterms	Contextsimilarity
Chédiak	Chediak higashi syndrome	5.5815
higashi syndrome	hermansky pudlak syndrome	3.2683
	wiskott aldrich syndrome	2.4093
	naevoid basal cell carcinoma syndrome	2.9550
	...	...

(ts), by multiplying appearance similarity *(as)* and context similarity *(cs)*. In other words, we have prepared 171 pairs *(p)* which are expressed to *p(vt, nt, as, cs, ts)*. By manual evaluation, the result shows that 40 pairs (about 23.4%) are correctly normalized. As described in Section 2.1 for construction of NTS and VTS, all elements in VTS are not kinds of variant. In order to check the effectiveness of the *as* and the *cs*, we assign threshold values to each similarity from 0.1 to 0.9 and evaluate each result, totalling 81 results.

In the research, we deal with term normalization and it should be performed carefully like knowledge enrichment [6] because the result influences its application area. In other words, these kinds of research guarantee that the resulted data should be pure. Therefore, precision is the most important factor among evaluation methods. We evaluate our method and Table 8 shows the result in detail from this point of view.

In the table, *c_p* means count of pairs which remain after applying TV_AS. Table 8 summarizes the cases on 0.5 and 0.7 of TV_AS which attain the best performances on F1 and precision. In the case of F1, it could reach 76.7(%) when 0.5 and 0.1 are given to TV_AS and TV_CS respectively. However, the research was not designed to have a wrong result, but pursues perfect precision with the maximum count of right pairs *(vt, nt)*. Accordingly we could find the result having 19 correct pairs with 100(%) at TV_AS 0.7 and TV_CS 0.2. Through the evaluation, we could confirm that the method proposed in the paper has positive normalization. In future, by concentrating on terminology construction when processing large amounts of data, it could help extract a high quality of

Table 8. Performance evaluations on precision, recall, and F1 rates (TV_AS: threshold value of appearance similarity, TV_CS: threshold value of context similarity)

TV_CS	TV_AS=0.5						TV_AS=0.7					
	c_p	O	X	Pr.(%)	Re.(%)	F1(%)	c_p	O	X	Pr.(%)	Re.(%)	F1(%)
0.0	63	39	24	61.9	100	76.5	34	29	5	85.2	100	92.1
0.1	47	33	14	70.2	84.6	**76.7**	27	24	3	88.9	61.5	72.7
0.2	34	27	7	79.4	69.2	74.0	19	**19**	0	**100**	48.7	65.5
0.3	24	19	5	79.2	48.7	60.3	12	12	0	100	30.8	47.1
0.4	20	17	3	85.0	43.6	57.6	10	10	0	100	25.6	40.8
0.5	18	17	1	94.4	43.6	59.6	10	10	0	100	25.6	40.8
0.6	13	13	0	100	33.3	50.0	7	7	0	100	17.9	30.4
0.7	13	13	0	100	33.3	50.0	7	7	0	100	17.9	30.4
0.8	12	12	0	100	30.8	47.1	6	6	0	100	15.4	26.7
0.9	11	11	0	100	28.2	44.0	6	6	0	100	15.4	26.7

knowledge, because the normalization helps to prevent unnecessary information extraction. However the research depends on the term appearance, rather than the context information or its semantics. We will prepare another method for better performance.

4 Conclusion

This paper proposed a normalization method of term variations which is necessary in constructing knowledge from large amounts of data. To do this, we divided technical terms into a normalized term set (NTS) and a variant term set (VTS) through Wikipedia concept matching, constituted context information for each term, prepared candidate terms for original forms, and finally found normalized terms based on the appearance similarity *(as)* and the context similarity *(cs)*. In the experimental evaluation, we could have the maximum count of correct pairs of *vt* and *nt* under the condition of 0.7 and 0.2 of threshold values for *as* and *cs* respectively.

In automatic knowledge construction, term normalization is a significant requirement, to avoid generating unnecessary information. To this end, this research is expected to contribute to diverse fields of knowledge mining. However it still has a limitation, which is that it cannot find 'Vitamin C' as an original form from 'L ascorbate' or 'L ascorbic acid' because the work depends with more weight on the *as*. We will continue study for the solution which is based on semantics.

References

1. Dowdal, J., Rinaldi, F., Ibekwe-SanJuan, F., SanJuan, E.: Complex Structuring of Term Variants for Question Answering. In: Proc. of the ACM Workshop on Multiword Expressions: Analysis, Acquisition and Treatment, vol. 18, pp. 1–8 (2003)

2. Ibekwe-Sanjuan, F.: Terminological Variation, a Means of Identifying Research Topics from Texts. In: Proc. of Intl. Conf. on Computational Linguistics, vol. 1, pp. 564–570 (1998)
3. Porter, M.F.: An algorithm for suffix stripping. J. of Program 14(3), 130–137 (1980)
4. Toutanova, K., Manning, C.: Enriching the Knowledge Sources Used in a Maximum Entropy Part-of-Speech Tagger. In: Proc. Joint SIGDAT Conf. Empirical Methods in Natural Language Processing and Very Large Corpora, pp. 63–70 (2000)
5. Hwang, M., Kim, P.: A New Similarity Measure for Automatic Construction of the Unknown Word Lexical Dictionary. Intl. J. on Semantic Web and Information Systems (IJSWIS) 5(1), 48–64 (2009)
6. Hwang, M., Choi, C., Kim, P.: Automatic Enrichment of Semantic Relation Networks and its Application to Word Sense Disambiguation. IEEE Transactions on Knowledge and Data Engineering 23(6), 845–858 (2011)
7. Brank, J., Mladenic, D., Grobelnik, M., Milic-Frayling, N.: Feature Selection for the Classification of Large Document Collections. Journal of Universal Computer Science 14(10), 1562–1596 (2008)
8. Duong, T.H., Jo, G., Jung, J.J., Nguyen, N.T.: Complexity Analysis of Ontology Integration Methodologies: A Comparative Study. Journal of Universal Computer Science 15(4), 877–897 (2009)
9. Jung, J.J.: Semantic business process integration based on ontology alignment. Expert Systems with Applications 36(8), 11013–11020 (2009)
10. Hwang, M., Choi, D., Choi, J., Kim, H., Kim, P.: Similarity Measure for Semantic Document Interconnections. Information-An International Interdisciplinary Journal 13(2), 253–267 (2010)
11. Hwang, M., Choi, D., Kim, P.: A Method for Knowledge Base Enrichment using Wikipedia Document Information. Information-An International Interdisciplinary Journal 13(5), 1599–1612 (2010)
12. Bawakid, A., Oussalah, M.: Using features extracted from Wikipedia for the task of Word Sense Disambiguation. In: Proc. of IEEE Intl. Conf. on Cybernetic Intelligent Systems, pp. 1–6 (2010)
13. Fogarolli, A.: Word Sense Disambiguation Based on Wikipedia Link Structure. In: Proceedings of IEEE Intl. Conf. on Semantic Computing, pp. 77–82 (2009)

Stabilisation and Steering of Quadrocopters Using Fuzzy Logic Regulators

Boguslaw Szlachetko[1] and Michal Lower[2]

[1] Wroclaw University of Technology,
Institute of Telecommunication, Teleinformatics and Acoustics,
ul Janiszewskiego 7/9, 50-372 Wroclaw, Poland
Boguslaw.Szlachetko@pwr.wroc.pl
[2] Wroclaw University of Technology,
Institute of Computer Engineering, Control and Robotics,
ul Janiszewskiego 11/17, 50-372 Wroclaw, Poland
Michal.Lower@pwr.wroc.pl

Abstract. The cascaded fuzzy controller system for quadrocopter was developed on the basis of computer simulations. The mathematical model of quadrocopter and its cascaded fuzzy controller were simulated using Matlab Simulink software. The proposed controller was tested in most frequent flight circumstances: in hover, in rectilinear flight with constant speed, in climbing and in rotation. In all these situations the proposed controller was able to provide foreseeable behavior of the quadrocopter.

1 Introduction

Several quadrocopters have been constructed recently. Most of them utilize the classical control theory, so they are controlled by proportional integral derivative (PID) feedback controller [1,2,5,4,8]. The other very promising method is based on the foundation of fuzzy logic [3,10,11]. The main advantage of fuzzy logic, in compare to classical method, is the ability to develop controller using simple transformation of rules expressed in natural language. The good example of this methodology was demonstrated in our prior publications [6,7,9].

2 Quadrocopter Model and Flight Control

Quadrocopter, called in some publications "quadrotor" [2,5], is a flying object with four fixed-pitch propellers in cross configuration. Driving the two pairs of propellers in the opposite directions removes the need for a tail rotor. Usually all engines and propellers are identical, so the quadrocopter is a fully symmetrical flying object. It is possible to use different configuration of rotors e.g. when the variable pitch propellers are used or different size of propellers are configured but the complication of the model dramatically rises, so the most frequent configuration uses the same engines and propellers.

The main effects, acting on a quadrocopter, witch have to be taken into account are:

L. Rutkowski et al. (Eds.): ICAISC 2012, Part I, LNCS 7267, pp. 691–698, 2012.

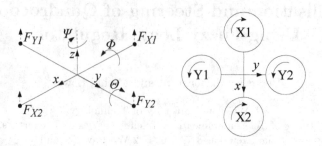

Fig. 1. The coordinate system of quadrocopter

- gravity effect caused by quadrocopter mass,
- aerodynamic effects of each of the propellers caused by rotating propellers,
- inertial torques of each of the propellers,
- gyroscopic effects of each of the propellers,
- joint aerodynamic effects in all three axes, causing linear movement,
- joint inertial torque causing pitch, roll and yaw angles changes.

All four torques caused by rotors add one to another and a join torque about mass center of quadrocopter is arising.

$$T_z = d(X_1^2 + X_2^2 - Y_1^2 - Y_2^2) \tag{1}$$

where d is a so called drag coefficient and X_1, X_2, Y_1, Y_2 are rotation speeds of propellers according to the Fig.2. Usually two opposite rotors have clockwise rotation and two others have counterclockwise rotation. If no rotation of quadrocopter is required we have to compensate left and right torques to each other according to the formula (1).

Change in the joint torque mentioned in formula (1) lets quadrocopter move around OZ axis and as consequence the angle called yaw Ψ is appearing.

$$U_z = b(X_1^2 + X_2^2 + Y_1^2 + Y_2^2) \tag{2}$$

where b is so called thrust coefficient.

The move around OY is caused by converse changing the propeller speed of the X pair of rotors. As the consequence the angle Θ called pitch can be observed.

$$U_x = b(X_1^2 - X_2^2) \tag{3}$$

The move around OX is caused by conversely changing the propeller speed of the Y pair of rotors. As the consequence the angle Φ called roll can be observed.

$$U_y = b(Y_1^2 - Y_2^2) \tag{4}$$

Mathematical model of quadrocopter is complicated, especially if all physical effects have to be modeled. Nevertheless previous researches [2,5,8] in this field let us infer the following system of equations:

$$\begin{cases} \ddot{x} = (\cos\Psi\sin\Theta\cos\Phi + \sin\Psi\sin\Phi)U_z/m \\ \ddot{y} = (\sin\Psi\sin\Theta\cos\Phi - \cos\Psi\sin\Phi)U_z/m \\ \ddot{z} = (\cos\Theta\cos\Phi U_z/m) - g \\ \ddot{\Phi} = \left[\dot{\Theta}\dot{\Psi}(I_y - I_z) + lU_y\right]/I_x \\ \ddot{\Theta} = \left[\dot{\Phi}\dot{\Psi}(I_z - I_x) + lU_x\right]/I_y \\ \ddot{\Psi} = \left[\dot{\Phi}\dot{\Theta}(I_x - I_y) + T_z\right]/I_z \end{cases} \tag{5}$$

where m is the mass of quadrocopter, g is the gravity acceleration, l is the distance between the rotor and center of quadrocopter, I_x, I_y, I_z are the inertia moment along proper axes, Φ, Θ, Ψ are roll, pitch and yaw angles, respectively. Presented model ignores aerodynamic drags and gyroscopic effects but it is good enough to model quadrocopter's behavior in hover and low speed circumstances.

3   Quadrocopter Controller

Generally quadrocopter is the object equipped with microprocessor, four propellers, four engines joined with ECS (Electronics Speed Control) circuits and bunch of sensors like: accelerometer, gyroscopes etc.

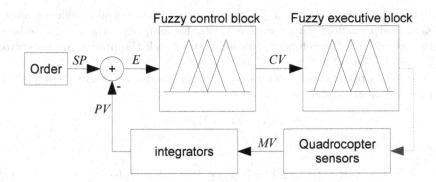

Fig. 2. The block diagram of proposed system

In Fig.3 the system block diagram has been presented. In diagram, solid line means the connection realized in microprocessor, usually by the message passing mechanism or shared buffer in memory. Doted line represents the "physical" connection. It means that executive blocks control the rotation speed of propellers which affects the sensors (particularly accelerometer and gyroscopes). Thus doted line represents the physical feedback to the quadrocopter system and executive output values $[X_1, X_2, Y_1, Y_2]$ control rotation speeds of propellers and sensors measure the linear accelerations and angle speeds $MV = [\ddot{x}, \ddot{y}, \ddot{z}, \dot{\Phi}, \dot{\Theta}, \dot{\Psi}]^T$. Because quasi integral relation between linear speeds U, V, W

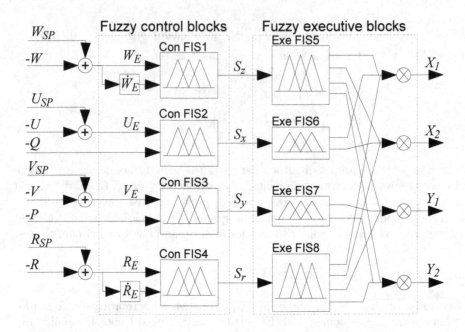

Fig. 3. The block diagram of fuzzy controller

and measured accelerations $\ddot{x}, \ddot{y}, \ddot{z}$ and between the attitude angle velocities P, Q, R and measured values $\dot{\Phi}, \dot{\Theta}, \dot{\Psi}$ exists, for simplicity, the integral substitution is inferred. Therefore, in the integrator block the process values vector $PV = [U, V, W, P, Q, R]^T$ is calculated.

The SP represents vector of desired values of speeds and yaw angle in quadrocopter coordinate system as follows:

$$SP = [U_{SP}, V_{SP}, W_{SP}, R_{SP}]^T \tag{6}$$

Consequently, the vector

$$E = SP - PV = [U_E, V_E, W_E, -P, -Q, R_E]^T \tag{7}$$

drives the fuzzy control block (see Fig.3). The values at output of control block $CV = [S_x, S_y, S_z, S_r]$ are used by fuzzy executives block which tries to imitate the movement rules defined in equations (1),(2),(3) and (4).

4   Fuzzy Rules

Fuzzy rules can be divided into two groups: fuzzy control rules and fuzzy executives rules, similarly to block diagram presented in Fig.3. The five linguistic values are used at the input of fuzzy control blocks. Let:

- $\{.\}^{++}$ - means large positive value,
- $\{.\}^{+}$ - means moderate positive value,

- $\{.\}^0$ - means neutral(zero) value,
- $\{.\}^-$ - means moderate negative value,
- $\{.\}^{--}$ - means large negative value.

The triangle membership functions are used in all cases except the end of the value's range where the trapezoid functions are used. The input and output values of the executive blocks are slightly different. Between the blocks (control and executive) the linguistic values S_x, S_y, S_z, S_r are defuzzified to obtain numerical values. Then the executive blocks use only two linguistic values: positive $\{.\}^+$ and negative $\{.\}^-$ (see Table 2).

The Table 1 contains rules for control blocks divided into four situations:

- if the error E is large or moderate and increases in time then the compensation has to be large,
- if the error E is large or moderate but decreases in time then the compensation has to be moderate or should stay without the compensation,
- if the error E is moderate and slowly decreases then the compensation has to be moderate,
- if the error E is moderate and quickly decreases then the compensation has to be moderate, too.

The Table 2 contains rules implemented in fuzzy executives blocks. As can be seen, these blocks try to mimic the general rules of quadrocopter movement mentioned at the beginning of the paper. From the functional point of view executives blocks can be seen as a kind of mixer, which mixes different control values of propeller angular speeds delivered to ECS.

5   Simulations Result

Simulation of the system presented in Fig.3 was provided. Some results are presented below. In each particular group the most representative results are chosen to be shown. First the hover state was simulated and results of simulation are presented in Fig.5. At the beginning the disturbance causing plunge in OZ axis was simulated. The reaction to this disturbance can only be observed on the rate of climb W whereas the longitudinal and lateral speeds U, V remain at $0[m/s]$, so the position of quadrocopter in OX and OY axes has not been changed. The right figure shows the angular speeds. Pitch and roll do not change but yaw reaches the constant speed about $0.002[rpm]$ which means the quadrocopter rotates around $0Z$ axis very slowly.

In the Fig.5 the simulations results have been shown. The left diagram presents behavior of quadrocopter at the start of the longitudinal movement. The speed U approaches desired speed $0.8[m/s]$ after two seconds and then it is oscillating around this speed. At the beginning of the movement the declining oscillations of the speed W (along $0Z$ axis) can be observed. In the right diagram the quadrocopter's behavior is shown at the beginning of the climb. The longitudinal and lateral speed do not change while the rate of climb achieves desired value $0.8[m/s]$ after half a second and then stabilizes at this constant rate.

Table 1. Rules of fuzzy control blocks

Con FIS1	Con FIS2
$W_E \cap \dot{W}_E$	$U_E \cap Q$
E is large and increases:	
$(W_E^{++} \cup W_E^+) \cap (\dot{W}_E^{++} \cup \dot{W}_E^+) \Rightarrow S_z^{--}$	$(U_E^{++} \cup U_E^+) \cap (Q^{++} \cup Q^+) \Rightarrow S_x^{--}$
$(W_E^{--} \cup W_E^-) \cap (\dot{W}_E^{--} \cup \dot{W}_E^-) \Rightarrow S_z^{++}$	$(U_E^{--} \cup U_E^-) \cap (Q^{--} \cup Q^-) \Rightarrow S_x^{++}$
E is large but decreases:	
$(W_E^{++} \cap \dot{W}_E^{--}) \Rightarrow S_z^0$	$(U_E^{++} \cap Q^{--}) \Rightarrow S_x^0$
$(W_E^{++} \cap \dot{W}_E^-) \Rightarrow S_z^-$	$(U_E^{++} \cap Q^-) \Rightarrow S_x^-$
$(W_E^{--} \cap \dot{W}_E^{++}) \Rightarrow S_z^0$	$(U_E^{--} \cap Q^{++}) \Rightarrow S_x^0$
$(W_E^{--} \cap \dot{W}_E^+) \Rightarrow S_z^+$	$(U_E^{--} \cap Q^+) \Rightarrow S_x^+$
E is small and slowly decreases:	
$(W_E^+ \cap \dot{W}_E^-) \Rightarrow S_z^+$	$(U_E^+ \cap Q^-) \Rightarrow S_x^+$
$(W_E^- \cap \dot{W}_E^+) \Rightarrow S_z^-$	$(U_E^- \cap Q^+) \Rightarrow S_x^-$
E is small and quickly decreases:	
$(W_E^+ \cap \dot{W}_E^{--}) \Rightarrow S_z^+$	$(U_E^+ \cap Q^{--}) \Rightarrow S_x^+$
$(W_E^- \cap \dot{W}_E^{++}) \Rightarrow S_z^-$	$(U_E^- \cap Q^{++}) \Rightarrow S_x^-$
Con FIS3	**Con FIS4**
$V_E \cap P$	$R_E \cap \dot{R}_E$
E is large and increases:	
$(V_E^{++} \cup V_E^+) \cap (P^{++} \cup P^+) \Rightarrow S_y^{--}$	$(R_E^{++} \cup R_E^+) \cap (\dot{R}_E^{++} \cup \dot{R}_E^+) \Rightarrow S_r^{--}$
$(V_E^{--} \cup V_E^-) \cap (P^{--} \cup P^-) \Rightarrow S_y^{++}$	$(R_E^{--} \cup R_E^-) \cap (\dot{R}_E^{--} \cup \dot{R}_E^-) \Rightarrow S_r^{++}$
E is large but decreases:	
$(V_E^{++} \cap P^{--}) \Rightarrow S_y^0$	$(R_E^{++} \cap \dot{R}_E^{--}) \Rightarrow S_r^0$
$(V_E^{++} \cap P^-) \Rightarrow S_y^-$	$(R_E^{++} \cap \dot{R}_E^-) \Rightarrow S_r^-$
$(V_E^{--} \cap P^{++}) \Rightarrow S_y^0$	$(R_E^{--} \cap \dot{R}_E^{++}) \Rightarrow S_r^0$
$(V_E^{--} \cap P^+) \Rightarrow S_y^+$	$(R_E^{--} \cap \dot{R}_E^+) \Rightarrow S_r^+$
E is small and slowly decreases:	
$(V_E^+ \cap P^-) \Rightarrow S_y^+$	$(R_E^+ \cap \dot{R}_E^-) \Rightarrow S_r^+$
$(V_E^- \cap P^+) \Rightarrow S_y^-$	$(R_E^- \cap \dot{R}_E^+) \Rightarrow S_r^-$
E is small and quickly decreases:	
$(V_E^+ \cap P^{--}) \Rightarrow S_y^+$	$(R_E^+ \cap \dot{R}_E^{--}) \Rightarrow S_r^+$
$(V_E^- \cap P^{++}) \Rightarrow S_y^-$	$(R_E^- \cap \dot{R}_E^{++}) \Rightarrow S_r^-$

Table 2. Rules of fuzzy executive blocks

Exe FIS5	Exe FIS6
$S_z^- \Rightarrow Y_1^+ \cap Y_2^+ \cap X_1^+ \cap X_2^+$	$S_x^- \Rightarrow X_1^+ \cap X_2^-$
$S_z^+ \Rightarrow Y_1^- \cap Y_2^- \cap X_1^- \cap X_2^-$	$S_x^+ \Rightarrow X_1^- \cap X_2^+$
Exe FIS7	**Exe FIS8**
$S_y^- \Rightarrow Y_1^+ \cap Y_2^-$	$S_r^- \Rightarrow Y_1^- \cap Y_2^- \cap X_1^+ \cap X_2^+$
$S_y^+ \Rightarrow Y_1^- \cap Y_2^+$	$S_r^+ \Rightarrow Y_1^+ \cap Y_2^+ \cap X_1^- \cap X_2^-$

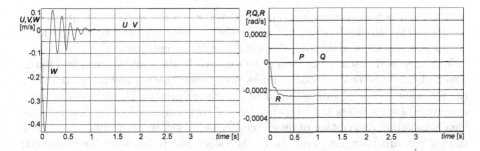

Fig. 4. Simulations results in hover state

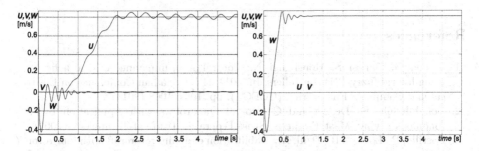

Fig. 5. Simulations results in horizontal movement (left) and during climbing (right)

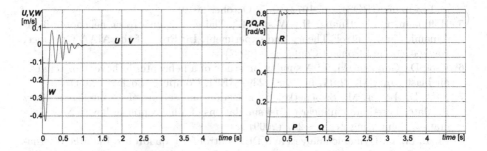

Fig. 6. UVW in rotation

The last presented results relate to simulations of rotation behavior of quadro-copter. The rotation speed R around OZ axis achieves desired speed 0.8[rad/s] (it is near the 8[rpm]) after half a second and then stabilizes. The only problem observed is the small declined oscillations of the speed W which means that during start of the rotation the oscillations of the altitude are appeared.

6   Conclusion

The proposed cascade fuzzy controller is well suited for controlling the hover and the flight of the quadrocopter. The control strategy was simulated for hovering, rotating and non-aggressive horizontal and vertical flight at constant speed. The results of the simulations are not worse then results achieved by conventional techniques (based on PID controllers [4,8]) or fuzzy logic ones.

The proposed cascaded controller lets us divide the problem into two parts. The first one - the control block - infers the general rules of movement based on the set-point vector of values (linear and angular speeds). The second one - the executive block - infers the proper values of rotation speed of propellers. This idea is based on description of quadrocopter behaviors in natural language. The simulations are promising and the further work has to be done. The cascaded fuzzy flight controller will be implemented in a quadrocopter test-bed specifically designed and built.

References

1. Arama, B., Barissi, S., Houshangi, N.: Control of an unmanned coaxial helicopter using hybrid fuzzy-PID controllers. In: 2011 24th Canadian Conference on Electrical and Computer Engineering (CCECE), pp. 1064–1068 (2011)
2. Bouabdallah, S.: Design and Control of Quadrotors with Application to Autonomous Flying. Master's thesis, Swiss Federal Institute of Technology (2007)
3. Castillo, P., Lozano, R., Dzul, A.: Stabilization of a mini rotorcraft with four rotors. IEEE Control Systems 25(6), 45–55 (2005)
4. Hoffmann, F., Goddemeier, N., Bertram, T.: Attitude estimation and control of a quadrocopter. In: 2010 IEEE/RSJ International Conference on Intelligent Robots and Systems (IROS), pp. 1072–1077 (October 2010)
5. Hoffmann, G.M., Huang, H., Wasl, S.L., Claire, E.: Quadrotor helicopter flight dynamics and control: Theory and experiment. In: Proc. of the AIAA Guidance, Navigation, and Control Conference (2007)
6. Krol, D., Golaszewski, J.: A simulation study of a helicopter in hover subjected to air blasts. In: SMC 2011, pp. 2387–2392. IEEE Computer Society (2011)
7. Krol, D., Lower, M., Szlachetko, B.: Selection and setting of an intelligent fuzzy regulator based on nonlinear model simulations of a helicopter in hover. New Generation Computing 27, 215–237 (2009)
8. Li, J., Li, Y.: Dynamic analysis and PID control for a quadrotor. In: 2011 International Conference on Mechatronics and Automation (ICMA), pp. 573–578 (2011)
9. Lower, M., Król, D., Szlachetko, B.: Building the Fuzzy Control System Based on the Pilot Knowledge. In: Khosla, R., Howlett, R.J., Jain, L.C. (eds.) KES 2005. LNCS (LNAI), vol. 3683, pp. 1373–1379. Springer, Heidelberg (2005)
10. Raza, S.A., Gueaieb, W.: Fuzzy logic based quadrotor flight controller. In: ICINCO-ICSO 2009, pp. 105–112 (2009)
11. Santos, M., Lopez, V., Morata, F.: Intelligent fuzzy controller of a quadrotor. In: 2010 International Conference on Intelligent Systems and Knowledge Engineering (ISKE), pp. 141–146 (2010)

Author Index